Susan Glaspell

Susan

Glaspell

Her Life and Times

LINDA BEN-ZVI

OXFORD
UNIVERSITY PRESS

2005

OXFORD
UNIVERSITY PRESS

Oxford University Press, Inc., publishes works that further
Oxford University's objective of excellence
in research, scholarship, and education.

Oxford   New York
Auckland   Cape Town   Dar es Salaam   Hong Kong   Karachi
Kuala Lumpur   Madrid   Melbourne   Mexico City   Nairobi
New Delhi   Shanghai   Taipei   Toronto

With offices in
Argentina   Austria   Brazil   Chile   Czech Republic   France   Greece
Guatemala   Hungary   Italy   Japan   Poland   Portugal   Singapore
South Korea   Switzerland   Thailand   Turkey   Ukraine   Vietnam

Published by Oxford University Press, Inc.
198 Madison Avenue, New York, New York 10016

www.oup.com

Oxford is a registered trademark of Oxford University Press

Library of Congress Cataloging-in-Publication Data
Ben-Zvi, Linda.
Susan Glaspell : a life / Linda Ben-Zvi.
   p. cm.
Includes bibliographical references and index.

ISBN 978-0-19-531323-9

1. Glaspell, Susan, 1876–1948 2. Authors, American—20th century—
Biography. 3. Women and literature—United States—History—20th century.
4. Women in the theater—United States—History—20th century. I. Title.
PS3513.L35Z595 2005
813'.52—dc22   2004010804

Printed in the United States of America
on acid-free paper

To Samuel

Preface: A Pioneering Life

In "Christine's" the party was in full swing. It was a Saturday night near the end of 1917, one of the coldest periods on record in New York; but those in the overcrowded, third-floor restaurant of the Provincetown Players, at 139 MacDougal Street, were generating their own heat. In the outer room Berenice Abbott, a young visitor, sat silently next to a table quickly filling with discarded coats and hats. In the main room Jig Cook, characteristically twisting a forelock of his white hair, leaned against the central mantlepiece booming out his plans for upcoming productions to no one in particular. In another corner, Eugene O'Neill, dark and brooding, sat at the feet of director Nina Moise, after having—uncharacteristically—perched on a chair to recite a poem. Arriving later than most, two women paused at the entrance to observe the group. One was the beautiful, red-haired Mary Pyne, a leading Players actor. The other was their central playwright, the novelist Susan Glaspell.[1]

Agnes Boulton, writing forty years later, could still recall her first impression of Susan that night: those quick, "expressive eyes" that seemed to take in the flowing life around her; the sensitive face; and the "gift of pointed and significant gaiety" that immediately attracted people to her. Susan was neither sensual like Christine nor beautiful like Agnes. Tall and graceful, with large hazel/brown eyes and short, dark hair that curled around her face, she still bore traces of her Midwest past, which made her look more like a sedate, visiting schoolteacher than a Greenwich Village celebrity. "A slight and girlish woman . . . an ethereal being, detached and yet passionate," Agnes described her.[2] Susan was, in fact, forty-one, a full decade older than most gathered that evening, but *girlish* was a word used by those who met her well into her fifties. *Ethereal* was another. In front of strangers and those who bored her, she might be silent, self-contained, seemingly even shy. Surrounded by people she found stimulating, she was witty, self-assured, a woman who "'kindled' to 'Feeling' when it was 'sincere.'"[3] There was also "a tang of wildness about Susan—something untrammeled, untamable"[4] that had marked her since her college days in Iowa, a fellow student recalled. A more recent acquaintance, Lawrence Langner, called her "Fragile as old lace, until you talked with her and glimpsed the steel lining beneath the tender surface."[5] He knew how Susan and her husband, Jig Cook, had mercilessly parodied the Village's obsession with Freudianism, in *Suppressed Desires*, a one-act play that Langner's Washington Square Players had rejected as "too special," and how she had written that great feminist masterpiece *Trifles*, about which the community was still buzzing. Villagers were surprised by the power of *Trifles* but not by the subject or Susan's interest in women's rights. After all, one of her first acts when she arrived in New York in 1913 had been to become a charter member of Heterodoxy, a club of "unorthodox women, that is to say, women who did things and did them openly," as Mabel Dodge, a fellow Heterodite, defined them.[6]

In her native Iowa Susan had long been used to breaking traditional patterns set for women, and so she fit in perfectly with Village life in that *annus mirabilis* that ushered in the first American avant-garde. After high school she had become a reporter for a local Davenport newspaper, and by twenty she was society editor and columnist, enjoining young women to give as much care to what they put into their heads as what they put on them. At a time when less than 2 percent of American women attended college, she put herself through Drake University in Des Moines, excelled in male-dominated debate tournaments, wrote for the literary magazine, and did freelance work for newspapers in the Iowa state capital, pursuing the same path as her Midwest contemporary Willa Cather. When she graduated, Susan got a permanent position as a reporter, rare for a woman, rarer still because she was assigned to cover the state legislature and murder cases—not the woman's page. After two years, she had amassed enough material to return home and begin writing fiction, her real calling. Success came quickly; within a year she was placing stories in leading national journals and winning prizes. While most of her Village friends were just embarking on careers, fresh from colleges or small towns, she was well launched in her profession. By the time she moved to New York, she had already published a book of short stories and two novels and was being heralded as a new, original voice in American fiction. She had also spent a year in Paris between 1907 and 1908 and been exposed to the new art, music, dance, and theatre that was only just coming to America in 1913.

Over the next years, Glaspell would solidify her standing as an important fiction writer, critiquing small town midwestern life, much as her friend Sinclair Lewis would do several years later. It was in theatre, however, that she made her greatest mark, heralded along with O'Neill as the country's most important playwright and credited equally with him for initiating "the entrance of the United States drama into the deeper currents of continental waters,"[7] as critic Isaac Goldberg described their epochal work with the Provincetown Players, the first indigenous American theatre company, which Susan and Jig founded.[8] It would be her plays, more than O'Neill's, which introduced this new American drama to Britain, where critics, such as James Agate and R. Ellis Roberts called her a genius and embraced her as heir to Ibsen and Shaw[9] and where actor Elizabeth Robins argued that "Beyond a doubt, Miss Glaspell is the most original mind" writing for the American theatre.[10] In 1931, her play *Alison's House* would receive the Pulitzer Prize.

The most important woman playwright of her time, a successful novelist, the mainstay of the Provincetown Players, a fine actor in her own works, and a leading writer chronicling feminist struggles of the period: Susan Glaspell was one of the most respected "strange bedfellows," as Steven Watson has called those who brought modernism to America.[11] And yet today she is virtually unknown. By the 1950s and early 1960s, when the myths and legends of this magical Greenwich Village period were being shaped, she somehow got lost in the telling. After her death in 1948, her plays and novels were forgotten and allowed to go out of print. In postwar America, works such as hers with strong female personas and feminist agendas were as outmoded as the overalls Rosie the Riveter had worn to work. Rather than a central figure in the Village story, Susan Glaspell became, instead, a bit player, given walk-on parts in other people's lives, usually identified as " . . . and midwestern writer Susan Glaspell." For instance, in Warren Beatty's film *Reds*, she is in crowd scenes, although she was a close friend of Louise Bryant and Jack Reed, and her life and Jig's were as much the stuff of celluloid fantasy as theirs. O'Neill's biographers do accord her one important footnote—the discovery of the playwright. Yet, after that moment, they, too, generally rush her offstage.

It was through O'Neill studies that I first encountered the name Susan Glaspell. Whenever I taught courses on American drama and theatre, I faithfully retold the seemingly magical tale of how young O'Neill had arrived by ferry in Provincetown, Massachusetts, in July 1916, at precisely the moment when a new, struggling theatre group—the yet-to-be-named Provincetown Players—was putting on plays on a fishing wharf and was desperately in need of material. The person credited with bringing the writer and the theatre company together was Susan Glaspell.[12] For several years I repeated the story of the advent of Eugene O'Neill without a thought to the woman who told it. I neither questioned her presence nor her subsequent disappearance from the rest of O'Neill's chronicle. For me, as for other American theatre historians, she simply did not matter. It wasn't until 1979, the year my feminism first intersected with my academic work, that the story suddenly took on new resonance; and I became aware of the disturbingly familiar roles in which Susan Glaspell was cast:

wife of George Cram Cook, *nurturer of* the Provincetown Players, *friend of* Eugene O'Neill, all traditional female parts. Knowing nothing more about her than a few references culled from O'Neill biographies, I was filled with curiosity—and questions. Did she willingly play Gabriel at the Annunciation and was she as enamored of the role as her words imply? Was she content to fade into the background? What about her own writing? What had happened to it? And what of her personal life and her relationships with O'Neill and with Cook? These questions converged into two overriding ones: simply put, who was Susan Glaspell and why had I, a professor of English and theatre, no knowledge of her or her work? They became the starting point for my research.

I can still clearly remember my shock and anger when, in the fall of 1980, while on a fellowship at the Library of Congress, in Washington, D.C., preparing a book on Samuel Beckett, I wandered over to the stacks that contained Glaspell material and realized for the first time the extent of her writing—over fifty short stories, nine novels, and fourteen plays—and the extent of her erasure from the American dramatic and literary canons. In that heady year of discovery, after reading Beckett in the morning, I would turn to Glaspell in the afternoon, conflating these two seemingly disparate writers into kindred spirits. Over the next several years I periodically returned to Glaspell, thinking I might someday write a critical study of her oeuvre, prefaced by a brief biography, following the signposts already set out by Arthur Waterman, Gerhard Bach, and Marcia Noe who had written about her in the 1960s and early 1970s. It was a 1987 symposium in Provincetown called "Beginnings: 1915—the Cultural Moment" that altered my plan. The year 1915 was chosen as the moment when modern theatre blossomed forth in America, and the person pictured in the center of the composite poster marking the event was Susan Glaspell, whose *Suppressed Desires* had started it all.[13]

For the first time, I began to realize her importance to American theatre and the key role she played in the creative revolution that occurred in Greenwich Village in the first decades of the century. I also became aware of the complex social, cultural, political, and artistic forces that shaped her writing and other forms of American modernist experimentation. If I hoped to understand her, I needed to study not only her works but her times. I also needed to strike up a first-name acquaintance with the woman herself. Provincetown gave me the opportunity. Walking "down along" Commercial Street, I visited the house where Susan had lived from 1914 until her death in 1948; O'Neill's apartment in Francis's Flats across the road, which still had the wooden rafters upon which O'Neill or a friend burned a Hindu inscription; the Hapgood/Boyce house overlooking the bay, where the first plays of the Provincetown Players took place in the summer of 1915; and the place where the Wharf Theatre had stood, now a vacant lot bearing a plaque commemorating the spot. I also began to meet people who remembered the writer and told me stories of her life and their own. Eighty-six-year-old Heaton Vorse, a local movie celebrity after his "testimony" and banjo playing in *Reds*, sang the socialist song he remembered Jig bellowing on visits to Heaton's mother, Mary, who lived nearby. Seventy-four-year-old Anna Matson Hamburger recounted how, at nineteen, she had fallen in love with forty-year-old Norman Matson, who left Susan to marry her. Anna thought her rival was fifty at the time, but Susan was actually fifty-six (having dropped six years from her birth date, as women in the bohemian community tended to do). This was heady stuff for someone who had assumed that research meant library stacks and archives. The problem was that such material was far too extensive and detailed for the general introduction I had imagined writing, too rich to be condensed into a short essay. Without meaning to do so, I found myself embarked on a biography.

I started my work with a clear scenario for the narrative I was creating. To me, Susan Glaspell was obviously a victim, beset by patriarchal villains (O'Neill and Cook) who were somehow responsible for her erasure; and I was the contemporary savior who would reclaim her. My story line fit perfectly the pattern Bell Gale Chevigny describes: A woman critic consciously trying to resurrect a forgotten woman writer, performing "an act of retrieval that is experienced as rescue."[14] I soon learned that I was repeating the very error that historian Nancy Cott describes when, in an earlier period, the young women of the 1920s "looked across the generational divide and saw Victorian sensibilities, as though the venturesome Feminists of the 1910s had never existed."[15] In desperately seeking Susan, I had sought her in my own times not in her own, when she was certainly no victim (and O'Neill and Cook no villains) but rather one of the most "venturesome feminists" of her era. As a corrective, I began studying the periods that influenced her, particularly the Midwest-settlement era in Davenport. The stories her paternal grandmother told her became the mythology that shaped her writing and her life, and she carried it with her when she joined the great reverse migration of writers, artists, and political activists moving from west to east in the early part of the twentieth century.

This research has followed her trail from Davenport, her birthplace, to her adopted homes in Greenwich Village, Delphi, and Provincetown. In each place the houses in which she lived are still standing, relatively unchanged from the time she occupied them. Of the woman herself, the evidence was less tangible and accessible. When her Provincetown neighbor and friend John Dos Passos was told that a certain writer intended to do his biography, he replied, "Someone has to do it." Susan, more modest, did not assume the necessity. She did not make genealogy charts like her husband Jig, nor mark a box of letters "to my biographer" like Edith Wharton. Not a weaver of her own legend like Katherine Anne Porter and Lillian Hellman, she seemed to assume that no one would come seeking her out and so tended to leave her papers and letters undated and uncollected. While Jig's and Norman Matson's correspondence to her survives (since she obviously kept it), hers—like that of far too many women—for the most part, does not. And while many of her friends wrote autobiographies detailing the events of those first two heady decades of the twentieth century and the roles they played in the period, or imagined they played, Susan Glaspell left only one published document concerning her life, *The Road to the Temple*, her biography of Jig, which she, as a consummate biographer, carefully shaped so that attention is riveted on her subject, a man she knew well and about whom she had no illusions. Her goal was to give him in death what he was never able to achieve in life: success and clarity. Toward that end, she often shifts details and embellishes scenes (as she did with O'Neill's discovery) to achieve her objective, purposely blurring chronology and facts to disguise events she felt were too personal and to provide a more lively, engaging story. She was, after all, a novelist and playwright. Anyone approaching her through this work, as I initially did, finds Susan Glaspell a constructed presence, carefully disguised and muted, certainly not the "venturesome feminist" and pioneer she actually was.

During the many years I worked on this biography, one word has remained constant: *pioneer*. Glaspell pioneered a new type of modern drama, extending the possibilities of what could be seen and discussed on the stage and what forms could be used. Finding few native models from which to draw, she created her own. She also pioneered in her depiction of the lives and struggles of women. Her writing is constantly marked by the presence of strong female characters whose consciousness of themselves and their world shape the works. The plots invariably turn on their experiences, relationships, and attempts to wrest at least a modicum of self-expression and fulfillment in societies that impede, if not prohibit, such possibilities. Cutting across geographic and class lines, Glaspell's women display what Carolyn Heilbrun has noted as "the major, perhaps single, mark of a feminist life: resistance to socialization."[16] Like all pioneers, they don't stay where they're put; they venture out. *Pioneer* also defines the direction of Glaspell's own life and the ways in which she continually pushed against fixed boundaries, assuming an independence that she saw as her legacy from her ancestors. Unlike O'Neill, who blamed the failure of American society on its inability to set down roots, Glaspell saw roots as marks of fixity and stagnation, choking off the free growth of an individual, institution, or society. The most consistent theme in her writing is the drive of her protagonists to escape the structures holding them in place; their direction is invariably toward some ill-defined but freer "outside" that has yet to be explored. In different ways, these women, like the author herself, are pioneers who come to recognize that the common sign of a society gone rigid or an institution gone cold is the way in which women are expected to hew ever more closely to narrowly defined gender roles and to stay within enclosing circles defined by family and custom.

Their desire to move beyond traditional boundaries becomes a comment on, as much as a rejection of, such rigidity and conformity.

Repeatedly, Glaspell uses pioneering imagery when she describes events in her own life, such as joining the Monist Society, a group of Davenport free-thinkers in 1907 or heading the Midwest Federal Theatre Project's Writing Bureau in the mid-1930s. In a notebook from the 1930s, she jotted down a quotation from the philosopher Whitehead, "the leap of the imagination reaching beyond what is then actual,"[17] and appended her own comment, "Adventure beyond the safety of the present," the motivation which drove her ancestors and would drive her characters and herself. She never defined precisely what she meant by the term *pioneering*. In fact, she steadfastly eschewed all definition. Like Samuel Beckett, who warned, "The danger is in the neatness of identifications,"[18] she was wary of the tendency toward taxonomy, explanation, and closure in writing and life. *Fluidity, openness,* and *otherness* are her most often-used words, the dash her most consistent punctuation mark. Although she was aware of the impossibility of keeping life and art free from fixed forms and even parodied fuzzy-headed dreamers in her works, she held to the belief that ideas should not be "shut up in saying,"[19] as her persona Claire Archer realizes in *The Verge*, and that "We need not be held in forms molded for us."[20] Like a pioneer, she kept moving forward, breaking with anything that was too comfortable, just as she broke with any writing style that seemed too "patterned" and "predictable." The verge for her was that place separating conformity from discovery, and it was there that she fixed her sights and from there that she sent back her writing.

Unfortunately, this writing is virtually unknown today. In the late 1960s and 1970s, with the reemergence of a feminist movement similar to her own, Glaspell's one-act classic play *Trifles* and its short story offshoot "A Jury of Her Peers" were reprinted and became central texts in gender studies, performed and read around the world.[21] Yet, for the most part, even those familiar with these works have little idea about the rest of her canon or its originality. This biography attempts to broaden the picture by offering samplings of her writing. They provide important documents of life in America as seen through the eyes of a pioneering woman in the first half of the twentieth century.

While constructing the story of Susan Glaspell, I found that I was simultaneously developing two other, intersecting narratives: the rise and fall of the Provincetown Players and the life of its founder Jig Cook—Susan's husband. Both are part of her story, but can be approached as discrete histories in their own right. The Provincetown chronicle has been told before, usually by biographers of O'Neill. This study seeks to correct the creation myth of American drama that posits it came full-blown from the brow of one creator: Eugene O'Neill. It does not question the greatness of O'Neill but describes the contributions of Glaspell as cofounder and female progenitor of American drama, a story until now written out of the myth. It also argues for her central role in the Provincetown Players' success and in the introduction of modern drama to America and the world. In addition, the study attempts to correct the errors that have sprung up concerning the company, some emanating from Glaspell's own literary flourishes when telling its story.

This biography also presents a portrait of that complex, brilliant, failed genius Jig Cook, who led the Players. He is one of the great, larger-than-life characters that America has produced. It was Jig in Davenport who sat by the Mississippi dreaming of Greece and died in Greece imagining how he could recreate ancient forms of arts and culture on native soil. For him, the Provincetown Players was his Greek-inspired "beloved community of life givers," amateurs creating through their art a better, more humane world. In 1915, it was a dream that fit the times. By 1922, when the theatre was finally on the verge of succeeding, he felt it had failed and left for Greece with Susan, since success seemed to destroy the communitarian ideal he sought. Naive some called him, crazy, a drunkard; others labeled him a dreamer, an impractical idealist. After carefully reading through his papers and constructing the biography of his life as it relates to Susan's, I have come to have a great appreciation for Jig Cook and his vision. He deserves to be more than a footnote in Eugene O'Neill's story—the surrogate father in decline, denied by the son in ascendancy—or even in Susan Glaspell's life, as her greatest love and the partner in her greatest adventure, the Provincetown Players. In this book, I suggest the outlines of a study someone else may choose to write.

Susan wrote one version in her biography of Jig, *The Road to the Temple*, revolutionary in its form, combining as it does narrative and citation, breaking chronology, shifting perspectives, interlacing Jig's ideas with her observations of them both. The result is finally limited by her wish to burnish the image and by her desire to keep herself from obstructing his story and from telling too much of her own. Yet, in the work, she provides an important example for biographers, which I have tried to follow. She recognized, long before Roland Barthes and others, that the biographical tendency toward coherence can distort the life described in the desire to give it a form that is ultimately a fiction. She writes in her "Foreword": "Perhaps [biography] is a form a little like life itself—rude breakings in, shattered coherence, unexpected pauses and defeated climaxes. Life, too, is combinations that baffle classification."[22] Taking my cue from Glaspell, I have also resisted easy explanation and summary—the overarching thesis so often found in contemporary biography—and, instead, have allowed the "rude breakings in" to remain. They are the mark of a pioneering life and of writing set on the verge.

Contents

A photo gallery appears after page 216

Susan Glaspell

Introduction: Blackhawk's Land

There was a deep obligation to make a good life, as a great wrong had been done in getting this land.

—Susan Glaspell, *Judd Rankin's Daughter*

Davenport was draped with lights and colored buntings on the day Susan Glaspell was born, in anticipation of the great event that would occur three days later: the centenary of America. In individual towns and in the official venue in Philadelphia, the country did not turn back to its past, as the bicentennial would do, but used the occasion to proclaim its future. The Philadelphia Centennial Exhibition was a celebration of a society coming of age, advertising—as much to its own people as to the world—the technology, produce, inventions, arts, and possibilities of America at the end of its first century. Over a period of 159 days, almost 10 million visitors journeyed to Philadelphia's Fairmount Park to see what was called "the greatest gathering of wonders in the world": a 284-acre field transformed into a Victorian pleasure park, with elaborate lawns, flower beds, trees, waterfalls, and fountains surrounding the 249 ornate iron and glass buildings that held the exhibits. Machinery Hall contained the leading attraction, the Corliss engine, the biggest steam engine in the world, whose twice-a-day start-up was heralded as a marvel of the coming generation. More specialized exhibits of produce and technology were housed in the 24 state and 9 international venues. In the Iowa building, for instance, the Gaume electro-motor, produced in Davenport, was placed next to a display of Reids Yellow Dent-corn pioneer hybrid.[1]

Along with the commercial enterprises, there were buildings dedicated to the arts, the most dominant of which was the huge Memorial Hall, whose display of European paintings and drawings would not be matched again in America until the Armory Show of 1913. There were also buildings designated as "special interest," the largest of which was the Women's Pavilion, devoted to technology, products, and arts, complete with its own, separate steam engine and a printing press that put out *The New Century for Woman*. Over the entrance of the pavilion were the words of Proverbs 31, "Let Her Works Praise Her in the Gates." Judging from the fair, it would seem that 1876 was a good time for a writer—a woman writer—to be born.

Yet, there was another side of the exposition and of the centenary celebration itself. Like the Vienna Exposition, three years earlier, which had seemed to be the quintessential moment of Hapsburg *Gemütlichkeit*, but had only temporarily masked cracks in a society that would take another forty-two years to collapse, the American celebration also pointed to fissures in societal structures that would widen over the coming years. The same banking failures that marred the Vienna fair had their equivalents in America, the related scandals in the Grant administration causing the president to make a hasty exit at the opening ceremony without taking full advantage of the political opportunities such an event offered. On the Fourth of July, the day that was to be the high point of the entire celebration, Frederick Douglass attempted to speak about the problems of racism in the country and was turned away. So were suffragettes, led by Susan B. Anthony, when they tried to present a petition to President Grant, in which they denounced the separate and not equal Women's Pavilion and the hypocrisy of the forthcoming Woman's Day fete, scheduled to occur on November 4, an election day in which they could not participate. Most damaging to the fair's luster was news that reached Philadelphia on July 5 of an army defeat in a western town with an incongruous name: Little Big Horn.[2]

Susan Glaspell was born at precisely the time when the United States was rushing determinedly into the next century, banners proclaiming prosperity and power furled out to temporarily block signs of discontent and inequality. So intent was the country on casting its eyes forward that the accomplishments of the preceding century were barely acknowledged at the celebrations. Progress seemed to require jettisoning the history of the past or at least refiguring and domesticating it to fit the patterns imagined for the future. In Davenport the original settlers, among whom were her family members, still received respect, but they had ceased to be figures of emulation. Successful entrepreneurs were the role models now. Business had usurped for itself the word *pioneer* and affixed it to all that was new, modern, and different. The schism between her own pioneer family, economically reduced in subsequent generations, and rising dynasties such as the Deeres of Davenport may help explain in part Susan's desire to cast her eyes back, not as a conservative who wished to keep progress at bay, but as someone desiring to reconnect with an earlier time and the dynamism and values that had shaped it.

In a period set on fast-forward, her tendency to gaze back to the future placed Glaspell at odds with her Davenport community, where the second generation had already forgotten what had motivated their pioneer parents and were hard at work replacing their families' log cabins with "big square ugly expensive brick houses," just as they were transforming "a society unconscious of social distinctions," into a class system demarcated solely on money.[3] This angle of vision also set her apart from her later Greenwich Village friends. While they saw themselves at odds with Progressivism, as Theodore Roosevelt was loudly bellowing it, they also had little interest in, or understanding of, their own pasts, preferring to think of themselves as self-created. The biographer of Susan's close friend, the journalist Jack Reed, could write that for Reed Greenwich Village was a "'homeland of the uprooted where everybody you met came from another town and tried to forget it; where nobody seemed to have parents, or a past more distant than last night's swell party.'"[4] Susan would never frame her own rebellion in such terms. For her, the life she established in her new home was less a rejection of the past than a reaffirmation of the pioneering thrust that had motivated her antecedents to move west in the first place. She describes her friends in the Village and in Provincetown not as the "Bohemians we have even been called," but rather as "a particularly simple people, who sought to arrange life for the thing we wanted to do, needing each other as protection against complexities, yet living as we did because of an instinct for the old, old things."[5]

Susan never lost her connections with her ancestors or with her birthplace. "The Middle West must have taken strong hold of me in my early years for I've never ceased trying to figure out why it is as it is," she wrote to her Provincetown neighbor and sometime tenant Edmund Wilson in October 1945, three years before her death.[6] The occasion was the publication of *Judd Rankin's Daughter*, the last of her novels. In it, as in the majority of her writing, she was attempting to explain, as much to herself as to her readers, the powerful influence Iowa still exerted on her, although she had left the region thirty-two years earlier to settle in a far different place. Fellow Iowan Carl Van Vechten could dream of escaping his origins and remaking himself in a new, different world. ("Everything that took Carl farther away from Cedar Rapids was desirable to him at the time," Mabel Dodge wrote.)[7] Glaspell carried in her luggage the sights, sounds, memories, and myths of her past. And the most powerful myths of all were the ones connected to her pioneer antecedents.

Born only forty years after Davenport was incorporated, thirty years after Iowa became a state, in 1846, Susan grew up on the tales of early settler life told by her grandmother, the first Susan Glaspell, who lived with the family from the time Susan was six. So compelling were these stories that they often overshadowed the actual experiences Susan would have in her own life in Davenport. "My grandmother made the trip from Maine to Iowa in a 'prairie schooner'," she explained. "As a little girl she knew the Indians. With what regret I think that although I used to hang upon her words when she told of pioneer days and of pioneer upbuilding of a democracy, I did not learn more from her."[8] What she did learn were the importance of hard work; the necessity for humor, courage, and tenacity; and the need for community. Women of her grandmother's time made their own clothes and soap. They also reached out to others, often leaving a light on in their cabins, although it exposed them to Indian attacks, so that passing travelers might know that they were welcome to stop and share an evening meal or rest until daylight.

What fired Susan's imagination were those stories her grandmother told about the settlers' relations with the Indians, particularly those concerning Blackhawk, the chief of the Sacs who, with the Fox Indians, held the land that today comprises much of Iowa, Illinois, and Wisconsin. To those who saw him as he was paraded through the cities of the East after his defeat and capture at the end of what became known as the Blackhawk War of 1832, Blackhawk was exotic and regal, his aristocratic face often likened to that of Sir Walter Scott. The Iowa settlers who had direct contact with him and wrote histories of the settlement period described him as far more "promotive" of bravery and fair-mindedness than those who eventually wrested the land from Indian control.[9] In Blackhawk's *Autobiography*, written three years after his defeat and dictated to one of the first settlers of Davenport—another larger than life figure, Antoine LeClaire—is found the chief's unshakable commitment to pacifist means. He also expresses his helplessness against the unstoppable hordes of whites who came and coveted the land where his villages had stood for 150 years, at the junction of the Mississippi and Rock Rivers, at a point below the present site of Davenport, on the Illinois side. "Poor old Blackhawk—what he didn't know was how many white man [*sic*] there was,"[10] Grandmother Morton says succinctly in Glaspell's historical drama *Inheritors,* in which Glaspell borrows from the history of her family and of Blackhawk. Blackhawk put it this way: "The white people speak from a paper; but the Indians always speak from the heart."[11] Clearly, the heart was not enough.

By the time Glaspell was born, much frontier experience had already lapsed into set patterns. Indians were depicted as savages intent on killing whites or as simple denizens of an Edenic land displaced by western incursion; settlers were portrayed as valorous, Christ-like figures bringing civilization to depraved heathens or as bloodthirsty pillagers whose sins could only be expiated by sacrifice and death. Iowa for the most part seems to have escaped these rigid dualisms. There was neither "The Indian ambuscade, the craft, the fatal environment" nor "the cavalry companies fighting to the last in sternest heroism" that Walt Whitman described in a poem written immediately after Custer's defeat.[12] There was also none of the "Doom! Doom! Doom! . . . whisper[s] it in the very dark trees of America" that D. H. Lawrence labeled as the American literary legacy of its frontier days.[13] The stories her grandmother told of the early settlers and of Blackhawk, in addition to her own reading of Blackhawk's *Autobiography* and the histories that settlers published, provided Glaspell with different narratives and notions about America. Her settlers are human, neither saints nor sinners, and her Blackhawk, while associated with nature, is also the repository of moral values and intellect, noble but in no way a savage. From her ancestors she gained a sense of adventure and possibility; from Blackhawk, a respect for the sanctity of the land, a reminder of the injustices associated with its acquisition, and a desire to be a worthy inheritor of that which she saw as held in trust from him. It is telling that when Glaspell wrote *Inheritors* in 1920—in a period when America was in the throes of another kind of "Red Scare," brought on by the excesses of post–World War I fanaticism that spawned the 100 percent American movement—she had a character with her grandfather's name say, "Sometimes I feel that the land itself has got a mind and that the land would rather have had the Indians."[14]

It is an idea that Susan returns to often. In *Judd Rankin's Daughter*, written twenty-five years after *Inheritors*, she contrasts a father's life "out there" in the Iowa of 1945 with his daughter's life in Provincetown, Massachusetts, Susan's own home at the time. Again she uses the image of Blackhawk to make the point that the post–World War II society, like the earlier period, needs to consider those values for which wars are fought. Describing Judd Rankin, his daughter Judith says: "He had always liked the feeling that this black and giving earth might pay a debt—debt long deferred, which couldn't be paid to the ones owed, not Blackhawk, whose heart we broke, but in the long run, long span, might be paid to the distant and unforeseen."[15] Paying a debt to the "the distant and unforeseen" may sound like a way of morally sidestepping the initial act of settlement; but in the philosophy that Glaspell wove from her Midwest history, Blackhawk becomes not only a symbol of white injustice done to Indians but the standard against which subsequent generations must measure themselves. To stop with the present, to become content, to keep from progressing or moving beyond what others have done, would be a betrayal of all those pioneers who came before as well as a betrayal of the Indians who first held the land. Glaspell's argument in *Inheritors* takes the form of a kind of American idealism, overt in this play but implicit in many of her other writings. As a true daughter of Iowa, she bases her formulation on corn. Just as its pollen does not "stay at home" but fertilizes neighboring fields, creating better strains, individuals have the responsibility to progress, move on, and better the human and spiritual strain, lest they betray the struggles that brought them to this point.[16] "The world is all a—moving field," Madeline Morton proclaims at the end of *Inheritors*. "What you are—that doesn't stay with you. Then . . . be the most you can be, so life will be more because you were."[17]

Like Faulkner's Bear, Glaspell's Blackhawk is the embodiment of that which once was and remains unaltered by time, continually growing in stature and symbolic association as society changes and becomes more material and alien to this spirit. Her own commitment to anti-militarism and pacifism in World War I, her struggles for the environment, her abhorrence of discrimination in any form and her tendency to speak—and see—from the heart and not from the head, have their roots in her Davenport heritage, in her grandmother's stories, and in the imaginative figure of Blackhawk. "'Twould 'a done something for us to have *been* Indians a little more," Silas concludes in *Inheritors*, the play in which the two strains—the personal saga of the Glaspell pioneers and the saga of those they displaced—converge in a young woman hero.[18]

Midwest Beginnings, 1876–1907

A Town Springs Up

1

The prairie schooners were ferried across the Mississippi in the spring of 'thirty-six, and that fall hauled corn to crib from virgin soil.
—Susan Glaspell, *The Road to the Temple*

When J. M. D. Burrows stepped from "the magnificent steamer *Brazil*" that brought him up the Mississippi River from St. Louis on July 27, 1838, he looked out on a scene that delighted him. "The sloping lawns and wooded bluffs, with the sea of beautiful wild flowers were a picture of loveliness such as I never had beheld before." After concluding his business in Rock Island, the town originally settled by Colonel George Davenport in 1832, he decided to take one of the wooden flat boats across the Mississippi to the "beautiful little hamlet of fifteen houses, with a population of about one hundred fifty people," which Antoine LeClaire had first plaited in 1835, called Davenport in honor of the colonel. Recognizing that his enthusiasm might be questioned, Burrows forestalled such criticism: "The natural beauty of the site is not exaggerated by our author."[1] Like many settlers he had come from Cincinnati to take advantage of public auctions that sold large tracts of land to settlers coming up the river on specially charted ferries. The brochures for these sales described the virtual paradise Burrows encountered. "We have a pure atmosphere, a salubrious clime, good soil, large potatoes, fat beef, unctuous venison, milk and honey. . . . our country abounds with inexhaustible sources of lead and most excellent springs are seen rippling from the crevices of the rock."[2] It is no wonder that among the first buildings to be established were churches in what must have seemed to many like a New Jerusalem.

Davenport today retains little that sets it apart from other midwestern towns; yet, in its early years there seemed to be something about the place that led to hyperbole. Situated in a lush, wide bend of land bordered by high bluffs that sloped down to the shores of the Mississippi—the only spot where the upper river runs from east to west—Davenport in the 1830s was an unspoiled valley. A correspondent from the New York *Star*, seeing the town for the first time, corroborated for his readers the impact of the place: "In the beauty of the scenery . . . I have found imaged all the charms I had pictured in my youthful imagination while reading a description of the Happy Valley in *Rasselas*, but which I never expected to see in the world of reality."[3]

Susan's forbearers may have been moved by a similar, if less rhapsodic, feeling. It was their third, and final, stop on a continuing voyage westward. In the seventeenth century the Rickers, along with the Jewett and Chippman families, antecedents of the first Susan Glaspell, came from various parts of England and settled in and around Boston: the Chippmans tracing their lineage back to four passengers on the Mayflower, the Jewetts listing a drummer in the Ninth Massachusetts regiment in the Revolutionary War.[4] Of the three branches, it was the Chippmans (or Chipmans), particularly great-grandmother Lydia Chippman Ricker, who caught Susan's imagination. It was through her that Susan could claim to be descended from Pricilla Bradford and thus eligible for membership in the Daughters of the American Revolution. Although she never became a "Daughter," she did use the name Lydia for her protagonist in the novel *The Morning is Near Us*, portraying her as a woman of strength and great determination, who returns after many years to the Iowa of her birth in order to reclaim her ancestral home and discover her history. The name also appears in the novel *Fugitive's Return*: "Irma remembered that her father's mother's people had come from Cape Cod, that Great-grandfather Chippman's father had gone there in the first days of America."[5]

That her family roots in America were first planted in Massachusetts gave Susan pleasure when she made the reverse trek across the continent and settled in Provincetown. Taking her paternal grandmother's spinning wheel from Iowa and placing it in her front room on Commercial Street, overlooking the Provincetown bay, was fitting, she would tell friends—she was merely returning it, as she herself had returned, to the place from which both had started out. Susan saw herself as completing a circle, uniting the two locales of her family past. Her love affair with Provincetown and the entire Cape region stemmed in part from her keen sense of family history, particularly her identification with the lives of the women, embodied in the figure of her great-grandmother Lydia.

Just as there was a certain migration pattern for Glaspell and her literary compeers in the first decade of the twentieth century, traveling from the Midwest through Chicago in its renaissance en route to the East, there was a certain pattern for her ancestors moving westward.

For the Ricker branch of the family, the journey began in Poland, Maine, where in 1815 Lydia Chippman married Rufus Ricker. Two years later, accompanied by Rufus's parents, Susannah Jewett and Samuel Ricker, the couple migrated to Ohio, around Cincinnati, following the trail of others who wished to try their fortunes in a new frontier. Before the Rickers left Maine, Lydia and Rufus's daughter Susan—Glaspell's grandmother—was born, on July 31, 1816. Grandmother and grand-daughter would share the same month of birth sixty years apart. The Rickers prospered in their Ohio home, and Rufus was appointed justice of the peace and postmaster. Later he would become judge of the Probate Court of Iowa. What prompted the family's second move after twenty years is unclear. Again, they were following migration patterns of the period: settlers from the Northeast moving first to Ohio and Kentucky, establishing lives there, and then moving further west, this time to the recently opened Blackhawk territory. The Rickers arrived in Davenport in 1836, drawn by the first auctions of land in the area.

The Glaspell family followed a similar route. Enos Glaspell arrived from England or Wales in 1755 and settled in southwestern New Jer-sey, where the family name appears under the several spellings—Glaspell, Glasby, Gillespie, Glassell—all of which would be adopted as variations in future generations. A family bible describes these first American Glaspells: "Enos had light hair, sandy whiskers and was of fair complexion; his wife Sarah had black hair, dark eyes, dark complexion."[6] A Glaspell tradi-tion was to identify which members resembled their paternal, which their maternal side. In the case of Susan, the genes seem to have split evenly: her fair, almost white skin was set off by her dark hair, determined in no small part by her own mother's Irish heritage. In April 1789, "The same month that Washington was first inaugurated president," the family bible records, Susan's great-grandfather, James Glaspell, was born in New Jersey.[7] In 1817, a year after the Rickers, he, too, moved west with his wife, Jane Stathem, and two children, Elizabeth and Silas, first to Hamil-ton County, Ohio, and then across the Ohio River to nearby Covington, Kentucky, where six more children were born. Family genealogy studies indicate that James was an educated man; he ran one of the first village schools in his home and was said to have compiled "the Glaspell speller." After twenty years the pull westward moved him again, and he and his family headed to Davenport, arriving in August 1839.

Neither the Rickers nor the Glaspells left written accounts of their first years in their new home; however, Burrows's history provides a picture of the period. Life was not easy; 10 percent of the population died in some years, but it was a lively community. Itinerant preachers held forth on Brimstone Corner, so called because of the "hot style of preaching,"[8] and speakers debated at the Lyceum on topics including "love or revenge?" "general happiness," and "Has the Negro Race Received More Harm From the White Race than from the Indians."[9] (The consensus was yes.) There was also an active social life, Burrows reporting that it was not unusual for settlers to drive bobsleds twenty-five miles to spend the day with other pioneer friends. Alcohol was plentiful, with stores keeping barrels of whisky and tin cups under the counter for all to help themselves. Looking back from the vantage point of fifty years, Burrows concludes that "the old settlers were a much more social and liberal community than the population of the present day."[10]

They were also more helpful to each other. One of his examples of generosity has to do with James Glaspell, Susan's great grandfather, whom Burrows calls "the progenitor of the Glaspell family . . . an excellent man; one of the salt of the earth—a man in whom there was no guile." Glaspell lived at the time below the Davenport bluffs, and Burrows tells that when he returned briefly to Kentucky, Mr. Glaspell asked if he could get money owed to him for some sales. Burrows reports that the money he collected allowed him to return "with the largest and best selected stock of goods in Davenport," and begin one of the most successful businesses in the community. Glaspell refused to take interest for the loan "considering that I was doing him a favor."[11] Almost a hundred years later, Susan, refusing interest on a loan, would repeat the act. James, too, initially prospered in his new home. He soon purchased a large tract of land on the scenic bluffs and a portion below for farming. The size of the property is unclear; one account indicates that at his death he held 120 acres, but it originally may have been much larger. The location was in the western part of Davenport, near the end of present-day Harrison Street, on what was known as Telegraph Road, because it was the first spot where the telegraph crossed the Mississippi River. The name Glaspell (spelled Glasspell) still appears on the map given out by the Davenport Chamber of Commerce, indicating a street in front of Fejervary Park.

Since the family home was outside the town limits at the time, roaming Indians would stop by asking for food. One family legend tells of a certain young Indian visiting on Thanksgiving Day, who wanted to buy one of James's daughters and made an offer of a fine collection of furs. When he saw that James was not interested, he upped the bid; "the final offer was said to have been the furs, plus two squaws, a papoose, and a fine Indian pony," Susan recorded.[12] Another family story tells of James's going to his smokehouse for a ham at the same time Indians came for food. That night, he discovered that someone had emptied the smokehouse of all the contents. The Glaspells were not certain if the Indians had taken the hams, but evidently the event was serious enough to be written down in the family Bible. Susan varies the story somewhat in *Inheritors*, stressing cooperation and reciprocity. Grandmother Morton tells of a young Indian who appears at the farm one day, watching her from a bush. She decides to offer him some cookies, and the next day he returns with a fish to trade. In an autobiographical sketch she wrote in 1942, Susan sums up such encounters, "Men of good will on both sides failed to stand off the Blackhawk wars."[13]

One of the first activities of the Glaspells when they arrived in Davenport was to join the First Christian Church, organized a month earlier by settlers from the Cincinnati area. James became an elder, and the Glaspell family continued their affiliation during the next two generations. It was there that Susan worshipped, sitting between her grandmother and mother. A 1904 article in a local newspaper describes a typical service in which sermons sometimes ranged from forty-five minutes to twice that long, with people "seldom growing tired of listening."[14] Parishioners were also in the habit of carrying copies of the New Testament and reading it at leisure moments in order to meditate upon the lessons while at work. It was such religious fundamentalism that Susan in later years would throw off, feeling the pressure of its practices.

A year after Iowa became a state, James Glaspell died, and Silas, his eldest son, received forty acres on which he established a fruit farm. It was there that he took his bride, Susan Ricker, in 1841, immediately after their marriage, and it was there that they resided until his death forty-one years later. The farm was known for its produce and Silas for his experimentation with new varieties of fruit. Susan would use the image of the farmer who develops new strains of corn and the biologist who experiments with new types of plant life in *Inheritors* and *The Verge*, perhaps remembering stories of her grandfather and her own childhood visits to the Glaspell farm. In *Inheritors* the homestead stands in contrast to the encroaching town and its changing mores. This conflict was also taken from personal history. Whereas the fruit farm in its first years was like many in the area, except larger, forty years later it had become anachronistic in Davenport's rapidly expanding economy.

This economic boom was fueled by the second wave of immigrants who began arriving in the late 1840s as a result of the upheavals in Europe. On a map the town of Davenport, situated on the banks of a great river, must have reminded many immigrants of their native cities situated on the Danube, the Rhine, and the Liffey and seemed like a congenial place to settle. It was this immigrant population that provided Davenport with the flavor Floyd Dell noted when he arrived in 1903. Unlike Rock Island or Moline, Illinois, the other tri-cities, Davenport seemed to him "golden," with "the bravado of an old Mississippi river port and the liberal 'cosmopolitan' atmosphere"[15] developed "because it was so largely German and Jewish, with an 1848 European revolutionary foundation and a liberal and Socialist superstructure" and with "some native American mysticism in the picture."[16] Typical of the settlers from Schleswig-Holstein were the Fickes who arrived in 1851, husband, wife, eight children, and the wife's piano. Thirty-three years later Arthur Davison Ficke would be born into one of the wealthiest families in the city and become, a poet, critic, and international expert on Japanese art—another writer springing from the rich Davenport soil.[17] When the Fickes arrived, Davenport already had four theaters, two of them exclusively for German-speaking audiences.

In Lahrman's Hall, between imposing busts of Schiller and Goethe, audiences in 1856 could hear a variety of concerts and see plays, some originating in New York and stopping in Davenport en route to Chicago, or vice versa. In 1867 the Burtis Opera House opened, providing an even more elaborate setting for legitimate theatre and opera. With its 1,434-seat auditorium and forty-three-foot ceilings, it was considered one of the three finest opera houses in the United States.[18]

By the time of Susan's birth, the cultural life and ethnic mix were even more diversified. Along with Catholic, Protestant, and Unitarian groups of German speakers, came a sizable group of German and Austrian Jews. Facing little of the anti-Semitism that would mark their entrance into other communities, they became part of the cultural mix that Floyd Dell noted. Jewish peddlers were a familiar sight on the streets, and particularly Rabbi William Fineshriber, a friend of Glaspell, Cook, Dell, and Ficke, later became part of the intellectual elite.[19] The revolutions of 1848 in Hungary brought Davenport another wave of immigrants, including Nicholas Féjerváry, a lawyer from Budapest, whose liberal activities had forced him from his homeland. He and his family came to Davenport in May 1853 buying a large tract of early settlement land adjoining the original Glaspell homestead on Telegraph Hill. On his death this land was willed to the city and became known as Fejervary Park, in which the family house still stands.[20] In *Inheritors* Glaspell honors him directly (omitting one *r* in his name). It is Féjerváry whom Silas Morton credits with bringing European culture to him and the Iowa farmers. Irish settlers also immigrated to Davenport in this period, including the family of Susan Glaspell's mother, Alice Keating, who arrived in 1854. By 1858, about 12 percent of the town was Irish, a population that was well represented in elected positions and on the city council.[21] Each of the ethnic groups set up life in its own districts, which remained clearly demarcated through much of Glaspell's early years. Even today some Davenporters still use ethnic designations to describe the sections of the downtown area along the Mississippi.

These different waves of settlers caused Davenport and the entire Blackhawk purchase to grow with amazing speed. Rapid change, however, was not universally applauded or desired. It soon gave rise to a class-based society in the second generation, in which farmers like Silas Glaspell were no longer as relevant to the society as business people and developers and in which the sense of land held in trust from the Indians was a rapidly fading concept. Such changes were noted in one of the first travel accounts of the area, Margaret Fuller's *Summer on the Lakes in 1843*. Fuller's eye is sensible to the alterations white settlers had already wrought in the years since settlement began. She writes, "Their progress is Gothic not Roman, and this mode of cultivation will, in the course of twenty or ten years, obliterate the natural expression of the country."[22] As in so many other areas, Margaret Fuller proved prophetic.[23]

While many old-timers had changed with the times, building thriving businesses and moving from sod and wood houses to large imposing mansions situated on the bluffs overlooking the Mississippi, the Glaspell fortunes diminished in subsequent generations. From owning large tracks of land in western Davenport, Susan's family, by her birth in 1876, was reduced to living in a rented house in an area of poor dwellings in "the flats," near the river, which often flooded its banks. These changes in her family's finances and prestige in the community created in Susan contradictory feelings about wealth and status, and the schisms appear when she discusses her youth or that of her protagonists. On the one hand, she is fiercely proud of her ancestors and their pioneering. Theirs are the primary stories of her childhood, which remain potent inspirations throughout her life. In fact, the decline of her family seems to have heightened their mystique and allowed her to interpret their acts as heroic affronts to wealth and position. In *The Road to the Temple*, her biograhy of her husband George Cram Cook, Glaspell writes, "Iowa went in fifteen years from settlement to statehood, and in about that time from primitive democracy to a class-conscious society with land speculator, banker, legislator at the top and the American farmer at the bottom."[24] Among those farmers were her grandparents.

At the same time there are notes of shame and resentment about her family's fallen state that run through *The Road to the Temple* and her other writing, particularly when Susan comments on the class differences that made her an outsider in the very community her ancestors first settled. These sentiments are expressed forcefully in *Fugitive's Return*, one of her most autobiographical novels, written in the late 1920s. In it, Susan describes Irma Lee's embarrassment that her family, who had owned considerable land, had lost it and now lived on a farm out of town, "which would seem desirable, but in this town it was not desired."[25] She wants to be friends with the girls from wealthier families but is painfully aware that her family's station precludes such intimacy. She does not dress the way they do, and she cannot offer them the foods they are used to receiving in each other's homes. There is no indoor plumbing, and when her classmates come to visit she is ashamed to tell them that they must go "outside." Irma's family life is similar to the Glaspells' position at the time of Susan's birth. She does not use a fictive surrogate in *The Road to the Temple* when she discusses Cook's wealth, and she clearly expresses her youthful feelings of inferiority because of her family's diminished status in the community. Writing at one point of the pride and confidence displayed by the young Jig, who, when teased by the boys in town for still wearing knickers, retorted that they were "artistic," Glaspell comments: "My own grandfather remained humbly on his fruit-farm—sheltered by no mansard roof, and had my clothes been jeered at on the street, my feelings would have been hurt."[26] A few pages later she returns to the same theme: "But George Cram Cook grew up in a town that had a Cook Memorial Library, the Cook Home, and a Cook Memorial Church. I am constrained to say again—there having been no Glaspell Home for the Friendless—these things are relevant."[27]

How relevant is a question that Glaspell would continue to explore in her life and her writing.

Families in Fact and Fiction

2

Yet of all the two hundred and fifty-five matings necessary in these nine generations, if a single one had not taken place, it would not be I who would be here.
—George Cram Cook, quoted in *The Road to the Temple*

Unlike her husband, Susan never formally traced her family's lineage, but its history had a great impact on her. If the first generation provided a reified version of pioneer life, the next generation deconstructed the tale. While her grandfather Silas may have been a fine horticulturist, he was not a good businessman. At his death, little remained of the original family tract, and it was finally disposed of in 1882, when his widow Susan came to live with her younger son Elmer and his family, including six-year-old Susan. In the Glaspell line the men were less physically robust than the women and died sooner. In the case of Silas and Elmer, they also showed signs of mental as well as physical breakdown years before their death. Although depression at the time was deemed a "female ailment"—newspapers running numerous advertisements for remedies to "cure the ladies of their disposition"—it was the Glaspell men who suffered from a mental state far more debilitating than such euphemisms imply. Silas's obituary indicates that after years of "nervous attacks" he was "glad to go, and so he died because he was literally worn out."[1] Elmer Glaspell, Susan's father, was even less of a businessman than his father and seemed less mentally able to withstand the stresses he encountered. He worked at a number of trades—farmer, teamster, contractor, and hay and straw wholesaler—but for the last six years of his life he, too, would be an invalid, after suffering a "severe mental breakdown."[2] Susan seems to have had her father in mind when she describes Irma Lee's father in *Fugitive's Return*, a man who worked constantly but never seemed to have any success: when he did get a job as a contractor, he would underbid it and lose money; when he finished the work, someone would find something wrong with the construction, and it would be rejected. Rather than mental collapse, it is a fire that incapacitates Mr. Lee. Even given fictional license, the sense of frustration and lost opportunities Susan describes could well have come from her early family life. The same feelings of failure would color the lives of the two men she loved in later years: Jig Cook and Norman Matson.

While Silas and his son Elmer were physically and mentally unsuited for the demands of life in the societies in which they found themselves, Susan Glaspell, the writer's grandmother and namesake, loomed larger than life. She was a woman of enormous energy and health, who became one model for the powerful women in her granddaughter's writing, a spinner of a mythology of pioneering that these works retell. A niece writing to Mrs. Glaspell in the 1890s observed, "you seem as young at heart as ever to me."[3] Elmer agreed with this assessment. When his family was away and he stayed with his mother, he informed his wife: "I never had any idea how strong cheerful and healthy mother is. . . . I wish you and I had as much life and health as she has."[4] This abiding vitality remained until a day or two before Mrs. Glaspell died, at the age of eighty-nine, of what the obituary listed as "natural causes."[5]

Although it was the Glaspell side of the family that Susan mentioned most often in the biographical essays she provided in later years, the woman who exerted the greatest influence on her, after her grandmother Glaspell, was her own mother, Alice Keating Glaspell. The Keatings, unlike the Glaspells, left no family histories tracing their antecedents. Of her mother's people, the only thing Susan told interviewers was that they came from Dublin. When a critic noted that in one of her books she displayed a clear insight into the Irish, Susan wrote to her mother, pleased to share the appraisal. She often liked to say that she was "one small embodiment of the English Irish question"[6] but that the battle had little place in her Iowa home, since there were more pressing things to engage the family. Alice Feeney Keating was just barely born in America, arriving in 1849 only a few weeks after her parents landed. Five years later the family moved to Davenport. The city directory, begun the same year, lists several Keatings—the men as masons, laborers, harness makers, the women as laundresses and seamstress—though none reside at the residence that Alice would later share with her mother and at least two sisters, Ellen and Lizzie. The name Alice Keating appears in a separate listing twice: in 1860, when she was eleven, as a servant, and in 1873, a year before her marriage to Elmer, when she is identified as a teacher. After 1874 she is listed, as was the custom, under the general heading of her husband.

Alice's mother, Susan's maternal grandmother, must have been a formidable person. Her letters to Alice indicate her considerable facility with language, despite grammatical errors. They also testify to the close bond between mother and daughter and the pressure put on the young woman to have a career and "improve yourself" as Mrs. Keating continually reminds Alice. These admonitions were usually followed by vivid descriptions of how much Mrs. Keating has suffered, both financially and emotionally, by sending her daughter away to school in order that she will get "a proper education" and become a teacher, and complaints about being alone, despite the presence of her other two daughters. No mention is made of a Mr. Keating. When Alice and Elmer married, the wedding announcement on the front page of the *Davenport Democrat* describes the ceremony as taking place at the home of the bride's mother. Whether she was a widow or divorced, it is clear that Mrs. Keating raised her daughters alone and was particularly close to Alice, whom she repeatedly prompted to succeed for them both—a theme that Alice Glaspell would repeat in her own correspondence with her daughter. "To know you are well is all I live for,"[7] Mrs. Keating writes in one letter, revealing a dependency on her daughter that would also be repeated in the relationship between Alice and Susan. Besides self-improvement and motherly self-sacrifice, three other topics fill Mrs. Keating's letters: her daughter's health, future teaching position, and beau, Elmer. She continually chides Alice to conserve her small reserve of strength if she wants to advance in her work. "If you can improve as fast and well as you can I hope there is a bright picture before you."[8] Concerning Elmer, rather than push the match, she does her best to discourage it at every turn, reminding her daughter that teaching is prohibited for married women. She also slips in hints that Elmer may be unreliable and seeing other women in her absence. From these letters, it is clear that Mrs. Keating saw marriage as a dead end for her frail, talented daughter and teaching as a more promising future, certainly not a commonly held notion in Davenport nor in the country at large in the 1880s. Alice would also encourage and actively abet Susan in pursuing a career, repeatedly mentioning work but never marriage in their correspondence.

In contrast to the letters of mother and daughter—voluble if awkward—Elmer's letters to Alice are testaments to the difficulty he had in expressing himself. One begins: "It's fearful hot today and writing is warm work so you must excuse writing please." He tries to indicate his devotion to her but is distracted, fearing a member of his family might come in and find him "writing such a note." The letter is signed "your love Elmer S. Glaspell."[9] Elmer retained the formal signature in letters to Alice, even after they were married, only preceding it by "your husband." Yet despite such epistolary reticence, after a two-year courtship he was able to convince Alice to give up her teaching. They married in February 1874. She was twenty-five, he thirty-six, both considerably older than couples marrying at that time. Because of their ages, they immediately began a family: Charles (known as Ray) born in 1875, Susan in 1876, and Frank in 1879.

The actual date of Susan Glaspell's birth has been in dispute. At the point in her career when she began giving interviews and was asked to write biographical essays, she followed the pattern of women she knew in Greenwich Village including Louise Bryant, Agnes Boulton, Emma Goldman, Georgia O'Keeffe, and Mary Heaton Vorse and subtracted several years from her age. Therefore, all her official biographies up to recently have listed her birth date as July 1, 1882. "Women do sometimes have to lie about their age," she explained when she presented her goddaughter Susan Marie Meyer a silver mug at birth but did not date it.[10] In the matter of ageing as in so many other areas of life, Susan was aware of the societal pressures on women. Although her birth certificate has been lost, there are at least three sources indicating that 1876 is the correct year. First, the Scott County census of 1880 lists a four-year-old Susie, a five-year-old Charles, and a one-year-old Frank living with their parents, Elmer and Alice Keating Glaspell, at 502 Cedar Street, Davenport. Second, her college records, when she entered Drake University in Des Moines in September 1897, indicate her age as twenty-one. Finally, the most reliable evidence available is found in the holograph diary of her great-aunt Lydia Ricker, who lived nearby, saw the Glaspells regularly, and kept a daily list of family activities from January 1, 1882, until her death in July 1888. "Ray sick, Susie said," appears on April 1, 1882. Here Lydia writes "Susie," the name the family used to differentiate the granddaughter from her paternal grandmother of the same name. On April 8, 1882, Lydia reports, "Susan made Susie a bonnet"; in August, "Alice and Susie went with me to the church meeting." On the supposed date of birth, July 1, 1882, Lydia makes only this short note: "Susan quite sick. Maria [her sister] and I worked all forenoon, men came again to settle Mr. Glaspell's affairs," referring to the death of Silas.[11]

To the interviewers who would query her about her early years, Susan invariably replied that her childhood was a happy one and provided many memories. The most vivid concerned the Mississippi flowing beside Davenport. One evening at a party in New York, when a woman challenged her story that the river would often freeze, making it possible to sled across it, Susan reacted with uncharacteristic vehemence. In a note about the exchange, she writes, "But why wouldn't I have feeling about it? Those are the sparkling memories of my youth . . . why I had skated miles down the Mississippi. You remember the freedom—free as a bird—your blood running swift and your self all fluid and sparkling. . . . The Mississippi was as *I* knew it—anyway it was to me."[12] Judging from the entries in her aunt Lydia's diary, Susan's other activities as a child were dominated by Sunday family dinners, usually prepared by Lydia and her sister; visits to neighbors, accompanied by her grandmother, aunts, and mother; picnics in summer—and church. Given Lydia's own bent, it is not surprising that the diary gives the greatest attention to activities related to religion. Alice also had a strict religious upbringing that carried over to her adult life. Among Susan's books at her death was a copy of her mother's Bible, inscribed to Alice "as a reward for committing to memory the Book of Matthew."[13] Besides Sunday services, there were weekly prayer meetings, lectures by visiting missionaries, and the Ladies Lend-a-Hand Club, a social service organization that Alice Glaspell attended until her death. Alice always took her children to church, but Elmer would manage to arrive for Sunday lunch at his aunt's home or his mother's after the women and children had returned. He was attentive to the family, but not to his "religious duties," as Lydia put it. Susan's notes for a biographical sketch indicate that while her father was often dogmatic in his beliefs, he was also something of an iconoclast in his practice, less concerned with communal activities than with charting his own particular course even when it came to prayer. "He prayed and he swore"; he also was "just crazy about racehorses," she wrote.[14]

Besides religion, three other themes recur in Lydia's diary: Alice's precarious health, her poor housekeeping skills, and Elmer's precarious financial situation. There are repeated references to Alice's unspecified illnesses and her inability to cope with the demands of home and family. Often Lydia and her sister Susan helped with the house and chores and invited the family for dinner so that Alice need not cook. Their concern was shared by other family members. A letter Mrs. Susan Glaspell received from her nephew dated January 6, 1881, begins: "I am sorry Elmer's family have so much trouble. Oh that they may cast their care on Jesus: He alone can make the dark days bright."[15] The particular nature of the "trouble" is not mentioned, but it seems to have concerned Alice's health. At one point Alice left home, taking Susan and Frank and leaving Ray with Elmer. "I am very sorry you are not feeling any better try and keep up your spirits as best your poor health will permit you," Elmer wrote to her. "I am sure everybody will welcome you back joyfully and that your health and spirits will improve when you are in your own home and with all of your children with you again. For we will try to make it as pleasant for each other as possible."[16] Not strong before marriage, Alice must have suffered physically from the burden of having three children in four years, particularly when the family lived in cramped conditions and there was no money to provide for help. They were only able to purchase a home in a more affluent section of town, on the bluffs, when Mrs. Glaspell came to live with them and provided the money. Alice may have had second thoughts about giving up her teaching career to marry. Elmer's letter seems to suggest that in addition to physical ailments, she was suffering from some form of depression. By the time Lydia Ricker's diary ends, however, most references to Alice's ailments or to the family's problems have disappeared. In her later years Alice Glaspell's health was robust, so much so that during her last illness in the late 1920s, which resembled Alzheimer's, Susan comments on how strange it is to see her otherwise healthy mother so feeble. Yet in Susan's impressionable early years, her mother's poor health, housekeeping struggles, and low "spirits" must have had an impact on her.

Susan would repeat the same pattern of health problems in her own first years of marriage to Jig and at the beginning of her relationship with Norman Matson. Although her illness, like her mother's, was never clearly diagnosed, Susan, and those who knew her between 1914 and 1918 in Provincetown, spoke of "heart problems," which came and went. So feeble was she in 1914 that she found it difficult to walk up the steep stairs in their home, and Jig built an elevator to transport her. However, four years later, her health, like her mother's, revived, and she was able to make periodic treks over the Provincetown dunes to the coastline fronting the Atlantic. Even for a healthy woman, that walk is not easy; for someone with "heart problems," it would have been a great strain, unless the problems were temporary, or psychological, as may seem to have been the case for Alice and, perhaps, for her daughter. In his unpublished autobiographical novel, Matson also refers to the same problem early in his relationship with Susan that afflicted her surrogate Ruth: "It was dreary in those late afternoons until Ruth was beside him, walking with a strong and happy stride (the heart cured, or forgotten)."[17]

If Susan inherited her mother's frail constitution in early marriage, she also inherited her mother's and grandmother's dreams of a career for a woman. Mrs. Keating had encouraged Alice, and Alice, in turn, supported her daughter's ambition, becoming the greatest champion of her writing. She seemed determined that Susan be given the opportunities she did not have to fulfill herself through work. When Susan's first novel, *The Glory of the Conquered*, appeared in 1908, she wrote to her mother thanking her for this unwavering support: "I never could have done it without you—I know that. You have always been wonderfully good to me about my work, made every sacrifice that I might have opportunity for working, and have always sympathized and helped as no one but you could."[18] Alice continued steadfastly to devote herself to Susan's career, as her mother had to her own aborted one. Her obituary notes: "She is credited by a circle of intimate friends with the nursing of her daughter's talents through the years of her adolescence and is regarded as a source of great encouragement in later years."[19]

Susan was the middle child, the only girl sandwiched between two boys, and her education might have been considered less important than that of her brothers had her mother been less determined to foster her daughter's talent. School records indicate that of the three Glaspell children, Susan was by far the most gifted and the only one who graduated high school. She opted for Latin, the most rigorous study track, which required courses in Roman history, classical rhetoric and literature, geometry, physical geography, and physics. Registered in 1890 as Susie Glaspell, she compiled only an average record her first year; however, in the next three years she excelled, receiving E+ in literature in her final year, only one of three in her class to receive such a grade in any subject.[20] Of the fifty-three graduates in the Davenport High School class of 1894, she was one of six who gave a commencement address; her subject was "Songs that Live." By comparison her brothers did not do well. Ray, who failed all his subjects in 1890, dropped out the next year. Frank did satisfactory work in the first year of the commercial track, but he did not return for a second year. By 1905 both held jobs at the Rock Island Arsenal.

While crediting her mother as her chief support, Susan had far less to say in public about her father. She seems to have affixed to Elmer some of those qualities his mother exhibited: tenacity, dreams, and good-natured acceptance of situations. "My father was a rugged man who had imagination. He worked very hard but it rested him to look ahead and dream of what one day might be," she wrote about him. Elmer would sometimes lease tracts of land and plant hay and grain for shipment to Chicago; and, as one of her most vivid memories of youth, Susan describes traveling to northern Iowa or South Dakota to visit him when he was working. "Sometimes we would stay at a raw little hotel in a town and other times were in tents on the land. The people I knew through that experience have remained very real to me. Their hard work was livened by a dry sly humor. There were the mean and the stubborn and the cranky too, but for the most part they took life as it was for them very good-humoredly; simple and good—very American."[21]

This description seems to apply to Elmer, at least as his daughter saw him, easy going and hardworking—a contrast to her ambitious, thwarted mother. One of his passions was the airplane, "when a few people were tinkering with it and most people were laughing themselves sick." This obsession Susan later used in an unpublished play, "Wings [Over Obadiah]."[22] In it she shows admiration for the "queer" man who dares to dream what others ridicule. In her life and that of her protagonists, the word *queer* would be a mark of respect. An interest that bound father and daughter was a love for animals. In one letter, written from Provincetown in 1915, Susan commiserates with Elmer on the death of the family dog, Patsey: "I do not suppose anyone but ourselves could understand just what Patsey means to us all, how much—how completely—he was one of us, so that losing him is indeed losing one of us."[23] Her tendency to rescue stray animals, a trait she seems to have inherited from her father, extended to people as well. A 1932 article printed in the *Davenport Democrat* carries this brief anecdote: "Miss Glaspell's early connection with Davenport makes her literary achievement and herself the object of unusual interest to old friends in her home town, some of whom recall the precocious, pretty little girl with a penchant for bringing home the ragged and hungry and making such queer friends in odd place."[24] Susan's first published fiction, a Christmas tale entitled "Tom and Towser," written when she was just out of high school, tells the story of a stray dog and an orphaned boy, saved from freezing on a busy street corner when a young girl takes pity on them both and gives them shelter.[25]

When studying the fictive families in Glaspell's short stories, dramas, and novels, it is not surprising to find that grandparents are generally revered, as they were in her own life. They are usually mythic figures who represent an earlier, idyllic time, which the protagonists attempt to recover. More complex is her handling of parents. One of the most significant patterns in Susan Glaspell's writing is the absence of mothers. Male writers may efface or neutralize mothers, the better to demarcate their own maturity and independence. However, in the case of a woman writer who goes to such pains to create strong, independent female figures and who displays such sensitivity to relationships between women characters, the absence of mothers is striking and perplexing. In Glaspell's thirteen produced plays, only three mothers appear: Mrs. Root, a mouthpiece for conformity in the one-act comedy *Close the Book*, Claire Archer, who disowns her daughter in *The Verge*, and Eleanor in *The Comic Artist*, whose baby is never seen. While it is true that there are only three fathers in these dramas—in *Bernice*, *Inheritors*, and *Alison's House*—and that none show particular sensitivity to their daughters or their needs, they are depicted with care and love. It is in Glaspell's nine novels that the absence of mothers and the dominance of fathers is most pronounced. *Judd Rankin's Daughter* and *The Morning Is Near Us* describe a daughter's attempt to come to terms with the father or the father figure she loves but cannot reach. In *Morning*, it is the specter of the absent mother that precludes this bonding; in *Judd Rankin*, the mother's presence is so irrelevant to the daughter that, after a few cursory references to her, she disappears entirely from the novel, her death not even noted by her otherwise sensitive daughter, who in all other aspects of her life is acutely attuned to interpersonal relationships. As the book's title clearly indicates, she is "Judd Rankin's daughter." Usually, the female protagonist does not even mention her mother; neither does the narrator. Glaspell's persona is raised by an aunt and father in *Norma Ashe* and by male figures in *The Visioning*, the novel that Glaspell dedicated to her own mother. When mothers do appear, they tend to be women of conformity, mouthing the values of the society, like the mother in *Ambrose Holt and Family*, a novel in which a father-in-law and mother-in-law become the surrogate parents of the female protagonist.

The most detailed analyses of mother/daughter relations are found in *Fugitive's Return* and *Brook Evans*. In *Fugitive's Return*, Irma resents her mother's smothering need for her, just as she resents the family's poverty. Somehow conflating the two conditions, Irma often focuses on her mother's inability to cope with domestic chores, like Alice Glaspell, and accuses her of being "not a good enough housekeeper to contend with difficulties."[26] When Irma matures, her infrequent visits home are difficult for the mother who so clearly adores her:

> Each month her mother longed for that time when Irma would
> come home. She counted the days, the hours. . . . But when her

daughter came, the excitement, the added strain of trying to have things nice for Irma, was too much, so that it would be to her father Irma would go, as for refuge, for quiet visits.

She saw that this was cruel, and she was miserable that some difficulty in expression, some lack of power kept her from putting her arms around her mother, saying: "Mother, I know! I'm sorry. Don't *try* so hard." Mother's whole life had gone into the trying, until she did not have left in her that which could have formed into understanding.

"Soon I can help more," would be the most Irma could say.

"Oh I don't want you to!" her mother would cry. "I don't want it to ruin *your* life." And Irma knew this was her greatest fear, her torment, that the daughter she idolized, for whom she would have worked to the death, might be sucked into a life from which she could not escape.[27]

The emotions that Irma displays are complex and often contradictory: she understands her mother's predicament, loves her, pities her, but resents her mother's disparagement of her father and her weakness and inability to cope with, or to conquer, what life has given her. These descriptions may well have sprung from Susan's own ambivalent feelings about her mother, who so tenaciously lived through her, and may explain her stronger tie with her father, who asked less and accepted her, no matter what her achievements. Her admiration of men with great imagination and failed promise must also have harkened back to him.

An even more powerful depiction of thwarted mothers whom their daughters cannot embrace, and fathers, shown to be weak but loved because of their vulnerability, is found in *Brook Evans*. In an early scene, Naomi Kellogg, a pregnant young woman, whose lover has been killed, turns to her father for understanding, begging him not to force her to marry a much older man who is willing to claim the child as his. "Her mother," she thinks, "was loving about many things, but she had no courage when it came to what people would say."[28] Naomi feels a closer bond to her father and tries to explain to him the great love she has felt for the boy who has died. The scene takes place in the barn, Glaspell introducing a dog, named Patsey, that keeps licking the hands of father and daughter. Near the end of the novel, Brook Evans—the child on whom Naomi has lavished all the love she could not give to the husband whom she had been forced to marry—thinks back on her own betrayal of her mother. Like Irma, Brook describes the responsibility that unconditional love demands, particularly when it comes from a mother who lives so completely through her daughter: "Did she feel herself surrounded with love from too lonely an intensity, and was that why she liked the easier give-and-take with her father and other people?" Brook concludes that "Girls are different now," but still wonders, "Were there daughters now who were at ease with their mothers?"[29]

For Susan Glaspell—judging from her writing—the answer was no. Too many thwarted dreams seem to have stood between Alice and her daughter, making the relationship tense. Also, Alice hewed closely to strict religious practices and midwestern models of social behavior, which became anathema to Susan, whose own lifestyle extended far beyond anything her mother could have imagined. Yet, like fellow-Davenporter Jig, Susan found it difficult to break completely with her parents. Over the years she resolved the problem by compartmentalizing her life. She continued to sign her letters "Susie," shared her professional successes with her family, but told them only those details of her personal life about which she thought they would approve. In her writing she would continually focus on the schism between those who believed in conformity and those who tried to escape it, those inside the circle and those on the verge struggling to get out. Central to her work is the idea that if women are to progress and find their voices, they must finally overcome or ignore those loving, but constricted, figures who stand most threateningly in their way: their mothers. It was easier for Susan to salvage fathers in her work, since they are usually described as benign and nonthreatening. Virginia Woolf could write that the death of her father Leslie Stephen allowed her, finally, to live. Susan did not have a successful, authoritarian patriarch who overshadowed and silenced his daughter; her father's shadow did not blot out her own. Her mother, on the other hand, was a constant reminder of how the best of women can be cowed by circumstances, feel weary and defeated, in lives that did not nourish or stimulate them. In her writing, it was the image of the stereotyped mother, wife, and care-giver against which Susan Glaspell struggled and which she effaced from the script of her fictive daughters' lives.

Society Girls

3

Oh, these Society girls. Primping their way through life. If they only knew how shallow their efforts, how limiting their vision.
—Susie Glaspell, Society Editor, *Weekly Outlook*

In 1891 the Glaspell family moved into the house that was to remain their home throughout Susan's life, and which still stands today, at 317 East 12th Street, on the bluffs of Davenport, a few blocks from the crest. It was a white-wood, two-story, five-room house, set back from the street. The front sitting room was a good size and was heated by a large fireplace; behind it was a combination dining room and kitchen. A steep flight of stairs led to three bedrooms, the back one Susan would later turn into her study, since it afforded a glimpse of the Mississippi. The immediate neighborhood was middle-class, but within walking distance were the large mansions of the Fickes and Frenches, the leading families in town, who would also produce writers. In order for Susan to get to her high school, she would pass by these opulent Victorian homes, taking the same route her protagonist Irma Lee follows to school. As a protection against rejection, Irma immerses herself in the stories of her pioneer grandparents and imagines herself a queen still ruling "all the land between here and Scott Street."[1] Susan may have had many of the same feelings she attributes to Irma; but instead of masking her thoughts, she found an outlet to express them through her writing, positioning herself as the outside observer of Davenport society, able to satirize and expose the foibles of its lifestyle.

In 1894 Charles Eugene Banks, who had recently moved to Davenport from Clinton, Iowa, and would soon make a name for himself in Chicago as a journalist and novelist, started the short-lived *Davenport Morn-*

ing Republican, to which Susan, just out of high school, contributed, for $3.00 a week. Two years later he began another publication, the *Weekly Outlook*.[2] The paper, published every Saturday, was a blend of society events (the teas, dinner parties, weddings, and charitable affairs of the wealthy), commentary on local news, reviews of the latest performances at Burtis's Opera house and at the many small theatres and amateur dramatic clubs in the tri-cities, human-interest items, occasional fiction, and history of the city. On the masthead next to the names of Banks and his wife, Carrie Wyatt, appears that of their society editor: Susie Glaspell.

Susan's weekly column, under the heading "Social Life," appeared in the first issue on July 11, 1896, and continued through July 1897. "Column" is rather a misnomer for the odd, two-part structure. The first section was a series of paragraphs, sometimes joined to a central theme, but more often separate vignettes on a wide range of issues, similar in format to what the *New Yorker* would popularize in its "Talk of the Town." Sometimes these vignettes focused on contemporary issues such as the debate over euthanasia or the introduction of private kindergartens, the socialist agenda, or even the philosophy of Emerson. More often they described a specific concern of what Susan called Davenport's "upper ten": the rich, famous, and the would-be-so. The tone is usually sarcastic, Susan taking obvious joy in disclosing the silly customs she observes around her, positioning herself outside the circle of Davenport "high society," and lobbing some powerful volleys at the foibles and banalities of the members. If Irma Lee yearns for acceptance by the wealthy, Susie Glaspell in 1897 is generally dismissive of them, making clear that if she had such wealth she would certainly not spend it on the "flim flam" that she reports about in her weekly columns. Immediately following these general topics, however, she was called upon to report on what this same Davenport society actually busied itself with during the past week. A column about parties, where invitation lists were made out, "using the utmost caution in putting down only such as had the money and social position to reciprocate," is followed by a description of the Library Ball, where "all the society people of the three cities were in attendance and it was universally acknowledged one of the greatest social successes of the season."[3] A sarcastic description of how young women are expected to be "mechanical dolls" hanging on the conversation of rich, eligible bachelors leads into an engagement announcement of "yet another popular young society lady" to a man who "received the contract for the building of the City Hall."[4] That Susan was not fired for her parodies of the rich may be explained by the tendency of social leaders to skim through the first part of the column quickly on their way to the second, where their names appeared. In addition, in her parodies, Susan never referred to specific people but types.

Because of its dual mandate, "Social Life" may have been a strange column, but it was also surprisingly effective, considering the age of the writer and her inexperience. Glaspell maintains a strong, consistent voice and a good eye for the concrete details of setting and character that would later mark her fiction. Certainly, the readership would have been surprised to know that the writer, who in one essay describes herself as "a very commonplace old maid," "an old woman and maybe an . . . old foggy"[5] and in another speaks about a time "many years ago when I was young and went to school"[6] was actually under twenty; that her numerous references to social customs in Paris, New York, Washington, D.C., and Chicago were gleaned solely through reading the national papers and magazines; that her unending string of stories and anecdotes beginning, "I know a man who thinks . . ." or "I went to lunch this week with a girl who knows . . ." were mostly inventions, based either on her imagination or on her recent experiences as a young reporter.

Her favorite subject for satire is "the society girl." Addressing these young women in an informal, conspiratorial style, she inquires: "What think you of the fall styles? . . . Whether McKinley or Bryan be the next occupant of the White House and what the coming financial policy of the country will be are concerns altogether secondary in importance. And rightly is it so, too. For the color of money is not nearly so vital as the color of your gown and the size of the tariff dwindles into insignificance when compared with the size of the winter hat."[7] Sometimes to vary the format, she creates stories to make her point. In one issue, she introduces the country girl who comes to "big city" Davenport to "make the rounds." She follows her through a typical day of parties, gossip, and social conventions, which ends with "her first ball where she was overawed for the first two hours, bored for the third and conscience-smitten for the fourth." The next night the girl makes a hasty retreat home, where she goes to "a literary society and was the happiest girl the town contained."[8] Some of the women she describes are aware that they are playing roles. "I'm tired of pouring tea for dead men, I'm tired of dancing with dead men, of having dead men in our theater boxes and at our table," one moans.[9] In another, "a society girl with very pink cheeks and a big plumed hat" seriously attempts to ponder her situation: "I am like the flowers in the hot-house, a forced production. Two-thirds of me has been made to die out, and the other third abnormally developed."[10] The metaphor of a woman as a cultivated plant shaped by society is one Susan will return to in her most experimental play, *The Verge*, in which her central character is a botanist who attempts to cultivate her own growth.

In many of her columns, the advice is more practical than parodic. In one written around Easter, she suggests that while "taking invoice of your wardrobe so thoroughly, you might look over the stock in trade of your brain and heart a little." She does not ask for miracles, only small improvements, chiding young women to read more so that they can know more and become "intuitive, penetrating, discerning . . . and self-possessed." Those qualities Glaspell will later assign to her protagonists."[11] Often given to finger wagging, she readily admits that for women life is never easy, so their concern with personal beauty is not necessarily wrong. "Women have such a hard time getting along in the world anyway that if

I had the ordering of things every blessed one of them should be a ravishing beauty . . . because nine-tenths of the difficulties along the way are smoothed out for the woman with the pretty face."[12]

Although clearly the work of a young, inexperienced writer, these articles already show a facility with language and an ability to uncover those same characteristics of snobbish, small-town life that Sinclair Lewis would point out twenty years later in *Main Street* and *Babbitt*: pseudo-intellectuals, who read only the book reviews not the books; gossips, who make "evident all that is littlest and narrowest and meanest in society"; and those who take pride in their genealogy. "A true aristocrat looks little to the past and much to the future . . . what our fathers did yesterday reflects small credit on us. It is what we ourselves accomplish today that we are going to be marked by."[13] For someone like Susan, who had to remake her family through her own efforts and not through inherited fiat, the words are more than passing rhetoric; they are a prescription to follow. Pride in what a family stood for was one thing; pride in what they accumulated in material goods was something else.

Equality among people is an idea that sometimes emerges from the banter of her column. In one issue, she suggests that despite their material possessions, the wealthy and the poor may not be so very different, a fact they would recognize if people could only transcend the things that keep them apart. Anticipating a major theme in *Trifles*, she writes, "The melancholy thing of it all is, when you come to think seriously on this subject, how very slightly we know one another." She particularly denounces the snobbery that causes the working girl to be excluded by "high society," since "nobody is supposed to have a soul that works week days."[14] Susan, unlike most of the women her age in Davenport's middle and upper classes, did work, and her mind was more concerned with deadlines and paychecks than with dance cards and parties. Her sensitivity about being shunned because of her social class shows through when she writes, "Do not be too pleased with yourself. You are not superior in your individuality. It is only that fortune has favored you with worldly things. Your position gives you so many opportunities and you utilize almost none of them."[15] Her empathy goes to those who are "outside," a word she continually uses in her writing to signify both alienation from society and freedom from the restrictions it imposes: "Half of us don't have to sit back under the galleries and watch the other half fill up the reserved seats in the front row. The whole world is the birthright of everyone and no box parties are allowed."[16] Her later embracing of socialism must have been informed by these early experiences in class-conscious Davenport.

That she should use imagery connected to the theatre is not surprising, since part of her job on the *Weekly Outlook* was to cover plays. Although today it is hard to think of Davenport, Iowa, as a national center of cultural activity, in the late 1800s it had a reputation as a theatre town. In 1887 Sarah Bernhardt had made Davenport one of the stops in her American tour of the play *Fedora*. A summary article on the 1896 theatre season, written either by Banks, his wife, or Glaspell, lists thirty-nine plays given at the Burtis theatre alone, including *Hamlet*, *Cymbeline*, a variation of *The Merchant of Venice* entitled *Shylock*, *Rob Roy*, *Charlie's Aunt*, and *The Prisoner of Zenda*. All of these productions were by professional companies and included established actors such as Otis Skinner, Chauncey Alcott, Lillian Russell, and Thomas Keene. So numerous were the productions and the stars that one well-known actor whom Susan would meet twenty years later barely gets more than a passing reference: Mr. James O'Neil (spelled with only one *l*) in *The Count of Monte Cristo*.

Susan in her writing is able to show the shallowness of life for a "society doll," but is also aware that the alternatives are not clearly defined: "if you're going to give up society you've got to have something right at hand to substitute for it."[17] In one of her more serious columns, she presents a viable alternative to the Society Girl for her readers to consider. She calls her "the New Woman" or "the Bachelor Girl," a woman who has chosen not to marry, but can not be dismissed as the stereotyped "old maid," since she may be "twenty as well as forty."[18] She must have had herself in mind when she described this new type of woman: "First . . . you must be . . . clever; you need not be pretty, but you must be bright, vivacious, interesting. You are not expected to spend your life buried in an encyclopedia or a treatise on the Origin of Man, but . . . be able to talk with intelligence and wit on anything from the penal laws of Russia to the latest production in the farce comedy line. You must have sufficient resources within yourself not to be afflicted with *ennui* every time there is no man in sight, and when the man does come into view, you must stand ready to cope with him on his own grounds rather than docilely and demurely wait for him to fill your ear with pretty nothings."[19] The description illustrates that by this date Susan had already begun to work out for herself qualities she would later develop in her life and give to her female protagonists.

However, while Davenport's elitist ways might be easy to identify in print, they were not that easy to overcome for those born there, whether inside or outside the circle of power. In a June column she indicates some of the problems a bright young woman, like herself, faces when trying to plot an alternative lifestyle: "When you are twenty and graduating with high honors you are very strong and self-sufficient, your ideals tower miles above the earth and you believe implicitly that . . . you are going to rise quickly out of the ranks of mediocrity." However, what the unnamed "you" discovers is that "true intelligence consists in knowing how much you do not know."[20] By the summer of 1897, Susan had reached this point. In one of her last columns, she denies the claim that "the new women" who went to college were no longer women but merely "sexless exponents of higher education." She writes, "If I believed this it would make me most unhappy and I would feel compelled to start to-night on a holy pilgrimage to burn all the women's colleges in the land."[21] Instead she began a different kind of pilgrimage: not to burn colleges that admitted women, but to enroll in one, Drake University, in Des Moines, where she began to study in September, at the age of twenty-one. Although she was to return to Davenport throughout her life, she never again returned as the outsider placed there by circumstances or the attitudes of others; she became an outsider of her own making. At the end of July 1897 her name stopped appearing on the masthead of the *Weekly Outlook*; by November, the paper was writing about her in the social column: "Miss Susie Glaspell, formerly society editor of the *Weekly Outlook* wrote an essay on 'The American Girl,' which was highly complimented by the professors at Des Moines [*sic*] university."[22]

Delphic Days

4

She wanted to go to college because that would open out from what she had.

—Susan Glaspell, *Fidelity*

Des Moines, the capital of Iowa, is only 106 miles from Davenport, but for Susan the distance must have seemed much further, because her move took her out of a familiar environment and launched her into a world no longer circumscribed by the peccadilloes of Davenport society or the preoccupations of her own family. Distance may, in fact, have prompted her decision. It would have been more natural for her to select the University of Iowa, in Iowa City, closer to her home and less expensive, but instead she chose private Drake University, founded in 1881. She entered as a junior, waving two years because of her Latin certificate, and in two years more she received a bachelor of philosophy degree. She was an excellent student and took a rigorous program, including Greek, French grammar and literature, history, English literature, ethics, Biblical literature, psychology, and philosophy in her first year. For her to have gone away to college at all was an unusual step; to take such a curriculum was even more extraordinary. Most young women who wanted postsecondary education opted to remain in Davenport, where there were a number of institutions whose curriculum was directed toward turning out women prepared to take up their places as wives and mothers in society. Elizabeth McCullough Bray, in a series of articles on the literary life of Davenport, published in the *Davenport Democrat* in 1929, describes the rare woman who broke the mold and sought more academic pursuits, perhaps with Susan in mind: "This girl brought home a bachelor's degree. She was regarded somewhat askance, people wondered if it wasn't possible she was a little queer. For a time her health was said to be wrecked from over study, but she led an active life for many long years."[1]

Queer is exactly the word Susan, in her later writing, would have her arbiters of society use in disparagement to describe female protagonists who break with convention or have women proudly apply to themselves, when they wished to distinguish their lives and values from those they observed around them. *Inspirational* is the word used by a fellow class-mate, thirty years later, to describe Susan, "my first heroine in the flesh, a glamorous presence of poetry and romance who fired one's imagina-tion and made all glorious things seem possible. A flame in the life of the student body [which] affected us like heady old wine. . . . She had a rare faculty for beautiful friendship, and for making others feel that life was beautiful and big."[2]

Two of the activities that occupied Susan during her college years were writing and oratory. The center of literary activities on campus was the *Delphic.* To be elected editor of this journal was the highest honor that a student interested in literature could attain, and the yearly elections were fiercely contested political events. In 1899 two women ran: Susan Glaspell and Lucy "Lulu" Huffaker. Lucy, originally from Cleveland, was a tall, pretty, angular woman, whose hair had already begun to reveal the first wisps of premature gray that would become one of her most striking fea-tures. Like Susan, she abhorred frivolous coeds and was already dedicated to pursuing a career in the arts. Their friendship was immediate and sur-vived the *Delphic* election campaign, which Lucy won. Both had been the "queer" ones in their hometowns; now they found reinforcement in each other. Lucy would remain Susan's closest friend, and their lives dovetailed over the next fifty years.[3]

While she was a student, Susan contributed four pieces to the *Del-phic*—the first three short fictions and the last a memorial on the death of a fellow student. Compared to her *Weekly Outlook* writing, "His Lit-erary Training," about an aspiring writer, and "The Tragedy of Mind," concerning an aging professor, are stilted and show signs of a new writer trying too hard, most nouns preceded by two obligatory adjectives, with little concrete detail and awkward dialogue. However, "The Philosophy of War," published in the *Delphic* in October 1898, is more successful. In it she presents a narrator who argues that the Spanish-American War, pres-ently being fought, is less the "war for humanity" and "the golden chapter of American history" that newspapers were touting than a terrible waste of young lives. In this early story, Susan already reveals her distaste for jingoistic language and displays a pacifism that she maintained through World War I and expressed in her dramas and fiction. Interestingly, the story parallels the experiences of Jig Cook, who volunteered for the war and suggests that the two may have had contact at the time, as Cook indicates in his unpublished novel "The Pendulum," in which he describes being interviewed by a young reporter, who may have been Susan.

While her attitude toward war went against popular sentiment, her religious beliefs still bore the marks of her family's conservative influence. In the memorial for the daughter of the chancellor of Drake, she continually refers to the death of the young woman as the will of God, her classmate now warmed by God's smile, and given "reverently up to God."[4] It is one of the only times in her writing that Susan invokes a deity as such.[5] One event that may have influenced her shift away from traditional religion was a controversy at Drake near the time of her graduation. Dr. Morgan, a professor of biblical studies, was removed from his duties for advocating in class that the inspiration of the Bible could best be determined not by an a priori designation of its authority but by the observation of how it affected people; in other words, that the Bible was not so much an inspired but an inspiring book. The position was considered heretical by the administration; and in the ensuing controversy, the majority of students favored the professor's dismissal. Although there is no record of Susan's position, she had taken a course from him and might well have been among the small number of students who protested the ouster. Twelve years later, she would be at the center of another debate involving religious censorship, when the Davenport public library attempted to ban a book by an author who took a similar position. In *Inheritors* she would also portray an embattled professor asked to change his views or lose his position. His only defender is a young woman, Madeline Fejevary Morton, a student exactly the age of Susan when the Morgan controversy broke at Drake.

Susan certainly could have roused the student body to the professor's cause, since she had already distinguished herself on campus for her oratory skills, a foreshadowing of her considerable success as an actor in her own plays for the Provincetown Players. In her senior year, she won the right to represent Drake at the state debates, although she was later dismissed on a technicality. Her talk, printed on the front page of the *Delphic*, was entitled "Bismarck and European Politics." Her thesis was that one must evaluate a figure like Bismarck not by some arbitrary standard but by an analysis of the times and conditions under which he functioned. Such a relativistic and pragmatic reading of history may seem strange for one who later espoused idealism in the face of historical necessity, but it does indicate that, even at this young age, Susan already recognized a counter-thrust: the necessity of wielding power in order to coalesce a group in order to achieve a common goal. Jig Cook is far removed from Bismarck, but two attributes that Susan would cite in her biography of her husband are mentioned in the Bismarck essay: the ability to put self second to the furthering of a cause and the jettisoning of democracy if need be in order to achieve the goals of the group.

Susan's success at Drake is indicated by the frequency with which she participated in the graduation activities of the class of 1899: At commencement exercises, she presented the only short story; and at the official banquet the next evening, she was one of three students who delivered essays. The *Des Moines Daily News* printed a description of the ceremony, in which the university's founder and ex-governor of Iowa, Francis Marion Drake, presented the diplomas and the current president, John Lacey, exhorted the students to pay attention to "trifles" for "trifles make perfection, but perfection is no trifle." Accompanying the article were brief paragraphs about the twenty-three undergraduate students, identifying their future plans. Most of the male students indicate that they will go into the ministry, the women that they are considering teaching or "will be at home next year." Glaspell's reads: "Susie K. Glaspell has been a student at Drake since the fall of '97. In that short time she has been easily recognized as a leader in the social and intellectual life of the university. Miss Glaspell will pursue a course in literature at Chicago University.[6]

This may have been her long-term goal, but first she needed to make money. Therefore, the day after graduation, Susan began to work full-time for the *Des Moines Daily News*, where she had been a stringer throughout her college years. She had two assignments: writing a weekly column, this time under the byline "The NEWS Girl," and covering the state legislature and murder cases. That she was able to get a reporter's job is an indication of her writing skills even at this young age, since, as fellow Iowan Edna Ferber learned ten years later when she attempted to get work at the *Chicago Tribune*, most newspapers had a men-only sign in the newsroom. In all of America in 1900, there were only 2,000 women journalists, and few of those covered political news. In Susan's case her fellow reporters were helpful, and she soon found them sending leads her way.

For the most part her column is a variation on her *Weekly Outlook* work, and she may well have sold the idea to the larger Des Moines paper. This time the running persona is a "greenhorn" naïf, awkward but daring, who gets the assignments that no one else will take, such as interviewing a clairvoyant to discover who had committed a celebrated murder. The column also covers a number of current issues, ranging from what city folks think of farms—too much mud—to the advantages of eating in a cafeteria run by the YMCA where "every girl waits on herself . . . and all seemed to have a feeling of proprietorship."[7] When she turns to the social foibles of Des Moines, the essays are far more controlled than those she wrote two years earlier about Davenport's society; there is less chiding at the wealthy than tongue-in-cheek jabs at carefully delineated types. In one she describes a group of unflappable Des Moines Law School students, whose chief characteristic is their amazing ability to be unimpressed, even by their own ignorance. After accomplishing that feat, she concludes, "all others must be easy."[8] In another she describes covering the National Congress of Mothers, which held a six-day convention in the city. While she makes it clear that she does not mean to belittle all the participants, she has a fine time describing those who stay at the best hotels, change their outfits six times a day, and wear "diamond studded creations of satin" and whose experiences with mothering are limited, since their children are probably "turned over to nurses and kindergartens from the day of their birth and have only a speaking acquaintance with their fond mamas." Becoming serious, she argues that, "The Congress of Mothers is not strong enough at the present moment to carry frauds on its back. In fact the backbone of the Congress was one of the last of its organs to develop and is still in a formative condition." Her suggestion for them: "come off the perch, my friends, or you'll never in a thousand years revolutionize the world."[9]

The NEWS girl was not above making fun of herself, and she often describes outings in which she is caught in embarrassing or uncomfortable situations. In one column she describes being coerced to attend her first football game. She suffers through the first half, but finally is won over by the sport, admitting "there was more to it after all than getting in one big heap and rolling over each other."[10] An "outing" of another sort, and one of her best articles, concerns theatre. Under a double-column headline "Glimpse Behind the Scenes," she describes filling in for a missing woman who played a small part in a pageant depicting the charge up San Juan Hill in the recent Spanish-American War, complete with soldiers fighting and girls waving white handkerchiefs. In a lively narrative, she describes in great detail how she got the job and what it was like to be "behind the scenes," with live dynamite positioned to go off. However, after surviving the experience and her stage fright, she decides not to continue her acting career. "Undoubtedly this was my first and last of life behind the scenes. I was not sorry I was not coming back and yet I was not sorry I went," she concludes. "It had been an experience and we are all living for experiences." Besides, she notes, "I must not forget to tell you I had earned fifty cents."[11] The next time Susan Glaspell would act in front of an audience would be exactly sixteen years later, in the Provincetown living room of Neith Boyce and Hutchins Hapgood, in the play *Suppressed Desires* that she and Jig Cook had written; and while she would still be nervous, this time she would not be paid.

Her work on the *News* and, later, on the *Des Moines Capital* gave her discipline, since she was expected to produce material on deadline; and the training served her well in her later career. No matter where she was—in her second-floor study, either in Davenport or in Provincetown; in a shack in the woods in Truro on Cape Cod; or in a hut halfway up Mt. Parnassus in Greece—Susan was conditioned enough by her newspaper experiences to spend part of each morning writing, whether she felt like it or not. Newspaper work also provided her with a style and a voice. The succinctness of her later descriptions and the directness of her narratives owe much to the format she learned in these apprentice years. One has only to look at her 1927 biography *The Road to the Temple* to appreciate the way in which she captures in a few simple sentences the mood of a period or the measure of a person—as in her description of the flavor and rhythm of life in Greenwich Village in 1913, the year she first moved there:

> Every once in a while, in the Sunday paper, I read of Greenwich Village. It is a wicked place, it seems, and worse than wicked, it is silly. Just what Greenwich Village is now, I do not know. Through the years I knew it, it was a neighborhood where people were working, where you knew just which street to take for good talk when you wanted it, or could bolt your door and work all day long. You had credit at the little store on the corner, and the coal man too would hang it up if the check hadn't come. I never knew simpler, kinder or more real people than I have known in Greenwich Village. I like in memory the flavor of those days when one could turn down Greenwich Avenue to the office of the Masses, argue with Max or Floyd or Jack Reed; then after an encounter with some fanatic at the Liberal Club, or (better luck) tea with Henrietta Rodman, on to the Working Girls' Home (it's a saloon, not a charitable organization) or if the check had come, to the Brevoort.[12]

Used to writing for a mass medium, Susan had little trouble directing her first stories to the mass audience that bought the national, popular magazines in which her work was printed. Although she tells of other reporters getting "thick envelopes" with returned manuscripts, she was able, almost immediately, to place her stories and usually had more requests than she could meet. Reporting also allowed her to be a paid observer, and the many events she covered provided a rich store of material she could draw from when she finally quit her job and began to turn her newspaper experiences into fiction.[13]

The Genesis of *Trifles*

5

When I was a newspaper reporter out in Iowa, I was sent down-state to do a murder trial, and I never forgot going into the kitchen of a woman locked up in town. I had meant to do it as a short story, but the stage took it for its own.

—Susan Glaspell, *The Road to the Temple*

Besides writing humorous columns and covering the state legislature, Susan often reported on court cases, particularly sensational ones that involved sex, scandal, and murder—and there were many. The Iowa of 1900 may not have been more violent than it is today, but it certainly was no less so. Sandwiched between ubiquitous advertisements for "Female Nerve Cures" and romantic accounts of the courtships of Vanderbilts and Rockefellers were a whole range of lurid tales that would keep a contemporary tabloid busy and happy. But, of all the cases reported in the *News*, the one that stands out from all the rest, both for the extended length of its coverage and its vivid detail, is the Hossack murder case, in which a mother of nine children was accused of hatcheting her husband to death while he lay in bed asleep. Susan covered the case and it became the source for her masterpiece *Trifles* and its short story offshoot, "A Jury of Her Peers."[1]

The case at first glance seemed simple. Sometime after midnight on December 2, 1900, John Hossack, a well-to-do farmer, was stuck twice on the head with an ax, while he slept in bed. Margaret, his wife of thirty-three years—who claimed to be sleeping beside him—reported that a strange sound, "like two pieces of wood striking," wakened her. She jumped out of bed, went into the adjoining sitting room, saw a light shining on a wall, and heard the door to the front porch slowly closing. Only then did she hear her husband's groans. Assembling the five of her nine children who were still residing at home, she lit a lamp, reentered the bedroom, and discovered Hossack bleeding profusely, brain matter oozing from a five-inch gash, his head crushed. One of his sons claimed that the mortally injured man was still able to speak. When the boy said to him, "Well pa, you are badly hurt," Hossack replied, "No, I'm not hurt, but I'm not feeling well."[2]

It was assumed that prowlers committed the crime; but when a search of the farmhouse failed to reveal any missing items, a coroner's inquest was called. Its findings were inconclusive. However, after discovering the presumed murder weapon smeared with blood under the family corn crib and listening to reports and innuendos from neighbors, who hinted at a history of marital and family trouble, the sheriff arrested Mrs. Hossack, "as a matter of precaution,"[3] while the funeral was still in progress—or, as Susan more vividly reported later, "just as the sexton was throwing the last clods on the grave of her murdered husband."[4]

Employing the techniques of Gonzo journalism sixty years before Hunter Thompson, Susan filed twenty-six stories on the Hossack case, from the fifteen-line item on page three, dated December 3, 1900, that summarily described the murder, to the full-column story on page one, dated April 11, 1901, that reported the jury's decision at the trial. Most of these articles are indistinguishable from her unsigned "NEWS Girl" feature running at the time. They make ready use of hyperbole, invention, and supposition, all filtered through one of Susan's most common journalistic devices: a lively, often opinionated persona. Whether labeled "your correspondent," "a representative from the *News*," or "a member of the press," she is a constructed presence who invites the reader to share privileged information, intriguing rumor, and running assessment of the case and of the guilt or innocence of the accused. In her first extended coverage, under the headline, "Coroner's Jury Returns its Verdict this Morning—Mrs. Hossack Thought to be Crazy," Susan announces the imminent arrest of the woman, a fact "secretly revealed to your correspondent." She also provides the first of many rumors that become increasingly more prominent in her coverage, although never attributed to specific sources: "Friends of Mrs. Hossack are beginning to suggest that she is insane, and that she has been in this condition for a year and a half, under the constant surveillance of members of the family," and "the members of the Hossack family were not on pleasant relations with each other," information which comes as "a complete surprise, as Hossack was not supposed to have an enemy in the world." She concludes by citing the most damaging evidence used against the accused woman throughout her trial: Mrs. Hossack's claim that she lay asleep beside her husband and was not awakened while the murder was taking place.[5]

Susan continues to mix fact, rumor, and commentary with a superfluity of rousing language and imagery, opening her next report with the reminders that Mrs. Hossack has been arrested for the death of her husband "on charge of having beaten out his brains with an axe"; that the accused woman has employed the legal services of Mr. Henderson and state senator Berry; that when arrested she showed no emotion and absolutely declined to make any statement concerning her guilt or innocence; and that, while her family supported her, "the public sentiment is overwhelming against her." How Susan gleaned this information or arrived at these conclusions, she does not say. She does, however, provide her first description of the accused woman: "Though past 50 years of age, she is tall and powerful and looks like she would be dangerous if aroused to a point of hatred." She again repeats the rumors of domestic tensions and quotes a neighbor named Haines, a witness at the inquest, who implies that Mrs. Hossack had years before asked him to get her husband "out of the way."[6]

"Public sentiment is still very much against the prisoner," the December 8 news story begins, reiterating the claim that Mrs. Hossack wanted "to get rid of her husband" and had been willing to pay liberally for the services of anyone undertaking the task, a story "the public generally accepts" and will, therefore, "sympathize with the county attorney in his efforts to convict the woman." In an added development, Susan reports that Mrs. Hossack had left home a year before but had been persuaded to return "with the idea of securing a division of the property, but this division had never been made." Although the sheriff had refused all requests to see photographs of the murdered man, Susan announces proudly that "a representative of the *News* was accorded this privilege though it must be confessed there is little satisfaction in it."[7]

Waiving a preliminary hearing, Mrs. Hossack's attorneys decided to take the case directly to the grand jury, which bound her over for trial in April. In the interim, the defendant requested and was given bail. The story Susan files immediately prior to the release contains a new element. The reporter, who only days before had called Mrs. Hossack cold, calm, and menacing, now describes her as "worn and emaciated" as she was led from her cell, with "red and swollen eyelids indicating that she had been weeping." Since Mrs. Hossack was immediately released after this date and remained in her home until the trial, it is likely that what caused Susan to alter her description was her own visit to the Hossack farm, the event she uses as the basis for *Trifles*. From this point on in her reporting, her references to the accused woman become more benign, the "powerful" murderer becoming with each story older, frailer, and more maternal.

Susan made her visit to the farmhouse probably to gather material for the front-page, double-column feature that appeared on December 12, the most extensive coverage of the pretrial events. It began with the headline "Mrs. Hossack May Yet Be Proven Innocent," followed by the subheading "Tide Of Sentiment Turns Slightly In Her Favor—Notified Today That She Will Soon Be Released—First Photographs Bearing On the Tragedy."

The photographs turn out to be three simple pencil drawings: one of Mrs. Hossack, sitting in a rocking chair, her head bent down, her eyes closed; one of her dead husband with the two gashes to his head; and one of the ax, complete with four dots representing blood. Captions indicate that the first is "sketched from life" and the second "from flashlight photograph of the dead man" that "others tried to obtain access to . . . but failed." In more detail, Susan describes her revisionary image of Mrs. Hossack: "the aged prisoner . . . looked up into the officer's face, smiled and remarked that she would be glad to get home again with her children but did not manifest any great degree of joy at the news." Bail, the reader is told, will not be excessive because the accused "is an aged woman and one who would not try in any manner to escape."

As much as Susan may have altered her own perceptions of Mrs. Hossack and may have tried to influence her readers, she still had the job of keeping them interested in the case. Borrowing devices from popular detective fiction of the time, she dangles tantalizing details. The test on the murder weapon may now be known, but the readers will have to wait until the trial to learn the results, the same for the blood stains on Mrs. Hossack's clothing. Susan does hint that the results substantiate the claim that the blood on the ax comes from slaughtered fowl; she continues, "if that is true one of the strongest links in the chain of circumstantial evidence is broken. If the blood is human, it will look bad for the accused." If still not intrigued, the reader is given a gruesome detail—a "substance resembling brains" has also been found on the ax—and a rumor that the defense will enter a plea of insanity if efforts on behalf of their client fail. Mrs. Hossack must be either crazy or innocent, "the best people of Indianola" surmise, since visits to the home in the past few months did not indicate problems. Of Mrs. Hossack's character, these unnamed sources reveal, "She is said to be a woman who is quick tempered, high strung, like all Scotch women, but of a deeply religious turn of mind."[8] In the months before the trial, Susan filed only three small articles about the case, each one using the opportunity of reporting new information to summarize the details of the murder, the grisly events becoming more grisly with the retelling. On March 23, she reports that new evidence has emerged "and that in all probability it would result in Mrs. Hossack's acquittal at an early date." She does not say what the evidence is but she offers an important turn in the case: Mr. Haines, the primary source of information about trouble in the Hossack home and the party to whom, it is believed, Mrs. Hossack turned to get rid of her husband, "had gone insane brooding over the tragedy, and was yesterday sentenced to the insane asylum."

Although there had been talk of moving the venue of the trial because of the strong feelings against Margaret Hossack and the fear that an impartial jury could not be found, the trial finally began in the Polk County Courthouse on April 1, 1901, and was held every day except Sundays for the next ten days. Susan had apparently been successful in stirring public interest; she reports that over 1,200 people attended the first day of the trial, far more than the tiny rural courtroom could accommodate, and that more than 2,000 were present on the day the jury returned its verdict, over half of whom "belong to the gentler sex." Describing the opening session, she adds, "The bright array of Easter hats lent a novelty to the scene, giving it much the appearance of some social function."[9] The seventy-eight witnesses, fifty-three for the prosecution and twenty-five for the defense, focused on seven specific questions during the trial:

1. Would it have been possible, as his son testified, for John Hossack, who had sustained two traumatic blows—one made with the ax head, the second with the blunt handle—to call for and talk to his wife and children?
2. Were the blood found on the ax and the hairs later discovered nearby human, or were they, as claimed by the family, the residue of the turkey killed two days earlier for Thanksgiving?
3. Was the ax, which the youngest son said he placed inside the corncrib after killing the turkey, moved by the murderer from its usual place?
4. Were the ax and Mrs. Hossack's nightclothes washed to remove incriminating stains of blood?
5. Was the dog, which always barked when strangers appeared, drugged on the night of the crime, as family members testified?
6. Were earlier domestic troubles and dissension in the Hossack house resolved over a year before the murder, as the family stated?
7. Was it possible for an intruder or intruders to enter the house through the bedroom window, stand at the foot of the bed, and reach up to strike the fatal blows without rousing the woman who slept by her husband's side?

An eighth question—that is, what prompted Mrs. Hossack to leave home and wish her husband "out of the way"?—only entered the testimony twice. The wife of Mr. Haines stated that she and her husband had come to aid Mrs. Hossack, who thought her husband would kill the family.[10] Another neighbor testified that he had to act as protector when Mrs. Hossack returned to her home "in case her husband again maltreated her as she had reason for believing."[11] Susan's reports do not suggest that the prosecution or the defense pursued the possibility of violence in the home, and she does not broach the subject herself. Instead her stories of the trial tend to be summaries of testimony by experts and lay people who describe the structure of the brain, the disposition of the body in the bed, and the configuration of the blood spots on the walls. She does pause to describe the shock caused when the Hossack bed was brought into the courtroom, complete with bloodstained bedding, and when two vials of hairs were displayed: one found near the ax, the other obtained by exhuming John Hossack.

Interspersed between these accounts are Susan's descriptions of the accused and of those attending the trial. During the first day, as the counts against Mrs. Hossack were read, "Her eyes frequently filled with tears and her frame shook with emotion."[12] About the second day, when the murder scene was again invoked, Susan notes that Mrs. Hossack, who occupied a seat beside the sheriff's wife, surrounded by three of the Hossack daughters and all but one of the sons, broke down and wept bitterly: "Grief was not confined to her alone, it spread until the weeping group embraced the family and the sympathetic wife of Sheriff Hodson who frequently applied her handkerchief to her eyes."[13] Since there were no witnesses to the crime, the prosecution's case was based entirely on circumstantial evidence, and Susan often stops in her narration of testimony to weigh the success of the unsubstantiated arguments and to prod her readers to keep following the case. About Mrs. Hossack's taking the stand in her own defense, describing how she and her husband had spent a typical evening together on the night of the crime: "He sat in the kitchen reading . . . later played with his whip . . . [while] I was patching and darning"—Susan observes, "When she left the stand, there seemed to be the impression on the audience that she had told the truth."[14] Earlier questions of Mrs. Hossack's sanity apparently were dispelled by her composed appearance in court.

Like the novelist she would soon become, Susan saves her most impassioned descriptions for the summations by the lawyers. Of state senator Berry, the defense counsel, she writes: "It is said to be the master effort of his life . . . at times the jury without an exception was moved to tears. Strong men who had not shed a tear in years sat in their seats mopping their eyes and compressing their lips in a vain effort to suppress the emotion caused by the Senator's eloquent pleas." This lachrymose display, she notes, even extended to the prosecution attorneys who were "seen to turn away their heads fearful lest the anguish of the family would unman them and the jury would have an impression which they could not afterward remove." The spectators were also moved. When the court was adjourned at noon, she writes, "fully two thousand people went out in the sunshine, their faces stained by the tears which had coursed down their cheeks." Aside from tears, Berry's chief strategy was to charge that Mr. Haines, "the insane man," was the real murderer. When he had been asked by the Hossack children to come to the house on the night of the murder, he had refused, saying that there were tramps about. It was he who had first implicated Mrs. Hossack by suggesting that she had wanted her husband dead and had sought his aid. And it was Mrs. Haines who had provided some of the most damning evidence about dissension in the Hossack home. As successful as Berry may have been in concluding for the defense, Susan warns her readers that "it is certain that when attorney McNeal closes the argument for the prosecution the effect of Senator Berry's eloquence will have been lost and the verdict, if any at all is reached, can hardly be acquittal."[15] Why, she does not say.

On the last day of the trial, county attorney Clammer and Mr. McNeal summarized for the prosecution; and, as Susan predicted, McNeal was able to rouse the audience with his indictment—"She did it, gentlemen, and I ask you to return it to her in kind . . . she has forfeited her right to live and she should be as John Hossack, who lies rotting beneath the ground." He too had his own bombshell: Margaret Hossack had been pregnant and given birth to a child before their marriage. This, McNeal claimed, was the dark secret often referred to in the trial, the story Hossack said he would take to his grave and the reason for the unhappiness in the Hossack home. Just how a pregnancy thirty-three years earlier could have been the sole cause of trouble in the marriage and how it proved Mrs. Hossack's guilt in the murder of her husband was not clear; but, as Susan reports, it provided the jury with the impression that the accused was a woman who could not be trusted. On this revelation the trial ended.[16]

The case went to the jury on April 10, the judge presenting the following charge: "When evidence consists of a chain of well-authenticated circumstances, it is often more convincing and satisfactory and gives a stronger ground of assurance of the defendant's guilt than the direct testimony of witnesses unconfirmed by circumstances."[17] In less than twenty-four hours, the jury returned its verdict: Margaret Hossack was found guilty as charged and was sentenced to life imprisonment at hard labor. Susan reported the outcome, but made no comment on the finding. It was the last story she filed in the case; it was also the last story she filed as a reporter for the *News*. Immediately after the trial, she resigned and returned to Davenport to begin writing fiction, and by the summer of 1902 she had moved to Chicago and enrolled in the graduate English program at the University of Chicago. Therefore, she may never have learned the final disposition of the Hossack case, for the story was not yet over. In April 1901 lawyers Henderson and Berry lost an appeal with a lower court, but in April 1902 the supreme court of the State of Iowa agreed to hear the case. Citing several instances where the trial judge had ruled incorrectly on the evidence, the higher court overturned the original conviction and requested a new trial.[18] A second trial took place in Madison County in February 1903. This time the jury, after twenty-seven hours of deliberation, was unable to reach a verdict: nine voting for conviction and three for acquittal. In papers filed in April 1903, the prosecutor stated that, since no further information had surfaced, it would be a waste of taxpayers' money to ask a third jury to hear the case. Mrs. Hossack, then near sixty and in failing health, was ordered released and was allowed to return to her home, her guilt or innocence still in question.

Eight years earlier, a court in Fall River, Massachusetts, had freed Lizzie Borden because they could not imagine that a refined, New England "maiden" who wore demure silk, carried flowers, and wept copiously in court could wield the ax that slew her family. So strong were the prevailing views about femininity that even the prosecuting attorney found it hard "to *conceive*" of the guilt of "one of that sex that all high-minded men revere, that all generous men love, that all wise men acknowledge their indebtedness to."[19] What is striking in the Hossack case is how ready the community was to assume the guilt of "one of that sex." Unlike Lizzie, who quickly read the signs of the time and played the part that was demanded of her—she learned to cry in court—Margaret Hossack, for all her tears and despite Susan's midcourse correction and subsequent, embellished descriptions of "the frail mother of nine," did not win over the jury. They may not have been convinced that she was guilty of murder, but she certainly was guilty of questionable female behavior: She had left her husband, discussed her marital troubles with neighbors, and—most damaging—had been pregnant before marriage.

To have found such a woman innocent or to have explored the question of justifiable homicide would have been unthinkable in the Iowa court of 1901. Such an argument would have necessitated an investigation of the family, the power wielded by the husband, his physical abuse over a long period, and the circumscribed lives of the wife and children. Both the prosecution and, tellingly, the defense seemed loath to pursue this direction. Instead, as Susan's accounts indicate, their cases were built on small, tangential points, few of which addressed the central issue of motive. Even the state supreme court ruling, which acknowledged John Hossack's repeated beatings of his wife—with his hands and with a stove lid—couched its findings: "The family life of the Hossacks had not been pleasant perhaps the husband was most to blame. He seems to have been somewhat narrow minded and quite stern in his determination to control all family matters."[20] However, absent from the seven points on which it reversed the lower court decision was abuse. In fact, the court argued that prior relations in the family should not have been introduced in the original trial since harmony had been established for over a year. Domestic life, thus, remained sacrosanct. John Hossack had been a pillar of the society, nominated "for some of the highest offices in Warren County," and "the twelve good men" Susan describes as sitting in judgment of Mrs. Hossack were all men who knew John Hossack well and had a vested interest in protecting his name if they could no longer protect his person. The women attending the trial in their Easter finery, perhaps even the sympathetic sheriff's wife, might have been able to offer a different reading of the case, but they were not accorded the opportunity in the court or in the newspaper accounts Susan filed. Sixteen years later, in her play *Trifles* and in the 1917 short-story version, "A Jury of Her Peers," Susan would give them the opportunity to be heard.[21]

In the wake of the Hossack trial, Susan returned home to Davenport. Although she does not mention the case specifically, she indicated in later interviews and biographical essays that by 1901 she had already accumulated a sufficient horde of experiences and stories so that she could now turn full time to what she really wanted to do: write fiction. "I was assigned [on the *Des Moines Daily News*] to the State House and covered the Legislature when in session. There I was always running into things I saw as short stories, and after less than two years of newspaper reporting I boldly gave up my job and went home to Davenport to give all my time to my own writing. I say boldly, because I had to earn my living."[22] As it turned out, her "boldness" was well founded. For the rest of her life, her writing supported her and the men in her life.

Susan's family was delighted to have her home once more, and her mother enthusiastically became the guardian of her time, explaining to friends who called that "Susan is writing now. Will you call later?" In a biographical sketch she wrote several years later, Susan would remember her mother's words. "Easy enough to say that when something has happened about your writing. Sheer faith, and love, while there is still no telling." But soon enough things did happen—her short stories were sent out to leading Eastern periodicals; and one morning in the mail, she found an acceptance and a check for seventy-five dollars, no small amount at the time. When she showed it to her grandmother, Mrs. Glaspell gasped, "Why, they must be crazy." She was a pioneer woman, who called "real" the work of making her own soap and providing for strangers traveling through the territory; she felt it dishonest of her granddaughter to keep the money. "You know as well as I do that nothing you would write could be worth seventy-five dollars." However, Mrs. Glaspell "quickly put on her bonnet and went out to tell the neighbors how wonderful I was," Susan recalled. Other checks arrived, and Susan kept the money. Grandmother Glaspell's exhortations about the successes of her talented grandchild reached such proportions that Susan was forced to remind her that others might not be as fascinated as the family had become with the subject. After that, whenever Mrs. Glaspell would be asked, "And How is Susan doing?" she would "primly fold her hands and say, 'I am not permitted to mention her name.'"[23]

Susan's talent had already been recognized beyond the Glaspell family. In 1897 Elmer reported to his daughter that "Miss French said you were the smartest the [*sic*] brightest girl in the city.[24] The compliment carried weight. Alice French, whose massive Victorian mansion was in walking distance from the Glaspell house, was not only the doyenne of local writers, but had a solid national following. She was a friend of Andrew Carnegie, who had donated $50,000 to build a public library in town at her request; and was admired by Theodore Roosevelt, who had invited her to visit the White House when he was president and had packed her *Stories of a Western Town* when he went on his first, celebrated safari to Africa.[25] Even when young, photographs show her as a buxom dowager with strong features, hair piled on top of her head, a formidable presence in pearls. She was a striking contrast to Glaspell, who continued to wear her hair in a long, girlish style for several years, and dressed in loose-fitting outfits. Their century and class seemed to divide them: on one side the aristocratic woman of letters who supported the privileged position of the wealthy, on the other the working woman writer who challenged it. French wrote under the pseudonym Octave Thanet, which conveniently hid her gender.[22] Her fictionalized Davenport was called Fairport; Susan's was Freeport, a town she believed had the possibility of becoming a more egalitarian community. French wrote twenty novels and numerous short-story and essay collections, becoming one of the earliest American writers to offer realistic touches of place and to focus on contemporary issues, particularly labor unrest and socialism, both of which she, the daughter of a capitalist father, abhorred.

Because of her vantage point from within her society, French was attacked by another Iowa writer, Hamlin Garland, who also depicted small-town life—but from the other side of the fence. In a talk he presented at the 1893 World's Columbian Exposition in Chicago, he argued that "every novelist should draw his inspiration from the soil, should write of nothing but the country he was bred in and the people most familiar to him." But when French agreed with his position, he retorted: "What do you know of the farm realities I described? You are the daughter of a banker in a county town riding up our lane in a covered buggy. Yet you look across the barbed-wire fence and you see two young men binding grain on a Marsh harvester. 'How picturesque,' you say. 'How poetic.' But I happen to be one of those binding the grain. I have been at it for ten hours."[26]

It is useful to consider the works of French and Garland, because Glaspell's writing falls between these two opposing poles. While serving as society editor for the *Weekly Outlook*, she had observed Davenport's upper class and had little sympathy with it. Yet she also did not tend to idealize the poor as Garland often did. Her trips with her father had given her opportunities to meet workers in rural areas of the region, and she found them "simple and good"; but her fiction concentrates on small-town, middle-class life, on people who work in offices, not on the land. They have enough to eat, but they still worry about mortgages and retirement. If they have rank, it is gained not through inheritance but through their own achievements. Most importantly, while her characters are true to themselves and their backgrounds, their perceptions of truth are not predicated on status or status quo, nor are they shaped by some revolutionary agenda, as in the case of Garland. Rather, like Willa Cather, Susan illustrates that perseverance not pedigree can mark success.

Her first stories, based on her state-legislature beat and written in Davenport between 1901 and 1902, reflect her direct observations of the political system and her sensitivity to the abuses of power and the folly of bureaucracy. They usually involve important decisions that the central character makes: a legislator must decide, when voting for a particular bill, whether to follow his conscience or choose an expedient position that will further his career; a governor must decide whether to appoint his predecessor to fill a vacant senate seat, as the party dictates, or follow the desires of the people of Iowa and himself; another governor must weigh whether or not to pardon a convicted embezzler whose wife is dying and face criticism for his lenient behavior; a legislator must decide if he is to pardon an eleven-year-old murderer or uphold the sentence as his home district wants.[27] There is a set pattern in these stories, with the protagonist torn between public reputation and private conscience. In all cases he— for they are invariably "he"—decides to follow the dictates of his heart. Unlike French's people, who return to the fold, to Harvard and father, her protagonists break with the status quo, demanding of themselves and of their world a higher standard.

When she turns to female personas and to material not connected to politics, Susan is even more successful in her writing. At the time, the short-story periodical *Black Cat* offered large cash awards, trips around the world, and automobiles for the best stories received. As a sign of how well launched she was, Susan already had sufficient material that she was able to submit by the contest closing date of February 26, 1902. Her story "The Work of the Unloved Libby" was awarded $150 and was published in their August 1904 issue. In it Susan is able to capture the pathos of the life of forty-year-old Libby Anderson, "unredeemably plain, and hopelessly conscientious," whose total dedication to her elderly mother goes unrewarded.[28] So controlled is the writing that the ending, in which Libby allows her mother to die peacefully without discovering her son's betrayal, avoids cheap sentimentality and is a genuinely moving moment. Since Libby is not accustomed to speech, her words come haltingly, like those of Glaspell's later, inarticulate stage characters. Compared to the rest of the stories in the same issue—about a young woman putting cotton into the ears of a nervous racehorse to drown out disruptive noises; about a man and a woman, accidentally locked into a tower with no food; abouit a ghost who returns to haunt her former family—"Libby" is sophisticated, both in language and subject matter.

Judging from the number of short stories Susan published in the following three years, her time back in Davenport was well spent. Eastern periodicals, whose swelling readership was voracious in its demand for fiction, readily accepted her work. Her former paper, the *Des Moines Daily News*, found her successes significantly noteworthy to run a feature on her, complete with a two-column photograph using her Drake graduation picture. Under the headline "Susan Keating Glaspell," the story summarizes her career at Drake and the *News* and points with pride to her acceptance as a short-story writer. It ends with a brief description of Susan—"She is a strikingly handsome young lady with a nobility of character and charm of manner that command more than passing attention"—and with her current location: "Miss Glaspell is now in Chicago."[29]

Chicago

6

I know one doesn't usually associate love with Chicago, but I love even its abominations.
— Susan Glaspell, *The Glory of the Conquered*

"Chicago is many things to many people and to me it is a place where you can write," Susan jotted down in notes for an autobiographical essay in the late 1930s.[1] By then the city was like a second home to her; however, in the summer of 1902, when she enrolled at the University of Chicago, it was more foreboding than familiar. Holding sway at the time were Robert Herrick, William Vaughn Moody, Robert Lovett, Henry Fuller, and Clara Laughlin, the first generation of Chicago literati, whom the critic Bernard Duffey dubbed the "Genteel writers." Eight years later, after winning major prizes for her short stories and publishing an acclaimed first novel, *The Glory of the Conquered*, set in Chicago, she would return there and be welcomed by a quite different group—Vachel Lindsay, Edgar Lee Masters, Sherwood Anderson, and Floyd Dell—who constituted the second generation of Chicago writers. In 1902, however, she was a twenty-six-year-old graduate student with a few published stories, a budding celebrity at home but an unknown in the largest city she had lived in to that date.

Her choice of the University of Chicago was not as unusual as her choice of Drake had been. For midwestern writers Chicago was the sought-after Mecca, promising freedom from the boredom and alienation of small-town life. Floyd Dell, Glaspell's friend and fellow Davenport writer, in his autobiographical novel *Moon-Calf*, describes seeing a map in a railroad station, "a picture of iron roads from all over the Middle West centering in a dark blotch in the corner. . . . 'Chicago!'"[2] Another Iowa writer,

Carl Van Vechten, whose life would intersect with Glaspell's in Greenwich Village ten years later, also saw Chicago and the university as natural havens after a youth spent in Cedar Rapids. As Van Vechten's protagonist explains in *The Tattooed Countess:* "I want to know everything, *everything* . . . and . . . I'm going to. . . . I want to visit the theatre and the opera and the art galleries. I want to meet people. I want to learn. Somewhere there must be more people like me."[3] There were. Van Vechten entered the University of Chicago in 1899, taking courses in French and German.

Like so much in Chicago at the turn of the century, the university had a brashness and a history that seemed new-minted and larger than life. It had opened its doors to its first class on October 1, 1892, ten years before Susan arrived. By 1901 its enrollment was 4,550, on a site that spread over thirteen blocks and included sixty acres situated between Washington and Jackson Parks, fronting Midway to the south. The university was new and so was the philosophy upon which it was based. Classes were held on a quarterly system during the entire year; they were coeducational; and there were branches situated in the center of the city, accessible to people who worked during the day and might wish to attend in the evening and on weekends, a forerunner of later continuing-education programs.

In the 1902–03 *Academic Register for the University of Chicago*, the name Susan Glasspell, with an additional *s*, appears, under category II: "Students Not As Yet Admitted to Candidacy in the Graduate Program." She is one of 912 students (591 men and 321 women) in this category, by far the largest number in the graduate school, which had only 131 students formally admitted to the master's program that year (96 men and 35 women). To the left of her name is an *s*, indicating that Susan attended during the summer session, but not during the fall, winter, or spring terms of 1902–03. Following her name are her major and minor subjects: English and philosophy, respectively. While there she took two courses, on the English essay and American literature, both taught by Oscar Lovell Triggs, an eclectic, widely known scholar, who edited, among other studies, the the fifteenth-century anonymous poem *The Assembly of Gods* (1897), *Tales from Totems of the Hidey* by James Deans (1899), the *Complete Writings of Walt Whitman* (1902), and the *History of Arts and Crafts* (1902), based on the teachings of William Morris, and went on to found the journal *To-morrow* to disseminate Morris's philosophy. Four years later he would be dismissed from the university charged with questioning the sanctity of marriage and advocating free love and socialism. He provided Susan with a grounding in Whitman, who became a central influence in the lives and works of the bohemian community in Greenwich Village. He probably was the first to introduce her to socialism, through the writings of Morris, a thinker whose ideas about the importance of work would have been congenial to Susan. She would have also shared his fascination with native American folklore. He provided one more model for the outspoken, beleaguered academic she would present in *Inheritors*.[4]

Although it is finally unclear just why Glaspell attended for only one quarter, such stays were by far the most common residency at the time. The statistics provided in the university catalogue indicate that during the 1902–03 academic year 665 students stayed one quarter and only 76 remained for all four quarters. Even though her time at the university was brief, it provided Susan with important material for her later writing. It also exposed her to some of the most illustrious writers in America, who had been brought together en masse from eastern schools, particularly Harvard and Yale, to form the nucleus of the eighteen-member Chicago English department, in which she studied. CTC—"called to Chicago"— became a familiar acronym for this migration westward, the faculty lured by an administration interested in assembling a department of writers not researchers. At the time she took courses, the English department was headed by Herrick and included Moody, Lovett, and Frederic Carpenter.

Susan left no personal record of her actual experiences at the university. However, glimpses of the institution during the period can be found in *The Glory of the Conquered* (1909), begun just after her first stay in Chicago, and in *Norma Ashe* (1942), written after she lived there in the 1930s. Both describe an intellectual haven and an idealized community. Interestingly, neither of her female protagonists in these works actually attends the university, both having graduated from small, western colleges similar to Drake. Ernestine, in the first novel, is married to one of the most famous scientists teaching at Chicago; Norma, who had won a scholarship to do graduate work there, marries instead and returns there only in later life to marvel in rhapsodic monosyllables at the opportunity she missed. Ernestine is a more sophisticated observer. She sees the university's mission as part of the thrust of "great Chicago": "the Chicago which had fought its way through criticism, indifference and jeers to a place in the world of scholarship."[5] Robert Herrick provides a far less idealized picture. In his novel *Chimes*, one of the first American "university novels," he describes his impressions of the University of Chicago during the period Susan was there. If she sees the university as part of the larger, dynamic temperament of the city, Herrick depicts it as exactly the type of university Chicago deserves: dirty, restless, sacrificing the quality of a Harvard in its dedication to an egalitarianism that leavened the student body and diminished the instruction. It even required that he teach women![6]

Attitudes toward the city and the university obviously depended on the direction from which one approached them, the period in which one arrived—and one's gender. Herrick and others from the East never got over the perceived barbarity of what William Vaughn Moody called "out here." Glaspell and those who formed the second generation of Chicago writers, beginning in 1902 and swelling after 1907 during Chicago's Renaissance, were all children of the region who had no preconceived notions of cultural refinement and were willing, even eager, to experience all that was offered. The city Susan first encountered was one about to happen and at the same time one already disfigured by what had happened to it. She reacted to both in her writing. The Chicago fire of 1871, which had destroyed 1,700 buildings and $200 million in property, had left in its wake both devastation and possibility. In 1893, as if in fulfillment of this possibility, Chicago became the unlikely site of the World's Columbian Exposition, an international fair to celebrate the 400th anniversary of the coming of Columbus to the New World. However, instead of building on the old city or creating a new one in its wake, the fair chose to build a temporary city alongside the real one, a city manqué. Paul Bouget, a French journalist sent to cover the event, labeled the two cities the "White City" and the "Black City," names that critics of the period still employ. The "White City" consisted of those buildings specifically designed for the fair, filled with technological wizardry that pointed to a new future for the area and the country. The "Black City" was the city still bearing the scars of the fire, where people actually lived their lives in 1893, a place of decay and hopelessness. Ten years later, when Susan lived there, conditions had improved somewhat, but for the working class life was still grim, as she shows graphically in her novel *The Visioning*.

The very roughness of the city, its violence, contradictions, and brashness attracted writers, who either satirized and condemned it, as Herrick did, or marveled and praised it, as its home-grown observers tended to do. A year after Susan arrived, Henry Fuller, a local novelist, was asked by William Dean Howells, the leading arbiter of literary values in the country, to send him names of Chicago novelists. A week after receiving the list Howells wrote back, "Your group is not a group, but an army. I give up in despair."[7] He did publish an article on the subject in the *North American Review* that year, in which he lauded the language of the nascent Chicago school of writing, singling out for praise two newspapermen: George Ade and Finley Peter Dunne.[8] Howells was particularly struck by their use of dialect and the verve with which they painted the contemporary scene, indications that a new language was springing up in the city, one directed at a reading public that had little time, or patience, for arcane phrases or academic prose. Although he doesn't mention Theodore Dreiser in his article, Dreiser also came out of the Chicago newspaper school, which demanded that its writers "jazz up" their accounts, "not so much bare facts as feature stories, color, romance."[9] It was this Chicago "newspaperese" that moved H. L. Mencken to proclaim: "I give you Chicago. It is not London-and-Harvard. It is not Paris-and-Buttermilk. It is America in every chitling and sparerib, and it is alive from snout to tail."[10]

For Susan, who, in her Davenport and Des Moines journalism work, had already shown a distinct flair for idiosyncratic speech patterns, slang, and colorful settings and details, the Chicago style reinforced her natural bent and was an important element in the development of her fictional voice. Over the next few years, she periodically wrote for the *Chicago Daily News* and freelanced for other local Chicago newspapers. In this work and in her fiction, the Chicago stylistic influences can be found. In a period in which stories often employed one voice—the writer's—Susan's writing invariably offered a variety of discourses and vocabularies: school children's sing-song phrases, ethnic dialect and diction, consciously used grammatical errors to reflect class distinctions, and, most noticeably, slang. This rich mélange gave her work its color and helped make up for her banal story lines at the time and her overly-sentimentalized themes. In her later, more mature writing, she would continue to make use of current idiom, a talent that critics today often overlook. For example, in her 1920 play *Inheritors*, with a phrase, "You can pick 'em off every bush—pay them a little more than they're paid in some other cheap John College,"[11] she deftly delineates the values of a state senator who sees professors and universities as commodities. With the latest slang—"Matthew Arnold. My idea of nowhere to go for a laugh"[12]—she illustrates the decline in literature and culture expressed by the son of the president of the university. Claire Archer's "Choke that phonograph!"[13] in the play *The Verge*—a request to stop offending music—carries the shock of the new to an audience unused to women speaking in slang and delineates Claire as someone "on the verge" in her language as well as in her lifestyle.

If Susan's populist style places her closer to the news writers of Chicago and further removed from the "genteel" novelists, her particular angle of vision in her writing sets her apart from both groups. When she focuses on the teeming life of the "Black City," outside the walls of the university, it is not with the muckraking zeal of an Upton Sinclair or with the obvious condescension of a Robert Herrick, but with a compassion that would mark all her subsequent fiction. Her Chicago-based short stories and her first two novels are amalgams of the period and its concerns, seen through the eyes of young women like herself, newly transplanted from small towns in the Midwest. However, while Chicago is the setting, it is not usually the subject. Her emphasis is on the private lives of these women: their work, friendships, family ties, loves, and marriages. In this respect, she is close to other women writers in the city, including Elia Peattie, Clara Burnham, Edith Wyatt, and Clara Laughlin, who were ensconced as "cultural leaders," but who also tended to write from a more personal point of view than their male counterparts. However, unlike these women, Susan knew first-hand the effects of the struggles and alienation awaiting a young woman from a small town who dared to come to Chicago. As Ann, in *The Visioning*, explains: "If you believe in praying—pray sometimes for the girl who goes to Chicago to find what you call the 'joy of living.' Pray for the pilgrims who go to the cities to find their Something Somewhere."[14] Glaspell's women characters usually come to the city not, as Henry Fuller argued in his novels, with "the one common avowed object of making money,"[15] but to learn a craft, enrich their spirits, and fulfill the dreams promised in "moving-pictures" or in the books they have read. These women seek new opportunities for themselves, beyond the limited possibilities offered them in marriage and motherhood.

In *The Visioning*, Susan's protagonist, Katie Waynesworth Jones, lives a safe, regimented life in a fictionalized Rock Island, Illinois. From a military family, she has courage but has not had to display it until she saves the life of Ann, a young woman who has tried to kill herself. Through this contact, Katie is made aware of the dangers and challenges awaiting women who dare to break free of stultifying lives and head for Chicago. The novel's descriptions of squalor and danger, presented through the Ann's narratives and commented on by the more astute but no less vulnerable Katie, must have derived from Susan's own observations, because they parallel images appearing in her short stories set in the city. Although the novel has certain points in common with Dreiser's *Sister Carrie*, written eleven years earlier and also set in Chicago, Glaspell does not focus, as Dreiser does, on those things that can befall a young, eager woman, but prefers to concentrate on a socialist argument for a more benign work ethic, better living conditions, and a realignment of resources and priorities in society. Unlike certain socialist novelists of the period, however, Glaspell is not interested in turning her story into a polemic. Instead, she filters the scenes through the eyes of young women and men who display instinctive moral outrage at injustices they observe around them.

Near the end of *The Visioning*, for example, Katie's brother, Wayne, an army officer, who has fallen in love with Ann, comes to Chicago to find her after the young woman has run away. Even when interjecting this male-narrative voice, Glaspell does not display the cynicism or contempt used by many male writers who described similar scenes. Instead, as she often does, she employs a playful, ironic tone, not toward "the poor and unwashed," at whom Herrick sneered, but toward the values of a society that created such conditions. She also invokes pioneer imagery. When Wayne sees the poverty of the area, he thinks that "there was still a frontier—and that the men who could bring about smokeless cities—and odorless ones—would be greater public servants than the men who had achieved smokeless powder. Riding through that part of town it would scarcely suggest itself to any one that what the country needed was more battleships."[16] Climbing the stairs of the poor rooming house in which Ann lives, he continues, "The matter would be solemnly taken up in Congress if it were soldiers who were housed in the ill-smelling place. Evidently Congress did not take women and children and disabled civilians under the protecting wing of its indignation."[17]

The same tone of pointed irony and social commentary colors Susan's Chicago-based short stories written between 1902 and 1907. For the most part they are still formulaic, with manipulated, simplistic plots, but they demonstrate a growing facility with language and interesting details, as well as clearly delineated central characters. Several deal with homesickness, which Susan may herself have felt. In "At the Turn of the Road," subtitled "A Christmas Story," a man provides a young female art student the money for her return home for a visit and advises her not to cut herself off from her roots, as he has done in his own search for success. In

"For Love of the Hills," later anthologized in Glaspell's 1912 collection of stories, *Lifted Masks*, a young woman organizes a group to aid an older woman return to her home in Denver so that she can see the mountains she loves before going permanently blind. Instead of the tag happy ending she tended to use at the time, Glaspell abruptly shifts her concluding scene to a Denver newspaper office, where the woman has gone to inquire about placing a notice for her Chicago friends, saying she had arrived safely. When the city editor and the reporters in the newsroom hear her story and her request, they decide to do even more: they write a feature article about this singular act of human kindness, the editor telling his reporters: "The biggest stories are not written about wars, or about politics, or even murders. The biggest stories are written about the things which draw human beings closer together."[18] This is a typical Glaspell message.

Her theme of human connection seemed to touch the reading public. By 1904 she had already been able to place her work in the leading magazines in the country, including *Harper's*, *Munsey's*, *Frank Leslie's Monthly*, and *Youth's Companion*. *Harper's* accompanied one of her stories with a short piece describing this new style of writing, "bringing us next to the very pulse of life and its implicit meanings."[19] "For Love of the Hills" was also published by *Black Cat* magazine in 1905, with a note that said, "The writer of this story received a cash prize of $500 in the *Black Cat* story contest ending October 12, 1904." This first-prize award was a handsome sum at a time when a pair of shoes cost $1 and the expenses for thirty-six weeks of tuition, room, and board at the University of Chicago was $396. It was impressive enough that when Floyd Dell first met Susan in Davenport two years later, he reported that he had met the writer who had won "all that money." It was a mark of her growing competency that by the time the story was reprinted in *Lifted Masks*, she had shed some of its worst stylistic excesses, omitting overblown phrases, such as "sobbing with a quiet tragicalness"; she had also struck many words describing sympathy and suffering, preferring, instead, to show the actions rather than tell about them.

A far more complex, successful, and, possibly, autobiographical Chicago story is "From A to Z," published first in 1909 and also anthologized in *Lifted Masks*.[20] In it Susan describes another would-be idealist only a few months out of the University of Chicago, who has a clear sense of where she wished to be—in a big publishing house, situated with a view of Michigan Avenue—but who, instead, finds herself looking down on dingy Dearborn Street, in a semi-partitioned cubicle adjoining a room whose sign stares directly at her: "Dr Bunting's Famous Kidney and Bladder Cure." Rather than publishing books, she is working on a dictionary; and her boss, a man "in a skullcap," kindly reminds her of only one commandment: "*not* to infringe the copyright." In this story, the theme, however, is not loneliness or selflessness but LOVE, fully capitalized for emphasis. The young woman, Nora, has fallen in love with an older man with whom she works. His brooding eyes, cough, and alcoholism—which is never directly described—seem to thrill her, and a connection is formed between the two as they work their way through the alphabet, devising definitions for basic human feelings. At the end of their work, Z completed, the man disappears, unable to provide the love he assumes she seeks. His reaction makes Nora angry. "What he did not know was that she was willing to *pay* for her happiness. . . . What did men think women were like? Did he think she was one to sit down and reason out what would be advantageous?" In the *Lifted Mask* version she adds, "Better a little while with him on a slippery plank than forever safe and desolate upon the shore." That Susan is so willing to have Nora enter a sexual relationship without marriage may be an indication of her own private life at the time; in two unpublished novels that Jig writes about a thinly disguised Susan, he indicates that when they met in 1907 she was recovering from "a great love affair" with a married man she had met in Chicago, much older, who tragically died. "From A to Z" itself appropriates details from Jig's first job in Chicago in 1901, and it may have been Susan's own comment on her still-unnamed love for him in the year she published the story.

Jig never names the man with whom Susan had her first love affair nor does she, but it is clear from *The Glory of the Conquered* that her time in the city was marked by love and its loss. The central plot of the novel concerns the marriage of Ernestine Stanley, a painter, and Karl Huber, a leading cancer researcher, his blindness, and her sacrifice of her own career to become "his eyes" in an attempt to allow him to continue his work. Much of the novel's shape would come from Susan's reading over the next several years; however, the idea that love transcends all other emotions, that it is the central force controlling lives and that the bravest person is the one who is willing to risk all else for it, was already fixed by the time Susan left Chicago and would remain constant in her life and her writing for most of her life. At one point in the novel, Ernestine's young cousin, a newspaperwoman strikingly like Susan at the time, contemplates marrying a sensible, practical man, whom she likes but does not adore. Ernestine tries to dissuade her, arguing that marriage must be based on more:

> "You wouldn't be willing to lay down your life for intellectual companionship. You wouldn't be willing to go barefoot and hungry and friendless for kindred tastes. Don't for one minute believe you would! The only thing for which you'd be willing to let the whole world slip away from you is an old-fashioned, out-of-date thing called love—just the primitive, fundamental love there is between a man and a woman. If you haven't it, Georgia—hold back. If you have"—a wonderful smile of understanding glowed through a rush of tears—"oh, Georgia, if you *have*!"[21]

Susan and Jig, 1907–13

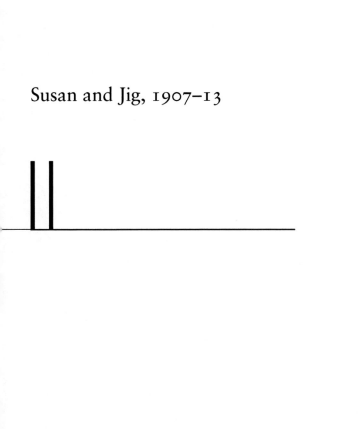

A Greek Out of Time

7

He was a strange person to be produced by the United States of America. He was a Greek born out of his time, and frustrated by the alien circumstances of his birth. At last he found his way back to his real home, in Greece, and died there.

—Floyd Dell, *Greek Coins*

It is impossible to trace the life of Susan Glaspell without discussing in detail the life of George Cram "Jig" Cook. She was his third wife; he was her only husband. They were married just eleven years, but their lives were connected far earlier and the ties between them carried on long after his untimely death. Davenport was their shared birthplace, three years apart. Susan's first direct contact with Jig probably occurred in 1895, when his name and that of his mother began appearing in her *Weekly Outlook* society column: items about their travels to Chicago, entertaining out-of-town guests, going on ice-skating parties. She also covered the opening of Jig's play *In Hampton Roads*, which he co-authored with Charles Eugene Banks in 1897. They may have been friends from this period, ten years earlier than the first meeting she cites in *The Road to the Temple*. In notes for his unpublished, autobiographical novel, "The Pendulum," Jig introduces a character he describes as a young newspaper woman, born in 1876, whose mother has Irish roots and who put herself through college and wrote short stories. The protagonist meets her when she comes to interview him on his return from study abroad in 1895. As a result of the meeting, the reporter completely changes her direction in life: She quits her job, enrolls in the state university where he is an instructor, and becomes his disciple and prize student. Her successes are marks of his tutelage. The interview may be a fictional device, similar to several Jig weaves through his outline, either to disguise the identity of the woman or to reshape facts to his liking. While the details do not reflect reality—Susan was never his student or his disciple—they do indicate Jig's need to see himself as someone who could inspire others and inflame them with his own vision of beauty, including Susan.

Throughout his life Jig Cook attempted to be the conduit through which others realized their inner potential. In a note among his papers, written when he was still a young man, he points to this goal: "I do not aspire to be, in the great sense of the word, a scholar. I hope to prove some day, writing and teaching, a person of tastes and talent, able to help people understand and love rightly the things which are beautiful."[1] This he tried to do for Susan, the Provincetown Players, and Eugene O'Neill: to inspire them to be the best they could be. Their successes would validate his beliefs. Such a goal may seem the mark of an egocentric who wished to bend others to his will. In practice Jig seems to have been the true idealist, desiring to fire others with his passion rather than aggrandize himself in the process. Susan understood this need in her husband and respected it. By the time she fell in love with Jig, she was already over thirty, a strong, successful woman. This did not change. Her individuality was not altered by their marriage, rather her life was enhanced by their love. There is a difference. Jig was not an easy man to live with; his passions were numerous and scattered, his attention span short, his frustrations over his failures great. But Susan, confident and steady in her own life, was able to provide ballast for her husband. It was she who supported the family through her writing; he took little money from his wealthy family and brought in little himself. It was also she who dealt with many of the more mundane elements of their joint project: the Provincetown Players. He inspired the group; she soothed it and helped it run more efficiently. There seemed to be little competition between them. Those who knew them mentioned their rare compatibility.

A man of great passion, Jig Cook thrust himself into each idea and relationship with his whole being, but never for long. His interests were too diverse, his "enthusiasms"—to use his word—too short-lived. He was a great talker and a catalyst for great talk, whether at his cabin in Davenport in 1907, with the young Floyd Dell and Susan, discussing the ideas of Ernst Haeckel and the possibilities of free love; around a table at Schlogl's in Chicago over drinks, trading stories and ideas with newspaper people; or at the Liberal Club, with his Greenwich Village friends and members of the Provincetown Players, planning for a new theatre in America. He was also a great doer and encouraged others to take on similar projects. He would write to his friend Neith Boyce, giving her precise instructions about the mix of cement and sand needed to obtain the right texture for outdoor stairs and directions about molding a sundial similar to the one he had recently constructed in his Provincetown yard, enclosing a "diagram correcting the sun," along with the endorsement, "Mine here works very accurately throughout the year, but it has the disadvantage that I am the only person who can read it."[2] He could also passionately attack the problem of vegetable production, designing and building a greenhouse that would allow him to get crops to market well in advance of those using conventional farming methods. His greenhouse was functional; it was also decorated in gold paint with designs of ancient Greece and Greek dithyrambs of his translation as well as original material. He explained, "You will look between golden bars through nice clear glass and see the green things growing against the black background."[3] Susan would pattern Claire Archer's greenhouse in *The Verge* on the one Jig designed, and the couple would use the sundial as the basis of their one-act comedy *Tickless Time*. When early in their marriage Susan was ill and couldn't navigate the stairs of their Cape Cod house in Provincetown, he broke the ceiling and made her a make-shift elevator so that she could ascend "like a queen on a throne," she would say. The elevator was still functional when she died in 1948. These talents for building and carpentry also allowed Jig to offer Eugene O'Neill "the world," or at least the illusion of infinite expanse created by the dome or *kuppelhorizont* he constructed for *The Emperor Jones* on the twenty-two-foot-wide stage of the tiny Playwrights Theatre on MacDougal Street, the first such structure in America.

Such projects received his total attention, but only for the moment; one love remained constant in his life and that was his romance with Greece— not modern Greece but the Age of Pericles, the Golden Age he dreamed of entering. If there was direction in the life of George Cram Cook, it was his movement toward this country of the mind. His was a steady trajectory on "the road to the temple," the title Susan wisely chose for his biography. If his life seemed to leave no great monuments or achievements as one ordinarily employs the words, it is because of his inability to do what others do: set down roots and specialize. He didn't have time. As Glaspell observed, "he was always on his way."[4]

Friends and critics invariably resort to hyphens when trying to describe Jig: novelist-philosopher-teacher-playwright-farmer-poet-soldier-violinist-actor-revolutionary-socialist-carpenter. In *Road* Susan adds to these, "great lover and a lusty enthusiastic drinker," writing that, "Drinking was one of the things in which Jig succeeded, in which he realized himself as human being and artist."[5] Some simply employed the word *dionysiac*. However, those who knew and understood Jig did not use the term as Dr. Relling does in Ibsen's *The Wild Duck*, to provide a comforting excuse for a wasted life. Jig's great desire was to inspire others; and alcohol flamed his speech and their interest, he claimed. Arthur Davison Ficke also invoked the word *failure* in describing his friend, but qualified the term: "George Cook's failure was of a kind considerably more interesting and useful than most men's successes; and one thinks of him along with such other abject failures as Blake and Shelley. His genius was not as great as theirs, but his passion was the same."[6] In passion, Jig was unparalleled. He lived passionately, thought passionately, loved passionately, talked passionately, and failed passionately.

George Cram Cook was always called Jig, a childhood name given him by his mother, Ellen Dodge Cook. "It seems so strange to me to be calling a grown up man by a childish nickname," a young woman who was introduced to him remarked.[7] He was a big man: over six feet and 180 pounds that he fought to keep from heading toward 200. He had a powerful, athletic body and a large head, with abundant hair, prematurely white, a lock of which fell directly over his forehead. When in thought or troubled, he developed the habit of unconsciously pulling on and twisting the lock. Those who wrote about him usually referred to this distinguishing habit as well as his striking countenance and size. When a fellow Iowan entered a *taverna* in Delphi, in 1922, he was awed by a tall man in traditional Greek garb: "A magnificent human specimen," the personification of Greek power and beauty just as he had always imagined.[8] His "ideal Greek" was Jig Cook, an American from Iowa. Photographs of him in Greece, with long, white hair and beard, dressed in his native Greek costume appear in the first edition of *Road*. In one, he sits in a wine shop, at the center of a table surrounded by four local men. He is the only one not in Western dress, and he is probably the only one who could quote excerpts from the classics of the country in ancient Greek.

A grown man who would dress in traditional Greek attire complete with tasseled footgear leaves himself open to ridicule. Edmund Wilson, who hardly knew him, called Jig "part professor, part Messiah and part drunken bum."[9] Others were kinder and more sensitive. After Susan, the colleague who knew him best and loved him earliest was Floyd Dell. He describes Jig's temperament not as childish but as childlike: "He made friends with the youth in us . . . with all that was eager and beautiful. Here was a man who felt profoundly and whose mind played. . . . We have all dreamed such dreams; but I think they were harder for Jig to give up than for anybody else. He wanted them to be."[10]

Jig sought to shape his life to fit some cosmic plan. Among his many papers are numerous diagrams of all sorts of things: plans for future days, lists of heroes, books, vegetable and fruit plants, evolutionary connections among species, and elaborate genealogy charts. He would employ these to help illustrate his ideas. In *Moon-Calf*, Dell has Tom Alden, the Cook persona, write a document, entitled "Girls," which starts with a few sentences and then moves to names, organized into groups, next to which he would put Greek letters, mathematical and algebraic signs, stars, crosses, and unknown hieroglyphics to distinguish them. Alden explains to young Felix/Dell the purpose of this list: "Instinct doesn't work—Not in matters of love. So I've been trying to use reason. I've been trying to review my experiences with girls, to see if I have really learned anything about them—and myself."[11]

Genealogy charts were his favorites. He was taken with the subject of evolution, and he liked to imagine his family as part of an evolutionary process leading to himself. Tracing back 512 people through nine generations of his family in America who went into making him what he was, he reveled in connecting his character and physical attributes to specific forbearers. From Ebenezer Cook, a Revolutionary War captain and a great athlete, who stood six feet and who, in his later years, weighed 300 pounds, he traced his physique and girth; from his great uncle with "a rousing voice" and from another relative who "could pick up a whiskey barrel and drink out of the bunghole," he inherited his "Herculean thirst!" He credited his grandfather, the scion of the Davenport Cooks—known as "the legal vocalist of the day" and something of a poet—with passing on to him musical and literary talents. These ancestors filled an enormous chart four sheets long on which Jig worked out dates, occupations and relationships, a small sampling of which he sent in a letter to Dell, describing his classification system, which identifies Benjamin Franklin as "my father's mother's mother's father's father's father's father's son's son." He could not resist bragging, not about the illustrious antecedent, but rather about *his* system for identification: "Do you note the ease, the nonchalance, with which I can run up the family tree two generations higher than necessary in order to land on Benjamin from above? Such agility is positively simian."[12]

One generation after Susan's ancestors arrived, Jig's family, bearing three coats of arms, came to America, settling, like hers, in New England. "A son of New England" he called himself years later when he wrote to Rudyard Kipling. Francis Cooke was the seventeenth signer of the Mayflower compact; Ebenezer Cook was a drummer in the Revolutionary War, and among family heirlooms passed down through the generations was the gold piece he received for his services. Jig's family also arrived in Davenport in 1836, but unlike Susan's, they prospered in subsequent generations and became leaders in the community. The first burial ground of Davenport was the Ira Cook farm; great-uncle Ebenezer had been on the board of directors of the Chicago and Rock Island Railroad, as well as alderman and mayor of Davenport; Ebenezer's widow, Clarissa Cook, became the major philanthropist of the city; and grandfather, John P.—who established the family law practice into which the subsequent three generations entered, including Jig's older brother Ruel—was elected to the state senate and to the U.S. Congress as a thirty-six-year-old Whig. The very successes of his family made his own accomplishments by comparison seem to him uncertain and questionable. At one of his low periods, he wrote to his second wife, Mollie Price, "Just now momentarily for the first time I feel a little regret that I am not as my father a trial lawyer." He immediately retracted the thought, "No I regret nothing. I am glad my life is now what it is—plus what it may become."[13] However, there remained a note of wistfulness about the way not taken.

Edward Cook, Jig's father, expanded the practice and the reputation of the Cooks in the community. "No man in the history of Davenport has been held in closer esteem or has enjoyed the respect and confidence of his fellow men to a greater degree than Mr. Cook," his 1914 obituary read.[14] The accompanying three-column photograph shows a man of stern demeanor, with wire glasses and short-cropped hair. As much as their temperaments and lifestyles differed, Susan attests to the great love between the indulgent father and his talented, iconoclastic son. It is clear in Jig's papers if not in Susan's biography that the son was desirous of pleasing his morally correct father, and even as an adult Jig hesitated to confront him. Several times in his voluminous correspondence with Mollie Price, when discussing whether the couple could live together without benefit of marriage, he remarks, "One person happier if with marriage than without—my Dad." He goes on to call him, "A great hearted man, but after all, in spite of eminence in his profession—a provincial lawyer—a man formed back in the 50's and 60's—with those ideas."[15]

A loving father, morally upright and correct, is balanced in Cook's life by the person most like, and closest to, him: his mother Ellen. Susan suggests that the father may have been the "practical man" precisely because the mother and younger son were not. Jig retained the childhood name she gave him, and she was called by his name for her, Ma-Mie. "It seems odd to hear a man call his mother Ma-Mie," said the same young woman who disliked the name "Jig." Ellen Cook would also be an important influence on her future daughter-in-law, Susan Glaspell, who shared many traits in common with this powerful, albeit retiring Davenport woman. When, in a letter to Edna Kenton, Susan accidentally typed an asterisk next to Ma-Mie's name, she continued, "I hadn't meant to give her a star, but she deserves one."[16] Woven through the early pages of her biography of Jig are tributes to Ma-Mie Cook. "Of all these people behind Jig, she was the significant pioneer for she broke a trail of self out of the life around her."[17] In her portrayal, Susan indicates how conditions that impinge on a woman's life—the time and place into which she is born, the predisposition of society—shape the possibilities of the life led, even though they need not completely quench intellectual thought. "One feels that a richer personality would have resulted from a richer soil—a little too much energy burned up in just keeping alive."[18] She credits Ma-Mie with overcoming her situation and, like so many of Glaspell's women characters, shaping a different course in her life, something Susan's more conservative and less-educated mother was unable to do. Traces of Ma-Mie can be found in Grandmother Morton in *Inheritors* and in the strong but thwarted women in *The Outside*. Louis Sheaffer, in his two-volume biography of Eugene O'Neill, also pays tribute to "Mamie Cook," who in her last years, after her husband's death, was assistant stage manager, wardrobe mistress, and general factotum for the Provincetown Players. Sheaffer suggests that O'Neill used her as one of his models for Deborah Harford in *More Stately Mansions* and Mrs. Shaw in *Strange Interlude*.

If Ellen Cook was the model for others' creations, her own great creation was her son Jig. Unlike Ruel, who entered the Cook law firm and Davenport society life, Jig was shaped by his mother's eccentric ways, her own inheritance from a grandmother who was a religious fanatic and from a mother, beautiful and delicate, who died when the child was three. Ellen's father LeRoy Dodge was a teacher before "footing it" from Ohio to Detroit, and eventually to Davenport, where he became a riverboat captain. His determination, widow's peak, and "thwarted poetry of the eyes" were his legacy to future Cooks.[19] Eventually, he was successful enough to buy a 640-acre tract of land in Buffalo, on the Mississippi, nine miles outside of Davenport. Ma-Mie, seeking refuge from the practical, Yankee schoolteacher who became her new stepmother, created on the Dodge farm what she called "a fairyland" of books and an inner life made rich by poetry and philosophy, which she later shared with her equally unpractical son and others, like Susan, who loved literature.

In 1866 Ellen Dodge married Edward Everett Cook, and the couple established a residence in Davenport, eventually settling at 128 West 6th Street, which would be Jig's home while in town. They visited the Buffalo property from time to time but did not spend complete summers there until 1882, when Ma-Mie had the Cabin, which had been built inland, moved to the wide sloping banks of the Mississippi, an act, Susan says, "which, if the cultural history of the region were written, would be an event of many radiations."[20] At that time people did not live in log cabins, much less spend money to move them to more scenic locations. Her act was one of the things that caused her to be called "queer" and "odd." "I feel sometimes like a prophetess of old who must cry out to the nations and the cities of the earth," she wrote to Jig, in a long letter chronicling her life. "If I had lived a hundred, two hundred, three hundred years ago and more I should have been burned as a witch—if I had lived two thousand years and more ago I should have been a Sybil with a tripod. If I had lived seven thousand years and more ago I should have been a priestess of the Temple of Isis."[21] It is no wonder that her son became a man who expected much from the women he loved.

The Cabin, usually referred to with a capital letter denoting a proper name, was actually a rambling, two-story plantation house with dark-red roofs, built in the 1830s. In 1902, Jig, assisting his friend Charles Eugene Banks in writing the book *Beautiful Homes and Social Customs of America*, provides a photo and a description of the "elegant" atmosphere and "cozy room of Mrs. Cook."[22] The place and the woman became inextricably intertwined; those who visited the spot went away enchanted by both. Dell writes about them in *Homecoming* and *Moon-Calf*, as well as in an unfinished novel; and Jig uses them as subjects for an essay for a composition class at Harvard, noting "The house was planned and decorated by a quiet dark haired little woman who reads and thinks a great deal."[23] It would be a place that the young Susan Glaspell would have naturally sought out even if Jig Cook had not lived there.

Jig's early memories are related to the Cabin and to books read there, particularly his father reading to him *Paradise Lost*, with illustrations by Doré. He read to himself *Sanford and Merton*, in which he particularly liked the name Stephen, which was divided by a hyphen, "so I called the story Step-hen," a detail he and Susan would use in their first play, *Suppressed Desires*.[24] Bible reading was also an early experience, Jig commenting in an autobiographical sketch that by nine or ten he had already hunted for those passages dealing with sex. His formal schooling began at Miss Kneeland's Kindergarten, and it was there he had his first theatrical experience: lying on the floor while his friend Popeye Morton, playing "a spasmodic beast," kicked him in the head. A few years later, his second appearance on stage also featured a kick; a walk-on part in Sheridan's *The Rivals,* in which he had to stand in a line and relay a kick to the next person. Such early stage experiences did not deter him from acting in later years. Jig was tall for his age, but he did not suffer because of the differences between himself and his friends, as some young children do. In fact, he courted difference, convinced by his mother's insistence that he was "special."[25] In a 1923 letter to his daughter Nilla, who questioned studying Latin, he referred to his own pride in knowing he was the only student at Griswold Preparatory School who could read Livy in the original. At his June 1889 graduation, he, like Susan, read a valedictory speech, his appropriately entitled "Enthusiasm"; and that summer he developed his own enthusiasms: for theosophy, Emerson, and vegetarianism. He later came to believe that he would have been even taller had he not stunted his growth by banishing meat from his diet.

He entered the University of Iowa at the age of fifteen, because of a letter from the head of the Davenport Board of Education attesting to his accomplishments at Griswold. His early years at SUI (State University of Iowa) seem to have been good ones. He first thought of becoming a university president, since the job gave him the possibility of changing the souls of people; he wrote of his plans in an autobiographical fragment in 1904, which attempted to trace his earliest memories of people, places, and ideas. What he does not list was an epiphany Susan describes in *Road*, when, in the university library, the book he was reading by Plotinus suddenly fell open on the floor, and he had a revelation of the oneness of the universe.[26] By the time of his graduation, he had somewhat modified his earlier plans: he was now eating meat and had fixed on literature as his calling, a doubtful occupation he knew, since "I have lived in a country not very favorable for culture."[27] Seeking a more favorable clime, he enrolled at Harvard, receiving a second B.A. at the age of nineteen, at the time the youngest person in the school's history to do so. He writes of this year in the opening section of his diary, which he kept periodically over the next twelve years and which would reach six volumes. He also saved the essays he was required to write each week in English class. Some record his impressions of Cambridge; others present his impressions—from this remove—of his early days in Iowa and of his family.

Throughout his life, Jig would repeat this habit of looking back over his shoulder at the place from which he had come, comparing the past to the present locale in which he found himself: in Buffalo he dreamed of Greece, in Greece of Iowa, in Provincetown of both.

It was Greece that remained his life-long passion. "I think America is a good place to metamorphose Greeks. Emerson was about that," his mother wrote to him from Buffalo.[28] After graduation he hoped to travel there with a friend, but a gold mine in which his father invested failed and Jig, instead, did the next best thing. He went to Europe in 1893, first to Heidelberg and then to Jena, Frankfurt, and Geneva, accompanied by Ma-Mie for part of the time. In his eighteen months of study and travel, he received two more B.A. degrees. From this period two events stand out. On the voyage to Europe, he was introduced to socialism through long conversations with the American painter George de Forest Brush; and on the return with Ma-Mie, he met the most celebrated English writer of the period, Rudyard Kipling: "A quick, noiseless, dark-faced man, his stoop the stoop of strength." Jig had with him a volume of Chaucer from which Kipling read "in short dips." Remembering the words of his former teacher, Charles Eliot Norton, "From Chaucer to Kipling," Jig took understandable delight in hearing "this latest English poet reading the work of the first."[29]

Davenport looked especially dreary after such adventures. In the spring of 1895, he decided to accept a position in the English department of the University of Iowa. He taught there for the next four years. He was not cavalier about his teaching; his introductory lectures indicate a sound pedagogical approach to the subject, arguing for the importance of writing and its connections to literature and to life.[30] Not reticent about displaying his interests in class, he would periodically play his violin and read excerpts from Dante, whose *Purgatorio*, with extensive notes by Cook, was part of the American literature curriculum for his course. After students were tested on writers such as Joaquin Miller, they would encounter one of Jig's extra-credit questions for the final examination: "Have you felt anything in Dante's poetry, its modes of thought, its hopes and fears, which relates to life in Iowa City or does it seem the dusty relic of a dark age?" Rarely has an instructor written a more loaded question. What bothered him most about his students was their pragmatic approach to their education. He called the State University of Iowa "a scientifically minded university in the midst of a methodistically minded population. . . . The facts of the inner life and the facts of poetry, of imaginative beauty elude the Iowan." He wanted to imbue his students with different goals: "It is what you are in yourself that counts," he told them, quoting Ruskin: "The first duty of young people is to be delightful and delighted."[31] Even at this point in his life, he believed his mission was to inspire others.

When the Spanish-American War broke out, Jig decided to enlist in Davenport Company B, 50th Regiment, Iowa Volunteer Infantry. To the president of the university, he wrote, "Let me express again my regret for the disorganization of my courses in the English department. . . . At present I have no heart for anything that does not bear upon the coming struggle."[32] To his classes, he simply wrote on the board in April 1898: "No class to-day, I've gone to war." The war may have been an excuse for a bored young man to leave his "disorganized classes" and seek some adventure; but the reality turned out to be far less exciting than Kipling's writing promised. Cook's war experiences were closer to Glaspell's ironic description of the actualities of enlistment in her short story "The Philosophy of War," written for the Drake *Delphic* the following year. Malaria-infested camps in Jacksonville, Florida, were dirty and damp, with the only danger the possibility of being fired upon by the sentry if one returned late and intoxicated from Jacksonville—which Jig often did. Five months later Corporal Cook was home, confiding to his diary: "It's all over. We did nothing. I wrote nothing. . . . Some died but uneventfully, quietly of typhoid. The rest returned . . . inglorious. We might as well have stayed at home."[33] His assessment is not exactly accurate. One tangible result was a brief history of the unit entitled *Company B of Davenport*, which he published in 1899. Susan also makes use of the experience in her 1942 novel, *Norma Ashe*. In a scene in which Norma's boyfriend visits her family for the first time, they discuss his war experiences: "Was it dangerous, the war, her grandmother was asking solicitously. 'Well—yes,' he said. 'The mosquitoes attacked us without mercy. We were wounded time and gain and suffered horribly.' 'But what did the Spaniards do?' her grandmother pursued. It seems they had never seen a Spaniard. 'They just kept us in a Florida swamp.' 'And what good could you do there?' Aunt Nettie asked. 'We used to spend hours wondering about that,' he said."[34]

Jig had one spoil of war. As he was about to enter his unit, on a whim he wrote to Kipling, admonishing the writer to see America's conquest of Cuba as an indication that it had also entered into the business of shouldering "the white man's burden." To Jig's surprise, the famous author wrote back. Addressing "Dear Corporal Cook," Kipling begins, "You are on the threshold of your work which, thank god, is the white man's work, the business of introducing a sane and orderly administration into the dark places of the earth that be to your hand." He personifies America and England as two correspondents, you "70,000,000 Americans, I, 800 year old England" and predicts that "you" will "fail, succeed, and fail again but in the long run you will come out all right and *then* you will be a nation indeed, but if you evade your responsibility toward lower ignoble races, if you try to patch up some compromise with half-breeds. . . . In plain English if you don't annex and administer the Philippines, you ought to be hung." His letter concludes: "I am curious to see now whether the younger singers will take hold of the affair and whether out of the stress and strain of it all, some good literature will be born . . . you've come into the tribe of keepers and no one is more pleased than yours always, Rudyard Kipling."[35] Jig made several attempts to answer the letter. In one draft in 1900 he tells Kipling that he had been offered $500, almost his yearly salary, to allow the letter to be published, but that he has refused to sell it. He also reports how far short his experiences were from his romantic expectations of war, that all he got was mumps and a near miss from a sentry. While he would not part with the letter, Jig does indicate that he would have been pleased to take the proffered $500 for his essay on the writer, a version of which he presented under the title "The Prose and Verse of Rudyard Kipling," on March 16, 1899, at the Contemporary Club in Davenport. The paper was published in its yearly publication. In Greece, twenty years later, having long since renounced his early embrace of colonialism and Kipling, he penned another unsent letter, addressed "To you, England, who, spiritually inferior, have owned India."[36]

In October 1898, Jig, now twenty-five, was back teaching at the University of Iowa, even more disconsolate about his situation and prospects for the future. In 1897 he and Charles Eugene Banks had written the play *In Hampton Roads*, recounting the battle of the first ironclads, the Merrimac and the Monitor.[37] They later turned it into a novel, published in 1899 by Rand and McNally, and still later into a re-dramatization. But Jig was interested in more challenging and more profitable writing. At the end of the 1899 academic year, while Susan was still a student at Drake, he quit the University of Iowa—for good this time—and made plans to go to Mexico, which he had decided would be the locale for his novel, *Roderick Taliaferro: A Story of Maximilian's Empire*. For two months he toured the country, meeting people and taking notes on the scenery and sites that he planned to use in a book, which he had already sketched out before he left. By April 6 he was back in Davenport and considering abandoning the project because of a young woman he had met.

The book had provided a reason for travel, just as his brief act of patriotism two years earlier had provided a temporary escape from a not-too-successful teaching career. But each foray inevitably deposited him home, once more confronting his own inability to find a focus in his personal and professional life. In 1901, recognizing that he could not continue to take support from his father, Jig left for Chicago, one year before Susan moved there and just about the time she returned from Des Moines to start her writing career. He began working at a publishing company, very much like the one Susan describes in "From A to Z," and was having his own love affair. Soon after his arrival, he met Sara Herndon Swain, and on May 12, 1902, they were married and returned to Buffalo for the summer, living in a small house, newly renovated for their use, next to the Cabin. There he completed the final draft of *Roderick Taliaferro*, which was finally accepted for publication by Macmillan and released in 1903.

The problem of how to support himself and Sara was solved when his former Iowa professor Wendell Anderson asked Jig to join him in the English department at prestigious Leland Stanford University in California. A new wife, a new book, and a new position boded well for the future. From his home in Palo Alto, he was able to travel to nearby San Francisco and meet with writers who provided the camaraderie he needed in order to feel secure about himself. Yet he realized that if he were to continue to write, he must find a way to make money that would not siphon his intellectual energies. Returning to Buffalo in the summer of 1903, he decided that the answer to his predicament lay at home. Influenced by Tolstoy and Kropotkin, he would become a truck farmer, using his fertile farmland to grow vegetables in the spring, sell them in the summer, and have the fall and winter for writing. For him the solution seemed perfect. When his novel was released, the local paper ran a story accompanied by a photograph of "Twenty-nine year old Mr. Cook and his youthful wife at the picturesque summer home of the former's parents near Buffalo. The two seem like a youth and the maiden who might have stepped down one day from Keats' Grecian Urn or the Frieze of the Parthenon."[38]

Looks were deceiving. For Jig this life may have seemed desirable; but it did not suit his wife. Susan, in her typically charitable way, tries to explain her predecessor's predicament: "A young woman of social gifts who has married a university man has perhaps a justifiable grievance when she finds herself the wife of a farmer."[39] In many of his writings, Jig also attempted to analyze what went wrong with his first marriage. "I have distorted her motives and character exactly as she has distorted mine," he jotted on a piece of paper, writing in the margin, "Main thing: not who began but that we can't be together."[40] There was something undermining the marriage besides money, which Susan may not have known or knew but chose not to mention in *Road*. Jig wanted a child. He later made this want clear in his letters to Mollie Price. "I'd like to make as many of said babies as please you," he wrote three weeks after their first meeting.[41] When Mollie feared she might be pregnant, he cautioned that the one law he held inviolate was "not to kill the unborn."[42] He is careful to add to Mollie, who was an anarchist, that there was another law that he also held sacred: "non-interference with decisions of others." Perhaps it is that which kept him from intervening when Sara decided to have an abortion, which probably took place in May 1904, when he marked in his dairy that he needed $500 for Sara's "sickness" and later that he took her to Mercy Hospital. In 1907 he still felt great anger over the loss. "She killed my daughter in her womb. She killed *all* of me that she could and it was her instinct so to kill."[43]

As so often with Jig, the details of his personal life became the material for his fiction, barely disguised. The many notes and sketches he made for "The Pendulum" are an excellent source of material concerning his marriage to Sara and also his subsequent relations with Mollie and Susan. To each Jig swore undying love, but until his relationship with Susan turned to love, he was unable to sustain any feeling for very long. The end of his first marriage was particularly painful. It seemed to confirm his fear that he could fix on nothing and on no one. "He wanted to wipe it all out of his life—both women, Fairview, everything! He wanted oblivion, deep, age-long," he wrote in another unpublished novel he penned during the period, "The Balm of Life."[44] The actual balm came to him the next year. Susan puts it this way: "There was much lonely thinking. But that year two things happened to change the years ahead."[45] One was his meeting with Mollie Price; the other was his friendship with a seventeen-year old boy who "had a name like a story-book": Floyd Dell.[46] Susan omits mention of his meeting with another person who would shape Jig's future even more than these two: Susan Glaspell.

The Monist Society

8

There are moments that remain as pictures, and he who filled those moments is a living person as long as the mind in which they live has life.
—Susan Glaspell, *The Road to the Temple*

In 1904, exactly at the time that Jig's marriage was unraveling, Susan returned to Davenport from Chicago, moving back with her parents, brother Ray, and grandmother, Frank having left the previous winter for Lewiston, Montana, to try his hand at lumbering. Three years earlier she had come back to launch her writing career; this time she was already something of a celebrity, at least in her hometown. The *Trident*, the tri-cities' weekly literary newspaper, edited by feminist Ella G. Bushnell-Hamlin was now referring to "Miss Susan Keating Glaspell" "prominent among Davenporters who are 'doing things' and coming to the front"; and by March 1905, when her grandmother Glaspell died, the obituaries referred to "the well known author Susan Glaspell."[1] Such praise was not unwarranted. She had already amassed an impressive publication record for her fiction and continued to do freelance work for Chicago newspapers, writing feature stories on regional political figures. However this growing reputation did not necessarily free her from conventional Davenport life. At home, her mother once more coddled and protected her, and her father bemusedly observed her progress. Even the news articles about her work struck a proprietary note, describing a bright girl whom "our city is proud to claim as her own."[2]

Davenport, however, was not quite the small pond she had tried to stir with her *Weekly Outlook* columns six years earlier. Money continued to dictate social standing, and young women were still expected to marry well and raise families—but at least they could read about options possible elsewhere. Bushnell's progressive journal repeatedly ran stories about the activities of Susan B. Anthony, Elizabeth Cady Stanton, Lucy Stone, and Maria Mitchell; and articles headed "The New Woman," "The Bachelor Girl," and "The American Woman" were now common. However, it was one thing to read about women actively working for women's emancipation and moving into professions previously closed to them; it was another to be the iconoclast in one's own community. Susan was indulged as an exception—a "queer" unmarried writer nearing thirty—but she had no illusions about how she was expected to behave and how far she could venture at home. Therefore, over the next three years, as she concentrated on solidifying her writing career and completed her first novel, she outwardly appeared to follow the path of Alice French: a big fish contentedly floating in home waters, careful not to splash too much. She gave talks to her mother's Lend-a-Hand Club; sang with the Harmonie Society, one of the more prestigious Davenport organizations, in which she had been inducted in 1895; and attended regional literary gatherings. Yet, if anything, she was even further removed from staid Davenport life. Too much had happened in the intervening years, including her love affair in Chicago, which had ended with the man's sudden death. Why then the double life: Susie at home and Susan away? It was a question she was to ponder the rest of her life and not fully answer.

At the same time Jig, living alone at the Cabin in Buffalo after the collapse of his marriage, was searching for something that would get him back on track and into the world. He began reading Nietzsche, a philosopher who exerted a great influence on him and later on Susan. He could easily relate to the idea of the lonely intellectual, misunderstood because of his differences. That was exactly how Jig felt: an outsider, shunned by the good citizens of the community because he was getting a divorce and had chosen to earn his living by farming. A man who has four degrees and is the son of the most respected lawyer in town is expected to do much better. "It is a miserable fate," Floyd Dell observed, "to be a non-producing 'man of genius' anywhere, but it is perhaps worst of all in one's home town."[3]

It is Dell who offers the best descriptions of the life in Davenport between 1902 and 1908, particularly the years in which Susan and Jig began the relationship that would eventually lead to their marriage. Today Dell is considered by critics to be a minor writer and is virtually unknown to the general reading public; but during the first decades of the century, it was impossible to read national newspapers, literary magazines, or book reviews without coming across his name. If anyone could be said to be the early chronicler of modernism in America and of the great migration of writers and artists from the Midwest to Greenwich Village, it was Floyd Dell.[4] And his journey to Chicago and New York began in Davenport, fostered to a large degree by his friendship with Jig. But rather than the teenage Floyd following the older Jig, it was boy who, in 1907 and 1908, served as master to the man. Because of the importance of this first literary relationship—what he called his high school and college education—Dell returned to it often in his writing. It became the locus of his bildungsroman *Moon-Calf* and his autobiography, *Homecoming*. Variations on it can also be found in fragments of two novels, one by Jig and one by him, that they wrote together during the fall of 1907, when they lived together at the Cabin.[5] These records fill in the areas sanitized in Glaspell's "official version" of Jig's life, *The Road to the Temple*.

In the margin of one of his lists for future novels he would produce, Jig wrote, "Floyd the savior." When the savior arrived, he did not come down from the hills; he arrived from Quincy, Illinois, on the steamer the *Bald Eagle*, "hatless into Davenport." The Dell family was poor; his father and siblings worked in factories, and he foresaw the same future for himself. Among the best known of his works is the often-anthologized section from *Homecoming* in which he first makes the discovery that he is one of those poor children for whom his school class is collecting money. Dell's primary escape from poverty and from an educational system that bored him was the Davenport public library. Librarian Marilla Freeman, a remarkable woman, took charge of the painfully shy young man, who secretly wrote poetry and was clearly a prodigy. Under her direction, he began a program of reading, which became even more vital when he left school to work in a local candy factory. After a day of carrying heavy barrels of sugar and pulling the still-burning spun candy with his bare hands, he would shower and retreat to the library, where he immersed himself in a world shaped by books.

In his abandoned novel about Floyd, Jig describes one day when his own persona, the vegetable seller/writer Nathaniel Burleson, comes into the library and learns from the librarian, Winifred Curtis, that she has discovered a sixteen-year-old poet in their midst. "[R]un the flag up over the public library of the city," Burleson advises her—which she promptly does.[6] The first meeting between Dell and Cook, arranged by Freeman, was less auspicious. At a dinner party in Buffalo, described in *Homecoming*, the diffident teenager talks incessantly but incoherently to an indifferent Jig, whose mind is elsewhere. Of his first reaction to Jig, Floyd writes: "A romantic-philosophical novelist of whose reactionary Nietzschean-aristocratic conceptions of an ideal society founded upon a pseudo-Greek slavery, I as a Socialist had totally disapproved." Jig for his part found the young man "excessively bookish and rather 'inhuman'"—or so Dell believed.[7] Three years later the shy boy, then nineteen, had left the candy factory, secured a job on a local newspaper, meeting trains and reporting on religious events, and had published a few poems in *Harper's*, the *Century*, and *McClure's*. He and Jig now became friends; and although thirteen years separated them, the young man was in many ways the more settled and mature of the two. So inseparable and so odd were the pair—one slight, the other towering—that Ma-Mie Cook remarked: "Jig and Floyd—it's like a St. Bernard following a little terrier around."[8]

When Floyd first came to Davenport he heard rumors that, despite the town's conservatism, a socialist group met in Turner Hall. Positioning himself outside, he finally was able to identify the "radicals" and joined their ranks. Fred Feuchter was the leader of the group, a dynamic speaker, theoretician, and practical thinker, who was also the local mailman. Then there was William Fineshriber, a young Reform rabbi, whom Dell first met when, as a reporter, he covered a service in the rabbi's synagogue. So taken was he with the worldly, erudite rabbi and his fine oratorical skill that he became an unofficial member of Fineshriber's eclectic congregation, which consisted to a considerable extent of "Gentiles, Socialists, Atheists and other heretics."[9] Another socialist was Jig Cook. By 1907 this nucleus of free thinkers decided to create yet another group, the Monist Society, based on the writings of the philosopher Ernst Haeckel. On December 27, 1906, Jig had presented a paper on the subject of evolution to the staid Contemporary Club of Davenport. His thesis, supporting Haeckel's monism concept, was that the theories of evolution need not undermine religion. On the contrary, the links among all forms of life are the best proof for the existence of a master plan and for a master creator. In his argument for monism, Jig presented a strikingly contemporary discussion of the dangers in dualistic thinking. If God is one thing and the world is another, how can one take heart in the beauties of the world as a manifestation of a higher order and in the nature of the self as manifestation of some divine hand?[10] Soon after, in a letter sent to Charles Eugene Banks, who had moved to Chicago, Jig reports: "Floyd Dell and I have formed— or *are*—the Monist Society of Davenport—for the propagation of our philosophy in the guise of religion, or religion in the guise of philosophy. That too is a seed. What it will grow into no one knows."[11]

For at least one person in Davenport in the winter of 1907, the formation of the Monist Society lived up to Cook's expectations, and even exceeded them. In the exact center of *Road*, Susan devotes an entire chapter to her encounters with the group and with the man who led it. Using the second person, as she often does to depersonalize the discussion, she tells of "you" declining to go to church with parents and heading instead for the Monists "down an obscure street which it seemed a little improper to be walking on . . . upstairs through a sort of side entrance over a saloon." Gathered there were an odd assortment of Davenport people who did not usually mix. "Some of us were children of pioneers; some of us still drove Grandmother to the Old Settlers' Picnic the middle of August. Now—pioneers indeed, that pure, frightened, exhilarating feeling of having stepped out of your own place and here, with these strange people, far from your loved ones and already a little lonely, beginning to form a new background." The "new background" began with talk—"the most interesting that had been in Davenport up to that time"—and then led to action. People changed their lives, she claimed. The group provided courage to "tell your father what you thought now, fortified by these oth-

ers, who, fortified by you, would go home and tell what they thought."
She concludes, "Supper-tables of Davenport would be different that night
because of the Monist Society. Courage being struck alive, no telling what
would be done with it."[12]

Although Susan certainly knew Jig earlier, she indicates that it was
the Monist Society that brought the two together, his speeches about the
oneness of life arousing in her something akin to a religious experience.
"Never had it happened in church. There the forms were of little use to
me, for my heart had not enough to flood them; but now, the worm, the
fish, the ape, and on and on until, as the crashing chords of an orchestra
that is mountains, torrents and great trees-'And thine shall be the power,
and the kingdom, and the glory, for ever and ever, Amen!' So sang one
heart, lifting to the courage of life and the glory of the world, down a
side street in a bare room over a saloon, in Davenport on the Mississippi,
in the year of our Lord nineteen hundred and seven."[13] The words are
reverential, a novitiate finding a calling and a god. Some critics, taking
their cue directly from this chapter's tone, have tended to see Susan this
way and have assumed that in their relationship she played Galatea to
Jig's Pygmalion. However, this section needs to be set in the context of
the work as a whole and of her motivation when she wrote the biography
between 1925 and 1927, immediately after Jig's death. In many ways, his
leadership of the Monists foreshadowed Jig's role as leader and catalyst
in another "beloved community" ten years later: the Provincetown Players. More than anything else, Susan wished to secure Jig's position as
the founder of modern American drama. His role had been effaced by
the internecine wrangling that accompanied the demise of the Players in
1922, when she and Jig left for Greece and, later, by what she perceived
as the usurpation of the group and its name by Eugene O'Neill and those
running the theatre at the time the biography was written. Yet, rather than
overtly foreground his messianic sway in shaping the Players, she instead
displaces it onto the Monists and, through them, displays his inherent zeal
and inspirational stature—and impact on her own life.

While she embellishes the details—she was, for instance, no longer driving her grandmother to pioneer meetings, since Mrs. Glaspell had died
two years earlier, and her father was himself not a churchgoer—it is true
that like many Monists, including Jig, she was leading two lives: with her
staid family and with her intellectual compeers; and despite her belief in
unity, she was not able to bring the two worlds into conjunction. The need
to escape being Susie and to get on with her life must have been strong
in her. Yet in 1907 she was still "at home"—as the phrase went—and
seemed, at least from her fiction, to find life away from Davenport lonely
and friendless. Therefore, the Monists presented a temporary alternative.
It could provide the congenial companionship of those other "queer fish"
who, once a week in a small room in Turner Hall could talk about socialism, anarchy, monism, Nietzsche, literature, evolution, and sex and still

return home for supper to families only partially aware of the "heresies" occurring in their midst.

One thing the Monist Society did was introduce Susan to the ideas of Ernst Haeckel, available in 1907 in a newly translated version by Wilhelm Bölsche. Even if there had been no Jig to draw her to his writings, she would have found Haeckel's ideas appealing, since she had already studied German philosophy at Drake, particularly the works of Goethe, many of whose ideas were incorporated by Haeckel. She had also read widely in American transcendentalism and had closely studied Emerson, whose arguments about the universe being composed of both nature and the soul and the "mind is a part of the nature of things" and thus "there is something of humanity in all, and in every particular"[14] were taken up by Haeckel. In certain respects, monism was a extension of these earlier philosophies. Both matter and spirit were one, Haeckel argued, part "in the process of evolutionary transformation," the nature of which was provable if one followed Darwin, who substituted "an intelligible natural law for unintelligible miracles."[15] Today Haeckel's work on what he called biogenetics is identified with the Third Reich's use of such theories, and few study him. However, in the first decade of the twentieth century, he drew a wide audience. For Susan, who continually invokes the spirit of her early pioneer ancestors, the idea of mutability was appealing: one could imagine oneself part of a continuum, which connected matter and spirit to the past as well as the future. One need not stop with the present. She also found a validation of her tendency to see the soul as part of the material world and the spirit central to daily life and social betterment. If, as she argued, each is part of each, then each generation bears the responsibility of bettering the race so that past struggles are not forgotten or nullified and social progress can occur. She knew that corn varieties can develop and thrive if put in contact with the best forms in the field; if plants could do it, so can people, she intuited. For an Iowa woman, monism was writ in the world she observed and made perfect sense.

The immediate impact of monism can be found in *The Glory of the Conquered*, the novel Susan was completing in the winter of 1907. In it she attempts the incongruous act of grafting the theories of Haeckel to the romance genre. In the marriage of young, idealistic artist Ernestine Stanley and cancer researcher Karl Huber, their choice of locale, the environs of the University of Chicago, is determined by his work and fame. However, Susan is at pains to make clear that Ernestine is equally talented, her art complementing his science, and that Karl learns to value and encourages her work as she does his. In their library his Haeckel sits next to her Maeterlinck. "I often think of the different ways Goethe and Darwin got at evolution. Goethe had the poetic conception of it all right; Darwin worked it out step by step. Who's ahead? And which has any business scoffing at the other," Karl says.[16] For Ernestine's parents there had been no such meeting ground: her father was a scientist who believed that life "could be reduced to a formula" while her mother was a lover of poetry and music, unable to accept the world of her husband, with whom she felt in mortal combat. Susan attempts to break such dualities by applying monistic paradigms to bridge the dualities of science and art, material and spiritual, and male and female. "Ernestine," Karl asks, early in the novel, "Do you ever think much about the *oneness* of the world?" "Why, yes,—I do," she replies, "but I didn't suppose you did."

Karl initially is the more famous of the pair, but soon she, too, is recognized for her work, chosen to have a painting hung in a Paris Salon, a great honor for an American artist. The successes of both feed their love, their fulfillment in their own accomplishments deepening and enriching the marriage. However, when Karl loses his sight, Ernestine decides to give up her own career at its zenith and study in his laboratory in preparation to become his eyes. The theme of raising up the conquered is foreshadowed in the title of the work, taken from the name of a sculpture executed by the French artist Antonin Mercie, which Susan reproduces on the cover: a winged woman, standing on one foot, lifting aloft a dying, vanquished soldier who clasps a broken sword. Ernestine's small bronze replica is one of her prized possessions. When chided by Karl and their friends for possessing "so Christian" a statue, Ernestine retorts: "It is more than the glory of the good fight. It is the glory of the unconquerable will." Her response is Susan's attempt to wrest self-sacrifice from Christianity and to wed it to a monistic belief in continual development of the soul and exercise of the will that transcends material victories or accomplishments.

In its execution the novel teeters on the brink of clichéd idealism. There are just too many glazed eyes, choked words, and obvious plays of light and dark. It is also far from a feminist scenario, since it is the wife not the husband who makes the sacrifice. Yet, Susan tries to weave into her romantic plot the power of Ernestine's *will*, a word italicized whenever it is used to describe her protagonist. Hoisting up the fallen Karl is not an act of Christian abnegation, she implies, but a sign of a woman who has strength and can offer the vanquished man what he himself cannot provide (a prescient comment on Susan's marriage to Jig and her later relationship with Norman Matson). Although Ernestine chooses to give up her own work, Glaspell makes clear that work is of equal importance for women and men—a radical idea in 1907. At one point, just after Karl has lost his sight, Ernestine asks what troubles him most. "'Is it—the work?' 'Yes!'—the word leaped out as though let loose from a long bondage. 'Ernestine—no one but a man can quite see that. What *is* a man without a man's work?'" This exchange takes place around the middle of the novel. By the end, Glaspell puts forth the argument that love is predicated on mutual, shared goals, and on the centrality of work in the lives of women as well as men: "For she must work,—theirs a love which made for work." This concluding sentiment in the novel would echo in Susan's life as well.

The Monist Society had a great impact on her life and writing, but it did not resolve the immediate dualities Susan faced in her daily life. She became a monist at the same time she accepted an invitation to join the Tuesday Club, the female equivalent to the all-male Contemporary Club. Her inclusion marked her acceptance by the Davenport literary establishment. Ellen Dodge Cook was a member, so were Alice French and various women from the French, Ficke, and Deere families. It was a serious organization, not like the frivolous social gatherings Susan had so derisively scorned in her earlier writing. But there was still an air of solemnity and respectability about the club that contrasted sharply to the freewheeling exchanges of the Monists. Susan was not the only one who had difficulty balancing rebellion and conformity in Davenport. Jig was also caught between his world and his father's. Dell describes an evening when Jig had been invited to defend socialism at the Contemporary Club against Arthur Davison Ficke, still a lawyer in the family firm. Jig, with his indulgent, straitlaced father in attendance and with friends Dell and Feuchter politely at attention, could not carry the radicalism of the Monists into the enemy camp. In pained tones Dell describes "the George who had been brought up as a gentleman, whose father was there looking on and wishing to be proud of his big, handsome, brainy son—it was *that* George, never clearly seen by me and Fred before."[17] While Susan was tied to her family by bonds of affection, she had less standing and privilege to lose; and she had long been used to viewing Davenport society from the outside. Yet, even she was wary of public censure, particularly when it might hurt those she loved. In *Road* at the point at which she introduces herself into Jig's life, she carefully telegraphs events and blurs dates so as not to call attention to the actual chronology of their growing love affair and its impact on Jig's second marriage.

Letters to Mollie

9

Love is moral even without marriage but marriage is immoral without love.

—George Cram Cook, Diary, 14 February 1911

The documentation of the beginnings of the love affair between Susan and Jig is unusual because it exists almost entirely embedded in the love letters of another couple: Jig and Mollie Price. Jig began to write to Mollie on August 1, 1906, four days after they met in Moline, Illinois, at a Chicago Press Club outing, and he continued the correspondence until she arrived in Davenport in February 1908 to become his second wife and sporadically thereafter until their divorce in April 1911. This collection of 106 letters is fascinating, since it reveals not only their personal love but also the mores of the time concerning sexuality and divorce. Iowa then required a two-year period after divorce before individuals were free to remarry. For the thrice-married Cook that meant that between 1902 and 1913 he was married for a total of seven years and was awaiting divorce decrees for four. With birth control virtually nonexistent, and with the possibility of pregnancy being grounds for criminal charges against the divorcing party, not to mention the scandal of illegitimacy, it is not surprising that Jig saw himself as someone hounded by society and deprived of sexual relations on the turn of a law. His letters to Mollie reflect his state. They are erotic, highly charged, and explicitly sexual, giving vent to deep frustration and lashing out at the community that had ostracized him because of his marital position. To make matters worse, the waiting took place while he lived in plain view of the Davenport community. One of the only people who sustained him and was a confidant during this difficult period was Susan.

What the real Mollie Price was like is hard to say, since her part of the correspondence is lost (just as Susan's letters to Jig do not survive). Mollie seems to have been an independent, vivacious twenty-one-year-old woman, who loved Jig but was not willing to give up her own life or lifestyle while waiting for him to win his divorce. An anarchist, espousing free love, she practiced what she preached, having sex with him at their first meeting, even before she knew his name. The setting was near Blackhawk's Watch Tower, on the Moline side of the Mississippi, a spot that Susan and Jig would also seek out when they wanted to be alone. For the lonely Jig, who had taken time out from his summer farming to attend the Press Club meeting, she seemed like a miracle sent to save him. "I'm good for nothing—nothing but one thing," he writes her a few days after they met. There is no salutation or signature on the letter, but on the reverse side he has drawn the signs for male and female and added the words, "There is destiny that shapes our end."[1] Two days later he writes, "It cannot be possible that I went with a girl at sunset down the woods to the river bank. She didn't sit on a rock unbound and speak my language . . . her arms opened and locked me in. . . . I never wanted anything so much in my life. I did not think a man *could* get so excited." He is suddenly alive with plans for the future: He will meet her in Chicago, although he knows that he shouldn't, since this is his busy period on the farm. Yet, he can't be reasonable now: "I love you gently, tenderly, reverently. At this moment passion sublimates itself to pure spirit. My body thinks one thought—you. . . . I am not merely happy. I am in bliss."[2] Even in love, Jig is Jig. He cannot resist making lists. Lest she forget, he enumerates the number of times she "felt the fluid jet." He also assigns names. His penis is William, her vagina is Peggy—coincidentally the name of his favorite dog—allowing him punning latitude. Ever exact, he also offers the specific size of his member: "six and a half inches in circumference."[3] Passion does not deflect habit (but it may exaggerate it).

From Jig's letters it is clear that he was more infatuated with his image of Mollie than with her actual person. For him she is first of all a sexual object whose body he desires, a femme fatale, an "obsessor or rather obsessoress of virtuous minded young men."[4] At the same time, she is his goddess: "the vital power of the earth concentrated and unveiled. Aphrodite come to life."[5] While she is his "blithe religion," she is also to be his companion and fellow worker. He asks, "Wouldn't you like to don men's clothes and work with me up there this winter chopping?"[6] In other words, Mollie is to be lover, goddess, earth mother, field hand, as well as someone who will love him without reserve, while still retaining her independence, and be a collaborator and inspiration, who will spur him to achieve great things. The actual Mollie who appeared in Buffalo in the early spring of 1908 could not help but disappoint her husband-to-be who had invested her with every conceivable stereotype of womanhood.

The courtship is almost completely epistolary; the couple met only six times in the eighteen months prior to their wedding. Although Jig often asked her to travel to Buffalo, Mollie avoided his suggestions. She did, however, travel—but on her own terms and for her own reasons. Against his protestations, she acted in a road company of a popular play, *The Land of Nod*, crisscrossing the Midwest and South. His letters of early 1907, at the same time he is founding the Monist Society, are constantly filled with fears that she is not receiving his mail and with reactions to the sordid descriptions of life on the road, which she must have been writing. As the divorce date nears, she showed little rush to join him, preferring instead to move to New York, where she began working on Emma Goldman's anarchist magazine, *Mother Earth*. Jig, taking his cue from her anarchist views, had proclaimed, "no shackles for Mollie." But when she takes him at his word and tells him of her affair with a man named Tom, he is, despite his initial protestations to the contrary, inconsolable. In his letters of November 29 and 30, 1907, he tells of his sorrow, "as if a dear friend had died," and of his fears that she no longer wants him now that her passion is slaked. It is not only her infidelity that troubles him. He only mentions it after enumerating the other people who have abandoned him, including Floyd and Susan Glaspell who "cancelled her engagement to come down today . . . saying on the telephone that she would explain later. Meaning: the same old thing—the incredible attitude toward a man undivorced that prevails in this provincial place." Susan's name had first appeared in the correspondence on November 25: "Am to call on Susie Glaspell tonight and hear about you. I telephoned her last night and said, 'I understand you have something for me.' She laughed and said, 'Isn't she a terrible girl?' 'Yep,' I said proudly." Evidently Susan had recently been in New York and had seen Mollie. How she knew her is not clear, but the literary circles in Chicago and New York were small enough so that their paths could easily have crossed.

Jig mentions Susan again in a letter written the next day: "Saw Susie Glaspell last night. 'Twas great to get such new mental pictures of you, also the girl herself is charming. I never realized it. She is to come down here to supper Friday with Floyd and Lillian" [Dell's friend]. Indicating that his thoughts are still focused on Mollie, he explains that the mark on the paper is not a blot of tears but rather another bodily fluid. On November 30, he is still brooding about Mollie's affair. However, part of Jig's desolation seems to involve Susan's aborted trip to the Cabin and his revived spirits in his December 2 letter is probably due to the fact that he has seen Susan again: "Susan Glaspell is *not* taboo. She couldn't come down here to be sure, but last night my mother had her at our house in town—or rather I did, for Susan and I talked and read most of the evening up in the attic den, I walked home with her, and am to go see her."

He moves from this account to a discussion of marriage plans, suggesting that if necessary he and Mollie should go to another state, if Iowa will not allow them to marry after two years, as he fears.

Despite talk of marriage, it is clear in his letters that there is a direct correlation between his growing involvement with Susan and his distancing from Mollie. Were he charting the emotional course of his love, as he liked to chart other events in his life, lines indicating his feelings for the two women would probably intersect during the next week, with those for Susan in ascendancy, although he does not acknowledge the realignment, perhaps even to himself, at this point. Jig did not write to Mollie again until December 9—one of the longest lapses in his correspondence—and when he did the tone was very different. He no longer makes any attempt to hide his anger and hurt over her affair and begins by telling her that he has burned all his letters to her during the past week; yet, he is not prepared to end their relationship and still holds out hope for some happiness for them. He explains that he would be desolate were it not for Floyd, who has agreed to come live with him. This letter must have been written mainly during the day; in a note at the bottom, marked "December 9 evening," after he had received a letter from Mollie telling him that her love is still constant, he is exultant: "I am an eternal thing today . . . heaven is mine." The importance of the letter is not so much in what Jig writes but in the situation that led to his writing of it. His joy may well come in part from Mollie's assurances that he had been replaced in her bed but not in her heart, as he feared. But there was another source. On that same evening, after he had written the first part of the letter and before he wrote the second, Jig had an engagement in town: he and Floyd visited Susan.

Floyd describes the meeting in *Homecoming*: "We called also upon Susan Glaspell, a young newspaperwoman who had begun a brilliant career as a novelist. She read us some of her just-finished novel, *The Glory of the Conquered*, the liveliness and humor of which we admired greatly, though George deplored to me on the way home the lamentable conventionality of the author's views of life."[7] Jig also refers to the novel in a letter he writes to Susan on the morning following the visit.[8] In it—the first letter of their own correspondence—he omits the reservations that Floyd indicates. "That your book deals truly with fundamental things (as *Hedda Gabler* does) is evidenced by the long discussions Floyd and I are having about it," he begins. "You probably don't know how we admired it either. This shows in the fact that when I was picking out elements and things in it and saying I coveted this and that, Floyd answered 'I made one fell covet of the whole thing. I covet her ability to write a novel.' There is no question as to the covetability of *The Glory of the Conquered*." After making one codicil—the Christianity implicit in the title—he excuses her even that and explains that he may be overly sensitive to self-sacrifice because he has so recently fallen into exactly "that pit of self-annihilation," something the young Dell has never experienced, "being an atheist." However, rather than chastising her for incipient religiosity, he decides that the book reflects her own battles against "the inmost essence of Christianity (the thing that was so nearly fatal to me) but without at the same time throwing off certain externals, certain virtues for instance commonly associated with Christianity but not essentially Christian." After other uncharacteristically rambling sentences of qualification and evasion, he returns to his initial praise: "I will not let Floyd have the honor of loving that book any better than I do. I love it for its throbbing vision of life—made more beautiful by the film of tears that floats across the eyes."

From Dell's comments it is clear that Jig's admiration is addressed more to the writer than her writing. He conflates them by making references to Susan's own experience of love, about which she must have told alluded during their meeting. "I feel in it your own heart's knowledge of love—saddened by knowledge that love is less strong than death—and often less strong than life itself." He concludes: "After all I'd better not boast of loving your book. Love is involuntary." The book thus discussed and praised, he turns directly to her: "You don't know how good it was to me to sit and talk last night with a really truly girl—oh a most wonderfully nice girl too. Weren't we all scared when we found out the time? Guilty wretches. I hope Public Opinion in none of its forms will punish any of us, Susie." He signs the letter, "yours sincerely, George C. Cook."

Susan's name now begins to appear with increasingly regularity in Jig's correspondence with Mollie. It is rare to find love letters to one woman so vividly outlining the growing attachment the writer feels for another. Reading them with hindsight, it is obvious that, as he continued to visit her, Jig became more and more intrigued by Susan and that the attraction grew, fed by his extended period of enforced celibacy and the discussions of sexuality and free love evolving naturally from Jig's relation to Mollie.[9] Mollie may well have been able to read the signals—as perhaps Jig, in retaliation, meant her to—because in one letter Jig assures her that she is still the only woman for him, adding, "You probably won't agree with me, but in my mind now the only justification for my flirting or having relations with anyone but you is some possible good effect on our relations, yours and mine."[10] Jig continues to chronicle his "flirting" with Susan. In a long letter on December 17, in which he belatedly recounts his visit with Floyd to Susan's house, he writes, "Susie terrifies me with her overpowering ideal of life-long constancy to an early and vanished love. I couldn't help observing apropos of it that I myself was 'so fickle.' 'You *are* rather dreadful,' she said I wasn't quite so much afraid of her just then, but golly! Sweet as she is, she inspires such an attitude that to think of my kissing her is as though a devout Catholic should picture himself flirting with the Virgin Mary. Not but what it would be nice." He ends, "I'll be glad when I lay eyes and lips on you." Nine days later he returns to the subject. "If I weren't so terrified by Susie I would try to kiss her to see how'd she'd take it." He ends this letter by warning Mollie, "If you don't come pretty soon William will forget what he's for."

Had Jig not been waiting to marry another woman—"An Anarchist Girl" who believed in free love—perhaps the openness of his discussions with Susan might not have occurred. The fact that he intended to wed also made it easier, and more acceptable, for the pair to meet. Jig's "undivorcedness," which made him "taboo" in other homes did not apply to Susan, who could entertain him freely as a friend of his betrothed, a fellow writer, and growing soul mate. She could commiserate with his situation, confide in him about her own great love, and even banter with him about sex. The situation provided them with a license that would have been difficult to obtain if Jig Cook had come to court Susan Glaspell in her parents' home, a place he describes as a "bourgeois parlor where something Presbyterian constrained their minds."[11]

In addition to his correspondence with Mollie Price, Jig's unpublished autobiographical novel, "The Pendulum," offers his version of his growing love for Susan, whom he calls Miriam, Eloise, and, most frequently, Edna Welling. In the novel Jig's surrogate is alternately named Benjamin, Harold, Arthur West, or Thorward Hillard. The "other woman" is a composite: part Sara (his first wife), part Jan (a local woman), and part Mollie. Although the nine extant fragments of the novel offer several versions of similar events and are rough notes that Jig never moves beyond brief sketches, the texts are important for they present a mosaic of the years 1907–1911 from Jig's point of view and depict the way he saw Susan. Repeatedly he describes her spirituality, fancy, wit, and charm. He also refers to what was the central event that shaped her prior to their meeting and to which he attributes her keen sensitivity to his suffering and need for love: "Edna Welling is having a deep life-experience with Clinton Hardwick, an older man, a newspaper owner. She is divinely happy. Her nature soars." In another fragment he writes, "Edna Welling's novel appears. A great one. Well veiled, but the story of her own love for Hardwick and its breaking."[12]

Another element that runs throughout the fragments of "The Pendulum" is also relevant to the way that Jig perceived Susan at this time. Unlike Adelaide, the name he gives to his composite Mollie, Edna "*is* of herself without tinkering." In three or four months they have developed a tender and beautiful friendship based on an instinctive understanding of and sympathy for each other. However, "he does not think of her as an object of physical passion," while she being in love with Hardwick does not, as she could have by a touch [the word *slightest* is crossed out] make him love her in that way." Jig adds, however, "their being man and woman added an unavowed interest and tenderness to their friendship." In a sentence that may explain why Jig continued his relationship with Mollie, despite his attachment to Susan, he writes: "He had a theory that like ought to marry with unlike, that a literary man ought to marry an unliterary woman. And he, before anyone else discovered it, knew that

Edna Welling had a rare and beautiful literary talent. He came to love her greatly, but was not kindled into passion."

From both the incomplete novel and the Jig/Mollie correspondence, it is clear that Jig was attracted to Susan and that had she given him any sign of her love—"the slightest touch"—he probably would have at least rethought his coming marriage. Evidently she did not, and he continued to write to Mollie through the first month of 1908, balancing every reference to "Susie said" with impassioned pleas for Mollie to hurry to him, perhaps his way of indicating that if she did not come quickly he might succumb to weakness and give in to his idea of "kissing Susie." In his last letter before her arrival, he asks Mollie to wipe the slate clean, and he will do the same. However, by the time she arrived in Davenport to become Mrs. George Cram Cook, Jig was already deeply connected to, if not passionately in love with, Susan, and her name was not so easily erased.

As for Susan, when, in *The Road to the Temple*, she comes to this part of Jig's life, she makes no mention of the flirtatious talks and growing verbal intimacy between them. Her most powerful passion is displaced onto the founding of the Monist Society and her enthusiasm for the genius of its founder. Of their personal relationship, she says simply, "Jig and I became friends. He would come to see me, or we would take walks, and talk of all things there were to talk about." It is only when she recounts their last meeting, just before Mollie arrived, that the powerful feelings between them become apparent. "Now life was taking us different ways," she writes, careful not to clarify the date, but specific about the place and time: Central Park [now Vanderveer Park] in Davenport in winter. "I was about to embark on my first visit to New York [an error since she had been there earlier when she met Mollie]. He would be married within a few months. But that last night something outside ourselves brought us together, and there was a new thing between us ever after."[13]

Rather than continuing her account of the evening in her own words, she quotes two fragments from "The Pendulum," thereby making clear that the story of Edna Welling and her friend Mr. West with the shifting first names is essentially the story of Susan and Jig. Together, on a night lit by the Pleiades, the characters in Cook's novel look out "through the cone of night," he sharing with her the ecstatic feeling of oneness with the universe that he first felt in a university library. She omits his awareness that the ecstasy is sexual in origin—"the imperative impulse to love taking the starry universe for mistress." Instead, she offers a more reserved description from the novel, powerful in what it does not say: "His hand moved suddenly toward her in gratitude. She drew hers from her muff. There in the starlit night their fingers exchanged a quick pressure. It sealed something between them—wide as the stars, long as time."[14] She does not comment on the import of the moment in both their lives. In sharp contrast to the elevated language used by Jig, she says simply: "The next few years were full ones for the two who had looked out through the cone of night with a cosmic emotion neither could have felt alone, but they were not experiences shared. And yet, separated though we were—I in New York, then Paris, and Jig married and living at the Cabin, we were never really separated after we came together that night of snow and stars."[15]

Travel at Home and Abroad

10

*Love had not failed—nothing had failed—and life was wonderful,
limitless, a great adventure for which one must have great courage,
glad faith. Let come what would come!—she was moving on.*
                                                    —Susan Glaspell, *Fidelity*

After the required two years "of solitary confinement," as he called it,
Jig was granted his divorce from Sara at the end of January 1908; and in
early spring, he finally married Mollie Price. Floyd stayed on at the Cabin
to greet the newlyweds on their return from their Chicago wedding. Only
one year younger than Mollie, he was immediately drawn to the young
woman who, with great vigor, threw herself into the role she was expected
to play. In fact Mollie was double cast: as the wife of an iconoclast poet-
cum-farmer, a socialist like herself, indifferent to bourgeois values, living
on the outskirts of staid Davenport, and as the wife of the scion of a
distinguished family, who had not decided himself which script he was
going to follow. In *Homecoming* Floyd describes Mollie when she arrived,
"happy and sparking and delightfully talkative." But soon—under the
pressure of societal approbation, immediate pregnancy, and life with her
thirty-five-year-old, brooding husband—a new Mollie emerged. "Marriage had tamed this wild bird," Floyd observed.[1] It was one thing to be
an anarchist and advocate free love from afar, quite another to fit this
philosophy into the Iowa she encountered.

If, as Susan indicates in *The Road to the Temple*, she and Jig were
already deeply connected before Mollie arrived, why did Jig go through
with the marriage? It is hard to say. Perhaps that basically conservative
element in his nature made it impossible for him to alter his plans; per-

haps he still held out the hope that "his anarchist sweetheart" might fulfill his deep needs. They were already sexually united, and Jig had invested much time and thought in concocting idealist fantasies about the perfect love that would spring up between them once they were finally together. Besides, Susan had been his friend, confidant, soul mate, but—judging from his writing and hers—the relationship was still platonic. She may have already been in love with Jig, but she did not seem prepared to stay in Davenport and attempt to win him from Mollie. Her own idealism, expressed in *The Glory of the Conquered*, demanded a love that must be total and not shared. It would also have to be a love with no conditions, an all-consuming love that was not shaded by apprehension and doubt, such as Jig evinced at the time. Therefore, Susan left Davenport before Mollie arrived. The trip was planned suddenly. She had agreed to deliver the paper "Socialism—Present Day Theories and Activities" to the Tuesday Club in mid-February 1908, but sent it with apologies and a request that someone else read it. Her first stop was New York, where she went over the proofs of *The Glory of the Conquered*, scheduled to be published by Frederick A. Stokes the following spring. At the beginning of March, she and her Drake University friend, Lucy Huffaker, now a journalist working in New York, embarked on a year-long trip to Europe. Her ostensible reason for the journey was to have a vacation and change of scene after her exhausting work on the novel. A more pressing reason was to allow herself time and distance away from Jig, to see if his marriage would work.

Paris, her final stop after a three-month tour through Europe, was just becoming a destination for American artists and students in 1908. They came because it offered "a simplified plan of existence amid delightful surroundings, on a less ruinous basis of expenditure than confronts one at home," journalist Anna Bowman claimed.[2] Carl Van Vechten, who had been sent by the *New York Times* to cover Paris during the year when Susan was there, filed a story on a typical young woman attempting to live in Paris on ninety-four cents a day while studying—it was possible, he said, if one were willing and able to climb seven flights of stairs to a room in a pension, do one's own laundry, and eat poor food.[3] Van Vechten, who was then receiving fifty dollars a week and living in comparative luxury with his wife on rue Jacob, advised women who came there to share living expenses and to stock up on items before their departure. While not on a large expense account like Van Vechten, Susan and Lucy had sufficient money to afford more than a poor student's life. Lucy received payments for a series of articles she wrote for New York newspapers and periodicals during the period, and Susan supported herself from advances on her book and fees from her short stories.

The pair found lodging in the Latin Quarter, near the Sorbonne, a district filled with newly arrived young people from many countries, interested in studying art but either inhibited by the presumed debauchery of

Montmartre or the higher prices of Montparnasse. In an interview upon her return to Davenport, Susan would describe her Paris flat as "cozy" and "homelike." The tenor of the interview must have been prompted in part by her wish to dispel any notions of the bohemian life popularized in America by the 1894 publication of George du Maurier's *Trilby*. In addition to trying to domesticate Paris for Iowa consumption, her words reflect her tendency to establish patterns and familiar routines wherever she lived and to see her new environs as a kind of idealized small hometown. People in the Latin Quarter, she said, were a serious group with simple needs. "Every one is doing something."[4] It was just easier and more stimulating for a woman to be doing that "something" in Paris. (She would say the same of her Provincetown friends.) Gertrude Stein, an earlier émigré from America, described her own living arrangements in Paris in a similar vein: "If you are way ahead with your head you naturally are old fashioned and regular in your daily life."[5] Susan, less "ahead" than Stein, still tended toward regularity in domestic and work routines, even in Paris. However, the general appeal of the city in the first decade of the century, like Greenwich Village in the second, was not regularity and order but the opportunity to experience "the new" in ideas, arts, social institutions, and, above all, lifestyles, freed from those societal pressures that limited Americans in general and women in particular. Susan certainly was exposed to a far more exciting mix than her interview would indicate.

She had already displayed both an interest in, and a knowledge of, French art in *The Glory of the Conquered*, making Ernestine a painter who had studied in Paris and sent her work there to be hung. "It's considered rather superior to disdain the Salon . . . but Paris seems to be only way of proving to Americans that good can come out of America," she has Ernestine say, even before she herself saw the new art that was filling the salons and galleries.[6] In her first five months in Paris, the sixth Salon d'Automne at the Grand Palais showed over 2,000 works by more than 600 artists, including Matisse, and leading galleries such as Kahnweiler, Druet, Bernheim-Jeune, and Notre-Dame-des-Champs offered paintings by Braque, Odilon Redon, van Dongen, Dufy, Derain, Marquet, and Picasso. On Christmas Day 1908 Matisse published an essay in which he described the art he was creating: "What I am after, above all, is expression. . . . I am unable to distinguish between the feeling I have for life and my way of expressing it."[7] Five years before the Armory Show brought this new art and theory to America, Susan was able to see it and to read about the assaults upon form and subject matter and about the ascendancy of expressionism, which would find subtle parallels in her own work when she turned to the stage and wrote some of the earliest expressionist dramas in America.

Art was thriving in Paris and so was theatre, the most popular form of entertainment at the time. The plays of Ibsen, Strindberg, Hauptmann, and Maeterlinck were already familiar to the French public, presented by pocket theatres such as Aurélien Lugné-Poe's Théâtre de l'Oeuvre, André Antoine's Théâtre Libre, and Paul Fort's Théâtre d'Art. Like the Provincetown Players, which modeled itself after them, these small theatres sought "new plays, new sight lines, cheap seats, ensemble acting."[8] Manifestos for new, alternative, small theatres proliferated at the time. In 1909 Jacques Copeau, with Jean Schlumberger, André Ruyter, and André Gide founded the *Nouvelle Revue Française*, which published articles attacking popular theatre in words similar to those Glaspell would use in writing about the Broadway theatre she discovered in New York in 1913. Susan had covered theatre for the *Weekly Outlook*, so it is probable, that even with her two years of college French, she went to the theatre in Paris whenever she could. The theatre choices were many; in fact Van Vechten, whose main assignment was to cover a wide variety of human-interest stories, filed so many stories on theatre and opera that the *Times* recalled him, accusing him of being too narrow in his reporting.

The playwright whose works would most significantly influence the direction of Glaspell's own dramas was Maurice Maeterlinck, the Belgian winner of the 1911 Nobel Prize for Literature. In the 1908–09 season his opera *Monna Vanna* and play *The Bluebird* were staged in Paris. In *The Glory of the Conquered*, Susan had already referred to Maeterlinck, placing his works in Ernestine's library. In 1896, in his work *The Tragical in Daily Life*, Maeterlinck described a theatre in which the soul took precedence over the material, and dramatic action centered on conflicts within the self and marked by no external action. As he put it, a person sitting alone in a room, motionless, might "yet live in reality a deeper, more human, and more universal life" than those engaged in violent actions on the stage. Against the argument that such brooding, static plays are "impossible" to create, Maeterlinck put forth the argument that the greatest drama has always relied for its power not on movement and events but on words, divorced from and not subordinate to action, forming an inner dialogue addressed directly to the soul. In such a theatre this "unnecessary dialogue" whose addressee cannot be seen "determine[s] the quality and the immeasurable range of the work."[9] Susan would embrace Maeterlinck's model in many of her plays, most notably *The Outside*, *Bernice*, and *The Verge*. In them she would attempt to create what Maeterlinck called that "intangible and unceasing striving of the soul toward its own beauty and truth," moving beyond even language to the silence used to convey inner struggle, the unsaid more eloquent at times, and more significant, than the said. For both playwrights, the writings of Emerson provided a philosophical underpinning for their work, Glaspell drawn to Emerson's idealism and belief in oneness of the physical and spiritual, Maeterlinck praising Emerson's belief that knowledge of self and the world can be gained by intuition that transcends language and that the little things of life could carry the weight of the universe.[10] Maeterlinck also argued that movement, not as an end in itself but as a visible sign of some invisible struggle, might be used on the stage when words and silences did not suffice. Susan would ascribe to the same ideas, employing an upturned palm, a bent neck, a glance, or closed eyes to indicate inner struggles in her characters or changes in the direction of their thoughts. In later years, Maeterlinck would reject the term *static theatre*. Writing to Barrett Clark in 1913, he explained that the concept was "an invention, a theory of my youth, worth what most literary theories are worth—that is, almost nothing. Whether a play be *static, dynamic, symbolistic,* or *realistic,* is of little consequence. What matters is that it be well written, well thought out, human, and, if possible, superhuman, in the deepest significance of the term. The rest is mere rhetoric."[11] Susan agreed, denying any fixed doctrine in life or in theatre that implied dogmatism, while trying in her plays, especially *The Verge,* to point to that "superhuman" sphere that eludes fixed representation of any sort.

Art exhibits and salons; operas, plays, French lessons, and lectures; "afternoon tea hours when the day's work is done, and friends congregated informally to visit over the 'cup of cheer'"—these filled Susan's "delightful year"—she told the Davenport interviewer. But while Paris might provide "perspective" and "atmosphere," it did not eradicate home. Two friends from Davenport visited, bringing news of Jig and Mollie and of the birth on December 4, 1908, of their daughter Nilla, named after an aunt of Jig's who had died in childhood.[12] There were also letters to and from Floyd, who had left for Chicago in November 1908 and was beginning his career at the *Chicago Evening Post.* "Isn't it great about Mollie's baby," she wrote him. "Suppose Jig is so happy that he won't think of doing any work for a year. But then it's better to be happy than to work, isn't it?"[13] She didn't need Floyd's answer; she was writing directly to Mollie. "Susan and Lucy write me from Paris that they are near socialists," Mollie reported in her own a letter to Floyd.[14]

For all her banter, Susan was not as casual about Jig as her letters imply. Her feelings at the time can be glimpsed in her novel *The Visioning,* begun the next year. Although it in no way furthers the plot, she has her protagonist briefly visit Paris, "the laughter-loving city," and she describes the feelings of loneliness she suffers there because her love is not with her: "The city's streets had always been for her as waves which bore her joyously along. But after a time, perhaps just because she was so live, it made her unbearably lonely. The things they might do together in Paris! The things to see—to talk about."[15]

On March 12, 1909, *The Glory of the Conquered,* subtitled *The Story of a Great Love,* was published. It is dedicated to Dr. A. L. Hageboeck, "who made this book possible," a reference to a well-known and respected Davenport physician, who supported the arts and probably provided Susan with funds to complete the book. Reviews for the novel were laudatory, the *New York Times* critic noting, "Unless Susan Glaspell is an assumed name covering that of some already well-known author—and the book has qualities so out of the ordinary in American fiction and so individual that this does not seem likely—*The Glory of the Conquered* brings forward a new author of fine and notable gifts."[16] Two weeks earlier, her parents had received an advance copy, and her mother immediately wrote to congratulate her daughter on this new arrival: "I . . . thought of all it meant to me this book born and growing amid great physical pain and labor as a mother suffers at childbirth so you my dear one many times suffered while bringing this book to life and none knows this better than your mother, but now the time of travail is over and we will enjoy the fruit." Praising Susan for "so many lovely thoughts, high, pure ideals," she also expresses her fears for her safety away from home, "a bright attractive girl like you exposed to so many temptations, but you know dear I believe a girl with such high beautiful pure thoughts as those portrayed in this book could never come to harm surely her Maker would protect and guard her and give her strength to resist all such." Her mother's letter ends with her desire to see Susan and share this victory with her: "I felt I must have you just to sit and look at you and thank God for having you. Papa thought I would send for you but no I won't I will wait till you are ready to come and then I will have my girl."[17] The letter vividly reflects the contradictions and ironies in Susan's double life. She was a thirty-two-year-old woman, living in Paris; yet to her adoring, churchgoing mother, she was her "precious girl," whose "lovely thoughts and high, pure ideals," she prayed, would protect her daughter from all "temptations." Susan was also a successful writer with a growing reputation; yet, as her mother's description implies, either the book had caused her to sacrifice what should have been her primary calling, motherhood, or—following the pattern Alice's mother had urged—maternity could best be fulfilled through work not through marriage.

In Susan's response she adopts her "Susie" persona, writing on the day the novel was published. After thanking her mother for her letter and for the sacrifices she made to bring the book to completion, she informs her that she has decided to sail home in June, but would be returning to Paris in October. "We want another winter here, not here perhaps, but in Italy. Lulu [Lucy] has work promised, and I want to write another book over here." She tries to soften the news of her extended stay by adding, "now that I have been here once I am sure you will feel better about my coming again"; and she promises to bring her mother to Europe the following spring "so that the separation will not be as long next time as it was this." But the main news is her trip home "and I hope you are glad, for if it weren't for you I do not think we would do it. . . . I am so anxious to see you all."[18] While Susan may well have missed her family, an equally compelling reason for her temporary return must have been to see Jig and assess the situation. By indicating that she planned to return to Europe, she left herself latitude. If the Cook marriage was solid, she could gracefully withdraw; if there were problems, she could decide what to do next.

What Susan discovered on her return was far from clear. Mollie had taken a long time to recover from Nilla's birth, which had been difficult. Happy with motherhood, she, nevertheless, felt physically drained and frustrated, since she burned to be writing "the books and plays and poems and thoughts [that] are begging me to write them," as she confided to Floyd. She also had little time or energy left for a husband who by necessity "lost his title of 'angel child' . . . the title . . . falling, perchance, upon the latest acquisition."[19] In one letter to Floyd, written at the beginning of June after describing her exhaustion, Mollie adds, "Susan has had it pretty hard, too, since her book came out, and by the way I phoned Susan today and she will be down to visit us Thursday. Have you by any chance seen her on her way to Davenport?"[20] Susan, when she arrived at the Cabin, must have been a sharp contrast to Mollie. She was now a genuine celebrity with a highly praised novel, wore the latest Paris fashions, and talked animatedly about the latest intellectual trends abroad. It is no wonder that Jig was awed by her presence. He records his reactions in one fragment of "The Pendulum," in which his protagonist and Edna Welling meet unexpectedly in Davenport. He is wearing corduroys; she is dressed in her elegant new clothes. He notices for the first time her lovely hair and eyes. There seems to be a bond between them; his state, which he calls "emotional hyperaesthesia," "sweeps her like a wave." In the same section, Jig has his hero think about his wife: "She is not what I took her to be—a free, generous and noble woman." He crosses out the next sentence, "She is a malignant woman," continuing instead with, "I am coming to hate her as I hate no other person, simply because I am bound to her." The wife cannot compete with Edna, who makes the hero see life and love in new ways. "The parasite woman and you—an economic Amazon, clearing your own way through our jungle."[21]

While the Cook marriage may have been strained in the spring of 1909, it had not yet reached the breaking point that Jig's later written fiction implies. What Susan discovered when she visited them was Jig displacing onto his writing the frustrations he may have already felt with Mollie, and Mollie struggling to keep the marriage going. Susan thus found herself thrust back into the role of friend and confidant to them both. In *Road* she makes no reference whatsoever to the fact that she returned to Davenport briefly after Paris. Instead she writes of Jig's situation at the time in the most enigmatic terms. "*The Chasm* had not been accepted. Farming was much work for little pay; Buffalo and Davenport seemed far from the centers of life, and despite the things he now had which he had long wanted, it would not seem that the light of imagination was playing over life."[22] Mollie offers a more positive picture in her correspondence to Floyd. Commenting on his recent marriage to Margery Currey, a Davenport teacher whom Mollie had introduced him to before he left for Chicago, she writes, "I asked Jig what drawbacks he found to marriage and after allowing himself sufficient time for reflection he said: 'Can't think of any.' There now—ain't he grand? and don't you wish that you had a husband like that, Margery?" She also tells Floyd that she and Jig would be visiting Chicago in the winter. There is no mention at all of Susan. Mollie, however, does betray her envy of Susan's freedom when she muses: "I wish Jig and I and Margery and Floyd could be in Paris together. Wouldn't it be jolly."[23]

In the fall of 1909, Susan did not return to Europe, as she had written that she would. It was too far away from Jig. But she also could not remain in Davenport, which was too close. Instead, until the situation cleared, and either she got over her feelings for him or his marriage ended, Susan decided to go to Monte Vista, Colorado. Her Davenport friend Mabel Brown worked there as a stenographer for the Rio Grande National Forest Employees and got Susan a temporary job as clerk for the U.S. Forest Service. "Monte Vista," from the Spanish, means "mountain view," an appropriate name for a town situated at 8,000 feet above sea level, in the center of the flat San Luis Valley, in south-central Colorado, with the 14,000-foot Sangre de Cristo range to the east, blood-red at sunset, and the equally massive San Juans to the west, snow-covered most of the year. The train that deposited Susan in Monte Vista ran from Denver to nearby Creede, the destination then for 300 passengers a day. It would be the same train that Ruth Holland would take in the novel *Fidelity*. Although Monte Vista was light years away from Paris, it was already an established community in the midst of a land boom, with a well-developed agricultural base, three newspapers, two hospitals, eight churches, a post office, library, and opera house. In some ways Monte Vista was similar to Davenport at Glaspell's birth, the second generation only just beginning to spoil the terrain, but the few mansard-roofed houses incapable of blocking the view.

While not the frozen wasteland that is implied in her use of the locale in *Fidelity*, the town was the most physically challenging place Susan had lived. She responded positively to the rigors of the life, the beauty around her, and the classless, open lifestyle, where institutions were still in the making and not fixed, as they had been in the Davenport of her youth. There was a camaraderie that appealed to her. Life was hard, the winters harsh, but the people working for the Forest Service were drawn there for a purpose: to protect the land from despoliation at the hands of water barons, who even then were attempting to cut the forests for their own gain. In her second novel, *The Visioning*, Monte Vista and the Forest Service are set in apposition to Government Island, a thinly disguised version of Rock Island Arsenal in the Mississippi River; and Katie, the sheltered, pampered protagonist of the novel, is compared to Helen, the Forest Service clerk, who is good at her job, plans to work after marriage, and even finds time to read Whitman (an author Katie's girls' school never offered her). Helen is even able to vote, living in a state that in 1893 enfranchised women. In the novel, which she began while in

Monte Vista, Susan also contrasts the environmental war being waged by the Forest Service against the militarism embodied in Government Island society. Katie's brother, a career officer, admits that he would gain "more satisfaction in constructive work than in work that constructs only that it may be ready to destroy" and would prefer "to help give my country itself—through natural and legitimate means—than stand ready to give it some corner of some other country."[24] By the end of the novel, Wayne has resigned from the army and moved to Colorado to bring his expertise to bear fighting water barons not foreign troops. Susan is thus able to present one of the first arguments in modern American literature for the importance of conservation and for social service as an alternative to military service.

Susan also uses her Colorado experience in her 1915 novel *Fidelity*. A mountain retreat becomes the refuge for her lovers Ruth Holland and Stuart Williams, who have become pariahs because they have placed love above duty and have chosen to live together outside of marriage. This time the Colorado setting is harsh, cold, and bitter, much like the lives of the couple worn down after eleven years of hiding and drudgery. Glaspell is realistic about the effect of enforced isolation from family; however, Ruth has no wish to return to the security and warmth of the inner circle in a fictionalized Davenport. At the end of the novel, when she finally extricates herself from Colorado and the now-loveless union with Stuart, it is not back home that Ruth travels to but to New York. Susan in Monte Vista in the winter of 1910 was less sure of her direction as she waited to see what would happen between Mollie and Jig.

In *Road* Susan condenses this waiting period and its end into a few brief sentences describing a letter Jig wrote to her and his cryptic appeal from Davenport.

> I had come home from Paris and was spending a winter in Colorado. One day I got through the drifts to the post-office and in my box, nine thousand feet [*sic*] above the sea, found this letter: "Have you ever had a feeling that there are loose ends—important strands slipping out of grasp—essential elements evaporating? It was in some such darkness this morning that I came out of sleep and found my mind's hands groping for a lost, important strand in the dwindled rope of life, and came with a splendid shock and sense of salvation upon the thought—Susan!"[25]

The letter, or at least her transcription of it, does not overtly focus on her but on Jig's thwarted book, which he hopes she will help him complete. It is in keeping with the tenor of the entire biography: circumspect and vague about details too personal to share. Only indirectly might it be construed as a love letter. It was, however, the signal for which Susan had been waiting. She had made every effort to distance herself from Mollie and Jig during the past two years, presumably unwilling to be the active agent in the rupture of their marriage. But Jig's letter implied that the union—or at least his life—was foundering of its own accord, without her intervention, and that he needed her. She immediately returned to Davenport and to him at the beginning of January 1910. This time she did not leave.

"Though Stone Be Broken"

11

Her life itself mattered more than what any group of people thought about her life.
　　　　　　　　　　　　　　　—Susan Glaspell, *The Visioning*

What Jig had omitted from his letter was that Mollie was once more pregnant, but that fact did not alter his determination to end the marriage. A young wife who suffered from morning sickness, fatigued by caring for a toddler, and frustrated by her inability to recapture her own sense of vitality and self was hardly the muse Jig needed. Susan was ready and willing to provide a different kind of inspiration. At first, they were discreet. Their meetings were ostensibly to discuss his stalled novel and her new one. Soon, however, they took on a project that provided them opportunities to be together under the guise of social action. During the winter of 1910, the Labor Lyceum of Davenport sponsored a series of Sunday lectures. The speaker at the February 14 meeting, presided over by Jig, was Rabbi Fineshriber, whose talk "A Study in Religious Liberty" outlined the gradual encroachment of religious institutions in secular life and warned of such creeping theocracy. It was Susan who stood up at the end and described an example of just such an encroachment in the community. Recently the library board, appointed by the mayor, had voted to censure head librarian Marilla Freeman's request for the purchase of a highly praised book entitled *The Finality of the Christian Religion*, written by George Foster, professor of the philosophy of religion at the University of Chicago. A newspaper reporter attending the lecture printed Susan's criticism of the board, and it became the opening volley in what came to be known in Davenport as the "library controversy." Responding in the *Davenport Democrat* to her comment, Mr. E. A. Sharon, who had voted against the book, admitted that he hadn't read it and that he and the majority of board members were swayed in their vote by the criticism of the work by Father Ryan, one of four Catholics on the board of nine, who believed the book would be harmful to Christian values in the community. How could Professor Foster have anything positive to say about religion, Sharon suggested, when in a recent sermon, he had praised the feminism of George Sand and taught in an institution supported by Standard Oil money![1] Susan answered in a long letter to the editor, arguing that books which open readers to challenging ideas should be part of any library list. She also questioned the authority of the board to censor books.[2] Her words against religious coercion parallel the similar debate that occurred while she was a student at Drake and to which she refers in *The Glory of the Conquered.*

To carry on this fight, a new group was formed, the Ethical Society of Davenport, whose prime objectives were "the promotion of benevolence and practice of the highest ethical conceptions in all walks and phases of life; the study of facts and laws of nature as the only infallible guide in the search for truth, and the free development of each individual self into the realization of its loftiest ideals."[3] Its leaders were Susan Glaspell and George Cram Cook. The group's activities took place in the months leading up to city elections and became a rallying call for those working to oust the incumbent Democratic mayor, George Scott, who had appointed the library board. When the election results were tallied on April 3, despite a Democratic landslide, which returned all six aldermen to office, Scott was unseated by Alfred Mueller, an "inexplicable" result, the newspaper proclaimed. Susan provides her own explanation: "We wrote the papers such stinging letters, both Monistically and individually, that the short-sighted candidate for mayor who had first defended the Board was quite snowed under by enlightenment."[4] Five days after the election, the paper announced that "the library matter had been amicably settled and that Professor Foster's book was now on the shelves of the library."[5] Susan, as she usually did, put experience to good literary use. The library controversy became the subject for one of her most delightful, tongue-in-cheek short stories, entitled "Finality in Freeport: A Great Agitation That Proved 'A Tempest in a Teacup.'" In it she pokes fun at the conservatism of the community as well as the righteous indignation of the opposition, including herself.

The library controversy was the first time that Susan and Jig had worked on a project together, and the results had been successful, reinforcing their sense that they belonged together. Their public stand against conservative elements in the community and religious intolerance was also an indication that together they dared to challenge Davenport institutions more openly than either had done up to now. After the mayoral dust had settled, they devised mutual writing projects that allowed them to continue their collaborations. Mornings they would walk along the Mississippi or hike beside the creek that wound its way toward the woods behind the Cabin in Buffalo. In a shady place, they would sit and create elaborate scenarios that might serve as the basis of a joint book. Jig described one scene to Floyd: "Susan and I had a day of creative energy here about a girl going to the city to seek her social salvation—a *questess*—you will recognize the model. We telephoned the model to come down and tell the story of her life—we wanted to put her in a book. She did—and somehow the reality—graver, weightier than our incipient dream, overwhelmed us." He also relates another scenario Susan wanted to explore: "a socialist-individualist contrast between the girl and the man."[6] Jig imagined having the two trade places, each having converted the other.

The day in question may not have proved successful, but both ideas are similar to those the pair incorporated in the two novels they were separately working on at the time and which they published the following year: Susan's *The Visioning* and Jig's *The Chasm*. In both a young woman, an articulate representative of her class—rich, lovely, protected—is attracted to a man who stands outside of the society she knows and is a socialist who works with his hands. Susan calls him Alan Mann, "the man who fixes boats"; Jig makes him a gardener, Walt Bradfield. In both plots the man introduces the woman to ideas related to socialism, evolution, poetry, and radical new books. "From the first it had been as if the things of which they talked were things sweeping them together, they were in the grip of the power and the wonder of those things," the protagonist of *The Visioning* thinks, probably putting into words Susan's own feelings at the time.[7] The meeting place for the couples in both novels is described as an island retreat in the Mississippi, away from the prying eyes of those who live on shore or in army compounds. Floyd Dell, in his 1920 novel *Moon-Calf* uses exactly the same setting for a love tryst; however, in his abandoned novel of 1907, based on the same love affair, he does not bother to camouflage the locale. It is actually the Cook cabin in Buffalo—where Susan and Jig worked on their books and which they used for their fiction.

Although "the man who mends boats" is almost a duplicate of Jig's rugged socialist gardener, Susan does not accord him the role of central catalyst for the change in her protagonist, Katie, as Jig does his Marion. Instead she creates a doppelganger in the person of Ann, the young woman whom Katie saves from an attempted suicide in the Mississippi. Ever prone to bringing strays home with her—much like Susan did as a girl—Katie treats Ann at first like another saved creature, installing her in her home and creating a new identity for the young woman. Initially, her actions are motivated only by charity and curiosity. Soon, however, she becomes deeply connected to Ann. If Helen in the Forest Service in Colorado offers one point of reference for Katie, Ann, the psychically and physically abused, love-starved young woman, offers another. Questions that had not concerned Katie before, such as the daily drudgery of life for poor working women, the double standard of a society that condemns women who "fall" but does not condemn the men who seduce them, and the limited choices such women have, now intrude in Katie's privileged, sheltered life. By the end of the novel, Katie gains a new understanding of the world around her and of her potential to break free of those things that hold her in place. Unlike Glaspell's first novel, in which love is idealized and portrayed as all-consuming, *The Visioning* presents love as an outgrowth of comradeship and shared social awareness, mirroring the nature of the growing bond developing between Susan and Jig, as both wrote their books.

Jig was anxious for the literary and personal collaboration to continue. As he wrote Floyd that spring, "The writing will of course be its own reward, but Susan is on the verge of writing to you, and if you wrote a valuably suggestive letter to me about *this*—do you see? she'd fall off the verge."[8] Dell was enthusiastic, at least about their writing merger: "Each had something the other tremendously needed—Susan's humor, story-telling capacity and sheer literary expertness, conjoined with George's magnificent ideas and brave truthfulness, should make a masterpiece. . . . Never were there literary needs which had a happier fulfillment than in such a collaboration, I thought."[9] What he did not suspect was the implication of Susan's falling "off the verge."

By the summer of 1910, it became obvious. When Floyd and Margery returned to Davenport, they discovered that the relationship had moved beyond fiction. Mollie was about to give birth, and Jig and Susan were deeply—and openly—in love. While Margery sat with Mollie and heard her story, Jig and Floyd walked the familiar fields around the Cabin, and Jig told him that that he now realized that he had been in love with Susan even before he married Mollie. As Floyd assessed the situation, "Mollie, who would really have been glad to settle down in respectable bourgeois monogamy with Jig for good and all, had in this emergency at first fallen back on her old Anarchistic ideas, and was prepared to be tolerant of Jig's affair with Susan. But Susan was a full-fledged romantic, and she wanted Jig all to herself, never mind the consequences."[10] Floyd had little sympathy for his friend; he particularly resented the blithe way Jig seemed to cast off women. He also could give little sympathy to Susan because, as he writes in *Homecoming*, she had hurt his feelings "very badly" before he left Davenport, and he had not yet gotten over the incident. He does not explain what she had done to him, but it is likely that Gloria, in the opening scene of *The Briary Bush*, the sequel to *Moon-Calf*, is Susan, just back from Paris with her friend, wearing the latest Parisian fashion and assuming a sophisticated air (a temporal distortion since she returned after he left). Gloria chides the protagonist to read from his new novel, saying that nothing in it will shock her; but when he does, she takes offense at something in it and, worse, tells the entire community, betraying him and wounding his pride. Although Susan and Floyd would remain friends in later years, the event, much disguised, and described in the fiction was evidently too close in time to allow him much generosity when it came to Susan as the other woman.

On August 23, 1910, Mollie gave birth to a son, Harl, the name again chosen by Jig, who claimed to be honoring Harl Meyer, his college roommate at Iowa, who had first taught him about "the art of kissing."[11] Mollie by now was finding it impossible to pretend that she didn't care about the affair Susan and Jig were having. She had written to Floyd that, "the value of sexual love is very much overestimated and holds too consuming a place in the scheme of things. The old fashioned God of Repression has a wise purpose behind him."[12] Mollie was not the only one to call for repression and to question the couple's unbridled passion. Jig had long ago written off the Davenport community and knew well their views about his unconventional life style and his reputation. He had hopes, however, of receiving a sympathetic ear from his few close friends, particularly Rabbi Fineshriber. With Dell gone to Chicago, Fineshriber had become indispensable to Jig, visiting him often to discuss poetry and philosophy. However, he, too, criticized the love affair on the grounds that Jig was destroying his marriage and affecting the lives of two infant children. "He knows no one in whom he is so keenly disappointed as in his friend G.C.," Jig confided to Floyd in July. "He has reluctantly come to the conclusion that G.C. is a monumental egotist, the most self-centered man of his acquaintance." Jig also passes on the rabbi's advice: "Every man is by nature a polygamist and would like to have passionate love affairs; but most men who have taken upon themselves the responsibility of a family take these impulses in time and nip them in the bud." Jig resented the criticism. "A situation that has made me ten years older in two months is not one that facile people like Fineshriber have any power of conceiving."[13]

Floyd was receiving letters not only from Jig and Mollie, but also from Fineshriber. In one dated October 11, the rabbi expresses his disgust for "this whole miserable conventional liaison." Although he accuses Jig of insensitivity and of being "a child who tires of his toys too easily, and who won't even attempt to mend them when they crack or break," it is Susan he most vehemently condemns, calling her "an amateur vampire." He tells of lashing out at Jig during a recent visit to the Cabin but of remaining silent about Susan—the actual source of his anger—because "chivalry . . . debars a gentleman from speaking of an absent lady, who is embroiled or stewed with the man to whom the aforesaid gentleman is speaking." He reports to Floyd that her name came up only once and then "by the Injured Party who remarked sadly that there was a Third Party too who was to be considered. I was stupefied and denied her existence."[14]

These correspondences offer some sense of the situation in Davenport as the Cook/Price marriage unraveled and the Cook/Glaspell love affair developed. As usual, Susan's only record of her thoughts can be found in her writing. Katie's words at the end of *The Visioning*, when she states that she will no longer be influenced by what other people say, must have come directly from the situation Susan faced when she wrote the book. Even more, her next novel, *Fidelity*, addresses this period, from a distance of five years. However, these are works of fiction and are layered and disguised for art and anonymity; *The Road to the Temple* purports to be "true." In "Though Stone be Broken," one of the briefest chapters in the biography, Susan succinctly alludes to the affair: "I was in Davenport not long after this and would visit the Cabin. We talked about *The Chasm*, which Jig was rewriting. We talked of what the last few years had been to each of us. One spring evening we were following the creek up the woods. We paused, listening to water falling over stones. Through a tree we saw the first star of night. We spoke of that night of stars in Central Park, when the world was so still that the silence was as something coming in from the sky. His hand moved again to my hand, again our fingers clung. This time they did not draw apart."[15]

Susan continues with one of her most candid glimpses of the love that, even metaphorically, could now speak its name. It is no longer the companionate feeling of *The Visioning* but rather the consuming passion she describes in *The Glory of the Conquered* and at the beginning of *Fidelity*: "Love may be strong as death. Death you will face easily for love, for that somehow does itself. Even more than disgrace you will face for love. You will risk hurt and shame to those you love. You will violate your own sense of fairness and right. In a world that is falling around you love dwells as sure, as proud, as if life had come into being that this might be." She follows with a detail about herself and Jig, omitting mention of Mollie and Jig's two children:

> I was going away. It was the last evening we would have together—
> for we did not know how long. We met at Black Hawk's Watch
> Tower—a few hours together on that bluff of Rock River, where
> the Old Indian chief had watched in other days, where Indian lov-
> ers, too, had known the sweetness and no doubt at times the pain
> and terror. It seemed now that life was driving us apart, and out of
> the anguish of that, from the rending of much we had held dear,
> in the crash that was the years, glowed a love which gave life to
> the love of vanished women for men long in their graves. We knew
> who we were, we knew what it all was, and that is why I mur-
> mured: "I wish we could die now."[16]

Unlike many sections of the biography in which Susan telescopes or alters events or conflates fiction and fact, the evening she describes actually took place, on June 28, 1910. As she indicates, she was planning once more to leave Davenport for an extended period, but this time their love was acknowledged and Mollie, about to have her second child, also knew. The question was whether Jig would be able to extricate himself and whether they would eventually be free to marry. The chances of both seemed slim at the time. After leaving her that night, he returned to his parents' Davenport home for a few hours of sleep before heading to Buffalo, and immediately he began a letter to her which starts, "Tonight when you spoke of dying thus together was the first time I have really felt the lure and beauty of death." His penmanship is sure when he writes these words, but the paragraphs which follow, written the next day, are filled with scrawls and erasures. In disjointed words, he tells her that when he woke after a brief sleep, he finally felt the full weight of her departure and was overwhelmed by their love, and he begs her not to let his "old fickleness" stand in her way. Continuing later in the day, he describes himself now sitting in the Cabin dining room, Mollie singing "Goodbye Sweet Day" on the piano nearby, "every note and word of it expressing my sorrowing love of you." He then turns to their present situation, indicating that Susan had finally revealed that she had loved him ever since 1907: "Those hours and times you've told me of through two and a half years which now, looking back on, seem hints and premonitions of your love for me—how can I make you feel how beautiful the thought of them is now?" And of the evening they have just spent together, he tells her: "Dear: if it weren't for my hope of seeing you again before so terribly long and finding that lovely love alive in you through all bitterness and hurt—then I would regret beyond every other regret that we did not carry into act that feeling that it was best to lie down together in our last beautiful union and never rise again from each other's arms."[17]

Three months later the Cook marriage was over. Mollie, taking Harl with her, went east, leaving Nilla in Buffalo with Jig. Although she had struggled to accept the situation, Mollie had been terribly hurt. She still loved him and tried to dissuade him from seeking a divorce, but Jig was adamant. "We did enough debating, Lord knows, and it never did anything but create bitterness," he wrote to her in New York, where she was staying.[18] Money created an added strain. Mollie's letters are filled with images of her plight, now alone with two small children to support. His own possibilities for money hinged on the success of *The Chasm*, which Stokes had finally accepted for publication. He had already received one positive letter from a young editor working there, Sinclair Lewis, and he hoped it augured well. Mollie eventually was forced to return to Davenport. Few were yet aware of the impending divorce. Ma-Mie knew, since Mollie had written to her from New York requesting car fare home; however, even in April 1911, a month after he had finally left Davenport himself and moved to Chicago to work with Dell, Jig was still asking his mother to keep the news from his father. Once more, the rebel Cook found it impossible to disappoint his father.

Jig agreed to a divorce on the grounds of desertion, arguing that an adultery charge would undermine his means of earning money for the family. He also suggested that Mollie consider working, since it would end "the injurious self pity and restore some of the self respect which you seem to have altogether lost." He even describes work that would be suitable for his ex-wife to perform: "I ask you not to rush into floor-scrubbing or something of that sort. Stenography for instance, would sound better if my present or prospective employers come to hear what you are doing; and you'll see that impressions on my employers have a relation to the welfare of Nilla and Harl." Seeking once more to clear his own conscience, he warns her against laying on him the blame for the "situation that arose in your life," that is, "the loss of character, the deterioration that threatens to swamp you and that will swamp you if you don't face things as they are and meet them."[19] His attitude toward Mollie reveals an ugly side of Jig: egotistical, given to self-justification, totally insensitive to all but his own needs and wants. If Mollie had ceased to be his ideal love, then for him, as he writes in "The Pendulum," she ceased to matter.

It is this aspect of Jig's personality that Floyd abhorred, that under the cloak of the ideal of love he justified abandoning Mollie and his children. However, Floyd's feelings were hardly objective either. In an unpublished work, he admits that he had been in love with Mollie himself, since she first came to the Cabin, and he relates the events of the summer of 1911, when, at the urging of Margery, he spent his vacation in Davenport alone and visited Mollie at the Cabin. Jig had already moved to Chicago, and Susan was in New York. He recounts that Mollie, "after entertaining me with some marvelous stories—she was a wonderful story-teller—proceeded cheerfully to take me to bed with her."[20] For Floyd the event was shattering: It was something he could not share with Margery, and it illustrated by its passion and naturalness both the staid sexuality in his own marriage and the possibilities and ease of sexual adventures outside its confines. The experience, much disguised in *Homecoming*, provides the initial impetus for his future casting off of Margery and for the beginning of a ten-year period in which he far outdid his "spiritual father" Jig both in love affairs and in the romanticization of them. Mollie and Floyd stayed friends throughout her life, although they agreed that their sexual encounter would not be repeated. After living for a period of time with the Cooks, Mollie moved to back to Chicago to be with her father and made plans to move to California with the children, where she took up teaching. Dell, writing of her in 1949, recalls, "She was one of the sweetest girls that ever lived, and life dealt her hard blows."[21]

For Jig, Mollie's departure from his life made little difference once the "tangles" of divorce were unknotted. He now had a new love to sustain and support him. However the breach between Jig and his children was not so easily dismissed, and it never completely healed. From time to time they would visit him in Provincetown, where he lived with Susan; and Nilla spent time with them in Greece. But a basic antagonism created by his desertion of their mother remained, most acutely in Nilla. In a letter to Hutchins Hapgood her father's close friend, written in the 1930s, she confesses: "As to Jig, he was a perfect stranger to me until long after he had died";[22] and in May 1960, almost fifty years after the divorce, in a letter to her son, Sirius, Nilla still displayed her resentment. She describes to him the beauty of the Cabin and the extraordinary nature of her grandmother, whom she called Bom Mie, her own childhood variation of Ma-

Mie. She urges Sirius to visit Buffalo, although by now the Cabin, sold by Jig's brother Ruel to a cement factory, bore no trace of its former beauty. Mentioning the paltry $300 Mollie had received as her share of the sale, she recalls that her mother's alimony settlement included an office building in downtown Davenport to be held in trust for the children: "She was wheedled into giving away [its] rights and set out for California alone with two children and no money but ten dollars from my bank. Because she was an idealist so sensitive and noble that she asked for nothing." Of her father she writes: "It was such a scandal that after all his education he had given up teaching in Leland Stanford to drive a vegetable cart to town. It was then that Susan broke into the blissfully happy life he had with Mollie, and Mollie, hurt and adoring, wanted to 'free him for his happiness.' Losing her the whole reason of shaping his earth in Iowa was suppressed by him but remained always the dream of a seer."[23]

It is understandable that Nilla would choose to see the breakup of her parents' marriage as Susan's fault. However, judging from Jig's voluminous diaries and his constant attempts throughout his life to chart his mental state, had it not been Susan who came to him at this time, it would most likely have been someone else. He had idealized the free-spirited Mollie; and when she revealed her human side, he lost interest. At the same time, Mollie reversed the equation and began to see her husband in godlike terms. What Jig now sought was someone who understood and accepted him, with all his many failings, someone who would be both helpmate and ballast for his own, often wavering self-image and fortunes. Susan provided all this. The youthful, vibrant, earth-grounded Mollie was not ethereal enough to fit the mold Cook imagined; neither could she mother and nurture him. Susan Glaspell could do both. Believing herself in the possibility of total love, she could understand and appreciate the neediness of Jig for passionate love. At the same time she was a woman who had already forged her own personality before she met him. The responsibility for her soul and life need not be his; she was more than capable of fending for herself—and for him—both economically and spiritually. He knew this and admired her for her independence. Mollie was twenty-two when she became Mrs. George Cram Cook. Susan was thirty-seven when she and Jig married. And she remained Susan Glaspell, never taking his name, for the rest of her life.

The question can be asked: What did Jig give her in return for her love? From the few glimpses Susan allows into her private relationships, it is evident that he provided the type of love for which she was looking, not one which required self-abnegation, even of the variety Ernestine espouses, but one which offered a meeting of two souls in understanding and passion. One of her notebooks contains a fragment describing such a marriage: "the islands join beneath the sea. . . . They knew that underneath the things that went on in life was that open way between them."[24] In addition to a spiritually open way, there was also sexual passion. Many people throughout Glaspell's life pointed to the seeming contradiction in her demeanor. On the surface she could look like a benign schoolteacher, as writer Arnold Sundgaard described her;[25] but she also possessed a smoldering sexuality evident to her close friends. She also believed in the primacy of passion. Without it, marriage cannot survive, Ernestine argues. When Ruth Holland discovers that hers has burnt itself out, she has no problem leaving Stuart Williams—the man for whom she has sacrificed her family and home—and going off on her own, so fiercely does she connect sexual love to the life force and the life force to the very essence of her being. Susan felt the same. Once she knew she loved Jig and he loved her, there was nothing that would stop her from having him. To have done less would have been for her to be untruthful to life itself.

For Jig's part, after their evening at Black Hawk's Tower, he wrote a poem, one of his most sustained and polished works, expressing his emotions and his hopes for their future love. It is titled "Though Stone be Broken," the title Susan chooses for the chapter in *Road* that chronicles the growth of their love. The setting is the creek behind the Cabin, Buffalo creek, the place where Jig had dreamed of Greece as a boy, where he and Susan had first revealed their love, and where Jig had shared this news with Floyd, who had refused to offer solace to his friend. All these experiences are woven into the poem. Susan, omitting cumbersome or too revealing stanzas, includes a portion in this section of the biography. In it, Jig watches the water gradually wearing down the rocks as he questions his own despair for the things not done and the friends not faithful. It is only his new love that sustains him. The poem concludes with two stanzas she omits in the biography: "Love, dearest love, whom bitter barriers keep / In loneliness afar, / Oh bear it till the surging waters sweep / Away the bar. / Barrier and bar go down beneath love's force / Between the shaken shores; / Though stone be broken, down his destined course / The torrent pour."[26]

Staging Area for the Future

12

So many of us began there, got our early impressions of life there, made friends there. Had we stayed in the home nest, in Chicago, when it all began for so many of us, the Robin's Egg might have hatched.
—Sherwood Anderson, *Memoirs*

While Jig was waiting for his divorce, Susan spent most of her time writing and traveling. Although her family and Jig's were not yet aware of their affair and their intention to marry, she was slowly disentangling herself from Davenport and home and moving physically and psychically closer to New York and the life they intended to establish there. She met with publisher Frederick A. Stokes to see about the publication of *The Visioning*, which appeared in April 1911. It is dedicated to her mother, and the epigraph, taken from Proverbs 29 reads, "Where there is no vision, the people perish." The response to the book depended on how the reviewers measured this work in relation to her first novel. Those who admired *The Glory of the Conquered* found *The Visioning* less satisfying, its scope more diffuse, and its central character less idealistic and "understandable." Those who recognized Glaspell's criticism of war and the military, her championing of women's roles in society, and her argument for socialism praised her efforts in furthering the possibilities of what women might discuss in a novel. One New York critic, overlooking this social agenda, concluded that no matter how readers compared the two books, "All must admit that it does prove Miss Glaspell's staying power, her possession of abilities that put her high among the ranks of American storytellers and at the same time set her a little apart from any of the others. For she sees the world more as spirit than as material fact."[1]

Although the royalties of both novels provided her with income, her main source of money continued to come from her short stories. She published six between 1910 and 1912. In addition Stokes brought out *Lifted Masks* (1912), a collection of thirteen stories: four new works, the rest a sampling of those she had published as far back as 1903. Again, setting the idealistic tone, she chose as the motto for the book a line from Browning: "Loftier than the World Suspects."

Their love propelled Jig as well as Susan out of Davenport. While she was traveling, he severed ties, gave up his truck farm, and moved on to Chicago, where Floyd Dell had gone two years earlier and was enjoying a success that read like a Hollywood scenario. At twenty-three Dell had become the editor of a prestigious weekly, the "Friday Literary Review," published by the *Chicago Evening Post*. The newspaper had launched the "Review" in March 1909, under the editorship of Francis Hackett, a brilliant journalist from Ireland with skills at turning a phrase and uncovering a new talent or trend and a belief that American letters, now coming of age, deserved a criticism that spoke its language. Hackett tended to chide new writers to abandon old forms. For example, his review of *The Glory of the Conquered*, argued that the book was only moderately successful because of its emphasis on what he saw as self-sacrifice. "However it is only fair to say that the author has chosen the romantic rather than the realistic métier and those who like the former will not object to the insubstantial character of the scene."[2]

The "Review" soon became one of the most respected and influential molders of literary taste in America. The writing was lively and erudite without being pedantic, introducing readers to homegrown writers, important works published abroad, and contemporary readings of classic literature. When Hackett went to New York in 1911 to help start the *New Republic*, Floyd took over the editorship. The trickle of new, socially progressive writers—Frank Norris, Upton Sinclair, Jack London, Jig—soon became part of an outpouring of modern literature, not all good but at least interesting enough for Floyd to use as a forum for his own theories of what should be written and why. He would "briefly" review one hundred books a week and write an extended column on one; he would also enlist others to carry similar loads. Margaret Anderson, in her memoir *My Thirty Years' War*, tells of having fifty reviews waiting to be written over a weekend and still having time to go to the Chicago Symphony. She had begun to review under Hackett, who tried to curtail her exuberance. "Why all the big words? I have to cut half of them out. A little simplicity, please, and at intervals a great word for beauty." Dell's instructions differed: "Here is a book on China. Now don't send me an article about China but one about yourself."[3]

One who had no trouble personalizing his writing was Jig. After moving to Chicago, he readily took over as associate editor of the "Review" under Dell. "Sometimes I wish the Provincetown Players had been a magazine," Susan wrote in the section of *The Road to the Temple* she called simply "Chicago," which recounts events of this period.[4] If it had been, Jig's ability to inspire others with his vision might have left a more lasting testimony to his genius. In a period when, as Susan noted, criticism was dreary, Jig brought his passions and intellect to bear explaining the merits of those writers he personally loved: Nietzsche, Strindberg, Homer, Henry James, d'Annunzio, and H. G. Wells.

While Jig's contributions to the "Review" were important, it was Floyd that many in the arts community and in the old-guard Chicago establishment wanted to meet. Although Dell was basically shy, particularly in large groups, Margery Currey, his wife, loved entertaining, and had a natural talent for bringing diverse people together. Their apartment on Morse Avenue in the Rogers Park section of Chicago became a meeting place, equivalent in spirit if not in size to the salon Mabel Dodge would institute in New York three years later. It grew even larger when, in 1913, they moved to Fifty-seventh Street and Stony Island Avenue, an area just starting to be used by artists. By then Susan and Jig were already living in Greenwich Village; but between 1911 and 1913 the Rogers Park apartment became a second home for Susan. She arranged to pass through Chicago as much as possible on her trips back and forth between Davenport and New York, often visiting her Chicago-based dentist and staying on to spend time with Jig. During these visits, she got to know many of the writers who became part of the Dell/Currey group, including Margaret Anderson, Martha Baker, Witter Bynner, Augusta and Lucian Cary, Marjorie Jones, Harriet Monroe, John Cowper Powys, and Eunice Tietjens. Some, like Edna Kenton, would remain lifelong friends; others, including Lucian Cary, Theodore Dreiser, Edna Ferber, Florence Kiper Frank, Kirah Markham, Cloyd Head, and Brör and Margaret Nordfeldt would be associated with the Provincetown Players; and still others such as Maurice Browne and his wife, Ellen Van Volkenburg, would provide models for the work she and Jig were about to undertake.

Browne had recently arrived from England, bringing with him a résumé that attested to his own peripatetic background and interests: educated at Cambridge, tutor in India, volunteer in the Boar War, and founder of a small, prestigious publishing house, the Samuri Press, which brought out poetry, including *From the Isles*, by Arthur Davison Ficke, whom he had met in India. While in Florence, Browne had fallen in love with Van Volkenburg, a young Chicago actor, and had followed her home in 1910. Nellie Van, as Browne called her, had already made a reputation for herself through her unique ability to see one performance of a play and then, in a trance-like state, remember all the parts and play them faithfully from memory. She had been presenting these one-woman recitals but wanted to become a "real" actor and have her own theatre. Chicago already had one "little" theatre company, which Laura Dainty Pelham had begun in 1900 under the auspices of Jane Addams's Hull House.[5] In the fall of 1911 the Abbey Players of Dublin came to America, performing Synge's *Playboy of the Western World*, which they brought to Chicago after stops on the East

Coast. Lady Gregory, who accompanied the troupe, met with Browne and Van Volkenburg and encouraged them, advising: "Engage and train, as we of the Abbey have done, amateurs: shopgirls, school-teachers, counter-jumpers; cut throat thieves rather than professionals. And prepare to have your hearts broken."[6]

The new theatre took the name the Chicago Little Theatre: "a small theatre would cost less than a large one; therefore ours was to be a *little* theatre," Browne explained.[7] Its prospectus indicated two objectives: "to create and produce a poetic drama" and "to promote free discussion of life and the arts." Heeding the suggestions of Lady Gregory, Browne chose amateurs, almost all of whom were women, since few men were willing or able to undertake the long rehearsal process he required. For their per-formances, they rented a fourth-floor space in the Fine Arts Building on Michigan Avenue, across the street from the Chicago Art Institute. The address was impressive, the theatre minuscule with ninety-two to ninety-nine seats, depending on the critic describing it, and a stage measuring fourteen feet across, twenty feet deep, and eight feet high. If the toilet flushed, everyone in the auditorium heard the sound. Although the theatre made only a limited impact in the general Chicago community, its influ-ence reached far beyond the city. Jacques Copeau would acknowledge the debt his Vieux-Colombier owed to it. In *Road* Susan only mentions the Little Theatre in passing, giving credit instead to the Irish Players for inspiring the Provincetown Players. She may not have wanted to deflect glory from Jig's creation, yet Browne's experiment was a model of what little theatres could do and be.

He was not the only one at the Dell/Currey evenings intent on start-ing something new and "little," by dint of limited finances and a natural abhorrence for material bigness. The idea for the *Little Review* came to Margaret Anderson in a dream; and the next evening at the gathering she announced her plan to start a publication in order to share her love for the new poetry, literature, and ideas discussed around her. When it ceased publishing fifteen years later, the *Little Review* could claim to have brought American writers such as Sherwood Anderson to prominence and introduced America to the best writings of Europeans, particularly James Joyce. In this period, when the arts seemed to be bursting forth in Chicago, other magazines sprung up which were also dedicated to dis-seminating the works of new writers. Harriet Monroe, with connections to wealthy Chicago patrons, and herself a poet, started *Poetry*, which quickly became a launching pad for the works of a group of midwestern writers including Carl Sandburg, Vachel Lindsay, and Edgar Lee Masters, all of whom were part of Dell's circle. Monroe's assistant at *Poetry* was Eunice Tietjens. In her autobiography, *The World at My Shoulder*, Tietjens describes her first evening at Rogers Park as an awakening, particularly through her meeting with Jig, "who said the thing that released me, as the right thing said at the right moment has the power to do."[8]

Sherwood Anderson, another midwesterner, fed up with bourgeois life in a small town and yearning for the collegial warmth of other writers, found his way to the parties on 57th Street, and soon designated Floyd as "a kind of literary father." In later years, when preparing his *Memoirs*, Anderson made a list of the significant people he had met and where he had met them. Next to Cook, he writes "an empty room"; next to Glaspell (which he spells with one *l*), "New York." Although Susan only met Anderson a few times, something about his person and their shared background touched her deeply. Born two months before him into a similar midwestern family and community, she recognized the pressures that weighed him down and his struggles to turn them into art. When Anderson told the New York literary critic Van Wyck Brooks, "You know a man cannot be a pessimist who lives near a brook or a corn field," Susan understood what Brooks could not, that the beauty of the Midwest stayed with one who was born there.[9] There is another aspect of Anderson's life that must have roused Susan's empathy. Dell makes the connection, when he describes the similar way in which Cook and Anderson in 1912 turned their backs on wives and children who stood in the way of their desires or careers. Susan, knowing how his divorce had severed the ties between Jig and his children understood what Anderson's freedom cost.

Although Susan visited Chicago as much as she could, most of the time between 1911 and 1913, she was either in Davenport or New York. However in the summer of 1912, she and Lucy rented a cottage from *McClure's* magazine editor Viola Roseboro in Provincetown, the small Massachusetts fishing community on the tip of Cape Cod, which Greenwich Village writers and artists were beginning to use as their summer retreat. Jig, during his vacation, visited them there and felt equally taken with the place. This was an extended reunion; usually they could only eke out a few days together. Jig calculated—as was his wont—that they met 12 days out of the last 108 before his divorce became final. As difficult as this time was, Jig, for the most part, was sanguine about their separation, knowing that they were about to begin a life together. Jig's letters to Mollie during the waiting period before their marriage spoke of sexual yearning and created erotic scenarios that he imagined them performing. His letters to Susan describe his great love for her and the pain caused since they must "abstain from love." But they are also filled with news and gossip about mutual friends and publishers, and with mundane concerns of daily life: how happy he is that her new typewriter works, how comfortable he finds his new chair. Susan and Jig already had common experiences and interests; she was not entering his life for the first time, as Mollie did. They were building a life together that already had a good foundation. Passion is there, but it is a passion tempered by what they both had gone through to reach this point. In one letter Jig writes, "The desire to be good to you and make you happy is a deep instinct, one that has deepened and grown and struck roots everywhere in my nature until it is the center of all things—the center of me myself. I cannot think 'Jig' without thinking 'Susan's.'" In the same letter he tells her: "You and I are lucky, dear Susan, both of us, that the power to love was not killed in us, but remained alive until we found each other deepened by sorrow and capable of giving each other such intense joy."[10] He begins to use the pet names that they were now calling themselves: she is the Little Bear, he the Big Bear.

As the date of his divorce decree neared, Jig moved to New York to find an apartment and set up contacts for them. He also began a series he called "Letter from New York," which he filed for the *Post*. To have remained in Chicago would have been easier; they knew the city and felt at home there. But in 1912, the direction for most midwestern writers was eastward, particularly toward Greenwich Village. On Memorial Day 1912, a few months before his departure, Jig wrote Susan about what he expected their new life to be. Typically, he did not confine himself to their personal love; he was already imaging their role in a larger community, a "beloved community of life givers." He laid out his plan or this new group he imagined: "An American Renaissance of the Twentieth Century is not the task of ninety million people, but of one hundred. Does that not stir the blood of those who know they may be of that hundred? Does it not make them feel like reaching out to find each other—for strengthening of heart, for the generation of intercommunicating power, the kindling of communal intellectual passion?"[11]

His divorce became final in April 1913. The couple planned to marry in New York and leave immediately for Provincetown, where they had rented the Roseboro cottage for a second summer. Jig counted down the days in daily letters written to Davenport, where Susan was staying in the last six weeks before her departure on March 30. By now her parents were aware of her plans to move east and marry Jig. Whether they knew how far back the relationship went or of Susan's hand in the breakup of his marriage is not clear. Susan's brother Ray wrote to Jig congratulating him and praising his sister: "She has had the courage of her feelings."[12] As usual, it took Jig a longer time to share the news with his own family. One week before Susan arrived, he informed his mother. "It made me wish that I had been telling her about our marriage five years ago," he confided to Susan.[13] When Susan wrote that she had also shared the news with a friend from Chicago who congratulated her, he commented: "I think there's hardly anybody that you could tell of it who wouldn't get your feeling and be in sympathy. That might have happened even with some of those shallow prejudicers [*sic*] from hearsay."[14] (Jig was overly optimistic about the sway of love on Davenport. The Tuesday Club, to which Susan had belonged and to which her absence made her inactive, did not make her an honorary member until 1932, after she was no longer "Mrs. Cook" and, therefore, no longer the "other woman.")[15]

Finally the countdown was over. On Sunday, April 13, Jig wrote to Floyd, telling him his weekly column was in the mail. In the second paragraph he announces: "But tomorrow, Floyd dear, I shall be on the Fall

River boat en route to Provincetown. With Susan. The mayor of Weehawken across the river is going to give us permission at noon tomorrow at the house of Blanche Norton's sister, Mrs. Dr. Fredrick, ex-Davenporter. They won't let Justices marry people anymore in New Jersey. Our prejudice against the theological would probably bar preachers even if their prejudice against marrying divorced persons did not bar me. Hence the mayor. It's his first job. Susan and I are happy people." He closes by inviting Floyd to visit them in Provincetown: "There's going to be a bully atmosphere for work there or I miss my guess."[16]

The wedding announcement that appeared in the Davenport paper was edited for local consumption. It made clear, lest anyone wonder, that Miss Glaspell had left home two weeks before the marriage and had gone first to Chicago and then directly to Weehawken, where she had been joined by her bridegroom on the day of the wedding. Once this point was clarified, the remainder read very much like a professional résumé, with the numerous publications of each duly listed. No mention was made of Jig's previous marriages or his two children. In the accompanying photos, the bride and groom look exactly like other couples in the "Just Married" section that week. Susan is posed demurely, one hand to her cheek, hair up, not yet bobbed, wearing a white ruffled dress, one of two photos taken during her Drake college years, fourteen years earlier. Jig is stiff and dour in a white shirt with rounded collar and tie, hair parted in the center, accentuating Cook's widow's peak and distinct heart-shaped face. Although they were writers and lived in far-off, suspect places, they visually passed the test as proper Davenporters. As a further bow to convention, the newlyweds even sent out wedding announcements. In a tongue-in-cheek version to their friend Charlotte Rudyard, a New York–based editor of *Harper's* Magazine, Susan wrote: "This is to tell you that two of your admirers got married last week. I am one of them. George Cram Cook is the other. We married each other. I guess that tells it. I've already dated wedding announcements, such solemn, pompous looking things."[17] It was mailed from Provincetown.

Interlude 1

Greenwich Village, 1913: The Joyous Season

*I want more life—more things from life. And I'm going to New York
just because it will be so completely new—so completely beginning
new—and because it's the center of so many living things. And it's such
a wonderful time.*

—Susan Glaspell, *Fidelity*

The spring of 1913 was a perfect time to start a new life, and Greenwich
Village was the perfect place to do it. Other midwestern writers, artists,
political activists, and seekers of change, like Susan, were heading there
for many of the reasons that had motivated the original westward thrust:
new opportunities, new freedoms, and new frontiers to conquer. As Ruth
Holland explains in *Fidelity* about her own decision to restart her life in
the East: "There were new poets in the world; there were bold new thinkers; there was an amazing new art; science was reinterpreting the world
and workers and women were setting themselves free. Everywhere the old
pattern was being shot through with new ideas. Everywhere were new
attempts at a better way of doing things." Besides, Holland adds, in New
York City—unlike Freeport, "Nothing is mapped out."[1]

    To the critic Van Wyck Brooks, such an inchoate whirl of forces might
be likened to a vast Sargasso Sea, but the very openness and lack of boundaries were seen by most as the period's most important, defining elements
and as a continuation of the spirit embodied in the man who became
the symbol of this new age: Walt Whitman. Floyd Dell called Whitman "the great Liberator," who "freed us—from whatever chains most
irked."[2] Although dead twenty years, Whitman was still remembered in
Greenwich Village at an annual dinner in his honor at the Brevoort Hotel

and in lectures his biographer Horace Traubel gave at the Liberal Club. Whitman's famous dictum—"if I contradict myself, very well I contradict myself"—had emblazoned Mabel Dodge's writing paper at Villa Curonia in Florence, even before she arrived in Greenwich Village; had shaped the photographer and curator Alfred Stieglitz's belief that "Static consistency is contrary to life";[3] and would frame Susan's later contention that biography could not be neatly packaged since "life, too, is combinations that baffle classification."[4] Ex–philosophy instructor turned editor Max Eastman said that he shaped the editorial policy of the journal *The Masses* after the model provided by Whitman: eclectic, physical, celebratory; and Jack Reed, who was responsible for writing the actual manifesto printed on its masthead—just as he would later be charged with writing the constitution for the Provincetown Players—declared that the magazine would be "sensitive to all new winds that blow, never rigid in a single . . . phase of life. . . . And if we change our minds about it, well—why shouldn't we."[5] The French painter Marcel Duchamp, who sought a temporary home in New York at the outbreak of World War I, gave the idea a Dadaist twist: "I force myself to contradict myself so as to avoid conforming to my own tastes."[6] Even Eugene Debs, who ran as Socialist Party candidate for president in 1912, 1916, and 1922, referred to "the divine Walt" who was not bounded by dogma. The bardic yawp drowned out the Progressive bugle in Greenwich Village, and the sound resounded outward from there. As Floyd Dell recognized, "we had something which it seemed all bourgeois America—sick to death of its machine-made efficiency and scared respectability—wistfully desired to share with us: we had freedom and happiness."[7]

This outpouring of people settling in Greenwich Village at the beginning of the second decade of the century has now become part of the country's legend, mythologized and romanticized in histories, fiction, and the personal accounts of those who participated in one of the most exciting periods in American cultural history. Ten years later, similar groups would settle abroad, usually in Paris; this group, with a few notable exceptions, visited foreign shores but quickly returned home. "Tether yourself in native ground," Henry James had advised Edith Wharton, although neither had physically done so. Susan and her friends in Greenwich Village and Provincetown took the advice and attempted to establish communities styled in many ways on the ones their own pioneer forbearers had fashioned; but rather than "tether" themselves to anything, they saw their activities as freeing and revolutionary, their lives and work unbounded.[8]

"I am part of the avant garde," twenty-three-year-old Mary Heaton Vorse had exclaimed when she moved to Greenwich Village in 1897, one of the earliest of Glaspell's circle to arrive.[9] The area in which she lived was still for the most part a quiet, backwater of New York City, kept quaint and enclosed by the configuration of the streets, winding haphazardly back upon themselves. First American Indian village, then Dutch farm, English hamlet, military post, fashionable enclave, city ward, and immigrant haven, Greenwich Village—or simply the Village—gracefully evolved into the form for which it is still known: the haven for bohemia in America.[10] Its geographical boundaries were debatable. Maps indicate an area from Fourteenth Street on the north to Houston or Canal on the south and from Broadway to Tenth Avenue; but John Reed, journalist, poet, adventurer, and "our 'marvelous boy'"—as Floyd Dell called him[11]—drew the parameters differently in his satirical poem "A Day in Bohemia." Just out of Harvard, where he had been a cheerleader, and living at 42 Washington Square South with other writers, he could claim with equal vigor that "within a block of my house was all the adventure of the world; within a mile was every foreign country."[12] For him the Village was more a state of mind than an address, and he celebrated it in poetry: "Yet we are free who live in Washington Square, / We dare to think as Uptown wouldn't dare, / Blazing our nights with arguments uproarious; / What care we for a dull old world censorious / When each is sure he'll [sic] fashion something glorious? / Blessed are though, Anarchic Liberty / Who asketh nought but joy of such as we!"[13]

Dell, who arrived six months after Susan and Jig got married, and who, as he did in Chicago, almost immediately fell into a job and a position of power, fixes on one event in 1913 that heralded the establishment of the latest "Greenwich Village of which all the world has heard."[14] It was Henrietta Rodman's break from the staid Liberal Club, a lecture society and gathering place for reform-minded intellectuals established in 1907 in the Gramercy Park area. Because of its refusal to open membership to blacks or allow anarchist Emma Goldman to speak there, Rodman— called "a *Candide* in petticoats and sandals"—organized a more radical faction on MacDougal Street in the heart of Greenwich Village, above a restaurant run by Polly Holladay and her brother, Louis. In one move, Villagers had two things needed for the cohesion of any group: a place to meet and a place to eat. "Why shouldn't intelligent people to-day have the same chance to know each other that the church and the tavern gave their grandparents," Rodman argued. Rodman's Liberal Club also offered a variety of lectures on new movements of interest: Goldman spoke on free verse as an integral part of the anarchist program, on sexuality, and on homosexuality; the visiting English suffragist Christabel Pankhurst discussed women's rights; Vachel Lindsay read his verse poem *Congo*; and an unnamed lecturer demonstrated the beauty and sensuality of the tango.[15] Susan and Jig, on their arrival, immediately became charter members and fixtures at the club. When the one-legged poet Orrick John first visited New York, he proudly announced to people back home that "in the course of a few evenings at Polly's, I met Lincoln Steffens, Theodore Dreiser, Bill Haywood, Joe O'Brien, and Susan Glaspell."[16]

One-Thirty-Seven MacDougal Street, the building housing both the club and the restaurant was owned by Mrs. Jenny Belardi, an aspiring actor, interested in the arts and willing to deal with tenants often unable to pay the rent on time. Along with her sister, she also owned the buildings at 133, 135, and 139. These three-story brownstones became the heart of cultural life for the Village: the first floor of 135 housed the Washington Square Bookstore, opened in 1913 by the brothers Charles and Albert Boni and soon incorporated into the Liberal Club when—with Mrs. Belardi's permission—a dividing wall between the two buildings was broken and club members could freely browse in this bookstore-*cum*-library. In 1916, when Jig was looking for a likely spot to establish theatre for the Provincetown Players, it was logical that he, too, would settle on a Belardi establishment, first choosing the ground floor at 139 and later moving to a larger space at 133.

Another quite different gathering place, drawing most of the same people who frequented the Liberal Club, was the salon established by Mabel Dodge in late January 1913. Mabel's "evenings" were carefully directed by a woman with a flair for theatricality and a genius for creating decors against which any discussions gained in intensity. In Florence, where she had lived for the previous seven years, she had taken the old Villa Curonia, carefully redecorated it to recapture its Renaissance beauty, and then invited her friends including Gertrude Stein, Alice B. Toklas, Jack Reed, and Carl Van Vechten to play out convoluted dramas in this setting. In her apartment at 23 Fifth Avenue, between Ninth and Tenth streets, decorated completely in white (to counteract the grime of the city, she maintained) and lit with a central Venetian-glass chandelier that created "exquisite shadows on the white ceiling,"[17] she was determined to create a similar ambiance. She wanted to bring together the most important, interesting people in New York; and with the help of Hutchins Hapgood, who wrote a general column for the *New York Globe*, and Van Vechten, who now covered the New York music scene, she did. Anarchists, labor leaders, birth-control advocates, suffragists, writers, artists, teachers, lawyers, doctors—whoever rang the bell and took the elevator to her second-floor apartment—were welcome as long as they were involved in the new movements afoot and able to discuss them with wit and verve. Later the salon became more selective in order to monitor the overflow crowds and more structured, usually organized around a central topic, presented by invited guests. Emma Goldman and Big Bill Haywood, the head of the International Workers of the World (IWW), debated anarchism and the labor movement with English Walling, a well-known socialist leader. Walter Lippmann, another young Harvard graduate recently arrived in the Village, organized a program on psychoanalysis, a topic of much interest, in the wake of the recent combined visit of Sigmund Freud and Carl Jung to America. On one evening, artists for the radical magazine *The Masses* confronted mainstream editors; on another, Van Vechten arranged for two black musicians from Harlem to play the banjo and dance. In one carefully invited event, peyote was introduced by a cousin of Hapgood who had been doing ethnological studies with Native Americans in Oklahoma.

Most social and cultural historians of the period have tended to disparage Mabel Dodge; she is an easy target because of her tendency for self-parody, exaggeration, and her unbridled enthusiasms. However, her idio-syncratic memoirs make fascinating reading, as do her numerous articles on everything from the writing of her friend Gertrude Stein to interior decorating and psychoanalysis, which she knew firsthand, as a patient of not one but two of the leading followers of Freud in America: A. A. Brill, who spoke at her salon, and Smith Ely Jelliffe. She was also important because she presented a case study of a woman of accomplishments and interests still not free of a Victorian upbringing, which had taught her to question her own talents and to live vicariously through a man. Lincoln Steffens thought he was complimenting her—and so did she—when he observed, "Men like to sit with you and talk to themselves!"[18] Susan and Jig knew Mabel both in New York and in Provincetown, where she spent several summers, beginning in 1914. She became the model for Mrs. Patrick in Glaspell's play *The Outside*, and her chandelier with its expressionistic shadows was one of the inspirations for Susan when she created similar effects with a lantern in Claire Archer's tower in act 2 of *The Verge*.

Mabel's was unquestionably the most famous salon of the period. A more informal meeting place was the home of Marguerite and William Zorach, later active in the Provincetown Players and the only husband and wife represented in the famous New York Armory Show. They had both studied art in Paris, where they met, and had returned to America in 1910 to continue their work, he turning to lithographs and sculpting, she to textile design. In their small apartment at 123 West Tenth Street, the Zorachs held open house against a backdrop of elaborate, stenciled wall hangings, hooked rugs, embroidered decorations, lithographs, and furniture painted in vivid Fauvist hues: lemon yellow, purple, cobalt, and vermilion. Susan and Jig would use a similar palette to decorate the first house they owned in Provincetown, called Gay House by their friends not only for the happiness of the inhabitants but also for its intense col-ors. Marguerite's art extended to clothing; she created hand-dyed designs, which would become associated, in the 1960s, with bohemian dress fads and which some Village women adopted, in 1913, as an alternative to the natural burlap sack dresses, sandals, and brown socks of Henrietta Rodman. While Susan followed the Zorachs' lead in interior design, she, like many of her professional women-writer friends, sidestepped the dress of both Zorach and Rodman, opting for corset-free middie blouses and dark skirts. She did follow one Village trend, bobbing her hair in 1913. Her thick brown curls were cut short and curled around her ears. Most who describe her mention this luxuriant, short hair as one of Susan's most striking features.

In addition to the Liberal Club and various Village salons, there was another important group Susan joined, although she does not mention it in her biography of Cook, nor does it appear in most chronicles of the period. It was called Heterodoxy, an organization that drew together the leading feminist activists at the time. It was the earliest of the Village avant-garde institutions, starting in the summer of 1912, and it lasted the longest, until 1940, long after Dodge's salon had succumbed to her waning attention in 1914, the Liberal Club to the economic pressures of war in 1917, and *The Masses* to political attacks in the same year. Heterodoxy was begun by Marie Jenny Howe, a former Unitarian minister, who wanted to provide women with a place to meet and freely discuss any issue or topic that interested them. "It was the easiest of clubs. The meetings were addressed by members. It entailed no duties or obligations. There was no press. Everything that was said was off the record," its unofficial historian Inez Haynes Irwin maintained. "The only quality demanded of a member was that she should not be orthodox in her opinions."[19] Luncheon meetings took place every other Saturday at Polly's and later, when the restaurant moved and dining out became too expensive, in a meeting room in Town Hall. Susan was one of 25 charter members. Over the years the group's numbers grew to around 110, according to Judith Schwarz and Kate Wittenstein, who have written contemporary studies of Heterodoxy. The roster of member reads like a Who's Who of those involved in the central issues concerning women at the time: suffrage, birth control, sexuality, careers, work opportunities, family organization, socialism, education reform, and the arts. More than half of the members were in some aspect of theatre; however, any attempt at classification does a disservice to the range of interests and accomplishments of Heterodites. Ida Rauh, for instance, who would become a leading actor with the Provincetown Players, was also a lawyer who studied with Crystal Eastman at NYU; a birth-control advocate, arrested for distributing pamphlets in Union Square with Margaret Sanger; a socialist, who introduced her future husband, Max Eastman, to Marx and Engel's writings and influenced the direction he would take as editor of *The Masses*; an accomplished sculptor, who worked with Jo Davidson; as well as a painter and a poet. Other Heterodites were equally talented and diverse.

Meetings consisted of "background" talks, an early example of what, in the 1970s, would come to be known as consciousness-raising groups, in which the personal became the political. Since it was all "off the record," women talked freely about their personal lives. Many, like Susan, came from the Midwest and described what it was like to grow up in that part of the country. Irwin recalls one talk in which a woman openly admitted that she would not have married her husband had she not lived with him for a year prior to marriage. "It was the first time that I had ever heard any woman make a statement that, in my childhood and girlhood, would have been described as 'compromising.'" At Heterodoxy, women put aside the notion of the double standard and challenged concepts such as "woman's honor" through their candidness and scathing wit—a technique Susan would also employ when she reduced "woman's honor" to parody in a play by that name. As one member's anthropological satire proclaimed, "The tribe of Heterodites is known as a tabooless group. There is the strongest taboo on taboo. Heterodites say that taboo is injurious to free development of the mind and spirit."[20]

In her notes about the club, Irwin gives short biographical sketches describing a few prominent members, including Susan. Writing that to praise Susan for her career as both playwright and novelist would be "a work of supererogation," Irwin begins by commenting on Susan's successful marriage to Jig. One-third of Heterodites were divorced, and most who were married made it a point to go by their own names and stand on their own accomplishments. Therefore, it is significant that Irwin focuses on the close relation between Susan and Jig, noting "There was an exceptional congeniality between them." They are only one of three couples whom she cites as helpmates and partners: the other two were herself and her second husband, Will Irwin, and Charlotte Perkins Gilman and her second husband George Houghton Gilman. Irwin also records an interesting anecdote about Susan. At the time, a popular pastime at evening parties was a kind of "who done it." Someone was designated "the murderer" and another "the murderee," lights were put out, the condemned "killed," and when lights came up, guests had to discover the "killer" with the aid of an assigned "judge." Irwin reports that Susan was such an expert judge, "conduct[ing] the whole trial with what seemed perfect understanding of the law and with a psychological deftness which ultimately revealed the murderer and his motives," that no one wanted to replace her.[21] Her time spent covering the Hossack case proved useful.

Of all the groups with which Susan was associated in her first years in Greenwich Village, Heterodoxy was the most significant for her theatre work. There she found women who, as Irwin described them, were the most open, least prejudiced she had encountered. They were at home with ideas. All could talk; all could argue; all could listen. They would become a ready inspiration and audience for her plays. Also, by the very fact of being an active member, Susan made clear her own political, feminist predilections. Not every member picketed and got arrested, but all supported suffrage, birth control, and women's rights; and most supported socialism and antimilitarism. It was in her writing that she, as much as any other Heterodite, expressed her dissatisfaction with women's roles in the society, using her pen to blast the stereotypes and rhetoric of patriarcial society.

Another institution that played an important role in Village life was *The Masses*, which became the official news organ for the community. It was not enough to have places to meet; if a society wished to forge a new lifestyle and revolt against traditional forms, it needed a publication in which to disseminate its ideas. *The Masses* provided that function once Max Eastman, a young Columbia University philosophy instructor, took over as editor of a narrowly defined socialist publication at the end of 1912 and, with the help of Floyd Dell, who became managing editor the next year, shaped it into the central organ for creative experimentation and social change published in New York between 1913 and 1917. Its masthead proclaimed it "A Revolutionary and not a Reform Magazine." It espoused most of the same radical positions discussed at Heterodoxy including suffrage, feminism, and birth control—as well as supporting radical socialism, the IWW labor movement, and, after the outbreak of World War I, pacifism and antidraft protests.

Two celebrated and revolutionary events occurred during 1913, the year Susan moved to the Village; and the effects of these events were felt for years and would influence the work Susan was about to undertake. The first was the famous Armory Show, the second the Paterson strike pageant. Susan was still in Davenport when Jig wrote her about "the picture exhibition" that he and Edna Kenton had attended for two evenings in a row, causing him to miss dinner and for his feet to hurt "something scandalous."[22] Like many, they had waited until the closing nights of the event, March 14 and 15, and thus became part of the 10,000 spectators who jammed the Sixty-ninth Regimental Armory Hall, on Twenty-fifth Street and Lexington Avenue, to see the largest gathering of art ever presented in America. In eighteen banner-festooned exhibition areas, decorated with live pine branches replicating the logo of the show, an uprooted pine tree, were 1,300 carefully chosen pieces. They ranged from Old Masters, strategically placed near the entrance doors, to the new artists beginning to sweep Paris—Picasso, Matisse, Braque, Cezanne, Brancusi, Duchamp—who were displayed in the back exhibition space, nicknamed "The Chamber of Horrors" by detractors. This new art, virtually unknown in New York and not seen outside of Alfred Stieglitz's tiny gallery 291 and the pages of his pioneering journal *Camera Work*, created an explosion. *Cubism* suddenly became the term of the moment, guaranteed to raise blood pressure and debate, while Marcel Duchamp's *Nude Descending a Staircase*, the single most controversial and sensational work in the show, spawned a cottage industry of those seeking a sufficiently derisory title for a painting in which, they argued, there was neither a nude nor a staircase.

By the time the Armory Show closed in New York, after its month-long run, more than 90,000 people had seen it, and smaller traveling versions presented during the next two months in Chicago and Boston drew another 210,000 visitors; but its impact went far beyond the numbers who actually attended. Mabel Dodge, a sponsor of the exhibition and one of its most ardent supporters, claimed that the Armory Show was the most important event in America since 1776, and, as often in her writing, although hyperbolic, she cannily touched on a central point. In his *New York Globe* column, written the month before the Armory Show, Hutchins Hapgood declared: "There seems a vague but real relationship between all the real workers of our day. Whether in literature, plastic arts, the labor movement . . . we find an instinct to blow up the old forms and traditions, to dynamite the baked and hardened earth so that fresh flowers can grow."[23]

Creativity, spirit, and *freedom* became words equally applied to the new paintings displayed in the Armory Show and to the revolutions occurring in a wide variety of social and political experiments during the period. Establishment America had depicted anarchists, such as Emma Goldman and Alexander Berkman, and labor leaders, like Big Bill Haywood, with sticks of dynamite protruding from their pockets, ready to literally blow up buildings and institutions. But now conservative leaders were becoming aware of the explosive power inherent in words and pictures. Goldman in her 1914 study *The Social Significance of Modern Drama* illustrated the ways in which the plays of Ibsen, Strindberg, and Shaw were also providing "the dynamite which undermines superstition, shakes the social pillars, and prepares men and women for the reconstruction."[24] Such playwrights were not interested in merely "patching up" society, like Progressive-era reformers; they insisted on completely throwing off "the dead weight of the past." Susan and Jig joined this radical revolution, both in their personal lives and in the direction of their work.

The second event in 1913 also had all the hallmarks of the radicalism of the period: It was explosive, revolutionary, and creative; its goals were diffuse and sometimes contradictory; it celebrated freedom and championed a new social order; it was run by amateurs, who had more enthusiasm than experience; it drew together diverse people from different social, cultural, and political streams; and it didn't make money. It was the Paterson strike pageant. Like the Armory Show, it crystallized "the new spirit" and brought many of the same people together. Susan missed the first event, but was in the audience with Jig to see the second and worked herself to create it. If the Armory Show introduced the new art to America, the pageant introduced the possibility of what a new theatre could be and helped pave the way for the one Susan and Jig would soon create. It also illustrated what could be accomplished if working people and intellectuals banded together in a common cause. "We have the feeling that we want to go out and fight on the barricade. But there is no barricade," Floyd wrote when he arrived in October 1913.[25] Had he come six months earlier, like Susan, he could have found a cause: the silk workers' strike in Paterson, New Jersey.

The strike was only one of several that took place in America between 1910 and 1913, the most successful of which was the Lawrence, Massachusetts, weavers' strike of 1912. It had been a great victory for the IWW (or Wobblies, as they were called); and when the Paterson silk workers struck for better working conditions and wages, the IWW assumed that the strike would be equally successful, since the numbers of strikers were greater, reaching 25,000, and their skill levels higher than those in Lawrence, making it more difficult for mill owners to replace them. Paterson is only fifteen miles away from New York, and Villagers slowly began to learn of this latest union struggle through its leaders Big Bill Haywood and Elizabeth Gurley Flynn, well-known and popular Village figures (he frequented Dodge's salon, and she was a member of Heterodoxy). On

April 28 Jack Reed visited the strike for the first time and, while talking to workers on the picket line, was arrested at the same spot where an onlooker had recently been killed. When asked what was his business there, Reed had misunderstood and answered "poet." Although he served only four days of the twenty-day sentence he received, the "poet" had sufficient time to learn firsthand about the workers and their cause, and he turned his experiences into an article for *The Masses*, which began, "There's a war in Paterson, New Jersey."[26] Judging from his article, the events of Paterson already seemed stageable. Dodge in her memoirs takes credit for actually suggesting that the strike be performed. "Show the whole thing: the closed mills, the gunmen, the murder of the striker, the funeral,"[27] she suggested one evening to a group meeting at Haywood's apartment. When he asked where such a hall could be obtained, Mabel suggested the one place big enough for such a pageant: Madison Square Garden, an ornate building then located on Madison Avenue, between Twenty-sixth and Twenty-seventh, ironically appropriate as a venue to fight Big Business since the land had been owned by a Vanderbilt and the building was developed by Carnegies and Mellons. Reed, also present that evening, loved the idea and shouted, "I'll do it." Soon the former Harvard cheerleader was leading 30,000 strikers and their families in union songs, even using the tune from "Harvard, Old Harvard" for one chant. The pageant forged what one contemporary critic has called "the fragile bridge" between labor and artists, who for that rare moment in American history worked seamlessly together for a common goal.[28]

In less than three weeks, Reed, aided by his fellow Harvard classmate Robert Edmond Jones, Dodge, Margaret Sanger, and more than eighty Heterodoxy members, including Susan,[29] created one of the largest and most successful pageants ever presented in America. On the afternoon of June 7, 1,200 workers, arriving by train from Paterson, joined an additional 800 supporters in triumphantly marching up Fifth Avenue singing the *Internationale* and the *Marseillaise* and carrying red banners emblazoned with union slogans. This was the unofficial first act of the pageant. When they entered the auditorium, more than 15,000 people, most standing, greeted them with cheers as the strikers made their way down the red carpet "road" that Jones had installed and marched up to the stage. This blending of spectators and performers underlay the entire event, with Reed and Jones skillfully staging the scenes—the workers entering the factory, their call for the strike, the death of one of the bystanders, his funeral, and the union speeches by Haywood and Flynn—so that the audience became one with the workers, angry at the closing, silent at the death, cheering and singing at the demonstrations that followed. Dodge reports that she was on her feet the entire two hours of the performance—shouting, booing, and singing—and had "never felt such a high pulsing vibration in any gathering before or since."[30] Others who attended found it equally exhilarating and unforgettable; it showed the potential for theatre to be participatory, political, and relevant. New York newspapers and journals, even when they were critical of the strike and the strikers, generally praised the power of the pageant. For the strikers, too, the event was extraordinary. As one explained, "We were frightened when we went in, but we were singing when we came out."[31]

The union never received the amount of money they had hoped the pageant would generate and some, like Flynn, cited the workers' participation as the cause of the eventual defeat of the strike the following month, criticizing Reed and Dodge for immediately leaving for Florence and showing indifference about the results. However, the effect of the pageant was long-lasting and positive for the Villagers who had seen and worked on it. One year later, Jig would look back on it as "the dramatic expression of social ideas which made this the most interesting winter New York has known" giving rise to the "staging [of] ideas in the streets and squares of Manhattan."[32] In *The Road to the Temple* Susan mentions the evening as directly inspiring the theatre she and Jig dreamed of creating. What struck her as most important was the fact that Reed had been able to capture the actual experiences of the workers. "He put into it the energy of a great desire, and in their feeling of his oneness with them they forgot they were on a stage."[33] She describes sitting up late with Jig after they returned from the event, talking "of what the theatre might be." Three days earlier, Jig had written in his column: "It is possible that this pageant with a purpose may fail suggestively—that the impulse it generates may later be refined by greater artistic skill."[34] Three years later it was.

The Provincetown Players, 1914–22

A Home by the Sea

13

Life is beauty and change and interest in a house by the sea.
  —Susan Glaspell, *The Road to the Temple*

At 5:00 P.M. on April 14, 1913, after a festive luncheon at the Brevoort
Hotel with friends, Susan Glaspell and Jig Cook, their marriage sanctioned by the mayor of Weehawken, New Jersey, walked up the elegant
gangplank of the side-paddled steamship *Priscilla* at Pier 14 in the lower
Hudson River for the trip to Provincetown, the first place in which they
would officially live as man and wife. They could have taken a variety
of routes to this small fishing village on the tip of Cape Cod. The New
England Steamship Company went to Boston, and the steamer from there
connected to Railroad Wharf in Provincetown. Alternatively, a train from
Boston to Fall River met a local train running through the length of the
Cape. But Jig, who had tried several combinations, settled on the most
expensive, $3.00, and the most romantic. With mahogany paneling, gold-
leaf filigree, and mirrored salons, the Fall River Line was more than a
means of transportation to a distant point; it was, as one contemporary
critic describes it, a "convenient extravagance."[1] The traveler could leave
New York City in the early evening, have a fine dinner served by "two
of the most perfect headwaiters in the world,"[2] walk the promenade
deck serenaded by a live orchestra playing the "Pilgrim's Chorus" from
Tannhäuser "very decently,"[3] retire to the comfort of a private albeit small
stateroom, and awake in Fall River, Massachusetts, in time to be escorted
to the waiting train, which would connect to one that delivered its passengers directly into the center of Provincetown the next afternoon. This
line would become the most often-used means of commuting for Susan,

Jig, and their friends, all of whom fell into the routine of summers in Provincetown, winters in Greenwich Village, and falls and springs sometimes in one place, sometimes in the other, abetted by the Fall River Line.

Provincetown can be imagined as an arm, jutting out from the mainland twenty-five miles into the Atlantic, bent at the elbow, the wrist curved inward with fingers at right angles to the hand. At the fingertips, Long Point Lighthouse; at the bend of the wrist on "the outside," Race Point; along the length of the outer arm, the duned coastline facing the Atlantic; on the inside arm from hand to curve of wrist, the town itself, "three miles long and two streets wide"[4] spread round a harbor, with small lanes zigzagging between the streets and connecting to the sand dunes and low scrub brush that separate town from ocean. Approached by sea from Boston, it appears to be a wide maw of bay in the center of which is MacMillan Dock separating the west end of town from the east. Directly behind the docking station is the Town Hall, and towering over all is Pilgrim Monument, commemorating the first landing of the Pilgrims in the new land, built to duplicate the Torre del Mangia in Siena, Italy. At 252-feet high, it is tall enough to be glimpsed on a very clear day by those in Plymouth across the Cape Cod Bay, a reminder that they may have received history's nod but that Provincetown knows better. However, the most spectacular first view is the one Susan and Jig had from the window of the train that brought them there on that April afternoon, similar to the one Henry David Thoreau described. From adjoining North Truro, he wrote, it looked "like the richest rug imaginable spread over an uneven surface."[5] Susan would be fascinated by this same stretch of nature between town and tide and use it in several of her works, particularly in the play she called *The Outside*.

The town itself also had a powerful beauty: Fishing boats bobbed in the wide harbor; whitewashed, wooden Cape Cod houses lined the narrow streets; swatches of flowers appeared in the hard-won soil; front yards were decorated with whale bones and other prizes given up by the sea. Most striking was the special light that bathed the landscape. It was a perfect place for artists to work. Charles Hawthorne had established the Cape Cod School of Art in 1899 and quickly gained a following of would-be painters who came each summer to sketch the models he had pose on the beach along the bay shore. By 1914 there were enough painters living permanently in the community to justify the establishment of the Provincetown Art Association, which held balls and parties and presented their first exhibit in the summer of 1915. Mingling with these artists on a Sunday in the summer would often be sailors on shore leave from the North Atlantic fleet, whose home port was Provincetown. Sometimes more than 4,000 sailors would crowd the narrow streets. Despite journalists' romantic descriptions, touting the community as "tiny," "undiscovered," "isolated," it was not as bucolic in 1913 as such romantic hyperbole suggests. Young Sinclair Lewis, in a letter to his West Coast friend Jack London, written in the summer of 1911, already complained that "Provincetown got too rich for my blood, while writing, with about 10,000 sailors and their "cute" officers especially in the harbor."[6]

Yet for all its activity, Provincetown on most days still had the feeling of a compact, friendly small town. All activities of daily life centered along Commercial Street, sometimes called Front Street, a twenty-two-foot-wide thoroughfare that followed the curve of the bay. Walkers in Provincetown either went "up along" toward the West End or "down along" toward the East End. Susan and Jig lived in the East End; if they visited Mary Vorse, for example, they had to go up along Commercial a few houses. If they wanted to go further west, they might consider taking the public transportation, the "accommodation," that slowly made its way along the sand-covered street. For five cents they could ride from one end of town to the other, getting weather predictions, local gossip, and sage advice from one of the regular drivers who steered its course. Walkers could rely for news on the town crier. In 1913 George Washington Readey retired after seven years of ringing his bell, announcing "No-tiz, No-tiz," of the daily events in the community, which people paid him to share. Heaton Vorse, Mary's son, remembered Readey bragging that before taking the job he had traveled all over the world and "a good many other places besides." Seen it all, done it all, and happy to be back in Provincetown.[7]

Susan liked to tell reporters that, for her, coming to Provincetown was actually a case of "coming home." "I'm what they call 'real old Yankee' myself. My father's people came over with the first English settlers."[8] So did Jig's. This connection with their antecedents might in part explain how two children of the Midwest so readily embraced not just the lifestyle of Provincetown but its physical setting. She, however, could not help comparing where she lived to where she came from, often imagining that the moving dunes of the outside were the rippling corn fields of Iowa in a good wind, an analogy Thoreau also used.

Susan was immediately drawn to the town; it was small but seemed freer than class-conscious Davenport. Above all Provincetown was a fishing community, and the sea seemed to be the great social leveler, providing riches or wrecking havoc equally on its inhabitants: the early English settlers and the later-arriving Portuguese. The Portuguese community, mostly from the Azores, began settling in Provincetown in great numbers around 1850, after fishing the Great Banks or working on New England whalers, which routinely plied waters off the coast of Portugal. At the end of the nineteenth century, half of the population of Provincetown was Portuguese, giving the town a special European flavor and vitality that immediately appealed to the latest arrivals from Greenwich Village. By the time Susan made her home in Provincetown, the distinction was less between old-time families and Portuguese arrivals than between the community as a whole and the newcomer artists. Grace Collinson, a local historian whose family emigrated from the Azores, remembered her mother walking to work and encountering some writer or artist just returning home, leaning over a white fence along Commercial Street, after too much liquor and too much partying. Jig, in this condition, was a common sight. There were other sights that gave the locals pause: women entertaining men who were not their husbands; men walking with open bottles of alcohol in their hands; women with cigarettes; both sexes sometimes swimming without bathing suits. Grace's mother "would cross herself with her left hand as much to say, 'This America, This America. What ways.'"[9]

A number of young Portuguese women worked for the summer community and for those who made Provincetown their permanent home. "Blessed Annie" Silva came to work for Susan and Jig when they first arrived and stayed with them until 1916, when she married. It was Annie who helped get the house ready each spring; cooked during their stay; assisted Susan in "getting into her costume," as she called her corset, which she put on whenever she made the trip back to New York; and cared for their animals and found them temporary homes when they couldn't be taken along. When Jig left his good shoes behind in a closet, it was Annie who sent them on so that he could attend *The Masses* Christmas party. Rachel White, Annie's daughter, grew up on stories of the household, particularly the kindness of Susan, for whom Annie was determined to name her first child. Because it was a boy, she settled on Michael Glaspell Silva "since he wouldn't have wanted to be known as Susan." His sister believes that his love of writing was a result of his sense of connection with his namesake.[10] Over the years, several local women would work for Susan. With each she developed close relationships, and they felt a special bond with her that remained. "There was nobody who was ever kinder and more helpful to me," her last employee Francelina Sousa Hubbard said, forty years after Susan died.[11]

The Roseboro house they again rented, faced the harbor at the end of the East End and had a large balcony overhanging the beach. From it they could see the quick daily retreats of the tide that are unique to Provincetown, "as though someone has pulled the plug as the water drains out of the harbor,"[12] leaving such wide flats at low tide that "the fishermen walk in across these flats and their dogs run out to meet them."[13] Emma Goldman, who sometimes visited her niece Stella Commins and her husband Eddie "Teddy" Ballantine, tells of one afternoon strolling out into the harbor with a friend while the tide was out and being struck by the beauty of the scene. But as they walked back to the beach, they heard the sound of gurgling water and turned to find the sea rapidly making its way once more to land. Immediately they began to run as the water quickly advanced toward them. "Now and then our feet would sink in the soft sand, but the foaming peril at our back kept steeling the instinctive will to live."[14] What the combined force of the New York Police Department, the U.S. government, and, later, the Soviet regime could not accomplish, the seemingly placid Provincetown harbor achieved: It put fear in the heart of "Red Emma." Every six hours Susan and Jig witnessed these dramatic shifts of water from the safety of their cottage or as they took their daily strolls along the beach. It would be the sea that Susan invoked when trying to explain what prompted her friends and her to turn to theatre there: "Perhaps we wanted to write plays and put them on just because we knew, more intensely than the fishermen, that the tide comes, the tide goes. You cannot know that and leave things just as they were before."[15]

They also heard the sound of the sea at night. Hutch Hapgood, who with his wife, Neith Boyce, and their children were spending their second summer in the town in 1914, wrote to his friend Mabel Dodge in Florence about becoming friendly with "two or three brides and their grooms, [who] have invited me to a couple of simple affairs. They seem unaccountably gay about nothing." About one particular couple, Susan and Jig, he writes: "His bride asked me if I liked the sound of the sea at night. I replied that I did, that it was beautiful, but like all beautiful things, also melancholy. He then said, 'I could not stand sleeping by the sea if she were not with me.' I knew well what he meant, and I remarked lightly that all companionship was intended merely to dull the emotions which we would otherwise get too intensely from solitude and nature. His bride didn't like that! I don't think she cared to regard herself as a buffer between him and Life."[16]

Hutch and Neith soon became close friends of all the "unaccountably gay" brides and grooms spending that summer in Provincetown. Besides Susan and Jig, there were Margaret Thurston, a painter, and Wilbur Daniel Steele, a short-story writer. He was a distant cousin of Bert Vorse and had traveled with Bert and Mary in Europe in 1909 and then boarded with Mary in Provincetown, profiting from the writing advice she provided to him and to his roommate, Sinclair Lewis, when both lived on nearby Avellar Wharf: "Place your unpaid bills before you, then apply the seat of your pants to the seat of the chair—and write."[17] Steele soon became one of the masters of the American short-story form, a much-honored writer for his realistic tales, before the sparer, more experimental work of Hemingway and Fitzgerald eclipsed his art.

Mary Vorse was also a bride that summer. Her first marriage to Bert Vorse had been unhappy, and they had separated in 1909, a year before his sudden death. She met Joe O'Brien when both journalists were covering the Lawrence strike, and they married the next year. The couple shared a passionate interest in labor movements and suffrage causes, as well as a great love for Provincetown and the Vorse house, which O'Brien made his own, remodeling and expanding it to accommodate Mary's two children from her first marriage and Joel, born to them in the winter of 1914. Joe was big, friendly, and easy going. His Irish humor particularly appealed to Susan, and she relished his friendship as she did his stories and yarns. She had first gotten to know Mary and Joe when she had lived in Provincetown the previous summer with Lucy Huffaker, and by 1913 she considered them both her dear friends. The four couples formed the nucleus of the transplanted Villagers. For Mary and Joe and Susan and Jig, Provincetown became their primary residence. For the others, it was one of several homes they occupied, but the friendships begun there in 1913 were long-lasting and important in all their lives.

For Susan to suddenly be surrounded by a group of like-minded people, who understood and encouraged her, as her own, well-meaning but conservative family could not, seemed like a miracle to her. In *The Road to the Temple* she describes the special closeness of the group: "None of us had much money, these were small houses we lived in: they had been fishermen's before they were ours. Most of us were from families who had other ideas—who wanted to make money, played bridge, voted the republican ticket, went to church, thinking one should be like every one else. And so, drawn together by the thing we really were, we were as a new family; we lent each other money, worried through illnesses ate together when a cook had left, talked about our work. Each could be himself, that was perhaps the real thing we did for one another."[18] The life she and Jig established that summer was exactly what she had been seeking. She had found a home.

Outwardly, however, Susan did not alter her daily rhythm nor the work habits first established when she was sixteen. No matter how she felt, she would write every day, "keeping hours—just as if it were a job (which it was—as I had my living to earn, as well as liking to write.)"[19] Each morning after a simple breakfast, she moved to a quiet space, preferably in a second-floor room, where she felt protected and cut off from the outside. There she worked until lunch on short stories and the beginning draft of *Fidelity*, her third novel. Afternoons she and Jig took long walks on the beach or over the dunes to the outside fronting the Atlantic; sometimes he swam and she sat, shaded in the sun, reading. Evening meals were usually eaten with friends, either at someone's home or shared around a fire on the beach. Jig continued his New York column for the *Chicago Evening Post*, and, against local predictions of defeat, successfully turned the vacant lot next to them, which he had "leased" for one dollar, into a successful vegetable plot. Writing to Mary and Joe who were in Europe at the beginning of the season, Susan reported with excitement about the cauliflowers Jig had grown. She also reported on their first month of marriage: "It is very important that you come home and see how happy we are. True, we expect to go on being happy for quite some while, but we grow impatient to have you come home and behold our bliss."[20] Their lives in Provincetown were simple, at least as Susan chose to describe them—a far cry from the popular images of what bohemian Greenwich Village did on holiday. "We were supposed to be a sort of 'special' group—radical, wild," she writes, but in fact what drew them together were simple needs: "to have a garden, and neighbors, to keep up the fire and let the cat in at night."[21]

Within the group, Hutch and Jig, who were alike in background, outlook, and personality, naturally bonded. Both came from well-established, prosperous families of the Midwest and had turned their backs on family businesses, preferring instead the world of ideas. Both were voracious readers with seemingly unquenchable enthusiasms for a wide range of subjects. What Hutch loved to do more than everything else was to talk; it was "his principal outlet," Mabel Dodge reported. In this he found a soul mate in Jig. The painter Marsden Hartley recalled how when he and fellow artist Charles Demuth first came to Provincetown in the summer of 1914, they would often find the pair together engaged in one of their endless dialogues "and as it wore some of us down so, if we saw Hutch and Jig coming up along, Demuth and myself would say—let's scoot, here come Hutch and Jig talking about the universe—and it always seemed so odd that they could find so much of it to talk about, and nobody knows if they ever came to perfect and definite conclusions."[22]

The women writers in the group were born within six years of each other—Neith the oldest, Susan the youngest—and physically resembled each other. All were tall, slender, and graceful, with finely chiseled features, expressive faces, and large, arresting eyes. Between Neith and Mary the resemblance was so striking that townspeople would sometimes be shocked to see "Mr. Hapgood escorting Mrs. O'Brien home late at night, with his arm wrapped around her waist."[23] Of the three, Susan was the only one who had gone to college and the only one who at the time had already reached national prominence; however, each was a serious, disciplined professional, happiest when she could be left alone to write fiction and prose. All three kept their own names and wrote under them. They were all highly ambitious; their independence and personal space vital. They were also early champions of suffrage and women's rights, Susan and Neith expressing their politics mainly through their fiction and drama, Mary increasingly turning to journalism. None relished traditional female roles or duties. All had help to do the cleaning and cooking, but they did not seem to see this arrangement in any way contradicting their feminist or socialist beliefs. They were workers, too, their money earned by their pens. In fact, each woman was the central financial support of her household, since none of the husbands held any sustained paying jobs for very long. Hutch suffered a severe writer's block in 1914 and did not publish anything for twenty years; Joe was soon taken ill and even when temporarily recovered was more content—like Jig—to putter around the house than to take on the arduous assignments Mary sought. In the case of Jig, the only money he earned when they married was the five-dollar salary he got for his *Chicago Evening Post* column. Any other funds came from family accounts or from Susan's short-story and book royalties. Mabel Dodge, who spent time in Provincetown each summer from 1914 to 1916, marveled about the seriousness of these women, who would usually drink along with their husbands at night but were still able to work the next day.[24]

Yet for all the women's independence, there was a double standard practiced among the group when it came to sex. Hutch called himself a "spiritual monogamist," but his monogamy was in spirit only. Mabel and others who knew him well believed that the only woman he ever loved was Neith; and yet, in his quest for all-consuming experiences, he was constantly driven to experiment with other women. In this he was not unique. Floyd Dell labeled the adultery he saw around him in the Village and Provincetown as "polite adultery": "any extra-marital sexual relations which involve a *tacit* or *express agreement* that they are not to be *taken seriously*. Polite adultery recognizes the permanence of the existing marital relation of the partners and promises not to disturb them."[25] However, as Dell was well aware, this arrangement invariably worked to the benefit of the man, allowing him guilt-free sexual experiences. He admitted, "We were content about what was happening to woman because what we wanted was something for ourselves—a Glorious Playfellow. . . . But they wanted something different—something for *themselves*."[26] These words were written in 1926, after Dell had already married again and had time to reflect on the clear double standard at work in the Village life he knew. In 1914, in *The Masses*, he could only revel in the situation: "Feminism is going to make it possible for the first time for men to be free."[27] Certain women, however, saw the situation differently. In a letter to Neith marked confidential, Mabel describes her pain over Jack Reed's refusal to be monogamous in their relationship: "Women *have* always asked men to be faithful—will men change and become so if women *won't take less*? Or are women to get over asking it? To whom is this victory to go? . . . *Why* should I *accept* being unhappy when I don't believe in it? Yet have I the right to ask him at his age to forgo any part of experience? . . . To him the Sexual Gesture has no importance but infringing upon his right to act freely has the first importance. Are we both right and both wrong and how do such things end? Either way it kills love—it seems to me. This is so fundamental—is it what feminism is all about? . . . I know all women go through this—but must they go on going through it. . . . what do you think?"[28]

Mabel's answer to this dilemma was to leave a faithless lover and seek another, hoping each would offer the desired total commitment. She married four times and only with her last husband, Tiwa Indian Antonio Luhan, did she seem to find what she sought. Neith stayed married to Hutch, and her attempted experimentation with another man, urged on by Hutch, caused a nervous breakdown in 1915, due more to its impact on her own sense of self than to its effect upon her husband. For Susan, who had been "the other woman," the idea of seeking others, even if Jig did, seems to have been too contrary to her vital belief in the force of love that joined two people and which demanded total honesty between them, as long as it lasted. As for Jig, although he had many women friends, after they married, his name was linked only once with another woman: Ida Rauh, after 1917.

There was also another area in which Susan's relationship with Jig differed from that of the other couples she knew. In the case of Neith and Hutch, Hutch was the son seeking a self-effacing, all-embracing mother whose total dedication to him would provide a fixed point from which he could freely and joyfully roam.[29] Mabel was willing to play mother-*cum*-muse, but it was Jack Reed who bridled at being smothered by such an all-embracing relationship.[30] Even Emma Goldman had repeated love affairs in which she took on the role of mother to a series of younger men, most prominently Ben Reitman, whom she addressed as "my boy," "my child."[31] All these women were well aware of the irony of their position: strong women who were cast as mother figures to men who reveled in their attention while feeling free to find pleasures elsewhere. Susan may have adored Jig, supported him materially and emotionally, but—with the exception of her attitude toward his drinking—she was not a passive, all-giving, and forgiving mother. She had no problem making clear her own desires and needs in a relationship that sustained its sexual edge for a considerable time. Hutch, in his autobiography, recounts an incident when Susan and Jig first married. Besides talk, both he and Jig shared a great fondness for chess. One evening a game at the Hapgoods continued into the early hours, and Neith, "more tolerant of the ways of men than Susan," silently went off to sleep. "Suddenly Susan darted in, with blood in her eye, and hauled off the recalcitrant player in the midst of the game." Later that night, when Hutch was unable to sleep and took a walk past their house, he heard "Susan's happy voice cry out from their upstairs bedroom 'Now, darling, don't bite!'" Hutch ends his account with the comment: "This little incident, recalled in later years, made Susan laugh and blush."[32]

Susan was not always so successful in dislodging Jig, and he was not always so amorous. During their second year of marriage, Jig's absorption in chess and in drink so infuriated her that she fled their cottage, not telling him where she was going—a tactic she would repeat when she and Jig (or later Norman Matson) had a serious fight. In his letter begging her to return and asking for forgiveness, Jig copies a poem that Mary Vorse had written about his behavior:

> Jig
> The Pig
> Not eating
> Or sleeping
> Or stopping
> Or speaking
> But chessing
> and messing
> All night
> at noon
> at morning!
> Oh listen
> Take warning
> You dull
> Old gull

Take warning
Cease scorning
The Act
In fact
Be human
Love Woman.

Jig adds, "She seems to have inferred sex-starvation." Indicating that Susan's anger was prompted by more than his inattention, he begs her forgiveness and asks her to return: "Wish I hadn't spoken that inebriate falsehood which hurt the little bear so unwarrantedly and sent her flying off on the lonesome train to the lonesome hotel. What I hope most is that the little bear will forgive me for it. He was bad—The Big Bear."[33]

As he admits in his letter, part of his behavior was colored by drink. From his days on the farm in Buffalo, Jig drank to excess. He claimed he needed it to loosen the words that flowed so powerfully from him when he was warmed by its influence, sometimes so "warmed" that he lapsed into insensibility. Alcohol also helped when depression threatened to overwhelm him or his own sense of failed accomplishment and wasted talent became too great. It was Jig who first introduced red Italian wine to dry Provincetown, importing it by the barrel from Brooklyn. He even gave the barrels names; one he christened Sappho, another Bacchus, a third Aeschylus. In their first summer in Provincetown, social drinking was a pleasant stimulation for good talk about shared interests. In subsequent years drinking accelerated, ironically brought on by Prohibition, which made it more covert and serious.

This first summer of their marriage brought them good friends and great contentment. Only one thing more was needed. They both desired children; and because of their ages, they wasted no time conceiving a child. By early September Susan was pregnant. She describes her joy in a scene in *Road*: "'Well, you didn't lose much time, did you?' said the jovial doctor who came to our house that first year, the year of the rented house on the shore. 'Oh, no,' said I, jovial too, 'there isn't too much time to lose.' A friend sends a little muslin dress; a sister-in-law knits pink boots." However, several months later, while they were still in Provincetown, she miscarried: "But the doctor is not jovial that day in the fall. The other doctor is out of town—no one to give an anesthetic; the nurse has not come from Boston. Jig helps the doctor. I was turned the other way, but saw his face in the glass, as he was carrying things away. . . . 'Another time,' we said. 'It will be different another time.'"[34]

War and Peace

14

From the very beginning we felt the war as social upheaval rather than as war. . . . It was personal and impersonal, a turmoil from within as well as from without.

—Hutchins Hapgood

Susan and Jig returned to Greenwich Village for the winter of 1914 but continued to consult realtors in Provincetown, looking for a cottage to buy. In the middle of May the *Provincetown Advocate*—which always referred to Susan by her married name—announced that "Mr. and Mrs. George Cram Cook have returned from New York and will occupy the Roseboro cottage, their last summer's residence during the coming season."[1] Soon after their arrival, however, they purchased a home of their own, at 564 Commercial Street. It remained Susan's residence for the rest of her life. In appearance it was typical of the houses in the area: a one-and-a-half-story Cape Cod "half-house," resembling cottages in Cornwall and Devon. Katie Dos Passos, who later lived across the street with her husband, John, described such houses as deceiving. "They seem frail but are sturdy, look small but are larger than they look, they are plainly built out of plain materials, and their chief beauty is their proportion."[2] The entrance, situated on the side, led immediately into the dining area; to the left was the living room/sitting room, facing the street and running the width of the house; to the right was a large rectangular kitchen. Between the two rooms, facing the door, were enclosed stairs that led to the second-floor sleeping rooms above the parlor and dining room. Behind the house was space for a garden.

To have a home of her own was immensely important to Susan. In several of her plays, married women live in houses that they alone own. It is their space, which they often struggle to control against those who attempt to invade their territory, even their husbands. In one unpublished fragment entitled "On Home," Susan writes, "Home—more than a house. Home of the spirit. Home is what we want to be. Where we feel at ease with ourselves. Home is faith—purpose. Many are homeless. Must get back home."[3] Perhaps place meant so much to her because she had such an acute spatial sense. Whenever she would recount a particular memory, it was invariably associated with a concrete image of place. For example, in letters to both Sherwood Anderson and Arthur Davison Ficke, she could recall exactly where a sofa they sat on was placed and where a lamp stood in a room in which they had had a conversation twenty or more years earlier. The topic of conversation forgotten, it was the spatial details that stayed with her. Susan also liked the idea of ordering and protecting her space. Even in a temporary home in Delphi, in the 1920s, she experienced "that sense of a household which one keeps safe, that it may move on its destined way," calling such a feeling "more than other satisfactions."[4] She shared with Mary Vorse the belief that for women it was essential to have a house—not just a room—of their own. "Our houses are our biographies, the stories of our defeats and victories," Vorse wrote. "To any woman who has not a house I would say, 'Go and buy one if it be but two rooms.' Not to have a house is to fail to share the history of your race. Women are meant to have houses as they are meant to have children of their own."[5] Susan did not yet have children, but she had her house in Provincetown, a place in which she could create. As she wrote in *The Road to the Temple*, "You make your house, then you sit down to write in your house."[6] The house and the town became for her fixed points of reference in her travels, places to which she could always return. The fact that her home was on the furthest verge of land, far out in the sea, also appealed to her. To its back was what she had left, facing it the vast expanse of what could be.

When Susan and Jig moved, one of their first acts was to unpack their cartons of books, so that, like Ernestine and Karl, they could merge their libraries. Another act was to knock down the enclosure around the stairs to let in light. They also added color: window frames were painted bright red, flower boxes green, against the white, wooden house. The inside was even brighter. By now artist Charles Demuth was a close friend, and he was pressed into service to help with the interior decoration. Jig had decided that the upstairs walls should be orange. Demuth agreed, "But the slope must be yellow," he insisted, referring to the special nature of the Cape Cod house, which had sharp angles in the upper story. "'And the floor green,' Jig added. 'But the woodwork black.'" Thirteen years later, Susan still marveled at the way the orange wall, which was actually many shades, lovingly applied by Jig and Demuth in the summer of 1914, still glowed when the sun hit it. And the blue that Jig had chosen for one of the many upstairs doors—"that blue which later he loved on the dome at the Provincetown theater, the deepest blue of the sky, blue of eternity it seemed to him"—still vibrated with the sun.[7] Demuth further decorated the house by painting the raised, cross moldings on Susan's bedroom closet door in the form of a crucifix. The recessed panels of the cross were painted in gold leaf (or gilt), the Corpus Christi in flesh colors, and other portions of the door in scarlet and purple. The crucifix was eventually destroyed "with paint remover" by someone who rented the house for the summer and who refused to occupy it until this work, executed by one of the great American artists, had been removed.[8] Upstairs one of the funny bedroom doors was painted purple. It was the color Ma-Mie Cook selected. In June 1914 just before she and Dad Cook visited, he suffered a massive stroke and died. Ma-Mie, who had been considered "queer" in Davenport, came alone to Provincetown and immediately fit in with the life there.

During this summer Susan began suffering from what she called a "heart lesion," which weakened her and made it difficult to walk upstairs to work, a sore disappointment because her second-floor workroom/bedroom afforded a view of the bay. However, the ever-resourceful Jig had a solution. Always an adept carpenter, he sawed through a square in the back west corner of the kitchen ceiling and with assorted bolts, lead pipe, and rope made a pulley elevator. Contrary to her friends' warnings that the thing would never work and would be "worse for her heart than stairs," probably shooting her right through the roof, the elevator fulfilled its function perfectly. Thirteen years later, when she wrote, *The Road to the Temple* she could report that she still rode her custom-made elevator, though she could now climb stairs.

In the late summer, after he and Susan became settled in their new house, Jig tried his hand at sculpture, something he had never done before but took to quite naturally. His favorite subject was his wife. In one of his letters to Susan after seeing the Armory Show, he had mentioned a nude by the sculptor Robert Henri that haunted him, adding, "I know about a lovelier nude than Henri's. Through the one I know and Henri doesn't know a lovelier spirit shines."[9] Now he took to sculpting a nude Susan. She obliquely refers to the work in her biography: "When you are happy, you may dance round the upstairs of your house before you get dressed. 'Hold that!' Jig commanded. Too hard to hold, except at moments, so he could 'check up,' feel it anew."[10] Later four nude sculptures of her became the base of the sundial that would eventually be placed in their backyard. In Chicago, when Floyd and his wife Margery had been painted in the nude, a discreet fig leaf covered each, and the drawings were placed in an out-of-the-way spot in their apartment. Jig and Susan seemed confident enough to place sculptures of her unclothed, lovely body in their garden.

If the original Provincetown group of 1913 was, as Susan described them, "particularly simple people," leading generally conventional lives, the group that congregated in the summer of 1914 was, for the most part, more rowdy, less family-minded, and more directly at odds with conventions of all kinds. Polly Holladay and her then-lover Hippolyte Havel transplanted Polly's MacDougal Street restaurant to Provincetown for the summer; and it became, like its Village parent, the meeting place for the bohemian community. The group this summer included IWW activists Joe O'Carroll and Fred Boyd; poet Baynard Boyesen; painters Charles Demuth and Stuart Davis; Helen Westley, Robert Edmond Jones, and Lee Simonson, who would all later make names for themselves in theatre; Lucy Huffaker; Louis Holladay, Polly's brother; and Floyd Dell, who, with Max Eastman, edited *The Masses* from there. At nights, there was always a party, depending on where the latest imported bottle resided. Often, it would be at Susan's and Jig's new home.

As the summer wore on, more people arrived on the Fall River Line. In July Mabel Dodge and Jack Reed appeared, still maintaining the tenuous affair they began during their work on the Paterson strike pageant. They stayed in a small house in town, but often took walks to the outside, that strip of beach along the Atlantic coast. On one such walk Mabel spotted an abandoned lifesaving station at Peaked Hill Bars, a large two-story building half-buried in the dunes. The place became her latest obsession, and she immediately started to make plans to create yet another ideal environment there. Eventually she would enlist the aid of amiable John Francis, the kindly local storekeeper, real-estate agent, and general factotum to the Village community in Provincetown, and he arranged the details in her absence. She even managed to get a wealthy New Yorker, Sam Lewisohn, to actually make the purchase and allow her to decorate it in exchange for temporary occupancy the following summer. Lewisohn eventually sold Peaked Hill Bars to Eugene O'Neill, who benefited most from Mabel's consummate skill and wrote many of his best plays in the "sea chamber"[11] environment she created. Susan also used the station as the setting for her play *The Outside*. Mabel did not stay long during the summer of 1914; Hutch had had yet another love affair, and Neith, angry and hurt, accepted Mabel's invitation to accompany her back to Florence in August. Before they arrived in Italy, however, they received news that war had broken out in Europe. Neith, her children, and Carl Van Vechten, another of Mabel's guests, returned home. Mabel remained, awaiting Reed, who immediately went over to cover the war zone; however, she was furious that the others had abandoned her. "It had never occurred to me that anyone would treat me so. I had been so accompanied all my life!"[12]

In Provincetown, the news of war brought forth equally egotistic outbursts. A comic-opera bravado immediately took over. The responses were befitting the mood of August in a resort where a recent case of rye had just washed ashore. A hurriedly called conference of the "elder statesmen" of the group, including Hutch, Mary Vorse, Ma-Mie Cook, Boyd, O'Carroll, and Eastman, could not agree on the wording of a statement calling on the working classes of the world to refrain from fighting this capitalist war. That evening O'Carroll roused himself from a drunken sleep, jumped over a balcony naked, and ran down the beach declaring that he would throw himself into the sea and drown. After subduing him with some effort, the men were confronted soon after by Polly, dripping wet at the window, saying that she, too, had tried suicide, but had found the water "too cold." And so the night progressed: the Greenwich Village vacationers, prodded by the news of war, alcohol, and their own particular angst, trying to find appropriate responses to the momentous events. By morning, the news went around that Fred Boyd, brandishing a gun, had entered the local telegraph office in order to send the group's resolutions against the war to the Kaiser, the Czar, and other heads of state. Even for the tolerant Provincetown townspeople this was too much; and Boyd and Hippolyte Havel were asked to leave.[13]

While all of these people were committed to social change—Boyd, an IWW member, had served time in jail during the Paterson strike—their histrionic response to war portended the end of the dreams of change that had so inflamed them all in 1912 and 1913. It would be three years until America joined the fighting, but in the summer of 1914, something in the fervor of the first Greenwich Village years had already dissipated. Vorse, an onlooker on this infamous Provincetown night, sadly recalled, "The more sensitive and least stable of the group reacted to the world eruption by going on a strange binge. . . . The normal and tougher-minded people merely looked on the world with unbelieving eyes. It meant a complete readjustment for those of us who were brought up to believe that peace was now a permanent thing."[14] Hutch saw his battles with Neith as a microcosm of the larger conflagration, going as far as to declare, "We were the Cause of the war: the violence and inconsistency of our emotions, the impotence of our ideas."[15] He was talking, of course, not only of himself but of the entire group of Village radicals whose socialist dreams were sundered by a war that was not being fought along class lines, as they had anticipated, but rather in the name of nationalism. He felt that the war turned his group inward, made them take protection in their own, isolated worlds, in their personal relations, in their marriages and betrayals. The writing of the next year would reflect this shift; many, including Susan and Jig, would write of individual relationships, often parodies of their own group, while the world in Europe was crashing down. Yet, during their first summer in their new house, Susan and Jig still talked about socialism and loved to sit around the wood table that Jig had built and lovingly polished singing socialist songs. However, from August 1914 until the Russian Revolution three years later, the possibility of such a revolution seemed very unlikely. Revolutions, if they were to come, had to occur at home, perhaps on a creative rather than a political level. Jig, always prescient, wrote in his August 7, 1914, New York letter for the *Chicago Evening Post*: "Life goes on for us not visibly changed, as yet, but the European war cannot leave it unchanged. After that we may find ourselves living in a world that has changed fundamentally—another epoch of human life."[16]

Life in Provincetown quieted once the summer crowd left. Joe O'Brien, who had been ill in the spring, went to Boston, for an operation, and Mary went with him. To cheer her friends, Susan wrote of Jig's "stunning" forty-first birthday party on October 7, he bedecked in a white suit, with turban and sash of orange calico, and red carnations and decorations snatched from Neith's cake. "Before the night was over Jiggie told us about our souls and was altogether wonderful."[17]

Now all that was needed to complete their happiness was for Susan to be pregnant once more. When they returned to New York in the late fall, the couple turned for advice to Dr. Harry Lorber, whose sensitivity to the needs of the Village bohemian community made him much loved, and whose skills made him much in demand.[18] He believed that her miscarriage could have been caused by a fibroid tumor that was pressing on her uterus and causing Susan painful back problems. He also diagnosed the uterus as prolapsed or displaced, sometimes the result of earlier mishandled births or abortions, but at that time common as a general diagnosis for problems related to reproduction.[19] When she once more miscarried in her early term, he recommended that the tumor come out as soon as possible and that the uterus be repaired at the same time to improve the chances that she could carry to term.

From the beginning of her marriage, Susan had decided that one way of keeping contact with her family was to make a yearly trip home at Christmas, a celebration that meant nothing to her and Jig, but meant a great deal to her parents. Back in Davenport at the end of December, she considered staying and having the operation there where her family could care for her. Then, too, there were money problems. She had published only one short story in all of 1914, devoting most of her time to her novel *Fidelity*. Jig's salary was negligible, and other monies from her royalties and investments was not sufficient to support them. There were also difficulties in the marriage. In one letter Jig writes that he is glad that "the L.B. has figured out . . . that maybe the B.B. does love her after all. Well, I should say so!"[20] In another, he tells her of his conversations with Dr. Lorber and discusses where she should have the operation, urging that she return to New York to be with him. "I'm sorry you went there at all," he writes; "It hasn't been good for the little bear. And lately she seems to be forgetting that she is the little bear. Will she remember again—with the ceasing of worry and pain? Or is she cross at the big bear and not going to love him any more?"[21] On February 2, after she finished a round of dental work in Chicago, Susan finally returned to New York. In her absence Jig had rented an apartment for them at 4 Milligan Place, on a tiny cul-de-sac, near Sixth Avenue and Tenth Street. At sixteen dollars a month, it had two large rooms with a kitchenette between and "perpetual care"—that is, a woman came in every day to make the fires as well as clean up. This street would be their New York address for the next three winters.

Soon after her return, Susan entered Woman's Hospital (now the New York Ear and Nose Hospital).[22] The operation was successful in removing the tumor, but it did not lead to further pregnancies. In *The Road to the Temple* she briefly mentions the operation and powerfully evokes her sorrow that she and Jig could not have children of their own. "I do not know how to tell the story of Jig without telling this. Women say to one: 'You have your work. Your books are your children, aren't they?' And you look at the diapers airing by the fire, and wonder if they really think you are like that. . . . There were other disappointments, and Jig and I did not have children. Perhaps it is true there was a greater intensity between us because of this. Even that, we would have forgone."[23] Twenty-seven years later, she still had the baby clothes, sent as gifts, which she had kept wrapped in tissue paper in a chest standing at the foot of her bed in the front room of her Provincetown house.

Numerous references appear in her fiction concerning children. However, in *Fidelity* the novel she wrote immediately after it became apparent that she would never have any of her own, Susan makes clear that motherhood is in itself not the only way in which a woman can live fully. The protagonist, Ruth Holland, who, like Susan, does not have children and probably never will, tells her friend Annie that maternity seem to make life worthwhile. Annie replies: "Not in itself. I mean it's not all. I think much precious life has gone dead under that idea of children being enough—letting them be all. *We* count—*I* count! Just leaving life isn't all; living it while we're here—that counts too. And keeping open to it in more than any one relationship."[24] Yet, despite these and other such comments sprinkled through her novels, Susan repeatedly told friends that the great regret in her life was that she had never been a mother. Motherhood—the desire for it, the compensations to replace it—becomes a repeated motif in her work.

Perhaps because of their failure to have children, Susan and Jig lavished great love and attention on the many animals that shared their lives. Two chapters in *The Road to the Temple* are named after their dogs, Nezer and TòPuppy, and throughout the book, Susan describes her pets with a flourish worthy of any proud mother. Like Edith Wharton, who near the end of her life also indicated a "great grief" over not having children and who, when drawing up a list of her "ruling passions" in life, listed dogs—particularly Pekinese—behind justice and order and just before books, Susan had a "ruling passion" for her animals, which Jig shared. In the summer of 1913, there was Copy-Cat, whom Jig swore would not be neutered but would "live to the fullest all his days." But "one pays a price for the fullness of life," Susan writes in *Road*. "Copy-Cat, out one night in the cat world, was killed by dogs."[25] His offspring Carbon-Copy and Mimeograph, or Mimi, took his place in their household. A love of animals had also united Susan and her father. Soon after her first miscarriage, when she wrote to him over the loss of the family dog Patsey, she could draw from her own pain:

> I have been thinking this morning of how, when we let ourselves care deeply for anything, we lay ourselves open to being hurt. Love always . . . means pain as well as joy. And yet . . . to let our affections go out is to shut ourselves off from life and lose what is best in it. And that very pain—the loss and grief that comes in the wake of love—has something to yield us if we have the courage to take it. It brings us new thoughts, a new way of looking at things, a deepened understanding and freshened sympathies. . . . Things that we love can be taken away from us; but what that loving had made of us is a thing we do not lose.[26]

In the early spring of 1915, still weak from the operation and her second miscarriage and still suffering from a heart problem that further sapped her strength, Susan was, nevertheless, determined to throw her energies into her life with Jig. What their difficulties had been—whether infidelity, drunkenness, or lack of communication—is uncertain. What is clear is that these problems were not serious enough to permanently endanger their marriage. That winter in Milligan Place they would become even closer, fed by a new interest they could share: theatre.

A Theatre on a Wharf

15

We went to the theater, and for the most part we came away wishing we had gone somewhere else. Those were the days when Broadway flourished almost unchallenged. Plays, like magazine stories, were patterned. They might be pretty good within themselves, seldom did they open out to—where it surprised or thrilled your spirit to follow. They did not ask much of you, those plays.

—Susan Glaspell, *The Road to the Temple*

Just after New Year's Day 1915, while Susan was still in Davenport, Jig wrote to tell her of the latest buzzing in the Village. A group calling itself the Washington Square Players had been formed and was planning to produce plays; they had even asked him to perform. "I said yes. You know I harbor a belief that maybe I can act."[1] Since he arrived in New York, Floyd had been in charge of play offerings at the Liberal Club, written by him and performed by a group nicknamed the "Dell Players," including Helen Westley, Sherwood Anderson, Edward Goodman, and Kirah Markham. The audience, all Village friends, were greatly amused by the clever parodies of themselves and their lifestyle, and most seemed unconcerned by the lack of production values. However, there were some who longed for more. The 1911 Abbey Players tour of America had shown what theatre could be. Robert Edmond Jones had seen the Irish company and marveled at its skill in moving an audience: a fisherman's house evoked by the mere placement of a net; peasant women indicated simply by bare feet and homespun skirts. Returning from Berlin, where he had worked with the legendary director Max Reinhardt, Jones dreamed of creating *"images of magnificence"* instead of the recipe-theatre he found on Broadway, where "we are given a cook-book to eat instead of a meal."[2] In comparison the Dell Players was an embarrassment.

There had been some attempts to start a more serious theatre, but none succeeded until the Washington Square Players, whose originators differ depending on the teller. Most credit Jones with providing the needed impetus. One day in the Boni Brothers bookstore, when several Villagers were discussing their failed attempts, Jones argued that real theatre required few trappings, and he proved the point by taking a volume of Lord Dunsany's *The Glittering Gate* and "staging" it on the spot with two speakers and a set constructed from what he found lying around the store.[3] Lawrence Langner, however, writes that the idea was his and Ida Rauh's, both tired of Dell's amateurish work.[4] They met that fall with Albert Boni at Ida's house to sketch out plans for a theatre patterned on Maurice Browne's Chicago Little Theatre. Among those suggested for the group were Susan and Jig. After dismissing several locations for their new theatre, including "an old cellar on MacDougal Street, which smelled most appetizingly of old wine" but was too small (two years later it was big enough to accommodate the Provincetown Players), the group fixed on the Bandbox Theatre on Fifty-seventh Street off Third Avenue. Goodman was named director, Boni and Langner business managers. Their manifesto acknowledged the sad state of American theatre and pledged to find works of sufficient "artistic merit," giving preference to American dramas as well as those important European works overlooked by Broadway.[5]

In the small community of the Village, news traveled fast. Now that there was to be a theatre, people began in earnest to write plays. "There are several plays I want to write at once!" Neith wrote to Hutch that fall.[6] Almost immediately after she returned to New York, Susan and Jig also decided to try their hand at writing a play together, on the subject of Freudianism, which was then sweeping through the Village. Freud, accompanied by Carl Jung, had come to Clark University, in Worcester, Massachusetts, in September 1909 and given a German-language address in celebration of the school's twenty-fifth anniversary. To his surprise, Freud found that "in prudish America it was possible, at least in academic circles, to discuss freely and scientifically everything that in ordinary life is regarded as objectionable."[7] Avant-garde circles were quick to embrace his ideas. While still in Chicago, Floyd was already proselytizing for the new psychoanalytical treatment, and whomever visited him was in danger of "getting psyched." "It was a time when it was well for a man to be somewhat guarded in the remarks he made, and what he did with his hands," Sherwood Anderson, a frequent visitor, remembered.[8] When he moved to Greenwich Village, Dell, like several of his friends, entered therapy, and he, along with Eastman and Dodge, did much to popularize psychoanalysis by writing extensive articles in leading newspapers and magazines describing their treatments and encouraging others to follow their examples.

Susan had already revealed knowledge of the new psychology as early as 1911 in *The Visioning*, and she had turned a skeptical eye on its excesses and the glibness of those using its terms. Her protagonist, Katie, bridles at the use of the word *neurotic* as a generic term of condemnation for all acts that the general society does not approve: "I think it's such a fine thing we got hold of that word," she says. "Since we've known about neurotics we can just throw all the emotion and suffering and tragedy of the world in the one heap and leave it to the scientists. It lets *us* out so beautifully, doesn't it."[9] By the winter of 1915, psychoanalysis had become such a popular subject in the Village that Susan complained that it was impossible "to go out to buy a bun without hearing of some one's complex." It was a natural topic for parody. "We thought it would be amusing in a play," she explains in *The Road to the Temple*, "so we had a good time writing 'Suppressed Desires.' Before the grate in Milligan Place we tossed the lines back and forth at one another, and wondered if any one else would ever have as much fun with it as we were having."[10] Although both she and Jig were given credit for the play, when Edna Kenton, in her history of the Provincetown Players, called it Glaspell's first play, written in collaboration with George Cram Cook, Susan made clear that the idea was Jig's and his name should come first. Kenton also indicates that the play was not actually written down until just before it was first performed.

Suppressed Desires is a deft comedy, poking gentle fun at Village faddists who, with a bit of knowledge and more jargon, were hard at work ferreting out their friends' complexes, reducing Freud to a late-night party game of "you tell me your dreams and I'll tell you mine!" Henrietta Brewster, the devotee, is a patient of Dr. A. E. Russell, and she is certain that the good doctor can interpret the meaning of her husband Stephen's recurrent dream of evaporating walls. Stephen's explanation for his restlessness at night is simple: "How can I sleep, Henrietta, when you're always waking me up to find out what I'm dreaming?"[11] When Mabel, her younger sister, arrives from Chicago, Henrietta finds a fresh subject ready for "psyching," particularly after Mabel admits to having a dream in which she is a hen who is told to move quickly through a crowd—"Step, Hen! Step, Hen!" Henrietta asks Mabel if she knows anything about psychoanalysis. "Oh—not much," Mabel admits. "No—I—[Brightening] It's something about the war, isn't it?" When she is told that it concerns forbidden impulses, which must be unmasked lest they drive a person insane, her first response is, "I don't believe they have them in Chicago." Henrietta assures her they do; they exist "wherever the living Libido—the center of the soul's energy—is in conflict with petrified moral codes." That's enough for Mabel. She consents to see Dr. Russell; and to get some peace at home, Stephen secretly goes as well.

Scene 2, set two weeks later, finds Henrietta busily writing a paper on psychoanalysis to be delivered to the Liberal Club, when the two patients enter separately to tell her what Dr. Russell has determined. Stephen, the architect who dreams dissolving walls and forests, desires to be free of his marriage, and Mabel, the Chicago housewife married to a dentist, who dreams she is a hen, desires her brother-in-law, Stephen, the "Step-hen" of her dream. The first revelation shakes Henrietta—"Did he know who you were? . . . That you were married to me?" she asks. The second entirely destroys her faith in the merits of analysis and the power of Dr. Russell, and she fights back, arguing that Mabel need not follow his advice. What about Bob "out there alone in Chicago, working his head off, fixing people's *teeth*—for you!" she demands. However, Mabel, who has been a diligent student, counters with Henrietta's own words: "Yes, but think of the living Libido—in conflict with petrified moral codes?" In frustration, Henrietta can only cry as she rips up her paper on psychoanalysis. "Look at all I've done for psychoanalysis—and—[Raising a tear-stained face] what has psychoanalysis done for me?" Vowing to burn the "Journal of Morbid Psychology" and cease interpreting dreams, she embraces her now-satisfied husband, who makes her promise to stop studying psychology. "But what about me," Mabel asks. "What am I to do with my suppressed desire?" Stephen, now satisfied that peace has returned to his home, has his own medical advice: "Mabel, just keep right on suppressing it!"

For a first attempt at drama, the play is surprisingly polished. Henrietta's protestations about the power of analysis in scene 1 are played against her quick retreat in scene 2; repetitions and echoes are subtly orchestrated, the humor pointed without bludgeoning the theme. Susan's ability to use irony was apparent as far back as her early newspaper and short-story work. Here it hits its target and deflates the pretensions of those who use jargon and seek quick cure-alls from the new science. In addition, although she and Jig conflate *suppression* with *repression*, the more appropriate Freudian term in this case, nevertheless they display considerable knowledge of the subject of psychoanalysis and its misapplication.[12] Two other elements already present in this first play, which will appear throughout Susan's dramatic work, are social relevance and topicality. Besides enjoying the satiric rending of their latest fad, the audience of Villagers would immediately remember the furor the preceding year at the Heterodoxy-sponsored first feminist meeting at Cooper Union, concerning an article by a Professor Sedgwick that compared women to hens. Most would be familiar with Edwin Tenney Brewter, an ardent proponent of Freudian analysis, whose last name the playwrights use for their protagonists. They would also be amused by the name Mabel, borrowed from the famous Village analysand Dodge and affixed to the dumpy bumpkin from Chicago. Dr. Russell is called A.E., a possible reference to the Irish writer, George William "Æ" Russell, well-known among Villagers, and perhaps a nodding acknowledgement to the George who penned the work. What they would not have gotten was the in-joke between the authors: Jig's childhood habit of reading the name Stephen as Step-hen. "Before the grate in Milligan Place,"

Susan and Jig created the first American Freudian play,[13] a small gem destined to be one of their most well-known works. However, despite the call of the Washington Square Players for experimental plays with artistic merit, the group found *Suppressed Desires* "too special." The play was rejected—as was *Constancy*, written by Neith Boyce; *Freedom*, by Jack Reed; and a manuscript entitled *Thirst and other One Act Plays* and a one-act play called *Bound East for Cardiff*, both submitted by an unknown, young man, Eugene O'Neill, whose father was a leading Broadway actor.

Jig did not act in the first production of the Washington Square Players, but he and Susan were in the audience on February 19 when they opened. Indeed, Susan reports that it was Jig himself who actually uttered the first words of the evening—proclaiming from the audience, "I've had enough of this," when the curtain failed to rise on cue. Confusing chronology and detail as she often does in the biography, she is most likely referring to an incident that actually occurred on the second night of the opening program, during the performance of Langner's *Licensed*, when Otto Liveright, who played a corpse, found lying on the stage when the curtain went up, decided to expand his part by beginning in an upright position and then ceremoniously dying and putting a cloth over his head. The audience went into such fits of laughter that the curtain had to be brought down, and the star of the play, Ida Rauh, refused to go on, claiming that her lines about her dead husband would be ridiculed, and she, a serious actor, would be humiliated. After a twenty-minute debate, she was convinced to perform, but soon after—perhaps because of this experience—she severed her connections with the Players. Since it was Ida who had the closest ties with the Provincetown group, her departure made it more difficult than ever for their plays to be accepted by the new theatre. Perhaps had Liveright been less of a ham, the Provincetown Players might not have been formed.[14]

That spring Susan had little time to think of the rebuff *Suppressed Desires* had received. For her, writing a play was an evening's entertainment; writing novels and short stories were her profession and the couple's only source of income. In May *Fidelity* appeared, dedicated to Lucy Huffaker. Its protagonist, Ruth Holland, like Ernestine Stanley in *The Glory of the Conquered*, is willing to follow her heart. However, in this novel the loved one is a married man, whose wife will not give him a divorce. "The law is the law," her sister reminds her (a phrase Susan will use again in *Trifles*), and women who go off with other people's husbands are breaking it.[15] Ruth does not listen; her desire for Stuart Williams is too great. "Nothing could have stopped her; she was like a maddened thing—desperate, ruthless, indomitable. She would have fought the world; She would have let the whole world suffer." She secretly runs away with Stuart, and for her actions, she is cut off from her family and not invited back for eleven years, until her father, near death, requests to see her. By describing the various reactions people have on her return—similar to those her own love affair with Jig engendered—Susan offers a scathing portrait of bigoted, blighted small-town life. But the novel, one of her most successful, displays how far she has come since her first novel. This time there is no triumph of love or glory in sacrifice. Instead, in the seven concluding pages, she makes a strong case for the rights of a woman to get on with her life once love has died or cooled. Even more shocking than living with Stuart without marriage is her decision to leave him when his wife finally grants him a divorce and they are free to wed. Her belief in love is so absolute that if it no longer exists in her relationship with Stuart, she cannot stay with him. "Some people, I know, could go on with the life love had made after love was gone. I am not one of those people—that's all," she explains to her brother Ted. What pushed her to risk all to live with Stuart, now drives her on to seek out a new life. The message Susan offers is that the most important act of honesty is finally being true to oneself. When Ibsen's Nora slammed the door on her husband and children, she at least had the decency not to crow. Ruth, as she prepares to board the train that will take her to New York and her new life, explains to her brother, "Lots of things have happened to me, Ted, and I've come through them somehow. . . . There's just one thing might happen to me that I haven't the courage to face. . . . Nothing happening." Unlike Nora, a very popular figure in 1915 Greenwich Village circles,[16] Ruth is bursting with energy to start a new life and the prospects look good. Susan herself had already shown that such a life was possible.

Four months after the book appeared, a young art student who had read *Fidelity* recommended it to her friend, a fellow artist, who was then living and working in Charlottesville, Virginia.

> I read a novel that you might be very interested in if you could get hold of it. Read it all day yesterday and finished it before bedtime, which I postponed indefinitely till I finished the book. It's "Fidelity" by Susan Glaspell a brand new modern novel. It left me full but not satisfied—In fact I felt as tho [*sic*] I'd eaten lots of stuff between meals and didn't like the taste anyway—It's very well written but I think Life would be quite a mistake if we liked it like that—For I do believe we have characters & can decide things—Mr. Stieglitz would approve—Pat—I'm sure of the author's pt. of view—but I don't think it's fair for one person—just because she loves—to make everybody so unhappy—Read it & tell me what you think—It upset me quite a little.[17]

What Georgia "Pat" O'Keeffe would have understood that Anita Pollitzer, her friend, did not was that the strongest message in the book was not undying love at all costs but rather self-realization. The next year, when Pollitzer took her friend's drawings to Stieglitz's gallery 291, he immediately recognized this power in O'Keeffe's works: "O'Keeffe seems to feel what women are feeling but have not been able to say. She is a spokesman [sic] for feelings that have not been expressed."[18]

So, too, was Susan Glaspell, and nowhere more directly than in the closing pages of *Fidelity*, which too few critics at the time—or since—have fully appreciated. The *New York Times* review, which praised the novel, as it had her first two, calling *Fidelity* "a big and real contribution to American novels,"[19] specifically criticized the ending, assuming that Susan was writing about love against all odds, rather than life against a dead love. The reviewer did cite her careful depiction of small-town life. Like Sinclair Lewis later, Susan reveals the prejudices and bankruptcy of such communities. However, unlike Lewis's Carol Kennicott in *Main Street*, Ruth does not settle for small victories. In the last pages of Lewis's novel, Carol can take comfort only in some distant future when her daughter may act as "a bomb to blow up smugness" in a Gopher Prairie. Glaspell's Ruth explodes things herself. *Fidelity* ends with four revolutionary words: "She was moving on."

Life in Greenwich Village in the spring of 1915 was moving on, too, although still relatively unaffected by the war. *The Masses* published articles about the need for socialists to unite against imperialist forces driving the conflagration; but since America was not involved, these issues were of less pressing interest than domestic concerns such as birth control, suffrage, and labor disputes. In fact, the Village was the beneficiary of the war, welcoming recent émigrés from Europe including Marcel Duchamp, Francis Picabia, Mina Loy, and Edgard Varèse, who had come to get away from the fighting. In the spring, the young doctor-*cum*-poet William Carlos Williams wrote to the editor of the British little magazine the *Egoist*, "Due to the preoccupation of Paris and London in cruder affairs, New York has taken over those spiritual controls for which no one had any time in the war-swept countries. Here was a chance to assert oneself magnificently."[20]

Susan also had a sense of new possibilities. The operation she had undergone rid her of the physical pain she had been experiencing, and she soon regained her strength. Her heart troubles also abated. Although it was clear that she would not be able to have children and though the disappointment was great, now that she knew, she could turn her energies elsewhere. She was thirty-nine, and life seemed to be brimming with new possibilities. Jig, as usual, was also searching for some project to absorb his great drives. He had thought of starting a small literary magazine, but could not get funding. He then turned to the formation of a College Teachers' Union, laying out his ideas in an essay entitled "The Third American Sex," in which he depicted the status of American professors as "under the thumb of business men and capitalists who control the university purse."[21] (Susan would use this essay and Jig's ideas about the need for independent college teachers when writing *Inheritors*.) The Washington Square Players might have provided Jig with the project he sought, but it already had a full complement of leaders. Jig needed something that could bear his personal mark.

In June 1915 Susan and Jig returned to Provincetown. Now that Gay House was completed, their lives settled into a comfortable rhythm, their friends providing the ready audience Jig needed and the companionship Susan craved in order to feel connected to the world. This summer season the Village community grew so large that there were sufficient customers to fill both Polly's and a second restaurant opened by Christine Ell and her husband Louis. There were the regulars: Neith and Hutch, the Steeles, Floyd, Ida and Max, and Mabel and Jack (but not together). Leo Stein, Gertrude's brother, was also a visitor, drawn by the burgeoning Provincetown art community. Margaret and Brör Nordfeldt and Charles Demuth were back, and they were joined by the Zorachs and Marsden Hartley, in addition to the regulars who taught in the various art schools. The Glaspell/Cook house rapidly became a center of social life in the East End. Friends and acquaintances flowed "in and out," staying for a shared dinner, usually Susan's famous "ice-box specials," drinking the last of a bottle someone had brought with them from the city to the dry community.

Often dinners were held on the beach around a fire. It was natural that during one such evening, the talk would turn to the plays rejected by the Washington Square Players. Who had the idea first is not clear; later accounts have Neith and Jig coming to it together, sitting around a bonfire one evening at the beginning of the summer. "Well, if no one else was going to put on our play, we would put it on ourselves," Susan writes, not attributing the line to any specific person.[22] And that is how a performance of *Suppressed Desires* and Neith's *Constancy* happened to be presented in the living room and open veranda of the Boyce/Hapgood home on the evening of July 15. Susan's description of the event in *Road* is almost offhand, just six lines of short, simple sentences. Judging from the rhythms of the rest of the book, always carefully crafted to fit the mood of the moment, the style reflects the offhanded way the group approached their first endeavor. Neith echoes this nonchalance, in a letter to her father-in-law two days after the event: "Nothing happens. One day is like another—except that the sea and sky are never the same. . . .You will be amused to hear that I made my first appearance on the stage Thursday night!! I have been stirring up the people here to write and act some short plays. We began the season with one of mine. Bobby Jones staged it on our veranda. The colors were orange and yellow against the sea. We gave it at 10 o'clock at night and really it was lovely—the scene, I mean. I have been mightily complimented on my acting!!!" After telling him about local gossip, she apologizes: "I wish I had more interesting things to tell you—but as I said, nothing happens here, and that is one reason I like it so much! We do talk, however, or some of us do!"[23]

The house Neith and Hutch had rented that summer, at 621 Commercial, on the bay side near the Roseboro cottage, provided an excellent view of the water; and Jones, with "a candle here and a lamp there," turned the porch into the setting for Neith's play, a barely fictionalized account of the love affair between Mabel and Jack, his character entering by boat from the bay below and climbing up to his waiting lover. For the second work, Jones asked the audience to turn their seats inward to the living room behind them, which, with a few pillows strategically placed and a table strewn with books, became the set for *Suppressed Desires*. Neith and Joe O'Brien starred in the first one-act; Susan, Jig, and Lucy Huffaker as Henrietta, Stephen, and Mabel in the second. "A few minutes before it was time to give our play," Susan recalls, "Jig and I took a walk up the shore. We held each other's cold hands and said, 'Never mind, it will be over soon.' But when it was over we were sorry. People like it, and we liked doing it."[24] Over the years, whenever she would be asked by interviewers what had first prompted the Provincetown Players to begin their revolutionary work, she would say because "we liked doing it." Edna Kenton, who did not see this first *Suppressed Desires* but saw all of the restagings over the next seven years, argued that no one but Susan ever did her own plays justice. She was a natural actor in her own work, and her performances in subsequent plays would be equally praised for their naturalness and power. William Zorach, present at the first performance and a member of the Players in its early years, believed that Susan had "that rare power and quality inherent in great actresses. She had only to be on the stage and the play and the audience came alive."[25] Others would share his assessment.

Since the community was small, word of the evening spread quickly; and those friends who had not been invited on the first night demanded that they, too, be given the chance to see the plays. The following day, Jig went over to Mary and Joe's house and demanded that they come to his aid. The summer before Mary had purchased Lewis Wharf, at 571 Commercial Street, directly across the street from Susan and Jig's house. It had once been used by local fisherman in the days when cod fishing off the Grand Banks flourished. Now abandoned, the wharf contained three weathered gray structures: a two-story fishhouse, measuring approximately 25-by-35 feet, at the back lefthand corner and two smaller structures, one behind the other, on the right.[26] In addition, at the foot of the wharf, there was a small property called the Arequipa cottage. During this summer, the Modern Art School held classes on the second floor of the "scrubbed out" fishhouse and Margaret Steele set up her easel on the ground floor. Jig proposed that Margaret's studio be turned into a space for the theatre. In the face of his persistence, Mary agreed, and the friends immediately went to work: "We dragged out the boats and nets which still stood there. We all made contributions to buy lumber for seats and fittings. We made the seats of planks put on sawhorses and kegs. We ransacked our houses for costumes and painted our own scenery,"[27]

Vorse writes in *Time and the Town*. Even with alterations, the theatre was tiny, the stage measuring only 10-by-12 feet; the seating space could fit ninety people.[28] Jig, who had been designing stages in sand and in his head since his childhood, constructed a four-tiered platform, sections of which could be shifted for effect, thus creating one of the first moveable set designs in American theatre. The central feature of the stage was provided by the enormous sliding doors in the back wall, designed to lower boats into the water. Opened, they now provided a natural backdrop of the sea.

On August 28, the temporarily named "Provincetown Players at the Wharf" again presented *Constancy* and *Suppressed Desires*; and on September 9, they offered two new plays: *Change Your Style* by Jig, and *Contemporaries* by Wilbur Daniel Steele. Once more the subject matter was topical, Jig parodying the debate raging in the local art community between the Moderns, represented by Nordfeldt, who championed the cubist and postimpressionist work shown at the Armory Show, and the Conservatives, such as Hawthorne, who taught traditional forms in his famous school. Steele's more serious work derived from the arrest of an IWW worker, Frank Tannenbaum, who had led a group of homeless into a church to seek shelter the previous winter. Near the end of the play, as the lights finally brighten, it becomes clear that the setting is not New York 1914, as assumed, but Jerusalem and it is Christ who has led the movement into the church. Both plays were slight works, but the audience's enjoyment stemmed from the fact that they knew the people being parodied or the events on which they were based. As for the performers and writers, they had been friends; now they were collaborators in the very best sense of the word, working together to create something that none of them could do alone. And Jig finally felt that he had found his calling. "I must act, organize, accomplish, embody my ideal in stubborn material things which must be shaped to it with energy, toil," he wrote at the end of the summer, as the nascent theatre took shape, at least in his imagination.[29]

Many in the group lingered on in Provincetown through the fall. Nilla and Harl, who had been spending the summer, returned to Iowa with Ma-Mie at the end of the season. In the ensuing quiet, Susan relished the life around her, especially now that the tourists had gone and Provincetown took on the splendor of autumn, the season she loved best. This contentment was destroyed in October when Joe O'Brien became ill and was taken to New York. He died suddenly on October 27. For Susan, the loss was a deep blow. She loved Joe, who had a way of looking at the world straight, unadorned by book knowledge, like her father and herself. Unlike Jig and Hutch, he did not "philosophize," he simply lived. She memorialized Joe in her only published poem, a forty-line tribute that appeared in *The Masses* soon after his death. The simplicity of the imagery and the everyday objects she describes capture the nature of the writer as well as her subject. She writes:

Much I do not know, but this I know—
You saw things straight; nobody put it over very hard on you.
The thing in you that thought was like a knife blade,
Muddling and messing made you sick.
Your scorn put the crimp in a lot of twaddle that goes on
    among our kind of folks—
How I'd like to hear you cuss some of them out again!
Graceful levity—fiery dissatisfactions.
Debonair and passionate.[30]

Throughout November, after Joe died, Susan and Jig remained in Provincetown. Now that they had their own house, they could use it as a base, moving more easily between the Cape and their Milligan Place rental in New York. Many of their close friends remained, too, and they would meet at their house, or Mary's, or Neith and Hutch's sharing the whisky that someone had ordered, or, when Miriam Hapgood got whooping cough on her eighth birthday and couldn't have any friends to celebrate the day, filling in for the invited children. More and more the group became Susan's family. In December, when she made her yearly trip back to Davenport, she needed this ballast because she found conditions particularly difficult. Her father had recently had a mental breakdown that left him a virtual invalid, and the responsibility for aiding the family fell on her mother and brother Ray and his wife Florence (Flossie) who lived nearby and could visit him. Frank had married, and he and his wife, Hazel, were still in Montana. Susan felt guilty about her physical and psychic distance from the family, especially now that her mother was in full charge of the household and needed assistance. Yet she was fearful, lest she be pulled back there. Each of these trips underlined the differences between life in Davenport and the new life she had fashioned for herself in the East. But, as usual, her mother encouraged her to continue her career and indicated that she could manage.

By February 1916 Susan had returned to New York and was staying at the Marlton Hotel in the Village, awaiting Jig who was still in Provincetown battling five-foot-high snow drifts that blanketed the town and making arrangements for Copy-Cat to find a temporary home until they returned. Alone in their Wharf Theatre, Jig "stepped" the stage, imagining renovations that might squeeze two more feet of playing space the next summer. Often he and Susan had discussed what was most important in the establishment of a theatre. Now he believed he knew. When Jack Reed had returned from Mexico in 1914, after interviewing Pancho Villa, he had described a native miracle play he'd seen, the mythic tale springing from the communal experience of the audience and performers as a kind of rite. Susan and Jig, who shared the heritage of Indian lore, were thrilled by Reed's stories of this native drama. It was exactly the type of theatre they envisioned—one that tapped a people's mythic horde, as the Greeks had done. Recently they had seen such a theatre in New York, when the Neighborhood Playhouse in the Lower East Side of New York did *Jephthah's Daughter*. "Full of strong inherited religious feeling beyond the command of any commercial manager, danced the Jewish youths and maidens of that neighborhood, their drama, much of it taken from the Hebrew ritual, full of feeling immeasurably old, the tribal religious feeling of the ancient Jews still a living thing to some of the Jews of Henry Street," Jig wrote.[31] It seemed to him that their Provincetown friends in their miniscule theatre might be able to make similar magic, arising from America, "a spirit of this continent that needed only liberation."[32]

Summer 1916, Two Playwrights

16

It was a great summer; we swam from the wharf as well as rehearsed there; we would lie on the beach and talk about plays—every one writing, or acting, or producing. Life was all of a piece, work not separated from play.

—Susan Glaspell, *The Road to the Temple*

It seemed that everyone in Greenwich Village wanted to get to Provincetown one way or another in the summer of 1916. Harry Kemp, the self-proclaimed tramp poet, who had a keen sense of where things were happening and an inflated appreciation of his own work, put an ad in the *New York Times* in May, asking for the use of a cottage there in exchange for "the manuscript of a well-known poet, an unpublished volume of verse. Leaser would receive any royalties that might accrue from the volume."[1] There is no record of how many responses Kemp received, but John Francis arranged for Kemp and his wife, the actor Mary Pyne, to stay in Francis's Flats, the studios above his grocery store. Whether money changed hands is doubtful; Francis's usual arrangement for impoverished writers to whom he took a fancy was to ask, "Oh, twenty-five dollars from now until the snow flies." Francis provided similar rooms under similar terms for Eugene O'Neill in the following years and became his devoted friend, taking charge of repairing and renting O'Neill's property, paying the taxes, securing domestic help, and handling other problems that came up. He fulfilled the same services for Susan and for other writers and artists. His grocery store was their meeting place, a sign entreating and inviting: "Please loaf in the rear." Selling for him was less interesting than listening to the stories and ideas of those who gathered there.

Newspaperman Ernest Meyer, who later summered in Provincetown and became Susan's good friend, recounted in his 1937 obituary of Francis an anecdote Susan told him, reflecting Francis's priorities. One day she spied an English marmalade she particularly liked on a top shelf in the store. The rotund proprietor dutifully climbed up to retrieve it for her and for others she recommended to buy it. But when the supply was gone, and she asked for a new order, he adamantly refused. "Sure it sells good, but it's too much bother fetching it down from the top shelf."[2] He was the only person whom Susan allowed to address her as Mrs. Cook. A married woman should be called by her husband's last name, the courtly and correct Francis assumed; and she was loath to argue the point and probably could not have dissuaded him if she tried. Only when Jig died did she venture to suggest that he might now use Miss Glaspell.

When Harry Kemp and Mary Pyne arrived in Provincetown that summer, they found the "regulars" already there. Susan and Jig had returned in early May, in order to enjoy the spring and get settled before the summer activities commenced. Ma-Mie, when she arrived from Davenport, brought Nilla and Harl with her. She occupied the Arequipa cottage at the foot of Vorse's wharf, and the children, eight and six, stayed with Susan and Jig. While all the theatre activity swirled around, Susan was in the unaccustomed role of parent, a time-consuming activity, with no help from Jig, and she forged even closer ties with the Boyce/Hapgood, Vorse, and Steele households, all of whom had children of similar ages. Nilla and Miriam Hapgood became particularly close friends, and Nilla also formed a bond with Hutch that lasted for many years.

By July most of the Villagers from the previous summer were back and even Emma Goldman appeared, taking a temporary respite from her anarchist activities to visit niece Stella and her new baby. In her autobiography, Goldman describes making "frequent calls of persons of outstanding individuality, such as Susan Glaspell, George Cram Cook, and my old friends Hutchins Hapgood, and Neith Boyce."[3] She also makes reference to Louise Bryant and Jack Reed, another couple recently ensconced in the community. Jack's affair with Mabel had ended the previous summer; and during the winter, on a trip back to his native Portland, Oregon to see his mother, he had met "her at last." "She's two years younger than I, wild and brave and straight, and graceful and lovely to look at," he reported to friends.[4] By all accounts Louise Bryant was even more beautiful and vivid than Reed described; she was also four years older than he knew. Heaton Vorse, a precocious fifteen-year-old in 1916, was smitten by the dark-haired, gray-eyed woman who had "the reddest, natural cheek color I had ever seen then or since. I wished I were older, but I would have had to stand on line that summer no matter what my age. She had too many admirers."[5] For the summer, Jack had rented a good-sized cottage for them at 592 Commercial Street on the same side and slightly down from Gay House. To it he had invited everyone he knew, and they came. Presiding over this all-male enclave was Louise, who had left her dentist husband and Portland to live with Jack. Hippolyte Havel, a Village character, recruited as cook for the group, called it "the dove cottage." After his tempestuous affair with Polly Holladay, he proclaimed that he was happy to find one couple who seemed truly in love. Ida Rauh and Max Eastman lived across the street but were slightly put off by the chaos of Reed's place. "Ida and I felt more at home a stone's throw down the street in the other direction where Jig Cook and Susan Glaspell had just bought [sic] a tiny house with a yard," Eastman recalled in his autobiography.[6] The atmosphere of love might have also distanced him; Ida and he were in the process of separating and had only joined for the summer because of the illness of their son, Dan. They were also closer in age to the "old-timers," whose lifestyle was less frenetic than that of the younger group. Susan and Jig, however, loved having Louise and Jack in their company, and soon the couples were seeing a great deal of each other, and Louise was reporting how happy she was that Susan had made her feel welcome in the community.

When Jack left for Chicago with *The Masses* artist Art Young to cover the national political conventions and to interview Henry Ford in Detroit, Louise was left alone to oversee the vacationers, and she wrote him daily, chronicling life in Provincetown at the beginning of June, as the tourists entered. One of her subjects concerned Jews. In one letter she writes of her landlord, "He is a little . . . Jew and Hippolyte almost dies when he's around. He says he forgets about the brotherhood when fresh Jews appear."[7] In another she reports: "Hippolyte and I have been to Mary's for dinner and at Jig and Susan's for a 'waffle' party. We have called on Stella and got reports of the Jewish invasion soon to take place in Provincetown. . . . It's going to be a sort of New Jerusalem at the end of town."[8]

Eugene O'Neill would echo similar questionable sentiments when, in March 1919, he wrote to John Francis to be careful about making a specific inventory of effects in Peaked Hill Bars before he moves in lest the owner, Samuel Lewisohn, remove items. "This may sound mean Mr. Francis, but I have had too many dealings with Jews, and millionaire Jews, too, in the theatrical business, to trust one of them any farther [sic] than I could throw your store with my little finger."[9] Elements of anti-Semitism would continue to fester throughout the twenties, breaking into print in an article entitled "A Jewish Symposium" in the September 1933 issue of the *American Spectator* in which the editors of this short-lived publication, including Theodore Dreiser, George Jean Nathan, James Branch Cabell, and O'Neill turned their attention to what could be done to alleviate "the Jewish Problem," O'Neill suggesting, tongue in cheek, their removal to "just north of British South Africa."[10] With the spectre of Hitler throwing an ever-increasing shadow over Europe and the world, such comments, even if written facetiously, as the editors claimed and the tone implied, made the virulent anti-Semitism of the period far easier to catch. Hutch Hapgood, author of *The Spirit of the Ghetto*, the first study of the contributions of the Jews to American life and its culture responded most vociferously, attacking Dreiser directly in a letter, rejected by the *American Spectator* but finally published under the headline "Is Dreiser Anti-Semitic?" in April 1935 by the *Nation*.[11] Susan, in her last novel, *Judd Rankin's Daughter*, written in 1945, finally discloses incipient anti-Semitism among some Provincetown intellectuals, making it one of her main themes. As she explained, by introducing the subject via the thoughts and actions of the main character, she could have a platform to express her feelings about "race prejudice" and "the menace of it to the world we are trying to shape."[12] In 1916, however, it was a nonissue, even to Stella Commins Ballantine—who was herself Jewish.

Provincetown was inundated with people of all persuasions in the summer of 1916. Local historian Leora Egan has painstakingly reconstructed the mix and activities: more than 600 artists attended the burgeoning art schools along the bay; two large public exhibits were held to celebrate the diversity of their art; 1,650 tourists debarked daily at Railroad Wharf from the iron excursion boat *Dorothy Bradford*; and sailors routinely went on shore leave from the carriers doing exercises in the surrounding waters. "Provincetown is full; Provincetown is intoxicated: full of people; intoxicated with pleasure," the daily newspaper proclaimed during the summer.[13] If the description fit the general community, it fit even better the group of friends who would become the Provincetown Players. They, too, seemed intoxicated, sometimes with liquor, more often with creativity, and the former helped to fuel the latter. During the winter, Jig had kept kindled the fire of their first Wharf season. While friends turned to other concerns, he sketched plans for the theatre that would bring about the "American Renaissance of the Twentieth Century" that he had described to Susan in his 1912 Memorial Day letter. Just as he had by chance picked up some clay one day in Freddie Burt's studio and begun to shape it, he now turned his attention to the theatre, hoping to mold it into a cohesive group whose plays would spring from the soil of America and embody the spirit of the country, as he imagined it. During the winter he had written: "One man cannot produce drama. True drama is born only of one feeling animating all the members of a clan—a spirit shared by all and expressed by the few for the all. If there is nothing to take the place of the common religious purpose and passion of the primitive group, out of which the Dionysian dance was born, no new vital drama can rise in any people."[14] The Provincetown Players would be his new Monist Society.

Not everyone who worked on the productions on the wharf shared Jig's sense of mission or zeal, but all could be swayed, if only for a short time, by his fervor. In later years the dream of community would fade; but in Provincetown, in that heady summer of 1916, it almost seemed possible to those Jig infused with his vision. Jig was the catalyst. When imaginations flagged, or when the fire provided by alcohol was in danger of running low, he would cry, "Give it all to me . . . and I guarantee to intoxicate all the rest of you."[15] And he usually did. In good times, he would make sure that all had enough to enliven the spirit. His "Fish House Punch"—four quarts of three-star Hennessey brandy, two quarts each of rum, peach brandy, and lemon juice, mixed with ten pounds of sugar, and poured over an immense block of ice placed in the largest punch bowl available[16]—became the ritual drink at opening night parties on MacDougal Street, where the budget for liquid refreshments sometimes surpassed the profits for the run.

Jig may have been a visionary, but when needed, he also displayed a practical bent. In order to support the theatre for the summer, he drafted a circular to his friends, asking for subscriptions: for $2.50 patrons received two tickets each for four bills planned for the season, with individual tickets priced at forty cents. Edna Kenton, in her history of the Provincetown Players, reports that eighty-seven subscribers responded, bringing the treasury to $217.50.[17] The appeal must have been sent in late May because by June 8 the *Provincetown Advocate* ran a short notice about work being done on the wharf by "hands of carpenters, who are making sundry interior changes."[18]

On July 13, the 1916 summer season at the Wharf Theatre opened with a triple bill: a revival of *Suppressed Desires* and two new works, Neith Boyce's melodrama *Winter's Night* and Jack Reed's parody *Freedom*, rejected by the Washington Square Players. Although a sudden fire in the theatre two days before the announced July 13 opening almost cancelled the season, Jig and company were able to do some quick repairs to the charred western wall, staining the other walls to match the new colorations, thus—as he would do so often in the history of the Provincetown Players—applying artifice to cover disaster.

The performances went off well, and again Neith wrote to her father-in-law reporting the results: "Amusements are scarce here and our little theatre has made a sensation. We give our next bill in two weeks and are all working like beavers."[19] Unfortunately, when Jig did the books, he realized that the subscription money would not cover the rest of the season. Again he wrote, as he would write repeatedly to patrons over the next six years, asking that they "rally without delay around the standard of the native American playwright."[20] Enough money came in to continue. The issue now was: To continue with what? Even before the first bill opened, play readings had been taking place. Bobby Rogers, a friend of Jack Reed, complained, "We recently heard six one-actors read at one fell swoop. Nearly passed out. And they will have to be acted or their authors will know the reason why. Yes, indeedy."[21] Despite the readings Rogers had endured, evidently none had produced works of sufficient quality to warrant production. It was here that fate seemed to intervene—at least as Susan relates the tale, which has become the most often-told story in Provincetown Players lore, repeated as gospel in histories of American drama and theatre: the discovery of Eugene O'Neill:

We gave a first bill, then met at our house to read plays for a second. Two Irishmen, one old and one young, had arrived and taken a shack just up the street. "Terry," I said to the one not young, "haven't you a play to read to us?"

"No," said Terry Carlin, "I don't write, I just think, and sometimes talk. But Mr. O'Neill has got a whole trunk full of plays," he smiled.

That didn't sound too promising, but I said: "Well, tell Mr. O'Neill to come to our house at eight o'clock to-night, and bring some of his plays."

So Gene took *Bound East for Cardiff* from his trunk, and Freddie Burt read it to us, Gene staying out in the dining-room while the reading went on.

He was not left alone in the dining room when the reading had finished."

Then we knew what we were for. We began in faith, and perhaps it is true when you do that "all these things shall be added unto you."[22]

It is a wonderful scene. Susan, a natural playwright, conjures up mood and drama in a few simple lines, a conflict climaxing in Eugene O'Neill, a *deux ex machina*, descending to save the day. Yet, as she often does in *The Road to the Temple*, Susan shifts chronology and detail in order to achieve a more striking effect. The description implies that O'Neill arrived after the first bill, right on cue; however, when Hutch wrote to Mabel Dodge on July 1 he listed O'Neill as one of those "enthusiastic in our circle."[23] Also, Susan probably knew O'Neill by face if not by name, since for the past year he had been spending most of his time in the Village, drinking at the Hell Hole bar, which she also frequented. His two close friends, Polly and Christine, were Village fixtures, as was his roommate that summer, Terry Carlin. It is likely that O'Neill had heard about the work of the Provincetown group from Carlin, who was a close friend of Neith and Hutch, and suggested going himself there so that he could find out what this new group was doing and whether they might perform one of his plays.

By 1916 O'Neill had committed himself to playwriting, but the road leading to Provincetown had been circuitous, to say the least. As the son of the famed actor James O'Neil, he was literally "born into the profession," as he liked to tell people, his mother giving birth to him in a Broadway hotel, nearby the theatre in which his father was performing. His own childhood had been shaped by his father's continual tours with *The Count of Monte Cristo*—that "damned play," James Tyrone would curse in *Long Day's Journey into Night*—which had brought money and fame, but ended the elder O'Neill's dream of becoming a great Shakespearean actor. Early on, the son had spurned the theatre as a calling, just as he spurned his parents' attempts to compensate for their nomadic life by adopting the trappings of bourgeois respectability. Such semblances of normality were undermined by Mrs. O'Neill's periodic morphine addiction, begun during Eugene's painful birth. To spare him the knowledge, his family sent him away to school at a young age, and by 1912 the twenty-four-year-old O'Neill could look back on a life that included expulsion from Princeton; an early marriage, fatherhood, and annulment; stints on ships sailing to Honduras, Buenos Aires, and London; and a year of drunkenness back in New York, where he lived at a bar and flophouse in lower Manhattan, among those sailors and drunks who became the surrogate family he would honor in his plays. It was in that epochal year of 1912, commemorated in both *Long Day's Journey into Night* and *Ah, Wilderness!*, that O'Neill began to see some way of reconciling his theatrical heritage and his hard-won personal independence. During a six-month period spent recuperating from tuberculosis, he began to write one-act plays, using settings and characters from his sea and hospital experiences. Two years later he had enough material to publish, at his father's expense, the plays that the Washington Square Players had rejected. Committed now to becoming a playwright and undeterred by his year in George Pierce Baker's famous 47 Workshop, where his writings were critiqued as "not plays at all," it was natural that O'Neill would eventually gravitate to Provincetown, to the people putting on their own works that were considered too "special" even by the avant-garde theatre of the time.

Others beside Susan wrote of that first reading of O'Neill's play, and their accounts differ from hers. Hutch remembered O'Neill coming to one play-reading session, sitting silently, as was his way, and then giving his play to Neith, who urged Jig to produce it.[24] Harry Kemp writes that O'Neill's first submission, *The Movie Man*—one of his "lost plays"—was actually rejected by the Players, and only then did he offer *Cardiff*, reading it to them himself.[25] However, all agree with Susan's assessment that the group immediately recognized the genius among them. If her story of the discovery of O'Neill is not exactly true, it lends the scene the exact power and solemnity needed and creates the effect she wanted. As she had done in describing the Monist Society meetings of 1907, embellishing details in order to suggest that her own intellectual awakening was due to Jig, she again makes use of religious, highly charged language to describe O'Neill's discovery, less to herald the playwright than Jig, who fervently believed that destiny had brought the young Irishman and the nascent American theatre company together. Susan's account reinforces this sense. "You don't know Gene yet. . . . You don't know his plays. But you will. All the world will know Gene's plays some day. . . . Gene's plays aren't the plays of Broadway; he's got to have the sort of stage we're going to found in New York," Jig told Edna Kenton, when she first arrived in Provincetown at the end of the 1916 season.[26] In notes written in 1920 for an article on the Players, Jig proclaimed, "Had O'Neill not been a member of the group which he knows to be ready to make any interesting new departures, to attempt the untried, he would have had no incentive to write *The Emperor Jones*."[27] O'Neill, for his part, while crediting the

Players and Jig in particular for unstinting efforts on his behalf, confided to Barrett Clark, "I cannot honestly say I would not have gone on writing if it hadn't been for them. I had already gone too far ever to quit."[28] In *Road* the discovery of O'Neill was not simply one more piece of reflected glory Susan could attach to the life of Jig. It was the most important validation of his faith in the entire Provincetown Players experiment: if we build it they will come.

Bound East for Cardiff appeared on the second bill at the Wharf Theatre, beginning on July 28.[29] It was unlike anything the Players had produced—not a parody of the group's foibles or passions, an inside joke, or a thinly disguised piece of local gossip. It was a mood piece, with virtually no plot, a scene set in the forecastle of a British tramp steamer, the Glencairn, with a group of sailors coming in from or going out to their watches, while one of their mates, a sailor named Yank, suffers his last few moments before he dies. Jig played Yank, Freddie Burt his buddy Driscoll, with Reed and Nordfeldt and O'Neill as members of the crew. The simple, functional set consisted of three-tier bunks, a small table in front, and painted portholes, constructed by Jig and his "carpenter" assistants. The language, too, was simple: rough, rhythmic, powerful speech, able to create the world of the men and the sea on the tiny stage. Such language illustrated the potential for a different kind of stage dialogue, spoken by virtually inarticulate characters.

With the second bill a great success, the by-now familiar question once more surfaced: What next? For Jig, the answer was simple; Susan would write a play. In *Road* and in countless interviews and articles, she would retell the story of how she came to write *Trifles*, "because my husband forced me to." In the face of her protestations that "I have no play!" that "I did not know how to write a play," that "I had never 'studied it,'" Jig replied, "Nonsense . . . You've got a stage, haven't you." That was the purpose of the Players, after all, to provide writers with a space that they could use for creative experimentation; and Susan's description of the process of writing her first and most famous play is carefully crafted to illustrate that the central tenant of Jig's faith worked. "So I went out on the wharf, sat alone on one of our wooden benches without a back, and looked a long time at that bare little stage." She began to see a kitchen and the exact location of a stove, table, and stairs to a second floor. She could also visualize the men and women who entered the space: "two or three men, I wasn't sure which, but sure enough about the two women, who hung back, reluctant to enter that kitchen."[30] Given her vivid spatial recall, she was able to reconstruct not only the events of the Hossack case but the configuration of the farmhouse she had entered sixteen years earlier, in Indianola, Iowa, to gather material for her articles about the case. The writing of the play went swiftly. Whenever she became stuck, she would walk across the narrow street that separated her home from the wharf and sit once more in the theatre until she could visualize the scene;

after structuring it on paper, she would test it in the actual space where it would be played. And so *Trifles* was written, under conditions most playwrights would envy.

In *Road* she indicates that it took her ten days to write *Trifles*, and it went into rehearsal immediately. Here again Susan must be altering chronology, because if she is correct and began working on it after the second bill began on July 28, that left only one day for rehearsals before the August 8 opening, an impossible schedule, even by Provincetown standards. What did hasten rehearsals was the fact that Susan and Jig played Mrs. and Mr. Hale. Even if more than ten days were needed to write *Trifles*, the creative process brought forth a work that seemed to have been nearly fully formed in the mind of the playwright. While the draft and two holograph copies with her corrections indicate that she altered wording and phrasing—plum preserves became cherry preserves, long comments about the canary were pared—the basic structure was there from the beginning.

Trifles takes only thirty minutes to perform, but in that time Susan is able to offer one of the most powerful plays ever presented by the Provincetown Players, a work that riveted the first audience who saw it in the summer of 1916 and is still able to speak as forcefully to audiences around the world in the twenty-first century, a credit to its author's skill and a mark of how little has changed in the intervening years. It begins as five characters enter the kitchen of an isolated, rural farmhouse where a murder has been committed. A man has been strangled while he slept; and his wife, who claimed to be sleeping beside him at the time, has been accused of the crime and taken to jail to await trial. Those prosecuting the case, County Attorney Henderson and Sheriff Peters, have returned to the scene to search for "something to make a story about—a thing that would connect up with this strange way of doing it."[31] Accompanying them are a neighbor farmer, Mr. Hale, who found the body; Mrs. Peters, the sheriff's wife, who has the task of bringing the accused woman some things; and Mrs. Hale, who keeps Mrs. Peters company while the men move around the upstairs bedroom and perimeter of the farmhouse searching for clues.

Left alone in the kitchen, the women, with furtive glances and few words, slowly construct their own theories about the crime. As they imagine her, Minnie Foster Wright is a lonely, childless woman, married to a taciturn husband, isolated from neighbors because of poverty and the rigors of farm life. When they discover a birdcage, its door ripped off and a canary, its neck wrung, they have no trouble making the connection: the husband killed the bird, the wife's only comfort, just as he strangled her birdlike spirit. She, in turn, strangled him—a punishment to fit his crime. The motive and method of murder become as clear to them as the signs of sudden anger they infer from the half-wiped kitchen table and Minnie's erratic quilt stitching.[32] Based on such circumstantial evidence, the women try the case, find the accused guilty, but dismiss the charges, and hide the evidence from the men, since their verdict is justifiable homicide. By so doing, Susan is able to create a new type of modern theatre, not based on actions observed by characters or audience but on the "reading" of actions and the construction of narratives depending on individual interpretations and subjective frames of reference. The question of truth becomes moot in the play. Minnie's guilt is not the issue; the real focus is on the ways in which the women are able to intuit her motives, drawing their interpretations from their own lives. In the ways in which they bond together and take action, the women become a true "jury of her peers."

While she keeps many of the details of the original Hossack case, Susan makes certain alterations. Of the original names of the participants, only Henderson is used, assigned to the country attorney rather than the defense lawyer. Margaret Hossack has been renamed Minnie Foster Wright, the pun on the surname marking her lack of "rights" and perhaps implying her "right" to act against her abusive husband. Susan adds Mr. Hale, a composite of the Indianola farmers who testified at the Hossack trial. She also changes the murder weapon, from an ax to a rope, the perfect dramatic correlative for the strangulations the play depicts. Her most striking alterations are her excision of the wife and the change of venue from the courthouse to the kitchen. In the play Minnie never appears. Since the audience never sees the accused woman, it is not swayed by her person but, rather, by her assumed condition, that of an abused wife, driven to commit a terrible act.

Susan displays extraordinary skill in constructing this brief play, her first independent theatre work. With only a stove, chairs, and assorted kitchen items as props—those "trifles" the men derisively dismiss and overlook—she creates a powerful mise-en-scène that uses expressionistic touches to externalize Minnie's desperate state of mind. Things are barren, broken, cold, imprisoning, and violent. Susan also moves beyond realism by choosing a conventional form, well-known to her audience—the detective story—and then systematically dismantling it.[33] In her version the lawmen are quickly shunted offstage to roam about on the periphery of the action, their presence marked theatrically by their shuffling sounds above the heads of the women, another expressionistic touch. She thus undercuts the male authority wielded in the original case and throws into question masculine-sanctioned power in general.

Mrs. Hale may be a surrogate for the young reporter Susan Glaspell; perhaps that is the reason Susan chose to play the role in the original production. It is she who becomes aware of her complicity in Minnie's situation because of aid withheld. "We live close together and we live far apart. We all go through the same things, it's all just a different kind of the same thing," she says, summarizing her insight about "how it is for women." In light of the Hossack case and Glaspell's role in sensationalizing the proceedings and in shaping public opinion, the lines could be confessional; so too her question, "Who's going to punish that?" Mrs. Hale's words seem to indicate Glaspell's awareness in 1916 of her omissions and commissions in 1901, of her failure to recognize and respond to Mrs. Hossack's disenfranchisement at the trial, and the implications of the woman's situation in relation to the lives of all women. Given this awareness, it may seem strange that when she has the opportunity to retry Margaret Hossack and change the outcome of the case, she does not acquit the woman or give her "her day in court" to prove her innocence. Instead she has Mrs. Peters and Mrs. Hale assume Minnie's guilt and, as in the original trial, base their findings on circumstantial evidence instead of incontrovertible proof. However, acquittal does not seem to be Glaspell's intention in the play. Whether Margaret Hossack or Minnie Wright committed murder is uncertain; what is incontrovertible is the brutality of their lives, the lack of options they had to redress grievances or to escape abusive husbands, and the complete disregard of their plight by the courts, by society, and even by other women. At stake is the need to confront female powerlessness and disenfranchisement and to rectify it. Yet she does not actually present the victimization of women or the violence they may suffer; instead, she stages the potential for female action and usurpation of power. By having the women assume the central positions and conduct the investigation and trial, she actualizes this empowerment and at the same time suggests that there are other options short of murder that can be imagined for women. These themes would be apparent to the Provincetown audience, both men and women, who in 1916 were working for suffrage and protection for women under the law. They would also understand that Susan was deconstructing the very assumptions about the incontrovertibility of the law and about all absolutist ideas. Mrs. Peters and Mrs. Hale, by suturing into their deliberations their own experiences and fears—just as the men in the Hossack case had done—illustrate the subjective nature of the reading of evidence and the essentialist nature of all readings of facts.

That Susan was able to reshape the events of the Hossack case in order to focus on gender issues can be explained by the personal changes she had undergone in the sixteen years separating the trial from the play. In 1900 she had been a twenty-four-year-old, right out of college, who, for all her advanced ideas of women's rights, had never left Iowa and had had little opportunity to test her beliefs. When she wrote *Trifles*, she had just turned forty and had already published three novels, thirty-one short stories, and a collection of short fiction, all focusing on the lives of women and their movements toward independence. She had also spent a year in Paris and lived in Chicago, Greenwich Village, and Provincetown, surrounded by other avant-garde women, who reinforced her basic feminism and anti-establishment views. The society, too, had changed in the intervening years. Certainly not all groups held her beliefs, but a growing number were at least aware of the movement to enfranchise women and to redress their positions in marriage and civil arenas. And if audiences did not share her ideas, Susan by this time was a consummate enough writer to find ways of swaying them to her position. For instance, when she wrote the short-story version, "A Jury of Her Peers," the following year for a more conservative readership around the country, she added certain details designed to gain their empathy for Minnie. "The law is the law," Mrs. Peters says early in the play, when she is still parroting the ideas of her husband; "A bad stove is a bad stove, how'd you like to cook on that," Mrs. Hale responds in the story version.[34] Women would get the point.

One of Susan's most impressive accomplishments in *Trifles* is her use of stage language. The speech patterns derive from the simple cadences of the Iowa farmers with whom she grew up, just as O'Neill's dialogue derived from the actual speech of sailors he knew. Both playwrights dared to place stammering inarticulates at the center of their plays. However, whereas O'Neill's men are rendered so by the limits of their education and class, Glaspell's women struggle against the gender restrictions that have silenced them in the past. They are unused to public speech and all too aware that the words they utter may be leading them into areas they are hesitant to explore. For O'Neill, the most common mark of punctuation is the exclamation point; for Glaspell the dash, as used in Mrs. Peters' revelatory speech: "When I was a girl—my kitten—there was a boy took a hatchet, and before my eyes—and before I could get there—[*covers her face an instant*] If they hadn't held me back I would have—[*Catches herself, looks upstairs where steps are heard, falters weakly*]—hurt him." Mrs. Peters's words are punctuated by long silences, and Glaspell resorts to pauses and silences throughout the play to indicate the hesitancy of the women to face the implications of what they are discovering. This use of silence as a stratagem to convey meaning is one of Susan's great contributions to drama, a legacy to later playwrights such as Samuel Beckett and Harold Pinter.

One other innovation that she introduces in *Trifles* and which will also be employed by later playwrights is what can best be called the technique of mutual monologues. Rather than have the two women respond to each other, as would be expected in dramatic dialogue in which speeches are given in the presence of another character, the playwright repeatedly has her women speak their thoughts not to an addressee but to herself, marking the fact that the real drama finally resides in the separate minds of each woman, a technique Glaspell borrowed from Maeterlinck, whose *The Tragical in Daily Life*, had just appeared in English in 1916. For instance, Mrs. Peters's reverie about her cat is spoken in the presence of Mrs. Hale, but not to her. And instead of responding, Mrs. Hale verbalizes her own thoughts in another self-addressed monologue: "I wonder how it would seem never to have had any children around. (*pause*)" While contemporary audiences have grown accustomed to such theatrical devices, the audience who first saw the play was introduced to an entirely new type of theatrical communication, one presented by a woman who had never before written a play on her own.

The immediate success of *Trifles* reinforced the sense that something magical was happening in Provincetown. Unfortunately, few other plays matched its power during the rest of the season, which concluded on September 1 with a reprise of *Suppressed Desires*, along with Louise Bryant's *The Game*, and O'Neill's *Thirst*, to raise money for the Provincetown coffers. Even before this date, Jig had been thinking about the future and the possibilities of taking the theatre with them when they returned to New York in the fall. Jack Reed supported the plan. They were strengthened in their determination when they received their first publicity, a *Boston Globe* article accompanied by photographs of the leading participants, including Susan, and a view of the interior of the Wharf Theatre. Two weeks earlier, a longer *Globe* article titled "Biggest Art Colony in the World at Provincetown" praised their work.[35] Buoyed by such notice, Jig was even more determined to move the group to New York, but Susan was appalled, aware that the burden for the theatre's success would fall completely on him, with others enthused only as their time and daily inclination allowed. But Jig persisted.

At 8:00 pm, on September 4, a meeting of twenty-nine active group members was held in the theatre, Bobby Rogers presiding. The first business was to choose a permanent name. The Provincetown Players—one of the titles sometimes used during the summer—soundly beat out Tryout theatre. The vote was also unanimous for Jig as the first president, a title carefully selected to sidestep the dictatorial sound of the word "director." Reed, Eastman, Burt, and Dell were charged with drafting a constitution, and by the next evening they presented it to the reconvened group. It began with a credo: "that it is the primary object of the Provincetown Players to encourage the writing of American plays of real artistic, literary and dramatic—as opposed to Broadway—merit. That such plays be considered without reference to their commercial value, since this theatre is not to be run for pecuniary profit." It committed the theatre to seeking out and producing new writers as well as plays by members. The constitution created three categories of participation: active members directly involved in production; associate members who would purchase seasonal tickets, necessitated by the zoning laws in New York City requiring that no theatre calling itself a club could sell tickets at the door; and club members who were involved, but less so than the associates, and who would pay dues and receive tickets. It also set forth the duties and responsibilities of the active members; outlined the procedures for play selection, membership, and dismissal; and described a procedure "to guard against an indiscriminate flood of plays." Each playwright was expected to oversee production of her or his play, and no member could be refused a reading. Finally, they planned a new bill of plays every two weeks of a season. Although neither of the extant copies of the Provincetown minutes or scrapbooks indicates it, Edna Kenton records one additional decision adopted: O'Neill's proposal that the full name of the theatre building itself should be the Playwrights' Theatre to indicate the emphasis the group placed on the primacy of the playwright as experimenter. The constitution resolved and executed, the individuals who now constituted the Provincetown Players made their several ways back to New York.[36]

The summer had been exciting but tiring for Susan, who was physically stronger than in the past two years but still not robust. In addition to participating in all the activities of the theatre, she also had kept Jig going—no easy task—overseen Nilla and Harl, and provided money for the family. Jig had given up his *Chicago Evening Post* column, and would not be receiving his fifteen-dollars-a-week salary as president of the Players until the fall. Only her short stories kept them solvent, and so she continued to write them: "Agnes of Cape End" and "The Manager of Crystal Sulpher Springs" in 1915, "Finality in Freeport" (based on the Davenport library controversy of 1910), "Unveiling Brenda," "The Hearing Ear," "Miss Jessie's Trip Abroad," and "Her Heritage of Ideals" in the last six months of 1916. By September she was exhausted and needed a break. Friends suggested Gates Farm, in North Harland, Vermont. She went there in October, while Jig stayed behind in Provincetown, waiting to hear from Floyd, who had been charged with finding a theatre venue in New York. In one letter Jig proudly informed her that the stamp he was using came from a Boston autograph seeker. "Such is the fame of the Provincetown Players," he proclaimed.[37]

When Floyd's leads were exhausted, Jig decided to go to New York himself, and he wrote Susan that he could not wait for her return. En route, he deposited Ma-Mie and the children at North Station in Boston for their trip west. Only when he arrived in New York did he discover that at the very moment when he was sitting in the Essex Hotel, waiting for his train to New York to depart, Susan, who had begun her trip back to Provincetown from Vermont, was in the same hotel. "And to think of the poor little bear being upstairs there in a room all that time! Susan, you simply have no conception of how glad I would have been to see you then. I was just aching for you."[38] She does not use this comedy of errors in *Road* when she describes Jig's departure, which ends the Wharf Theatre period and begins the New York years. Instead, she creates an even more dramatic scene, one that has all the ingredients of film fantasy. She places Jig on the back platform of the moving train, waiving to her as it departs, and shouting something she can barely hear as she runs after him. "He cupped his mouth with his hands to call back 'Write—another—play!'"[39]

A New Kind of Theatre

17

P.S. 139 MacDougal Street leased by Provincetown Players! Hurray! Paid $50.00 first month's rent from October 1st. So that much is settled!
—Jig Cook to Susan Glaspell, September 19, 1916

Susan returned alone to Provincetown to put the house in order and to plan for the next several months. She and Jig had talked vaguely about spending the winter in Dobbs Ferry, New York, with the Hapgoods, Jig making the trip into the city from there and Susan joining him occasionally. After their separation, the idea sounded less appealing to both, despite its financial benefits. However, as she had been in 1914, Susan was hesitant about joining Jig, either an indication of recurring tensions or her ongoing concern about money. "Of course I want you to live in New York with me. . . . I feel terrible cut off from the Little Bear," he assured her soon after he settled into his temporary quarters in one of Jack Reed's rooms at 43 Washington Square South.[1] Jack had offered the place because he and Louise were now living in the house he had just purchased in Truro. They became the first of the Provincetown crowd to seek the quiet of this smaller nearby community. Susan and Jig would follow them a few years later. Jack's purchase, however, had not ended the Bryant/O'Neill affair that had begun during the summer while Jack had been in Chicago and would continue during the coming fall when he went to Baltimore for a kidney operation.

Half in jest, Jig had written Jack that one possibility for a home for their theatre was his Village apartment, but the suggestion was not well taken. Jig had in his pocket $245 of the $320 in the theatre treasury, raised by the special last performance on the wharf and by the contributions of thirty dollars each from eight "rich" patrons. The first choice in this price range—which had also been considered by the Washington Square Players two years before—was the old bottling works at 139 MacDougal Street. Unfortunately, it was presently occupied; but the landlady, Mrs. Belardi, said she'd try to see what she could do. When Jig visited her, she was frankly charmed, so much so that twenty-four years later, when she was awarded a trophy by the Residential Information Bureau for "improving relations between tenants and landlords," she could remember the event: "I thought Mr. Cook was a handsome fellow and the actors wonderful. My husband thought they were just actors. But he couldn't kill my feelings for the theatre." As an aside, she added that it was ironic that she should receive the award just when the second mortgage on her property was due. "Maybe some of my old tenants who are doing well will notice it. Maybe they'll realize that the money they owe me would come in handy now."[2] After meeting Jig and listening to him describe his dream theatre, she displaced her former tenant—her brother-in-law—and let the Players take the entire parlor floor space at 139. Mrs. Belardi became what Edna Kenton would refer to as "our endowment," waiting patiently when the rent was overdue, trusting the good faith of the group, and becoming a subscribing member. "Without her interest and her patience we could not have survived," Kenton believed.[3]

By the standards of other acting spaces in New York, 139 was spartan; in fact, it wasn't a theatre at all but a series of three rooms, two parlors and a dining room, twenty-four-feet wide and eighty-one-feet deep, with a narrow hallway running along the side, used later for access to the auditorium and stage. The stage was 14-by-10 1/2 feet, only a slight improvement over the Wharf Theatre's dimensions of 10-by-12 feet.[4] The hall parlors, converted into the seating areas, accommodated 150 people perched on stilt-raised circus chairs, which soon became known as *the* most uncomfortable seats in Manhattan, with their small strip of wooden backing, a concession to sore backs, digging painfully into shoulder blades. There were no dressing rooms. Players were forced to scatter to the apartments of nearby friends to dress, hardly an ideal solution, particularly in rain and snow, when just-applied makeup would wash away from swarthy "sea men," revealing soaking Provincetown actors. To keep the group spirit so vital to Jig's concept of community, a clubhouse was required. They could get none this first year, and so they made do with the stage, on which meetings and parties were held after performances. They also had no office; Margaret Nordfeldt's kitchen table in her nearby apartment sufficed. And yet, these limitations did not seem to dampen the ardor of the group, who set about preparing for their November 3 opening night.

Disaster almost occurred when, in the process of breaking down the walls dividing the rooms, Jig discovered that he had also broken a building code and incurred the wrath of the building inspector, who was adamant that a steel girder must be installed to support the proscenium arch.

At $200, this unexpected expense dangerously depleted the treasury, which now had only $70 left for the completion of the renovation and for running of the theatre. But even with this setback, the group was not devastated. "I remember that the chief topic of discussion during those tense days was not money—oh no! The chief topic of discussion—and dissension—was the right decoration of the proscenium arch," Kenton recalled.[5] This was not just any paint job, and the "painters"—Demuth, Nordfeldt, Zorach, and Joseph Weyrich—were not just any painters. The results were striking. "The benches painted lavender, the walls dark dull gray, with emerald green doors and paneling, the arch-way over the stage, gold squares and purple design at each side, and the curtain a wonderful royal purple affair with a cerise band across it."[6] With equal fervor and brighter colors, the group attacked a second project. Nani Bailey, a trained nurse, and one of the Provincetown group during the summer, decided to open a small restaurant around the corner on Fourth Street. While not the official club the group sought, the Samovar, her tearoom, soon became their home away from home, providing them with a communal kitchen, which offered some of the cohesiveness Jig desired, along with inexpensive food.

A day after he wrote to tell Susan that he had found a home for the Provincetown Players, Jig reported that he'd found an apartment for them, again on Milligan Place, but this time at number one: five "'rooms' for twenty-one dollars a month, if you want to call two tiny hall-bedrooms rooms." If she will send her bed, he will buy one, and they can move in. On October 1, when he took possession, she and her bed were still in Provincetown, but he prodded her to come quickly because Floyd wanted her to play Guinevere in his *King Arthur's Socks*, slated to open the first bill, along with Louise Bryant's *The Game* and *Bound East for Cardiff*. "L. B. [Little Bear] has charm, has never had a chance to show it in a play, and could show it here. Does the L. B. want to do it? She would have to come to N.Y. right away."[7] There is no record that Susan read for the part; however, Louise, in a letter to Jack the next month, reports the gossip that Susan cannot forgive Floyd "since he put her out of his play."[8] Whether she means the Guinevere part is uncertain. In any case, soon after Jig's appeal, Susan found temporary arrangements for their cats and headed for New York to help launch the theatre.

In *The Road to the Temple* she describes what she found when she arrived: Jig on the stage, surrounded by bags of cement and lumber, deep in conversation, explaining the concept of the theatre to a policeman and a building inspector. Again the scene is probably a condensation, Susan splicing together events of the first few weeks of frenetic activity and near disaster, shaped into a vivid moment: "'Now here is Susan Glaspell,' he said, as if I had entered for just this. 'She is writing plays and there is a young Irishman, O'Neill'—turning to the Irish policeman." Tucked under her arm in the scene, is her play *The People*, "dutifully written."[9] Since the play was not read to the group until February 17, 1917, and since they were suffering from a dearth of new material—Jig cajoling her in December to produce something—the likelihood is that here, too, she is fictionalizing for continuity and effect. What she did discover when she arrived in New York was that tensions had already begun to surface among the Players, even before opening night. On the one hand Hutch was warning about "a decadent spirit in the P.P. in the form of a certain longing for efficiency," a claim Jig immediately dispelled.[10] On the other hand, people such as the Nordfeldts and Freddie Burt were calling for more organization and professionalism. What had seemed possible to a group of vacationers sitting around a fire on a secluded beach in Provincetown, fortified by Italian wine, was not exactly what the same group imagined or desired, once the vacation was over. Mary Pyne, in a letter to Mary Vorse, who was still in Provincetown, describes the differences a month can make: "Provincetown seems like a land of dreams—infinitely far off and unattainable—there one approached the illusion of life having some sort of form—but here . . . its an awful helter—but a gay thing after all—requiring many virtues. Trust patience courage and all that."[11]

These virtues were being sorely tried. The constitution, lovingly crafted by Reed and friends, had called for weekly meetings of the entire active membership, at which there would be readings of, and voting on, plays submitted. Between October 5 and 17, despite their frantic rush to meet the announced opening night, the Players miraculously held five meetings, at which—besides settling pressing business and approving new members—the group read, discussed, and voted on nine plays, in addition to making suggestions for casting and performance schedules. By the October 22 meeting, however, it became clear that too much time was being spent listening to plays and making group decisions about all elements of production, causing members to become restless and bored. Even before opening night, a schism was forming between those who wanted less involvement and those who sought more. Slowly during the year, the community would give way to the committee, and the number needed for decision-making would shrink to a majority of a quorum of twelve and later of seven. By 1922 Kenton reports that almost all decisions were made by Jig, Gene, Susan, and herself; and of this group, only she and Susan actually read through the initial piles of manuscripts submitted.[12] Other changes occurred out of necessity. The original plan was to have ten bills running for twenty weeks, two weekend nights each. But almost immediately it became clear that two consecutive days would be simpler and allow more preparation time between bills. Then "a miracle" changed even this plan. A representative of the New York Stage Society received the circular Jig had sent, visited the theatre, and immediately embraced the new experiment, arranging to take over two of the evenings of each run for the membership, purchasing 200 subscriptions, or 400 tickets, for a total of $1,600. Buoyed by this show of faith and by the numerous individual subscriptions that came in, the Players scheduled bills to run from Friday through Tuesday, the first and last days reserved for the Stage Society. Later in the year, unable to keep up the frantic pace, they introduced new programs every three weeks, offering a total of eight plus one review bill, rather than ten.

Part of the problem from the beginning was the difficulty in finding good plays. Of the six works on the first two bills, only Dell's *King Arthur's Socks* was new. There was also the problem of temperamental playwrights. Padric Colum's *The Betrayal*, scheduled to be on the second bill, was withdrawn by the playwright two days before opening, and *Suppressed Desires* was put on in its place—Susan, Jig, and Margaret Nordfeldt rehearsing until just before the curtain went up. On the third bill, difficulties arose from temperamental group members unwilling to have poet Alfred Kreymborg's stylized farce *Lima Beans* on a bill with O'Neill's realistic *Before Breakfast* and Boyce's new play *The Two Sons*. Kreymborg convinced them to let him produce the play and enlisted the services of avant-garde poets Mina Loy, recently arrived from Florence and soon part of the transplanted Dada group in New York, and William Carlos Williams, a young doctor from New Jersey who came to the Village on weekends. The play was successful, demonstrating that nonrealistic works could find an audience, thus paving the way for experiments by other poet/playwrights, such as Edna St. Vincent Millay, who arrived in 1918.

Before the fourth bill, on December 15, the Players experienced a bit of extra-theatrical excitement, which led to their first newspaper headlines: "Schoolboy, Lured by Stage, Takes Part Under an Assumed Name in Mac-Dougal Street Theatre, but not for Long."[13] Richard Mansfield II, the son of the famous actor, had run away from his boarding school in Connecticut and made his way to the theatre, which he had read about in a circular sent to his mother. Hiding in the last row of seats while a rehearsal was in progress, he could not stifle groans as he listened to the struggling actors. In response to Jig's "Who the deuce are you?" the boy revealed his name and his dream. He wished to become a Player, but requested that his presence be kept a secret from his mother. Jig was enchanted and allowed him to attend rehearsals, eat with the cast at Nani's, and spend one night at O'Neill's apartment and one night with him. For young Mansfield, this may have been enough, because he then sent his mother a telegram reading, "Mother! I have run away. I have joined the Provincetown Players. Rescue me for I am too weak to rescue myself." He was subsequently "saved." Two years later, barely nineteen, the would-be actor would die in an army camp in Texas.

Details of Mansfield's adventure in the Village made all the New York papers and gave inadvertent publicity to the group that did not seek any. Ironically, this shunning of publicity generated a sort of mystique of its own. When writing about the Mansfield affair, one reporter wondered how the boy was able to pierce the secrecy of the establishment "because nobody can get in to see George Cram Cook, Susan Glaspell, Mary Heaton Vorse, Wilbur Steele, John Reed, Eugene O'Neill or Mary Pyne writing, staging or acting in their own plays unless one knows a member."[14] While the description was hardly accurate—critics, like anyone else, were able to become subscribing members, and a few were—it was true that the Players had no press agent, provided no free press tickets, and did not court critics. Those who wanted to see their work paid, and those who wrote about them did so because they chose to, not because they were told to by their editors.

Susan did not get to read the Mansfield headlines; she'd left for Davenport on December 9, the day they appeared. She was also spared from seeing the next bill, which Kenton called an "air hole out of which we did not climb on the current of this or the two succeeding bills."[15] No play emerged strong enough to carry any of the programs, and the players for the first time began to feel anxious about their future. "If we don't get them we're going to peter out," Jig wrote to Susan, repeating what by now had become a familiar refrain: "You must write one." In a following note he entreats her, "Hope the L.B. does a nice funny play. We need a nice funny play." Turning to personal matters, he begs her to return as soon as possible, since he misses her and feels lonely, attributing part of his sense of unease to O'Neill, who had stopped seeing Louise once more, now that Jack had returned from the hospital. O'Neill is "nearing the snapping point of suspense and tension," Jig reports, "and the mood is contagious."[16] Susan wrote Louise a Christmas note and asked about Jack's health, reporting that in Davenport it was "10 below zero" and that "having nothing else to do, I have written just today a comedy which I am hoping is funny."[17] Evidently it was. At the December 27 meeting of the Players two plays were read: *The Sniper* by O'Neill and *Family Pride* by Glaspell, the "nice, funny play" she had evidently written while in Iowa and sent ahead to be read before her return. Following a new policy calling for voting at subsequent meetings after initial readings, the group accepted her play unanimously (an unusual event) on January 17. For some reason, *Family Pride* (the title later changed to *Close the Book*) was not staged until the first bill of the next season. Instead, another Glaspell play, *The People*, was read on the January 17 by the author and at the next meeting was unanimously accepted and placed on the eighth bill, beginning March 9.

The People broke new ground for the Players. Its cast of twelve was the largest assembled on the tiny stage (one more than O'Neill introduced in *Bound East for Cardiff*); it was also the first play since *Suppressed Desires* to receive an extended, positive review in a New York newspaper; and it took on a Village sacred cow—the radical magazine *The Masses*. The play is set in present time, March 1917, in the offices of the newspaper *The People*, on the morning after its editor, Edward Wills, a fictionalized Eastman, has returned from an unsuccessful cross-country trip in search of funding. Gathered to hear if the journal will continue are its staff and four others identified only by type—the Earnest Approach, the Light Touch, the Firebrand, and the Philosopher. Each provides an explanation as to why *The People* has not been successful and all suggest cures in keeping with their particular predilections. In her handling of the melee, Susan gleefully critiques *The Masses*'s internecine feuding, which she knew well from her close relationship with its editors. She also parodies similar battles within the Players.

When editor Wills, played by Cook, enters and hears the babble, he can only comment, "Everybody plugging for his own thing. Nobody caring enough about the thing as a whole."[18] The words are directed not only to the assembled characters on the stage but to members of *The Masses* and Players in the audience, a serious rejoinder lobbed in a comedic form, a familiar Glaspell technique. While she delights in depicting a periodical that purports to speak to "the people" but cannot even create a dialogue among its own workers, Susan's goal, finally, is to provide an impassioned reminder about how a revolutionary group, *any* revolutionary group, dedicates itself to certain goals at its inception and then loses sight of them along the way. In order to link this serious theme with the comedic opening, she introduces a new group who have heeded the editor's message, even when he himself no longer believes in it. They are "the people"—the Woman from Idaho, the Boy from Georgia, the Man from the Cape—who have come demanding "the rest of what you've got." In keeping with her tendency to place women at the center of her plays, Susan has the Woman from Idaho speak for them all, just as she has Sara, an office worker, be the most committed to the perpetuation of the journal. After describing where she has come from—"a flat piece of land fenced in"—the Woman from Idaho tells Wills that his words have been for her "like a spring breaking through the dry country of my mind." With her hands outstretched "in a gesture, wide, loving," she asks him to continue his magazine: "Let life become what it may become!—so beautiful that everything that is back of us is worth everything it cost."

Susan played the Woman from Idaho. French director Jacques Copeau, who was spending the war years in New York, directing performances of his transplanted theatre company, Théâtre du Vieux-Colombier, happened to be visiting the Players and saw Glaspell perform the part. He describes how greatly moved he was by the experience:

Recently I attended a performance of one of your little theatres
and I observed on the stage a young woman of modest appearance,
with a sensitive face, a tender and veiled voice. She was absolutely
lacking in technique. She did not have the slightest notion of it. For
example, she did not know how to walk on stage or how to enter
or exit. She did not know either how to accompany her words with
the gestures appropriate to the action of the dialogue, and she kept
constantly her two arms a little feverishly against her body. And
only at the end of her speech, she reached out her two arms simply,
and she became suddenly silent, looking straight ahead as if she
was continuing to live her thoughts in the silence. Well, that ges-

ture was admirable, and there was in that look a human emotion that brought tears to my eyes. I had a real woman before me, and the tears which she made me shed were not those involuntary tears brought on sometimes by the nervous excitement of theatre. They were real tears, natural, human as she was.[19]

Editor Wills is similarly moved by the simple, yet impassioned speech and rekindled by her message that "*Seeing*—that's the social revolution."

In this early example of expressionist theatre, in which she replaced characters with types, Glaspell creates a new hybrid, which blends humor and social drama, a form she will refine in *Inheritors*. Moreover, she illustrates that she is a sensitive reader of the times. Only a few weeks after the opening, both *The Masses* and the Provincetown Players were to experience putsches, predicated on the very squabbles depicted in her play. "With tomahawks and axes we cleared away the illusions that had made us not see the forest for the trees," Kenton reports.[20] Jig running against Freddie Burt, was reelected president, but not unanimously; Margaret Nordfeldt was defeated for secretary by Dave Carb; her husband Brör, one of the great irritants to Cook and others because of his irascible personality, was asked to resign; and three original members—Eastman, Dell, and Hapgood—who had proffered their resignations earlier were officially removed from the membership. In *The People*, idealism carried the day; in the Players, expediency seemed to dictate. Before the first year was over, the community had retrenched, moving away from Jig's original idealization of amateurism and the assumption that all elements of production would naturally arise from the group dynamic.

Descriptions of the first six bills indicate that even had the players received excellent plays, the mostly amateur actors would have had problems, as Copeau's comments indicate, since none had any sense of even simple stage business. And then, just as with O'Neill's arriving as if on cue, the Players obtained the services of Nina Moise, a trained director, who began to take over many of the productions, beginning with the seventh bill of the 1916–17 season. When she began, she found the theatre in chaos. "If people stood in front of each other and bumped each other in a room, why not do it on the stage, which was exactly what they were doing. I didn't know much about stage direction, the rest of them knew less." When Moise met Susan, she made the mistake of calling her Mrs. Cook. Despite this faux pas, the two women soon began to work well together. During her eighteen months with the Players, Moise directed *The People*, *Close the Book*, *The Outside*, and the second New York production of *Suppressed Desire*. Years later, after she had moved to Hollywood, she commented that Susan's and O'Neill's plays were the most important the group mounted and that "for her own plays, [Susan] was a very interesting actress and was a joy to work with and interfered very little in direction," an unusual quality among playwrights in the early Provincetown history.[21]

Part of the success of the eighth bill, including *The People*, comes from Moise's work. Reviewer Heywood Broun, who wrote detailed descriptions of the three plays (including Harry Kemp's *The Prodigal Son* and Pendleton King's *Cocaine*), had no criticism of the acting, a sign that it had improved appreciably. While crediting each playwright, he offers particular praise to Glaspell "who has done more for American drama than any playwright of the year." Arguing that *The People* could stand cutting, he still praises its "gorgeous plan," which is "developed with humor and telling eloquence." Broun only wishes he had a copy so that he could print verbatim the stirring editorial of the editor, "for it sounds like a capital piece of writing."[22]

Broun would soon get the opportunity, since Frank Shay, who now ran the Washington Square Bookstore, started publishing the plays of the Provincetown Players, first in single volumes, later in collections. *Trifles* appeared in 1916, *The People* and *Close the Book* in 1918. By 1920, Small and Maynard took over from the enthusiastic but quickly impoverished Shay. Their publication of *Plays* by Glaspell, including all her one-acts and her first full-length play, *Bernice*, was widely distributed and reviewed in the leading New York newspapers and magazines, bringing her further attention and praise. Many critics joined Ludwig Lewisohn in citing *Trifles* as "one of the best one-act plays to appear in America." In his review in the *Nation* he wrote, "the life [in her works] is strong, though it is never rich. In truth, it is thin. Only it is thin not like a wisp of straw, but like a tongue of flame."[23] Lewisohn would become one of the most insightful and enthusiastic of Glaspell's critics. Others offered uniform praise for her entire oeuvre: "Here is a little body of work—far too small to suit me, for one—that seems to prove us less poor than is generally thought," Edwin Björkman wrote in the *Freeman*. "An American Shaw—but quite original," he called her. He also found Synge's hand in *Trifles*, despite the meagerness of the prose. "Iowa farmers do not talk like Aran Islanders. If they did, Miss Glaspell's credit would be less than it is. The tongue of Ireland breeds poetry naturally and almost mechanically. It has to be wrung by hard labor and unusual vision out of the thrifty soil of the Middle West."[24] The impact of these early publications of the Players' plays cannot be overestimated. Few got into the miniscule theatre, but many read the plays and were introduced to the works of Glaspell and O'Neill long before they ever had a chance to see them performed. Susan's reputation would spread in Britain in the same way, through the later publication of her full-length plays by Ernest Benn, before they were mounted there on stage.

As the Players moved through its first New York season, events in Europe were becoming increasingly desperate; and the war, which had seemed far away, was suddenly brought home. Susan and Jig, like most of their friends, were socialists and had voted for Eugene Debs for president in 1912. However, carried by the enthusiasm of Jack Reed, who had met

President Woodrow Wilson and believed he would do as he said—keep America out of war—they supported Wilson's candidacy in 1916. When, in April 1917, Wilson went before Congress asking it to declare war on Germany, many in the radical community felt betrayed. *The Masses* took up the fight against U.S. involvement and against the draft law, which was instituted on May 8. During the first induction round, Jig was too old to serve; O'Neill was also exempt because of his earlier tuberculosis. But other Players were called or volunteered. Pendleton King was drafted immediately. Nani Bailey gave up her tearoom the Samovar and returned to nursing. She would be killed in France in 1918. Eventually seven Players served in France. Slowly, over the next two years, the climate that the war created reached into all aspects of Village life. "The country which had so little wanted war went mad for war," Mary Vorse wrote.[25] Those who opposed the war were increasingly isolated, branded as subversives, traitors, and—after the revolution in Russia in the fall of 1917—as Bolsheviks, or Reds. In September 1917 Jack Reed noted: "In America the month just past has been the blackest month for free men our generation has known."[26] By that time, *The Masses*, along with seventeen other radical periodicals around the country, had been closed down by the government for antiwar and antidraft positions. Eastman, Dell, Reed, Art Young, and three others were tried twice in celebrated cases against *The Masses* that finally concluded in hung juries but ended its publication.

Other radical Village institutions also ceased operation, due in part to fiscal problems brought on by the pressures of the war. The Washington Square Players closed at the end of the 1917 season; the Liberal Club ceased to function in July 1918. Of all the groups that began with calls for a new openness in society, only Heterodoxy and the Provincetown Players made it through the war period. What makes the accomplishment of the Players so remarkable is that it occurred in a climate so antithetical to any form of radical endeavor. Perhaps because its antiwar protests were often muted by transference to another time, as in Cook's *The Athenian Women*, or another place, as in Susan's *Bernice*, the authorities saw little offense. It might be that any institution that claimed, as the Provincetown did, that it was a "little theatre for American writers to play with" was not to be taken seriously.

Not all the Villagers who had shared a desire for social change and had worked together to cobble an agenda of reform were universally opposed to the war. Charlotte Perkins Gilman, for example, tendered her resignation to Heterodoxy because the majority of the women were antiwar. This schism also carried over to families. When O'Neill visited his parents in New London, Connecticut, in May, he and his father argued strongly about the younger O'Neill's antiwar views. In the case of Susan, her parents seemed to share her antipathy for fighting and for the war hysteria. When Jig visited them in the fall of 1917, Mr. Glaspell commented that Christ would have been antiwar, an argument the elder Glaspell probably did not realize was being put forth in a stirring series of cartoons in *The*

Masses, one picturing Christ in front of a firing squad, with the caption "Deserter," another arrested for draft resistance, because he would not kill.[27] Despite the differences in their lifestyles, it seems that Elmer and Alice were not that far removed from their daughter's basic beliefs (or she from theirs) when it came to war. Susan was not a pacifist. She simply believed that America was not best served by its intervention, particularly since it deflected attention from pressing issues at home such as suffrage, child care, and labor rights; and it caused the government to stifle debate and trample free speech in the name of patriotism. Her protests, however, were carried out in her writing, not on the street. During World War II, she would be an active proponent of the war effort, as were her friends Vorse, Eastman, and Dell. Her last novel *Judd Rankin's Daughter,* places a pro-war daughter, living in Provincetown, in opposition to her isolationist father in Iowa. Had Elmer Glaspell lived, he might have been the model for the father.

In May 1917 despite the war hysteria, the Players were primarily concerned with the aftermath of their own internal wars. The season ended on a high note with the great success of the review bill, including *Suppressed Desires* and *The People*; but the group was "literally spent body and spirit" after the great accomplishment of surviving the year in New York. "Even knowing we did it, I am disposed to say what we did that first year couldn't be done," Susan writes in *Road*.[28] They had overcome building inspectors and court orders requiring that they desist from performing on Sunday. They had overcome sloppy performances and weak scripts. They had even overcome the trials of wartime. A few critics were now traveling downtown, paying their own way, and those who wrote about them praised the young upstart company, at least its most prominent playwrights Glaspell and O'Neill. Burns Mantle, for one, saluted them: "With no desire to invade the splendid exclusiveness of the Provincetown folk, we count it a civic duty to report that their season's achievement is as sound as it is modest. We never thought anything could live a year in New York without a press agent."[29] Susan was all too aware of the poor acting and often badly written and hurriedly produced plays. But she and O'Neill had shown through their work that it was possible for America to produce a theatre worthy of the country. With a positive balance in the bank, subscription renewals coming in at a brisk pace, and plans for the next season well under way, the Players took a well-earned break.

Fire from Heaven on MacDougal Street

18

We will let this theatre die before we let it become another voice of mediocrity.

—George Cram Cook, "Provincetown Players Circular,"
1917–18 season

The summer of 1917 in Provincetown was different from the last two. The Wharf Theatre was still there, but no longer being used for productions. The focus of the group was now New York, and there was no time or energy to plan a summer season, even if the inclination had been there. The Hapgoods were in town, but Neith had stopped writing plays after negative reaction to *The Two Sons*, which Louise Bryant reported caused the audience to burst into laughter. Mary Vorse, who from the start was peripheral to the group and had written nothing the Players would accept, was busy packing to move to Washington, D.C., where she would work for the Committee for Public Education during the remainder of the war. Wilbur Daniel Steele had just returned from the Caribbean and was completing short stories based on his experiences, while he and Margaret awaited the birth of their second child. And Louise Bryant and John Reed, progressively limiting involvement with the Players throughout the winter—Louise announcing that they "give me a pain in the stomach"—had married the previous November and taken up residence in Croton-on-Hudson, a community that other Villagers, including Mabel Dodge, were using as a city retreat. In the summer the couple was preparing to travel to Russia where, to the delight and amazement of the Village radical community, a revolution of the proletariat had actually taken place. O'Neill, still in love with Louise and suffering over her rejection, was in Provincetown, living with Terry Carlin and others at Francis's Flats and spending most of his time swimming, having completed that spring several of the Glencairn plays and *Ile*, which would appear in the coming bills. As for Susan and Jig, the summer was a time for writing: for him the first draft of his Greek play, *The Athenian Women*; for her a new play based on local themes.

After their day's work, both enjoyed taking long walks. One of their favorites took them to the outside, that stretch of beach that faced the Atlantic Ocean, a place cut off from the rest of the town by shifting dunes, on which rough sea grass and odd-shaped vegetation acted as buffers between the woods backing the community and the ever-encroaching sand. The lifesaving station Mabel had refurbished and temporarily occupied in 1915 stood there, once more abandoned and more deeply buried in the sand because of a sudden gale that had recently struck the Cape that summer, capsizing three schooners and taking the lives of thirty-five Provincetown men. It may have been this tragedy, together with the image of the station gradually being covered by sand that prompted Susan to begin work on *The Outside*, the play which bears the most direct stamp of her adopted home.

It is the shortest and most lyrical of her one-acts, its idiomatic rhythms, spareness and subject matter showing, even more than *Trifles*, the influence of Synge. Like *Trifles*, it presents the separate worlds and ways of women and men, closed off from each other. In contradiction to what French theorist Hélène Cixous claims—that a woman must die before a play begins—Susan begins both plays with the death of a man. This time he is a drowning victim, brought to the former station by lifeguards, who struggle to revive him as they have done for so many in the past. While they work in a side room from which part of the body can be glimpsed, two women enter: Mrs. Patrick, the present owner, a New Yorker who now lives year-round on this isolated stretch, and her servant, Allie Mayo, a local woman, who has "a prejudice against words," and has barely spoken since her own husband died at sea twenty years earlier.[1] Both have sought refuge on the outside, escaping from lives too painful to bear. "They're *both* crazy," the men conclude; they certainly don't act like women. "A woman—she makes things pretty." Here "things—do not hang on other things." After introducing the two groups, Glaspell, as she does in *Trifles*, dismisses the men and focuses her attention on the world of the women. In the process she once more overturns the expected direction of the plot. It is the lifesavers who fail to revive life, while Allie Mayo, moved by the struggle and by the presence of the dead young man, painfully and successfully enacts a lifesaving ritual of her own. Aware that her employer has stopped up the channels of feeling, just as she has attempted to do, Allie empathetically reaches out to Mrs. Patrick, as Mrs. Hale belatedly did to Minne Wright. "For twenty years, I did what you are doing. And I can tell you—it's not the way," she says, once the men have left, sharing her own story with the woman she assumes is also grieving over the death of a husband. When she discovers that abandonment, not death, has driven Mrs. Patrick to the outside, Allie, nevertheless, persists, arguing that life cannot be denied. Just as the vegetation surrounding them fights to survive against the forces seeking to bury it, all life must struggle to exist, even on this "edge of life," this verge, where, as Mrs. Patrick claims, "life trails off to dwarfed things not worth a name."

In their debate, both women resort to staccato-like phrases, sometimes mere ejaculations of words, spoken in counterpoint, particularly melodious and poetic in performance:

> MRS. PATRICK: A line of land way out to sea—land not life.
> ALLIE MAYO: A harbor far at sea. [Raises her arm, curves it in as if around something she loves.] Land that encloses and gives shelter from storm.
> MRS. PATRICK: [Facing the sea, as if affirming what will hold all else out.] Outside sea. Outer shore. Dunes—land not life.
> ALLIE MAYO: Outside sea—outer shore, dark with the wood that once was ships—dunes, strange land not life—woods, town and harbor.

In such exchanges, and in the visual and verbal imagery of the play, Glaspell once more attempts to move beyond realism, invoking through the cadences of the language and the echoing sounds a topology of the persistent struggle for life, even in such an inhospitable place. The dead body provides one locus, the battling scrub bush another. Again, as in *Trifles*, the dialogue takes the form of self-discovery, a process being worked out seemingly by improvisation, the women stumbling over words as they make their way to some new awareness. She also makes extensive use of carefully modulated body movements, reminiscent of Maeterlinck: an outstretched hand and open palm denoting both the need for contact and the fear of returning to life. To make the gestures more poignant, Susan once more starred in the production, playing Allie Mayo to Ida Rauh's Mrs. Patrick.

Despite its brevity, *The Outside* took Susan far longer to compose than her previous one-acts. By September, when Jig left for Davenport with Nilla, Harl, and Ma-Mie, to see the children half-way along on their trip to Mollie in California, he had already read a draft and wanted it for the opening bill. Yet, on October 1, after he had returned to New York and the Players had met to plan the season, the play had not yet arrived. Neither had Susan, who was still in Provincetown working on revisions. This pattern would be repeated in coming years: Jig imploring her to finish a play and she resisting his pressure, feeling she needed more time to complete her work to her satisfaction or at least time to be alone before facing once more the tumult of production and politics at the Players. At the end of the month, she finally brought the manuscript with her, and it was read and approved, but too late to be included in the first program.

Instead, the 1917–18 season began on November 2 with her "nice funny play" *Close the Book* written the previous season, along with O'Neill's *The Long Voyage Home* and poet James Oppenheim's *Night*.

Close the Book harkens back to the parody of *Suppressed Desires* and again brings up issues related to the period, Susan relying on humor to make its points. Written and set in Iowa, her first play to specify her native state (the stage directions for *Trifles* only mention a kitchen, not where it is located), it also presents her first upper-class family, appropriately called the Roots, whose antecedents go back to the Revolutionary War. Three generations have gathered to celebrate the engagement of Peyton, an activist professor of English, to Jhansi Mason, a student radical who claims to have descended from gypsies. His family is confused by Peyton's activism: "What business has a Professor of English to say anything about society; it's not in his department."[2] About his intended marriage they are more sanguine, since they recognize that Jhansi "won't be in a position to say so much about freedom after she is married. . . . She won't be a gypsy after she's Peyton's wife. She'll be a married woman." With one sentence, Glaspell is able to point to the conformity expected of married women, gypsies or not, and the ways in which propriety and its purveyors control dissent merely by imposing their values on new arrivals to their ranks. The "flat land fenced in," which the Woman from Idaho fled in *The People*, is reduced in *Close the Book* to a well-appointed parlor, no less enclosed; and its inhabitants are equally at odds with new ideas. Rather than venture out from behind the walls of respectability they have constructed, toward some further verge, these second-generation inheritors smugly plot to draw outsiders "within the gates." This is a familiar Glaspell theme, more politically charged since the play opened just as America was being drawn into a war that Glaspell and most of her friends opposed.

Yet, she also levels her satire at the would-be bohemian, similar to many she knew in the Village, who took pride in their newly formed identities, which separated them from their forbearers and from bourgeois society. The young woman is too much captive of her own romance, assuming that she can only be a nay-sayer as long as she is a gypsy. To be yourself and to critique your world from within is a far more difficult role, as Glaspell well knew and depicted in other writing. Initially it seems that Jhansi holds the moral high ground, but as usual in a Glaspell play, all is not what it seems, and radicals are held up to parody as well as conformists. In a wonderful reversal, Susan has disaster occurs when, during the course of the evening, a genealogy book is produced, indicating that Jhansi is not only *not* a gypsy, but that her father was a milkman, her mother helped in missionary causes, and that they were even married in the Baptist church! This is too much for the "disgraced" young rebel, who releases Peyton from his vows, since she is not what she claimed to be. However, after they read the small print of the book, both discover hidden skeletons in their families: the fortune of the Roots came from a man who sold guns and liquor to the Indians, and Jhansi's grandfather torched his neighbor's house for shooing his pigs away. Now neither need be held in check by family pride, since both have "crevices in these walls of respectability."

Those who reviewed the play in its MacDougal Street premiere and in the production at the Comedy Theatre, which the Washington Square Players mounted on May 13 as part of their final bill, recognized the Shavian social parody at work. Edwin Björkman, reviewing the printed version in 1920, noted that "The laugh she draws from us may appear to be at the expense of respectability or of its opposite: in reality, it is always directed at the self-satisfied superficiality of both sides"[3] Again Susan shows herself to be a keen reader of the times, even anticipating events. Before the Espionage Act put tight restrictions upon what could be said and the Alien and Sedition Act of 1918 put limits on those who were not natives, she has Peyton denounced as an "Untrue American" for questioning the direction of modern literature, and she reveals the incipient racism in his "all American family," who are fearful of aliens in their midst whether "the gypsy" or "the Negroes."

With two plays in production in two months and acting in both (she played Mrs. Root in *Close the Book*), Susan had little time for much else during the winter of 1917–18, one of the coldest in New York history. For Jig and her, home was the theatre and their social life revolved around the newly opened second-floor restaurant Christine Ell established, where they would usually dine, meet friends, discuss theatre business, and socialize over a bottle of wine. Their apartment for the season was outside of the central Village area, at 41 Charlton Street, on a broad block still lined with large, well-preserved houses and private gardens, a five-and-a-half-minute walk from the theatre, Jig calculated. Its two large parlors provided more work space than they had the year before. Susan took over the back room for her writing, and entertained guests around the fireplace in the large front drawing room. The predominant population of the area was Italian, even more so than on MacDougal Street. "Those who have gone down there feel as if they were going through the high adventures of pioneers when they undertake to create a home in the midst of an alien civilization," a visiting reporter wrote when she came to interview Susan after the December opening of *The Outside*. The thrust of her article concerned Susan's own pioneering roots, her work habits, methods of composition, and attitudes about contemporary events. "The war must necessarily affect us all. But I find that I cannot do war work. I am entirely unfitted to public service in any way," Susan explained, making clear that in order to write she needed time and quiet "so that I can work away uninterruptedly until I have done all I can."[4] In a later interview, which appeared in 1921 after the openings of *Inheritors* and *The Verge*, she is more emphatic: "Of course I am interested in all progressive movements, whether feminist, social or economic, but I can take no very active part other than through my writing. One can't work with too many things. . . . When one has limited strength one must use it for the thing one feels most important."[5] These comments, which have been used by some contemporary critics to argue Susan's apolitical nature,[6] do not deny her activism; they indicate only that its most potent form exists in her writing.

Like her, Jig also felt that he could best address the war hysteria and suppression of radicals by shaping his protest in a play. His *The Athenian Women* appeared on the fifth bill, after three mediocre bills marked only by the success of *The Outside*. When Aspasia, the protagonist in the play, says, "O Kalia, do you not know in your heart that there is no other such disaster as this war of exhaustion which has become the nightmare of our lives,"[7] the contemporary references were obvious to Village audiences, although the authorities let the play run, put off perhaps by the ancient setting and the fact that Ida Rauh, who spoke the lines, was dressed in a Greek costume. The work was daring in its form as well as its message. It was the Players' first attempt at a full-length play, requiring changes of scenery and a cast of twenty-seven playing thirty-three speaking parts. Probably only Jig would have dared to write such a play for such a tiny theatre and assume that the group was up to staging it. When Moise suggested that perhaps a more experienced, professional company should take over the work—say the Neighborhood Players or the Stage Society—Jig responded, "I am confident we can rise to a big production of a thing people are intensely interested in."[8] He seems to have been right. The critics were generally positive, even though Heywood Broun thought the play flawed "from the too obvious attempt to state present-day problems in terms of Greece."[9]

The person who received the most glowing reviews was Ida Rauh, who had developed into the finest actor the Provincetown Players produced. She appeared in thirteen productions in the first two seasons, and was referred to in print as the Duse of MacDougal Street or an American Bernhardt. In life she displayed a similar power and sensuality. Mabel Dodge described her as "noble-looking, like a lioness."[10] To her husband, Max Eastman, she was beautiful and mysterious when he first met her—and clinging and dependent when he tried to leave her for a much younger woman in 1916. Dodge tells a different story, describing Ida's joy at the thought of finally being free to face life without Max.[11] Part of this post-Max life included Jig. Just when their affair began is not clear; but by March 1918, it was common gossip among the Players. "Jig and Ida breaking, it is said. Jig is jealous of notices of Ida in the papers—so they say,"[12] Hutch wrote to Neith from New York, referring to *The Athenian Women*, in which his own last-minute takeover of the leading male role brought him negative reviews as opposed to her accolades. Professional jealousy aside, the affair was still going strong two months later, when Hutch again reported to Neith: "Saw Jig and Susan for a moment at the Samovar. . . . Justus [Sheffield] said that Susan is 'hanging on' to Jig, a distant second in the race with Ida."[13] Just how serious the relationship was is hard to know. After her divorce, Ida had become one of the most dedicated of the Provincetown group, advancing to the executive committee with Edna Kenton, when Bryant and Reed resigned. Her administrative and acting work brought her into daily contact with Jig. Susan seems to have been able to rationalize the relationship—just as Jack seemed to do with Louise's attachment to O'Neill—perhaps convincing herself that a good friend could show devotion and attention to one's partner, but not threaten the relationship. Or she may have decided to do what other of her friends did in the face of clearly sexual liaisons within the group: ignore them and hope they will pass. During this same period, Hutch was carrying on an affair with Mary Pyne, who was still married to Harry Kemp, and Neith discussed the relationship in her letters to him. Susan, far less stoic and forgiving, wrote no such letter (that I have found). However, she continued to work with Ida, directing her in *Woman's Honor*, in which Ida played "The Scorned One," and Susan "The Cheated One."

The triangle was of sufficient importance within the Players for Harry Kemp to have created a fictionalized version in his almost unreadable 1931 novel *Love Among the Cape Enders*, a satire of the life and loves among the Players in Provincetown. In his treatment, Jim Dale, who "twisted his iron-gray forelock while he descanted," is clearly Jig, a man "happy platonizing."[14] Jane Enders, the heavily veiled Susan figure, is a painter and his student, who has a longstanding and platonic relationship with Dale, until the advent of Alva Jarvice, "an actress who had had a bit of professional experience." Steve Groton, Kemp's persona, describes Jane's growing discomfort over the affair but her unwillingness to do anything, since she had "deep convictions as to what civilized, enlightened behavior consisted in." Jane does not mind the physical relationship between the two; what she cannot tolerate is Jim's "sharing his career with her; her sharing her career with him." In the climactic scene, Kemp has the finally roused Jane storm into Alva's cottage, push Jim aside and deliver two well-placed slaps to her rival, who responds by wrestling Jane to the ground. The two are finally separated by Alma's wise, black maid, Eunice, who restores order, counseling the women, "Lawdy! Lawdy! The men! . . . chillun—cain't yuh see how they's gotta be managed." As the scene fades, the rivals are united by sisterhood, and an awestruck, chastened Jim can only think, that "some feminine miracle—had happened." Together, Kemp writes, the women become "aiding and abiding powers increasing the power of his Dream!"

When the affair was at its height, Susan produced her own version of female solidarity. *Woman's Honor* appeared on the seventh and final bill of the 1917–18 season, between April 26 and May 2, 1918, along with O'Neill's *The Rope*, and F. B. Kugelman's *The Hermit and his Messiah*.

Originally, the Players had cautiously announced six bills plus a review, not wanting to repeat the mistake of last year, when they were unable to offer the promised number. However, in the spring, they received Susan and Gene's plays and decided to end the season by once more featuring their two most successful and prolific writers. *Woman's Honor* is exactly the type of play one would expect from a charter member of Heterodoxy. Subtitled "a comedy in one act," it is a biting renunciation of that old chestnut from the Gilded Age, "woman's honor" still being held over the heads of women. Susan illustrates how it has allowed men to be chivalrous and keep women in line by forcing them to accept male protection—and advances. The plot is simple. A good-looking young man has been accused of murder; and the only way he can clear his name is for the woman with whom he has spent the night—the entire night—to provide an alibi. Refusing to name her, he proclaims his willingness to die rather than risk her "honor." His lawyer, not content to allow his client to sacrifice himself so that some woman can remain "safe in a sheltered home," leaks the story to the press, assuming that "the romantic sex" will flock to his aid and not let such "a chivalrous young man die."[15]

Flock they do. Through a continually revolving door of the jail (one of the sight gags in the play) come five women[16] who claim to be "her." As she has done in *The People*, Susan presents them as types rather than rounded characters, each one designed to expose the irony inherent in the idea of "woman's honor." The Silly One talks only in clichés about how "Love is conquers all." The Motherly One says, "It would be just like a lot of men to fuss around about a woman's honor and really let it hurt somebody." She has nothing to do before lunch, so she is willing to help. Good-natured as she is, she is not there to destroy the idea for men. "I suppose it really has to be kept up, as long as it gives men such noble feelings." It's not an easy habit to lose. "Like giving up cigarettes or drinking: you have to do it gradually, and there should be something to put in its place." The Scornful One cuts closer to the bone. Logically, she sets forth the hypocrisy of a man nobly defending the honor of a woman, when she no longer has it—thanks to him. If woman's honor is only about virtue, why die for something that is already lost. It is she who provides the central argument in the play: "Did it ever strike you as funny that woman's honor is only about one thing, and that man's honor is about everything but that thing?" She has come because, like the Motherly One, she has no use for honor and therefore has nothing to lose. And besides, she's sick of hearing men talk about it. Two other women also appear. The first has been stifled by "the horrors of the shielded life" and is determined to destroy hers and finally be free. The second has been doubly cheated by the term, first seduced by a man she did not love then forced to marry him to protect her "honor." While the women argue about who most deserves to shed her honor, others wait in the wings to enter the room. The young man, silent throughout the scene, can take no more. "Hell," he says as his curtain line, "I'll plead guilty."

Reactions to the play indicate how deep-seated was the mindset Susan exposed. Most critics found the play witty and clever, even acknowledging "a touch of Wilde,"[17] but failed to see the feminist agenda underlying the humor. They focused, instead, on women's tendency toward self-sacrifice and on their inability to get along with each other. A woman reviewer, seeing it on a review bill the following year, described the action as "half a dozen women who are altruistically ready to part with their [honor] to save the young man from his old-fashioned wrongheadedness," overlooking entirely the pointed messages imbedded in their speeches.[18] She does, however, find the play successful. A reviewer, who saw the play at the Greenwich Theatre, where it transferred after its successful run on Mac-Dougal Street, commented, "A feminine playwright might be expected to be the last person to extract humor from such a subject, but Miss Glaspell generally may be depended upon to do something in the nature of a surprise."[19] Another was not as kind. Commenting that a Schnitzler play had been substituted "in favor of some home made apple-pie riskiness," the reviewer finds that Glaspell's lines "are sometimes amusing sometimes shocking. But *often* they are just plain vulgar and not at all witty. . . . All of which is too bad because Miss Glaspell is a good writer and does not have to be either silly or crude."[20]

Edwin Björkman, one of the most astute Glaspell critics of the period, when reviewing the printed version, was one of the few to allude to the play's serious import:

> *Woman's Honor* is a farce that cuts more deeply than many trag-
> edies. Its main significance to me is that it shows woman speaking
> out of her own nature and not in hypnotized conformation to
> man's established view of her. Women have produced many fine
> things in literature, but the amount of genuine feminine self-rev-
> elation contained in their works is astonishingly small. Even when
> seeming to lay bare her innermost soul, woman has generally
> taken good care that the exposure should not deviate too shock-
> ingly from the conventional image of her created by man to suit
> purposes of his own. Now she is changing at last, in this as in so
> many other respects, and she is growing more and more deter-
> mined to portray herself as she really is rather than as man prefers
> her to be.[21]

As Björkman's review indicates, *Woman's Honor* marks Glaspell's emergence not only as one of the most significant new voices in American theatre but also as one of the playwrights most directly associated with questions related to women's experiences. His reactions are echoed by a review in the *Nation*. After observing that women in theatre are making inroads into a world in which "man is still 'the whole thing,'" it cites Glaspell as spearheading this drive, through her one-acts, which are "distinctively feminine in their social satire, keen observation and trenchant dialogue."[22] John Corbin, the theatre critic for the *New York Times* also applauded her female sensibility. On May 26, in a feature article on her life and work entitled "Who is Susan Glaspell?" he describes her as "one of the two or three foremost and most promising contemporaneous writers of the one-act play."[23] A week before, in a study of the form, he had asked, "Is there any dramatist of the Great White Way who equals Susan Glaspell in subtle feminine intuition, in keen social satire?"[24] To contemporary eyes, the repeated use by Corbin of the term "feminine" might seem a case of damning with faint praise, Glaspell's work assumed to be focusing on the narrow sphere of women's interests, particularly home and family, and, therefore, not to be taken as seriously as that of male writers—O'Neill, for example.[25] However, in the context of the reviews themselves, the word choice seems to reflect the writer's awareness that Glaspell was creating new types of women never before seen in American theatre: women who refused to comply with male fantasies of them, had the wit and audacity to satirize masculine pomposity, and who demanded that they be allowed to define their own lives and worlds.

Glaspell was not the only woman artist being heralded for bringing a female sensibility to her work. Georgia O'Keeffe, who moved to New York two months after *Woman's Honor* opened, expressed similar feelings. "I feel there is something unexplored about woman that only a woman can explore," she would write to Mabel Dodge in 1925.[26] When Alfred Stieglitz first viewed her works he proclaimed, "Finally a woman on paper!"[27] The same reactions were being expressed about Glaspell's writing and would continue to dominate the criticism of her plays as she embarked on full-length women figures.

In other ways, Glaspell and O'Keeffe share points in common. Both were from the Midwest, O'Keeffe born in Sun Prairie, Wisconsin, eleven years after Glaspell. Both moved to the East but retained their attachments to less urban places. ("In my mind," O'Keeffe would repeat about her later home, "I was always on my way back to New Mexico.") There was also a "demonstrable Americanness in their thinking despite their acute awareness of European innovations."[28] Both were also involved with strong, dominant men, but were able to maintain their own names and personalities. Serious professionals, self-assured, and completely focused on their work, they were comfortable with their more ebullient mates taking front stage. In many respects the energetic, charismatic Stieglitz and Jig were brothers: great, nonstop talkers about what they loved most; visionaries who believed that "without losing oneself to something beyond, one is bound to be disappointed"; and leaders in avant-garde movements, who saw their chief function as facilitating others in their work. Stieglitz's assessment of himself could well have been said by Jig: "At least it can be said of me, by way of an epitaph, that I cared."[29] And what O'Keeffe said about her genius husband could have been echoed by Susan: "He was the man and the idea."[30] For these men, their wives' successes were validations of their own beliefs. O'Keeffe drew before Stieglitz; Glaspell wrote before Cook; but both women were fortunate enough to find love with men who understood and did not feel threatened by their genius.

At the end of the Players' second season in New York, Susan had come into her own. Her plays and O'Neill's were the mainstays of the group. They had also become the most celebrated works of the Washington Square Players and Greenwich Village Players, both of which closed their doors permanently at the end the season running a Glaspell play. In comparison, the Provincetown Players not only survived in these critical times, but without a press agent and free tickets to critics, they had also built a reputation for excellence and were now the acknowledged leaders of the little-theatre movement in New York and the country. The question facing them at their final board meeting of the season was what to do next. The organization had already moved appreciably from its beginnings. With only fourteen active members listed, a quorum now reduced to seven, and the functions of president and treasurer combined, decision making was more centralized. Jig still held fervently to the group ethos, as he would until the end of the Players; but in practice, the marks of professionalism and organizational hierarchy were apparent. Nina Moise had left for Hollywood, but the precedent for paying a director had been established, the same for hiring a scenic designer.

Jig now unveiled a plan that might allow the theatre to succeed but still keep its experimental nature. For many years, tucked in the pocket of his work shirt, he had carried plans for his dream theatre to be located along Washington Square: a domed structure, seating 250 people, which a subscriber list of 1,000 would support.[31] It was to be the ideal workspace for playwrights, directors, and designers. He recognized that there would be criticism about seeking such a building when money and resources were so scarce that during that long, cold winter, Mondays had been designated "no heat days" to conserve coal for the war effort. However, he decided that the time was right to see if he could advance his idea, cautiously announcing in the spring subscriber circular that a special fund was being established for a new venue. When A. C. Barnes, the Philadelphia art collector who had been attending performances, suddenly sent a check for $1,000, asking that the donation remain anonymous, the dream suddenly seemed nearer. In the meantime, their present theatre was just too cramped to continue to use. Jig, Susan, and Edna, representing the executive committee, began scouring the neighborhood for places to move to until a further sum could be obtained that would allow them construction of their dream theatre. They finally fixed on another Belardi property at 133 MacDougal, a former stable where the smell of wine still stored in the basement by the most recent tenants, a bottling works, provided a salutary perfume. "Decide" is not exactly the right word, for the decision to move was actually made by Belardi, who, in her absolute faith that the Players could raise the needed money for repairs for 133, had already rented 139. Although it was not Jig's ideal theatre, in the short term it would do. The Players took an option on it and dispersed for the summer to plan for the future. Kenton, summarizing the group's second season in New York sounds—in hindsight—the warning note. "I suppose we could not, even if we had unanimously voted it, have kept ourselves any longer quite as we were when we came down from Provincetown in 1916. We had, in a sense, grown up."[32]

"Here Pegasus Was Hitched"

19

It is incredible that some enterprising manager has not seized upon the exceedingly high gifts of Susan Glaspell. She is a fresh and original genius in the theatre—shrewdly aware of human values, satiric and sensitive.

—Rebecca Drucker, *New York Tribune*, 20 April 1919

At the end of May, while Jig stayed on in New York, participating in "a couple of all night drunks with millionaires"[1] ostensibly designed to raise money for the new theatre, Susan returned to Provincetown to open the house for the summer. These summer periods were her time for short-story writing, still her steadiest source of income, since play royalties were only just beginning to trickle in. For the rights to do *Suppressed Desires*, the rate was fifteen dollars, or ten dollars if admission were not charged; for each story, she could expect to receive at least $350. *Harper's*, where she placed three stories this year, paid its writers $500 per story, and *Pictorial Review* offered writers $650. While her worry over money was not as severe as among some of her friends who had children, it was a concern and had been since her youth. She even considered using the topic for a future story, jotting down in a notebook, "The woman writer who is making the money for a husband who is sick. The strain of doing it alone, the fear."[2] As her dramas improved, so did her short stories, sometimes the one feeding the other. She had converted *Trifles* into "A Jury of Her Peers," which was selected by Edward J. O'Brien as one of the best short stories of 1917 and published in his widely read yearly anthology. Over the next two years, she would publish eight more short stories, five of them in *Harper's*. "The Government Goat" and "His

Smile" were chosen by O'Brien as best short stories for 1919 and 1921, respectively.

Nilla and Harl arrived in July and were delighted with the new addition to the household, a collie pup, a gift from the delivery man who brought eggs and vegetables. "He is a religious dog," Jig decided, "serious minded," so he was awarded a serious name, Ebenezer—after Jig's ancestor Captain Ebenezer Cook—which was immediately shortened to Nezer.[3] The dog took his place in the household alongside Carbon, offspring of the Copy-Cat, and became part of the Provincetown canine community, romping with Mary Vorse's Timmy and the O'Neills' Bowser. In *The Road to the Temple* Susan devotes an entire chapter to Nezer, condensing the next two years into one continuous narrative stretching up to 1920, the details of which are held together with a string of accomplishments of this most talented dog. His death from distemper a few years later was particularly painful for Susan and Jig. When the time came to put the dog to sleep, it was Gene O'Neill who performed the service. He would do the same for Carbon, who died while Susan and Jig were in New York. Writing to Agnes Boulton, O'Neill's wife, on that occasion, Susan expressed her gratitude: "You and Gene seem to help us at these hard times."[4]

By the summer of 1918, Susan had known Eugene O'Neill for two years; they were colleagues, fellow workers, and the leading playwrights of the Provincetown Players. At the outset of their relationship, the younger man had kept his distance, preferring to spend time with his male friends Terry Carlin and Hutch Collins or with a number of women, including Nina Moise and Dorothy Day, who served as surrogates for Louise Bryant. However, during the preceding fall something had happened that altered O'Neill's life and his relationship with Susan. The twenty-four-year-old writer Agnes Boulton, recently widowed, had come to the Village to try to sell some of her romance fiction, in order to support her daughter, parents, and the dairy farm she owned in Connecticut. Her only contacts were Christine Ell, whom she had met previously, and Mary Pyne. At a reunion with Christine at the Hell Hole, she was introduced to O'Neill, who was immediately taken with this dark-haired woman with large, soulful eyes. "I want to spend every night of my life from now on with *you*," he told her, at the end of their first evening together, as they stood outside the Brevoort hotel, where she was staying.[5] When Agnes came to a party for the Players at Christine's a few nights later, she also met Susan, who remarked on Agnes's striking resemblance to Louise. The romance between Gene and Agnes moved quickly; by January he had convinced her to go with him to Provincetown, since the battles being waged at the theatre were distracting him from writing, and the death from a heroin overdose of his good friend Louis Holladay, Polly's brother, was a shadow he wished to escape. After spending the winter together in a small studio that John Francis arranged for them, they got married on April 12, two days before Susan and Jig's anniversary—dates the two couples would celebrate jointly over the next few years. By the summer Agnes and Gene had taken up residence in Francis's Flats, across Commercial Street near Susan and Jig's home.

During the summer of 1918 Gene got into the habit of visiting Susan each day immediately after both had finished their morning's work. The visits, to which Agnes was not invited, made the young bride grumpy and quiet when Gene would finally return "having stayed in that quiet restful house for too long." Gene was thirty, Susan forty-two, but that did not quiet Agnes. Agnes was aware of the soothing quality Susan exuded, her "feminine inner spirit, a fire, a sensitiveness that showed in her fine brown eyes and in the way that she used her hands and spoke." She knew of "many men who found her conversation simulating and helpful," since she could discuss "everything that was going on in the world—economics, the rights of mankind, the theatre, writing, people—and she was able to talk of them when necessary with charm and interest." Agnes, in comparison, felt herself far inferior: unworldly and inarticulate.[6] She was then supporting Gene with her writing, mostly romance potboilers like "Ooh La La!"[7]; Susan wrote for *Harper's*. Agnes also knew it was always Susan, not Jig, whom Gene sought out for a talk. Whenever he wrote to the pair, he would invariably address the letter to Susan; his queries about his work and the Players were taken up with her. The critic Travis Bogard describes what O'Neill generally sought in friendships: "In a woman, performance of the functions of wife, mother, mistress, and chatelaine were sought; in a man, a combination of editorial solicitude, listening ability, financial acumen, and a producer's willingness to serve the demands of the artist were essential."[8] Susan was unique among O'Neill's relationships; all those qualities sought in men, he found in her, plus the decidedly feminine aura she radiated, which Agnes recognized.[9] They talked about their work, read each other's finished manuscripts, and assisted each other whenever possible. She was the only playwright with whom he forged such a close personal—and professional—relationship. The artist William L'Engle, Susan's neighbor, made a pencil drawing of the "Provincetown Theater Group and Friends" in 1920. O'Neill is in the center, with "Lord Christ O'Neill" emblazoned on it. Susan is situated just below Terry Carlin, with Agnes small and to the side, a halo encircling her head. Jig does not appear. The drawing indicates how others in the group at the time saw the relationship between the two writers. Susan, ever sensitive to the nuances of personality within the Players, seemed to understand the reticent O'Neill, and the affection and respect were returned. In notes for a talk she gave on his work some years later, she characterizes him in her usual succinct style: "Hands himself everything—sea—fate—God—murder—suicide—incest—insanity. Always the search for new forms. Because necessary to what he would express."[10] She also has a brief note, penciled into a notebook, under the heading

"Misfits": "Terry's philosophy on Gene 'Every souls is alone. No one in the world understands my slightest impulse.' Then you don't understand the slightest impulse of anyone else."[11]

Agnes and Susan eventually became close friends. During the summer of 1918, the couples spent most evenings together. It was to Susan and Jig's the O'Neills hurried so that Gene could read to them *The Dreamy Kid* as soon as he finished it; and they were the first readers of his *Where the Cross is Made*, since their function on the executive committee of the Players required that they read new plays before they were accepted. Gene was thus a first reader of Susan's works as well.[12] At a crucial time in their careers, when both playwrights were about to move to full-length plays, the special professional and personal relationship they enjoyed and their familiarity with each other's work was significant.

Although the war in Europe had been going on for four years, it only directly invaded Provincetown in the summer of 1918, when a German submarine U-156 shelled a passing tugboat and barges. Mary Vorse, who details the event in *Time and the Town*, reports that by the end of the war ninety-one ships had been sunk by the eight U-boats that operated along the East Coast, killing 435. For his part, during the summer Jig was less concerned with U-boats than with planning for his dream theatre. Most of his time was spent in sketching seating arrangements and stage configurations, including the dome he hoped to build, the first of its kind in America, which would provide the illusion of infinite space, even on a cramped stage. His other passion during the summer was work on a sundial, the calculations for which teased his mathematical skills. After the difficulties of working with a group, it was a relief for him to concentrate on a project he could do alone. He had tried his hand at sculpting in 1914, using Susan as his model; now he designed a base for his sundial that included four nude women, demarcated "Dawn," "Noon," "Sunset," and "the North Star," about three feet high, in various classic poses, all bearing a striking facial and bodily resemblance to her. They held up the rounded base upon which the sundial was carved. Susan also acted as Jig's assistant on the project, providing plaster and water at the correct temperature, ready to pour when required. "I do not know just what went on in the house of Benvenuto Cellini," she writes in *Road*, "but in our locked house you had the feeling death would be done for a slip of the arm." But after all, the work was serious. "And why not? Was not this the work into which the moods of the days had gone? Were not these the figures to support the sundial, and symbols of our relation to truth beyond our world?"[13]

The sundial placed in the garden that summer (and still standing there, without its dial) became the central image in Susan and Jig's one-act play that grew out of the summer experience. *Tickless Time* is a parody about a man who wishes to have "a first-hand relation with truth" not mediated by arbitrary devices such as clocks, which for him symbolize the standardization of modern life.[14] In her enthusiasm to also be in touch with the forces of the spheres, Eloise, his wife, rashly decides to gather up all their timepieces for burial behind the sundial. Almost immediately she regrets her exuberance when she learns that "Sun time" in Provincetown, the setting of the play, is twenty minutes ahead of Eastern Standard Time. She may choose to live "in direct relation to truth," but train schedules, dentist appointments, and visiting friends will be twenty minutes behind her. "But Ian, if the train is wrong we have to be wrong to catch the train," she laments. Besides, as their friends Alice and Eddy remind them, "you'll be awful lonesome sometimes," with all the world wrong—but wrong together. Finally, Eloise admits that sun time is not for her; she needs a tick. "I am afraid of tickless time!"

By carrying Ian's drive for truth to its extreme and situating it in opposition to the daily details of life, Susan and Jig are able to make a hilarious spoof of dreamers and the pitfalls they face. For example, how is Annie the maid going to time her cooking now that her alarm clock has been buried? Throughout the play, she frantically rushes out to the garden, pot in hand, to check the sundial for the recipe she is preparing. As the sun begins to set and she realizes that she is about to be pitched into clockless night, she decides she's had enough and decides to quit. What had begun as a philosophical quest for truth suddenly takes an ominous turn, now that the possibility of cooking one's own meals arises. Pulled between her unmovable husband and her unmovable cook, Eloise wavers, first toward love and absolutes, then toward practicality and the body politic. The clocks are unburied, then buried again; the sundial is accorded a similar fate. Finally, in the midst of all this furious comic activity, a neighbor Mrs. Stubbs comes along, converted to Ian's time scheme, and proclaims simply: "Let them that want sun time have sun time and them that want tick time have tick time," at which cue Annie, once more reunited with her clock, exits from the house and, in a flat voice, announces, "It's dinner time!"

This—the last Glaspell one-act and her last dramatic collaboration with Jig—became another hit, appearing on the second bill of the 1918–19 season, then on the season's special bill in Newark, New Jersey, and finally on Broadway as the opening play for O'Neill's *The Emperor Jones*. Although Susan and Jig got joint credit, hers was the dominant hand in shaping the work. He left Provincetown at the end of August to prepare for the move to the new theatre, writing her on October 24 that he had "announced a comedy by Susan Glaspell in the circular for first bill," but would substitute something else "if that hurries you."[15] Evidently, Susan once again needed more time, since *Tickless Time* did not appear until December 20. Had it been a truly joint venture, she would have probably come up to the city sooner, and he would not have forgotten to credit himself as co-author of the opening play in the new theatre.

During the fall, while working on *Tickless Time*, Susan was kept company by Gene and Agnes, who also did not hurry back to the flurry of activity surrounding the move. In New York, Ida was directing Gene's *Where the Cross is Made*, which was to open the season. The script had called for three "ghosts" to silently appear on stage, invisible to all but the central figure. Most of the Players, particularly Ida, were against the ghosts, assuming the audience would laugh at these very physical apparitions moving across the Provincetown stage in touching distance of the audience. Jig, still faithful to the concept that the playwright had ultimate control, wanted Gene to come and argue the case. He did, the ghosts stayed, and no one on opening night laughed when they appeared, squeaking floor and all.

When O'Neill arrived, he found Jig furiously working on the renovations for the new Playwrights' Theatre and dreaming of his ideal theatre yet to be built. Since every penny raised would mean another padded chair or an additional bit of scenery, Jig decided to forgo an apartment and, instead, had his Charlton Street possessions moved to the theatre, where for the month of September he camped out and contributed the saved rent money to the moving fund. Building was what he loved best, and again he had his chance. At the end of the previous season, just before he had left to join her in Provincetown, he had written Susan about his spells of hating the whole business of the theatre. "Then I start pulling new strings and take hope again."[16] To handle administrative details that he disliked, the Players now had the services of a paid secretary. "She is of much ability but isn't here enough." Jig told Susan. The "she" was Margaret Eleanor Fitzgerald, soon known to everyone as Fitzie and soon to be "around" even more than Jig. A tall, indefatigable woman, with a mane of red hair, she had been a close associate of Emma Goldman, sometimes called "Emma's wife," because of her work on *Mother Earth* and the Antimilitarist League. Fitzie had been with Goldman and Alexander Berkman in 1917, when they had been arrested by U.S. marshals, who suppressed *Mother Earth;* she'd struggled to keep an underground version of the journal going while both served jail terms and had even tried to join them when they were deported to Russia as "undesirables" under the Espionage Act of 1917. By then, Fitzie was such an integral part of the Players that the group would probably have blocked her had she been able to go. She began work for the theatre in the fall of 1918 and never left. She was there in 1922, when the original group disbanded; and she continued to work along with the reconstituted triumvirate who ran the Playwrights' Theatre until it, too, ceased to function in 1929. The acrimony accompanying the shift to the later theatre tended to throw a pall over Fitzie's relationship with Susan. However, until 1922, she was a mainstay and a godsend for Jig. He could now concentrate on productions, while she ran the office, which soon included an assistant, in charge of filling the growing number of critics' requests for free tickets. This policy had finally been approved by the members in the late fall, the final nail in the coffin of amateurism, as Edna Kenton described this capitulation to success.

If Jig was busy with plans, he was happy; and that fall he was so busy that in his letters to Susan he does not even mention Ma-Mie's sudden death at her cabin in Buffalo on October 6, one day before his forty-fifth birthday. The small, birdlike woman, "at war with the practical world," who had made her son feel he was special, and who herself was considered "queer" in staid Davenport had become, in the four years since her husband's death, an important member of the Players, spending their season in New York, overseeing costumes, and taking part in all meetings and discussions. She, thus, was able to witness her son fulfilling his dream: the establishment of a native American theatre, taking Greek theatre for its model. It was she who had told him long ago that he could find "beauty and art everywhere—under your feet and over your head."[17] He had.

The war ended officially on November 11, 1918. Eleven days later, the third season of the Provincetown Players in New York opened in their new theatre. The company finally had room for a basement workshop for scenery and a proper dressing room area (although the stored wine would only be cleared out the next year), a small office on the main floor off the auditorium, and a restaurant occupying the complete upper floor. The stage measured 22' 10"-by-22' deep. It could seat 202 people on numbered, cushioned benches with inclined backs (although a contemporary Federal Theatre Technical Survey of theatres lists only 184 places).[18] The seats were black; the walls, a rich, tawny orange/brown, a color suggested by Ida's leopard-skin coat; the proscenium, a neutral gray. There was now a proper curtain, which opened and closed without struggle and a lighting system that allowed for a variety of effects and was one of the most sophisticated then being used in New York. Inside, on the wall, under an old ring, once used for horses, Donald Corley had written, "Here Pegasus was hitched." The group also had their first official programs, a four-page format. The cover featured a linoleum-cut of the set for Louise Bryant's *The Game*, which had been created by the Zorachs; the inside cover provided the names of Cook, as overall director; the executive committee, including Glaspell, O'Neill, and Kenton; and the expanding staff. They still lacked a professional director and were making do with members of their company. Susan had taken over the direction of *Woman's Honor* when Moise left, and she and Jig were both listed as directors of *Tickless Time*. Ida began to direct more often, in addition to her acting work, whereas Susan gradually withdrew from acting altogether, spending more of her time writing longer plays.

Tickless Time was the first of her plays in which she did not appear; the two main women's parts were taken by the Millay sisters, arrivals the previous season. Norma Millay played Eloise, the wife, and Edna Millay, already fabled as a young poet and romantic beauty, miraculously became Annie, the nondescript, dowdy cook. Both remained active members of the Players for the next several years, Vincent—as Edna was called—acted in five productions and wrote two plays produced there, most notably *Aria da Capo*, one of the most successful works of the theatre company. Norma became the most active woman actor in the group. Beginning as the Silly Woman in *Woman's Honor*, she appeared in nine other plays, until her disappointment about not being selected by Jig to play the role of Madeline in Glaspell's *Inheritors* caused her to leave. "The Provincetown Players never recovered from this rebuff," she claimed in an interview seventy years later.[19] The reviews for the joint Millay performances in *Tickless Time*, directed by Glaspell and Cook, were generally quite good, so were reactions to the play, Broun calling it "easily the best of the three plays in the new bills," which included *The Moon of the Caribees*.[20] Opening a month after the war ended, the play seemed to be pointing to the next problems about to face the American society, mechanization and conformity, a comic rendering of what Fritz Lang would depict in his 1927 expressionistic film *Metropolis* with its giant clocks.

Tickless Time ended its run on December 26; on March 21, 1919, one-week late, the fifth bill presented Glaspell's three-act drama entitled *Bernice*, the only one of her plays written in New York, a place in which she generally found it difficult to write. The composition probably took place between the two dates; however, its genesis may have gone back to her daily talks with O'Neill during the previous summer, while he was struggling with his own first full-length play, *Beyond the Horizon*. After both writers had proven their ability to handle the one-act form, it seemed natural that they should explore the possibilities of longer works. In the case of *Bernice*, the experiment is particularly bold. Whereas O'Neill's play follows closely certain themes used by Neith Boyce in *Winter's Night*, including a conventional love triangle, Glaspell's *Bernice* totally abandons traditional dramatic action, along with the comedic devices that had served her so well in the past. This time she creates a mood piece, very much in the style of Maeterlinck, in which characters explore their own psyches in an attempt to come to terms with a situation they do not fully understand. This unceasing striving to understand, marked by silence not words, is the theme of *Bernice*.

In form the play resembles *Trifles* and *The Outside*, but is structurally more complex, Susan exploring the psychological states of her several characters, each responding to the personality and actions of a woman who does not appear. Susan must have had *The Outside* in mind when she wrote a twenty-one-page draft for a short-story version of *Bernice*, entitled "Faint Trails," which was never published. In the fragment, she describes the setting as Provincetown's outside, "this place of strange forms, brink, verge."[21] In the play, the setting is the living room of Bernice, a well-to-do woman who has died just before the play begins. Those closest to her—her father Mr. Allen, maid Abbie, husband Craig Norris, best friend Margaret Pierce, and sister-in-law Laura Kirby—have gathered for the funeral. What makes the situation even more painful is the suddenness of Bernice's death, after only a two-day illness, and the sense that they never really "knew" the woman they describe as "off by herself."[22] To her father, Bernice was his little girl, whom he loved unqualifiedly but never completely understood. Abbie and Margaret loved this special quality of Bernice that could not be possessed, while Laura, practical and conventional, sees the detachment as a mark of Bernice's failure as a wife to Craig and the implied reason he sought other women. "He is a man. He does want to affect—yes, dominate the woman he loves," she says. What for Margaret is wonderful about Bernice—"a life too full, too rich to be *had*"—is for Craig a sign that he was not really loved, since love for him means total possession.

The play takes a shocking turn when Abbie confides to Craig early in act 1 that Bernice did not die of natural causes but committed suicide. He immediately assumes that his infidelity was the cause. "You think I didn't matter," he shouts triumphantly to Margaret. "But Bernice *killed* herself because she loved me so!" It is now Margaret's turn to recoil. She cannot believe that her friend, who embraced life so deeply, could commit such an act; it makes a mockery of all she thought she knew about Bernice. Act 1 ends with Margaret's disbelief, act 2 with Abbey's forced declaration that what she has told Craig is a lie which Bernice, just before her death, demanded. Now, instead of a betrayal of life, Margaret must come to terms with what seems to be Bernice's act of malice and revenge. In act 3, before the funeral, she attempts to tell Craig the truth, in order to release him from the guilt he must bear, but is checked when she sees the changes in the man. No longer the shallow person whose stunted feelings have made his writing so banal, he has been transformed into a more confident, sensitive soul, measuring his own worth by what he sees as his wife's great sacrifice and validation of her love for him. Margaret finally pierces the truth, as her surname has promised. Bernice in death has given her husband what she knew he needed: a gift of love measured to the stature of the man. The fog, mentioned several times in the play, which had clouded Bernice's motives, suddenly lifts. Margaret "sees," even if she cannot put her discovery into words. "Only—there are things not for words. Feeling—not for words," she says near the end of the play.

Again Glaspell's special subversive style is at work. Taking the all-too familiar scenario of female suicide in the face of spousal betrayal, she upends the familiar tale as she did with the conventional detective story in *Trifles* and male chivalry in *Woman's Honor*, revealing the male need—and desire—for female self-destruction to abet masculine aggrandizement. Her agents in this male unmasking are Margaret and Abbie, sisters of Mrs. Hale and Mrs. Peters in *Trifles*. It is they who realize Bernice's motives and in the process reveal the culprit: not simply Craig, but the societal assumption held by most men, and some women, that complete love can only be predicated on a man's total control of a woman and the complete suppression, unto death, of her will. Craig is happy because he thinks Bernice died for him; and the audience viewing him is made aware that his acceptance of such an act as a sign of love is a critique of its own values, just as a later audience will be made aware that Willy Loman's unquestioning belief in the American dream is a comment on their values as well.

Susan presents other contemporary critiques in the play. Staged only four months after the war ended, the play already depicts certain aspects of life in the postwar era. Bernice's father, for example, has studied Sanskrit during the war, and he defends his choice. "Why not study Sanskrit while such a world is being made over—into another such world." (O'Neill would use this character as a model for Professor Leeds in *Strange Interlude*.) In this newly made world, the free spirit that Bernice represents also seems anachronistic. However, Margaret, who works to release conscientious objectors, makes a stirring appeal for the importance of Bernice's life-affirming spirit, needed now more than ever. "Oh Laura, we die so soon! We live so in the dark. We never become what we might be. I should think we could help each other more," she says, giving voice to a recurring Glaspell theme. Susan also focuses her ire on those writers like Craig who sidestep the issues of the day, in favor of glib stories, which may be popular but do not serve society. Margaret's words to Craig are Susan's to such contemporary postwar writers: "What is it is the matter with you—with all you American writers—'most all of you. A well-put-up-light—but it doesn't penetrate anything. It never makes the fog part." Such speeches become more frequent in Susan's works over the next few years and make clear her strong political bent and her ability to embed social criticism, even in a play as poetic as *Bernice*. It is interesting to note that, again, none of the critics reviewing the play caught her political message, nor do most contemporary critics. Also none but John Corbin discussed the ironic portrayal of the husband and the attack on his profession.[23]

The sixth bill, featuring *Bernice*, had purposely been postponed a week in order that the Players could adequately rehearse Susan's first full-length play, since they anticipated that the event would draw many people. They were right; on opening night, the theatre was packed. Kenton describes the scene: "Old subscribers, even after having called up for guest tickets and after having been told there were none, brought guests down anyway. 'We'll try to make the bench space for two do for three,' they would say. When the benches were packed, they still came in, the people willing to stand, and when these slipped along the aisle and sat down in it, others behind them crowded in to stand."[24] Critics shared in the excitement. The *New York Times* reviewer found the play "quite beautifully simple and deft, perfect in each of its several characters as in the great central person of Bernice. It is a play after Maeterlinck's own heart, and (although it bears no trace of its author's abundant humor) it is tender and heart-wise as Barrie at his best."[25] *Bernice* would become one of the most praised of Glaspell's works, Ludwig Lewisohn, in several of his book-length studies of American drama calling it not only her masterpiece "but one of the indisputably important dramas of the modern English or American theater."[26]

It is tempting to see *Bernice* in part as Susan's response to Jig's affair with Ida and as a general comment on the tendency of the men in her immediate group who sought liaisons with women as a way of proving themselves. While she is certainly not equating the banal Craig with Jig, whose idealism she shared and whose talents she respected, she does seem to be making a public statement about the fact that for "women of feeling" there might be "those things in her—even greater than loving. Those things in her even loving never—caught." Just as Bernice knew of Craig's affairs and was not touched by them, Susan may well be indicating that for her such affairs did not threaten the inviolate place that connected her to the fullness of life, which was undiminished by Jig's passing flirtations. From the beginning, when Susan and Jig's circle were still putting on plays just to amuse themselves during the summer, the subject matter fixed on current sexual adventures or misadventures of the group. Neith wrote about Mabel and Jack, Jack about Louise and Gene, Neith and Hutch about themselves. In *Bernice,* life and art also intermingled, at least in the casting. In the production, a white-wigged Susan playing Abbie towers over a small, dark-haired Ida as Margaret, thus visually presenting a female unity inherent in the script, between these two Heterodoxy women, who may have loved the same man, but who, like Bernice, did not choose to define themselves as rivals or as victims.

Whatever Ida's feelings for Jig were, one thing she shared with him, and with Susan, was a wholehearted acceptance of the group philosophy. At just the time when members of the Players were beginning to chafe at their amateur status and suggest the possibility of salary, Ida still argued in interviews that it was possible to "go uptown," gain fame, and still function as a beloved community of amateurs for whom work was play. However, by the end of the 1918–19 season, it became increasingly clear that the new members of the group no longer shared this vision. Many approached their work as a stepping-stone to Broadway. They wanted to support themselves from their work; but, as Jig realized, experimentation would be limited if the goal was only financial success. Eventually, he gave in to the pressure: runs were extended to two weeks to gain more revenue. Yet, he still tried to keep a modicum of the old language in the circular he sent out in the spring of 1919, reminding the subscribers, and perhaps the Players themselves, that "Taking chances is the best thing we do." However, since success and chances were not usually compatible, something had to give. Susan's advice was, as usual, direct and simple: "Why not let the younger members have the theatre for the year and see what they could do with it?"[27] Her words seem bland, but the constant meetings and battles had taken their toll on her, as she describes in a notebook, under the heading "the Provincetown Players": "Expressing beauty and becoming so nerve fagged in doing it as to . . ."[28] The sentence, like the experiment, hung in abeyance. Giving in to the building pressures, Jig decided to take what he called "a sabbatical" and turned the directorship over to Ida, who would, for the most part, represent the older spirit, and to Jimmy Light, a relative newcomer, who favored the younger contingent. Susan and he would take a leave and spend the year writing. For her, the break was a godsend. After three years of constant pressure to "write another play," she had the freedom and time to work out her ideas, and she and Jig would actually get to spend time together in Provincetown. After all, as she saw it, "We never meant to do it forever. . . . Now that we had shown our idea, set a number of things in motion, would we not rather return to our work as individuals? The theatre left small chance for Jig's writing, and took a great deal from mine."[29]

Although the leave was prompted by internal events, the pressures were symptomatic of the changes in the Village and in the country. The radicalism that had initially fostered the Players and had shaped the institutions of bohemia in 1913 had altered during the war years. Now a new generation was pouring into the Village. This "League of Youth," as Malcolm Cowley called them, "had lost our ideals at a very early age, and painlessly. . . . We were content to build our modest happiness in the wreck of 'their' lost illusions, a cottage in the ruins of a palace."[30] He describes the old guard who still remained as cynical, their illusions destroyed. It was true that several of Susan's friends, while not cynics, no longer embraced the radicalism, which had motivated them earlier. Floyd Dell, whose romances were so public and frequent that they could have occurred, his friend Dorothy Day noted, "on the stage of the Hippodrome before a packed house,"[31] finally found a soul mate in B. Marie Gage, married her in February 1919, and moved permanently to Croton-on-Hudson and suburban family life. Max Eastman, a co-conspirator with Dell in the famous *Masses* trials, also began his gradual shift from radical to liberal and, eventually, to the reactionary politics that marked his later years. For Neith and Hutch the death of their son in the 1917 influenza epidemic shaped their retreats from earlier social causes into forms of religious mysticism in her case and writers' block in his. Mabel Dodge, always a mystic of sorts, looking for what Hutch had labeled her "It" finally seemed to find it in Taos, New Mexico, with the aid of her final husband Antonio Luhan. Others remained part of the radical community, though not necessarily based in the Village, and were still committed to those dreams and beliefs that had originally drawn them to rebel. Louise and Jack had gone to Russia to document the events of the revolution and would later returned to promulgate it at home. Mary Vorse was more than ever committed to labor and social justice and would work towards those ends till her death in 1966. And theatre people such as Phillip Moeller and Lawrence Langner were simply retrenching before launching the Theatre Guild, another avatar of the Washington Square Players. What Cowley describes as the schism between generations was similar to what Susan, in all her writing, saw as the inevitable loss of pioneer values in subsequent generations. This theme of lost values in the new generation would become the subject she would explore during her sabbatical year.

Plate 1 [*top*]. Blackhawk Monument, Spencer Square, Rock Island, Illinois. Courtesy of the Putnam Museum, Davenport, Iowa.

Plate 2 [*bottom*]. Susan Glaspell, circa 1883. Courtesy of Marcia Noe.

Plate 3 [*facing page*]. Susan Glaspell, circa 1894. Courtesy of Marcia Noe.

Plate 4 [*this page, top*]. Susan Glaspell's family home, 317 East 12th Street, Davenport, circa 1986. Photograph by Linda Ben-Zvi.

Plate 5 [*this page, bottom*]. Alice French's family home, 217 East 11th Street, Davenport, circa 1986. Photograph by Linda Ben-Zvi.

Plate 6 [*right*]. A sketch from life of Mrs. Hossack at her preliminary trial. Drawing by G. A. Proctor.

Plate 7 [*bottom*]. Susan Glaspell, circa 1913, in front of her fireplace. Courtesy of the Henry W. and Albert A. Berg Collection, The New York Public Library, Astor, Lenox, and Tilden Foundations.

Plate 8 [*top left*]. Susan Glaspell, circa 1915. Photograph by Nicholas Muray. Courtesy of the University Libraries, University of Iowa.

Plate 9 [*top right*]. George Cram Cook, circa 1915. Courtesy of the Henry W. and Albert A. Berg Collection, The New York Public Library, Astor, Lenox and Tilden Foundations.

Plate 10 [*bottom*]. The Wharf Theatre, Lewis Wharf, Provincetown. Courtesy of Hazel Hawthorne.

Plate 11. The Provincetown Players' production of *Bound East for Cardiff* at the Playwrights' Theatre, New York, November 1916. Eugene O'Neill is on the ladder (at left); George Cram Cook is holding the pole (at right); and Hippolyte Havel is seated (in the middle). Courtesy of the Museum of the City of New York.

Plate 12 [*right*]. Susan
Glaspell, circa 1916. Courtesy
of the Henry W. and Albert A.
Berg Collection, The New
York Public Library, Astor,
Lenox and Tilden Foundations.

Plate 13 [*bottom left*]. Portrait
of Susan Glaspell, 1920, by
William L'Engle. Courtesy of
the Henry W. and Albert A.
Berg Collection, New York
Public Library, Astor, Lenox
and Tilden Foundations.

Plate 14 [*bottom right*].
Interior, Provincetown
Playhouse, 133 MacDougal
Street. Courtesy of the
Macgowan Papers,
Department of Special
Collections, University
Research Library, University of
California at Los Angeles.

Plate 15 [*left*]. Susan Glaspell, George Cram Cook, and dog Nezer, in front of their Provincetown home, 564 Commercial Street, Provincetown, circa 1918. Courtesy of the Henry W. and Albert A. Berg Collection, The New York Public Library, Astor, Lenox and Tilden Foundations.

Plate 16 [*bottom left*]. The sun dial sculpted by George Cram Cook, in the garden of Glaspell's Provincetown home, shown here in 1989. Photograph by Theresa Doyle.

Plate 17 [*bottom right*]. The Provincetown Players' production of *Bernice*, directed by E. J. Ballantine. Playwrights' Theatre, New York, March 1919. Ida Rauh as Margaret Pierce (at left), and Susan Glaspell as Abbie (at right). Courtesy of the Fales Library, Elmer Holmes Bobst Library, New York University.

Plate 18 [*this page*]. Provincetown Players' production of *The Athenian Women*, directed by Nina Moise. Playwrights' Theatre, New York, March 1918. Ida Rauh as Aspasia and George Cram Cook as Pericles (left corner). Courtesy of the Billy Rose Theatre Collection, The New York Public Library for the Performing Arts, Astor, Lenox and Tilden Foundations.

Plate 19 [*facing page, top*]. Pencil drawing of the Provincetown Theater group and friends by William L'Engle, 1921. The group stands in front of a poster of *Anna Christie*, featuring Pauline Lord. Those identified in the drawing (from top clockwise) are Terry Carlin, Susan Glaspell, Bobby Jones, Bill Zorach, Ida Rauh, Wilbur Daniel Steele, Eugene O'Neill, and Agnes Boulton O'Neill. Courtesy of Madie L'Engle.

Plate 20 [*facing page, bottom*]. The Provincetown Players' production of *The Verge*, act 2, directed by George Cram Cook. Playwrights' Theatre, New York, November 1921. Courtesy of the Billy Rose Theatre Collection, New York Public Library for the Performing Arts, Astor, Lenox and Tilden Foundations.

Plate 21 [*this page, top*]. Susan Glaspell and George Cram Cook, visiting neighbors' new-born goats at Delphi, with Tópuppy, fall 1923. Courtesy of the Cook estate.

Plate 22 [*this page, bottom*]. Nilla Cook, Susan Glaspell, and Jig Cook in Kalania, Greece, summer 1923. Courtesy of the Beinecke Rare Book and Manuscript Library, Yale University.

Plate 23 [*facing page, top left*]. George Cram Cook in the ancient theatre of Delphi, 1923. Courtesy of the Cook estate.

Plate 24 [*facing page, top right*]. Norman Matson and Susan Glaspell. Courtesy of Anna Matson Hamburger.

Plate 25 [*facing page, bottom left*]. Susan Glaspell. Photograph by Bachrach. Courtesy of the Henry W. and Albert A. Berg Collection, The New York Public Library, Astor, Lenox and Tilden Foundations.

Plate 26 [*facing page, bottom right*]. Susan Glaspell and Eva LeGallienne, publicity photograph for *Alison's House*, New York, December 1930. Courtesy of the Theatre Collection, the Museum of the City of New York.

Plate 27 [*top*]. Susan Glaspell with terriers Samuel Butler (on her lap) and Tucker, Truro, 1929. Courtesy of the Henry W. and Albert A. Berg Collection, The New York Public Library, Astor, Lenox and Tilden Foundations.

Plate 28 [*bottom*]. Susan Glaspell in her living room in Provincetown, 1940. *Life Magazine* (July 15, 1940).

Plate 29 [*top*]. Memorial stone for Susan Glaspell and Harl Cook, Snow Cemetery, Truro. Photograph by Linda Ben-Zvi.

Plate 30 [*bottom*]. Plaque above grave of George Cram Cook, in the old cemetery of Delphi. Photograph by Linda Ben-Zvi.

Inheritors

20

Fejevary: We've just fought a great war for democracy.
Madeline: Well, is that any reason for not having it?
                                    —Susan Glaspell, *Inheritors*

Now that she was on "sabbatical," Susan had the luxury of stepping back from the daily demands of the Players to think about new directions. "The Nervous Pig," one of the two stories she wrote during the summer of 1919, explores this question of "busyness" and what happens to a person when "the mechanics of living ate life up." The protagonist is a scholar who nervously burrows in details "in order to deepen his knowledge of life,"[1] only to find he has somehow forgotten to live. He is like the pig of the title, who, nervous over motherhood, has eaten one of her young. For Susan, too, during the past few years, the mechanics of establishing and running the theatre had made it impossible for her to do much else. She and Jig were now free to break this pattern. One thing they did was to buy a Model Ford to start enjoying the surrounding areas on the Cape. Susan approached the car with much trepidation as she did all mechanical things that required that she do something with them.

In July they made the short trip to Truro to see Louise Bryant and Jack Reed, who were vacationing there before Jack headed for Chicago and the national convention of the Socialist Party. The previous January, holed up on the second floor of Polly's Greenwich Village Inn, he had written *Ten Days That Shook the World*, his monumental story of the Russian Revolution, and in March his one-act *The Peace that Passeth Understanding*, a parody of the machinations at the Versailles negotiations, had been staged as the opening bill for *Bernice*. Although he was still showing the signs of his Russian ordeal and his hostile reception at home—called by many the most dangerous man in America—Jack still retained the vitality and charm that appealed to those who knew him. Susan felt a great affection for this man/boy, who, in so in many ways, reminded her of Joe O'Brien, another bigger-than-life character, and of Jig. Like them, he generated electricity and completely filled the space he occupied, making life somehow more alive because of his presence. Sitting outside the Truro cottage with his visitors that evening, Jack said, "I wish I could stay here," and confessed, "Maybe it will surprise you but what I really want is to write poetry." Susan was not surprised and asked why he couldn't remain. Reed's troubled answer was that he had "promised too many people." Recalling that evening Susan would write, "So he left the quiet little house in Truro, where he wanted to write poetry, went back to Russia, died there. First Jack and Jig and I sat under that tree; then Jig and I went there. Then one day I went alone, thought of them both—in whom had been so much of adventure, so much of faith."[2] Jack returned to Russia some months after this meeting. Louise followed and was with him when he died of typhus on October 17, 1920, five days before his thirty-third birthday.[3]

A couple Susan and Jig saw almost daily were the O'Neills, who had grown even closer to them since last summer. Agnes and Gene had purchased Peaked Hill Bars, the old lifesaving station Mabel Dodge had lovingly decorated, but they frequently walked into town to meet their friends or invited them to hike over the dunes to spend the evening. Agnes was pregnant, and in order to be near Dr. Daniel Hiebert—Gene's roommate during his Cambridge year and now Provincetown's permanent and only physician—the O'Neills rented a small cottage, Happy Home, directly behind the Glaspell/Cook house on Commercial Street, "so close that I could call to them from the window," Agnes explained.[4] Miscalculating the date of birth, Agnes waited all through September and October; Shane Rudraighe O'Neill finally arrived on the last day of October. Jig wrote to Neith to make the announcement: "Gene O'Neill's new son Shane O'Neill, not unlike other babies, cries. This causes his father to leave the house even in the five-day nor' easter we've been having."[5]

Gene may well have left home and sought out Jig in hopes of finding some alcohol to lull him if not the baby. Although the Volstead Act prohibiting liquor had come into effect in July 1919, Provincetown at first didn't feel it, because it had long been a dry town. However, by the fall, it, too, "had gone Sahara," as Harry Kemp described the situation. So had New York. At the end of November, Jig and Gene traveled there on the Fall River ferry, leaving Susan and Agnes in Provincetown. "There's nothing for me here now that Prohibition is in force," O'Neill wrote back. Things had gotten so bad that even in the Hell Hole, his favorite bar, "all the lads were drinking sherry. Even that 'ladies' booze is not to be sneezed at in the New York of today. Believe me, Prohibition is very much of a fact."[6] O'Neill had gone to New York to see his ailing father and to check on the status of two plays *Beyond the Horizon* and *Chris Christopherson*, the first version of his later *Anna Christie*, which he had optioned to Broadway producers. What Jig was doing in the city was less clear, but it involved Ida, who was still attempting to lure him from Susan by aiming her attack at his most vulnerable point: creature comfort. Jig had an intense dislike for the necessary labor of keeping stoves lit during the long, cold Provincetown winters. Ida had a heated apartment in New York. At least this was the excuse both Jig and Susan fixed on for his prolonged stays there. Agnes, writing to Gene, reported on Susan's reactions to the situation: "She was trying so hard to pretend *not* to mind.—But she looked *sick*—She said, 'Agnes, you know I think Ida's awfully selfish . . . without meaning to be so (kind Susan) but she's so fond of Jig in a friendly way . . . and now she wants him to stay down in New York and live in her apartment and *write*.' And then she said, 'She doesn't seem to consider how I feel about it at all.' Susan tried to keep it all, of course, on a very *friendly* basis." To Agnes, the situation was far clearer than Susan would admit. "Ida is a b—ch in my opinion. She's just made up her mind to keep him down there—somehow."[7]

From the beginning of their marriage, if Susan were angry at Jig she would not directly confront him; that was not her style. She would never have penned, as Agnes now did to the absent Gene, "When you don't write I feel sick like my backbone had been removed."[8] Instead, she usually chose withdrawal. She now mulled over plans to join the Steeles in Bermuda, while she continued to rationalize the ongoing relationship between her husband and Ida, being played out so openly at the Provincetown Players. A glimpse into her feelings is provided in a short story Susan wrote in 1918, entitled "The Busy Duck." The central figure is Mora Arthur, who bears Ida's salient physical traits: extreme intensity, flashing eyes, grieving mouth, and a vibrant, colorful voice. She comes from a rich, bourgeois family, like Ida's, and joins a group of radicals, similar to the Provincetown Players. In order to fulfill her unceasing quest to "[make] up for some fraction of her wasted years," she fixes her sights on John Hastings, the leader of the group.[9] He is Glaspell's most revealing and critical portrait of her husband, a man who "sees things in new combinations which startle you out of old ones" and who would be "an important writer if only he would write. But he'd rather entertain himself thinking new things than bother himself writing down the ones already thought." Although she describes this tendency as a sign of his total commitment to the thought and not to what he can receive by selling it, she wryly observes, "Laziness probably has something to do with it—impure souls really have to work" Yet, as her narrator, a man who admires him, observes: "Those of us who know him get a lot from him—busily lapping. . . . He's splendidly prodigal, not having the slightest instinct for keeping ideas to himself in order to do something with them." There are few instances in her writing in which Susan alludes so clearly to Jig's weakness and his greatness—as she perceives both.

Hastings is Mora's dream man, someone who can feed her voracious need for "lapping," and she set out to snare him, not because she loves him but because she must possess for herself the ideas he so freely dispenses. The narrator, who is in love with Mora himself, observes that in this single-minded quest, "She struck me then as the most cold-blooded creature I had ever known." Eventually Mora succeeds in marrying Hastings and cares for him when he becomes ill, by taking him to New Mexico (a place Ida often visited, staying with Mabel Dodge in Taos). Susan, ever kind and sensitive to people's strengths as well as their weaknesses, concludes her story by describing Mora's metamorphosis; through ministering to Hastings she becomes a person no longer self-absorbed. Thus Susan dismisses Ida's attachment to Jig as desire for the man's mind not the man, a tribute to the qualities she also prized, equating her rival to the busy Duck of the title, who frantically moves between sea and its own dish, attempting to carry beakfuls of water, in order to possess all that expanse. Ida, half-Nietzschean, half-Marxian—as Max Eastman described his ex-wife and as Jig described himself in *The Chasm*—remained Jig's soul mate and, perhaps, occasional lover. When Jig died, Susan made a point of requesting that word be sent to his friends then living in Taos, "particularly Ida, whom Jig knew so well."[10] For her part, Susan continued to stay friendly with Ida and married to Jig, and all three continued to work closely together. In the skirmish over stoves in the winter of 1920, Ida and her warm apartment lost. Susan cancelled plans for Bermuda; and by the middle of January, Agnes could report to Gene, once more in New York, that Jig had been "up all night with fires and longing desperately for a drink."[11] His desire was rewarded; forty cases of alcohol washed up on Provincetown beach.

O'Neill's letters to Agnes and Jig's to Susan during December and January recount other battles concerning Ida that were being waged at the Players. Originally the sabbatical-year plan had been for Jimmy Light, who had joined the group in 1917, to serve as codirector with Ida for the year. However, by the second bill, she had left in anger, and Jimmy and his wife (also named Susan) took charge for the remainder of the season—but with Ida in the wings, planning that control would return to her, Jig, Susan, and Gene the next season. Part of the problem, in Jig's opinion, was "'too much Millay' in the acting part of the players." Almost daily, Susan and Agnes in Provincetown met for coffee and avidly discussed the bits of theatre gossip each received from her husband. Much of the news concerned another newcomer that season, Djuna Barnes, who was reported to also be stirring up trouble. "What on earth has the fair but malicious Djuna has been up to," Agnes asked Gene in one of her letters. "Are Ida and Jimmy rivals? (Of course, Susan is no party to that evil thought.)"[12] Barnes, one of the most talented, enigmatic, and striking figures associated with the Players, had probably come to the theatre at the suggestion of Light, who sublet rooms to her in the building at 86 Greenwich Avenue, which he rented out to Village writers, many of whom associated with the Players.

During the 1919–20 season, the theatre presented three Barnes one-acts, *Three from the Earth*, *An Irish Triangle*, and *Kurzy of the Sea*, all highly experimental, echoing elements from Synge, but bearing Barnes' special sardonic humor.[13] "The greatest indoor sport this week is guessing what it means," the critic Alexander Woollcott wrote about the first,[14] but even he finally agreed with Lawrence Langner's assessment that Barnes's plays had an "incoherence of expression" that made them "both exciting and baffling at the same time."[15] It was unfortunate for the group, although few would have admitted it, that "the difficult Barnes" stayed only one year before moving on to Paris where she turned to fiction. From 1939, when she returned to the Village, until her death in 1982, at the age of 90, only one other new play of hers was produced, the equally incoherent and equally exciting *The Antiphon*, published in 1956 and premiered in Stockholm in 1961, translated by Dag Hammarskjold and Karl Gierow, of the Swedish Academy.

The year that Barnes was part of the Players she was twenty-seven, one of the older of the "new Turks," including the Millay sisters, Jasper Deeter, Lawrence Vail, and the Lights, who were running the theatre in Jig and Susan's absence. Those who observed their stewardship were split concerning the results. Edna Kenton, always Jig's faithful champion, chided them for breaking his two cardinal precepts: (1) not to stage a play first presented in another venue (they presented Harry Chapin's *The Philosopher of Butterbiggens*) and (2) not to stage a non-American play (they produced Arthur Schnitzler's *Last Masks*). The "transgressions" were in response to complaints that the Players were no longer offering the accomplished works of Glaspell and O'Neill but rather odd and incomprehensible plays. Helen Deutsch and Stella Hanau, publicists, who began working for the theatre under the reconstituted regime after 1924 and whose history of the group is marked by hearsay about the Cook years, saw the sabbatical break as the beginning of the subtle move toward more efficient organization and away from one-man rule.

Whatever the complex reasons for the sabbatical and its results, it gave Susan the time she needed to continue her experiments with full-length drama. Although some critics predicted that one-acts would revitalize along with the entire little-theatre movement, now that the war had ended, neither she nor O'Neill were any longer interested in doing them. By the middle of January 1920, Susan had completed a long comedy, and Gene eagerly advised her to get it typed and sent to him in New York, so that he could give it to his producer George Tyler, who had optioned *Chris Christopherson*. "Tell Susan I spoke to Tyler about her play and that he is genuinely eager to have a look at it. He said he had seen three of her plays at different times at the P.P. . . . He said, 'that *girl* has a reach touch of genius'—(He evidently thinks Susan is about as old as Helen Hayes,) and he added with a questioning misgiving: 'If the damned Greenwich Village faddists didn't get her into the radical magazine publications class.' I didn't disillusion him about Susan being 19 and at the mercy of the faddist world—it was too funny—but I did say she was married to a very sensible man."[16] She was then forty-four.

Although busy himself with the opening of *Beyond the Horizon*, and suffering from a serious virus that sapped his energy, O'Neill repeatedly mentions Susan's play in his letters to Agnes, expressing his willingness to read it and prodding Susan to send it to him as quickly as possible. For her part, she was grateful for her friend's assistance, because, as she admitted to Agnes, she wasn't sure where to place it. Since she had withdrawn from the Players for the year, she did not want to send it to them. Besides, she, too, was interested in having her work performed on Broadway. Agnes had quickly read the play and reported to Gene: "It's a corking idea and has all her fine characterization and delightful ironic fun making some delicious comedy."[17] Yet, Agnes felt it needed work and should be considerably cut. After her usual delay in letting go of a play, Susan finally sent the manuscript to O'Neill and two days later he turned it over as promised to Tyler, expressing regret that she had not delivered it sooner, since in the interim Tyler had three new productions. To Agnes he wrote, "I like her play tremendously and think it has fine chances either with Tyler or another producer."[18] At the same time, the newly formed Theatre Guild, a reconstituted version of the earlier Washington Square Players, asked to see it. Susan was skeptical, since they had planned to produce *Bernice* during the previous fall, but changed their mind due to the great success they had with the more accessible play, St. John Ervine's *John Ferguson*. She agreed with O'Neill that "you can't eliminate the weakness of the old Washington Square Players by merely changing the name."[19] The outcome of negotiations with producers was "in the lap of the gods of course," Gene warned;[20] and in this case the gods did not smile. Neither Tyler nor the Theatre Guild took the comedy, and Susan put it away and only reluctantly allowed the Provincetown Players to stage it two years later, under the title *Chains of Dew*, on their last bill of the 1922 season.

In addition to the "cluttered comedy" and an idea for a one-act play about a bedbug (inspired by one Jig had discovered), which got as far as a title, "The Chastening Bug," and a sentence, "But—now there was a bedbug in the ivory tower," jotted down in a notebook,[21] Susan began work on another play in the winter of 1920. On January 14, Agnes reported to Gene that Susan had "an idea for a new long play about which she says she's crazy—a real *American* play (serious)."[22] The date is significant, because it comes only three weeks after the most sweeping raids in a long series of abuses, which came to be known as the "Red Scare." Although the armistice had been declared more than a year earlier, the war at home had, if anything, accelerated.[23] The Espionage Act of 1917, calling for a maximum of twenty years in jail and a fine of $10,000 for anyone interfering with the operations of the military or opposing the draft, and the 1918 Sedition Act, making it a crime to use language that could be construed as being disloyal to the national cause or to that of an allied country, were still in force, except that now they were being used by politicians, business people, and self-appointed watchdog citizen groups to suppress any form of political, social, and cultural dissent. "Illiberalism at home to reinforce the man at the front," Woodrow Wilson had argued[24]; but when the man at the front returned, he was informed that a new enemy had been identified: the "Red." Jack Reed was branded "Red," so was Louise Bryant, who had published *Six Months in Red Russia*, IWW head Big Bill Haywood and Eugene Debs, four-time presidential candidate on the Socialist ticket, convicted under the Espionage Act and sentenced to two ten-year terms running concurrently. In addition to individual harassment and conviction, Socialist Party and IWW offices were firebombed and closed, active members dispersed or arrested.

In March 1919, the front page of the respected *New York Herald*, under the large headline "How is America to Stamp out Bolshevism," featured a cartoon of a three-headed dragon labeled Radical Socialism, IWW, and Bolshevism. All were described as enemies of the people, and threats to Christian America. Equally dangerous and "Red-inspired," the paper suggested, was the growing labor unrest, which marked the end of the war. In February, 60,000 workers in Seattle had staged a four-day general strike; on May 1, there were riots in ten large cities from coast to coast; and in September, 365,000 steel workers started the largest mass strike to date in U.S. history. Mary Vorse wrote to Susan to join her in Pittsburgh for two weeks aiding steel workers. Whether Susan went is uncertain; but she did not need to go to be aware of the plight of workers, the cycle of poverty and hopelessness feeding their actions, and the institutional responses, which, in turn, led to more civil violence and recrimination.

From her early Davenport days, Susan had seen and written about such abuses. She was also aware of the deportation of aliens. Under antiquated legislation and hastily passed laws, government agencies, often employing private detective agencies, began arresting those with foreign names and accents, since they were clearly not "100 percent American," an undefined litmus test that was sweeping the country in its Red panic. It was enough for someone to speak Russian to be targeted. In November 1919 there had been a particularly brutal attack at a New York school run by the Union of Russian Workers, in which people were beaten, arrested, and held for deportation. Across the country, the pattern was repeated over the next several months. In one case, a man in Gary, Indiana, was kept in jail for three months on the charge of possessing material in Russian thought to be a manual for undermining the government. The "offending" book turned out to be *Huckleberry Finn*. Not only Russians but any foreign group was suspect. In Braintree, Massachusetts, when a robbery and murder were committed, although there were no witnesses, police quickly charged two anarchist Italians Nicola Sacco and Bartolomeo Vanzetti with the crime. "The Red raids were a thug phantasmagoria ... made of chicanery, funk, political ambition and venality," Vorse called them.[25]

They reached their crescendo on January 1, 1920, when U.S. attorney general A. Mitchell Palmer, assisted by the head of the newly formed Federal General Intelligence Division, the twenty-four-year-old wunderkind J. Edgar Hoover, swooped down without warrants on seventy-seven cities across America and in two days arrested 8,000 people. Two weeks later, in the wake of these actions, Susan began to write her great American political drama *Inheritors*.

During the previous year, Jig had already expressed to her his uneasiness about the country's drift: "I have a feeling that a new tyranny is being born which will not permit us to live on our terms," he wrote, since "the world cannot subdue Prussianism except by becoming Prussia." Jig's advice was "to say no to it and let it do what it can."[26] Brave words, but not so easy to follow in such a climate. Even Susan and he were not immune from suspicion. After all, they were good friends with the number-one "Red," John Reed, and neighbor of labor activist Vorse, whose new lover Robert Minor, a self-declared communist, had been held in Europe for trial on espionage and was now in the country in hiding. They also worked with Fitzie, who had tried to accompany Emma Goldman and Alexander Berkman when they had been deported to Russia, along with 247 other exiles, the previous December on the old military ship, the Buford, with Hoover there to check that the "Red Ark" set sail. Besides, Susan and Jig themselves had been reported to the Justice Department as being members of a subversive organization. An undercover agent, posing as a Village bohemian, had once plied a susceptible Hippolyte Havel with alcohol, stolen his address book, and turned it over to government authorities, who discovered the name of the Provincetown Players, which they assumed was a "radical group." Although no action was taken, the designation was not far from the mark. They were a radical organization; like *The Masses* and Goldman's *Mother Earth*, they had presented ideas which could hardly have been seen as "100 percent American" by those who defined the label.

By the time *Inheritors* opened, in March 1921, the Espionage and Sedition Acts had just been revoked, but they were still in effect during the year Susan worked on the play, and the ideas she espoused in it could have made her liable for prosecution under their terms. She had been making quick hit-and-run raids against the armies on the right in her earlier plays, but it would have been easy to miss these attacks. Not so this time, since her play confronted head-on three blatant injustices of the time: intimidation of university professors and students; prosecution and deportation of aliens, often without due process; and incarceration and excessive punishment of conscientious objectors, still continuing after the cessation of the war. Each of these abuses, as described in the play, was based on an actual event.

Six years earlier, in his pamphlet *The Third American Sex,* Jig had described systematic attempts to undermine the moral and intellectual power of professors in American universities, a tendency that proliferated dangerously during and after the war. In one celebrated instance in 1917, two respected Columbia University professors, Harold Dana and James Cattel, had been fired for speaking out against the war. Ralph Bourne, one of the most articulate of the young intellectuals fighting such repression, interviewed Dana and asked whether he intended to make a scandal in the wake of his firing. "Certainly not," the distinguished professor replied, "I've given my word as a gentleman." Bourne's response: "That's the trouble. . . . You look upon all this as a gentleman's quarrel. You lack Homeric anger."[27] It was "Homeric anger" that led Jig, ever the Greek, to bemoan the passivity of teachers, whom, he argued, were complicit in the gradual erosion of intellectual pursuits in America. Professor Holden, in *Inheritors*, is Susan's example of the great teacher cowed into submission, and she borrows from Jig's biography certain salient features. Holden has been to Greece, and he dreams of influencing Iowa minds with the beauties of that ancient culture, just as Jig had tried to do in his short tenure at the University of Iowa. To this character, she grafts elements of Dana and others like him, who were being sacrificed by cowardly administrators fearful of criticism. She may also draw from her own memories of embattled professors she had known at Drake and the University of Chicago.

The model for the aliens in the play came from the numerous trials of Hindus widely reported at the time, against which Susan's close friends organized protests. A pamphlet issued in April 1919 by "The Friends of Freedom for India" movingly describes the life term in prison or execution awaiting Hindus who call for freedom against British rule; and it cites recent cases in San Francisco in which Britain spent $2,500,000 to secure the conviction of sixteen Hindu nationals and to revoke the American citizenship of others. Fitzie was on the Friends' committee; the pamphlet also remains among Reed's papers at Harvard, so it probably reached Susan as well. Her choice of Hindus as the alien group in *Inheritors* thus addresses contemporary injustices; it also allows her to draw parallels with native Americans, an earlier group of Indian "Reds," who, as Emma Goldman pointed out, might be next to be deported for not being sufficiently American. Given Susan's pioneer roots, she was particularly sensitive to the injustices done to them and to the debt owed to their leader, the mythic "100 percent American" Blackhawk.

As a model for the conscientious objectors in her play, Susan could use numerous cases that received widespread coverage.[28] In one case nineteen-year old Fred Robinson had been sentenced to twenty-five years in Leavenworth prison for his refusal to serve, a term reduced from the firing squad originally requested by the judge. In her play she uses Fred as the first name of her young objector, borrowing as well the details in another celebrated case involving Philip Grosser, sentenced to thirty-five years in prison, which he served in various facilities including Alcatraz, where he was often chained to his cell door and kept in solitary confinement in the hole for long periods of time. These measures, harsh enough in times of war, continued after the peace, since the United States, unlike its allies, did not pardon objectors. (The last of the 1,900 convicted under the Espionage Act of 1917 and the 500 found guilty under the Selective Service Act of 1917 were only released by the presidential clemency of Franklin Delano Roosevelt in 1933, fifteen years after the war ended.)

In *Inheritors*, the most politically overt and biographical of her plays, Susan weaves these three contemporary themes together against a backdrop of one hundred years of American history, from 1820 to the present, in the lives of two neighboring families: the Mortons, founding pioneers of their Iowa town, and the Fejevarys, Hungarian aristocrats, who brought their European intellectual heritage to their adopted country. Grandmother Morton is patterned on Susan's paternal grandmother and namesake as well as on Jig's mother, whose personality, like Grandma Morton's, was "ill-nourished by the life of that place in those days."[29] Silas, her son, takes his name and occupation from Glaspell's grandfather; and Nicholas Fejevary is closely modeled after one of Davenport's most prominent citizens of the same name, spelled Féjerváry with two *r's*, who left his native Hungary after the failed revolution of 1848 (but did not participate himself, as Glaspell's character did) and moved to a farm adjoining the Glaspells, where he soon prospered. It is the deep friendship between the sensitive farmer and his intellectual émigré neighbor that shapes the action and may reflect to some degree the relationship between the Glaspells and the Féjervárys.

The central theme of *Inheritors* is the loss of pioneering values in the second generation, the spirit for movement and change replaced by acquisition and fixity. "I'm of the second generation, dad, and the second generation has an ideal of its own, and that ideal is Success," says one of the young men in Susan's short story "His America."[30] She had seen the process at work in Davenport, where the second generation got rich and the third richer—and more conservative. Saved from this cycle by her grandfather's losses and her father's further financial decline, Susan came to believe that the price succeeding generations paid for their comfort was nothing less than the denial of their antecedents' dream and positive values. *Inheritors* traces this decline. The play begins appropriately on the Fourth of July, 1879, in the Morton farmhouse, as Grandmother Morton awaits the return of her son and Fejevary from a Civil War Veterans' parade and entertains a young salesman who has come to the Morton farm to convince them to sell land for development. He listens as she regales him with tales of the past—taken directly from Glaspell family legends—but is totally indifferent to her history or that of the community. "More people more homes,"[31] the cry of America in the postwar years, is his mantra, a phrase that must have resonated with the audience. Although the first act of *Inheritors* is set in 1879, Glaspell in these introductory speeches lays down the gauntlet against 1920 postwar jingoism and materialism, but does so while her characters munch on cookies in an old farmstead. Radical ideas are made palatable since they are spoken from a rocking chair not from a soapbox.

Picking up the challenge in acts 2 and 3, set forty years later, Glaspell presents her most appealing protagonist. Against second-generation pragmatists and third-generation Philistines, she might be expected to pick Professor Holden as her protagonist—the radical Grecophile who has supported the rights of student conscientious objectors and aliens. But he proves to lack "Homeric anger" and is finally cowed into silence. Instead, as she has done in her preceding plays and novels, Glaspell introduces a female protagonist, whose anger burns brighter and who withstands those who seek to quench it. Madeline Morton, in many ways, is the apotheosis of Glaspell's young women characters: attractive, lively, hair blond as the cornfields where she was raised. She is a lover of good times and a hater of cant, who would rather play tennis than attend ceremonies, and who resents the process that has turned her grandfather and his dreams into hollow phrases. Instead of pontificating, she acts, almost spontaneously, carrying forward the values of her antecedents, and becoming, Glaspell suggests, a link in a moral evolutionary chain. When she defends the Hindu students against arrest on campus by attacking a policeman with her tennis racket, she becomes an unlikely radical, opening herself to prosecution under the Espionage Act. Unless she recants, she, too, will face a protracted jail term.

In act 3, Glaspell creates one of her most powerful theatrical and political moments. While Madeline waits alone in the old Morton farmhouse, the setting of act 1, struggling to decide between her love of family and love for justice and right, she draws from her pocket a note from Fred Jordan, her fellow student, now in solitary confinement because of his refusal to fight in the war. With chalk, she carefully measures out the space of Fred's cell: two-and-a-half feet on one end, three feet on the other, and six feet high. She then enters the space. By this simple act, Glaspell takes all the lofty discussions about free speech published in 1920 and shows her audience what it actually means to act upon convictions. It is a powerful and convincing moment, the political made personal, a visual image that is moving because of its starkness.

In the same way, the unadorned simplicity of the play reinforces the sense of righteous indignation that is at the center of the work, expressed by Glaspell through Madeline. Others chide the young woman for being uninformed, emotional, romantic, young; yet they are finally rendered silent against her simple logic and language. Why aid aliens, they ask? Because "they're people from the other side of the world who came here believing in us." Why "go against the spirit of this country?" Because "America is a democracy." Why speak out when it can bring severe consequences? Because "Once in a while you have to say what you think—or hate yourself." It doesn't get much simpler and direct than that in theatre. *Inheritors* is not a great play. Far too many of the ideas seem to be spoken by those whose function it is to develop a position rather than to interact in a dramatic fashion. However, even its sometimes-naive form and diagrammatic structure do not destroy the basic power of Susan's historical chronicle of the American dream that could and the way it went off the track.

Susan had used the same theme in relation to the Red Scare the preceding summer, in a parable entitled "Free Laughter," parodying a controversy raging in Provincetown concerning how to celebrate the tricentennial of the Pilgrims' landing. Vying with Plymouth across the bay, the Provincetown city commissioners argued that they should be given equal funding, since it was in their town that landfall had first occurred and where the Mayflower compact had been written, before the boat ever turned to Plymouth and its rock. In a fifteen-page handwritten manuscript, never published or performed, Susan, whose ancestors had been on the Mayflower, ridicules those who seek an appropriation to build a "Wildflower" replica to be used in the celebration, at the very time they ignore the injustices rife in the country. In the play, an all-powerful dictator, named Trend of the Time, doles out money for the celebration but cannot act on the expenditure because he is distracted by laughter, which is growing louder around him. Declaring that only sanctioned laughter will be allowed, he forbids any other kind. "Laughter makes me nervous," he explains to another character, the Patriot; "Laughter is not good for law."[32] The Patriot supports the dictator's actions and is more intent on plans for commemorative, patriotic events than preserving free speech; however, Trend of the Time is challenged by two other characters: Foreign-born and Native-born. The former explains that he came to America precisely because it encouraged free laughter; the latter argues, "A land satisfied with what it has [is] a dying land." In words similar to those Madeline will use, Native-born proclaims, "I have dreamed of a state where all men might become the most those men might be." "He's dangerous," Executioner recognizes, scurrying off to introduce a law silencing and deporting Natives as well. The skit ends with Trend of the Time shaking his fist at the laughter that cannot be stopped, despite the new legislation forbidding it.

While Susan was writing *Inheritors*, Jig was busy working on *The Spring*, a full-length drama also interweaving philosophical idealism, current events, personal biography, and Blackhawk, but in very different ways. Each reflects the character of the writer. Susan's play shows men who build colleges and women who support the disenfranchised, Jig's presents a scientist, patterned after himself, who seeks to inspire others, particularly a young adoring woman, to develop their innate talents. Susan focuses on links with the past and on social and political amelioration of wrongs done, Jig on the mystical acceptance of life and the need to retrace paths into the self. With both absorbed in writing, they needed more quiet than Provincetown could supply, at least in summer. The number of vacationers walking by their house on Commercial Street had grown over the years, as had the general noise level of the town. On one of their car trips to Truro in the summer of 1919, they happened upon a group of abandoned farmhouses, spread out along a small wooded valley called Hingman's Hollow, with the sea over a low ridge. "The peace of God is in this valley," Jig felt.[33] Using some money he had inherited from Ma-Mie and royalties from their one-acts now being performed by small theatre groups around the country, Susan and Jig bought one farmhouse, which became their summer home, and soon purchased another nearby, to be rented or loaned to friends who might wish to join them. The house consisted of a single-story building, more than a hundred years old, and two later additions. It was surrounded by several acres of land, which gave them complete privacy and room to plant trees and a garden. In later years, Susan would seek even more solitude, taking over a tiny shack a few kilometers behind the house, which became her work place, somewhere she could be totally alone. While Susan needed privacy and isolation to do work, Jig, being Jig, immediately started dreaming of organizing a colony in Truro, perhaps even a Truro Players and "never taking it to New York."[34] There already was a nucleus: the Millays rented from them, and Jack Reed's now vacant house was not far away.

Like the house on Commercial Street, this one, too, became a communal decorating project. Jig and Don Corley, an illustrator, covered the dining room with silver paper and created a fresco on the history of theatre and church. The kitchen also bore Jig's decorating and organizational zeal. Each utensil was hung on the white-washed walls, Jig drawing its shape, so it could not be confused or replaced with any other object. As they had done in Provincetown, Jig and Hutch often played chess in the living room, except now the very floor had become an elaborate chessboard, not black and white, but shades of green, blue, pink, and red—"at first somewhat dismaying the little Cape house, but soon the color made itself at home," Susan felt.[35]

It was from their new home that Susan and Jig set out at the beginning of October 1920 to visit the O'Neills and to hear the new play Gene had just completed. In one of the most oft-quoted passages in *The Road to the Temple*, Susan alters the date, describing how they trudged over the dunes from Provincetown in August to the lifesaving station and listened as Gene read to them *The Emperor Jones*. "Then Jig knew he wanted to go back to the theatre," she continues. "He had been wavering." The picture is compelling, another one of Susan's theatrical moments: the couple who had battled a late summer storm the day before in order to get to the outside, now marching back to town resolute, pausing a moment at their favorite spot—the edge of the dunes—while a revitalized Jig indicates his determination to leave for New York immediately. "Here is a challenge! This is what I have been waiting for—a play to call forth the utmost each one can do, and fuse all into unity."[36] However, like O'Neill's discovery and Jig's cry to Susan from the back of a receding train to "write another play," this event is also fictionalized. By the preceding April, long before O'Neill had finished his play, Susan and Jig had already returned to New York to reclaim their leadership of the Players, Edna reports.[37] Agnes, who was visiting New York at the time, while Gene remained in Provincetown, wrote him that she had seen Susan, who had indicated that "the Players had a big new impetus and everybody's . . . quite wildly enthusiastic."[38] Soon after, the Players held their election for the coming year; Jig and Jimmy Light were voted codirectors and the executive committee, which included Susan, was expanded first to seven and later to ten. In the yearly circular that went out to subscribers in the late summer, Jig described the plans for the coming year and called for contributions for his dream theatre, an idea he had not abandoned. He also listed one or possibly two plays by Susan Glaspell as well as one or two new ones by O'Neill, "which will rank with his best."[39]

Therefore, when Susan and Jig heard *The Emperor Jones* for the first time, they already were actively planning the new season, in which they would once more resume their places in the Players. *The Emperor Jones* did not precipitate their return; but Susan does not exaggerate when she describes Jig's enthusiasm for the work and his complete dedication to producing it. *Jones* required a sense of infinite space, impossible to achieve on a stage of approximately twenty-two-feet square, with the first row of patrons only a hand's-breadth away. Traditional painted backdrops would not do, because the low ceiling made it impossible to mask the flies in conventional ways, as a publicity photo of the recently staged *Aria da Capo* reveals.[40] This structural problem was the impetus for Jig's most audacious act: the construction of a fixed plaster cyclorama, or *Kuppelhorizont*, similar to the moveable ones patented by the Italian Mariano Fortuny, around 1901, which had been installed in large public theatres in Europe, such as the Schauspielhaus in Dresden.[41] Modeling his dome after those designed for huge stages twenty times its size, Jig took the entire treasury of the Players, around $535 dollars and, with the assistance of Light, built the first plaster cyclorama in America, placing it on the raised stage of a back parlor on MacDougal Street. Only he could have conceived of such a project and pulled it off. The advanced lighting board also installed was state-of-the-art, allowing the Players to provide effects no other company in America could rival. Thus did *The Emperor Jones* have its space.

When the play opened the first bill of the 1920–21 season, on November 1, directed by Jig, the acclaim was immediate. Reviewers, while mentioning the inordinately long breaks between scenes, all cited the extraordinary silhouettes achieved and the sense of infinite space created. They also commented on the fact that a white company had, for the first time, used a black actor in a leading role. Who chose the great Charles Gilpin for the part of Jones—and later Paul Robeson, who took over the role—is still debated in Provincetown lore. Jasper Deeter, who played Smithers in the production, claimed that it was he who had to convince the company that a black actor, and not Charlie Ellis in blackface, must play the part. Kenton and others give the credit to Jig. What is clear is that three weeks before the play opened, there was still no Emperor and Jig wrote playwright Ridgely Torrance, asking how he could get in touch with an actor named Cooper whom he had seen in one of Torrance's productions. Eventually, Charles Gilpin, who had acted a bit role in a recent Broadway production, was selected, and as Kenton writes, "the rest is history."[42]

By the time the play closed—after an extended, fifty-five day, sold-out run—subscription lists for the Players had risen to 1,500, and Jig's dream theatre seemed at last a reality. Yet, to Kenton, this success was actually "the beginning of the end."[43] Although money was pouring in, it was as quickly flowing out. Salaries were now routinely paid, not much but something; new staff was required to meet the growing demand for tickets by the public and critics; and the Players had succumbed to the temptation they had been founded to reject: they were going to Broadway. The demand to see *Jones* was so great that they decided to allow it to be taken "uptown," which meant that two different companies had to be sustained, in order to continue with the season on MacDougal Street. Once the precedent had been established, "uptown" became the route that successful, and not so successful, Players' productions took.

Susan had no specific involvement in the group effort to produce *Jones*. While Jig spent much of October once more living on the stage of the theatre while he built the dome, she remained in Truro working on *Inheritors*, only coming to the city for the *Jones* opening, when she and Jig took over an apartment at 87 Bedford Street, which would be their Village residence for the year. She needed the time to herself, since the summer had been taken up with Nilla's visit. Whenever the children were with them, Susan had most of the responsibility, because Jig used the summer months to prepare for the next theatre season. It was not a simple matter to entertain Nilla, a lively, headstrong twelve-year-old. "The years in which a tomboy turns female are difficult years for all concerned," Nilla herself admitted many years later.[44] She was able to stir up enough mischief with Miriam Hapgood during this visit that Neith was forced to warn her daughter not to follow Nilla's example.

A different arrival was a copy of the recently released edition of Susan's plays published by Small, Maynard and Company, which contained all the performed one-acts plus *Bernice*. Now anyone with a creative bent as far removed from New York as Gopher Prairie could say, like Erick Valborg in Sinclair Lewis's 1920 novel *Main Street*, "I'd like to stage 'Suppressed Desires,' by Cook and Miss Glaspell."[45] Jig must be credited with understanding the importance of publishing plays, a practice that was not widely done at the time. After Frank Shay stopped publishing individual plays, it was Jig who sought contracts with Henry Holt and then with Dutton for a collection of representative Provincetown Players' plays, arguing the importance of letting the American public know of the great revolution in theatre. Finally, in 1921, Stewart and Kidd Company put out *The Provincetown Plays*, edited by Cook and Shay, with a foreword by Hapgood. Included among the ten selections were *Suppressed Desires*, *Bound East for Cardiff*, and *Aria da Capo*. Millay, appreciating the importance of the publication of her play, could write to a friend at the time predicting, "there is scarcely a little theatre or literary club in the country, so far as I can see, that isn't going to produce it or give a reading to it."[46] The same was true for *Suppressed Desires*. Royalties from it provided a steady income for Susan and Jig, bringing in forty dollars a week in the six weeks after it appeared in print. It would remain one of Glaspell's most lucrative plays.

By the end of November, Susan and Jig had changed positions; he retreated for two weeks to Truro where he worked nonstop on the final draft of *The Spring*, just before it was to go into rehearsals, and she went to their New York apartment to begin work on the second draft of *Inheritors*. "A big job—for there's so much to do. I hope I'll be better satisfied with it at the end of the second writing than I am at the end of the first," she wrote to Agnes, who was with Gene in Provincetown.[47] Much of Susan's time was taken up with the battles raging at the theatre. Around Thanksgiving she toyed with the idea of making a quick return to Truro, prodded on by Ida, to whom she'd said in jest that maybe they should surprise Jig with a turkey. She decided against it; there was still too much work to do on her play, and too many Players' troubles to mediate. The move uptown with *Jones* had, as Kenton predicted, splintered the group between those who wanted to continue pursuing their experiments on MacDougal Street and the majority who sought Broadway, professional standards, and sufficient pay. They were now running two venues and were, thus, understaffed, Jig needing to bring in new actors to play the many parts in *The Spring*, which he codirected with Jasper Deeter. Deeter would later claim that the play was unactable and was saved only by his skillful direction. No matter whose hand finally shaped it, the critical responses were surprisingly positive, given the esoteric subject matter and painfully awkward writing. Perhaps the theme of a Svengali male and passive woman appealed to critics. William Archer called it "a work of arresting theme and highly imaginative workmanship, despite its indifferent acting," and Kenneth Macgowan proclaimed it "a remarkable and arresting drama," illustrating that the Provincetown Players, after years of struggle, were with this work, and *Jones*, "almost upon their goal: certainly they seem at this moment the most creative single force in the American theater."[48] O'Neill, after reading the reviews, wrote an enthusiastic, congratulatory letter to Jig: "There has been nothing I have hoped for more . . . than that you, who have labored so long and unselfishly for the work of others, should enter into your own kingdom." He concludes his note with, "Now it only remains for Susan's play to finish us up in a blaze of glory. Which it will, depend upon my newly-proved gift of prophecy."[49]

Although *Inheritors* was scheduled to open on March 21, 1921, Deeter, who was directing it, had still not cast Madeline three weeks before opening night. Susan was particularly intent on finding someone who was young, spirited, and could convey a sense of midwestern pioneering stock and yellow, sun-drenched cornfields, not easy requirements to fill on MacDougal Street. Then one day, when time was running out, a young woman, bored with her job in an insurance company and wanting a little extra income, stopped by the theatre and asked to audition for a part. Deeter thought she might work for one of the "giggling girls"[50]—but when Susan saw her "swirl of pale gold hair," she asked her to read the lead, and after listening to the untrained, but impassioned delivery, she knew she had found her Madeline. Ann Harding's role in *Inheritors* was the first in a long, distinguished career on the stage and in films.[51]

Critics praised the acting of Harding and Cook, who played Silas, although one writer spent his entire review describing the appalling makeup that made it impossible for him to concentrate on the play. "A child with a box of paints could make something far more closely resembling a human face." This same reviewer was angered by Glaspell's defense of conscientious objectors, who are "being deprived of copies of the *New Republic*" he cynically suggested. "It's a bit late for the subject, but time means nothing down near Washington Arch, nor to the Provincetown Players. The play began at 8:35 and ended at 1 sharp."[52] Several reviewers, such as Alexander Woollcott, willing to accept Susan's position and acknowledging its "contribution to the literature of radicalism," still found the play too much a polemic for her ideas, "painfully dull, pulseless and desultory."[53] This is a position Kenneth Macgowan surprisingly shared, comparing it unfavorably to *The Spring*, a work far more didactic and devoid of action.[54] A much more sympathetic review came from Ludwig Lewisohn, himself a target of the Red Scare as a college professor at Ohio State. "If the history of literature, dramatic or non-dramatic teaches us anything," he wrote in his review in the *Nation* and later expanded in his book *Drama and the Stage*, "it is that Broadway and its reviewers will some day be judged by their attitude to this work."[55] Floyd Dell agreed. He believed that the justification for the entire Provincetown experiment rested on two plays: *Aria da Capo* and *Inheritors*. For him, *Inheritors* was "a high moment in American drama."[56] Even those who carped about its polemical nature admitted that *Inheritors* broke new, uncharted ground, since it claimed as its subject nothing less than the history of the country and its direction in the future. Underlying the various comments was the sense that Glaspell had introduced a new historical drama form, never seen before in America.

Inheritors proved to be a popular success with audiences, running an additional week at the Provincetown, then following *Jones* and O'Neill's *Diff'rent* uptown for a run at the Princess Theatre and returning to MacDougal Street, along with *The Spring*, in a special summer season that Deeter organized. Deeter would stay faithful to *Inheritors*, which he believed to be one of the most important political plays ever written in the country. As he explained to Susan: "Your vision taught me how to look; your insight taught me how to perceive; your words enable me to speak and your play gave me a life to live."[57] In his repertory company, the Hedgerow Theatre, in Moylan, Pennsylvania, which Deeter began in 1923 as an offshoot of the original Provincetown Players, he presented *Inheritors* on Memorial Day and the Fourth of July, every year from 1923 to 1954, except during the Second World War, when Glaspell denied him permission, explaining that some might confuse her antiwar sentiments concerning the First World War with her feelings about the present war.

The Verge and Beyond

21

Our minds go into grammatical grooves, and think in grooves worn by the ways of words.
—Susan Glaspell, *The Road to the Temple* Notebook

This should have been a happy period for the Provincetown Players. *The Emperor Jones* had put them on the map, brought in new members, and swelled the treasury to over $30,000 from the long uptown run and national tour. Critics who had previously looked askance at the little theatre in the Village were now clamoring for free press passes. Yet problems plagued the group. In response to the criticism that theirs was the work of amateurs—a mark of praise in its early days—they spent more on production values. A $1,500 set for Evelyn Scott's play *Love* did nothing to camouflage poor acting and weak direction. New personal jealousies also surfaced. Those performing uptown received salaries commensurate with Broadway standards; those who remained on MacDougal Street nursed the bruised egos that came with small paychecks. The Players' stage had been a laboratory for playwrights to use for their experiments; it was now a place to launch vehicles heading north beyond Fourteenth Street. Symptomatic was the warfare that broke out in May over who would be going to London when *Jones* made its debut there in the fall and who would play in *Suppressed Desires*, scheduled to open the bill. Susan was ill over the fighting and took to her bed, disgusted by the pettiness that seemed to have intensified along with the glory the company had garnered over the past year. In-the-trenches battles for a cause never frightened her, as her act of writing *Inheritors* during the height of the Red Scare illustrates, but this battling reflected how far short the group was from fulfilling the goal Jig set for them. Instead of a "beloved community of life givers," they were at each other's throats.

Jig shuttled between New York and the Cape during the spring and early summer of 1921, quelling the disputes; and from August on, he stayed in the city to prepare for the upcoming season and to oversee the production of *The Spring*, scheduled to begin a run of evening performances at the Princess Theatre on September 21. When he left Truro, he carried with him the proxy votes of "his camp," the newly constituted executive committee for the 1921–22 season—Susan, Ida, Edna, and Gene—giving him the power to stop any insurrection from the "Light brigade," who had threatened to curtail the *Jones* tour. It turned out that the war was already won: Jimmy Light had taken an unannounced, extended trip to Europe; Charles Ellis had become a full-time member of the Theatre Guild; and Jasper Deeter was on the road with the *Jones* company, leaving Jig in full control of the season. The London tour was finally cancelled not because of disagreements among the Players but because of the reported illness of Charles Gilpin, who by this time had been playing the part for almost a year in New York and on tour and had begun to succumb to the constant pressure. The press notice Fitzie prepared indicated that he would go to London next year and, after *Jones*, would play Othello opposite Mrs. Patrick Campbell. This never happened. By the time O'Neill's play was first staged in London in 1924, the original Players had disbanded, and Gilpin was on the tragic slide that would lead to his premature death from alcohol at the age of thirty-eight, one of the greatest actors the country had produced unable to find another starring role for a black man in white America. The part he created was filled by another great, but very different talent, the legendary Paul Robeson, who would play Othello in London, not opposite Campbell but Peggy Ashcroft.

Freed from what he called the "load of inert human dead wood" of the previous year, Jig began planning for the upcoming season, sending Susan notes about possible apartments they could occupy, one requiring a two-year lease. About the theatre, too, he was filled with hopes for the future. "There is a fairly clean slate for a new group. If we pick it well some clean work can be done."[1] At the same time, he continued to plan for his Dome Theatre, working on drawings and details for the repertory system he hoped to install there, which would allow the company to produce new works, while running earlier plays of distinction. Fitzie and he placed notices and short articles in newspapers in order to spur interest and financial support. To Agnes, Jig confidently explained that, if this theatre materialized, all Gene's new plays could be staged there, since he'd have no incentive to go uptown. However, as the season approached, Jig found little support for the project, and he put it aside once more, as he busied himself casting for *The Spring*. "I think Gene sees by this time that the uptown con game is no good," he had written to Agnes,[2] but this did not stop him from wanting to take his own play to Broadway, based on the surprisingly good reviews it had received. Although he discouraged the Players from putting any of their own money into a venture that might not return their investment, he and Harry Weinberger—a supporter of the arts and a lawyer for a number of radical movements and groups, including the Players—each invested $1,000 in the production, Jig's contribution most likely coming from his inheritance from Ma-Mie's estate.

Kenton, in her history of the Players, indicates that the uptown production of *The Spring* was a debacle, four tickets sold on the third and final day of the run.[3] This information, repeated by most subsequent critics,[4] is incorrect. While certainly not a success, the play did continue for at least a two-week run of twenty-four performances, and it did attract some attention. In a letter to Susan on October 6, Jig reports that the first week's take was $500, and the second's had jumped to $1,500, a steady growth, but far less than the $2,400 needed to keep the play running. He writes these figures in a side margin, as if an afterthought to a letter filled with plans for the coming Provincetown season. He displays none of the bitterness or regret about *The Spring*'s run—which Kenton implies, and critics of the theatre have assumed, is a central reason for his departure for Greece five months later.

Susan came down from Truro for the opening of *The Spring* but stayed only a few days before returning to complete *The Verge*, the play she had been working on during the summer—intermittently, for this had been a summer of interruptions. During May, in addition to dealing with the Players' disputes over the London tour, she had been asked by Agnes to spend two weeks at Peaked Hill Bars helping Mrs. Clark, the family nanny, take care of Shane, while the O'Neills were in New York. Then in June Harl had arrived. Jig was so occupied by the *Jones* tour that he had little time for his son; and once he left for New York at the end of August, the full responsibility for the boy's care and entertainment fell on Susan. She planned an eleventh birthday party for him, selected the gift his father had no time to purchase, and took Harl to Boston in September to catch the train back to his boarding school in Florida. "Do all the thinking you can for me about it," Jig wrote her from New York, "because I'll get caught here with no time to think."[5]

This injunction was a familiar one. From the inception of the Players, she had done most of the practical thinking for the group: reading manuscripts with Edna, when nobody else had time; taking care of details, before the advent of Fitzie; providing reasoned responses to problems, when there didn't seem to be any; and, most importantly, keeping Jig focused, when flights of fancy or alcohol threatened to veer him off course. If there were bouts of antagonism over the role she played, she left few indications, and none of those reporting on her character or the events of the period record any signs. In *The Verge*, however, she allows herself to display the frustration she must have felt at having to minister to Jig and the theatre, putting both before her own creative and personal needs and her fiction, which she continued to see as her main form of expression. In addition, while writing the play, she was occupied with caring for Harl. Susan had always been adversely affected by obligations that drew her attention away from work, and she would not brook any interruptions—even from her husband—when she was in the actual act of writing. Francelina Sousa Hubbard, who worked for her in later years, remembered only one occasion when Susan shouted at her. One morning, hearing loud talking coming from the bathroom where Susan was taking her morning bath, Francelina anxiously began knocking on the door to see if she were all right. She was severely rebuked by the author, who told her to go away. Susan was creating dialogue as she soaked in the tub and was furious over the disturbance. "Never never interrupt me when I'm working," she shouted back.[6] Leisure and quiet were crucial to her, and she stressed both needs repeatedly in interviews. "Not leisure to spend doing nothing, but time to think while at a given task," she told Chloe Arnold in 1917. "I usually wrote of mornings [sic], and I do not like to think that in two hours I must stop and see some one or go some place; but that I can work away uninterruptedly until I have done all I can."[7] Even an appointment late in the day could distract her. The interruptions occurring between May and October, while she was writing *The Verge*, must have worked their way into her play.

Susan never had to cope with the dual demands of family and career the way her friends Mary and Neith were forced to do. This summer she got a small taste of what it meant to balance competing claims for her time, something that constantly plagued Vorse, who placed her eldest son, Heaton, in boarding school and, put her younger children, Ellen and Joel, under the care of Joe O'Brien's sister in the southwest, whenever travel and work took her away from home. Throughout her long career as journalist, novelist, and political activist, Mary never escaped the guilt and frustration she felt by working when she thought she should be mothering or mothering when she yearned for the freedom to travel and write. She became one model for Claire Archer in *The Verge*. Susan concentrated particularly on Vorse's struggles with her daughter Ellen, seventeen in 1921, the same age as Claire's daughter Elizabeth, who was also being raised by a relative, not by her mother. Neith Boyce was another model for Claire. In her case, it should have been easier for her to write and take care of her family, because she had a husband to share the responsibilities. In fact, it was Hutch who made the greatest demands on her time and most resented her work. As he explained to a friend, "I want all essentially that there is of Neith, both for myself and the family."[8] Susan may also have drawn from birth-control advocate Margaret Sanger, another activist Villager she knew who struggled to balance motherhood and career. Although the main thrust of Sanger's work focused on the reproductive rights of women, she framed her agitation in broad revolutionary terms, choosing the name *The Woman Rebel* for her magazine. Its motto, "No gods, no Masters," was selected, she explained in the first issue, "Because I believe that woman is enslaved by the world machine, by sex conventions, by motherhood and its present necessary childrearing, by wage-slavery, by middle-class morality, by customs, laws and superstitions." Sanger's goal was for women to be able "To look the whole world in the face with a go-to-hell look in the eyes; to have an ideal; to speak and act in defiance of convention."[9] Glaspell's Claire would struggle to express similar needs and attempt a similar rebellion: to live "without gods or masters."

Claire Archer is not a writer like Mary, Neith, or Susan, nor is she an activist like Margaret, but she is a creator, an extremely vexed one. Her métier is plant breeding, and in her greenhouse laboratory she cross-fertilizes specimens in order to produce what she calls "the big leap," in which plants will "explode their species."[10] Her goal is not to create better, more useful varieties, not even more beautiful ones. What she wants is to see plants "broken from their form," displaying "strange new comings together—mad new comings together." As she explains, "Out there lies all that's not been touched—lies life that waits. Back here—the old pattern, done again, again and again. So long done it doesn't even know itself for a pattern." Edge Vine, which she has painstakingly cultivated, clings timidly to the familiar pattern of the species, as its name implies, and she destroys it. Breath of Life, the plant that is the focus of her work, holds out the hope that it is possible, as Claire imagines, to "get out" to "otherness" and move beyond "the verge" of the title, that position on the margin or brink, between the enclosing circle and that which lies outside any boundaries.

Claire is not a female Luther Burbank, as most male critics of the play assumed. Her work with plants is a dramatic correlative for the struggle to free herself from those customs, traditions, and expectations that similarly fix women in place, a theme Susan had touched on repeatedly in her earlier plays and fiction but never so directly and forcefully as in this, her most daring and experimental work. If Claire is able to succeed with plants, one character in the play suggests, perhaps she may not have to do it with her own life, that is, "open a door to destruction hoping to find a door on the far side of destruction." Yet, as her experiments have taught her, it is hard to "get past what we've done. Our own dead things—block the way." In one of her working notes, Susan describes her theme: "The story of a woman's adventure out of forms molded for us. In her experiment with plants she sees that they sometimes break themselves up, because something in them knows they can't go farther. Two acts of the play are in the greenhouse where she comes to see that these explosions may be expulsion of birth. She sees life with a clarity which leaves no satisfaction in which to rest. Like her plants she is on the verge—perhaps insane—perhaps saner than we dare to be."[11]

In her choice of botany as the means by which Claire hopes to free herself, Susan draws inspiration from her grandfather Glaspell, a self-taught horticulturalist and experimenter with new plant forms, and from her father, a breeder of plants. She also may have been influenced by the watercolors of flowers being executed at the time by her friend Charles

Demuth, whose highly evocative colors and shapes are like Breath of Life, "arresting rather than beautiful." Later, Georgia O'Keeffe would also depict flowers that many would see as representations of women's nature, vital, sexual, unfolding—qualities Susan ascribes to Claire and, by association, to Breath of Life. For the greenhouse setting of acts 1 and 3, she draws her inspiration from the structure Jig had built in Buffalo, whose walls bore his poetry, just as Claire's greenhouse bears patterns formed by the frost outside, "as if—as Plato would have it—the patterns inherent in abstract nature and behind all life had to come out." The reference to Plato also has connections to Jig, who, at the time she was writing the play, had called a meeting of the Players and had read them Plato as a reminder not to be so lost in the particulars of success that they forgot the ideal pattern that should motivate them. Susan called Jig's act "perhaps the bravest thing he ever did."[12]

Just as Breath of Life is Claire's greatest creation, Claire is Glaspell's, a larger-than-life woman with great charm, wit, gaiety, and a finely nuanced irony, able to cut through the banality around her. Not an absent presence like Minnie Wright or Bernice, she is very much *there*, animating all those with whom she comes into contact, particularly the three men who encircle her, appropriately named Tom, Dick, and Harry: soul mate, lover, and husband. Each is warmed by the "inner fire" Claire emits, but none is willing or able to allow her to journey outward toward the selfhood she desperately seeks. O'Neill, borrowing from Glaspell, uses the same configuration seven years later in *Strange Interlude*, in which Nina Leeds, his variation of Claire Archer, revels in the way men's desires converge in her. Glaspell's Claire knows better. She recognizes that to exist as merely the fulfillment of others' dreams and wishes is to cease to exist for oneself. She, therefore, rebels against the stereotypic roles she is required to perform—wife, mother, hostess, sister, good citizen—parts she is expected to play as written, leaving no room for interpretation or improvisation.

Claire has been twice married and twice a mother. Her son died in youth, and her daughter, Elizabeth, is being raised by Claire's sister, Adelaide, one of Glaspell's conventional foil characters, used as a contrast to her unconventional protagonist. Claire's age is not specified; but with a seventeen-year-old daughter, she is probably around forty, closer to Susan's own age of forty-five than any of her previous protagonists have been. She also bears other marked similarities to the playwright. Both come from New England stock, had Puritan ancestors, are witty and perceptive, and display refinement. It is the label of refinement that most irks Claire. She continually tries to shake it off by doing and saying outrageous things, such as openly flaunting her sexual liaison with Dick, telling him in front of her husband, "Harry will be suspecting that I am your latest strumpet," a word that was so shocking in 1921 that women trying out for the part of Claire often had trouble even saying it without blushing and lowering their heads, Jig reported.

Like Claire, Susan was also continually described as being ladylike and refined, sometimes too much so, and the label may well have irked her as well. Hutch relates an anecdote about a visit Susan paid one Christmas day to her Provincetown neighbor Alice Palmer, one of the most outspoken and independent of the bohemian community, who detested excessive shows of refinement in others. With many guests expected soon and the dinner not done, Alice was fortifying herself on drink and ignoring Susan, who finally got up to leave. "I just came in a friendly spirit to wish you a happy Christmas, I don't see why you feel this way," Susan remarked, her feelings hurt. "'Well, Susan', said Alice, 'You're too goddamned refined.'" Hutch indicates that it was Susan, "with her usual humor and generosity," who told him the story.[13] She often made fun of the fact that in her bearing she tended to seem conservative and restrained. For example in her 1920 entry in the "Heterodoxy Album for Marie," a collection of photographs and comments by the founding members of that most radical of feminist groups, she wrote under a photograph of a portrait of herself: "I am Susan Glaspell. I am from the painting by William L'Engle a friend. That is why I look so nice and refined."[14] In *The Verge*, Susan has Claire rebel against the labels "nice" and "refined" and against being categorized as "the flower of New England," tied to male forefathers who exact conformity. Claire creates a far different flower to represent her true nature.

Her marriage—the most important relationship in her life—must have also played a large part in the composition of *The Verge*. In a note intended to go into a future novel or story, Susan jotted down, "One can surely be amused by one's own marriage. Be it beautiful or ugly one thing is certain it—isn't what you thought it was going to be.[15] Jig was certainly not stick-in-the-mud husband Harry, detached artist Dick, or terrified soul mate Tom. He did not resent her work. She was his wife, but she was also one of two star playwrights of the Provincetown Players. Her successes, like O'Neill's, proved that his dream for American theatre was possible; and he often took credit for both playwrights in a gender-neutral way, as proof of his ability to inspire others to do their best work, the theme of *The Spring*. If anything, Jig himself became yet another model for the character of Claire. Like her, he was the possessor of a "life giving fire," who constantly inveighed against the commonplace and the traditional form. What Susan writes of his condition in the fall of 1921, echoes what she writes about Claire: "His spirit always asked more. Life, too, was experiment for its own sake." Jig's nature made him strain toward "the impossible," she writes in *The Road to the Temple*: "He would rather destroy himself than deny that need to make plastic the world which is and mold it new."[16] This desire she imparts to Claire. Susan also weaves into her play the present struggles Jig was experiencing with the Players. Just as those who saw their recent successes as the culmination of what they had been striving for all along, those around Claire see Breath of Life's breakthrough at the end of the play as an indication that she has achieved her end. As Harry tells her: "So you've really put it over. . . . I'm mighty glad—after all your work, and I hope it will set you up." His banal words, couched in the business jargon of the time, are Susan's parody of the words being spoken by those critics and Provincetown Players who felt they had "made it" by embracing and being embraced by Broadway. Claire, like Jig, was not interested in success and novelty; she wished to achieve in her experiment what she wished to achieve in her life: freedom and ascendancy. In many ways Claire's breakdown at the end of the play parallels Jig's failure in the fall and winter of 1921–22, and it suggests the general—and perhaps inevitable—failure facing those who attempt to break old ways of thinking and old forms, only to discover that instead of "getting out," they have been "taken in."

As with all her plays, many of the significant issues Glaspell addresses have to do with the political conditions during the time the play was being written. *Inheritors* was her response to the Red Scare; *The Verge* is her depiction of, and reaction to, the situation women faced now that suffrage had finally been achieved, with the ratification of the Nineteenth Amendment to the Constitution, in August 1920. Until then, the major feminist battle had been to secure the vote. Now the National American Woman Suffrage Association (NAWSA), which had supported the war effort, and the more radical, antiwar National Woman's Party (NWP) could not agree on a common agenda for the future. Without a uniting cause around which women could rally, the feminist movement began to come apart: NAWSA dissolved after 1920, while the NWP, in a skeleton form, redirected its efforts to the passage of the Equal Rights Amendment. No serious women's movement would surface in America for the next forty-five years. Although recent historians have cited the year 1925 as the date when the women's coalition finally collapsed and disillusionment over its accomplishments set it, Susan could see the direction to which women were heading—back to the kitchen—as early as the summer of 1921, when she was writing *The Verge*. She was also aware, through discussions at Heterodoxy and her own observations, of the widening gap between the older, radical feminists, like herself, who believed in a complete redressing of women's rights and needs, and the younger generation, inheritors of their successes, who, with great alacrity, once the vote was won, turned their backs on their foremothers and their goals. Asked in a survey in 1924 to name their female heroes, young women in New York and Tennessee listed Joan of Arc and Cleopatra; asked for their preferences in the future, 90 percent of the 1923 class at Vassar—where bohemian icon Edna St. Vincent Millay had graduated six years before—chose marriage over career.[17] The term the *New Woman* began to appear in the media as the generic label for this younger generation of postsuffrage women, in many ways far more conservative than their mothers or grandmothers. Glaspell's *The Verge*, written at this time, is the first drama to present "the New Woman" in the person of Claire's daughter, Elizabeth, and to stage the schism between this postsuffrage generation and the generation of feminists, like the author, who had imagined a complete revaluation of society not just freedom to do "something amusing," as Elizabeth says.

One of the key scenes in *The Verge* is the confrontation between Claire and Elizabeth, less a character than a cipher for the direction feminism had taken. Susan describes Elizabeth as "the creditable young American—well built, poised, 'cultivated' so sound an expression of the usual as to be able to meet the world with assurance"—in other words, the New Young Woman of 1921. She does what "one does," she studies "the things one studies," she follows "all the girls," and finds it "awfully amusing" that "values have shifted and such sensitive new things have been liberated in the world." Claire's aversion to Elizabeth and her violent rejection of her—she attacks her with Edge Vine, the plant she rips from its roots at the end of act 1—shocks audiences and readers today. Nora in *A Doll's House* leaves her children; she does not tell them, as Claire does: "To think that object ever moved my belly and sucked my breast." Although critics who first reviewed the play often disliked Claire and some ridiculed the play, none cited the abnormality of a mother who hates her child, as contemporary readers invariably do. They understood the function of Elizabeth, even when they did not fully understand the struggles of Claire or the import of Glaspell's play.

There is another way in which Glaspell addresses the battle between generations in the play, and that is related to sex. It was Mary Vorse, forty-seven in 1921 but admitting only to forty-one and in the midst of a passionate love affair with Robert Minor several years her junior, who bemoaned the way younger women tended to deny sexuality to older women. Isadora Duncan, the famous dancer, and friend of the bohemian community, echoed Vorse's feelings. "Especially do I resent the conclusion formed by so many women that, after the age of forty, a dignified life should exclude all love-making. Ah, how wrong this is![18] Glaspell's mature Claire clearly expresses her need for sex, turning from timid Tom to randy Dick to satisfy her. In staging Claire's unashamed sexual desire, Susan becomes one of the first American playwrights to finally give the lie to Hamlet's assumption about his mother, that "at your age / The heyday in the blood is tame, it's humble, And waits upon the judgment." Susan knew better.

Critics of the play tended not to mention Claire's overt sexuality or her treatment of Elizabeth. What they wrote about almost exclusively was the *The Verge*'s break with form and use of expressionism rather than conventional stage realism. Susan had employed certain expressionistic techniques in her earlier plays, such as *The People* and *The Outside*, but *The Verge* goes much further. It is the first full-length American drama to rely so directly on those expressionistic forms and themes being used by German playwrights and filmmakers, which were spreading throughout Europe. Like her German peers, Glaspell draws on Darwin, Nietzsche, and Freud, philosophical pillars of expressionism. She saw Darwin's theories as complementary to a thrust forward in moral development, which might enhance the race, a theme found in *Inheritors*. Borrowing from Nietzsche, she emphasized the philosopher's call for complete freedom and self-awareness and for a war against bourgeois values, even at the price of madness. Claire echoes Nietzsche's question, "Where is the madness with which you should be filled," when she chides those around her with having an "incapacity—for madness." Her use of Freud in the play is her most innovative touch. Presaging feminist theorists of the 1970s and 1980s, she upends Freud's dismissal of female rebellion as a form of hysteria, making the case that hysteria can be seen as a mark of rebellion in a society that does not allow other channels of expression for women. Susan stages Claire's struggle to become a new person, closely following playwrights such as Toller and Kaiser. However, her play focuses on a woman rather than on the Universal Man of German expressionist dramas; the generational battle is between mother and daughter not father and son; and the utterance at the end is not a *Schrei*, or scream, but a hymn, "Nearer My God to Thee," sung not in exultation but in madness, by a woman unable to triumph over societal forces assailing her.

What marks *The Verge*, as well, is the degree to which Glaspell makes use of scenic and linguistic devices to depict the state of mind of her female hero. Robert Wiene's *The Cabinet of Dr. Caligari* and Paul Wegener's *The Golem* had opened in New York in 1920, revealing how twisted, fragmented lines, shades of light and dark, highly stylized body motions, and visual imagery could reveal both madness and fear. Susan's play takes its leave from these revolutionary films, particularly *Caligari*. It is also shaped by highly stylized acting techniques used on the European stage at the time, which were being condemned by adherents to realism as narrow, neurotic, violent, and formless art, the exact criticism leveled against *The Verge*.

Susan's most successful blending of theme and expressionistic uses of lighting, scenic design, and dramatic language is found in act 2, set in Claire's "thwarted tower," an oddly shaped womblike structure that the audience views through a bulging window, with latticed bars, made by light and shadow. This interior is lit by a lantern from Susan's Truro home, and the "innumerable pricks and slits in the metal create a marvelous pattern on the curved wall—like masonry that hasn't been." The effect is heightened by the way the light hits Jig's dome, last used to suggest infinite space and a psychic interior in *Jones*. Cleon Throckmorton, who designed *The Emperor Jones*, also made the sets for *The Verge*. Susan also uses stairs to indicate levels of consciousness. In acts 1 and 3 they lead from the greenhouse down to her subterranean retreat, in act 2 from the main house up to her tower. She may have borrowed the idea from recent Broadway productions of Robert Edmond Jones, who also employed stairs in similar ways.

In addition to experimenting with expressionistic scenery, Susan also introduces expressionistic dialogue, consisting of those fragments of ideas and incoherent outpouring of words emanating from the mind of her troubled hero, unedited by the speaker—or the playwright. In Claire's attempts to share her desires, both sexual and intellectual, with Tom Edgeworthy, the only character who seems to understand her quest, she finds that language, too, is a prison-house. Claire's declarative statements in act 1, despite the vagueness of words such as *outness* and *otherness* still can be understood. In act 2, her sentences veer further away from traditional dialogue and closer to the poetic ejaculations of German expressionism, as she says to Tom: "Let me tell you how it is with me. / I do not want to work, / I want to be; / do not want to make a rose or make a poem— / Want to lie upon the earth and know." As much as the words take her to a level of heightened passion and near ecstasy in her efforts to break Tom's resistance to her physical entreaties, she is also the conscious artist aware of the limits of language, the speaker self-editing: "Stop doing that!—words going into patterns; they do it sometimes when I let come what's there. Thoughts take pattern—then the pattern is the thing." Like the skeptical nominalist philosophers of the period, such as Austrian Fritz Mauthner and, later, Ludwig Wittgenstein, and like later playwrights such as Samuel Beckett, who takes his leave from both, Glaspell realizes the impossibility of using language to critique language and attempts to reflect this impasse in her play.

In act 3, which returns to the setting and realistic tone of act 1, Claire recognizes that there is finally no escape from pattern in her experiments, her words, or her life. When Tom is finally emboldened to reach for the love she offers, he becomes demanding and possessive, like all the others who desire her, drawing her back rather than accompanying her through to freedom. Her anguished cry—"No! You are *too much*! You are not *enough*"—becomes, as playwright and critic Karen Malpede argues, the knowledge that plunders love in a world in which both partners are not free. "'You are *too much*'—I cannot be myself. 'You are not *enough*'—I cannot find myself in you."[19] Using an ending that O'Neill later appropriates in *The Hairy Ape*—the hug of death—Glaspell concludes her play with Claire choking Tom, as she realizes that it is finally he who is the greatest threat to her search for self. "You fill the place—should be a gate," she shouts, before lapsing into insanity, presumably the only way, aside from suicide, that a woman in 1922 and later may get "out."

Unlike the extant typescript copy of *Inheritors*, which has relatively few changes, the undated typescript of *The Verge* indicates that while Susan already had the three-act structure and details of plot fixed, she was still searching for expressionistic devices and dialogue at a late stage of the composition process. Repeatedly in the margins of the text, she indicates the need to heighten the tension and the inner conflicts of the characters. One note reads, "Claire's feelings about life—why she would go insane—now." Another, "In this scene Elizabeth musts glibly use words which to her mother have significance and she shows the pain every time they are thus used." A third reminds her to place "somewhere in this scene or in act 3 the phrase 'don't leave me alone with what you've let me know is there.'" A fourth simply indicates "heighten intensity."[20] Names also shift. In addition to the final title, Susan was still considering "Breath of Life" as a title; while "Rose of the Rainbow" appears as an early name for her final plant experiment. Only at the end of act 1 does Claire Given become Claire Archer, Tom Stanhope (the family name used in *Alison's House*) become Edgeworthy, and husband Stanley shift to the expressionistic moniker Harry, completing the male trio. These additions indicate that Susan was continuing to fine-tune the play, and they may explain her hesitation about setting a fixed date for its production, despite the usual pressure that Jig was exerting from New York.

From their first year in New York, the Players had opened every season with an O'Neill play. In the fall announcement to subscribers, which went out in August, Jig had indicated that O'Neill was working on *The Hairy Ape*, "a play of the length of *The Emperor Jones* and another one-act play";[21] but O'Neill only began *Ape* in December. Therefore, it fell to *The Verge* "as the P.P.'s best bet," Jig wrote Susan in August, reminding her to show the play to Gene, "in order to vote on it for P.P. production." As an indication of the new priorities of the Players, he already was discussing possibilities for taking it to Broadway. By October 6, Susan had still not finished the manuscript nor written to him about its progress, causing Jig to beg for some word or, better still, for her to come to New York and complete the script there. He was already casting, having interviewed more than "100 girls" to play Claire and was considering a number of established actors, including Alla Nazimova, the legendary Russian who had starred in the first American production of *Hedda Gabler* in 1907 (and would play Christine Mannon in O'Neill's 1931 *Mourning Becomes Electra*). By October 30 a notice in the *New York Call* stated that Margaret Wycherly, a respected Theatre Guild figure and later a distinguished Hollywood actor, would play Claire. An admirer of *Bernice*, she had told her fellow Heterodoxy member, Susan, she hoped to act one day in a Glaspell play that presented a strong woman. She got her wish.

The Verge, directed by Jig, opened the Provincetown Players' sixth season in New York on November 14, and it quickly became a cause célèbre in the press. The reviews, from vituperative condemnation to ecstatic praise, were the most extensive and varied any Glaspell play had received. Those critics who were uncomfortable with the shift from realism found it easy to disparage the character, the author, and the radical new form; those who appreciated Glaspell's groundbreaking efforts applauded her daring accomplishment—if not completely realized—and admired the complexity of the woman she created. Many echoed responses to German expressionistic drama a few years earlier, and anticipated criticism of experimental Absurdist works several decades later. "Insanity Acted Out," one critic proclaimed,[22] "Claire—Superwoman or Plain Egomaniac?" a second asked as a front-page banner.[23] Weed Dickinson in the *New York Evening Telegraph* subtitled his review "Bad Insanity Clinic," adding a barb directed at those who flocked to see it: "Nothing pleases the merry, merry Greenwich Villagers so much as a well misdirected idea which nobody understands."[24] Arthur Pollock, who appreciated the play, argued that it was "unintelligible only to those who do not think,"[25] while William Archer argued that the play was not nonsense but one presenting a problem with no exit, a blind alley, "incapable of solution or rather of which all possible solutions are equally unsatisfactory and undesirable." He concludes, "What is the artistic profit of letting the imagination play round with a problem which merely baffles and repels it?"[26]

Stephen Rathbun takes the opposite position, writing that attempts to deal with the inexplicable are needed, even if unsatisfying and unsatisfied: "Maybe . . . in the year 2021 or in 2121, 'The Verge' will be as much of a stage classic as 'Hamlet' is today."[27] Maida Castellun also praises Susan's attempt to offer for the first time on an American stage a superwoman, sister to those supermen found in Goethe, Strindberg, Nietzsche, and Shaw.[28] Usually it was male critics, feeling disparaged like the male characters in the play, who were most passionate in their condemnation of Claire and most revealing of their own fixed ideas about gender roles in art and life. Alexander Woollcott, in a vitriolic review in the *New York Times*, called Claire "a neurotic disagreeable cat," a woman from whom any sane man would escape "on the next train." Such a woman could appeal "only to the fervid brains of the faithful Greenwich Village intelligentsia," who are packing "the little theater in MacDougal Street to suffocation" in order to see a play "which can be intelligently reviewed only by a neurologist or some woman who has journeyed near to the verge of which Miss Glaspell writes." Woollcott also strenuously objected to the technique of stream of consciousness that Glaspell employs, calling Claire's speeches "miscellaneous, unselective, helplessly loquacious—like a stenographic report of someone thinking aloud"—exactly the expressionistic technique she was attempting to employ. Like almost every reviewer, he did find the play "gorgeously acted" by Wycherly and "beautifully mounted, a little art and a little skill creating a more satisfying suggestion of earth and air and sky than can be managed with immense expenditure by the allegedly wiser producers of Broadway."[29] Five days later, in his column "Second Thoughts on First Nights," Woollcott returned to *The Verge*, this time disparaging its vague language, particularly words such as *otherness* and *apartness*. When one character says he loves Claire's apartness, Woollcott says that he thought he meant he loved Claire's apartment.[30]

In response to his cynical dismissal, Heterodite Ruth Hale, head of the Lucy Stone clubs, which called on women to keep their maiden names, and herself the wife of critic Heywood Broun, wrote a letter to the editor of the *Times*, which was printed as a response to Woollcott's reviews. In it she admits that the play is overwritten and suffers from too much talk; however, she denies that Claire is unknowable. On the contrary, Hale writes, she is "as clear as glass" to those who will draw on their own experience of clashing with "accepted physical or social habit." Hale goes on: "Miss Glaspell is the only playwright I ever knew who can tell a story like this. If the surface of life changes by a hair's breadth, she not only knows it, but can convey it in words. She is the painter of those wisps of shadow that cross the soul in the dead of night. She can write great horrors in the terms of little ones—come to think of it, of course, she wrote 'Trifles.' I do feel strongly that, if we cannot always quite understand her, it would be smart of us to try."[31]

Stark Young, writing in *The New Republic* three weeks later also attacks those, like Woollcott, who were so dismissive. "No play of Susan Glaspell's can be passed over quite so snippily as most of the reviewers have done with *The Verge*; for Miss Glaspell is one of the few people we have in our theatre who are watching the surface of life to find new contents and material." He argues that a play which takes as its theme the groping of the mind will find it difficult to put in words its hero's struggles, but the attempt of the playwright is worth the effort "unless the theatre plans to go on dodging the modern ego." Certainly, this is a play that needs to be supported, he concludes. "Prattling about new forms in the theatre and then fighting any attempt to introduce new material is a poor game." Young does differ from other reviewers in one key point: he dislikes Wycherly's highly stylized body motions. "She fidgets her arms neurotically; she is a conscious oddity; she has force but it is an erratic force. She gets all the afflictions but none of the point."[32] His description indicates that Jig, as director, was making a conscious attempt to match body movement to theme, an acting style close to that being used in German stage expressionism. Another important theatre person of the period, Barrett Clark, did not publish on the play, but in a note to his own copy of *The Verge*, he, too, supports the effort of Glaspell, even if problematic in spots: "The attempt is what matters here making theatre stretch its limits."[33] Kenneth Macgowan also argues for the importance of the play; in his opening night review, he calls the work "the most difficult play that any American and perhaps any European has ever written. . . . Take "When We Dead Awaken," and the most devious play by Strindberg and go beyond it into dizzying distances and fogging depths and you have got very little closer to 'The Verge.'"[34]

It is true that the play's shifts from realistic to symbolic levels are often too jarring, the gears sounding too loudly as Claire goes from talking about breakfast to talking about destruction, but this is the problem of a play trying to show both surface and inner reality. O'Neill, in *Strange Interlude*, would attempt to solve the same problem by having action freeze, so that the characters could offer monologues, as in a novel, to indicate what is going on in their minds. Glaspell's solution is more successful. As Barrett Clark, an O'Neill biographer, explained, "Claire is the sort of person who in life does not say anything or but rarely though the play is based on the assumption that she is always willing to argue. Nonrealistic, but why not eh?"[35] Why not indeed. It is noteworthy that with the exception of Ruth Hale and the anonymous critic or critics in *The Greenwich Villager*, who created a skit of contrary reactions to the play, none fully grasped the political level of *The Verge* and how it, like *Inheritors*, was addressed to a current situation, this time the plight of women in postsuffrage America. Even Rathbun and Castellun, who praised Glaspell's work, do so on universal grounds, comparing Claire to a female Nietzchean figure. The women of Heterodoxy, however, had long been concerned with issues facing independent women, and their discussions certainly provided both inspiration for Susan's play as well as a ready, empathetic audience. It is not surprising, therefore, that this group heartily embraced her play and devoted an entire meeting to discussing it. Hutch Hapgood's embittered reaction to *The Verge*—"an expression of half-mad feminism"—grows out of his equal distaste for Heterodoxy and independent women in general. He writes in his 1939 autobiography, "This club was composed of women, many of them of force, character, and intelligence, but all of them shunted on the sliding path from the early suffrage movement into the passionate excesses of feminism, in which the 'vital lie' was developed, that men had consciously oppressed women since the beginning of time, enslaved and exploited them." For Hutch it was natural that the group would love *The Verge*; and he relates with relish the story that dancer Elsie Dufor told him about the meeting devoted to the play: "It seemed to me, while these women were talking about 'The Verge,' that I was in church, that they were worshiping at some holy shrine; their voices and their eyes were full of religious excitement. I was, I think, the only woman not under the spell. I tried at first to say a few things about the play that were in the line of ordinary dramatic criticism, which I thought had a reasonable basis; but when they all glared upon me, as if they thought I should be excommunicated, I spoke no further word.'"[36]

The End of the Dream

22

It's time to go to Greece.

—Jig Cook, quoted in *The Road to the Temple*

Because of the heated debate about *The Verge*, the run was extended to eighteen days, finally closing to make way for the previously announced second bill, Theodore Dreiser's twenty-seven-character play *The Hand of the Potter*, one critic noting that while *The Verge* was considered too vague, this play is all too clear in its degeneracy. Audiences agreed, and the Players found themselves with a depleted subscriber list, a deficit of $1,500, and a disgruntled Dreiser, in California, receiving periodic reports about the progress of the rehearsals and the debacle after the opening. In one note, Jig quotes a sentence from a review of *The Verge*: "On Broadway there is repetition. . . . On MacDougal street there is revelation. Let those go who are not afraid."[1] These words did little to quiet Dreiser, who blamed Jig, as theatre head, for what he believed was a sloppy production of his play. In contrast to this failure, *The Verge* continued to gather interest once the monthly journals began to appear, carrying more extended and generally positive reviews, such as those by Stark Young and Ludwig Lewisohn. In response, the Theatre Guild took over the production and moved it to the Garrick Theatre on December 6, where it began an eleven-matinee run. After *Potter* closed, it returned to MacDougal Street for holiday performances, December 26–31. While the entire run of the play never approached anything like that of *The Emporer Jones*, it did have its champions among respected critics and audience members, who were personally touched by Claire's plight and impressed by Glaspell's ability to stage it. A postcard Susan received from a young male admirer indicated that the play spoke not only to women: "The play has been the greatest inspiration of my life. . . . Nothing that I have seen or heard before has so stirred me," he wrote.[2] Another letter came from the president of the New York Drama League, who noted, "I doubt if any other theatre in this country would have had the courage to produce it."[3]

Courage was needed even more, now that the Players had to contend with an empty treasury, a road company of *Jones* still needing attention, and no idea how to fill the third bill. These troubles were also affecting relations between Susan and Jig. His frustration is apparent in a letter to the executive board, defending himself from their criticism over his failure to appear at a Drama League dinner, which he had promised to attend. His special wrath is directed at Susan, who evidently led the others in censuring him for his actions: "Susan did it and the other two of you backed her up in it, and if you are now feeling morally superior about your conduct I advise you to take another think."[4] A second brief note reinforces the sense that the theatre was becoming a battleground for them: "Telegram to the Executive Committee of Susan Glaspell 129 W. 13th St. I am at Brevoort writing Greek for the reason that I do not wish to hurt you—or be hurt."[5] The handwritten note is signed George Cram Cook.

The Players had proved that they could succeed in presenting daring works; the problem was that few such works appeared. At the beginning of 1922, they could muster only a weak trio of one-acts for the third bill, and nothing at all for the fourth, until the fortuitous visit of the Chicago troupe of Ellen Van Volkenburg and Maurice Browne took over the theatre and offered Arthur Davison Ficke's *Mr. Faust*. On the horizon, however, was O'Neill's anticipated play, *The Hairy Ape*, which Jig believed would save the day.

He and Susan returned to Provincetown in early January 1922, after the final close of *The Verge*, and almost immediately went over to the O'Neill's, who were living at the Monroe House on Bradford Street, to hear Gene read his newly completed play. It was a work with a long incubation. In 1917 he'd written a short story about the suicide of his sailing friend Driscoll and had been telling the germ of the idea to friends over the years, but had not found a way of transferring this highly personal work to the stage. Suddenly at the beginning of December he wrote to critic Oliver Sayler, "It is one of those plays where the word 'inspiration' has some point—that is, you either have the rhythm or you haven't and if you have you can ride it and if not you're dead."[6] Although critics have speculated on what suddenly provided the "inspiration" that finally allowed him to give form to the story—some mentioning his possible viewing of *The Cabinet of Dr. Caligari*, others his possible familiarity with German expressionistic drama, specifically Kaiser's *From Morn to Midnight* (which he denied)—none mention one of the most obvious catalysts: Glaspell's *The Verge*.

The similarities between the two plays are striking. Both make use of expressionistic settings, marked by a variety of spaces, including a sub-basement retreat or "home" for the central protagonist; both use light and dark to demarcate these spaces and externalize the hero's inner conflicts; both surround the central figure with stock characters representing ideological or social points of view; and both resort to sound effects emanating from unseen presences offstage. Claire's special buzzer code summons her assistant Anthony; a whistle from above activates the men in the stokehole. The most obvious similarity is "the hug of death" that concludes both plays, Claire's act a protest against those holding her in, Yank's against those keeping him out. Susan read *The Verge* to Agnes and Gene before it was produced (Agnes found her reading better than the staged production[7]), and Gene may well have found in it a possible key for telling the story of Driscoll, which had eluded him up to then.[8]

When Jig heard *The Hairy Ape*, he recognized it as a great play and assumed that he would direct it, since he had successfully directed *The Emperor Jones* and *The Verge*, two similar works in style and theme. And just as *Jones* had provided him with renewed vigor, this even more challenging play promised to do the same. However, O'Neill had other plans. In the middle of December, while he was still writing it, he had contacted Charles O'Brien Kennedy, a professional actor and director, about overseeing the production. Kennedy, an associate of Broadway producer Arthur Hopkins, had come down to MacDougal Street to direct *Diff'rent* and stayed to do a successful revival of *The Moon of the Caribees* in 1921 and Dreiser's play. Under Kennedy's hand, the rehearsals of O'Neill's plays had been meticulously run, with none of the laissez-faire attitude that tended to mark the work of the amateur group under Jig and other directors. O'Neill appreciated this approach and wanted it to insure the success of his new play, which he realized was still too special to go directly to Broadway, but which would move uptown, if it received a powerful production at the Players. To insure a possible move, O'Neill had also been in touch with Hopkins, who agreed to take it over after its opening and even offered to assist with the downtown production.

Edna Kenton once described Eugene O'Neill in awkward situations as taking three positions at the same time, lest he alienate competing camps. When Kennedy was forced to drop out because of other commitments, O'Neill indicated that Jig could direct the play, although he took on a more active supervisory role than he had exercised in the past, involving himself with the details of production, assisted by Hopkins, who began appearing regularly at the theatre. Gene had already fixed on Louis Wolheim to play Yank, and he had asked Robert Edmond Jones—absent from the Players since its 1915 summer inauguration—to do the complex sets. With these decisions taken out of his hands and more and more people appearing to give advice about the play, Jig found himself being shut out. He could have chosen to retreat quietly and, as overall director of the Players, take vicarious pleasure in the fact that his theatre made it possible for Yank to find a theatrical home. But Jig had been too taken with the work to accept such a passive role. He believed he had given life to *Jones*, (even when others, such as Deeter, questioned his role as director), and he felt capable of breathing the same fire into this latest avatar. Perhaps he could have hung on if it were just O'Neill and Hopkins shaping the play; but the final blow was the return of Jimmy Light. It was Light who had led the "Young Turks" during the 1919–20 season, opposed to what they considered Jig's overbearing rule. When it became clear that the executive committee for the 1920–21 season would consist of those supporting Cook, Light had retreated to the continent, without informing the group, and thus was suspended. Now back, he hoped to step in as director, after Kennedy's demise, and had O'Neill's blessing to do so. This was too much for Jig. He felt betrayed, most of all by O'Neill, whom he considered his friend. Jig felt that Gene, by supporting Light, was siding with those who cared more for uptown than the Village, for salaries than spirit, for professionalism than amateurism, for success than community.

In her chapter in *The Road to the Temple* describing the end of the Provincetown Players—pointedly called "The Beloved Community"—Susan makes no mention of the *Ape* imbroglio, just as she makes no reference to *The Verge* or to most of the productions at the theatre. What she does indicate is Jig's growing sense of failure over his inability to make the Players share in his vision. "I am sick of this New York hogtrough!" she reports him saying one day, as they walked down Barrow Street in the Village. "Let us withdraw into ourselves and form the thing that is ourselves—let come success or failure."[9] Earlier in her biography, she offers an anecdote that provides an explanation about why Jig could not abide the rejection, not only of himself but his dream. She tells of his chance meeting in Chicago in 1911 with a man with whom he and two Italians had shared a train compartment in Italy eighteen years earlier. The four had been students looking for adventure and had immediately bonded and decided to travel together for the next two weeks, recognizing that probably age and necessity would dampen their fervor in years to come. Before they parted, they made a pact: When and if they should meet again they would cheat time by immediately picking up the conversation on which they were then embarked—the question of the superiority of Dante over Shakespeare—thus illustrating that for them the fire of their youth had not been quenched nor its memory. Therefore, when Jig Cook, now a thirty-eight-year-old journalist in Chicago, spotted the man who had been his traveling companion, he immediately went over to him and without introduction began: "'But the trouble about Dante . . .' Nothing happened; bewilderment, a cold look." The man could not even remember the trip; for him, Susan explains, "Time won."[10] Not so for Jig. In 1911 and still in 1922, he retained the enthusiasms and fire of that young man of 1893, who carried a paper he had written even earlier that read: "Life is one long-drawn death and we must burn out white and fierce and joyous!"[11]

Such words may sound too naive—or too idealistic—to be taken seriously; however, many in Greenwich Village had used similar language in

1913. By 1922, the idealistic fever had run its course; the Jazz Age was beginning; and Jig Cook was an anachronistic holdover, chastising those with "little willingness to die for the thing we are building."[12] It is no wonder that many of the newly arrived Players found him at best out of step; at worst, a befuddled nuisance. However, it was one thing for people such as Charles Kennedy to say, "We thought he was a poseur, that he pontificated too much"[13]; another thing for Eugene O'Neill to dismiss Jig this way, especially since he had known him longer and better. For the sake of *The Hairy Ape*'s shift to Broadway, Jig was shunted aside as director in his own theatre, or so he felt. This was the main reason Jig could no longer stay in America.

While it may be clear why he left for Greece, it is less obvious why Susan went with him, cutting short a theatre career that held out great promise for the future. *The Verge* may have puzzled many critics, but even those most dismissive of its feminist theme and expressionistic form recognized the considerable talent of its creator. Those who embraced her vision, like Inez Haynes Irwin, saw her as "a sage, a seer, a mystic," for whom greatness lay ahead: "Nobody can say where she is going. She is so young that perhaps she doesn't know herself."[14] In his 1922 survey of modern world drama, *The Drama of Transition*, Isaac Goldberg ends his section on Glaspell with the sentence: "What she has already done pledges her to even higher things."[15] By 1922, at the age of forty six, Susan had succeeded in establishing herself as one of two central voices in American drama. The trajectory of her career was steadily rising. Like O'Neill, she had been forced to invent her own forms, since few existed, and every play only widened the dramatic landscape. Why, then, would she be willing to follow her husband on a quest that was his, not hers?

One answer is that when Susan left the Players, she did not intend to make the break permanent. The interim was to be one year, similar to the sabbatical season, which she had used for productive work. In her letters from Greece that first year, she mentions her intention to write more plays; and during her voyage there she worked on revisions of *Chains of Dew*, her play that closed the season, and sent them back to Edna, who was overseeing the production in her absence. She also took a lively interest in the play's casting, director, rehearsals, and reviews. Her mind was certainly still involved with the Players. Another reason she may have willingly left is that she welcomed the respite. *The Verge*, like all her plays, was created under tremendous pressure to get it on stage. She would now have time to think of what she wanted to do next and to write without hurrying the process. Also, she had not been abroad in thirteen years nor had she taken a real vacation from the theatre since its inception, seven years earlier. The previous break, while productive, had not removed her from the battles raging on the Cape and in the Village. Now she was taking a temporary leave from an impossible situation, from the even more rancorous squabbling at the Players over which direction to take: more professionalism or a return to the amateurism that lay at the heart of its inception. She also wished to regain some equilibrium and to restore the damage that had been done to her marriage because of these problems at the theatre. The most important reason she left for Greece probably lies in a simple fact: Susan loved Jig. She had left him when angry or when she wished to be alone to write; but from the time they had stood together on a winter's night in Davenport in 1908, she had not been emotionally separated from him. To have stayed behind in New York would most likely not have occurred to her, particularly now when he was so broken from his perceived failure with the theatre and needed her as never before. Also, unlike her protagonist Claire, Susan did not see her marriage as a bond she must sunder in order to be free; she had gained the freedom she sought when she broke from the restrictions of her family and community and chose to live in the East with Jig and create her own life. Seen from her perspective in 1922, her willingness to accompany him to Greece does not seem as antithetical to her feminist positions as it does to some contemporary critics today.[16] The theatre had been their joint work; it was now, at least in its present form, hostile to what both believed this theatre should be. It was as difficult for her to work there as it had become for him, at least under the present regime. So they left.[17]

On February 23, 1922, Jig and Susan went to the O'Neill apartment on West Thirty-fifth Street, and met with the other members of the current executive committee of the Players—Gene, Edna, Fitzie, Cleon Throckmorton, and lawyer Harry Weinberger—to incorporate the Players, a plan they had discussed informally the previous year. They now did so to preserve the name as a legal entity. Thus any other group wishing to take over management of the building during the one-year interim called at the end of the 1921–22 season would be required to take a different name. The incorporation went into effect on February 24, although they agreed to withhold news of their action until the end of the season, after Susan's *Chains of Dew* closed. With Jig's departure, Light was now free to return to the company and work alongside O'Neill and Hopkins to shape *Ape*; however, there was still not a clear sense of who, finally, was responsible for directing the play. When it opened on MacDougal Street on March 9, the director's line reads, "Produced by the Provincetown Players," without specifying who of the many who had their hand in the production should be given credit.[18] Susan and Jig did not wait for the opening; they sailed for Greece on March 1. Kenton, to whom they gave their proxies, recalls the bittersweet feeling of that premiere: "It was odd to hear on all sides unstinted praise and prophecies for the future knowing all the while we were finished, done for."[19] Not until the middle of the summer was the notice of incorporation and one-year suspension announced to the Players or made public. Many assumed that Jig had impulsively packed up and left, allowing the theatre to flounder unattended and limp through the rest of the season.

In fact, before he departed, he had prepared a final circular for subscribers, focusing on the accomplishments of the group and stating that in order to continue, a year of rest was needed before the Players returned in the fall of 1923. The only note of regret is reserved for the playwrights and their failure to take the opportunity the theatre provided for them: "We have given two playwrights to America, Eugene O'Neill and Susan Glaspell: we could have given a dozen by now if the other ten had appeared."[20] A more somber message that Susan prints in *Road*, is closer to the truth he felt: "Since we have failed spiritually in the elemental things—failed to pull together—failed to do what any good football or baseball team or crew do as a matter of course with no words said—and since the result of this is mediocrity, we keep our promise: We give this theater we love good death; the Provincetown Players end their story here. Some happier gateway must let in the spirit which seems to be seeking to create a soul under the ribs of death in the American theater."[21]

This note illustrates the insurmountable schism between Cook's vision and O'Neill's, between spiritual success and professional attainment. Certainly *Ape* was a great play, not mediocre; and Jig, more than anyone, recognized this. What he seems to label as "mediocrity" is not the product but the process, and for him the process of creation was always more important than its results. Jig's conception, therefore, was doomed to fail from the beginning: fail if the plays were no good, and the audiences did not support the experiment; fail if the plays were great, and the world rushed to their door. His was a dream that could only have flourished in that special soil cultivated in an earlier moment in Greenwich Village, when idealism was possible in America and *amateurism* was not a pejorative term.

They had already set sail when *Chains of Dew* opened. To complete the season when no other plays were available, Susan had allowed the Players to stage the comedy she had written in the fall of 1919 and Broadway producers had rejected. Unlike what some critics have assumed—that Glaspell wrote the play after *The Verge* or was retreating to realism because of the rebuffs it received[22]—the play actually preceded *The Verge* by two years. Her agreement to let the Players produce it was seen by Kenton as one more example of Susan's "sacrifice" for the theatre: allowing a play she knew was not fully developed and needed more work to fill the last bill because the theatre needed it. As Agnes had astutely noted, the work, while comic at times, is cluttered. Susan tries to do too much, grafting her variations of Ibsen's *A Doll's House* and *The Wild Duck* onto critiques of Greenwich Village enthusiasms and peccadillo's circa 1919 and of Davenport dogmatism. Given the many ideas she intertwines, the surprise is how well much of the play works. It displays the playwright's usual sly humor in catching the foibles of the characters, particularly the ponderous male protagonist and the general parochialism of the Village concerning its midwestern "cousins." It also explores political issues such as freedom of speech, birth control, and stereotypic roles foisted on women.

Act 1 is set in the cramped office of the Birth Control League,[23] in which posters, charts, exhibits, and large photographs are prominently displayed.[24] As the action begins, Nora Powers ("Powell" in the printed Playbill), League secretary, is busy mimeographing material for distribution. Nora, her name clearly intended to call up images of Ibsen, is Glaspell's thoroughly modern young woman: self-assured, sexually free, witty, bobbed-haired, and a committed worker for birth control. As she struggles with this new machine, which wheezes, chimes, and creaks throughout much of the scene, she also attempts to hold conversations with a trio of men who visit her, marginally more rounded characters than Claire's Tom, Dick, and Harry. There is Leon Whittaker, associate editor of *The New Nation*, a political and literary magazine; James O'Brien a young, visiting Irish essayist and fiction writer, whom Leon plans to interview, and Seymore Standish, a midwestern poet, making one of his infrequent visits to New York. Both Leon and James admire Seymore's work, but agree that there is something missing; it is so good that it should be better. Glaspell handles their rapid dialogue skillfully, illustrating her development from the set deliveries of the earlier one-acts. She has clearly mastered the realistic form.

Standish's entrance focuses their attention once more on an analysis of his work and what seems to keep it from greatness. He claims to be held by chains of responsibility and affection for his bourgeois family. Nora protests, "You don't have to be caught by living if you don't want to be," a familiar Glaspell theme; and to prove her point, she secretly decides to go the Midwest to rescue him and, at the same time, set up a Birth Control League there. In act 2 when she arrives in Bluff City/Davenport, she discovers that Seymore has misstated his life. His mother is independent and clearly aware of the shallowness of the community—and of the limitations of her son, which she analyzes with surprisingly clear eyes, And his wife desires to break out of her sheltered life as "Dotty Dimples" and become Diantha (her given name), a serious woman. Sick of the painting of the Sistine Madonna that graces the living room, in Seymore's absence she has slowly been loosening the nails that hold it, but is still unsure what to put in its place. Nora provides the alternative: birth-control posters. Dotty agrees; she also happily accedes to Nora's request that she become the president of the first Birth Control League of the Mississippi Valley. The elder Mrs. Standish is equally enthusiastic, donating $700 to the cause. Seymore, reeling from his wife's change and her now bobbed hair, is even more shocked by his mother's attitude—for, as he reminds her, he as the seventh child would not have been born if she had practiced birth control. "I know," she replies. In this new atmosphere, Seymore becomes a martyr with no one needing his sacrifice. It is his mother, Susan's most original creation in the play, who best recognizes his plight. Take away his cross and he is lost, his creativity thwarted. This underlines the dilemma Susan has Dotty face. She can pursue her emancipated life, but at the expense of Seymore and his art, or she can return to being

Dotty Dimple, rehang the Sistine Madonna, and regrow her hair. Despite Nora's indignation about the choices presented and her prodding that Dotty return with her to New York and not become once more "merely something to be superior to," Dotty cannot make herself abandon her husband, whom she loves. Through her tears, she agrees once more to become the cross Seymore has to bear.

The denouement of the play is Glaspell's reworking of the ending of *A Doll's House*, but instead of having the doll-wife reject the posturing husband she no longer idealizes, Glaspell's Dotty stays, fully aware of her husband's failings and of the fact that he needs her more than she needs him. She does, however, take what the stage directions indicate is "malicious satisfaction" in knowing that behind the Madonna "there will still be holes in the wall." She also extracts the promise that when he next goes to New York, she will go too.

Chains of Dew is an early comedic working out of the situation in *The Verge*, in which Edge Vine scuttles back from the verge. As she had done in *Suppressed Desires*, *Close the Book*, and *Woman's Honor*, Susan purposely stages the rationalizations and contradictions of her characters the better to direct the gaze of the audience at the societal critique her comedy is presenting. Dotty makes no speech proclaiming Seymore's shallowness; neither do Mrs. Hale and Mrs. Peters proclaim their own emancipatory actions in *Trifles*. In both cases, the audience is left to question the ways "the nail marks will show." As in *Bernice*, Glaspell also cuts her man to his true size, ironically naming her male figure who cannot see "Seymore" and widening the depiction by giving him a surname that calls up Puritan antecedents, to which he is the true patriarchal heir. Obviously, the play can be read as Susan's personal statement in 1919 about her own marriage and as eerily prophetic of her situation in 1922, when she chose to stay with Jig, who also displayed a penchant for martyrdom and was in need of constant encouragement. While Susan is not Dotty, as she was not Claire, she may be illustrating that even for a woman with her considerable talents and independence, total freedom is not possible—if one loves another person. Standing by your man when you have no illusions about your man is quite different than continuing to dream the impossible dream of Ibsen's Nora. One notebook reference Susan provides seems to make the point. Following an entry about Hutch, she writes, "The man (or men) who make the woman personify custom—holding them from their fullest selves. She lets them think so." She continues with another note: "Women invade their solitude. She keeps him from knowing that he is not equal to his solitude. As a part of Chains of Dew (The Lonely Soul)."[25]

Because of the complexity of the many intertwined themes and subtle ironies, *Chains of Dew* required a strong hand to guide it through production. Unfortunately, it did not get one. In a ten-page, single-spaced letter, one of twenty-three letters, duly numbered with carbons, which she faithfully posted to Susan and Jig in Greece, Edna Kenton outlines in copious detail the fate of the play she attempted to oversee in Susan's absence. At first she had hoped to secure well-known actors Roland Young, Mary Shaw, or Margaret Wycherly to direct and play leading parts, but all had other commitments. After running through several more possibilities, she finally settled on Ralph Stewart, who had directed the 1921 premiere production of *Trifles* at the Players. Since he was simultaneously directing another play, he had little time and relied on an actor to oversee rehearsals, while he arrived only the last week for intensive work. Casting the six lead roles was equally difficult, given that most Players were still uptown with *Ape* or on the road with *Jones*. The roles of Dotty and Leon were still unfilled six days before the opening, which had to be postponed for three days, until April 27, to give those finally recruited time to at least learn their lines.

Susan had wired two sets of play corrections from the ship, and these were incorporated into the six working scripts Kenton prepared; but without the playwright in attendance, Stewart had a free hand to make any cuts he wished. In her letter, Kenton apologizes profusely but argues that she had no authority to stop him, since there was no other director who could step in at this late stage. She reports that when Wycherly saw the performance, she was aware, from her earlier work on *The Verge*, what had been lost of Susan's subtle ways and what had been added, which made the final production far from its intended form. Among Stewart's cuts was the entire act 1 business with the mimeograph machine, because Marion Berry, who played Nora, could not master it. This cut completely altered the tone of the act, omitting the visual and auditory humor, which served as a running gag and an important corrective to the bombastic pronouncements of Seymore and the fervid proselytizing of Nora for birth control. At the end of act 1, other lines were substituted for the playful exchange that closes the scene; and even more disastrously, at the end of act 2, scene 1, Stewart cut Nora's triumphant curtain lines proclaiming that Dotty had agreed to become first president of the Mississippi Valley Birth Control League. As Kenton reports, "He could not and would not see Dotty as President of B.C. and so she wasn't."[26] Finally, at the end of the play, all references to Dotty's going to New York and her comments on love were omitted, so too the business of replacing the birth-control posters with the Madonna and discussion of the nail marks that remain. The last image in the performed version is of a pensive, silent Dotty staring off into space contemplating her future. She is not self-aware, as Susan wrote her, but rather a defeated, passive wife.

For her part, Susan could do little to affect the fate of her creation. With letters taking over three weeks to arrive, and cables not always reliable, the best she could do was respond long after the fact to the scenario Kenton tirelessly presented. In one note from Delphi, dated May 11, five days after Kenton's opus arrived, she describes "that sense of helplessness in being in heaven on Delphi and unable to raise a voice about the run of your recently abandoned life!" She thought to send Edna a cable reading,

"Not worth the struggle."[27] In a later note, she explains, "I saw there was nothing for me to do but get drunk and so deaden the first pangs," and she concludes, "Little do our subscribers know how much better is the comedy that is not being staged."[28]

Despite the chaotic rehearsal period, the excisions, and insensitive direction, the reviews for *Chains of Dew* were not as dismissive as might be expected. "I thought our friends the reviewers treated us very well. Giving the play pretty much all it deserved, I should say, and writing quite entertainingly about it," Susan wrote to Edna.[29] Alexander Woollcott called it "a wisp of a comedy" and found that "it is touched here and there with a charming fancy, lighted from time to time by gleams of the shrewdest and most subtle humor."[30] Interestingly, he thought the work more a rough sketch for a novel than a play, a keen observation, since Susan in 1931 would recycle the plot in *Ambrose Holt and Family*. Woollcott also felt that the play's concerns with bobbed hair and birth control give it "an anachronistic aspect," unaware that Susan had written it three years earlier. Again he misses, or refuses to acknowledge, Susan's ironic portrayal of men. Stephen Rathbun in his review illustrates how Susan's ending had been altered by Stewart's direction and cuts, for he writes that the play is another example of Glaspell's "thought dramas" in which "the players and the play, too, are, objectively at least, just where they were when the comedy started." For him, her designation of the play as comedy was mistaken. "To us it is tragic that a woman sacrifices her future and becomes a slave to her husband's career. It is just as tragic as though she had committed suicide. And yet, as wives are continually doing this sort of thing in real life, we might call it a grim, realistic comedy."[31]

Of all Glaspell's produced plays, *Chains of Dew* is the only one never in print, but filed in the Library of Congress.[32] Small, Maynard, and Company had thought to include it in the edition they were preparing of *The Verge*, but Edna decided that her masterpiece should stand alone. When Susan returned from Greece, the play was probably forgotten among the more pressing problems she had to face. She may also have decided not to print it because she wanted to make clear that she had written *The Verge* last. It, not *Chains of Dew*, was her last written work for the Players and stands as her greatest experiment and achievement.

The closing of *Chains of Dew* marked the end of the 1921–22 season, the seventh in the history of the Players (two seasons in Provincetown, five in New York). Rather than return the theatre to Mrs. Belardi, and let her rent it for the coming year, the corporation decided to retain its claim to the space, in order to recommence activities in the fall of 1923. Now the problem was for them to find tenants, an endeavor complicated by the question raised by one would-be taker: who has the right to use the name the Provincetown Players? This question put fear in Edna's heart. Were Jimmy Light, for instance, to be part of any consortium renting the space, she believed that this group might be tempted to simply call themselves Provincetown Players, and thus take over the theatre by default, leaving nothing for Susan and Jig to return to the following year. Given to intrigue and conspiracy theories, she paints a detailed scenario of plans attendant on finding a suitable tenant who did not have direct ties to the old group. After almost two months of uncertainty, on July 14, in letter twenty-one, Edna was finally able to announce to Susan and Jig that the theatre had been rented for one year to producers Alice and Ben Kauser, who intended to present the works of their friend Mercedes de Acosta. Thus assured, Edna left for the summer. The Players were officially on leave.

Interlude 2

Delphi, 1922–24: The Road to the Temple

Dreams for me have always had a peculiar reality, while the actual world has seemed extremely dreamlike.

—George Cram Cook, quoted in William Rapp,
"An American Apollo"

At 7:30 A.M., March 1, 1922, the small, ocean-going passenger vessel the *Themistocles* left New York harbor bound for Piraeus with Susan and Jig aboard. "Snow blowing canary singing," Jig noted as his diary entry for the day.[1] "The 'Themistocles' was less expansive than the man for whom it was named," Glaspell wryly recalled. Better equipped and far more spacious ships crossed to Greece, but a more comfortable booking would have meant a two-week delay; and Jig did not want to be in New York when *The Hairy Ape* opened eight days later. Because the ship was small, they were able to become friends with the ship's captain and at least two of their fellow passengers: Miss Eldridge, an archeologist, who was on her way to work on a dig at Calliphon, and William Rapp, who, like Jig, was a lover of Greek culture and was working on some writing projects in Athens and Istanbul. Susan loved the crossing, despite the wind and snow that followed the boat during the first weeks en route, and she spent much of her time on deck, talking with Eldridge and Rapp. Jig was usually holed up studying his massive Liddell and Scott Greek dictionary, which he had found on Fourth Avenue in New York two days before they sailed, and which he carried under his arm as he moved around the boat and later put in a place of honor in his room in Delphi.

When he was seven Jig had built the city of Troy on a beach in Nantucket; at sixteen, in Iowa City, he had written, "In Greece one's eyes can still be glad"; from Harvard, he had sent a letter home explaining that "Greece is becoming for me, as for so many others, as a lost Fatherland"; and as a college professor at the University of Iowa, he entered in his diary: "Why not be a Greek Thoreau?" He planned then to "go up Parnassos and live with the shepherds," but his father's financial setbacks had made that impossible. In recent years, the dream had grown, if anything, more intense. *The Athenian Women* arose from this longing. Now the time had finally come, and he was impatient to get there. For him the trip was the fulfillment of a lifelong dream; it also seemed a presentiment of imminent death or at least of fragile mortality, a feeling that had plagued him from his youth and had accelerated prior to the journey. Just after leaving New York, he scribbled, "Beat against me, East Wind, / Wane, Moon; / Do you think I do not know / I have to die?" His sense of failure over the Provincetown experiment traveled with him and exacerbated the sense of death, so too his feeling that somehow his talents had once again been misdirected and come to nothing. He was finally setting off to Greece, not as a young man filled with hope, but rather as a forty-eight-year-old man, who bore hurts and a great sense of defeat.

What going to Greece meant to Susan is more difficult to determine. "It is so exciting to see these things of which we have always heard, and particularly for George, who has always cared so much about them," she wrote to her mother the day they arrived.[2] "Particularly for George," would become the sub-theme of her letters to family and friends and bracket her descriptions of their life in Greece, so beautifully detailed in the last third of *The Road to the Temple*. The dream had been his not hers, but once there she shared in the splendor of the country and was usually drawn—as was her wont—to the beauty of the forms she discovered, rather than to the lore of ancient myths or historical events. "The Parthenon!" is the name she gives to the first of seventeen chapters in *Road* set in Greece. In it she describes Jig's euphoria as he actually climbed the steps of the Acropolis, like "one who at last comes home," and looked out through the columns of the ancient temple, not at modern Athens that lay below him but at the Greece of his imagination, fed by glimpses of Salamis where Aeschylus had walked and the Persian fleet had been defeated. Writing of herself in the third-person, Susan notes, "She who followed saw him reach over and pat one of the marbles as we pat what we love and are at home with," omitting her own responses, so as not to divert attention from the central figure in the scene she is creating, a technique that marks the book.

However, Jig's euphoria soon gave way to intoxication of another kind. Nowhere else in the book, or in private correspondence, does she so candidly address his drinking, which had progressed over the years from private bouts in Davenport, to elegiac group drinking in Provincetown and New York, and finally to almost daily inebriation during their last year in Greece. In a detailed anecdote, she describes how he spent one of their first afternoons in Athens drinking with a cab driver he had met, riding up on the top of the *amaxa*, or open carriage, with his new-found friend, while expatiating on the wonders of ancient Greece and the beauties of the Greek language still alive on the tongues of modern Greeks. Tired of remaining alone at the hotel waiting for his return, Susan went out, discovered the pair, and reluctantly got into the swerving cab. Jig planned to drink a final bottle of wine on the Acropolis, but constant stops at Roman ruins, which "should be torn down" since they marred Greek structures, took time. When they arrived, the gates to the ancient temple were closed, and no cajoling would prompt the gatekeeper to reopen them. At nightfall, reluctantly and unsteadily, he parted from the driver and allowed Susan to lead him back to the Hôtel Hermes. But once safely in their room, he insisted that he would sleep that night on the Acropolis and bolted, leaving her to spend a sleepless night alone. When he finally returned at 5:00 a.m., he related his adventures. Having fallen asleep on the grass in front of the National Library, he woke to discover that he had been robbed and sought the help of three passing men, who returned with him to the scene and found that his coat, used for a pillow, still held his wallet and valuables. "They came here to the hotel for coffee with me. I wanted them to come up and meet you, but they thought it was late," he explained. "Now you see, Susan, how easy it is to make friends in Athens." She ends the story by writing that the next day was one of their all-too-familiar "Hang-over days," which "have a subtle, fragile, sensitive quality. Satisfied by a violent encounter with life, one has a rarefied sense of being something nearer pure spirit. They are isolated days, no use trying to go on with things."

That she includes this story and other tales of long vigils alone, while Jig drank ouzo and retsina with new-found Greek friends, indicates something of the strain his drinking caused their relationship, particularly during the Greek period. Although she uses the pronoun *one*, the "violent encounters with life" in Greece were invariably alcoholic and his not hers. Whereas in America she could turn to friends and to work at such times, in Greece she didn't have the first to sustain her and found it more difficult than she expected to undertake the second. In general, making new friends was harder for her than for Jig, given her private, more reserved temperament; and now the instability of their lives and lack of needed privacy made it difficult for her to write. Yet, in keeping with the tenor of the biography, which is a paean to her husband, Susan adds a postscript to the description of the wild taxi ride: "I wonder if more eloquent words have been uttered for Greece than were spoken by this American to his drunken driver as we wound round the Acropolis." She also concludes the section with a comment that Upton Sinclair, a vehement anti-drinker and supporter of Prohibition, would call the greatest "piece of nonsense [to come] from the pen of a modern emancipated woman":[3] "A woman who has never lived with a man who sometimes 'drinks to excess' has missed one of the satisfactions that is like a gift—taking care of the man she loves when he has this sweetness as of a newborn soul." In Greece, she would often have this "satisfaction."

Even with his enthusiasm for the Acropolis, Athens proved to be a disappointment for Jig. It was too European. Susan was more tolerant of the city. To Neith and Hutch, then living in Florence—whom she tried to convince to visit—she wrote, "I wouldn't call any city that has the Acropolis, and the mountains around Attica, and that magical light from housetops at evening, second rate."[4] In order for Jig to discover some remnants of the classical world still preserved in present-day Greece, they left Athens after a month and made their way to Delphi.

"If you look hard at the left hand mountain, you see a town half way up. That is our Delphi,"[5] Susan wrote to her mother on a picture postcard in May, when they arrived in the place known in ancient times as the *omphalos*—the navel of the world—a sacred city to which rulers from as far away as Rome, North Africa, and Asia Minor had traveled in order to receive the messages of the oracle. In the summer of 1922 it was a village both new and old. Twenty-nine years earlier the inhabitants, living over the ancient ruins, were asked to leave and reestablish their community a few kilometers away, around the bend of the mountain, so that French archaeologists could excavate and reassemble the site. However, the villagers still returned to the ruins to tend the gardens they had planted there and to let their goats graze amid the toppled stones and drink at the sacred spring. The ancient city had not yet been ceded to the past; it still remained part of the ongoing life of the community.

Although devotees have long since vanished, Delphi still retains the majesty and spectacular beauty of the past. It is situated on a narrow ridge of a steep cliff jutting out precariously over a valley 700 meters below, which is filled with olive trees, thick as a carpet spreading down to the Bay of Corinth and the small seaport of Itea. Just visible on clear days are the mountains of the Peloponnesus beyond, while directly across from this narrow valley and seemingly enveloping Delphi on three sides are gray/green crags and outcroppings of mountains that lead to towering Mount Parnassus, 2,500 meters above the town. Although present-day Athens bears the scars of industrialization and the roads leading away from it are pock-marked with factories, making it almost impossible for a modern traveler to imagine its heroic past, Delphi, even today, preserves its unspoiled mystery and beauty. As Susan noted, the old Greeks certainly knew how to choose a place for their oracle to speak. "See Delphi before you die!" she wrote to Edna. "The valley and the mountains make such a stage set for the speaking of god that if he said nothing it would be bad art."[6]

They arrived by sea, sailing on a small steamer from Piraeus to Itea, and toward evening made their way up the zigzag sheep path that hugs the mountain, until they came upon Delphi bathed in moonlight. Immediately walking around the bend of the road and entering the ancient city, they came to the Temple of Apollo "eloquent in ruin." When she describes

Delphi, Susan often uses words related to form and how it speaks across time, a reminder to those who follow of the strength of the ancestors from which they spring. For her, the Temple of Apollo was "As if the gods had ordained form for the best man could dream"; the shepherd leads his flock home at night in front of the temple, and this too "has its form, its truth unto itself"; a mountain becomes "only the form on which falls the light from distant worlds"; and the view from her balcony, "on a scale for gods—exciting and satisfying in form, a breathtaking plunge and lift of the eye—a wideness to which you want to open your arms." To Edna she summarizes these feelings: "Form has its ultimate triumph here, and it is as if the light were grateful and does what light has never done before."[7] The words are similar to those Claire expressed in her unfulfilled quest in *The Verge*, when she described Breath of Life. In her ability to discover in Delphi the form that eluded her protagonist, it is possible to say that Susan, as well as Jig, found a home in Greece.

Their first address was the Pythian Apollo, the only hotel then in town, which still stands today, though abandoned, at the entrance to the new city. Jig was enchanted with the grandeur of the area and the simplicity of the daily life of the inhabitants; however, again he found the tourist experience intolerable. On their first morning, when the well-meaning waiter addressed him in English and served him an egg in a cup embossed with a picture of the Eiffel Tower, Jig exploded at him, explaining that he had not come all this way to have people speak to him in the broken English they might have acquired during a trip to the United States or eat his eggs from French crockery. Then for what? asked the waiter, Athanasius Tsakalos, who himself had only returned to Delphi from Manchester, New Hampshire, the year before, after several years abroad. Jig explained, "I wanted to walk where their feet walked and see what their eyes saw. . . . But I wanted more than that. I wanted you. I love the Greek words so much that I wanted for my friends men who have never spoken any other." Through Athanasius, whom they would affectionately call Thanasie, Susan and Jig were able to have the experience Jig desired: not as American tourists observing Greek culture, but as a couple choosing to live among the local townspeople and shepherds, eating what they ate, living in accommodations similar to what their houses contained, sharing with them the rhythms of their daily lives. It was Thanasie who introduced them to the village, quit his job at the hotel, and took up the task of overseeing their household. He found them living accommodations in a house at number 29 Paul Frederika Street, the main street of Delphi, on a lot sloping so precariously that the house, which opened onto the street, angled down two stories in the back to gardens sloping even further. Susan's room faced the street; Jig's room, the larger, was behind and had a small balcony, affording them a magnificent view of the valley of olive groves, the imposing, rounded mountain directly across, and, slightly to the right, and far below, Itea and the Corinthian Bay. The adjoining kitchen, dining area, and second balcony were entered from the street by a separate door, a hallway dividing this section from the other rooms. Today the space they occupied is one room, taken up by a gift shop, in the window of which are modern reproductions of Greek and Roman heroes; but it is possible to still see the remains of the wall separating the rooms, the balcony is the original, and the view is still spectacular. For Susan, the best part of the house was this balcony. In her first letter to her mother after settling in Delphi, she describes her pleasure sitting there: "There are difficulties about living here, but whenever they seem a little too much, I go out on my balcony and realize that what I have there is worth all the inconveniences and little hardships."[8]

Along with such grandeur, she also took pleasure in "the loveliness of little intimate things, how clarity can be so subtle." For example, next to the house was a steep sheep path leading down to the valley in one direction and up to the slopes of Parnassus in the other. Each morning and evening the flocks moved under their windows. In order for each shepherd to identify his own, he would attach bells of different tones and sizes to the necks of the sheep and goats. Susan came to love the sounds and to recognize their owners from the music. "Hardly any other music is so deeply real as that of this flock of sheep. You can't believe your ears. It is too beautiful to be true."[9] In letters to family and friends, and in her essay on Parnassus, she repeatedly mentions this special sound.

Their rooms were simple: bare floors, wooden tables and chairs, and an oil lamp, yet with the advantage of beds, something others in Delphi did not necessarily have. Breakfasts Thanasie would arrange for them, and their other meals they took directly across the street in the local wine shop, which also served as a restaurant/bakery and was the center of the social life of the village. It was owned by Andreas Korylss, whom Jig said reminded him of Aristophanes, because of his natural humor. Shepherds and villagers would sit there late into the night drinking Andreas's home-made wine from huge wooden caskets, sharing stories, singing, and, if enough had been drunk, dancing in a ring. Jig quickly joined the group that also included Elias Scarmouches, who kept his large flocks on Parnassus, but who often spent evenings at the wine shop, telling stories of life on the mountain. For Jig, it was the life he had sought: friends, wine, an audience, and the modern Greek language, which he rapidly acquired. By his second year in Delphi, he even began dressing in the traditional Greek shepherd costume, which suited him very well. Scarmouches personally took him to neighboring Amfissa to make sure he was fitted properly and not cheated. The dress, or *rouka*, consisted of small black skullcap, white wool leggings, made from the sheep of Parnassus, pointed shoes ending in big red pompoms, embroidered gray tunic fitted to the waist, and short skirt (*funestella*). Dressed in it, holding the long curved staff, which a peasant had given him because Jig had said it was the most beautiful he'd seen, and with his hair and beard now long and white, he looked like an idealized image of a Greek.

Susan, who spoke virtually no Greek, had a harder time making contacts. Only near the end of her time in Delphi did she interact with other women; and since it was a male-dominated society, she had little access to men as friends, as she did in Provincetown. Jig was Kyrios Kouk (Mr. Cook), she was the Kyria (his wife). Elias Tsakalos, the son of Thanasie, who was nine years old at the time, remembers Susan walking by herself, while Jig sat, drank, and conversed in the wine shop. "She was always reading, sometimes crying, and usually very sad."[10] What Susan enjoyed most was wandering around the ancient city. At the time, the restoration had not progressed far; the towering columns of the Temple of Apollo were still in pieces on the ground. No fences had been raised to separate the sacred way from the adjoining landscape, so townspeople and animals wandered freely through the scattered statuary, treasury buildings, ancient theatre, and stadium. One favorite destination for her daily walk was the Castalian spring on the far side of the ruins. In ancient times, when suppliants approached Delphi, they would stop there to wash and purify themselves before consulting the oracle. The spring was still an active center, and Susan loved the beauty and utility of the spot. In the evenings she and Jig went there to eat their dinner, fill their water jug for the night, and read until the light faded. They sat on the large flat rock under the spreading plane tree facing the spring, the two massive "shining rocks" from which it spilled towering just above them. The second place she loved to visit was the ancient theatre, which she describes to Edna. "To sit there alone, waiting for the play which will not begin, and thinking of the plays that are over, is more drama than one usually gets in theatre. I love it for the way it lies there alone, so undisturbed by its oblivion."[11] In the letter she encloses a tuft of gray herb that grew there. These words might indicate that her thoughts were of her own loss of a theatre, but Susan denies this mood in a letter to her mother at the end of her first month in Delphi: "What George wanted was to stay over here a year, and it looks now as if we would be here next winter. I am glad for him, and he needs an entire change from the things he has been doing in the last seven years and in many ways I am glad for myself too; the theatre has always made it hard for me to write, and now I will have a better chance for my own writing."[12]

No play emerged, but she used her Delphi impressions in a short story, essay, novel, and a rough draft of a poem, whose setting is the ancient city. In the poem, entitled "Stones That Once Were Temple," she presents her particular sense of the power of the ruins, which act as a conduit, uniting her with those who first walked amid their majesty. "Perhaps a hand that lay where mine lies now—it too forgot that it was resting there / Loving the living moments of flowers in grass and clouds on sea; / And because that hand was very still and was forgotten, And mine still and was forgotten, / I live again in what had lived then, and what lived then / moves now in me." Susan knew her Whitman.

In early June, when the village became too hot, those who could get away packed their food and household provisions on donkeys and headed up Parnassus to spend the summer months in Kalania, situated near the top of the mountain, a wide valley with three cold springs, surrounded by towering spruce trees. The route went up a winding mule trail, through lower mountain parks and thick forests, until—after a three-hour climb— it opened upon Kalania. "Ah Kalania, Kalania," was the cry Susan heard, almost like a mantra, as people breathed the special scent of the place. When I was taken there by Elias Tsakalos, the eighty-four-year-old son of Thanasie, who happened to be visiting Delphi on one of his infrequent trips from New Hampshire at precisely the time I was there researching this book, he, too, uttered those exact words, as did Elias Loukas, the grandson of Andreas Korylss, who accompanied us. Little had changed. Thanks to Mr. Tsakalos, I was able to see exactly where Susan and Jig had camped. Sitting on the stone bench that Jig had built seventy-five years earlier, I read them sections of *The Road to the Temple* that described Kalania, while Mr. Tsakalos pointed to the place where, for two summers, they had built their *kalyvi*—a small hut of spruce boughs—and where his father, Thanasie, had prepared their meals. The fireplace Jig constructed is still there, so too the rough stairs leading up the hill to his "studio"; and someone is still planting a small field of corn that Susan, ever a daughter of Iowa, mentions with some amusement. Jig had taken pains to make the spot beautiful by arranging large rocks for comfort. When Susan asked him why he bothered creating order and beauty for a temporary spot, which "we must go away and leave," he explained, "Men [sic] passing over the mountain will find it. Perhaps it will become a place to stop and rest. Perhaps it will remain." It has.

Even more than Delphi, it was Kalania—seemingly untouched by time and holding the origins of Greek culture in the lives of Parnassus shepherds—that most moved Susan. On its slopes, the natural, simple beauty allowed her to feel at one with Greece, as she had not yet been able to in Delphi, where the dirt, noise, and poverty oppressed her senses. "At Kalania" she writes in *Road*, "we knew, at least in part, the strange beauty of the days we lived." It is not surprising that the only writing she published during her stay in Greece was a short piece entitled "Dwellers on Parnassos," which appeared in the *New Republic* in January 1923. In it she describes their lives in Kalania and their friendship with Elias Scarmouches. The short story "The Faithless Shepherd," written in 1926, also uses the locale.

Two events marked their first summer on the mountain: Jig's taming of a wild bird and their brush with bandits. Whenever they would take their breakfast on the rock table, they noticed that a small robin, or *kombojanne*, would watch them. Placing crumbs and water on an adjacent rock, Jig patiently coaxed the bird down from its perch over a period of time and finally got it to take its breakfast inches away from them, while they ate. Soon the valley was filled with the story of how Kyrios Kouk could talk to and tame birds. For him, the bird came to represent a victory in communication: "I love him more than anything in Greece," he told Susan, as they got ready to leave in the fall. The only time Elias Tsakalos remembered seeing Susan angry is when he aimed his slingshot at birds. "She thought I might be shooting at Jig's bird by mistake."

The bandits, or *lystes*, were not so easily domesticated. Parnassus had been their haunt; there they lived, a law unto themselves, demanding money and goods from the locals, who had come to accept their threats as natural. "Perhaps they like this idea of a place beyond the law, to which one may go if there is need," Susan, typically broadminded, wrote. What she and Jig did not know was that Thanasie had been threatened by them and asked to turn over the rich Americans for ransom. He refused and was beaten. One evening at their camp, during a visit from Miss Eldridge and their Athens friend Leandros Palamas, the son of the Greek national poet Kostas Palamas, they were roused by a shot. Demetrius Komblss, the richest shepherd on Parnassus, had been shot by the *lystes*, who wanted ransom and revenge for past grievances with his family. He lay injured on the other side of the valley, but people in Kalania and doctors in Delphi were afraid to come to his aid for fear of retribution from the *lystes*. Jig immediately volunteered to lead his friends to assist, and the four walked through the night until they came to the hut, or *strunga*, where Komblss was. Chasing off fierce dogs that guarded it, they entered, found the man severely injured, bandaged his wounds, and stayed with him through the night until they could carry him down to Delphi in a litter, which Jig fashioned. While there, they heard stories of the intricate family feuds that led to the attack and the tales of bandit raids and responses, stories Susan relates in detail in *Road*. She and Jig loved to collect anecdotes about the *lystes*, which for them became part of the present lore of Delphi. Jig's response to Komblss's stories was to tell of legends from his own country and of the way horse thieves in Iowa were hunted by posses. He suggested forming one, but no one volunteered. Until they returned to Delphi at end of the summer, Susan and Jig would be nervous when they heard a twig snap outside their tent. Even the gun Jig always carried, which Susan eventually gave to young Elias Tsakalos, did not make them completely quiet.

Although Kalania and Delphi were far removed from the centers of Greece, and life went on there virtually undisturbed, tremendous upheavals were occurring in the region. In 1922 the historic enmity between Greece and Turkey boiled up once more, and with the defeat of Greek forces in Asia Minor, more than one million Greeks, who had lived outside the country for several generations, were repatriated. After coming down from Kalania in September, Susan and Jig traveled to Salonika and witnessed the pathos of dislocation. In "Dwellers on Parnassos" she writes movingly of this human misery: "I was on the dock the night the *Megale Hellas* brought nine thousand of them home to Greece. And when I saw them I knew them for the same people I had known in the olive groves watered by the Castalian spring; and knowing their way of life, I know that this exodus is their destruction."[13] To her mother she also described the desolation she saw when she tried to assist the refugees: "It was the saddest thing I ever saw in my life, and I shall never forget it." However, as in all her weekly letters home, she tempered the harshness of her experiences with a positive note, as she was wont to do with her family: "While this is harrowing to see, as long as there are such things in the world I don't know why I shouldn't see some of them. I am going to try and write something that might be of service in getting relief here."[14]

They had thought to spend the winter in Athens, away from the snows and cold of Delphi, but housing was almost impossible to find due to the numbers seeking shelter. Living arrangements for Susan became moot, when, in early October, after they had returned temporarily to Delphi, she received a letter from her mother informing her that her father had died on September 27 in Davenport. She answered immediately: "How terribly I feel about what you have all gone through, and that I should not have been with you. No one could have been better to another than you were to father, all those years he needed to be cared for."[15] There was little she could do for her mother or her brothers Ray, then living in St. Louis with Flossie, or Frank, who had moved back to Davenport with Hazel to be near home. Nevertheless, she decided to return to the States.

Throughout her first months in Greece, Susan's letters to family and friends had referred to trips she and Jig hoped to take: to Constantinople with Philip Moeller, to Egypt with William Rapp, a visit to the Hapgoods in Florence, the L'Engles in the South of France, Lucy Huffaker and Eddie Goodman in Paris. None had materialized, usually because of money. She also mentioned possible visits that these friends and others, including Agnes and Eugene O'Neill and Margaret and Wilbur Daniel Steele, might make to Greece. None came. She had already lived in Greece for six months; and while it had been exciting, it had also been difficult, physically and mentally. It is not surprising, therefore, that she took the occasion of her father's death to return home temporarily. By planning to stay for only a few months, she was not foreclosing on Jig's dream of Greece; yet she could get a respite from the isolation she must have experienced. She could also see firsthand the situation at the Provincetown Players and gain some sense of what might await them on their eventual return. She, therefore, wrote her mother that she would be returning: "I couldn't feel satisfied to stay here, feeling that I could perhaps help you if I were home." "Besides," she added, "I just love crossing the Atlantic! So the trip is no hardship for me."[16]

After several delays, she finally managed to book passage on an English boat, the *Constantinople*, which sailed from Piraeus around the Peloponnesus and stopped at Patras, where she embarked. Jig accompanied her that far, and on the way they visited Sparta and the ruins of Olympia and Mycenae. The Atlantic crossing was uneventful, and Susan stayed a few days in New York with Lucy and Edward Goodman, whom

Lucy had married, before heading to Davenport, where she spent several weeks with her mother and brothers. On her return East she went to Provincetown to check on her properties on the Cape and update John Francis about re-renting them for the coming year. From there she returned to New York and visited the theatre she had left almost one year earlier. When she arrived, none of the former Players were around. "I was down there just once," she reports in *Road*. "I looked at the stage where I had so many times found Jig working. I could not see him working there again. I felt he had indeed left it, was through with it, had gone far away." She carefully refrains from saying anything about her own future there.

Jig's separation from Susan was extremely difficult for him. Depressed before she left, he became even more so now that she was once more visiting the place he considered his great failure. His moods sometimes resembled those he experienced in the years immediately after the dissolution of his first marriage, when, alone in Buffalo, he skirted madness and questioned his life and purpose. A young Greek friend, Leandros Palamas, had finally found him a small cottage for the winter, in a new suburb of Athens, but Jig hated the place, since it had no connection to classical Greece and he could not even see the Parthenon from its windows. To make matters worse, he was having money problems. He had given a $700 check from his family bank in Davenport to a money changer who had absconded with the cash, and he was forced to write to his brother Ruel to stop payment and reimburse him. The negotiations took most of the winter, and details took up part of each letter to Susan. For Jig, the worst of it was that he had trusted the man. In Athens he was struggling to maintain the Greek romance, but it wasn't easy. Greek food, bureaucracy, and city life took an ever-increasing toll on his nerves. He was also drinking heavily; and his daily letters to Susan, some left unfinished and unmailed, are long, incoherent scrawls, filled with his love and need for her, regrets over lost opportunities with his family and the Players, his wasted talent, and talk of murder and death. In one he describes a dream in which he visualizes her copulating with other men. "It's not nice of you—when I want you so much. You do the things I have always wanted you to want to do with me—and you explain that this is what you have always wanted and I not. What kind of inside out transference is this dreaming?"[17]

His need for her had grown more acute because of their separation: "I had no idea what a lost soul I would be without you. It is ignoble." He marks her *Iliad* with the places they have visited together: "Now when I read those stories of our places—in three thousand years' old writing— well, what I think is 'that is *ours*'—Susan's and mine." He continues: "If I can't show them to you they are not very beautiful. They are beauty in vain. And that's why we need god so. As spectator of the beauty we discover in this mainly ugly world. And I, Jig, have weakly become dependent upon Susan as spectator (there being no God) of the world." He is particularly haunted by his failure to develop any relationship with his children and his fears for their safety. In one letter he asks in passing, "You couldn't bring Harl and Nilla with you, could you?"[18] Death is repeatedly on his mind: his own, Susan's, his children's and the eventual death of Europe. "I love you, knowing how dead we'll be for how long, and what a moment only there is left." The one bright spot was his Sunday walking tours with a group of students from the University of Athens. They provided a ready audience, which he so needed, and a promise of a future. With them he began to talk about a new theatre. "The old theatre of Dionysus in Athens might have a modest little Greek Provincetown Players activity in it," he wrote to Bill Rapp. "If there is anything here that wants to move I know how to give Greece a little theatre movement—or rather an art-theatre movement. What one did in the existing theatre of Dionysus could not be 'little.'"[19]

While he was alone in Athens, nearing fifty, age became a disturbing preoccupation. His greatest fear was losing his youthful vitality: "If I were cooped up with old people only I too would become old, a thing I have always considered impossible." When Susan wrote that she had been able to arrange with Mollie to bring Nilla with her and perhaps later to bring Harl, Jig was at first enthusiastic; but he could not help sharing his mixed feelings about being thrust again into the role of a father: "I am astonished at the different world which takes form from the fact of being responsible for a daughter. It instantly tends to make me the guardian of youth for its good. I won't! The last of me yet is my youth."[20] In Nilla's autobiography, *My Road to India*, she bitterly recalls her father's resentment of her youth, since it reflected on his own ageing; and in a letter to Hutch Hapgood describing her time in Greece, she writes, "There was considerable antagonism between us, as far as I can see, because I was young. The few months we lived together he was rarely if ever sober—hang over days he would show resentment of youth in general, and what particularly annoyed him was the budding of womanhood in me."[21]

Much of the unsettledness in Nilla's own life she attributed to the difficult years following Jig's divorce from Mollie. By the time she was twelve, she had crossed the continent ten times, "shipped back and forth between a father and a stepmother in Provincetown and a mother in California, or half way across to conservative relatives between." She soon discovered that "what was correct in Iowa was taboo in Provincetown. What was correct in Provincetown got me expelled from school in Chicago."[22] While her Iowa relatives would allow her to go to dances and parties, her bohemian family gave her curfews and scolded when she broke them. "The more radical the parent in public, the more reactionary in the privacy of the home," she complained.[23] Susan was the woman who had taken her father away from Mollie, and, therefore, try as she might, Nilla could never totally overcome her resentment. Although at times they seemed to arrive at an amicable relationship, it was often tinged with anger and guilt. The title of Nilla's autobiography tellingly echoes Susan's biography of Jig, but Nilla makes clear that the two stories differ: "Greece was my father's dream . . . Greece was no dream of mine."

For Jig, his failure as a father was connected in his mind with his general failure to accomplish any of the things he felt his talents had promised. In a poem written in New York in 1921, entitled "Nilla Dear," he expresses these feeling of frustration, and his desire that she might somehow learn from the near misses of her family:

> I wish you were here to pick up some golden
> fragments
> from the breakage of my life.
> Bommie [Ma-Mie] failed,
> But she dared the impossible.
> I have more richly failed.
> You dance like a person with courage.
> Don't let them break your will—which is your
> purity.

Although he attempts to focus on Nilla, Jig cannot help returning again and again to his own defeats: "If you could see how by a hair's breadth / I miss / Being a transforming force / In the theatre of our unrealized nation." He signs the poem "(with the outgrown kid-name, nice in its time) Papa Jig."[24] It was to achieve some rapprochement with Nilla and to share with her the great adventure of Greece that he had asked Susan to bring her. The two sailed from New York on the *Providence* on March 21, 1923. During the trip, Susan got a taste of what it meant to be *in loco parentis*. Nilla, wearing lipstick and dangling earrings looked—if not acted—much older than her fourteen years and drew the attention of an Italian royal commissioner and a Spanish diplomat, both of whom kept attempting to spirit the girl into the dark corners of the ship.

A month before their arrival, Jig had written to Hutch, passing on Susan's suggestion that they travel to Florence and put Nilla in a school with Miriam, "unless I could persuade you to bring your family to this spiritually deeper land."[25] Like other proposed trips, however, this one did not materialize. It does indicate that Susan was reluctant to stay alone with Jig and Nilla in Delphi for one more year. Instead of Florence, Jig met the boat in Palermo, and they went by land to Brindisi from which they sailed to Athens, staying only long enough to rest, before traveling to Xylokastro, a seaside town near Corinth. There they spent the month of May with close friends Eva Palmer, daughter of Courtland Palmer, of the influential Chicago Palmer family; her husband Angelos Sikelianos, later to be the national poet of Greece; his sister Penelope; and her husband Raymond Duncan, brother of Isadora Duncan. During this May idyll of friends and lovers of Greece, Nilla spent most of her time with fourteen-year-old Glaucos, son of Eva and Angelos, while the grownups swam, read, drank, and talked. It was a Greek version of earlier Provincetown days, spent dreaming and planning for a modern theatre that would have the spirit of the ancient, "beloved community." Although Nilla relates the details of the stay, Susan, for some reason, fails to mention it in *Road* nor in any of her other writing. Perhaps the omission is deliberate: of the group, only she was not a Greek devotee. During the stay, Nilla bristled at what she perceived to be her stepmother's overzealous chaperoning, particularly when Susan found the young people alone on the beach with Glaucos's hand on Nilla shoulder. "It seemed to me very peculiar," Nilla writes in her autobiography, "as the heroines of the books she wrote were always meeting people in the woods, even when they were married to someone else." She reports Susan's rejoinder: "'Love excuses everything,' she said when I mentioned that. 'But you are not in love with Glaucos, and so there is no excuse.'"[26]

Watching over an extremely precocious fourteen-year-old who told everybody she was eighteen was difficult for Susan, but she soon found Nilla a companion able to make her feel less lonely. "I often find myself talking to her as if she were much older," she wrote Mrs. Glaspell.[27] Susan particularly appreciated Nilla's studiousness, when it came to languages. A natural linguist like her father, Nilla would sit long hours with him pouring over the Liddell and Scott, and she was soon able to converse in the modern Greek of Delphi. Susan herself never formally studied Greek; her acquisition of daily words came by happenstance not design. "I would learn such words as I liked—the word for lamb, the sea, the shepherd, the trees, the Temple, the spring, the vineyard," adding to her list those words that came naturally from the life of the village. Her favorite sources of Greek were the inscriptions carved in stone in the ancient temple. She loved to stand before them tracing with her hand the letters that seemed to her to hold "the secrets of long ago." In *Road* she tells of one occasion in which she recopied an inscription she found, and she and Jig puzzled over its meaning, Jig deciding after five days of sleuthing that it actually contained not praise to some long forgotten hero's virtue but "a sensational accusation of unchastity." Susan transferred her fascination with ancient inscriptions to her protagonist Epimonondes Paraskeva, a young shepherd boy in her short story "The Faithless Shepherd."

Besides Nilla, the household now included a servant, Theodora, whom they hired in Xylokastro, on their way back to Delphi. She was a wild and exotic-looking woman, who had been repatriated from Smyrna, arriving without family or possessions and in immediate need of shelter and work. Other young women in the town had applied for the job, but they seemed docile, too shy to speak. "I am the one you should take," Theodora had said; "I am a great traveler."[28] Her audacity immediately impressed Jig, who was not deterred when she said that the only thing she knew how to cook was soup. Her stories of the murder of her brothers, which she witnessed, made Susan her immediate champion. Susan could imagine that in the dead of night Theodora might "run round and round the house with a torch, singing weird songs, and dancing madly."[29] Although she did not quite live up to this image, the young woman would sing for them and tell them stories as she danced around the fire—sometimes through it—in Kalania. Finally, before the summer was over, she left the mountains and disappeared, saying only that "the cosmos was not there."

After spending the month of May with the Sikelianos and Duncan families at Xylokastro, it was time to return to Delphi. Susan opted to make her way there by land via Athens; Jig, however, insisted that it was more practical to cross the Corinthian Bay to Itea, which was only eighteen miles away, rather than travel such a circuitous way to Delphi. Besides, one night at a local taverna, over a great deal of ouzo, "the Captain of the Drunkards" had promised to ferry them, and a promise made over ouzo could not be broken. Susan makes no mention of the dispute in *Road*, but Nilla describes it in detail. Susan, after purchasing goods for the family, arrived in Delphi and then waited for the others to join her. It took the captain four days to remember his passengers; and then, after many mishaps and much ouzo, when he finally got the group halfway across the bay, he passed out, and the boat drifted back to Xylokastro. Ten days later Jig, Nilla, and Theodora arrived by land in Delphi to meet a frantic Susan.

Almost immediately it was time to go up Mount Parnassus, since the days had already grown warm. Because of their experiences with the *lystes* the past summer, they decided to try the village of Agorgiani on the far side of the mountain, a six-hour ride by mule. Both Susan and Nilla describe the summer but choose very different details. Nilla's account focuses exclusively on her own budding sexuality and amorous suitors; Susan's describes their disappointment with the small village, the poorly equipped house they had rented, the bad weather, and scant food. Her mood was not helped by a fall from a mule en route that incapacitated her for three weeks with a dislocated arm and a bruised knee. The one bright spot was their adoption of a mongrel puppy who made his home under their balcony and whom they rescued from the landlord who abused him. They called him Puppy, Theodora adding the Greek article, *tò*. "He's not Nezer," Jig remarked, "but he likes to learn things." Although Jig, who was never happier than when he could teach, found diversion in training TòPuppy, he, too, was not as exuberant this summer as last. Susan had returned to Greece to find that he had lost considerable weight and was not well, but her entreaties that he go to a doctor went unheeded. More and more he talked of death. One day he told a group of drinking companions that, "I have come to Parnassos to die," and challenged them to join him in a death pact since, "it was hard to die alone." All politely refused. The story, which Susan relates in a humorous fashion, makes a good anecdote in *Road* and was later repeated in obituaries published on Cook's death, but it underscores the growing darkness that seemed to pervade his moods, even on his beloved Mount Parnassus. In an attempt to regain something of the harmony and joy of the previous summer, they decided in July to risk returning to Kalania, taking TòPuppy with them, since he had now become a permanent part of the family. Just before they left, Susan, who had quickly bonded with the funny-looking mongrel, showed a rare display of anger when Demos, the landlord, demanded they leave "his" dog. "That evening," she writes, "Demos was saying Americans were bad people. Even the women would shake a fist in your face and threaten to kill—just for something you had said about a dog."

Would their bird still be there, they wondered on their first morning back in their camp in Kalania. They once more set out the crumbs and water that had drawn it; and to their delight and amazement, after accustoming itself to the presence of ToPuppy, the bird flew down when Jig whistled, each day drawing closer, until it would alight when Susan or Nilla whistled and would perch on the table inches away from them as they ate, wrote, or read. Despite Jig's loss of weight and swings of moods, Susan seemed even more content this summer in Kalania than the last. For her it was the place that held all that was beautiful and special about Greece, not a place of ancient lore as much as a place of ongoing beauty that fed the spirit. She captures this mood in "The Faithless Shepherd," in which she is less interested in presenting details of place than in the effect of place on the beholder, in this case an illiterate young boy who first experiences a beauty that "he had surprised" in Kalania, but who becomes disillusioned when he can not find others who share his wonder.[30] She may well have patterned her hapless shepherd on Demos Zineles, whose love of English touched Susan, unaware that his true interest in sitting long hours alone with Nilla was not grammar. (I was told this by his ninety-five-year-old widow who still remembered "wild" Nilla.)

During the summer, Jig continued to lose weight and to show signs of fatigue and depression, at times retreating to his *kalyvi* to write long poems, often related to ageing. One of the subjects troubling him was loss of potency. In one of her most candid passages in *Road*, Susan describes a sleepless, lonely Jig coming into her hut one evening and telling her, "I do not want to live beyond sex." She writes:

> I cannot tell how things were with him, without saying something of this. He was unhappy because it was not as it had been in the first years. "We who were those mad lovers . . ." Was not that one of the things we had to accept, I said. After years together, something goes, yet is it all loss? Does not something also come? He did not care for that way of looking at it, he said. He was the lover. In his loving was all of himself, and without it himself was impoverished. He had a rare gift for romantic, intense love. It created a world in which his spirit could be. More than once he said to me, "But we will lie alone so long in our graves."

She ends this section with one of her most personal comments about their relationship: "To succeed in love is the greatest beauty in life. Love is fulfillment, and the great ordeal. We have our failures. Yet I think he always knew I loved him."

Jig being Jig, could still rouse himself from despair when a new project or idea occurred to him. That summer it was building a wall to surround their encampment. He and Scarmouches held contests to see who could roll the largest Cyclopean stones down the mountain to add to the fortification. When Susan entreated him to stop and conserve his energy, he explained, "If each man shaped one little piece of the earth, how beautiful the world would become!" A second project that lit his imagination more fiercely was the inauguration of the Greek Provincetown Players, the people of the village acting in a pageant taken from the story of their own lives. "It could become another Oberammergau. There are good poets of modern Greece who would write plays for it," he informed Hutch.[31] The subject matter he fixed on for the first production was the evolution of life in Delphi, beginning thousands of years before classical Greece, when shepherds, antecedents of those still working in Kalania, tended their flocks and fought any attempts at encroachment. A second play, in what he envisioned as a trilogy, would be set in the Hellenic world, the stones of the earlier time now taking on mythic import as they became part of rites codified and expanded in classical Greece. Finally, Delphi of 1892 would emerge, when the old lay buried by the new and the clash once more was between the living community and its past.

Talk of future theatres led to talk of theatres that had failed, and Jig once more turned back to the Provincetown Players and his assumed defeat there, a subject that continued to plague him. In a letter to Ida Rauh, which was never mailed, he began, "It seems to me that you, more than any other friend or lover of me, believed in my prophetic gift, owing that I knew—in flashes—what must be."[32] Throughout their stay in Greece, the pain of failure permeated his life, never more so than in the summer of 1923, when the immediate anger over betrayals and regret over miscalculations gave rise to a more general, albeit deeper, sense of wasted opportunity and loss. One day, in utter frustration, he stopped writing and threw a piece of bread at his bird. When Susan intervened, warning him that he would chase the bird away, he exploded in what she writes was "the worst quarrel Jig and I ever had." Grabbing her, with hate in his eyes, he shouted that he was tired of living with her and Nilla and made his way out of the camp heading back to Delphi. She admits that "there was a moment when I was afraid" and that her immediate thought was to leave Jig and take Nilla to Paris with her. "One of those things you think you believe, but which doesn't sound true as you hear it." She reports that Jig returned chastened after two days, but she may have foreshortened and edited the event or encapsulated several such outbursts, since Hutch, in his autobiography, mentions that she wrote a despondent letter mentioning her desire to leave and telling of the difficult time she was having dealing with Jig's outbursts and Nilla's care. In his consistent fashion of translating all relationships to parallel his own, and in his distrust of independent, creative women, Hutch comments, "Susan's letter was written in great distress. It was a typical situation between the poetic and idealistic male, seeking an impossible realization, and the woman, understanding all things except that."[33] On the contrary, the pages of *Road* make clear that Susan knew "that" all too well—it was "that" which had always threatened to swamp both her and Jig and which had accelerated in Delphi, driven by his unshakable sense of failure and loss and by his continuous drinking.

They stayed on in Kalania well into October, long after all the villagers of Delphi had gone down the mountain. On his fiftieth birthday, October 7, 1923, Jig wrote "At Fifty I Ask God," written in a minor key "But now, humbler with the down-slope of my life, / When power is not with every day increasing but declining." Its first line succinctly captures his mood: "Sought for a life-time and still unfound!"[34] Before breaking camp, they had to decide what to do with their bird. Last summer, they left it; this year they sent to Delphi for a birdcage and coaxed it inside. At first reluctant, the bird finally accepted the confined state. However, one day in Delphi, soon after their return, Jig let it out and it flew away.

For Susan, life seemed easier and more familiar this second fall in Delphi. The *Kyria*, as well as the *Kyrios*, had been accepted. People stopped in, bringing gifts, and included them in village festivals, such as harvesting the grapes in the vineyard. "Life in Delphi is quiet, but has its rhythm," she wrote to Edna Kenton that fall.[35] Mundane activities held a beauty for her, and many of her observations of daily life are of those simple things that brought order and happiness. In Provincetown it was fishing; in Delphi, the women spinning and the sheep passing. Jig now threw himself into his plans for the Delphi Players. Around the tables at Andreas's wine shop, the plot of their play was unfolding, between rounds of wine. Again, as in his early days with the Provincetown Players, Jig spoke with ardor to a listening and accepting group, calling them to his own vision of what they could accomplish if they only had faith—in him and in themselves. He spoke to them about their past, "they bending forward to listen as in the Greek language he told them what Delphi had been. Nobody had ever tried to relate them to it before." However, when he tried to draw Susan into his plans, she held back. "You belong to the Delphic Players," Jig told her one night. "Indeed I do not," she replied, "more hastily than convincingly, for I felt something like destiny in this. 'I am through with groups.'" But Jig still persevered with the Delphi Players, Susan or no Susan. Despite his deteriorating health, the thought of a new theatre set him afire once more, and he threw himself into the preparations. One evening in late November, Susan and he hosted a party for the villagers, overseen by Elias Scarmouches, at the Castalian spring under the large plane trees. "Fiddler and piper were there, and we danced in the moonlight," Susan reports. "We looked up at those black-mouthed caves of Jig's play, the caves from which man came." Although it had not touched Delphi, much of Greece was becoming enveloped in a revolution, and the party had contravened martial law and was reported as a possible insurrection by the Athens newspapers. Jig avidly followed the details of the revolution and was particularly moved by a letter from mothers of those fighting on both sides, which called for an end to the bloodshed. In his response, "Letter to the Greek Nation," sent to an Athens newspaper, he recalled *Lysistrata*, that call of women to end war, and asked that Greece once more "Let our mothers save us!"

Although active in spurts, Jig showed signs of fatigue. He was also drinking more, sometimes sitting at the wine shop all evening and then inviting whomever remained back to his house for dinner. Her attempts to draw him home were sometimes met with a blank stare. So intent was he on where he was that he often forgot her existence. Drinking, talking, dancing to the music of local fiddlers and pipers during that long, beautiful autumn, he was in turn Apollo and Dionysus, the two mythic inhabitants of Delphi, the gods of poetry and of wine.

Jig was anxious to experience the Christmas holiday in Delphi. At the end of November, Nilla, who had made great strides in Greek, was scheduled to enter a school in Old Phaleron, near Athens; and Susan and Jig were to help her get settled there. But at the last minute, Jig changed his mind, and Susan went alone. While she was away, Jig was kept busy with guests, including Clarence Streit, a reporter for the *Philadelphia Public Ledger*, sent to do a story on the new Delphi Players, and a young Greek from Athens interested in giving up his job at the American Express Company in order to become business manager for the Players and the new Pythian games to be staged in the old stadium. In letters to Susan in Athens, Jig related the news with which the town was buzzing: the kidnapping of Alexos Komblss, the son of Demetrius, the shepherd whom they had bandaged the summer before. The villagers around were reluctant to search for him, causing an exasperated Jig to say that he would go himself. Thanasie dissuaded him. Jig was also full of other news. First that he has been asked to run for president of the Delphi commune in the elections scheduled for December 16. "If they accept my political platform more and better plays in Delphi," he would consider the offer. That would mean that they would have to remain five more years, but he tells her he has heard of a house for sale. He also has news of another venture: a partnership in a new restaurant/hotel, which Thanasie wished to open. And if these options for the future were not enough, he concludes by notifying her that he has also applied to become monk of the nearby Prophet Elijah Monastery. "Write or telegraph whether you wish to become co-proprietress of hotel and theatre in Delphi and mayoress of the village or prefer to be grass-widow of monk in the monastery of Prophet Elijah, you can't be both, so decide at once, for events march."[36] Susan publishes part of this letter in *Road*; she also includes a letter written at the same time, in a much more somber mood, focusing not on the future but on the past, recapitulating once again the defeats of a lifetime: "Why, with so much beautiful power, was I nothing? Say exactly in answer if you can. Because you know, best loved of my whole life, these are real questions, such as we would ask from beyond the grave."

When Susan returned some weeks later to Delphi, Bill Rapp, their young friend from the *Themistocles*, accompanied her. The trip was arduous because the Corinthian canal had collapsed, and they were forced to come over Parnassus by car in a blizzard. Rapp had brought his camera, and during the weeklong stay he took pictures of Susan and Jig holding TòPuppy and of Jig in his *rouka* standing in the theatre he loved so much. Susan would use these photographs in her first edition of *Road*. After his visit, she came down with grippe, and TòPuppy also took sick. Although she recovered after a week, the dog did not. A disease had hit several dogs in Delphi; some had already died from what was presumed to be distemper. Susan and Jig, remembering their grief over the death of Nezer, tried everything they could to revive the dog: taking turns to walk him, despite the inclement weather; keeping him warm; giving him special food. On New Year's Eve, TòPuppy could no longer move. Jig asked Susan to leave the house: "There's no Gene O'Neill to help us this time." With Thanasie he buried the dog under a large boulder in the yard. The next day, saying that he was more tired than he had ever been, Jig took to his bed; nothing seemed to rouse him. When neighbors came in carrying a small box that contained a bird that had flown in through their window, Susan got out the cage and it immediately flew within, assuming the familiar perch. Jig accepted it as natural that his bird had returned, sensing that he was ill. Local doctors diagnosed his sickness as grippe and gave him medicine, but he did not get better. Because the roads were blocked by a continuing snowstorm, there was little that Susan or Thanasie could do during the next week. Sometimes at night Jig was delirious, talking of ancient Greece or of the Provincetown Players. One day Susan read to him a notice in the paper that *The Emperor Jones* was to be performed in Prague, and he murmured, "Some honest work." Susan responded, "Oh, much honest work," but in the biography she follows with, "He had left that, and me."

The villagers were preparing for Greek Christmas celebrations; and when they heard of Kyrios Kouk's illness, they insisted that doors be kept open so that he could hear their music and preparations. A doctor from a nearby town arrived and agreed that it was grippe, but Jig seemed to deteriorate. One morning he could not drink water; he asked Susan to go to the Castalian spring to see if that special water would help. "It is the most beautiful thing I have ever known in my life," he told her when she returned with it. He had a bowel hemorrhage, red discoloration appeared under his nails, blotches on his skin, his voice changed, he could not swallow, and his body ached. When the roads finally cleared, Nilla arrived for Christmas vacation with a few of her American teachers. Two days later, Dr. Jesse Marden attached to the Near East Relief Agency in Athens was able to get through. When he saw Jig's condition, he immediately ordered that he be moved to Athens, but in the night his condition worsened, and it became apparent that Jig could not make the difficult ten-hour trip. For two days he lingered. When word went out that Kyrios Kouk was dying, shepherds from the entire region left their flocks and gathered at the house; Elias Scarmouches, with tears streaming down his face, sat at the foot of his bed and refused to leave even when Thanasie said Jig needed quiet. "Quiet? What does quiet matter now?" From his earliest youth, Jig had thought of and written about death, and Susan was plagued by the sense that when it was finally occurring he should be made aware of it. Toward the end, he did wake and whispered to her two words: "Milligan Place," where they had first lived in Greenwich Village and where they had written their first play together, *Suppressed Desires*. "Yes, where we used to live," she responded; to which he replied, "I don't know if we'll ever get back to New York." Susan's answered, "And if we don't perhaps we don't want to. Perhaps it is better here." To this Jig said simply, "Yes, perhaps better here." These were his last words.

A few weeks earlier, they had read together a new book she had purchased in Athens: *Ariel*, André Maurois's life of Shelley in French. Although she doesn't mention it in *Road*, the two epigrams that Maurois chose to demarcate the early and later sections of the poet's life reflected on Jig's life as well. The first is from Blake: "So I turned to the Garden of Love / That so many sweet flowers bore; / and I saw it was filled with graves"; the second from *The Tempest*:

ARIEL: Was't well done?
PROSPERO: Bravely, my diligence. Thou shalt be free.

Reading of the many losses suffered by the poet and Mary Godwin prompted Susan and Jig to turn to a discussion of their own lives, their becoming lovers and their years together. Susan writes in *Road*, "After people have lived together a long time, it may happen that it is not easy for them to talk to one another. Living has built something around them. They have come to take much for granted. This night Jig and I could talk. It was as if we were lovers who had been long separated, though it was of experiences shared we talked. We talked of what it was we had wanted from life; of greater success we might have had, born of a searching, an asking, we had shared. We saw one another, and with tenderness." Jig was tormented by the idea that if one of them were to die, how would the other continue. "'We've grown together—way down deep. We *are* one. How can one of us go and—That *other* one. *What is that other one going to do?*'" Weeks earlier Susan had finally gotten the courage to enter the old graveyard next to the ancient threshing floor, which she passed daily on her walks to the temple and theatre. What she saw there shocked her. It is the Greek custom to disinter bodies approximately seven years after burial to make room for new graves. For someone not familiar with the custom, the sight of a caretaker laying out and cleaning the bones in preparation for placement in a communal charnel is frightening. Jig, however, liked the practical attitude the Greeks have toward death. He told Susan that he wanted to be buried in the old graveyard, whose ancient walls adjoin the threshing floor and temple.

A little after midnight, on January 11, 1924, Jig Cook died. Doctor Marden had originally diagnosed the illness as septic, possibly typhus. His final diagnosis was that Jig had died of glanders, a rare disease in dogs that in even rarer cases can be transmitted to humans. He also indicated that had he been taken to a hospital in Athens earlier, he could not have been saved, since there was no cure.[37] Jig, who had so totally embraced the people of Delphi, was embraced by them in death. Susan and Nilla could just watch as townspeople took over, according him a funeral as if he were one of their own. They washed the body in wine, as the custom demanded, dressed him in his *rouka*, went through the deep snow to alert monks from the nearby monasteries who would officiate and carried the uncovered body to the local church, where Jig—"who had dwelt upon Parnassos considering in its pagan past" and who had long since abandoned his own childhood Christianity—was given the last rites of the Greek Orthodox church. "They could withhold from him nothing they would desire for themselves. It would have touched and amused him," Susan writes. He was placed to rest in the far uphill corner of the small cemetery against the back and side ancient walls, which separate it from the sacred city.

Jig's fame in Greece had not been confined to Delphi. On hearing of his death, the Writers' League of Athens petitioned the government, which agreed to have a stone from the Temple of Apollo be taken from the ancient city and placed as his headstone. "I think it is a quite unprecedented thing and it moves me very much that the Greeks should do this for Jig. He would like it," Susan wrote to Bill Rapp from Athens, after the funeral.[38] Two weeks after his death, a large commemorative ceremony took place at the YMCA in Athens, at which Leandros Palamas read a tribute to Jig as well as Greek translations from *The Spring*, and Susan presented some of the poems Jig had composed in Delphi. The picture Rapp took of Jig in his *rouka* at the ancient theatre was projected on a screen during the ceremony. Several Athens papers carried articles about the event and Jig's connections to Greece. Palamas took it upon himself to organize a George Cram Cook club to honor his friend, and sixteen members, following the Greek custom, visited the grave on Easter. He wrote to Rapp about the visit and about plans for reinstating the Delphi games and theatre performances to be held once a year on Easter Monday, an honor "always conferred on a great man in ancient times."[39] He suggested that *The Athenian Women*, which Jig had begun translating into Greek and which Palamas finished, should be the first play presented. Rapp himself visited Delphi and the grave one year later and arranged for the carving on the ancient stone that acts as a headstone and bears Cook's name, place, and dates of birth and death. Ironically, though Greek letters carved on such stones two thousand years ago are still completely legible, those on the headstone can barely be deciphered after less than a hundred years. More distinct is the engraving on a slab of marble, which covers the grave. It contains the last stanza from "At Fifty I ask God":

I hear the mountain stream
Pouring in beauty.
That rhythmic water
Does not need to be
More than itself,
But I,
Spirit,
Have no reason for living unless,
    somehow, for spirit
somewhere,
Life is immortal.[40]

Under it in larger letters is carved "George Cram Cook" and under that
the figure of a small bird. Directly behind the grave, on the huge stones
of the back wall of the cemetery, are two other plaques. An oblong one
on the left contains two stanzas from his poem "The Shining Rocks," the
second of which reads: "More deeply here / In the heart that is us all, /
The instinct of the hollow of the hills, / Not knowing its own aim, / Built
blindly for the Greece which could not be."[41] Next to it on a smaller
plaque, placed there by Nilla years later, is written in large capital letters:
"In memory of Mollie Price, Susan Glaspell, and Ellen Dodge."

While Jig was being buried by the villagers of Delphi in an outpouring
of love, Susan thought how odd that these people should have made him
their own and yet knew nothing of his past life, while their close friends
abroad had no idea that he had suddenly died. Her first cables announcing the death were to her mother and to Lucy Huffaker, in New York.
Huffaker received the news on January 14 and immediately relayed it to
newspapers and to friends, which is why Cook's death date appears as
January 14, the date the reports were published in the States, rather than
January 11, the date of his death. The obituaries, carried by all leading
American newspapers, tended to take details from a long article by Louis
Weitzenkorn, appearing in the *New York World*, containing Edna's summary of Glaspell's letters from Delphi, comments by Fitzie, and a detailed
summary of his life. Accompanying this much-circulated obituary and
reprinted elsewhere were two pictures: a photograph by P. Thompson,
done in New York before their departure, showing Jig in shirt and tie and
Susan in a long, printed dress sitting on a sofa reading a script; and a photograph of Jig as Silas Morton, in *Inheritors*, that uncannily resembled the
white-bearded man who had just died in Delphi in a different costume.
Since details of the death were sketchy, several of the obituaries made
factual errors, such as listing his age at death as forty-five or expanding
and embellishing anecdotes, particularly Jig's challenge in Agorgiani to
have others join him in a death pact, or his burial of TòPuppy, which
one describes as a sacred burial on Mount Parnassus after which Jig died
while returning to Delphi. Those who knew him, however, were able to
offer moving testimony to the legacy he left behind. "He never realized

what he did," Fitzie said, "but it was his inspiration that built up the Provincetown Theatre, his shoulders that carried the burden, and to him alone the success of the experiment must be credited."[42] Floyd Dell wrote a special letter to the *Davenport Democrat*, describing his feelings on receiving news of his friend's death and enumerating the close ties that Jig had with his native town. "He was a lover of beauty, and of brave ideas, and a dreamer of what the world's wisdom calls impossible dreams. We have all dreamed such dreams; but I think they were harder for Jig to give up than for anybody else. He wanted them to be realities—here in America."[43] Dell tells of the last time he saw Cook, just before the trip to Greece: "He said, 'Let's go back to Davenport, and help make it another Athens!'" He omits the irony with which he relates the same story in *Homecoming*, particularly the drunken state of his former hero and Dell's dismissal of him.

Of all the tributes, the one that seemed to capture Jig best was the anonymous paragraph, which appeared in the *Nation*. The writer called him:

> a brave enthusiast, whose experimental eagerness helped break
> new paths for the American theatre and drama. He was a play-
> wright and novelist but, beyond these things, he was extraor-
> dinarily a person, exerting an incalculable personal force and
> influence. That influence is itself not easy to describe, except as a
> civilizing influence, or perhaps a Utopian influence; he made people
> ashamed of surrender to an ignoble world, he made them try to do
> the beautiful and impossible things of which they dreamed—and
> that attempt, which is often enough ridiculous, is the best the
> world has yet been able to offer in the way of civilization any-
> where. It was the Greeks of the Periclean age who went at it most
> eagerly and naively, perhaps; and in spirit George Cram Cook was
> a Greek of the Periclean age, strayed somehow out of his place and
> time into our more timid age; and after bruising himself by work-
> ing a lifetime against realities which he was too eager to reshape,
> he strayed back again to what must have seemed his own country.
> He will be buried, as he wished, at Delphi.[44]

A theme repeated in the press and by friends was the aptness of Jig's place of death; and the obvious question was whether he had gone to Delphi to die. In *Road*, Susan seems to hedge the question. She makes abundantly clear the hurt he felt concerning the Provincetown Players and his need to find some substitute "beloved community," whom he could galvanize and fashion to greatness. Without a group or project, he felt himself adrift. Jig had always suffered from mordant lows after euphoric highs, and in Delphi there were more of the former than the latter. There were also abundant quantities of alcohol to get him over the low spots, which was not available in Prohibition America. He may well have died from a disease contracted from TòPuppy; but as Susan herself repeats, long before the dog took sick, Jig had already shown signs of serious decline. Although she never brings herself to explain his health problems, they must have been abetted if not caused by his drinking. Did he die of alcoholism, then? His old socialist hero Upton Sinclair thought so. In his book *Money Writes!*, written in 1927, just after *Road* appeared, Sinclair devotes one chapter, entitled "Bacchus' Train," to those writers of genius who killed their talent and, ultimately, themselves, by drinking to excess, and he cites Jig as a prime example. His accusation that Jig drank himself to death is probably true, but he also drank himself to life, or at least he believed he did. In his Greenwich Village days, Jig would ask his friends to pass all the alcohol to him so that he could intoxicate them with the fire that sprang from his inebriated soul. When even this excess could not blot out the pain of the past, he succumbed, having failed to catch a star.

After Jig's burial, Susan returned with Nilla and her teachers to Athens, where she remained for several weeks, concluding their affairs and making arrangements for passage home. She now wrote to close friends about Jig's last days and the outpouring of grief in Delphi. To Neith and Hutch she expresses her regret that they had not seen their friend before his death. "Jig had become wonderful," she told them.[45] Hutch reprints her long, detailed letter about Jig's death and burial honors almost in its entirety in his autobiography, except for one sentence Susan asked him to remove, in which she implies that she thought about suicide at the time. She also wrote to her mother but avoided details about the funeral and burial, for fear of offending her Christian sensibility.[46] She also mentions Nilla's wish to remain in Athens to finish the school years, if Mollie approves, and her own plan to return to Davenport but only for a visit. If she is to continue with her writing and her life, she must be near friends in Provincetown, she explains. To Neith and Hutch she is more direct, indicating her obligation to her frail mother, whom her brothers have cared for in her absence. "I am the one to do something for her now, and I grasp at all the reasons there are for going ahead. But I cannot live in that place—Davenport." She recognizes how painful it will be to return to the Cape alone. "How can I ever walk into the Provincetown house—much less the Truro valley? But all of that is farther on. Now—just go ahead." Up to this point in her letter, she has written with great control, but near the end she breaks down, "But can you believe it, that Jig is dead? Just think—there is no place in this world where I can go and find him." She concludes with her hope that "you will all help me to come through to the place where I can perhaps make Jig realized by more people, and especially more deeply realized by all of us. And you will all do what you can to keep his memory in the life he loved." Even at this point, so soon after his death, Susan was already thinking how to honor him.

One friend who wished to write her a condolence letter knew very well what it was like to lose a husband on foreign soil. Louise Bryant was then living in Paris, and when Blanche Hays, a former Provincetown actor, told her of Jig's death, she immediately wrote to Neith, asking for Susan's address. "It can be so terrible—to lose someone—in an alien place. I know. One seems so far away and friends do not know one's address—no one writes. One gets a sense of being lost and forgotten. I always loved Susan and if there is any small practical thing I could do to help—I want to."[47]

Before Susan left Greece, she made one more trip to Delphi, arriving forty days after Jig's death, the day before a mass was to be said in his honor. She ends *Road* with a brief description of its service and of her final visit to the old cemetery: "As I stood there, though it had seemed I could not leave him, there came a feeling of its all being something bigger than I, than he. Our parting, a personal grief, became almost an intrusion. He had been taken into the great past he loved and realized. Below, on the road—the women spin, the sheep pass." She also tells how Jig was already becoming part of the lore of Delphi, with songs sung by shepherds on Mount Parnassus and tales told by patrons in the wine shop of Delphi describing this tall, white haired man from America—a tamer of wild birds—who had come to Greece because of his love for its culture and who had embraced the simple life of peasants, learned their language, dressed in their clothing, and taught them about themselves. And the legend has remained, at least among the old-timers who can still lead visitors like me to Kyrios Kouk's grave and point out the house where he lived or who can tell the curious how to find the grandchildren of Andreas Korylss, Thanasie Tsakalos, Elias Scarmouches, and Demitrius Komblss, who still live in Delphi. Of Susan they have far fewer stories or memories. Delphi, finally was Jig's dream; it was not hers.

There are two footnotes to Jig's Delphi years. In May 1927, Eva Palmer and Angelos Sikelianos finally arranged to hold a Delphi festival, just as Jig had dreamed.[48] Besides staging *Prometheus Bound* they organized an exhibit of Greek folk art and a performance of kleptic ballads and held the Pythian games in the ancient stadium, in Jig's honor. Nilla, who had returned to Delphi in 1925, and at seventeen had married Nikos Pro-estopoulos, a cousin of Sikelianos, worked with Palmer and Sikelianos to create the festival. At their house in Phaleron near hers, Nilla learned to weave the ancient Greek silk fabric that would fall in perfect folds for the authentic costumes they created. She watched as workers embroidered designs taken from ancient vases, depicting Dionysus, Attic images, and dolphins, the sign of Apollo. She also was part of the Oceanides group who presented Greek dances at the festival, accompanied by their own singing. In her description of the festival, however, she makes special mention of the athletic games, dedicated to her father: "With a clash of shields and blare of trumpets they danced the Pyricheion, the ancient war dance for fallen heroes, in memory of Kyrios Kouk. The drums and trumpets rang in the cliffs and the cheers of the stadium when the white silk banner with his name in gold letters was carried around it. What he would have liked best, I thought, was that the eagles came down from the peaks of Parnassus to see what was going on."[49] The games were held again in May 1930 and were equally successful, drawing over 3,000 participants from around the world. However, try as they might, Sikelianos in Greece and Palmer, who subsequently divorced him and returned to America, could not get further backing for the event, although Palmer spent the remainder of her life trying to interest Americans, including Eleanor Roosevelt, in sponsorship, so that the Delphi ideal of world understanding through beauty and moderation would not "fall from the high lookout where we had placed it."[50] In 1950 she returned to Greece; Sikelianos died that year, and she the year after. She is buried one grave away from Jig, along the same ancient wall. Neither grave has yet been disinterred. Jig's part in the reinstitution of the Delphi festival, however, has blurred with time, just as the letters carved on his grave have faded. In 1997, on the seventieth anniversary of the first event, the European Cultural Centre at Delphi sponsored an international symposium honoring the festival. Although there were papers and exhibits and performances concentrating on the work and life of Eva Palmer and Angelos Sikelianos, and though the Museum of the Delphic Festival honoring the couple and the festival was officially opened just yards from the old cemetery, there was no mention at all of Jig Cook. Like so many instances in his life, his inspiration and influence on others and his own work went unacknowledged.

There is one more footnote to Jig's life and death in Delphi. Nilla did not receive permission from Mollie to remain in Greece, and reluctantly she returned with Susan to America, sailing with her on February 12, on the *Byron*, another lover of Greece. She was met in New York by her mother, who was living in the city. Although Mollie attempted to show her daughter a brave face, she was shocked by Jig's death. They had been divorced for eleven years, but she still felt a strong connection to him and had never considered marrying again as long as he lived. However, Nilla, in her autobiography—in a brief aside from her preoccupation with tales of her own love life—mentions, when Bill Rapp stopped off in New York and visited her and Mollie on his way back to his own family, that "After all the years of refusing to marry, my mother thought Bill Rapp looked like Kyrios Kouk and married him. She was ten years older than he was, but did not look it, and they were ridiculously happy."[51]

Going On, 1924–48

IV

Picking Up the Pieces

23

I could have stayed with life gone dead; it would have been safer, as you say. But you see I'm not through yet.

—Susan Glaspell, *Fidelity*

Susan arrived back in the United States on March 16, 1924. She went first to Davenport to see her mother. She then spent a month with Lucy and her husband Eddie Goodman in New York, finally returning to Provincetown with Lucy to reopen her house and restart her life without Jig. Hardly had she time to unpack, however, when she was embroiled once more in an issue that had been simmering during her time away: the future of the Provincetown Players and her relation to the theatre. While she and Jig had been in Greece, Edna Kenton had acted as faithful proxy, keeping them apprised of the ongoing struggles on MacDougal Street through scrupulously detailed accounts, which would have done credit to any war correspondent. During the 1922–23 season, the Players had signed a two-year lease for the theatre at 133 MacDougal Street and had sublet it the first year. In the late spring of 1923, the lease once more reverted to them, and they once more had to decide who would occupy the space and what the group would be called. In June 1923, Edna reported that four of the seven corporation signators now wished to take over the theatre. She backed this move, arguing that it was better to allow them to do so than to return the property to Mrs. Belardi once and for all. Unlike other groups who had wanted to run it, they at least had some connections to the past and some claim to the name. And, besides, either the experiment would fail and prove that the company, particularly O'Neill, needed the vision provided by Jig or they would succeed and thus offer a place for

Susan and Jig to return to should they decide to do so. From Greece came the reply "Terminate." However, since they were overruled by the other members on the board, Edna argued that they practice "intense passivity" and "let the future take care of itself"[1] in order to keep options open. "Let me say that our own feeling remains what it was," Susan responded, "that the Provincetown Players was a unique group, with a very definite reason for existing, and that a quite other thing should have a quite other name." However, she added, "it is easy to talk, I know, when an ocean and various seas, not to mention a mountain lie between."[2]

Although the core of the original group would form the majority of the new organization, Susan was right that this theatre would be "a quite other thing."[3] In addition to Fitzie, Gene, Cleon, and Harry, several new people were added, most notably the critic Kenneth Macgowan, who was to become the undisputed general director with unlimited powers, and scenic designer Robert Edmond Jones, who would share with O'Neill the duties of assistant director. The triumvirate, as they were quickly labeled by the press—Macgowan, O'Neill, and Jones—had a clear vision of what they wished to accomplish, and it diverged radically from the original Provincetown mandate. They saw themselves as a professional theatre company, not a home for amateur productions; their emphasis would be on production values, on acting, designing, and directing, and not on play writing and playwrights; they would produce a variety of world dramas, not just American works; and they would present established playwrights and not function solely as a laboratory for new, untried American authors. However, the new members, particularly Macgowan, recognized that there were advantages in holding onto the Provincetown name and capitalizing on its reputation. Therefore, in the late spring of 1923, when it was suggested that the new group take the name the Playwrights' Theatre, the name originally affixed to the building, the motion was defeated, since the magical word *Provincetown* did not appear. A second suggestion, put forth by Macgowan, was that the group be called the Provincetown Playhouse, which would differentiate it from the Players but still keep the much-desired associations with the former organization. It was O'Neill who argued against this name, since for him, as Edna reported to Susan and Jig, "The close association of his and fame with the P.P. is galling."[4] Still unable to clarify what they would call themselves, the company sent out press releases indicating that the Provincetown *Players* were reopening, and in the fall they followed with word that the Provincetown *Playhouse* was readying plans for the new season. Whatever the final name, the group seemed determined to keep the link with its antecedent, and the press tended to see it as a continuation of the earlier theatre, now back in business after its announced one-year hiatus.

Kenton, in her zeal to make the best of the situation, continued to weigh in on the side she assumed to be that most advantageous for the return of Jig, changing her position regarding the name whenever she smelled conspiracy on the part of those not equally committed. Once she learned of his death, her goal shifted. No longer keeper of the faith, she saw herself, instead, as protector and chronicler of the legacy, along with Susan. For that purpose she now argued that a clear demarcation must be made between the Provincetown Players, which ended in spring 1922, and this new entity, which seemed determined to keep some ties with the past.

Almost immediately after Susan returned, the two women discussed tentative plans for memorializing Jig, Susan imagining a play she might write about him and present at the theatre. However, Edna thought this plan unlikely: "There's nothing to save—no theatre for Jig's play if you write it, with these new members added."[5] She was referring specifically to Jimmy Light, Jig's nemesis in earlier years, who was part of the new organization. Edna predicted that Light would be director of the new group in a year, and that meant that the new theatre would never continue the work of the old, and that all Susan could do was to see that at least it took a new name not associated with the past. Having accomplished this, she was prepared to "have done with it once and for all."

This was Edna's position. Where Susan stood is harder to determine. Later she would write, "I never meant to stay on after getting a few things straightened out."[6] But during April and May 1924, when intense negotiations over the new theatre were held, there might have been a possibility that she would join the reconstituted group, or at least keep some quasi-connection with them, had Fitzie, Throckmorton, Weinberger, Macgowan, and—particularly—O'Neill reached out to her and addressed the one sin she could not abide: disloyalty to the memory of Jig. On January 3, a week before Jig died, the company had opened its season in the rechristened and refurbished Provincetown Playhouse with August Strindberg's *The Spook Sonata*, a choice that clearly signaled its divergence from the earlier Players. By the time Susan returned, it had already mounted a second production, a highly successful revival of Anna Cora Mowatt's 1845 comedy *Fashion*, still without clarifying its legal status or name and still without mentioning in the expanded playbills anything about Jig's legacy or even his death. When *The Emperor Jones*, Jig's greatest triumph, was revived in May, the playbill made no reference to his direction of the first production and his building of the dome, which insured its success on the stage. The omissions seemed proof, as Edna had been arguing, that this new group was only interested in exploiting the past not in honoring it. To her, "the whole thing lay in Gene's hands, and he was temperamentally unable to deal with it. His whole sense of guilt over Jig lay too deep for him to work with it."[7]

Since Susan and Gene were the two central playwrights of the original Provincetown Players, they were charged with the final decision as to the name of the new group. Actually, their positions did not differ. In a letter written to Susan in January, after Jig's death, Agnes expressed the sorrow she and Gene felt and indicated that Gene also wanted to change the name of the theatre, since the current theatre "was to be a *new* thing."[8] Gene placed the blame for the continuation of the name on Edna and Harry Weinberger. In her letter to Fitzie prior to the decisive meeting in May, but intended for the entire group, Susan stated her position clearly, using many of the same words she had written to Edna from Greece. If the new group were to branch out in different ways from the original theatre, why not call itself by a new name, rather than court the inevitable confusion that the use of Provincetown in its title would cause? She explained: "There was never a more simple organization than the Provincetown Players. It seems to me there never was a more cumbersome one than you who call yourselves Provincetown Playhouse. We never went in for patrons and this and that kind of stock. We wrote plays and put them on. We did that for awhile because we felt like doing it, and we stopped because we were not sure we felt like going on doing it. That's that. And I wish it should stay at that." As much as she focused on the name, the real crux of the issue for her was the failure of the new group to acknowledge the contribution of Jig, the very issue which had driven him away in 1922:

> There was a man named Jig Cook. He gave some eight years of his life to creating the Provincetown Playhouse. If it had not been for him there would not be that place in which you now put on your plays. He worked until he had worked himself out, and then he went away, and he died. You are profiting by what he did, and you have forgotten him. It is not a spirit that will ever make the kind of place he made. He was, above all things, generous. That is why he is now dead in Greece. I know the story—the whole long hard story. I, for one, do not forget. And it is because you do not remember that I do not feel one with you.[9]

Although she does nothing to mask her hurt, even implying that the group had been the cause of Jig's death, she stops short of making a final break, leaving the way open for some sort of rapprochement. In fact, at one point in the letter, which Edna catches and asks her to amend, she seems to change course asking them either to "Use the name or don't use it." Had any of the group attempted to write her or had she decided to attend the decisive meeting and been in a mood to listen to what they said, Susan might still have become part of the new theatre and continued to write plays for them, or at least not totally severed her connections. They did not, and so she became as she put it "invalidated" from this theatre permanently.

When the executive committee met on May 28, neither Susan nor Gene was present, she remaining in Provincetown, he at his new home at Brook Farm, in Ridgefield, Connecticut. Edna describes in a long letter to Susan what happened.[10] She began the meeting by floating the possibility of both she and Susan cutting any association with the theatre if they would agree to come up with a new name and drop all references to Provincetown in its title. She indicated that she had not discussed this option with Susan, but assumed that she would agree. Macgowan took the opening to finally make his position clear. He wanted Susan in the new group. Next to O'Neill's writings hers were the most important that the original theatre had produced, and he wanted an option on her future plays. However, he didn't want Edna to have anything to do with the new corporation because of her "recalcitrance" over the past months and her attempts to block each action they took. He even questioned her right to the stock options that were being considered in the transfer of assets from the old to the new company. For her part, Edna again insisted that she and Susan would only withdraw if the group finally came up with a name for itself. After much prodding, they chose the Experimental Theatre, Inc., operating at the Provincetown Playhouse. However, no formal action on the proffered resignations was taken; instead Weinberger suggested that the new corporation create two dummy directors to be left unnamed for a year, the implication being that Susan and Edna might have time to decide if they wished to join at a later date, a move clearly designed to allow Susan a way to return to the theatre and continue to produce her plays there.

This option was closed once Susan received the five-page, single-spaced letter Edna sent off immediately after the meeting, minutely detailing what had occurred. Not surprisingly, Susan was outraged by the slight done to her friend and voiced her anger in her response, sent a few days later to Fitzie with copies to the others. In it she repeated what she had written earlier about the need for a clear demarcation between the old theatre and the new; but this time there was no "intense passivity" or ambiguity. "I think Edna was treated abominably. Even if I hadn't had it in mind to resign, I should certainly have done it on this. I herewith do so." She had waited to hear from the others to get their version of the meeting, but since none had written, she was left to assume that Edna's account of Kenneth's denunciation was accurate. It was Edna, she reminds them, who was most faithful to Jig. "That is why you couldn't have taken a better way of outraging me, outraging the deepest feeling about him, than in doing this to Edna." Renouncing her own stock entitlement, she concludes, "Fitzie, and all of you, for this letter is for all of you, from very deep down, I am through."[11]

In response to Susan's first letter, on May 23, O'Neill had written to Edna, saying that it seemed he and Susan agreed that the Provincetown name should not carry on. What he did not mention is the source of their positions; his desire to cut with the past, hers to honor it. In his own letter to Susan on May 26, prior to the meeting, he blames Edna for the battles and bemoans the fact that Susan "should be pestered with our bickering." Then he turns to the issue of Jig, which had put the greatest strain on his close relationship with her.

When I heard of his death, Susan, I felt suddenly that I had lost one of the best friends I had ever had or ever would have—unselfish, rare, and truly noble! And then when I thought of all the things I hadn't done, the letters I hadn't written, the things I hadn't said, the others I had said and wished unsaid, I felt like a swine, Susan. Whenever I think of him it is with the most self-condemning remorse. It made me afraid to face you in New York. The above is futile. I haven't said it at all. But I hope you'll understand. This is a late day to be writing to you but I couldn't before.[12]

The letter ends with a warm invitation for her to come to Brook Farm, but pointedly makes no mention of her decision to sever ties with the new theatre he will head nor requests that she reconsider. It may be, as Edna suspected, that his guilt over his treatment of Jig, declared so clearly in the letter, made such a request impossible. Or it may be that he wished to finally distance himself and his career from the past and from her. Either way, O'Neill's failure to act or to encourage Susan to join him in writing for this new theatre virtually sealed the end of her association with any remnants of the Provincetown Players. And with no group of colleagues waiting for her plays, it is not surprising that her focus shifted back to fiction. It was not the death of Jig that turned her from theatre as much as her alienation from the theatre he had established and for which she had played such a pivotal role.

But it was not over yet. In October 1924, when the Provincetown Playhouse began its new season on MacDougal Street and at the Greenwich Village Theatre—another venue the company leased for productions—Susan's name and Edna's still appeared as members in the playbills. Macgowan, perhaps entertaining the idea that Susan would one day reconsider, had never made her resignation official. Edna, ever smelling intrigue, assumed that he was trying to placate those subscribers who might have been unwilling to support a theatre that no longer included Glaspell's plays. In a further letter demanding that her name be stricken from the membership, Susan also complained that the company continued to use the word "Provincetown" emblazoned in large letters and made scant mention of the official name. However, even she found it difficult to break old habits, writing "Players" after "Provincetown," before crossing it out for "Playhouse." If she could not keep the old and the new names clear, it is not surprising that critics and audiences had similar difficulties; and the new company, despite O'Neill's objections, did not go out of its way to correct them. Solicitations for subscriptions and contributions invariably began with a glance backwards to its mythical point of origin when "a small group of writers, poets, and artists gathered spontaneously at Provincetown, Massachusetts,"[13] shifting the date yearly, until in its final promotion booklet in 1929, it began "Fourteen years ago," and listed all productions back to 1915. Even as it embraced the past theatre, it took pains to erase the name of its founder. Although the October brochure, which opened the 1925–26 season, referred to Jig as director of the Players, an article in the November playbill for *Desire Under the Elms*, meant to advertise the revival of *The Emperor Jones*, describes the first production occurring in a "made-over barn off Washington Square where *some people* [emphasis mine] were putting on a monolog with no love interest." The distinction between Jig's theatre and the present company disappeared entirely in the next line, which began, "The Provincetown Playhouse is famous now." As Edna foresaw, the Experimental Theatre, Inc. was eager to proclaim itself as an "offspring" of the Players, but unwilling to acknowledge its father.

Over the next two seasons, they mounted eighteen plays, but finally could not overcome the same financial and production problems that had plagued Jig. The Greenwich Village venue, headed by the triumvirate, lasted only until 1926, then became part of the Actors' Theatre; the Provincetown venue, headed by Fitzie and Jimmy Light, struggled along until 1929, producing three or four plays a year. Long before its demise, the group had run out of steam, lacking the very thing that many faulted Jig for having in excess: ego and enthusiasm. Even O'Neill, who had disparaged Jig for his dictatorial style and lack of discipline, eventually came to appreciate the work done under his tutelage. Right after Jig and Susan left for Greece, he had written to Fitzie, "As I look back on it now, I see where he drove all our best talent, that we had developed, away from the theater for daring to disagree with him—this is supposed to be democracy."[14] Yet, a year later he was advising Macgowan: "To hell with democracy! Director with a capital D!"[15] By 1925 he had come to better appreciate just how much had really been accomplished by the first Players and how "in comparison to our present productions, our first season at the Provincetown Playhouse was ten years in advance of what we are now!"[16] At one testimonial dinner, he stood up and muttered: "The Provincetown did its best work when it didn't have a dime"—to which Fitzie quickly added, "For the sake of Jig Cook's memory, let's not drop tears—let's drop dollars!"[17] an ironic illustration of just what Jig had come to mean for them.

One of the chief impediments against Susan's participation in the new company had been its failure to honor Jig. O'Neill, in a letter to Macgowan, urged him to remedy this for Susan's sake.[18] After the dust had cleared, this slight was formally ameliorated. On October 11, 1924, the playbill for the production of Stark Young's *The Saint* carried a brief essay by her entitled "George Cram Cook, Founder of the Provincetown Players."[19] In it she does not attempt to delineate the history of the theatre; instead, she tells of Jig's last days in Delphi, the honor the Greek government accorded him, and the love the simple shepherds of Delphi unconditionally gave him. The implication is that they appreciated him, even if his Provincetown colleagues had not. Another tribute, this time a plaque on the wall of the Playhouse, also honored Jig, inscribed with the words he wrote just before his death: "And we will make the cold world / Flame and music, / The dance of flame / Obedient to dream." In her testimonial Susan added tellingly, "Jig was obedient to dream."

She had agreed to the memorial plaque because she felt something of Jig should be in his theatre, but she wanted nothing else to do with the people who now occupied the place. "I cannot go on contending with them, and I am not part of them," she wrote Edna. "I have done the little I could, and now—that is over. To other things."[20] However, until the theatre's demise, she continued to feel resentment about the usurpation of the Provincetown name and its history. In 1929, when Fitzie asked her to contribute a brief essay for the "fourteenth anniversary" brochure, celebrating the theatre—a last frantic attempt at fundraising—Susan tried yet again to argue that the Players had ceased to function in 1922, and the brochure was, therefore, fraudulent, since it claimed a history that was not its own. She was particularly anxious that the book which Barrett Clark was to write about the group make clear the distinction between the two theatres, something he had failed to do in his biography of O'Neill, also written in 1929. It was Clark whom Fitzie asked to draft a formal reply to Susan in the name of the board, but he admitted to her that "Really, I think we ought to have Glaspell with us. Personally I'd like to have us review *Bernice* and maybe try out *The Comic Artist* her latest play."[21] The letter was moot; Clark's Players book was never written and the campaign for funds came to nothing in that October of the Wall Street Crash, a last flurry of activity before the lights went out permanently on the theatre.

Several other groups, with more limited goals and with varying success, tried to keep the early Provincetown spirit alive. On April 21, 1923, Jasper Deeter, the original Smithers in *Jones* opened Hedgerow Theatre, whose name derived from his claim that the company would perform anywhere, even a hedgerow. Amazingly, with short hiatuses over the years, Hedgerow is still functioning today as America's oldest residential repertory theatre, and Deeter's dedication to communal living and shoestring performances still drives the group. In addition to reviving *Inheritors* for runs on Memorial Day and the Fourth of July, he presented several of Susan's other plays including *Trifles*, *Bernice*, *The Verge*, and her later works *Alison's House*, and *The Comic Artist*. A series of small summer theatres in Provincetown were also modeled after the original Players, replicating as well its fractious history. In 1923 local resident Mary Bicknell enlisted the help of publisher Frank Shay to start the Wharf Players in an abandoned movie house. The following summer, Shay started his own, more radical group, the Barnstormers, in a reconverted barn, presenting for the first time the Glencairn-cycle sea plays on one bill. In 1925 Bicknell opened her own summer season in the newly rebuilt Wharf Theatre and ran it successfully for two years, until it too was taken over by others and became merely another summer theatre venue. The wharf itself was finally washed into the bay in the great gale of 1941. Periodically since then, one or another group has resurrected the name "Provincetown," or "Wharf" and attached it to its theatre, but not for long. Of those that followed, only Catharine Huntington's Provincetown Playhouse made a significant mark and had Susan's support.

As difficult as the break with the new Provincetown theatre had been for Susan, one burden of the past was lifted: she did not immediately have to turn out stories in order to support herself, as she had done when Jig was alive. Despite his indifferent attitude toward money, his estate totaled approximately $62,000, exclusive of royalties, thanks to the watchful eye of his brother Ruel, who had seen to it that the money Jig had received from their parents' estates had been well invested. It was a considerable amount in 1924, and Glaspell's share of the inheritance—at least equal to the $15, 000 each that Nilla and Harl received, and perhaps double—gave her the largest cushion of money she had had in her life. In practical terms, this meant that for the immediate future she was free to concentrate on the project that had occupied her since her return: honoring Jig through his writing. It proved to be a daunting task.

A man who had loved order in his surroundings, Jig had not been able to bring the same principle to bear in his writings, which tended to be scattered, fragmentary, some no more than short jottings made on scratch paper as a mood or thought took him. Going through the crammed drawers of his desks in Provincetown and Truro and the cartons of their papers stored in Lucy's apartment, Susan attempted to make some order and extract those worth publishing. She concentrated first on collecting Jig's poetry, which spanned the period from his youth in Davenport to the tormented days just before his premature death in Delphi. "They are not many," she wrote Edna, "but surely some profound beauty is here." [22] To Floyd she sent a manuscript containing twenty-seven poems and two translations, asking him to read it, write an introductory essay for the book, and assist her in seeing it through publication. She also hoped that Edna and Hutch might supply memorial essays as well as Gene who had told her he wanted to contribute. However, when *Greek Coins* appeared the following year, it contained just three essays: "A Seer in Iowa," by Floyd; "Provincetown and MacDougal Street," by Edna; and "Last Days in Greece," by Susan. Since the poems bear no date or place of composition and are not accompanied by any explanatory notes about the organization, the reader is left to puzzle over questions of positioning and poetic development. The first section appears to be mainly devoted to works written by a youthful Jig and bears the signs of traditional prosody, which interested him at the time, particularly the sonnet form. The later poems from Greece are looser, more idiosyncratic, and roughly formed free verse, carrying with them much of the pain and frustration, as well as the exultation, of those final years. They were usually penned in the night, while he was sleepless and drunk, as Susan admitted, and discarded at dawn. What is not apparent to the reader is the way in which she carefully encloses the collection between two poems especially important to her, written by Jig to celebrate the beginning of their love.

She opens *Greek Coins* with "Though Stone be Broken," first drafted in 1910, and closes with "That Winter Day," which refers to their walk in Central Park in Davenport in 1907.[23]

Greek Coins was simple compared to the larger project she now described to Edna: "I am beginning what I want to do more than I have ever wanted anything—to make this picture of Jig, not only in Greece, but in life." Her playbill memorial and her essay in *Greek Coins* had focused on his last days; now she realized that to do justice to his end she would have to trace his early years, since "Greece begins in Iowa." "I don't know that I can do it. I'm going to try. That's what I live for."[24] The problem was not too little material but too much—forty years of Jig's writing, in which he had tried to answer the central question that plagued him: "Why am I, with all my abilities, not able to marshal my talents to successfully fulfill some higher end?" She might not be able to provide an answer, but she was determined at least to present his thoughts and let people finally glimpse the measure of the man and derive their own conclusions. This much she felt she owed him.

Several months later Susan again wrote to Edna, describing the impasse she had faced: "Arrested, it seemed; terror stricken before the future because knowing all the time, I suppose, that what I was writing about Jig wasn't the way to make the picture of him. I suppose I began it too soon. Anyway I came to see it was my grief, rather than Jig, I was writing about—or at least I was too much writing from that, and that was all wrong." In reaction, she told Edna that she had burned a year's worth of writing, in case she might be tempted to use it, and was beginning again. "I think I can do it. If I can't I will have to do other things first, and give this its time to come. Just the knowledge that I can do that helps."[25] Although she candidly describes her initial failure, she makes no reference to what has given her the surety she will succeed and the patience to put the work aside, if need be, until she is ready to continue. What she does not tell her friend is that, in the interim between the two letters to Edna, Susan had once again fallen in love.

She had been back in Provincetown seven months. It had been a difficult time for her. Now that relations with the O'Neills were strained and they were no longer living nearby, and now that the Steeles had moved to the South, she was left with a smaller circle of friends to act as a support group and surrogate family. Susan continued to walk with Neith Boyce, drink with Hutch Hapgood, and occasionally visit with Mary Vorse, but the summer bore little of the joy that had marked earlier years. Hutch describes her at the time: "Lonely and unhappy after the death of Jig [she] drank in a different spirit from that of the old days, and a worker all her life, still worked, to be sure, but more chaotically and with frequent interruptions."[26] In addition to the pain of Jig's sudden death, the stress created by the battles with the Players, and the struggle to organize his papers and publish them, she had to contend with changes in the Provincetown community and society in general that had occurred during her two-year absence. Instead of the comfortable, familial lives the friends had shared, a new rhythm and lifestyle had taken over, one Hutch blamed on Prohibition. Drinking, which had been an accompaniment to social life, now became the reason for its existence; the less alcohol available, the more the obsession with getting drunk. The Jazz Age was in full force, and youth seemed hell-bent on simply having a good time, a far more self-destructive, vapid "good time" than the earlier bohemian community had sought.[27] It was not only the youngsters who were embracing this new spirit. Vorse describes her own age group, in which "Everybody joined the nation-wide strike against prohibition by drinking as they never had before." One sign of these "days of the locust," she noted, was that people engaged in "strange romances."[28] Although she does not mention it directly, one of the "strange romances" she must have had in mind was that between her neighbor Susan and Mary's boarder Norman Matson.

Susan was forty-eight, claiming to be forty-two, a widow of less than a year, when she fell in love with the thirty-one-year-old writer, in November 1924, at a party at the home of Neith and Hutch. In his autobiography, Hutch recalls the event: "With great vividness I remember the moment when Susan met Matson. I knew from her eager expression that something had happened, that by instinct Susan felt that here was a thread leading her back to life, a plank that would save her from the depths. Need and love—how closely you are related!"[29] Hutch makes no comment about the disparity in their ages nor the fact that Susan, in middle life, sought a new lover. Others he knew had done the same. Emma Goldman had taken younger lovers; Vorse, too, had known "autumn love" with a "summer man," ten years her junior. Even more than either woman, Susan bore her years lightly. Although her health had always been delicate, as she neared fifty she showed none of the physical signs of diminished vitality, and only a few strands of gray in her short-cropped, curly hair attested to the passage of time and to the arduous years of living with Jig. She still had the supple carriage and beautifully proportioned body of a much younger woman. Her unlined face was dominated by large, curious eyes, which might reflect past pain but also signaled the desire for future experiences.

Those who knew her at this time remember a woman still very desirable to men. Heaton Vorse, Mary's elder son, recalled, "Susan was not beautiful in the conventional sense, but she had something that held you and made you want to know her better, especially if you were a man."[30] Miriam Hapgood Dewitt had a similar recollection of Susan. "She wasn't glamorous but attractive. She was the kind of woman that men like—she was a man's woman."[31] Mary Hackett (known as Bubs), who came to Provincetown a few years later agreed, "She had that talent for making men feel appreciated, something they needed, and may not have gotten elsewhere."[32] If any of her neighbors thought the pairing strange, it had more to do with Matson's character than with Susan's age. Neither Neith nor Hutch particularly liked him. Not as "interesting, good looking, or attractive as Jig, they found it difficult to understand what Susan saw in him," Miriam remembered her parents saying.[33] In her novels, Susan's female protagonists repeatedly talk of sexual love as a way of opening them out to the richness of life. It was this need that led her to begin her love affair with married Jig in staid Davenport under the noses of her conservative family and his; and it was this desire—to continue living in the vital way she demanded—that probably drew her to Norman Matson in the fall of 1924. As she repeats throughout her canon, Life (capitalized) is too important to be daunted by life, and "With memory alone you cannot live."[34]

She and Norman were also drawn together by common interests and backgrounds. Like her, he was a child of the Midwest, born in Grand Rapids, Michigan, the second of five children, to Norwegian immigrant parents, his father an upholster by trade, who loved to read Dickens to his family, his mother a seamstress and a Quaker. At a young age, he began to draw cartoons, and he sold them locally in order to finance night school, which promised him escape from the lower-middle-class life of his childhood, a station similar to Glaspell's. His first work, like hers, was for small newspapers. Moving east, at about the time she did, he worked as a copyeditor for the socialist newspaper the *New York Call*, before going to Europe in 1919 as a foreign correspondent for the *New York World*, for which he wrote a weekly column. While there, he was joined by his lover, the feminist activist Clara Wohl, who died in Vienna giving birth to a son, who also did not survive. It was this tragic experience, Matson would later claim, that his friend Ernest Hemingway used as one source for a similar tragedy in *A Farewell to Arms*. When Matson returned to the States, he decided to go to the Cape, a place he had come to love when he had visited Jack Reed in Truro. In the winter of 1924, he arrived in Provincetown with the reporter Griffin Barry, who had introduced Mary Vorse to both Joe O'Brien and Robert Minor. Perhaps wanting to make a new match for Mary, Barry suggested that Matson board at Mary's house. Whether a romance occurred is unclear. Her biographer Dee Garrison indicates that he had a profound impact on her and was the unnamed "friend" Mary cites in her confessional essay "Why I have Failed as a Mother," who chides her for not controlling her own children. Vorse's collapse at the end of November 1924 and what she called "my tragic gesture of suicide," which led to a four-month rest cure, and her rehabilitation from morphine use came at exactly the same time Norman began his love affair with Susan and may have been a response to it.[35]

Norman was good with children, and Mary's son Joel O'Brien, ten at the time, spent a good deal of time with him and thus became a witness to the beginnings of the love affair. He remembered vividly the day Susan and Norman took him for a walk over to Peaked Hill Bars, and he lagged behind. When he caught up on a ridge, he found them in an embrace. "I fell down, as if I stumbled, so they might think I didn't see them. For their part, they didn't seem to be embarrassed at all. I certainly was."[36] Norman recounts the incident in the "Book of Days," which he gave Susan as a gift on their first Christmas together. In this narrow, miniature notebook, headed "40 days on 40 pages," beginning on November 22, 1924, he traces the small events of their first month together:

> December 13th. How it rained. You sang and splashed. In din-
> ing room your hair up differently and you were different. We agree
> that it was indecent to be so gay.
> December 2nd. Joe [Joel] in heavy boots ran ahead and hid.
> Pond in yellow clearing thinly iced. He said Goodby Norman and
> Susan. We walked the railroad tracks and talked about love.
> December 15th. The night, the first of your absence, I walked to
> your house and then alone, the wind sobbing outside. I knew your
> feeling still a little, I went upstairs and looked . . . in Jig's desk and
> the wind watched me.
> December 20th. Left you in front of big stove and I went to
> prove that I knew something about running my life.[37]

At first the lovers tried to keep Norman's nightly visits to Susan's house secret, but friends quickly became aware of the love affair. "I see Susan occasionally, but always with constraint," Neith wrote to her husband, "She is completely in love and absorbed in Norman, coos over him and flatters him, and he looks like a fat cat!"[38] As she had done with Jig, Susan found correlatives in nature for their shared secret life together. In Davenport it had been a winter walk at starlight and a stream in the woods behind the Cook cabin. Now, in Provincetown, it became the shared path the two discovered that pointed to the outside, a way, they believed, no one else knew, and which became their "secret way." Susan also repeated her act of making shared pets a conduit for love in lieu of children. Her wire-haired terrier given to her by Lucy, became Samuel Butler, named because he fought with his father, or simply Sam or the mule, and joined wire-haired Tucker and a cat called Camelot as part of the family she and Norman now shared. Their love for the natural beauty of the Cape, devotion to their pets, and physical joy in each other became the dominant motifs in the letters they exchanged. In one written from Boston on their first winter together, she tells of suddenly putting her hand in the pocket of her heavy coat and finding to her delight a sprig of wintergreen, which reminded her of him: "I don't want Boston or any other place on earth where you aren't. I want to be in my house now and hear you whistling. The whistling means that you will open the door. The door means you will call to me—and come upstairs and find me, and there will be hours together."[39]

For a young writer, who had yet to publish anything and seemed unable to finish projects he started, who had no money and no home and craved both, and who, by his own admission, was insecure around intellectuals he sensed were his superiors, a love affair with an older, successful, estab-

lished author provided security. As Norman candidly admits in the unfinished autobiographical novel he wrote about their lives together, in which
he is called Peter and she is Ruth, a good part of the initial attraction he
felt derived from "that comfortable glow of second-hand importance that
may be enjoyed only by the innocent—and the parasitical." He also relished the comfort of her homes in Provincetown and Truro and, perhaps
even more important, the praise she lavished on him, which bolstered his
self-esteem. Susan flattered him and encouraged and guided his writing
career. "She made a setting for him," Norman says in his novel, "and
was thoughtful of the angle of light so that the best glitter always rayed."
Unlike Jig, who was capable of radiating his own energy if not sustaining
it, Norman was lethargic and had need of Susan's experience and the surer
hand she proffered. She was a woman "innocent of self-doubt," he writes
of Ruth/Susan in a note for his novel. He was a man who did not seem
certain of his direction.[40]

Despite her two-year hiatus isolated in Greece and her break with the
Provincetown theatre, Susan was still a formidable figure in American
literary circles when she met Norman; and her fame began to spread to
Britain, where she was embraced even more enthusiastically than she had
been at home. In 1920 when Small and Maynard had published her collection of plays, it received considerable attention in London. There had
also been a few reports of her work and O'Neill's with the Provincetown
Players; and in 1925, Emma Goldman, in London after leaving Russia,
had advertised a series of lectures she was prepared to deliver in her capacity as "Overseas representative of the Provincetown Players," including
"Strindberg," "The German Expressionism," "Eugene O'Neill and his
Works," and "The Plays of Miss Susan Glaspell."[41] With the London publication of Bernice, Inheritors, and The Verge in June 1924, in the first of
Ernest Benn's series of modern plays, Susan's work became known to an
even wider audience. The critical reactions to these low-priced, popular
editions, each published separately and in one volume titled Three Plays
by Susan Glaspell, were the most laudatory she had received to date. "She
follows directly in the Ibsen tradition and may justify the description, I
think, as his spiritual descendant in America. In fact she is very much
more related to him than Shaw ever was or will be," the reviewer for the
Daily Telegraph exclaimed.[42]
    Although James Agate, one of the most influential theatre critics of the
period, writing in the Sunday Times had some reservations after reading
The Verge—"a work of either a wander-wit or a genius and I found it
difficult to decide which"—and felt that Bernice was over his head, like
Ibsen's Little Eyolf, he had no hesitation about Inheritors "which I take
leave to proclaim the best achievement of the American theatre." He, too,
equated Glaspell's writing to Ibsen's. "Certainly one would not rate it
below An Enemy of the People and for my own part I am inclined to think
that it ranks with The Master Builder. Has the reader ever tried to imag-

ine what kind of play Ibsen would have enjoyed seeing? This is one of that kind, and it would have sent the old man thoughtfully home."[43] Andrew Malone, writing a long piece in *Dublin Magazine*, lavished equal praise on all three plays. "So far is Susan Glaspell from that satisfaction with things-as-they-are, which is so markedly American, that Bolshevism seems conservative besides the revolutionary ardour of her Claire in *The Verge*," a play he calls "technically perfect" and likens to Ibsen's *The Wild Duck*. Like several other critics, he brings up the name Eugene O'Neill in conjunction with Glaspell's, and like the majority of British critics at the time, he prefers her dramatic writing to his: "In technique Susan Glaspell is undoubtedly the superior of Eugene O'Neill. There is no trace of O'Neill's loose construction about these plays; they are as perfectly constructed as a first-class watch."[44] When the *Manchester Guardian* in its end-of-the-year supplement for 1924 listed the leading plays published in the past twelve months, it selected *Three Plays by Susan Glaspell*, announcing, "Pirandello was last year's high water mark of significance; this year's chief invader is hardly a match for him, but emphatically in published drama of non-British origin—and we don't forget Turgenev—this is Miss Susan Glaspell's year."[45] To reinforce the claim, *Fidelity* was belatedly published in a British version, as her first two novels had been, and it immediately went through five editions in its first five weeks. "A year ago hardly anyone in England had heard of Susan Glaspell," one review of the book opened, "but the publication of *Fidelity* and her three great plays have given her an instantaneous fame in England, so that the best critics are loud in her praises."[46]

With all this interest in her plays, it is not surprising that offers for stagings soon followed their publication. On October 17, 1924, Susan reported to her mother that *The Verge* was to be done in London, starring Sybil Thorndike, "said to be the most interesting actress acting at present. . . . Isn't that great? They want me to come over for it, but of course I can't leave the work I am doing and can't afford it." On the back of the letter, Mrs. Glaspell penciled a note "Susie sent me a check for $25 dollars," from the 100 pounds for the rights, and she underlined twice the words "my girl."[47]

Although Susan's letter mentions the New Theatre, the venue for *The Verge* was the Regent Theatre, and the company spearheading the production was the famed Pioneer Players, a private-subscription society headed by Edy Craig, daughter of the great British actor Ellen Terry and sister of famed theatre theorist Gordon Craig. She had established the Pioneer Players in 1911 as a place to put on plays addressing feminist and socialist issues, and to act as a laboratory for new methods of direction meant to enhance such ideologies. Often controversial for its selection of material and mise-en-scènes, the Players had a dedicated following among those who searched for serious and innovative theatre experiences. In 1919, at the King's Hall, Craig had presented *Trifles*, as part of a series of one-act plays, its first production outside of America. The twenty reviews the bill received all cited Glaspell's play as the highlight of the evening. At the end of that season, the Pioneer Players, two years before their American cousins with the same initials, had taken a leave at the height of their considerable reputation and determined, like the Provincetown group, that the name be held and the current executive committee stand so that they might continue, if they found plays of interest. When Craig read *The Verge*, she felt she'd discovered a work worth doing, so well did it embody the feminist ethos of the company and provide an opportunity for her to experiment in nontraditional staging. On reading the script, Sybil Thorndike shared her enthusiasm. "Edie darling—I adore *The Verge* . . . we are mad about it. . . . I've never wanted to play anything so much." Thorndike, an outspoken feminist, felt Claire "says everything I want to say!!!"[48]

The play opened on March 29, 1925, in a performance for subscription members of the Pioneer Players, with Ellen Terry in attendance, and was given two additional open matinees on April 6 and 7. Extensive preproduction articles helped to rouse interest and heighten expectations about the author and her work. In one, Susan was identified as "scarcely 30" (she was almost fifty) and lavishly praised for her own pioneering work in theatre. In the same article, Thorndike was asked if Glaspell was a genius, and she replied: "I am not quite sure but at least in the part of Claire she has created a genius."[49] *Genius* was the word James Agate used to describe Glaspell, now that he had seen *The Verge* staged. "Nobody whose genius was less than Ibsen's could have hoped to tackle such a theme," he proclaimed. "I stand my ground. *The Verge* is a great play," describing it as "the work of a fine sensitive mind preoccupied with fine and sensitive things."[50] A few, of course, dismissed Claire as insane and decadent, as Woollcott had done in America. The founder of the Agrarian Party, Deputy Adams, felt compelled to warn his compeers: "Gentlemen, I speak as one horticulturist on another, do not visit this abnormality on an otherwise admirable vocation."[51] Most, however, were captured by the work and thrilled by Thorndike's performance, several claiming that it was the greatest in her career. "The Pioneer Players expired in a blaze of glory. *The Verge* is out and away the most interesting play that has ever been produced by any Sunday Society so far back as the present writer's experience takes her," the *Daily Telegraph* critic wrote.[52] The *Illustrated London News* devoted an entire article to Susan, comparing her importance in theatre to Charlotte Brontë's impact on the novel in that "she has broken away from masculine tradition."[53] Three years earlier the majority of New York critics had either ridiculed or dismissed Glaspell's play; now a number of British critics and audiences embraced it as one of the great works of theatre. In the *Manchester Guardian*, R. Ellis Roberts wrote, "Miss Susan Glaspell is the greatest playwright we have had writing in English since Mr. George Bernard Shaw began. I am not sure she is not the greatest dramatist since Ibsen."[54] In the wake of the excitement, articles about Glaspell continued to appear in Britain and as far away as India and South Africa, long after the Pioneer Players closed their run and their theatre.

Inheritors, thus, had a ready audience when the Liverpool Repertory Theatre Company produced it in September 1925 in its own theatre and, in December, transferred it to the Everyman Theatre in London. The *Manchester Guardian* praised the initial production: "Liverpool does a service to the theatre in producing for first time in this country Susan Glaspell's *Inheritors* for it takes rank among the most sincere and moving plays of our time."[55] The correspondent for the local newspaper was more specific: "This play will live when Liverpool is a rubbish heap."[56] By the time *Inheritors* opened in London, Susan's reputation had been established, and all the major newspapers and literary magazines ran extensive reviews, most unanimous in their appreciation of the work. She continued to find favor with British critics and audiences, even as her reputation as a dramatist began to fade in America. *Bernice*, produced by the Lena Ashwell Company at the Century Theatre in London in January 1927, while not enjoying the success of the preceding plays, found an appreciative audience as well. When the play was revived by the Rusholme Repertory Players in July 1928, it still retained its power. About the playwright, one critic noted: "She may not teach us how to live but, as someone wrote of Thomas Hardy, she certainly extends and deepens our knowledge of the mystery of life,"[57] a reaction that must have pleased Susan. In Britain she became the American playwright against whom other Americans writers were judged. When Edna Ferber's *Showboat* opened in London, the actor Elizabeth Robins noted that Ferber's work "has not shown Susan Glaspell's power of vivid generality, nor any touch of philosophical curiosity that shines through that play *The Verge*, nor the political sense reflected in *The Inherits* [sic]."[58]

During late 1924 and the first five months of 1925, while her plays were being published, produced, and discussed abroad, Susan remained in Provincetown, absorbed in her new love and in her "Jig project." She was also occupied with Nilla, who had been greatly affected by her year in Greece and dreamed of returning as soon as she could. The death of her father and her mother's recent marriage to William Rapp had made Nilla feel more unsettled than ever. She and Harl spent some time with Susan at the beginning of the summer of 1924, but Nilla got into trouble, and had to be taken home by Mollie. In the fall, she had notified Miriam Hapgood that she was going through the motions of preparing to enter Mount Holyoke College by attending a preparatory school in Cambridge, but that her real intent was to return to Greece as soon as she could. In the late spring of 1925, Nilla was again in Provincetown, accompanied by Glaucos Sikelianos, son of Eva Palmer and Angelos Sikelianos, with whom Nilla had played and flirted while visiting at their home in Greece.

When the young man returned to his parents, Nilla accompanied him. Soon after, she married, not Glaucos but his cousin Nikos Proestopoulos. Before her trip, she spent time in Greenwich Village, retracing some of the places her father and Susan had frequented, even agreeing to take a part in *Adam Solitaire*, the first production of the Provincetown Playhouse in the 1925–26 season—much to the publicists' joy, since it allowed them to tie the past and present together. The following year, back on a visit, Nilla had a brief love affair with Clifford Odets, a young playwright who dreamed of following in the footsteps of the great writers of the early Provincetown years. Odets in his diary records his experience with "Lovely wonderous Nilla!" For decades he kept a wrinkled scrap of paper on which she had written, "So sweet child do try to recover from your avowed passion and be my friend—and my nice kitten-cat."[59]

Susan and Norman had their own travel plans during their first summer together. He had finally been able to complete *Flecker's Magic*, the tale of a Minnesota art student in Paris, whose encounter with a young, beautiful witch would one day become a source for the long-running television series "I Dream of Jeannie." It had received favorable reviews, including a particularly encouraging one from E. M. Forster. Perhaps influenced by Susan's work on Jig's life, Norman envisioned a similar project for himself and decided to go to Norway, his parents' homeland, and gather material for a novel about a Norwegian-American family who attempt to establish a new life but bring with them the shaping influence of the past. At the end of May 1925, the couple, declaring that they were married in order to make travel less awkward, sailed for Norway, on a "honeymoon trip" that would extend for seven months and conclude in the south of France. For Susan it was a serious working trip, too; she took notes for her Jig book and spent the time completing it.

Arriving in Oslo on June 26, Norman immediately sent his parents his first impressions of their homeland. A self-proclaimed "racialist," who would have grudging admiration for the early nationalism of Hitler (though decrying his lack of religion), Norman was first struck by the lack of Jews on the streets. "To be in a land where there are no Jews makes one despise them. . . . In Oslo you are never pushed nor elbowed, nor shouted at. People do not show off. People need not be ill mannered to cope with the greed of Jews."[60] Susan must have been aware of Norman's anti-Semitism but makes no mention of it. However, it did not seem to rub off on her or her writing. In the three novels she wrote during her time with him, she presents two minor characters she identifies as Jewish—in *Fugitive's Return* and in *Ambrose Holt and Family*—neither of whom are stereotypes nor sources of derision or contempt.

Norman devotes a good portion of his autobiographical novel to the Norway trip and the beginning of his love affair with Susan, when "their senses were naked and the world each day was new."[61] He describes them taking long walks along glacier fjords, rowing on mountain lakes, going on picnics, sleeping "in funny hotels where the halls smelled of spruce," and, most of all, working every day, writing "pages and pages." In the novel, it is Ruth/Susan who loves Norway best, since she is unafraid of mountains, which Susan had loved since her time in Colorado. Peter/Norman feels closed in by them and needs the comfort Ruth provides. Peter is jealous of the time Ruth spends writing about her former life. While he takes weeklong trips through the valleys of his ancestral home, she, the older woman, the famous writer, sits "amongst her papers about her past." The difference in their ages is a subject Norman repeatedly brings up in the novel. Even in the Norway scenes that mark the beginning of the eight-year love affair between the couple, he has Peter think, "He felt ashamed because she was so much older than he." In the same section, he gives these lines to Ruth: "Our love won't last. . . . Life isn't long for a woman; and I am almost 42, darling. But when the end comes, I'll know. I'll know what I had."

When the cold made it impossible for them to stay in Norway, the couple went by train to Paris and then to nearby Senlis, a small village of cobblestoned streets and brick-walled gardens, which Susan particularly loved, despite the dampness of the house in which they lived. "I haven't done as much work as I hoped I would since I left Norway," she wrote to her mother at the end of November. "Now I am going to the south of France where the Steeles and other people I know are." As she sometimes did, she included a check, part of royalties she had received from Stokes. "It will make a Christmas present for you all, including Ray and Flossie. Soon I think I can do more, and next year we will all be together."[62] On New Year's she again wrote, this time sending greetings from Nice. Her pointed use of the first-person singular indicates that at this time she had not told her family about Norman. It was only in 1927 that the Davenport paper carried an announcement of their marriage, which Susan fabricated for home consumption. The fiction may have also included people in Provincetown, for many in later years assumed that they had wed. However, early in their relationship, Susan and Norman decided they would not go through a formal service. Norman was Catholic and felt strongly against divorce; later he would claim that they had known from the beginning that because of their age difference their relationship was temporary.

They returned to Provincetown in late winter 1926; but with the first thaw of the spring, they began motoring over to Truro each week to check on Susan's house. Norman immediately fell in love with the place and made the small shed next to the main house his workroom, while she took over the small ten-by-twelve-foot cabin, a fifteen-minute walk from the back of the house, for her own isolated writing sanctum. "It's just pine boards—not even painted," she described it to a reporter. "There's nothing in it except a table and a chair—not even a sofa or a book. Nobody comes there with me but my dog, and if I don't work I just feel silly."[63]

Norman, like Jig, loved gardening, and soon he was putting in a vegetable garden and planting fruit trees. Susan tended to the flowers, often checking with her mother to learn if varieties she discovered, such as arbutus, also grew in Iowa. She even attempted to match the house to its surroundings, painting the exterior a gray-lavender and the trim the green color of the moss.

The Truro house became the setting for the play the couple concocted during the summer and fall of 1926 after their return. She and Jig had liked to talk, smoke, and drink late into the night, after others had gone to bed, and from such talks, around a fire on Milligan Place, *Suppressed Desires* had developed. With Norman she continued the habit, and the result was *The Comic Artist*, its genesis "you and me, the room in Truro, the strange night, that play growing between us,"[64] she reminded him on reading the final manuscript. In a handwritten note among her papers there is a list of the characters: The Comic Artist; His Beautiful Wife; Her Mother; His Elder Brother; The Elder Brother's Serene, Humorous Wife; and Her Respectable Brother—the time, the present; the place, New York; and three acts, taking place in the home of the elder brother. In the final version the Respectable Brother is omitted, the place becomes Truro, and the home belongs to the elder brother's wife, Eleanor. She is identified as "somewhat older" than her husband, although she is still "serene" and "humorous" in the play and is still clearly Susan, just as Eleanor's husband, Stephen Rolf, is based on Norman. The source for the others is less certain; however, younger brother/artist Karl may be patterned on Harold Matson, Norman's sibling, who was a literary agent in New York; and his wife, Beatrice, renowned for her great beauty, may be the inspiration for either the beautiful wife, Nina, or her mother, Louella.

Like Norman, the character Stephen had spent time in Paris and been a socialist; he is also someone never able to finish any of the things he starts, and is unsure of himself—that is, before he meets Eleanor and becomes "settled" and "comfortable." "I feel a bit relieved," Stephen admits; "there's less responsibility in mediocrity."[65] Eleanor has persuaded her painter husband to take up residence in an old farmhouse in Truro, built by her ancestors 200 years ago. Before their marriage, Stephen had loved Paris and New York; now he seems content with the simple activities they share, which were central to Susan and Norman: walking in the woods and along the shore, brewing home wine from wild plums they gather, reading from their extensive library, and working. In the play Susan adds to their happiness a baby son, who is never seen. In his youth Norman had been a cartoonist, and he still liked to doodle. In the play this talent is given to Karl, the younger brother, the gentle comic artist of the title. Karl has married Nina, a vain, petulant beauty, who had once been Stephen's lover in Paris. When she and Karl arrive for a visit at the same time that Nina's mother, the much-married Louella, unexpectedly returns from Paris, the play begins to waffle between weekend-in-the-country romantic comedy and darker, heavier melodrama, as Nina tries to use her beauty to rekindle Stephen's ardor. He succumbs, convincing himself that he is "doing it for Karl," so his beloved brother will see her destructiveness. Only Eleanor and Karl seem above the fray; but they, too, become embroiled through love for their spouses. When Eleanor finally confronts her rival, Nina reacts histrionically, declaring she will throw herself in the sea if she cannot have Stephen. Only Karl takes her claim seriously and, rushing off to save her, dives into the ocean and drowns. Although the play was completed by the end of 1926, it would take another year for it to find a publisher. The production history of the play was even more difficult. It had several amateur productions, first in London and then in small venues in America, before reaching Broadway in 1933 for a short, disastrous run, in a revised form that differed from the printed text.

The Comic Artist was a diversion, something they could do together after separate workdays, spent trying to give shape to two very different biographies: his Norwegian-American saga, which would become *Day of Fortune*, and her story of Jig, called *The Road to the Temple*. At the time that she destroyed the first version of the book, Susan already had an idea of what the biography would contain. "The Iowa background Dad Cook and Ma Mie . . . the boy at Iowa City who dreamed of Greece—Harvard and Heidelberg; university teacher, gardener; and always the creative artist with life itself; hence the Provincetown Players; then knowing it was time to go to Greece—the American in Delphi."[66] This is the outline she follows, but instead of chronological order, she begins in Greece and interlaces scenes of their life there with those of Jig's early years in Davenport. As she indicates in her notes, the book is to be divided into three parts, similar to the three-act format she employs in her longer plays, each act ending in a moment of complication or sudden change, which invariably leads to the next disclosure and eventual climax. In the notebook, act 1 presents youth and marriage, culminating in chapter 25 and the Monist Society, when she comes into his life; act 2, their shared lives in Provincetown and Greenwich Village and their work with the Provincetown Players, ending with chapter 36 and the cessation of the theatre and Jig's self-imposed exile; and act 3, "Greece, despair and death," culminating in chapter 53, "The Women Spin—The Sheep Pass." Her goal is to provide a structure for Jig's writing and life. However, whenever she makes use of his unpublished manuscripts, most often during the years before she enters his life, the story bogs down, sometimes for pages at a time. Once they marry and move east, the work changes. Jig was too busy with the Players to do much random writing; therefore, she is not compelled to turn to him to fill in the interstices. She can tell it her way, and her great narrative skills take over. The result is a unique book: a biography in which a wife tells the story of her husband, his words as part of a narrative she creates and organizes. The impetus for the project was to reclaim Jig's legacy, which had been distorted, she felt, by subsequent events. She attempts to set the record straight, describing the unique qualities of the man and his many accomplishments. She is careful to place herself to the side lest she shift the focus away from Jig. Those sections that seem to lapse into hagiography are her attempt to reinforce her central contention that he was a man who deserved better than he got at the hands of the Provincetown Players. The foreword of her original edition concludes with these words: "Weaknesses—failures, they are here. But it is a man of vision of whom I write, and he was great because nothing could kill in him a sense of wonder."[67]

The Road to the Temple became one of her best-selling books. Because of her large following in Britain at the time, it appeared there first, issued by Ernest Benn in October 1926. The American edition by Stokes came out the following March, and by the end of the year had sold more than 30,000 copies. On both sides of the Atlantic, there were those who questioned the unusual format, but the majority praised it precisely for its unique organization and style, befitting the special nature of its subject. "A strong book, sincere and beautiful and frank, standing high among revelations of the secret story of a man's spiritual pilgrimage," the *London Daily Mirror* proclaimed, and Benn quoted the praise on the cover of the edition. In the States, several of the prominent reviews were written by Jig's friends. Arthur Davison Ficke in the *Saturday Review of Literature*, under the title "G.C. Cook: Mad Humanist," described Jig's "glowing, rich, child-sweet personality [which] haunts, like the echoes of a bell, the memories of all who knew him."[68] Floyd Dell's piece in the *Herald Tribune*, titled "A Living and Inexplicable Man," makes the point that Susan chose well when she titled the work to reflect the life rather than merely affixing his name, as in most biographies. "It offers no theories to account for him, it passes no final judgments. It recreates the man we knew."[69] William Rapp was less enthusiastic, arguing, probably at the instigation of Mollie, that a less subjective portrait would have emerged if someone else with objective distance had edited Cook's writing and shaped the book.

Another who had known Jig well and felt that Susan did not capture the man was Hutch. In his 1939 autobiography, he writes that the book Susan had intended to write was much modified after she met Matson. He felt she had omitted Jig's essential spirit. One evening, soon after he had read the copy Susan sent him, he told her how he felt. "Jig cared most intensely about the light that never was on sea or land, but much as you loved him, you didn't love that part of him. You perhaps, like most women, wanted him to be practical. He felt that before he left New York in despair." The next day, he received a note from Susan expressing her pain and asking him a question: "What would you feel if Neith had just died and I had said to you: 'You neglected the best part of the woman with whom you had been living so many years, and perhaps caused the death of her spirit?'" Hutch ends the recollection by describing the "complete" apology he offered. "Susan nobly forgave me. For, ambitious, self-absorbed, as she was, there was always a generous quality about Susan."[70] There was also a Victorian masculine quality about Hapgood.

When *Road* appeared in London at the end of October, Susan was in Davenport visiting her family. "How strange to think of *Road* out and people reading it," she confided to Norman in a letter. "And that they like it. That's strange, too, and beautiful; after all the uncertainties. I think of us, in the Provincetown house, in Norway, in France, of the many hard times when my honey was good to me." What worried her was the reaction of her family and Jig's to her candor. "Pray for me," she asked him, before she went to visit Jig's brother. "Melancholia and drinking, and irregular love affairs, they may make a fuss. As I read it I wonder how I had the nerve to do it, without their seeing. . . . Now here it is, and here am I. I don't believe I mind, except for mother, to whom it will bring pain."

Susan finally decided not to show the book to her family just yet, feeling that her mother's frail heath would be affected. "I hate to have her read the things I say about myself. It will really be very hard on her. All the family will blame me for having done it. Davenport will buzz, I fancy. I am glad I will be away then." She still found it difficult to face Davenport conventions, and this extended to her relationship with Norman. She spread the fiction that they were married, placing a wedding announcement in the local papers and taking the precaution of having Norman address all letters to her as Mrs. Matson. She also never allowed him to accompany her, fearing that there might, even at this late date, be pressure for them to remain there. Over the next few years, whenever she returned, she came alone, even though her mother asked her to bring Norman. It was not only her wish to keep her two lives separate; she also did not want the melancholy she experienced there to invade her life with him. Since Susan's father's death, her mother had not been well, and the responsibility for caring for her had fallen on Frank and Hazel, who now lived with her. Susan's brothers were not in good health themselves, and Susan knew that they could use her assistance, but she also knew that it was impossible for her to spend much time in Davenport, a place she might celebrate in fiction but which she found stifling and depressing in reality. As often as she could, she sent her family checks, so often that her mother cautioned, "You are too liberal with your hard earned money."[71] But sending money was easy compared to being there. This visit lasted two months, from Thanksgiving through the New Year, and Susan filled her letters to Norman with longing and desire to quickly return to their home. It was exactly two years since they had met, and she reminds him of that first Thanksgiving they shared: "We went home together and you stayed the night. A night of strange beauty." In answer, he writes of "nice Norman who loves you and will cherish you and tell you stories and boast and walk long walks with you in the woods; and sleep with you all night long or call through the open door goodnight, good morning."

For him, too, the receipt of *Road* had been a special moment. "I kept reading at it all that day and evening. Couldn't stop. I felt my old feeling of interest, sympathy, and profound initiation with Jig. I doubt if we'd been friends. But you've made him live. You've given him continuing life. What a beautiful thing for a woman to have done for a man." He admits a special connection to the work because of his part in the suffering that produced it. "Oh remember Norway! The pain, the fight you made, the days of despair buried deep in old old scraps of paper. Now . . . very finely received. Oh I'm so glad my honey's book is going over!"—words ironically reminiscent of what Harry told Claire in *The Verge*. His own Norway work was stuck, and he had little incentive to complete it, after his disappointment over the failure of *Flecker's Magic*, despite Forster's praise. One way of alleviating the sting was drinking. Throughout the summer and fall Norman made his own wine, and he gave her a count of the kegs he had filled with this home brew and the bottles he had decanted. "Even if we drink a quart a day it will last till May." While she had been away, he had kept himself busy by going to parties, mostly drunken revels. He had spent New Year's at Mary's, flirting with her daughter Ellen, a sign to Mary that time had finally caught up with her. For Susan, on the other hand, the beginning of 1927 seemed the start of a new life. She had love, and she was ready for a new project, now that she'd successfully paid her debt to Jig by bringing out the book of his life. "I want to write other things" and "I want to live with my Norman," she wrote from Davenport.

Novel Times

24

I am interested in novels these days, thinking about them.
        —Susan Glaspell, Letter to Norman Matson

Now that *The Road to the Temple* was behind her, Susan was anxious to return to fiction. In preparation she began avidly to read new novels—and there were many from which to choose. In the three years since her return from Greece, Willa Cather had published *The Professor's House, My Mortal Enemy,* and *Death Comes to the Archbishop*; Virginia Woolf, *Mrs. Dalloway* and *To the Lighthouse*; F. Scott Fitzgerald, *The Great Gatsby*; Ernest Hemingway, *The Sun also Rises*; and John Dos Passos, *Manhattan Transfer.* All, with the possible exception of Cather's, were examples of a new sensibility at work, a modernist bent, addressed to a postwar audience that no longer looked for, or believed in, one universal order or overriding belief system or ideal to guide their lives. Susan held to the idealist notion that love might meliorate the alienation of the present period and provide a lost generation with a compass pointing home. Rather than plots with complications and clear resolutions, these novels presented fragments of daily life and personal relationships without any attempt to systematize or explain either. For Susan, such writing was interesting, even admirable, but not what she wanted to do. She had begun her career as a newspaper writer at the beginning of the century, and she still believed in the efficacy of stories and the truths derived from them. She might believe that "Life, too is combinations that baffle classification,"[1] and she might desire to break forms and move her women characters out of confining circles, but as far as her fiction went, she was still wedded to traditional structures. *Mrs. Dalloway,* therefore, disappointed her: "I admire Virginia Woolf so much," she wrote Norman, "that I wonder why I don't like her more. She makes the inner things real, she does illuminate and she makes realities as well as people. But I remember the intensity the thrill with which I read *A Passage to India*, how I would have hated anyone who took the book away from me. In *Mrs. Dalloway* you can about as well read one part of the book as another. If one could have what she has, or something of it, and have also a story, that simple downright human interest."[2] In addition to Woolf, she had also been reading Cather. In *My Mortal Enemy* she found "too much is shut out. It is moving, has in it some great insight and beauty and wisdom but it doesn't do for one what *The Professor's House* did nor did it get me as *The Lost Lady* did." Sigrid Undset's *The Wild Orchid* was a novel she did admire. "It will complete the work of making you a Catholic," she told Norman. "She is a great wise woman. It makes Norway so real and so beautiful." While she makes no reference to recent Edith Wharton fictions, she did see the stage adaptation of *The Age of Innocence*, and found Wharton's depiction of society "cold and arrogant righteousness. We've got a better feeling about life now. If Mrs. Wharton doesn't know it she'd better stop," she reported to Norman.

It was not that Susan denied the importance of capturing the inner life of characters; after reading Stanislavski's *My Life in Art*, she had jotted in her notebook, "a conscious path to unconscious creativeness."[3] In her theatre work she had been at the forefront of those who attempted to stage the unconscious, but as a novelist, she was convinced that the reader deserved a good tale. The trick, she believed, was to balance inner and outer reality, giving equal weight to character development and plot. In notes for a talk about how one wrote novels, she explained: "If you made your plot and put your people in it your book would be dead as a doornail. It all has to grow along together—events shaped by what people feel and are. At the same time—form. People can't run wild all over the place. Direction; and proportion. But fluid—always fluid—that's the great thing—so that the turn things take can surprise even *you*."[4]

In the winter of 1927, back in Provincetown, Susan returned to fiction for the first time since *Fidelity* in 1915, and attempted to put her theories into practice. As she often did, she turned to earlier notebooks, where she had jotted down one or two sentence descriptions that might later be worked into stories. One notebook, dated October 16, 1915, begins with the entry: "The country boy and girl—lovers, he killed by farm machinery—she is pregnant, her family, his mother—the man who is willing to marry her."[5] This became the plot of the first section of *Brook Evans*, one of her most popular novels. The theme of this novel must have been influenced by her recent visit to Davenport, where Susan had once more confronted small-town conservatism, particularly when it came to sexual matters. Set against a series of landscapes she knew well, the story of *Brook Evans* traces four generations of one family who suffer the consequences of trying to break social patterns. The first section begins in 1888, in rural Illinois, on a farm similar to one on which her aunt Ruth lived and Susan had visited as a child. In the second and third sections, the story jumps nineteen years later, to the Colorado mountains, around Monte Vista. After another two-decade jump, the story concludes in the fourth section in Paris and Senlis, places where Susan and Norman had stayed during their European travels in 1925.

The initial protagonist of the first section is eighteen-year-old Naomi Kellogg, passionately in love with Joe Copeland, whose more prosperous farm adjoins her own and whose autocratic mother refuses to sanction the match. Undaunted, the young girl meets her lover by the brook separating their properties. When Joe dies in a farming accident and Naomi discovers she is pregnant with his child, she is convinced by her fearful parents to marry Caleb Evans, an older parishioner of their church, who is willing to raise the child as his own in the Colorado homestead he has purchased. Naomi's daughter, Brook, named after the place of love, is the focus of the next two sections. She is now a young woman experiencing her own first romance. Naomi does not want her to suffer the horrors she has had to endure in a loveless marriage and encourages her daughter's romance with a young man Caleb has forbidden her to see. When Brook discovers her true parentage, she turns on the mother she now reviles, embracing her father and his strict adherence to religion, convinced that her future lies not in personal happiness but in helping others through missionary work abroad. It is only in the final part of the book, set in the present, that the now-widowed Brook, an expatriate living in France, comes to realize the life-affirming experience of passionate love and decides to go off with a man she has just met, a wild, lusty Norwegian mathematician, Eric Helge. It is left to her teenaged son, Evans, to make their planned trip back to the family farm in Illinois and lay flowers on Naomi's grave, a sign that her daughter now understands and embraces the love for which her mother had been willing to risk all and that she tried to bequeath to Brook.

While Susan is not the first in her period to overturn conventional mores and show the woman who seeks love and sex as more moral and life-affirming than the one who denies both, she does break new ground by placing the scenes of lovemaking next to a midwestern brook rather than on a Long Island pier or at a Spanish bullfight, thus setting up the battle lines in the heart of the region she knew best and which was still so inimical to the message she delivered. *Brook Evans* is dedicated to Norman. In the concluding section, the very rapidity of Brook's affair with Helge parallels Susan's immediate attraction to Norman, although unlike her protagonist, she was reclaiming love, not experiencing it for the first time. Even the brook, which is the symbolic center of the novel, representing love, sexuality, and continuation, derives from the special brook the pair had discovered in Norway. "My brook," Matson has Ruth call it, "the one that came down through the birches," which she had cried over when it was time to depart.[6]

Susan's work on the novel was interrupted at the end of February 1927, when she was called to New York, to sit in on rehearsals of *Inheritors*, which Eva LeGallienne had selected to complete the opening season of her Civic Repertory Theatre. It had been Jig's dream to establish a theatre that could run its best productions in repertory and not be prey to the lure of Broadway. LeGallienne had the same dream. She had been impressed with the little theatres she found in New York, when she arrived from London in 1915, a sixteen-year-old with some experience on the English stage. In December 1925, when George Pierce Baker invited her to address his theatre class at Yale (where he was then teaching), she argued that the successes of groups like the Provincetown Players indicated that America had talent that could rival that of Europe. "Eugene O'Neill and Susan Glaspell have no superiors," she proclaimed. In words which would have thrilled Jig, she went on, "Let us make the theatre of America stand free and high up, with no world peers."[7] It was banker and patron of the arts Otto Kahn, whom Jig had half-heartedly approached for aid, who put up a portion of the money that allowed LeGallienne to start her own theatre, located on the north side of Fourteenth Street, west of Sixth Avenue. Before starting her company, LeGallienne had gained a reputation as a serious actor and had been acclaimed for her productions of Ibsen plays. In 1924 she had spent a summer working with Jasper Deeter at Hedgerow, and it was probably he who introduced her to *Inheritors*, a play he cherished and had begun producing the year before. Glaspell's stirring message of individualism and action in the face of "bigness" and "practicality" spoke directly to LeGallienne and her own fight against Broadway. In addition, she must have been drawn by the fact that the central hero is a woman, an important point for the feminist director/actor, a lesbian, whose administrative organization consisted only of women.

Unfortunately, tragedy struck the *Inheritors* cast. Just before the opening night, March 7, Sydney Machet, the young man scheduled to play the dual role of Silas and Ira Morton, committed suicide, throwing the cast into shock and requiring that his understudy play the role on opening night with script in his hand. Whether the reviews would have been better had this not occurred is difficult to say. Unlike the Liverpool production, mounted two years earlier, this one received only a lukewarm reception, critics calling the play dated. But while acknowledging "its too obvious effort to teach a lesson," R. Dana Skinner, in the *Commonweal* praised the "sheer poetry and an abundance of authentic feeling woven into the play, not to mention its sharp and often scathing social analysis."[8] Despite its tepid reception, LeGallienne did not regret her choice. In her autobiography *At 33* she writes that if she could, she would require all young Americans to read or, better yet, see the play: "*Inheritors* is not perhaps a 'good play,' but it is a burning challenge to America, full of indignation against the results of a too rapid, too greedy prosperity. . . . The play is a tonic, and I heartily recommend it as an antidote to incipient smugness!"[9]

Susan sat in on rehearsals offering suggestions, but she was reluctant to attend the opening night, disliking public occasions. However, at LeGallienne's insistence she came and was heartened by an audience, "young, keen, and responsive," who, the *Herald Tribune* critic reported, "listened with intelligence, and occasionally was so moved . . . that it interrupted the action with little bursts of applause."[10] In her notes about the opening, LeGallienne also describes the enthusiasm of the audience, their calls of "author, author," and a timid Glaspell, hoisted to the stage by four young men, who was only able to murmur, "I'm so glad you liked my little Play," before making a quick exit.[11] *Inheritors* ran for thirty-three performances in repertory, one of the less-acclaimed works in LeGallienne's successful opening season, but one that had a special meaning to the director, who played Aunt Isabel in the production. She continued to champion Glaspell, whom she called "the greatest of our American dramatists." As Susan's friends recalled, LeGallienne was the only person that Susan allowed to call her Susie. The two remained close friends; and whenever she was on the Cape, LeGallienne would visit her.

After this flurry of activity, Susan was delighted to return to Norman. Together, in April 1927, they opened the Truro house, which had become by this time their home, a place they both loved and shared. From New York, she had written him about the pain of separation and her desire to be together. "We will write; we will love each other and be happy, won't we dear? Spring will come and maybe we will fall in love all over again, as the bulbs come out in Truro." As much as she describes the solitary pleasures they would share, both also craved the company of others. In his descriptions of her, Matson points to this anomaly in Susan: At times, particularly in front of strangers who did not interest her, she might be silent, almost at the point of fainting from boredom, or reticent, self-contained, even shy, like the woman LeGallienne describes awkwardly standing on the stage trying to find words to address an adoring audience. However, surrounded by those she found stimulating, she was herself, a self-assured woman, alive to those around her. Toward her Provincetown friends, she felt a particularly kinship and warmth, and they responded in kind. In addition to Neith, Hutch, and Mary, by the summer of 1927, a younger group had formed and Susan became a central figure in this new constellation. Although over twenty years separated the first and second arrivals, they quickly formed a close community.

The center for this new group was the communal house rented by Katie and Bill Smith (siblings from Michigan who had grown up with Ernest Hemingway), Edith Foley, and Stella "Knobby" Roof, who became known as the Smooleys, a combination of their initials. The women were all close friends, unmarried, and in no hurry to change their status. During their first summer in Provincetown, the Smooleys rented one of the Hapgood cottages along the bay, but the next year Katie and Bill convinced Mary Vorse to sell them the Arequipa and another house that stood at the foot of the wharf that contained the original Provincetown theatre. Repairing the properties buffeted by the severe gales of the winter and combining the structures, the Smiths created a wonderful living space. Some dubbed it Bachelor Hall, since single men could come there without fear of complications from the women, who shunned serious relationships, but who were more than willing to suggest other mates for their callers. One who eventually found his way to the Smooleys and into the social group was John Dos Passos. Dos, as he was called, had by the mid-1920s established a solid reputation as a reporter, novelist, and nascent playwright and was looking for a congenial locale in which to write and engage in summer sports, which he loved. He also was drawn to Provincetown because his father was Portuguese. The group immediately embraced Dos, who was lively and passionate about ideas and about life, "as accessible as Eugene O'Neill was solitary," Mary Vorse wrote.[12]

Dos's passion during the 1927 summer was the Sacco and Vanzetti case. Seven years earlier, at the height of the Red Scare, Nicola Sacco, a shoemaker, and Bartolomeo Vanzetti, a fish seller, had been accused of the murder and robbery of two men in Braintree, Massachusetts, and sentenced to death. Attention fixed on the pair because they were known anarchists; even if not guilty of the crime for which they were accused, they were guilty of being "anarchists bastards," as Judge Webster Thayer, the presiding judge in at the trial, declared.[13] The case gained international attention, since it pitted those who championed workers' rights, immigration, and progressive policies against the supporters of 100 percent Americanism rampant after World War I. Susan, in *Inheritors*, had already addressed many of the issues the Red Scare raised and was, therefore, in total sympathy with the men and the efforts made on their behalf by the Citizen's Committee, headed by Dos. She became a signatory to a petition calling on the governor of Massachusetts to temporarily stay the execution, scheduled for August 10. When he did so, she traveled to Boston with Provincetown friends and joined others from her earlier Greenwich Village days, including Polly Holladay, Ruth Hale, and Edna St. Vincent Millay, who picketed during the next thirteen days, until the men were eventually executed on August 23.

Edmund Wilson was also a 1927 addition to the Provincetown group. His first wife was Mary Blair, a Provincetown Players actor; and although separated from him, she suggested he write Susan, when he was looking for a summer rental for himself and their young daughter, Rosalind. Susan had him contact John Francis, who arranged for them to take over O'Neill's Peaked Hill Bars home, when Jimmy Light suddenly had to cancel for the summer. From there Wilson would often walk over the dunes and mix in the social life of the town, attending parties and inviting the group to visit him. Wilson returned to Provincetown in 1930 and again the next summer, when he rented Susan's house, bringing with him his new wife Margaret Canby.

Of the two men, Dos was closer to Susan than Wilson was. After 1929, he made his home directly across the street from hers, and she saw him daily, when he was in town. Dos's intellect, stamina, and good spirits appealed to her, as Joe O'Brien's had. Wilson was less an intimate, and her main contacts with him were only during a few summers and through occasional letters over the next decade. He mentions her in his diaries of the 1920s and 1930s, but sometimes with condescension, as he tended to do with others, particularly women. One entry reads: "Dramatist friend who had formula: three points—condition at the beginning of play, 'which grows'—obstacle at end of second act, which is removed by surprise—ditto at end of third act." He also quotes her about the passage of time: "About our age—you know, there's the young thing, and then there's the middle-aged thing, and then there's the older thing—and then, after that, there's just mumbling and shaking the cane—this way."[14] Twice he refers to her use of the word *nice*, a tendency Glaspell was aware of and even defended in a poem, found in her notes, in which she argues that this much maligned word needed rehabilitation, because the world could stand a little more "niceness." *Nice* was not a Wilson word.

Susan formed closer bonds with many of the women of this younger Provincetown group. In addition to Katie and Knobby, she became friendly with Marguerite Kaselau, a beautiful and talented painter, much beloved in the community, who died at a young age and was eulogized by both Vorse and Hapgood in their autobiographies; Phyllis Duganne, a writer, who had arrived in town with her young daughter and mother and after several years married Eben Given, a local painter; Dorothy Smith, a dancer, who believed, as Hutch reported, that "no man and probably no woman was worth much who didn't drink to an extreme"[15]; and Bill and his wife Lucy L'Engle, whom most called "the duchess" because of her haughty airs, but whom Susan, ever the peacemaker, almost alone among their friends defended, because "she didn't think they ought to be discriminated against because they were rich."[16]

This new community would meet in the late afternoon for spontaneous meals, often at Susan's, where her "box suppers" of cold chicken and preserves were similar to what Eleanor offered in *The Comic Artist*. They were washed down by the latest cache of liquor bootleggers had abandoned and the tide had washed up on the Provincetown beaches or by the homebrew Norman and others were making. If it were an evening party, however, discussions of politics or literature usually gave way to wild dancing and more serious drinking, often culminating in fistfights and broken furniture. During this period Susan and Norman drank heavily, in keeping with the tenor of the times, when drinking became a way of asserting independence against governmental intrusion on private life—a rationale popular in Provincetown, which now had, as Neith Boyce put it, "an increasing number of drunks."[17] With the older group, Norman had been an outsider, only partially filling the huge place carved out by Jig. Years before, as if foreseeing such a situation, Susan had jotted down an idea for a story in one of her notebooks: "The woman who brings the man she is going to marry (or has) into a group, like ours. Their disappointment—bewilderment at his dullness. Trying to figure out why she married him. Feeling something wrong."[18] He was not much liked by the younger group either despite his closeness to their age. "He had a sloppy, loose mouth I didn't like," Miriam Hapgood Dewitt recalled.[19] When Edmund Wilson writes of him, he focuses on another physical trait: "his eyelids half drooped as if he were a sleepy child."[20] Often the look derived from too much drink. At one dinner party, which Susan and he attended, Neith reported to Marguerite that Norman "as usual got drunk early and left the party in peace," not before he had responded to a conversation Hutch and Susan had over Jig (possibly the one Hutch later describes in his book), saying, "in a pathetic alcoholic manner: 'It's *awful* nice to keep the dead alive. Life is so short and so sad, but let's dance.'"[21] When Susan was away from Provincetown, either in Davenport or in New York, Norman would write her almost daily, frequently complaining about their friends, either his alienation from them or his boredom with them. "The trouble with Provincetown people is this: they are all respectable. I'm not."[22]

Susan worked hard to encourage and promote Norman's work. During the winter of 1927, she made several trips to New York, during which she sought medical assistance for recurring problems with her teeth, kidneys, and legs. Despite a swollen, arthritic foot that caused her to wear a temporary brace, she still made the rounds of publishers, trying to interest them in both Matson's *Day of Fortune* and their joint work, *The Comic Artist*. In the spring Ernest Benn brought out the latter in his Contemporary Playwrights Series, prompted by Susan's growing reputation in Britain; and Stokes followed soon after in the States. However, she still could not find a major producer willing to stage it. She had more success with *Day of Fortune*, which Matson had completed by the middle of 1927 and dedicated to her. Unable to convince Farrar to take it, she turned to Stokes, who brought it out in 1928. Just as she had provided encouragement and practical help with the writing, she now turned her energies to promoting the book, contacting two acquaintances of earlier years, Sherwood Anderson and Theodore Dreiser. "The book is alive, so I feel an obligation to it, and at once thought of you in thinking of the people who should know about it," she wrote to Anderson in June 1928. To Dreiser she explained: "I would just feel more comfortable, somehow, to think you knew about it."[23]

In the late summer of 1927, after her activities for *Inheritors* and Sacco and Vanzetti, Susan returned to *Brook Evans* and completed it a few months later. On March 17, 1928, Victor Gollancz in London, who had published *The Glory of the Conquered* and *Fidelity*, published it, and an American edition by Stokes appeared three months later. On the dusk jacket Gollancz wrote: "I had always held, that if Susan Glaspell would turn again to a novel, choosing a theme of universal significance, we should have one of the great novels of our time. *Brook Evans* is such a novel. A book, profound, beautiful, fearless, and true in every page." Critical reaction, particularly in Britain, supported his enthusiasm. *The Statesman* proclaimed that "no one who is interested in the varied outgrowths of the American novel should pass it by,"[24] and the *Oxford Magazine* listed it as one of most successful novels written by a woman that year, along with works by Anne Douglas Sedgwick, Margaret Kenney, and Virginia Woolf. But *The Observer* cautioned that "Miss Glaspell has the mood, but not the machinery of greatness. She sees the high tragic fact, but does not always know what to do with it."[25] More positive was the long piece in the *New York Times Book Review* by John Chamberlain, accompanied by an ink drawing of Glaspell by Bernard Sanders, which reinforced the myth that Susan was still in her thirties although she had passed the age of fifty. *Brook Evans*, Chamberlain argues, is a response to the "commotion" recently made by Van Wyck Brooks, Sherwood Anderson, and Waldo Frank, against the incipient puritanism of America, which thwarts artists. "It plays love of life and of the beautiful off against the sour Protestantism of the rural mid-America of the '80s."[26] Although the reader might assume that Glaspell is delivering "a commonplace sermon on the superiority of the pagan ideal," Chamberlain is quick to add that the novel offers something more—namely, the story of the intricate relationship between a mother and daughter.

It is not surprising that Susan's own mother found the book disturbing. Unlike *The Glory of the Conquered*, which she felt captured her daughter's "high, pure ideals to life," this novel, with its cowering, vindictive, or sexually starved mothers and its open avowal of sex outside marriage and brutal sex within, shocked her; and she wrote Susan in June about her disapproval. In a second letter, written the next month, she modified her position: "Susie, dear, when I thot [*sic*] I had hurt you after all your hard work, I was hurt myself but I did not realize the story and after I read the different reviews I thot differently. I am old and my thots are slow and weak but I think you will understand. I am so thankful the book is so well received, and I think the reviews from London are very remarkable, from so far."[27] Sales of the book were good, although it was not the best seller the *Retail Bookseller* had predicted. Curtis Brown, Susan's agent, issued her a royalty payment two months after the British edition appeared for $5,878. One sign of its popularity was the fact that Paramount studios in Hollywood, on the lookout for material, now that *The Jazz Singer* had made movies talk, purchased the rights to the novel in 1930 and commissioned the playwright Zoë Akins to write the screenplay, entitled *The Right to Love*, with Ruth Chatterton, "the first lady of the screen," in the triple role of young Naomi and young and older Brook. The book was also translated in 1929 into German under the title *Narzissa* and in 1936 into Rumanian, entitled *Dreptul La Iubire* (*The Right to Love*), the title of the film. Atkins' screenplay was also published in both the United States and Britain. Why Susan was not selected to write the screenplay is not clear.

During the summer of 1928, now that *Day of Fortune* and *Brook Evans* were completed, Susan and Norman relaxed, but by the fall they were both on their next writing projects: he, a science fiction novel, *Doctor Fogg*, about a man who came from outer space, she, a story, as yet untitled, which drew on her Delphi experience for its locale. Again she turned to an earlier notebook for inspiration. Among her notes on Greece, she had described an actress unable to perform because she had lost her ability to speak. In the same notebook, she wrote the names of two women she had known in Delphi: Theodora, the young refugee from the Turkish expulsion, who had worked for her, and Constantina, an eleven-year-old shepherd girl who lived on the slopes of Parnassus and whom Jig had hoped to include in his Delphi Players. Her new novel weaves the stories of these three women together. Its protagonist, Irma Lee Shraeder, is not an actress but a former teacher, who stops speaking after her husband leaves her and her young daughter suddenly dies. Intending at first to take her life, Irma, instead, flees to Delphi, through the intervention of a well-meaning relative. There, "loosed from the scheme of things," she creates for herself a new identity among the people who call her with respect the Kyria Archai [ancient or sovereign Madame], believing that her silence indicates her affinity to the spirits of the place. The Delphi scenes take up approximately the first third of the story, although this time Susan neither divides the narrative into sections nor tells the events in chronological order, preferring to begin on the day of Irma's failed suicide and rescue, followed by her voyage to Greece, during which the silent, ghostly woman meets an archeologist, patterned on Miss Eldridge, and a strange ménage à trois: a young man clearly in love with the vibrant woman married to his friend. This part is followed by scenes in Delphi over a period of time, during which the Kyria becomes a much-loved figure in the village; it culminates with her sudden return to speech, when she witnesses young boys torturing a helpless puppy. "Was it for this Jesus died?" she shouts, saving the dog and thus breaking the silence which had sealed her past from her.[28]

The second section provides flashbacks to Irma's early years in a family, whose history closely resembles Susan's. Again, as in *Brook Evans*, she describes the difficulty a daughter has in showing affection to the mother, who clearly adores and lives vicariously through her, and her easier relationship with her father, who is less demanding in his love. Irma eventually marries Dan, a man bearing certain characteristics of Norman. Although he is an architect, it is she who selects their house in Truro, one her ancestors the Chippmans (Glaspell's own New England antecedents) had built. Thus the house once more is the woman's. "Even though it isn't my house, I will live in your house forever," Dan tells her. Forever, however, is only a few years. He loves parties, drinking, and dancing; she prefers her garden, child, and home. Tellingly, the one moment when their lovemaking finally involves her as much as him occurs when he returns briefly after their separation on news of the sudden death of their daughter from infantile paralysis.

Having filled in Irma's background, Susan returns her story to Delphi in the third, and least effective, section of the novel. Having regained her voice, Irma can now assess past mistakes and explore her future. In Glaspell's terms, she is ready to know love, and the novelist conveniently supplies a recipient: John, the man on the ship, who turns out to be her absentee landlord. Although the pair comes together in the shadow of the ancient stones, Susan withholds the expected ending; the man still loves another. Undaunted, Irma declares her willingness to be a mother figure for him, just as she becomes the mother figure for the shepherd girl, Constantina, whom she eventually takes back to America.

That her new novel starts with a woman's husband leaving home because he felt too confined by the life she has created for them seems to indicate her own awareness of Norman's feelings and her fear that her control of the direction of their lives might one day lead to the destruction of their relationship as well. Yet, she also includes the shadowy John, at the end of the story, who causes Irma to think, "It had seemed everything of life was behind her, and then so easily, naturally, had come the change. It made life as a miracle, and kinder than it had ever seemed before." This late love she describes as something different from early passion. "The urge in love is not only to bring the lovers together; it is to throw themselves against the impossible—to break down that last barrier—breaking down loneliness," an idea she often repeated to Norman in their correspondence, calling their love "salvation." Tellingly, the relationship with John ends with both declaring their deep connections, based not on physical but maternal love.

In *Road* the transitions between Greece and Iowa worked; in *Fugitive's Return* the shifts are artificial and jarring. It may well be that when she began the novel, in the spring of 1928, she did not intend to introduce material about Davenport. However, that fall, before she had gotten very far or even settled on a title, she was called back home because of her mother's failing health, and the place may have worked itself into the draft she took with her. Mrs. Glaspell was beginning to display signs of dementia, sometimes unable to recognize her daughter. At one point she asked Susan, "Were you in Greece when Susie was there?" and went on to admit that she "hadn't wanted Susie to marry George Cook but afterwards she liked him." That these moments would be followed by periods of lucidity made the experiences even more disconcerting. Susan confided to Norman: "It gives such a strange feeling to hear all this about Susie, as if I really were another person. She showed me my picture and said who is that? That's me I said. Oh no, she said: that's Susie. But I am Susie mother I said. Oh no, she said, you haven't the same characteristics." Often her mother would tell her stories about what "Susie did," incidents Susan had completely forgotten. These painful sessions of dredging up the past are similar to what she has Irma Lee Shrader experience in the novel, which Susan returned to several months later. They also must have been reminders to Susan of the double life she had always maintained with her family.

Susan spent a month in Davenport, returning to Provincetown just before Christmas 1928. She had not been well before the visit, suffering from recurrent bouts of arthritis, which swelled her leg, and bladder infections that sapped her strength. In addition, her old problem with her teeth flared up. After New Year's, she went to New York for treatment and was forced to stay there, at the Hotel Seville, for three to four weeks. Infected tissue in her gums required that she have three teeth extracted, and it would take time before she could be fitted with replacements. Her doctor also treated her bladder problems with silver nitrate and "put me on the wagon," she wrote Norman. Although she was ill, she did have time to write to Covici Friede, the publisher engaged in a highly publicized lawsuit about the American release of Radclyffe Hall's *The Well of Loneliness*, a novel about lesbian love. "Have read this serious interesting novel and action against it seems preposterous to me."[29] Although the letter showed her lifelong dislike for any sort of censorship, she was also recording her acceptance of women's rights to any form of sexuality they chose. Lesbianism was certainly not something new to her; several of the women in Heterodoxy had long-standing relationships, which they discussed in their meetings. She had also recently forged a close connection with openly avowed lesbian LeGallienne. However, during the past theatre season, when she had attended a performance of *The Captive*, the first Broadway presentation of lesbian love, she criticized it, not for its subject matter but for its failure to make contact with the audience, a need that was paramount to her as a playwright. "Drama should have its roots in everyone's experience," she felt. "Here you look on, finding out something about a thing quite outside from experience. It has thrilling scenes but leaves you quite cold." One point she fails to mention is the play's reliance on a central lover who is never seen but who sends violets to the woman she loves. The absent figure is a device she herself had used in *Trifles* and *Bernice*, and seeing it once more may have prompted her to consider using it again in the next play she was to write, *Alison's House*.

Susan was just back from New York, and still not well, when she received a cable on February 15 from her brother Ray telling her that her mother was near death. "Not more than one or two days." The next day he wrote, "Mother very low. The end within a few hours. She has no pain."[30] On February 17, 1929, Alice Glaspell died at the age of eighty. Her health had worsened during the previous two weeks, but no one expected her to go so quickly. Susan wrote explaining that she was ill, and Ray cabled back that it was not necessary for her to make the long trip, since she had recently been there to say her good-byes. Although Susan didn't attend the funeral, her name was much in evidence in the obituary, the headline reading "Alice Glaspell, Mother of Famed Writer, is Dead."[31] Frank and Flossie, Ray's wife, wrote her long letters describing in detail the funeral and burial. She also received a letter from her cousin Ruth. After telling Susan that her mother "did look so nice and restful," she writes, "How hard it is to have homes broken. . . . For of course Frank and Hazel will not want to remain here and that is another home that is a thing of the past."[32]

The death of her mother, her own health problems, and her accelerated drinking now made it difficult for Susan to work. In June, when she was interviewed for a full-page feature story in the book section of the *Boston Evening Transcript*, she was still struggling with *Fugitive's Return*, which "had been delayed by many interruptions," she told the interviewer, careful to avoid details.[33] During the summer, Norman set out on his own adventure. He had read a short article in the *Provincetown Advocate* announcing the final round-the-world voyage of the *Coriolanus*, a commercial, three-masted sailing ship similar to those once used to carry people and cargo between the Azores and New Bedford, Massachusetts. He decided to join the voyage as far as Cape Verde and record the event, the only passenger on the stately schooner that this time carried a modern cargo—used cars. With him away, Susan was able to quickly complete work on *Fugitive's Return*. It came out in America and Britain at the end of October 1929 and was less enthusiastically praised than *Brook Evans* the preceding year. Many critics noted the odd juxtapositions of story line and writing style. The *New York Times* review, reflecting her solid reputation by this time, was at pains not to openly criticize, but certainly hedged its words: "So much of an individual is Susan Glaspell one knows in advance that a novel from her pen will not be an ordinary book. This is not to say that it will necessarily be a notable book; it is merely to say that the narrative will reflect the individuality of the author."[34]

The novel appeared just as the American stock market crashed, sending many of Susan's friends into a financial decline. Hutch and Neith lost $30,000; $7,000 in just two days; and O'Neill, then living in France with his third wife, Carlotta Monterey, saw half his proceeds from the financially successful *Strange Interlude* disappear. Unlike them, Susan had not complicated her life by investing in the stock market during the boom years of the 1920s; therefore, she suffered little loss when the bubble burst. Actually, her tax return for 1929 lists a gross income of $20,064, a good year for her. Ten thousand dollars came from her sale of *Brook Evans* to Hollywood, which was the going rate for successful novels. (Pearl Buck had been offered the same for *The Good Earth*, but held out for and received $50,000.) She was also engaged in selling her one-act plays as possible scenarios for films. The year before, she had begun a correspondence with Barrett Clark, who had long admired her plays and suggested that *Trifles* would make a fine film and that he was willing to be her agent for the deal. Throughout 1929 they exchanged letters, Clark citing a possible $5,000 fee for *Trifles*, and she answering that she would take less, if it meant that the work could be sold. By December 20, Neith was reporting to Hutch that, in addition to *Brook Evans*, Susan had sold two short plays to Hollywood and that "she says they're crazy to get stuff."[35] "*Trifles* went for $2,000," she added. No film of it was ever made.

Alison's House

25

Alison said it—for women.

—Susan Glaspell, Alison's House

Even before *Fugitive's Return* was released, Susan turned her attention to a completely new project. Mary Vorse, who was spending the summer in Provincetown, recorded her friend's enthusiasm. "Seeing Susan in those days when she was first plunging her mind into Emily Dickinson's story was seeing a creative force at work."[1] Vorse left by the end of August and did not return until the following summer, so if she were present at the genesis of *Alison's House*, as she claims in *Time and the Town*, that means that Susan had already conceived of the idea as early as the summer of 1929, while she was alone, during Norman's sail. By February 1930 she had completed the play, and sent it off to the Theatre Guild. In April she received the news that they had rejected it. "It was disappointing," she wrote to Clark soon after, "but that disappointment was very much eased by your feeling about the play."[2] In the same letter she thanked him for suggesting that Samuel French, where he worked, might want to print it, but hesitated to do so until it was produced.

One of the factors which must have prompted her interest in Dickinson that summer was the activity associated with launching the celebrations leading up to the centenary of the poet's birth the following year, December 9, 1930. Several books were published to mark the occasion.[3] In 1929 Dickinson's niece, Martha Dickinson Bianchi, daughter of the poet's brother, brought out an edition of poems with the arresting title *Further Poems of Emily Dickinson: Withheld by her Sister Lavinia* to add to her co-edited *Complete Poems* and *The Life and Letters of Emily Dick-*

inson, both published in 1924. In 1930 additional Dickinson biographies by Josephine Pollitt and Genevieve Taggard appeared. Susan, who had recently completed Jig's biography, had long been interested in the form, particularly the lives of poets, and had avidly read Maurois's life of Shelley. She most likely read Bianchi's biography of her aunt, popular enough to have gone through six printings by 1929; and although Pollitt's and Taggard's books were published after Susan had completed her play, she might have seen the latter in manuscript, since Taggard was a well-known figure in Greenwich Village, whom she probably knew.[4] It was the Taggard biography that Glaspell selected, along with Virginia Woolf's *A Room of One's Own*, as reading material for her protagonist in *Ambrose Holt and Family*, the novel she completed immediately after *Alison's House*.

Pollitt and Taggard, following Bianchi, describe Dickinson as a recluse, marked by a great love for a married man, "instantaneous, overwhelming, impossible" and unnamed in Bianchi, posited as Edward Hunt by Pollitt, and as George Gould by Taggard. Susan makes him a Harvard instructor of English, whom the poet met when she accompanied her father to Cambridge and to whom she wrote her great love poems.[5] She also takes a page from the Dickinson family saga, introducing a protective brother, John Stanhope, called only "the Father," in the list of characters, but clearly patterned after Austin Dickinson, who was himself rumored to have loved a married woman, Mary Loomis Todd. In her play there is a spinster sister, Miss Agatha, who, like Dickinson's sister Lavinia, committed herself to the poet and to family honor; and a second-generation assortment of nieces and nephews who, like Bianchi, had a close relationship with their aunt. Susan also creates two additional characters: Anne Leslie, the daughter of Stanhope's lover, who now acts as his assistant, and whom he treats like the daughter she well may be, and Richard Knowles, a Chicago reporter, sent to cover the dismantling of the famous poet's home. However, missing from the play is the central woman herself. Alison Stanhope, the Dickinson surrogate, like Bernice before her, has died before the play begins, and it is the attempt of others to reclaim her through their memories and needs, which forms the central action.

Susan also shifts the time and locale of Dickinson's biography, setting the action on December 31, 1899, in the home where Alison Stanhope had lived, on the banks of the Mississippi, "with a village nearby and a small city ten miles up the river"—in other words, the Cabin near Buffalo, Jig's family home. Since 1881 Agatha has kept the house exactly as Alison left it. Now, frail herself, she is being moved to town to live with John, and it is to be sold to a couple who plan to make it a boarding house for summer tourists. Throughout two acts, as various characters pack and go through Alison's books and possessions, dredging up memories associated with them, Agatha sits nearby, clutching a small portfolio. It later proves to be a cache of love poems she withheld from the first posthumous publication of her sister's works—just as Lavinia withheld Emily's—fearful that their content would shame the family, since they suggest a love for a married man. Finally, at the curtain of the second act, Agatha discharges her duty. Handing the poems on to Elsa, her niece, she dies. The question the family now faces is what to do with them: destroy the poems, as the elder Stanhope counsels, or make them public, as the younger characters demand, Alison's "gift to the world," handed across the century from one generation to another, confirming the power of love, which does not die.

Susan did her homework well, reading all the source material available on Dickinson, and she was able to incorporate her research seamlessly into the writing. To supplement published accounts, she also had a firsthand source in Vorse, who had been born in Amherst to one of the prominent families in the community and had grown up with stories of the "queer" Dickinsons, particularly the reclusive "Miss Emily." Vorse may have shared her recollections with Susan, as she did with Taggard, who acknowledges her help in the biography.

Alison's House is Glaspell's only work directly inspired by an historical figure. That she should fix on Emily Dickinson is not surprising, since there are a number of connections between the two women writers. Both were keen observers of life and nature, able to weave the everyday and the extraordinary into their writing; they cultivated flowers and plants; wrote in an upstairs room; used frequent dashes to mark interstices, which should not or could not be filled; notated their much-loved editions of Emerson; and—as Glaspell believed—had the life-changing experience of great love for a married man. Both also came from small towns, which thrived on gossip, particularly when it involved sex. Susan knew only too well from her experiences with *The Road to the Temple* that families prefer to keep sensitive issues about their loved ones from appearing in print. Her revelations of Jig's foibles and her own had placed her on the side of the younger Stanhopes, who believe that the words that can convey the emotions of love and loss enrich all who read of them, even as they may shock the deniers of both. Dickinson also bore a resemblance to many of Susan's fictive women. Like them, she was thought *queer*, that word used to designate the brave woman rebel who fails to conform to the expectations of the society in which she lives. She was also reputed to have a special quality that set her apart yet drew people to her. This "apartness"—remaining inviolate, "uncaptured," and yet inspirational—was a trait Glaspell imparts to several of her women characters, particularly to her absent persona in *Bernice*.

The other characters in *Alison's House* echo earlier Glaspell women. Elsa Stanhope, who has disgraced her family by running off with a married man whose wife will not divorce him, bears a striking resemblance to Ruth Holland in *Fidelity*. For both, the moment of recognition comes suddenly at a dance, and they find that despite their strong moral principles, they must be true to the overwhelming love they experience, despite the consequences to themselves and others. In the novel, the father dies never having forgiven his daughter. In *Alison's House* the prodigal daughter returns and is embraced at the end of the play, through the agency of the ever-present Alison and the discovery of her poems, which give voice to Elsa's love and reveal the price Alison paid for denying hers.

Susan's recent loss of her mother and the breakup of her family home also influenced the play. As her cousin Ruth had reminded her "that is another home that is a thing of the past." The words must have struck a responsive note, for Susan had always displayed an acute sensitivity to homes, not merely as places of shelter and safety, but as material embodiments of, and links with, the past. *Alison's House*, as the title indicates, is as much about a physical place as it is about the woman who lived there. It is significant that a poem quoted in the play from Emerson is entitled "The House." A central question embedded in the work is: "What happens to the memories of lives lived and of loves felt, once others occupy the same place?" (A question Arthur Miller will later explore in *Death of a Salesman*.) In her emphasis on Alison's house, Susan takes her leave from Dickinson herself, who wrote in a letter, "Home is not where the heart is but the house and the adjacent buildings."[6] Of the many critics who reviewed the play, only one, a woman, noted this theme. Overlooked as well was Glaspell's originality in creating a play that moves outward from the story of one special dysfunctional family to point to the corrosive effects of all secrets buried in family life.

With so many details of the play directly connected to the life and writing of Emily Dickinson, the question remains as to why Susan chose to change the names, dates, and settings of the original biography. Both Arthur Waterman and Marcia Noe, in their earlier studies, indicate (without substantiating their claim) that the Dickinson estate refused the playwright permission to use the family name and story, and, therefore, Susan was forced to fictionalize the events. However, a few years later, Vincent York and Frederick J. Pohl in *Brittle Heavens* staged a version of Josephine Pollitt's biography, listing the members of the Dickinson family by name, including Emily and Captain Hunt. Barbara Ozieblo, another Glaspell biographer, also cites a letter from Bianchi to her publisher in October 1930 mentioning a play being written about Dickinson but making no complaint about it.[7] It is possible that the estate was simply not consistent since they forbid Pollitt the right to quote Dickinson's poems, but allowed Taggard to do so. Yet, had there been a dispute about using the actual names, it is certain that Eva LeGallienne, who finally produced the play, would have made much of the fact in the extensive pre-production material that her publicity people issued. It was they who promulgated the Dickinson connection, and it was immediately picked up by the New York Press, which reported: "*Alison's House* . . . purports to deal, rumors assiduously circulated by Miss LeGallienne's press department and others have it, with the effects on Emily Dickinson's family, after her death, of some of her poems previously unknown."[8] A dispute with the estate would surely have boosted interest in the play, but it was never mentioned, neither by the company nor by Glaspell in the several interviews that she gave prior to the opening and later, after it moved uptown.

In fact, in one published comment she made on the matter, Susan indicates her regret that it ever became known that she had read and admired Emily Dickinson. "The play was in no way founded on the life of Dickinson. It grew out of a feeling for her work and character," the *New York Times* reported her saying.[9] It may well be that she had no intention of making the connections with Dickinson overt and purposely chose to displace the action and change the names, lest the play be seen as a direct biographical study of the poet and not judged on its own merits. If this were her fear, her instincts were sound, because the Dickinson shadow almost completely obscured Glaspell's play. Despite the centennial activities, the poet was not sufficiently known to the general public to guarantee commercial success; and critics—strange as it may seem today—knew almost nothing about Emily Dickinson, except that she was the source for *Alison's House*, and they faulted the playwright for not telling them more. In addition, Susan must have been aware that a total identification with Dickinson, even if permitted, would too closely tie the play to the history of a specific woman and her time and make it impossible to introduce the many other issues that the play raises. She may also have feared possible litigation by the estate if she altered details or claims by biographers that she had co-opted their work. She certainly knew of the lawsuit instituted a few months earlier by a woman who claimed that O'Neill's 1929 Pulitzer Prize–winning play *Strange Interlude* was in fact plagiarized from her prior novel. In the suit, the woman charged that in addition to similarities between the two stories, O'Neill "took a beautiful ideal and brought it so low that I was shocked and scandalized."[10] The case was much discussed in Provincetown the summer Susan wrote *Alison's House*, and it could have prompted her to take precautions against facing a similar charge of distortion.

The play is set, like so many of Glaspell's works, on the verge, this time between one century and another; and the loss of the house becomes a metaphor for this change, just as it does in Chekhov's *The Cherry Orchard*, which was an important influence for the play. In her nod to Chekhov, Susan presents the youngest Stanhope, Ted, as the "modern" man, a cross between Lopakin and Yasha, espousing the mentality and language of the crass new epoch. He is interested in his poet-aunt only in order to curry favor with his English teacher at Harvard, himself an implied diminution of Alison's lover. The nature of the facts Ted is after—what did Emily eat, how did she sleep, was she a virgin—indicates that Susan is critiquing the tendency, already evident in 1930, for inquiring minds to want to know tidbits about the lives of famous persons. Any tidbits will do. Knowles, representing a newspaper, is also there to ferret out stories hidden in the house. Much ahead of its time, the play illustrates how the lives of artists tend to become fodder for a demanding public, a theme more recent audiences and critics have immediately understood.[11] Unfortunately, the press agents for LeGallienne—acting in the same spirit Glaspell critiques in the play—dangled the Dickinson connection and choice items in front of the press, who bit and structured their responses accordingly. In the fall of 1929, while writing her play, Susan had ample proof of how newspapers can distort the truth in their rush to sell papers and of how fact quickly became fiction and then myth. With the final collapse of the Provincetown Players, there was a flurry of articles on the original group, and she reluctantly agreed to be interviewed by the *New York Times*, which quoted her description of the 1916 season in the Wharf Theatre, when *The Emperor Jones*, *The Moon of the Caribees*, and *The Hairy Ape* were presented, by a company which included Edna St. Vincent Millay! Thus do myths grow.[12]

Norman had returned from his adventure on the *Coriolanus* in the late fall of 1929 with enough material for another book. *Doctor Fogg* had just been published, but quickly disappeared. Again, he began the painful process of composition, which came slowly and painfully to him, just as, he claimed, it flowed automatically for Susan. Ruth in his novel had no such trouble. "She writes novels and never re-writes a line, because if I thought it was right then how can I now change it? One must be loyal to oneself."[13] This ability must have been galling to him. Over the winter of 1930, they stayed in Provincetown, working and seeing a few friends who were now making it their permanent home, because of the economic depression. In the middle of March, they went to Chapel Hill, North Carolina, to spend two weeks visiting Susan's close friends Margaret and Wilbur Daniel Steele, who had recently moved there. Margaret had had two operations that winter, but was sufficiently recovered to take them to Charleston, South Carolina, where the Steeles had lived the previous year. On their return, Susan and Norman stopped off briefly in New York and were back in Truro by the middle of April, to open their house. Like a tourist who collects souvenirs to remind her of places visited, Susan tended to place cherished objects from trips in her writing. Therefore, in her next novel, *Ambrose Holt and Family*, she mentions a particularly lovely North Carolina vase and gives one of the characters a Charleston birth. The timing of their visit was fortunate; a few months later Margaret died, leaving Susan to mourn once more the passing of someone she had known well. Several months earlier she had received news that Mollie Price had died. "Somehow I didn't think of Mollie as one who dies," she wrote Norman when she got the news.[14] Harl was still living with his mother and stepfather at the time, but Nilla was in Greece and had given birth to a son, named Sirius, in December 1927. Five months later, Nilla went to India to become a disciple of Gandhi, on her own "road" quest.

In April 1930, with *The Comic Artist* and *Alison's House* still without producers, Susan returned to fiction; by November she had completed

Ambrose Holt and Family, based on *Chains of Dew*, her last-produced Provincetown play. The same characters appear in both novel and play, given different names, but in the novel instead of focusing on the misunderstood poet husband or the array of characters she introduces, Susan filters the action through the consciousness of the poet's wife, named Harriette but called Blossom, the flowerlike daughter of the richest family in town. She knows that she is "a woman who thought and felt," but "she had never succeeded in making anyone else know this; it must be her fault,"[15] she assumes, until she meets Ambrose Holt, her father-in-law, the new character Glaspell adds to the mix. He is a renegade, who many years before had escaped his own "fixed place" in the community, leaving his wife and young son behind. Susan provides three extended encounters between this odd couple, each debating responsibility versus personal happiness—the theme she developed in *Alison's House*—this time clearly coming down on the side of the rebel who leaves rather than the poet who stays. Although Susan makes it clear that Ambrose has the advantage of solitary travels and random life because he is a man, his actions still provide Blossom with a model that she can alter to suit her own needs. She does not desire to leave her convention-bound, pompous husband, although Ambrose and most contemporary readers wish she would. Instead, she realizes that it is sufficient for her to leave the old Blossom behind and assume her true identity as Harriette, still wife and mother, but now a more independent, self-assured person. Through her conversations with her father-in-law, she has, in fact, blossomed, Glaspell indicates. She has "gotten loose; she was out; she couldn't go back, for it would not be the same self she took back." In this resolve, she differs from her predecessor Dotty, who at the end of *Chains of Dew* allows her husband to assume she is unchanged. Seen in terms of Claire Archer's struggle in *The Verge*, Dotty had been an Edge Vine; Blossom is more a Breath of Life, but a less exotic variety than Claire hoped to cultivate. As for Claire's Nietzschean will to power, Ambrose rather ruefully says: "What is it the rather sentimental Nietzsche says? The pathos of distance. Don't take the unattainable from a poet." Instead, Blossom opts for what she considers the attainable following Ambrose's country wisdom: "See the world around you, Harriette. Love life and don't let any of them fool you." Unlike *Chains of Dew*, at the end of the novel, the husband, Lincoln, admits his weakness and his need to rely on his newly emancipated wife. Harriette, for her part, is positive about the prospects for their future. Since she has asserted herself and her husband recognizes and appreciates her strength, "she could be more patient now. She understood more, so she need ask less. It was all right. One took what was there, and went ahead. It was all a journey, a pretty good journey."

While the ending certainly is not a feminist triumph and is a far cry from the rebellion of *The Verge*, it is a more positive ending than Susan had offered in *Chains of Dew* seven years earlier. Such philosophy made the book a popular and critical success. John Chamberlain, usually quite favorable to her work, likened Ambrose Holt to many of Sherwood Anderson's characters and praised Glaspell's ability to offer comedy and then surprise. "If Henry Seidel Canby is still looking for the 'unknown man'—in this case the unknown woman—who consistently goes his own fruitful way through the waste land of the America that is to be beheld, let him turn and contemplate the career of Susan Glaspell."[16] Theodore Purdy in the *Saturday Review of Literature* invoked Henry James, who argued for "the profoundly ordinary side of life." It was this "which has so often stood Miss Glaspell in good stead, [and] has seldom been more in evidence than in this book in which no person or event is at all extraordinary."[17] This book of "profoundly ordinary" life proved to be one of Glaspell's better selling works.

While working on the novel during the summer, Susan still had time to be part of the active social life that had shifted from Provincetown to Truro. Katie Smith and John Dos Passos had married and purchased a house nearby. With them as neighbors, life became immediately gayer. Edmund Wilson and his wife, Margaret Canby, were occupying Peaked Hill Bars for the summer, Neith and Hutchins Hapgood were in Provincetown, and Ida Rauh, after several years in the Southwest, was back. Last summer's drinking went on unabated; so did the parties. It was the summer in which no one but Susan liked Lucy L'Engle, as Wilson reports, since they were unable to forgive her for visiting Katie and Dos's new house and announcing, "Why I don't think this house is so unattractive as everybody says it is!"[18] Norman by this time had become an accepted addition to the group, but the differences in the successes of the couple had become a topic of discussion—if not between Susan and Norman, then certainly among their friends. At one party Marguerite Kaselau was drunk enough to warn Susan that "it was a fatal mistake for a woman to make more money than her husband and would ruin any marriage, and the men always hated it." Kaselau reported to Hutch that "Susan was so upset she couldn't do any work today! But Norman seemed quite pleased."[19] That is not the image Norman conveys in his autobiographical novel. Often his fictive character Peter shows resentment at his inability to support himself and make his wishes known to Ruth. In a one-page fragment, possibly meant to go into the novel, Norman also describes this frustration. Out walking one day, his persona Peter discovers an old house near Wellfleet, which takes his fancy; but he is afraid to tell Ruth about his solitary find. She, however, senses something is afoot and is jealous. "In the night she comes to his bed and makes love to him. It is exhausting, and somehow desperate. They talk about their life together. Before they had been able to speak easily of the age difference but now, suddenly, it is not mentioned. A tacit understanding that they are to pretend that it doesn't exist."[20] Just as Norman reveals his own ambiguous feelings in his unpublished writing, Susan, too, expresses her feelings about the relationship in several undated fragments, one of which uses as its title the word *remember*, a common word used between them: "Remember what you loved in me I killed by loving you. . . . I believe there is a surge of life, like the tides, and when I go down to the shore I can no more hold back the tide than I can help loving you."[21]

With tensions surfacing, Susan held onto her work as ballast against the forces that seemed to be undermining their relationship. At the beginning of November, she received some welcome news. Eva LeGallienne had decided to stage *Alison's House*, and Barrett Clark had arranged for Samuel French to publish it immediately after the opening, scheduled for December 1, eight days before the centennial of Dickinson's birth.[22] By now LeGallienne had a devoted following who championed her work as the most significant alternative to Broadway available; however, December 1930 was hardly an auspicious time for an opening. The economy was worsening, and Broadway, in an effort to divert attention from the disaster, presented 190 plays during the year. A new play on Fourteenth Street that was not a musical or comedy could easily get overlooked, particularly during the holiday season—and particularly since it was a work about a dead poet, who does not appear and whom few in the audience would recognize if she did.

As she had done with *Inheritors*, once more LeGallienne asked Susan to attend rehearsals, at least those in the last two weeks leading up to the opening. Norman was already in New York, and their relationship was so troubled that she was not sure he would want to see her there. When she arrived in the last weeks of November, she stayed downtown at the Gramercy Park Hotel, in walking distance of the theatre, and Norman remained in the city, but not always with her. In preparation for the opening, she was photographed with LeGallienne. The two women, separated in age by twenty-three years, bear a striking resemblance to each other: They are similar in height and shape, with similar hairdos and in similar informal outfits. LeGallienne's hand rests on Glaspell's shoulder, while both gaze directly at the camera. Another photograph, taken by Helen Loehman on the day of the opening, was used in the subsequent news stories. This time, a more formal, remote Glaspell is seen in profile, bending down to read an open book in her lap, sitting on a rocking chair in front of a neatly arranged bookshelf. She is wearing a dark dress, with a wide lace collar running down the front, which gives the impression of a romantic, slightly old-fashioned bookish woman who might write a bookish play. Her appearance is still youthful for her fifty-four years, as interviewers noted, but it is altered by the removal of several teeth, that caused her mouth and jaw to sink noticeably.

In rehearsals Susan sat quietly in the back row of the cavernous theatre, making a few suggestions from time to time, but careful not to usurp the authority of LeGallienne, who believed in absolute control of her company. ("The whole company did what she did," recalled Josephine

Hutchinson, who played Madeline in *Inheritors*. "If she took high colonics, everyone did. She was like a guru. If she ate raw eggs, everybody ate raw eggs."[23]) One critic, in her review of *Alison's House*, remembered being touched by a glimpse of the playwright at one rehearsal, weeping silently as she watched the action on the stage. Whether it was in anticipation of the critical response, as this critic surmises, is not certain, but even before she came down to New York, Susan already had reservations about the production and its success. "I have cold feet about it. Don't believe it will get over—fear it won't be well played," she confided in a letter to Norman.[24]

Tears turned out to be the appropriate response. Despite fine acting by LeGallienne as Elsa, Alma Kruger as Miss Agatha, and Leona Roberts in the small role of Jennie, the maid, and despite the beautifully detailed Victorian sets, executed by Aline Bernstein, few critics praised the play. Ironically the Dickinson connection, the very gimmick used to get their attention, backfired. It was virtually the only subject critics discussed. Both Brooks Atkinson in the *New York Times* and Robert Littell in the *New York World* began their reviews with the same words: "For Alison of *Alison's House* . . . read Emily Dickinson."[25] Although all felt compelled to focus on Dickinson, few seemed to know very much about the poet; they either blamed Glaspell for not providing information or praised her for at least making them curious. Picking up the same theme, Burns Mantle in the *Daily News* writes, "If Susan Glaspell's play . . . does no more than send a lot of folk (like this reviewer) scurrying after Brentanos' new issue of Emily Dickinson's poetry it will have done something."[26] Atkinson at least recognizes that *Alison's House* is not to be seen as a strict gloss of the Dickinson story, yet he finds the drama "too abstract to evoke that image vividly" and "disappointingly allusive." John Mason Brown, in the *New York Evening Post* praises Glaspell for attempting to present a new idea, but also finds that the execution disappoints the expectations.[27]

The most dismissive review is from Robert Garland in the *New York World-Telegram*. Garland can barely hide his contempt for "Miss LeGallienne's non-commercial theatre," situated "beneath the 6th Avenue L." He states a feeling, implied by others, that Glaspell is talking down to the audience and critics, trying to foist a highbrow work on them, but he for one is not taken in. "Miss Dickinson, in case like me, you have not heard, was a lady poet whose I'm-sorry-for-myself verses rank high in the appreciation of the intelligentsia and who, when no one but herself was looking, suffered the pangs of unrequited love in the great open spaces of the American countryside. . . . She is a poetical prig who is dead but who will not lie down."[28]

There were a few who found the play moving. R. Dana Skinner, an earlier admirer of Glaspell, writing in the Catholic journal the *Commonweal*, congratulates her for invoking a character who never appears,[29] while Euphemia Van Rensselaer Wyatt, writing in *Catholic World*, mentions the "inanimate things" the family packs to move from their home.[30] Only she quotes Dickinson and seems to have some idea of the poet's work. The negative reviews took their toll: *Alison's House* was only performed twenty-five times over the next five months.

Susan stayed on in New York after the opening, meeting with Clark and conducting interviews, which she usually shunned but now undertook for the good of her play. By the holidays, she and Norman returned together to Provincetown. On December 31, she autographed a copy of *Alison's House* to Clark, "one of the first and best friends of *Alison's House* on this last day of the year, just thirty years after the time of the play."[31]

Needing a break after her New York experience and wanting a new locale to work out her problems with Norman, Susan agreed to take a vacation; and so, right after the New Year, the couple began a four-month trip to Mexico. The destination was not random. By the late 1920s, the country had become a haven for writers and artists seeking a warm climate and cheap, available wine. Mary Vorse had spent the preceding winter in Mexico City, where she met former Village habitué, Dorothy Day. Katie and Dos were also there in the winter of 1930 and decided to join Susan and Norman this winter, sailing to Mexico from Key West, where they first visited with Hemingway. "Mexico is beautiful, and most interesting. We are going to be down here until some time in April," Susan wrote to Barrett Clark from Cuautla.[32] In the letter she thanks him for letting her know of Walter Prichard Eaton's positive review of *Alison's House*. From Taxco, Norman wrote to Wilson and his wife, encouraging them to join them: "Quakes being put gradually under control. Tequila's strong and suave. . . . Maybe we'll never return."[33]

They did return four months later. Susan busied herself during her first week home answering the mail that had accumulated in her absence. On May 3, when she opened her mailbox and found a letter from Columbia University, she assumed it was yet another invitation to speak or an amateur theatre group seeking permission to do one of her one-acts without payment. Only later in the day, when she got around to reading the letter, did she learn that *Alison's House* had been awarded the 1931 Pulitzer Prize for drama. Her shock was as great as that of the critics, when they heard. She was only the second woman to receive the drama prize since its inception in 1917; Zona Gale was the first for *Miss Lulu Betts* in the 1921 season.[34] Among the other Pulitzer recipients for 1931 were Margaret Ayer Barnes for fiction, Charles W. Eliot for biography, and Robert Frost for poetry, each receiving $1,000. The newspaper announcements made virtually no mention that Glaspell had ever written other plays, the *New York Times* referring to "*Inheritors, Verge* [*sic*], *The Road to the Temple*, and *The Comic Artist*" without genre designation. The Pulitzer committee's citation is also a rather strange testament, praising her sincerity and choice of theme, which is "fresh," "taken out of American life," and "worthy of serious attention," while at the same time indicating that she had chosen the topic "quite apart from any considerations of temporal styles or box office appeal."[35] Despite the less than encouraging wording, Susan was delighted over the award, the first she had received for her writing since her Black Cat prize in 1905. Three days after getting the notification, she was back at the Gramercy Park Hotel giving interviews, which in print read like something Alison's nephew would crank out, focusing on what she wore and how she looked, rather than making any serious attempt to assess the play or the award. "Thirty years spent at the hard trade of writing have matured her beauty without destroying it," one unnamed interviewer notes. "Her graying hair carried a wind-blown cut, which could not be more appropriate and her hazel eyes are soft and sensitive."[36] For the first time outside of her native Iowa, Susan Glaspell was a celebrity, and women celebrities were described in terms of their appearance or by the number of their children (which, in fact, was the banner headline accompanying the parallel story on Margaret Ayer Barnes).

A few days later, however, the theatre critics began to be heard from and banal descriptions gave way to querulous and often vitriolic reactions. If Susan was elated, they were dumbfounded and indignant over the award, given to a play that had run only twenty-five times in repertory during the season—and then not on Broadway but on Fourteenth Street, where only a handful had even seen it. They scrambled to find out what it was about and why it had been selected over works such as *Elizabeth the Queen* by Maxwell Anderson, *Once in a Lifetime* by Moss Hart and George S. Kaufman, *Tomorrow and Tomorrow* by Philip Barry, *Green Grows the Lilacs* by Lynn Riggs, or *Five Star Final* by Louis Weitzenkorn. Bashing *Alison's House* quickly turned into a feeding frenzy, generating almost as much copy as that produced two years earlier, when the Pulitzer went to O'Neill's *Strange Interlude*. In Robert Garland's rehashing of his earlier criticism of the play, he takes comfort in the fact that at least "it's an improvement over *Strange Interlude*."[37]

That was about the most positive thing most of the New York critics could say. Not only was *Alison's House* attacked as the "Most Unsatisfactory Dramatic Award Made During the Past Few Years," in the opinion of Brooks Atkinson, but the three judges who had selected the play—Walter Prichard Eaton, Clayton Hamilton, and Austin Strong—were pilloried, the first two accused of being too old and out of touch with contemporary trends to recognize a good play, the third labeled a mediocre playwright himself. Atkinson's long discussion of the award, appearing on page one of the arts section in the Sunday *New York Times* and featuring a reproduction of the Loehman photograph, begins with several paragraphs attacking the committee who every few years "insists upon publishing its ignorance." He argues that since there were no plays worthy of the award this past year, it could have followed the lead of the 1918 group and refused to make a selection in the category or, if feeling it must, could have settled on the Hart/Kaufman comedy, which at least displayed a "versatile satire in the current American idiom." When he turns to Glaspell, he is far more deferential. "If the 1931 drama prize were for Miss Glaspell personally every one would purr with satisfaction," he opines. His support for a "lifetime achievement award" is for her fiction. He compares her to Willa Cather, noting that for over twenty-five years she "has been seeing life steadily and seeing it whole without sacrificing an artist's pride or a lady's decent sweetness." To Atkinson *Brook Evans* is her crowning achievement; had the Pulitzer been given for this, he would concur. When he briefly turns to *Alison's House*, he recycles his earlier reservations, once more repeating the assertion that Glaspell's intention in the play is to "recreate the spirit of a dead poetess."[38]

Again, there were a few who championed the play, particularly R. Dana Skinner in the *Commonweal*, who praised the award as he had praised the play when it first opened. So strongly did Skinner feel that he took the unprecedented step of writing a letter to Atkinson, attacking his criticism of the play. "The play says nothing more clearly than the simple fact that Alison Stanhope became great through denying herself a love which she thought wrong," he argues, and her act "rips to pieces the smug egotism of today."[39] While it may be unreasonable to expect drama critics to know about a poet, who in 1930 was still considered a minor figure in American letters, it is harder to understand why none seemed to know—or at least make no reference to—Glaspell's earlier theatre work. A few interviews after the opening had focused on the Provincetown Players, but these interviews tended to rehash the mythology of O'Neill's discovery and the Village bohemian lifestyle rather than to discuss the body of Glaspell's works and her reputation. It seems that the eight years that separate *Alison's House* from *Chains of Dew* had eclipsed her for this new generation of critics. The question is why. Why does an erudite critic like Brooks Atkinson, who started reviewing in 1925 but surely knew about American theatre history prior to that date, make no comment whatsoever about Glaspell's seven one-act or three full-length dramas or put *Alison's House* in the context of these earlier dramatic efforts? "Drama is not Miss Glaspell's most congenial medium," he concludes without attempting to make the case.[40]

One reason for this critical erasure seems to lie in the general cultural climate change in America in the preceding decade. As feminist historian Nancy Cott details in the conclusion to her book *The Grounding of Modern Feminism*, the post-suffrage Jazz Age and the Great Depression that followed ushered in a period of widespread " 'disremembering' [a] process by which Feminism was selectively absorbed and repressed." By the end of the 1920s there was a more conservative, traditional social climate present in the country, marked by "male aggrievement at women's failure to be satisfied" with their gains.[41] Something of this attitude can be seen in the wording of Atkinson's criticism. He praises Glaspell for her "lady's decent sweetness," using words that at first sound like echoes of the term "feminine" used by his *Times* predecessor John Corbin to describe Glaspell's one-acts. But Corbin was writing in 1918 in response to *Trifles* and *Woman's Honor*, and his criticism indicated his understanding, if not acceptance, of the strong, independent women in these plays who were, in fact, challenging traditional stereotypes of what it meant to be "feminine." Atkinson, on the other hand, sounds very much like certain social critics of 1930, happy to "purr" were ladies to act as they should. If he sees *Brook Evans*, not *The Verge*, as Glaspell's great achievement, then it is clear that he has "disremembered" the body of her work, in keeping with the tenor of the times.

That is not to say that he and other critics are wrong in faulting *Alison's House*, but not for the reasons they state. The play does not represent Glaspell at her best. It is far less focused and far more sentimental than any of her Provincetown works; the language at times is painfully wooden; and the structure, which resembles a series of debates, is less arresting than in *Inheritors*. However, given these near fatal flaws, the play does more than the critics indicate. So focused are they on the Dickinson ghost that they fail to see the possibility that the poet is less important than the characters who are actually present. Had these critics been familiar with *Trifles*, or even with *Bernice*, they might better have understood Glaspell's technique of focusing on an absent woman and responded to it. In addition, even Atkinson, who began as a newspaperman, entirely missed Glaspell's important attack on the celebrity-seeking media. Fixed on Miss Glaspell's "ladylike decent sweetness," he also overlooks one of her key messages in the play: that sexual love, which both women and men may feel, can be powerful enough to alter life, and that it does not dissipate in time, as Alison's poetry shows. In the case of Skinner, he praises the play for precisely the wrong reasons, assuming that Glaspell is saying that Alison's greatness comes from her self-denial, an idea that runs counter to all Glaspell's other depictions of love in her novels and dramas. To be fair, Susan courts such misunderstanding because of the vague dialogue that ends the play. The nearest she comes to addressing the subject is when Elsa—responding to her father's statement that "It is possible to love so much you can live without your love "—says pointedly: "I suppose it is possible, if you are a very great soul, or have a very stern sense of duty." Few people have either, Susan indicates, and it is for them, especially for women, that Alison speaks. When Skinner, later in the year, published his study *Our Changing Theatre*, the only fault he found in the play is this final act in which Elsa says that Alison would have wanted her to seek happiness, even if it meant going off with a married man. Skinner argues that Alison would never have taken such an immoral position and that, by implying that she does, Glaspell is distorting the nature of her absent character.

Because of all the publicity associated with the Pulitzer, LeGallienne, who had announced a one-year sabbatical at the conclusion of her regular season, agreed to bring *Alison's House* uptown to the Ritz Theatre for a limited run. She appeared as Elsa during the first week, and Gale Sondergaard took over the role during the second week. Critics who had not seen the first production, now reviewed it; and some of those who had seen the first production, such as Garland, returned to see if they could detect something that might have prompted the Pulitzer committee to make their award. They could not; and despite the hype, with some critics running second and third reviews of the play, it only ran two weeks. In October the same production, with Sondergaard, opened a short run at the Wilbur Theatre in Boston, where it received better reviews. Later, NBC presented it as one of their first radio dramas, with Mercedes McCambridge as Elsa.

The debate over *Alison's House* was one of the most vociferous in the Pulitzer's history. Writing fourteen years later, Walter Prichard Eaton, who had chaired the committee, still defended his decision, noting that those critics who found the play boring were always bored when they had to travel down to Fourteenth Street.[42] As usual, despite critical reactions, Susan's writing held immediate appeal for audiences and readers. LeGallienne described how those attending performances were always absorbed. Returning home after her difficult stay in New York, Susan found letters from many who had seen the play and wanted her to know how they felt about it. To one such letter, she replied, "The critics did not seem to take much pleasure in the award, I must say, but I'll try . . . and go on and do a better play."[43] A cable congratulating her for the Pulitzer came from an old friend, Eugene O'Neill, who called it "An honor long overdue!!"[44]

Break Up

26

Then her own pure strong instinctive love for the younger man. His love of her, but his leaving her for one who is younger and can give him the other things he wants.

—Susan Glaspell, Notebook entry

After the furor surrounding the Pulitzer, Susan felt the need to distance herself as much as possible from New York. Even Truro seemed too close. London had always warmly embraced her work, so she decided in the fall to finally visit there. Throughout the late summer of 1931 she made plans, trying to find a ship that suited their requirements—that is, a ready supply of alcohol. For Norman drinking was a way of dealing with his writer's block, and he would begin his day with a few drinks to fortify himself. Susan, more abstemious because less fearful of her skill, only began drinking in the early afternoon after putting in her usual workday. When she was in New York, she did not drink at all, finding it impossible both to "do New York" and to drink. Navigating in the city was difficult enough for her because of the recurrent problem with her foot, which required that she wear a special shoe and brace whenever she stood or walked for extended periods. Yet, for her, too, drinking had now become part of her daily routine.

One reason for the trip was to bring the couple closer together. As a sign of her commitment to Norman, Susan made a new will, deeding him the part of the Truro property on which her studio was located. But she still seemed tentative about their immediate future, even about his desire to accompany her to London. "Do you still want to go, or do you want to stay in Provincetown,"[1] she asked even as she made plans for both of them to sail. This hesitation and need for reinforcement were reminiscent of those times in her marriage to Jig when she doubted his love and his desire to be with her. Unable to progress on his book, Norman finally decided to accompany her to London, and they sailed from New York at the beginning of November 1931. On their arrival, they stayed briefly at the Hotel Abbotsford, before taking over the house she had rented from writer Richard Hughes for their three-month stay, at 21, Lloyd's Square, in Islington, near King's Cross, a location Susan selected because it had recently become home to a growing number of writers and artists. With the house came the assistance of Hughes's housekeeper, who catered to all their needs, leaving Susan free to fully enjoy the city.

The first part of Norman's untitled and unpublished autobiographical novel is set in London; and while he may have embellished a few facts, most details appear accurate. For instance, he mentions Ruth's desire to go to see the city of Keats and Shelley, but her inability to walk around the historical places because of trouble with her foot. He also describes their daily routine of completing breakfast with a shot or two of whisky that was always nearby. As they take taxis around London, they see placards pasted on buses advertising Ruth's newest novel. While the placards may be exaggerated, Susan was certainly a personage in the city. Almost immediately after her arrival, she received invitations for speaking engagements, including one from the local PEN chapter, all of which she declined, usually citing health problems. However, she did attend an evening in her honor given by her London publisher, Victor Gollancz, in his home. Among the invited guests were writers Rose Maccaulay, Elizabeth Bowen, and Hugh Walpole. When the American Women's Club organized a luncheon tribute to her as "one of America's outstanding women writers," she also participated. Those speaking about her work included Eva LeGallienne and Edith Craig. The report of the event, reprinted in the *New York Times*, described Susan's "modest account" of her work with the Provincetown Players and referred to the current run of *Alison's House*, at a drama festival in Cambridge.[2]

Although her stay was mostly low-key, Susan became embroiled in a controversy that had long-ranging repercussions. Nancy Price, who headed the London-based People's Theatre, decided to put on *Trifles* and asked her to play the role of Mrs. Hale, as she had in the original 1916 production. Susan agreed; however, she had to appeal to the Home Office to waive a law on the books since 1921, which limited the number of non-British allowed to work in the country. Using her case as a rallying point, a group representing a cross-section of the entertainment community demonstrated for a more flexible quota system that would allow more theatre people from abroad to work in the United Kingdom. Their protest was carried by newspapers in London and New York, along with articles about Susan's petition and the general issue of work restrictions. On January 21 the group met with officials at the Labor Ministry, and the following day the ministry announced that Miss Glaspell could act in

Trifles, since the ban somehow did not apply to her. While the ruling was a victory for those who sought to change the law, Susan finally declined to appear in her play, explaining that the management had already cast the part and she did not want to deprive someone of a role. On January 30, *Trifles* opened to enthusiastic cheers from the audience. In reviews Susan was given credit for staging the play, and Nancy Price with playing Mrs. Hale. Since Price was the producer, Susan's reason for not performing the role is curious. Either she felt unable to play it or the issue was only a pretext for testing the law.

While in London, she gave a number of interviews, one of the most extensive appeared in *Everyman*, on January 7, 1932. In it she traces her career, emphasizing her English and Irish roots, and mentions that she is thinking of a new novel. On a more controversial note, she points to what she sees as a tendency of some British writers to put their names to works not worthy of their talents, a situation, she suggests, that might be motivated by lower remunerations than commensurate writers in America receive. Using those familiar idealistic words that appear in almost all her writings, she explains her regret over the situation: "You *are* what you do, so you can't afford to do less than your best." As usual, the interviewer gives considerable space to describing the woman, indicating "a kind of spiritual incandescence about her which is almost a palpable thing," a quality she attributes to an American penchant going back to Emerson and Hawthorne, "a passionate aesthetic awareness burning luminously inside an unbearable shell of traditional morality."[3] The words approximate Susan's description of Breath of Life in *The Verge*.

In his novel, Norman indicates that Ruth and Peter finally got tired of London and decided to return home several weeks earlier than they had planned. But since their house was occupied (Glaspell had rented her Provincetown house to Edmund Wilson for the winter), on a whim they go to Paris for a week, before sailing to America. To make it more of an adventure, the fictive couple fly. "Ruth had written lyrically of the joy of flight but had never flown herself."[4] Neither had Susan, despite her description of flying in *The Verge* and her long interest in aviation, inherited from her father.[5] "I have never flown and am holding my breath," she wrote in her farewell letter to her landlord on February 27, the day the couple left London.[6] Unlike their fictive surrogates, Susan and Norman remained in Paris for two months, returning to favorite spots they had visited together in 1925 and meeting with friends, including Anna Strunsky and her husband English Walling, who, with their daughter, were spending a vacation in the city. Anna Senior, as she was called, was a writer, well known in the Greenwich Village community as one of the Strunsky sisters, her father the owner of several restaurants and rooming houses catering to artists. As a young woman, Anna had been close to Jack London, before marrying Walling, a noted socialist leader who had been on the editorial board of *The Masses*. Their daughter, Anna Junior was a nineteen-year-old college student, beautiful, strong-willed, and independent. Matson in his autobiographical novel calls Anna Junior Alice or "the Driscoll girl," whom Peter had admired on the beach in Provincetown two months earlier. In the novel, when he meets her at her parents' house in Paris, Alice is surprisingly mature and candid with Peter describing herself as "the very first product of a progressive education. . . . I've been emancipated. It was expensive, and here I am, and what shall I do with my emancipation?" Alice's answer is to immediately fall in love with Peter; Anna Junior's was to fall in love with Norman Matson.

"I knew from the first that I loved him. There was no doubt in my mind. He was much older than I but I didn't care. I would have done anything to keep him. There was nothing which could have stopped me," Anna, still beautiful, recalled some fifty years later.[7] Often the two would take long walks around the city, while Susan stayed with Anna Sr., unable to join them because of the recurring pain in her foot. Norman's account has Ruth warn Peter of the dangers of the flirtation. "You have it in you to make a great fool of yourself. She will cost you everything, do you realize that? Me, your work, friends." Judging from his novel, Susan must have known about the affair in Paris but initially dismissed it as a flirtation. She had prided herself on allowing Norman his space, an act made easier because over the their eight years together, he had rarely demanded it. Perhaps she assumed that Anna's youth precluded any serious romance. Although only Susan knew it, the seventeen years difference between herself and Norman was nearly that of Norman and Anna. In his novel, Norman manages to have Ruth conveniently called back to London to oversee one of her plays, leaving his persona free to pursue his affair with Alice. In fact there was a more prosaic reason for Susan's departure. Her kidneys, which had given her trouble in the past, began to cause her considerable pain, and she decided to return home. She could have been treated in Paris, but she seems to have used the illness as a pretext to pressure Norman to leave with her. He did not respond. Using the excuse of his still-unfinished book, he argued that writing would be easier in Paris. Instead, Anna Sr. accompanied Susan on the voyage. They sailed on the Hamburg-Amerika Line, and, although Susan always enjoyed sailing, this trip was hardly joyful. Instead there were days of sitting in a deck chair being an audience for Anna's long monologues on her life with her husband. To pass the time, Susan tried to imagine what Norman might be doing in her absence, possibly visiting the Luxemburg gardens and seeing the first chestnuts, thinking of her. "We were happy in Paris—so much of the time," she reminds him in a note written en route. "I won't try to tell you how much I've thought of you. You might say 'Why doesn't she think of something else? Well I've done that too.'"

When she arrived in New York, Susan checked into the Gramercy Park Hotel once more and immediately visited Dr. Lorber, who had been treating her since 1914. Her fear had been that she had cancer; but after tests, she was relieved to learn it was pus in the neck of the womb, and she could be easily treated. Another fear was not so easily dispelled. Waiting at the hotel when she arrived was a cable from her friend Dorothy Smith in Provincetown, informing her that Samuel Butler—"Sam the Mule" her much-loved wireless terrier—had disappeared. It had been Susan's great regret that she had been unable to take him with her, because of quarantine restrictions, and she mentioned the fact in several interviews and even selected a photo of Sam in her arms for the *Everyman* article. While she often repeated, "It takes a lot of dogs to run through a person's life," and had mentioned several in *The Road to the Temple*, Sam was special to her. Her friend Lucy Huffaker had given him as a gift when Susan returned from Greece, and he had been her central companion in those difficult days. She even explained that one of the reasons she had taken up driving once more was so she could take Sam for the outings he loved, when Norman, his usual chauffeur, was away. In every letter Susan wrote to Norman, she included some reference to Sam: what he was eating, what he was doing, how he was feeling. He was a central element in their "remember" game: remember how he found a place for himself under the elm you had just planted near the Truro house; remember how he leaped ahead as we walked down the path no one knew but us; remember how he stayed outside the door, when you first spent the night, as if to guard us from harm? There was Tucker, her other terrier, but he did not inspire the same feeling in them and in others. Sam was "the most loveable animal and the best sport and his affection meant so much because it took some time to get it," Dorothy wrote, explaining her own special fondness for the dog and her sadness over his disappearance.[8]

The news about Sam was a terrible blow for Susan. Lonely for Norman, she now felt totally bereft. She immediately called Dorothy to get details and learned that Sam had been missing three weeks; notices had already been flashed in movie theatres along the Cape, offering a reward for his return, and a search of nearby dunes had yielded no trace. Still in treatment for her kidney ailment, she had to stay in New York, but kept in constant touch with Dorothy, raising the reward money, in hopes that someone would respond. In a letter she had received from Norman when she arrived, he had written, "Nothing much has happened" since her departure. "I'm drinking about not at all, and seem to have 'control of the day.'" He signed it "Love to S. and T. (Sam and Tucker)."[9] On May 4, she cabled to tell him the news, and he cabled back on May 21, "Dearest poor foolish Samuel. Am sailing for home on about June first. All my love." Before he arrived, Susan returned to Provincetown and soon got a call from the Race Point Coast Guard that they had found Sam. Overwhelmed with joy, she asked if they could bring him. "Why, yes, if you want him. He's dead," the man on the other end of the phone explained.[10] Susan, Dorothy, and her young son, who was particularly fond of the dog, retrieved the body and took it to the Truro farm to bury under Sam's favorite elm tree. Her only comfort was the thought that Sam's mangled body was found in the water near home, a sign to her that he was trying desperately to get back. "Do you know," she wrote to Norman, "I think there is a pattern in life, and Sam, in my loneliness and need was sent home to me, and couldn't quite make it. Now laugh, with your Anna and your hopes, have a good laugh, but believe it. And he couldn't quite reach me. And nothing again, can quite reach me."

When Norman finally arrived in Provincetown in the middle of June, Susan tried to reestablish the pattern of their lives together, as if nothing had happened, but it was clear that the spectre of Anna fell between them and made the closeness she craved impossible. Just as she had done when tensions surfaced in her marriage to Jig, Susan escaped, this time going to Boston without telling Norman. He wrote in care of various friends, asking her to come home and assuring her that she had "won." He intended to write "to A.W." who was now visiting her family in Chicago and end the affair. "All the sadness and hurt and talk makes [sic] it not worth the effort." And yet he cannot keep from fixing blame. "But that's the way it's always been. Another case of 'man-failure.' It's a woman's world. I don't think it runs very well." He signs it, "Your own." The twenty-one extant letters that Norman wrote to Susan over the next two months and Susan's two to him provide a rare glimpse into the smashing of a relationship, conducted by two writers whose words sometimes sound as if they are carefully parsed from their books and at other times resemble incoherent ramblings and repetitions inspired by too much drink. His follow a clear pattern: comments on the weather, gossip about friends, both couched in light and friendly tones, and then some crushing details about his love affair with Anna, followed by invectives about women who don't understand men and are merely vindictive, and a closing in which he proclaims once more his love for Susan and his passion for Anna. Her letters respond to his and always include reminiscences of the love they once had. The letters are also marked by an insurmountable gender divide: he, self-righteous and preening in his newfound love; she, crushed and humiliated over his rejection and love for a much younger woman, still trying her best to "be fair," retain her dignity, and keep intact her belief in the primacy of love, which had always sustained her and her fictive women.

From the Hotel Bellevue in Boston, where she was staying, Susan answered his letter and agreed to return, now that he had decided to break with Anna. His immediate reply made her regret her decision. After opening pleasantries, he casually mentions that "Mlle X" had suddenly arrived in Provincetown: "Her coming here while you were gone was pure coincidence," he claims. In a tone of self-absorption and with complete indifference to her feelings—which mark his subsequent communications with her—he outlines what he and Anna have decided: She will go back to college to finish her last two years, and he will see her once or twice a month. He makes clear that he cannot give Anna up. "That life flows into me from her you know. It doesn't change, doesn't need to change the you-and-me at all. Why should it? Even if it shipwrecks her—it's her choice."

Susan's response was immediate, direct, predictable, and long: seven pages. His letter had come as a blow to her. She had believed him when he had assured her that this was a casual affair. Now it was clear that he and Anna were planning their future: "And what in that, do you think you have to offer me," she asks. "Not love, for you haven't had that for me since you came home from Paris. Not even tenderness, concern did you have when I was so hurt. Only irritation, harshness. Not companionship in the old way, for you were thinking only of this excitement, of yourself, and through it all was that falseness which puts a blight on all there was since you came home." As for his suggestion that the affair need not affect their relationship, she wonders how he would feel if in the future Anna were to pose the same arrangement to him. "You would not sit contently watching her go to her meetings, and welcome her home as if it made no difference. Not if you loved. You could not work that way, and I can not work that way. So let us not talk so foolishly." Responding to his words, carefully chosen to touch her, she writes, "You say life flows into you through her. Then you must have her. But do not, quite so facetiously ask me to do what I can not do." She explains that she will stay in Boston until she has had time to think. One thing she wishes to avoid is further ugliness and recrimination. "There has been a great beauty between us, a rare beauty, I think. It is better to save some of that in feeling than go on in a life that would destroy it." Again she explains that his proposal that she accept his love for Anna is impossible. "I could not go on this way, with you two planning the future, as if waiting for me to die. In that, I will die now. It is better. I cannot write more."

He responded this time without any opening pleasantries. Angry and bitter, he calls her attention to sacrifices he had made for her and indignantly chides her for not doing the same by overlooking "this first affair of mine" and responding to it "in the spirit of a grown woman and a realist." As he sees it, the fault is hers: she is acting "in the angry grief of the usual female vanity, who is smashing things and not me." He urges her to come home; and if she wishes to live alone, he will move to Truro, which will suit him, since he could live cheaply there. "PLEASE try to be sensible; PLEASE try not to thirst for my punishment; PLEASE come back and take over your house, and PLEASE don't parade our troubles."

Susan acceded to his request and returned to Provincetown at the end of July; but it soon became clear that reconciliation was impossible, and Norman stormed out of the house, going to New York to await Anna's return from Chicago. Susan's letter to him, written immediately after he left, begins like an essay; she even gives it a title: "With my respects to E.M. Forster, who suggested the form." She borrows a phrase from *Trifles*—"It was a strange thing happened in this house that last night"—and recreates the scene in *Fugitive's Return*, in which Irma sits up waiting for the sound of a car signaling that her estranged husband has come back to her. In virtually the same words she gave Irma, Susan describes her own vigil after Norman's departure, going over in her mind their last night together, each unable to bridge the distance. She "remembers" how special their love had been and calls the break a "sin against life, like cutting down a good tree." "How," she asks, can Anna, with all her "young love" and "exuberant admiration" of him ever replace what they had? Near the end of the letter, there is a time break. In the interim, as she ate lunch, a telegram arrived from him telling her that Anna is pregnant and that he plans to marry her as soon as possible and requests that she immediately divorce him. "It can not be true," Susan continues in the same letter. "So recently you said, I love you more than any one in the world. So how can these other words be true, too, so soon—I want a divorce, so I can marry her." However, she indicates that she will not make a fuss. "I will go through it with what pride and courage I can."

Slowly, like the unfolding of a rather trite, not very original romance novel, Norman in his next letters provides the pieces of the plot withheld till now. After he left Paris, Anna had quickly followed. They met in June in New York, when he first arrived; she became pregnant and came to Provincetown to tell him and to say that she would have an abortion, since, "You really don't want to marry me, do you? Because I'd be such a bother." Touched by her words and appalled by her intention, he declared that he loved her and would take care of her and that they must marry and have the child. She went to Chicago to tell her family the news; he waited in New York, fearful that she would be convinced to abort, yet wondering how he would be able to support her and the child.

During August, alone in New York, Norman wrote Susan almost daily, professing his sorrow that they had parted and describing in great detail his new, consuming passion. Anna, he knows, will never provide the same understanding and have the same shared interests; yet he cannot stop his love for her. "It is too intense for me; it is like a sickness; and the wrench of her going makes me helpless as when someone dies and you can't stop walking and walking and your head won't either think or rest." His dream, he admits, was that he could have them both. He now recognizes that this is impossible, but he still holds out hope that Susan and he can at least continue to write and perhaps, at some time in the future, to meet. Although they had never married, Norman assumed that their eight years together constituted a common-law marriage, which would require legal action to end—a situation he decries: "What was the sense of our not marrying," he asks, "if we couldn't separate without the disgusting mess of a divorce?" He also decries her feelings about the situation. "I don't see why you should feel 'belittled.' You knew it in Truro, in London, in Provincetown; you knew it in Norway and we talked of it; you have always known that we, our being together, could not last, would not." She denies his claim that theirs had not be a marriage. He agrees but adds: "it was strange: you supported me, you were successful, and I wasn't; and then the age difference and—no children."

What must have been most painful for Susan was his constant references to the baby he and Anna were expecting, a reminder of her own inability to have children. In one letter he informs her "the kid's to be named Peter if he's that kind." In a later note, he quotes at length from one of Anna's letters to him, describing her joy over the "Peter" she is carrying, a confirmation that "all our love has come alive—and it will walk and talk and look around and laugh." Norman scolds Susan for suggesting that the baby will affect so many lives, implying that an abortion should take place. He reminds her that in her writing her women always seek "Life," which he purposely capitalizes. Again, his attack is aimed at Susan's most vulnerable point, her idealism, and claims for the supremacy of life and love. He taunts her by suggesting, "Did you ever think of doing a woman—*a woman urging the good sense* of abortion in a play. Wouldn't it be marvelously revolting?"—forgetting that birth control, if not abortion, was her theme in *Chains of Dew*. When she asks in one letter if the child is worth it, he retorts, "You don't ask such questions in your writing. You say: Yes, yes, yes, yes. Life is Worthy. That's what you've always said." In fact, Susan resisted taking a stand on the abortion issue. When she received a letter from Anna Sr., on September 13, assuring her that "there will be no *consequences* for Anna," implying that her daughter is contemplating an abortion,[11] Susan wrote back that she appreciated the letter but did not want to be involved in this decision.

During September, Susan remained in Provincetown, not opening the Truro house, while Norman stayed in New York, arranging for an apartment for himself and Anna and trying, without success, to do some writing, which was essential now in order to earn money. He had discovered that Massachusetts did not recognize common-law marriages, so there was no need for a divorce before he was free to marry. When it became clear that Anna would have the baby and that the marriage would take place, Susan wrote another letter, this time to Anna Sr., in which she tried to summarize her feelings, using those very words Norman had belittled: the claim of life and of understanding between women. It is an extraordinary letter, which, perhaps, only Susan Glaspell could have written. In it she assures Anna of their continuing friendship. "As I grow older I think friendship between women is a thing to cherish." She also tries to alleviate the mother's fears about her daughter's future. "Knowing how good Norman has been to me, I know he will be good to Anna. You may worry, because she is not going back to college. Life with Norman is more than college. She has a chance for a deep sensitive feeling about life that will inform all her days. Because Norman is beautiful. I who have lost him, say that. I had eight years with Norman. I know him. Trust him, Anna." She then goes on to describe what Norman meant to her. "When Jig died, and I came home from Greece, I thought of myself as the observer. I thought, I will try to be brave, and I will write, because I love life, and want to celebrate it in expression. Then Norman came, and loved me, and instead of seeing life from death, again I saw it from life. I was again in life. That I owe Norman. And never will I forget it." And of the present, she can only write, "I am lonely, as you must know, but I want you to know—I have no resentment against Norman. I too was once nineteen. So were you, dear Anna." Up to this point, the typed letter has few erasures. In the last paragraph, however, the writing breaks down, Susan crossing out phrases and inserting others, indicating her difficulty in ending the message. She writes, mostly by hand, "I say a little prayer—Dear god, call me home. But I know he won't until he is through with me. So perhaps there is something in me still though hard to feel it at the moment." Her closing line, "Anna, be good to Norman. I ask it," is crossed out.[12]

Norman Matson and Anna Walling were married quietly on October 18, 1932. He was thirty-nine, Anna nineteen. He continued to write to Susan, telling her how much he missed her understanding. There were also practical matters between them that needed to be discussed, including *The Comic Artist*. Ironically, now that their relationship had ended, a producer, Arthur Beckhard, finally decided to stage it on Broadway. Over the years both had tried to tinker with the text during various tryouts and in summer stock, including a Westport Playhouse production, overseen by Lawrence Langner, and a short-lived London production at the Strand Theatre in 1928. The play, which opened at the Morosco Theatre on April 19, 1933, therefore, differs considerably from the printed version, published back in 1928. Instead of Karl drowning, he now goes off with Nina and Louella, while Eleanor and Steve are left to try to piece together their fractured marriage, much as the comic-strip figure Mugs, after the last frame, is always left with the disastrous results of his well-intentioned acts of kindness. Although Susan had hesitated about attending the opening, at the last minute she decided to go. It was a difficult evening, since Anna and Norman also attended, she three weeks overdue. They all exchanged a few words, but the tension was palpable. Anna remembers, "I could hardly sit through the play. I was just about to go into labor. And besides, there were some moments that were truly comic if they hadn't seemed tragic at the time. At one point, a scrim was to be lowered and moths flew out at the audience, almost causing outbreaks of laughter. It seemed just the right response for what was going on the stage."[13] She gave birth a few days later to a girl, and as he promised, Norman informed Susan, who responded with "God bless her." It was a sentimental wish, she admitted, adding "I wish I had had a child. I tried. It went wrong."

Virtually no one acknowledged Matson's hand in the writing of *The Comic Artist*, assuming that the strengths and weaknesses were solely Susan's. Of the twenty-one critics who reviewed the play, approximately half found the play intellectually arresting, even poetic, and praised her for challenging the usual complacent Broadway audience.[14] They also praised Beckhard's direction and the acting, particularly Blanche Yurka as Eleanor. Joseph Wood Krutch called it Susan's most successful play;[15] Percy Hammond applauded the writing, while recognizing that audiences would probably not enjoy it,[16] and Robert Garland, perhaps to make amends for his scathing critiques of *Alison's House*, raved, concluding that *The Comic Artist* "is the modern theatre in its more enlightened aspect."[17] There were an equal number who faulted the lugubriousness of the dialogue, its archaic language, and stilted exchanges. The play ran for twenty-one performances. Norman sensing it was heading for disaster apologized to her that their collaboration had produced her one failure. (This, however, did not stop him later from suggesting that her share of the royalties go initially to him, since he was in more need of money at present than she was.) In the same letter, he admitted that he is considering trying his hand at another play, this time dealing with anti-Semitism, since "at bottom I am, as you know, anti-Semitic." To prove the point, he describes his admiration of Hitler's nationalism, regretting however the "misguided atheism [which] is his 'flaw,'" and he ridicules "that fool Dorothy Thompson [wife of Sinclair Lewis] calling Hitler—a 'half-wit.'" Norman's play was never written; in fact, after he left Susan, he rarely published anything, since, as Anna readily admitted, he had difficulty finishing work. He also became an alcoholic, brought on, Anna believed, by the excessive drinking he began while living with Susan.

After Jig died, Susan had been forced to rebuild her life. That had been painful and difficult, but she was sustained by her memories of their lives together and her commitment to memorialize him through her writing. This period was different. She found it hard to salvage positive memories of her years with Norman; and, worse yet, she found it impossible to write. "Writing is not always easy, unless one feels the pulse of self-assertion and the conviction of purpose," she had told an interviewer the year before.[18] She now felt neither. Not only had Norman left her to marry a much younger woman, but he had also shaken her belief in love, central to her personal life and vital to her work. In a letter to him written just before Christmas 1933, she admits being terrified for the first time in her life, because she cannot pick up the pieces of her life and she cannot write. "I don't think a man has often been loved more deeply, more understandingly than I loved you," she tells him, "So bear with me, for just a time. It tore up the roots of my life. I am not a superficial person. I care, and it is my whole life." About her writing, she continues, "I have tried and tried, but written no line I would publish, and fear what writes in me died."

Adding to her concern was pressure about money. In the election in the fall of 1932, as the full impact of the depression began to be felt, she voted for Norman Thomas "because too many were hungry."[19] Again there were men selling apples on the streets of New York, in scenes reminiscent of those at the end of World War I, which she had described in a fragment found among her papers. She wasn't hungry; but she no longer had the cushion of ready cash that she had accumulated in the past decade. Used to living on little, she was not severely restricted in her daily life, as many were during these depression years; however, much of the inheritance Jig left her and his children had been wiped out when the bank in Davenport where it was deposited failed. She also felt a responsibility to aid Harl, who had gone to Greece and was now unable to return because of the bank collapse. "Someone has to look after him for a little while—And both my brothers are broke in the west, so if I don't write I'm a flop, even though I write tripe, though I'd rather die than write tripe. I still have my pride," she wrote Norman. To give her an added incentive to make money, she bought herself a Chevrolet Cabriolet on time, "a gay car" blue-green with beige and black trimming. The problem was that she had never been able to produce "lollipop stories" like Mary Vorse sometimes produced just to raise money, and she could not do so now, despite the goals and incentives she purposely set for herself. In the past she had required a congenial place to work—familiar, enclosed, and private—and interesting friends with whom she could establish connections when the writing day was done. Now, most of her friends were more intent on giving her advice than on providing companionship.

Even her own houses had turned against her, she felt, particularly the Truro farm, which carried so many memories of Norman that she feared she would never again feel comfortable there. Earlier, she had deeded him a section of the property as a birthday present. On the night he left, he had shouted to her, "Do I get Truro?" When she told him that it was his, he replied, "Hell, what good does that do me? You'll live longer than I will."[20] To clarify the matter, Susan consulted a lawyer soon after the breakup, to make sure that on her death it would still go to him, since she knew he would keep the property intact, unlike Nilla, whom she feared would sell off sections. She reported to Norman the lawyer's surprise: "I have had a unique experience. A woman has come into my office to will property to a man who has just deserted her." Norman declined the gift, and she, therefore, requested that he deed back the section in order to keep the parcel together. He acceded to her request. However, he told her that he and Anna intended to make their home nearby, occupying the house in Wellfleet he had discovered on one of his walks, which he describes in the fragment for his novel. Susan asked him to reconsider, since their proximity would "undermine the security of my home, all I have left," but he followed through with his plan. Soon after their second child, Peter, was born, the family settled there and continued to use it as a residence. Anna and Norman's marriage lasted thirty-three years, until Norman's death from emphysema in 1965. Anna described him as "an excellent, loving father. He was very funny, had a catholic taste, and was interested in any new idea."[21] After his death, Anna continued to occupy the house in summers with her new husband, the *New Yorker* music critic Philip Hamburger until her death in December 2002.

The Federal Theatre Project

27

The President of the United States in writing to me of his regret at the closing of Federal Theatre referred to it as a pioneering job. This it was, gusty, lusty, bad and good, sad and funny, superbly worth more wit, wisdom and imagination than we could give it.

—Hallie Flanagan, *Arena: The History of the Federal Theatre*

Like her homes, Susan's friends had been hers, and Norman had gained access to them thanks to her. Several, including the Hapgoods, only tolerated him for her sake. Mary Vorse, alienated from Susan during the Norman years, now, in 1933, picked up the threads of their relationship. Susan's closest confidants during this period were Katie and John Dos Passos, Dorothy Smith, and Stella "Knobby" Roof, a former "Smooley," who shared Susan's Provincetown house during the winter and spring of 1933. Susan was now drinking heavily and still unable to write. While she talked about the latter problem, she found it difficult to admit the former. She prided herself that she was able to keep up a good front and that friends assumed "Susan is fine." In fact news of her situation was well known. Even Blanche Hays, a former member of the Provincetown Players, now living in Paris, heard and wrote to Edna Kenton: "I am terribly sorry about Susan. It's too bad. She deserves better in life because she is a really lovely person. I hope she gets hold of herself but it is not easy at her age. If you see her, will you give her my love. Susan is one of my happiest memories of those days."[1] Ironically, it was Norman, still writing to her, who kept urging her to stop drinking, assuming the reason was her writing. "You say that with Jig, you knew about it, though you yourself never did it, you never had to do that, knowing better how to write, being more naturally a story teller and a far far better one than I—or he, either."[2] Edmund Wilson, in his published diaries of the thirties, makes frequent references to Susan's drinking problem. In one entry about them, he writes, "Susan . . . and Knobby living together and drinking constantly: name for female inebriates."[3]

At this time, Susan also became friendly with two summer-resident families: Martha and Ted Robinson and Dorothy and Ernie Meyer, both men journalists, and with year-round West End neighbors Mary "Bubs" and Chauncey Hackett. Another addition in the summer of 1933 was Langston Moffett, Mary Hackett's brother.[4] At thirty, he was a strikingly handsome man, a towering six-foot-six, with dark hair and imposing features. Their father Cleveland Moffett had been a well-known journalist associated with the muckraker movement, and he later wrote for Hollywood. After two years at Dartmouth College, Langston had dropped out of school, married Claudia Read, and moved to Paris, where he worked as a correspondent for the *Paris Herald*, often covering the activities of visiting writers, such as Hemingway and Fitzgerald, which meant joining them on drinking bouts around the city. Now back in the States, he brought with him a serious drinking problem, which caused Claudia to periodically leave him. Alone in Provincetown for the summer, he began spending time with Susan, who had moved back to the Truro farm and rented her Provincetown house to Wilson. Langston was twenty-seven years younger than Susan—ten years younger than Norman—but the extreme age difference did not deter him. Susan at fifty-seven still seemed able to attract men, because of the special quality of concern and attention she could lavish on them, qualities Langston apparently needed. As she had done with Jig and Norman, she grounded their relationship in a shared love of literature and animals. They talked about a shared writing project, but the best they could come up with was a scheme for a new journal to be called *The Provincetown Review*, which occupied their correspondence the following winter, after Langston had returned to Claudia and their children in Washington, D.C.

Letters were the only writing she was able to produce at this point, and even these usually began with descriptions about the difficulty of penning them. Her only published work between 1931 and 1939 was a brief 1934 memorial profile of Provincetown artist John Noble, a colorful local character, famed for his ten-gallon hat, cowboy attire, and obstreperous manner.[5] Her tribute to him is reminiscent of the poem she had written for Joe O'Brien twenty years earlier, revealing once more her own penchant for "characters" who dared to confront life on their own terms. "Remembering the dead, as I have been doing with Noble, I think of life and its infinite possibilities," she wrote Langston. "There never seemed a better chance for creative work, for expressing the past, and trying to shape the future."[6] Such sentiments, unfortunately, did not reflect her present condition.

If her writing was blocked, her commitment to social causes was not. At the beginning of 1934, a new rash of strikes hit America in response to the deepening recession. While Susan was staying at the Brevoort in New York that winter, the Amalgamated Hotel and Restaurant Workers Union struck, and she immediately joined the picket line. Newspapers reported her actions, particularly her wire to fellow Heterodite, U.S. secretary of labor Francis Perkins. She asked Perkins to intervene and help the New York strikers, who numbered around 25,000. Susan made clear that her stand was not against the hotel, which she liked, nor the manager to whom she showed the cable before she sent it."I didn't want him to think I was trying to do something underhanded. But I am convinced the strikers are right. I have visited their headquarters and talked with hundreds of the men."[7] She also indicated that she expected to get guests at other hotels to follow her lead.

Susan received a different kind of publicity that same winter, this time related to her family. She had managed to scrape together enough money to finance Harl's trip back to the States, and he had spent the previous summer with her. She was very fond of him, in part because he reminded her of Jig. She called him "the big bad Harl." She was always ready to forgive him his sins, support his whims, and overlook his shortcomings, even his own serious drinking problem. She did not feel the same about Nilla, and their relationship had steadily deteriorated since they returned from Greece together in 1924. Nilla had been living in India since 1929, one of only two Americans admitted into Gandhi's ashram, and as such her actions were widely reported by newspapers in the States. However, by 1933 the ascetic life began to pale. "My heart is leaping for thrills. I want speed. I want to fly," Nilla announced when she arrived in New Delhi.[8] She soon got both by running her car into a ditch at seventy miles an hour, prompting the British authorities to label her an undesirable alien and to request she leave the country. When she stepped down the gangplank of the *City of Elmwood* in New York in the winter of 1934 with her son, Sirius, she once more drew headlines. She arrived without any luggage, "except the flower seeds in my heart" and a new husband, "the messboy" on the ship, Albert Hutchins, whom she had married en route. Susan was in New York at the time, and reporters wanted to interview her about her flamboyant stepdaughter. Privately she confided, "I think that Nilla is crazy, but I don't know what Harl and I can do about it."[9] Her chief concern was to protect Harl and young Sirius. If it weren't for them she admitted, she would wash her hands of Nilla. She even considered raising the seven-year-old boy, whom she called Toppy, but feared that Nilla might accuse her of beating and starving him, in order to gain headlines for herself. "When I think of having taken her to Greece, of the effort I made with her—Oh well, wasted effort, of which life is pretty full," she wrote in one of her last letters to Norman, in the spring of 1934.

Despite her fear of Nilla, she willingly cared for Sirius that summer, just as she lovingly continued to care for Harl. When Harl smashed her car, she forgave him, grateful that he and Sirius had not been hurt and pleased that he insisted on paying for the secondhand Plymouth he bought her in its place. During the following year, when Harl had to be hospitalized for diabetes, she joined him on the strict diet that was prescribed.[10] She even assisted him in writing a series called the "Billy and Betty stories," which he published monthly in *True Story* magazine. The best memories that Harl's first wife, Leonora, had of her mother-in-law were these "lively séances," as Susan and Harl worked out the plots.[11] One, clearly bearing Susan's stamp, concerned an essay contest Billy wins, with editorial assistance from his sister, on the subject "the greatest person America had produced." The answer Betty supplies for him sounds like one Susan must have provided: "Those pioneers of the frontier who faced every imaginable hardship . . . And still greater than the pioneer men were the pioneer women—the wives and mothers who willingly and gladly left the comfort and security of their homes to aid their menfolk in the conquest of the wilderness."[12]

In the summer of 1934, in addition to Harl and Sirius, Susan once more made room in her life for Langston, who returned to Provincetown and became her lover. Marguerite Kaselau reported to Hutch that "he only stays at her house nights—to avoid any unnecessary talk or scandal."[13] Actually friends seemed less scandalized by this spring/fall affair than relieved, at least as Edmund Wilson explains: "Susan and Langston Moffett had united on an alcoholic basis. Charles Kaselau said it was a great thing for the rest of them, because now Susan and Langston could listen to each other where they had previously made other people listen to them."[14] Susan had a tendency when drunk to get into a groove, fixing on an idea or phrase and repeating it until her friends were driven crazy. Once when Wilson had read to her Shakespeare's sonnet with the phrase "death's dateless night," she made him recite it over and over and then asked others to read it when he became weary. The summer was filled with such stories of "Susan's repetitions," and how only Langston, himself too inebriated to care, had the patience to tolerate them. One tale concerned a celebrated dinner party Susan gave in August for her Provincetown neighbor, Commander Donald B. MacMillan, who had led the Crocker Land Expedition to the Arctic in the early 1910s. Langston played host, handing out drinks of pure alcohol, then retired to the stairs where he made a rambling speech to himself, while Susan held forth at length to MacMillan about the fact that we all come from ice, an idea she credited to Langston, who interjected that he certainly wouldn't consider going on a polar expedition, once he learned that no alcohol was allowed. "Susan called MacMillan 'darling.' He drank nothing and left soon."[15] Another who chimed in on the Glaspell/Moffett romance was Mary Vorse, reporting to her son Heaton that she had received an ecstatic letter from Susan who was with Langston in the Maine woods at the end of the summer. Mary's response was, "I wouldn't want to lie around with a pine cone up my ass no matter how young the man was."[16] On another trip, the couple went to the Laurentian Mountains in eastern Canada on St. Anne's Day, July 26, a date that took on special significance for Langston years later, his sister said, because Susan died on that date.

Mary Hackett was convinced that her brother was deeply in love with Susan and that he found a haven with her, after Claudia left him during his drunken bouts. "She gave men something that most women can't give, even though she was in her fifties and her clothes were decidedly old fashioned," Hackett claimed.[17] She also knew how to listen. Mary assumed that Susan's motivation for attaching herself to Langston was his courtly manner and good looks, also his youth. She felt that Susan enjoyed the fact that she, too, now had someone youthful; it seemed to take the sting away from her loss of Norman to a younger woman. Mary was with the couple one evening when they happen to sit directly behind Norman and Anna in the Provincetown movie house. She reported that Susan hardly showed any reaction because she was sitting "with a much handsomer, taller gentleman." During the summer Mary Hackett carried on her own romance, falling deeply in love with Harl. Susan encouraged the affair,[18] arguing that "the young people" should have time together, even though Mary was married with two children at the time. Fifty years later Mary would call Harl a "no goodnik," but she could still recall his eyes "like plums" and kept a photo of the handsome young man standing in front of the motorcycle he had ridden through the narrow streets of Provincetown that summer of 1934. Mary's marriage survived; Harl, in October 1935, married, the first of three women he would wed over the next twenty years.

In the fall Langston returned to Washington, but his relationship with Susan continued when he returned to Provincetown the following spring. In May 1935 it became public knowledge—and so did their mutual drinking—when police discovered his car parked in the center of the highway leading into town, the pair gazing at the moon, with Langston draped suspiciously over the steering wheel. He was arrested, and Susan was accompanied home by an officer. She could have chosen to retreat from public view after the scandal, but instead she typically faced it head on. When Langston's case was heard, she not only attended the trial but rose from her seat and demanded to be heard. Claiming that he was not drunk as charged, she explained that they had been merely "enjoying the scenery and discussing a new book she was writing when they were interrupted by the troopers."[19] She went on to take the offensive, telling the court that in her twenty-three years as a resident of Provincetown, she had never been "escorted home by a State trooper" and should this treatment continue she would leave the town for good. The Associated Press picked up the story, headlining it "Miss Glaspell Makes Threat," referring to her as "a noted writer and Pulitzer Prize winner, stepmother of Nila [sic] Cram Cook former Gandhi disciple, and aid to Eugene O'Neill on his road to fame."[20] Because of her defense, Langston was not fined, and at the end of the summer he went back to his family. The Moffett marriage survived the interlude, lasting for sixty-three years, until Langston's death in 1989. In 1940 the family moved to St. Augustine, and Langston took up painting. In 1947, finally free of alcohol, he wrote *Devil by the Tail*, his description of his recovery, for which Susan wrote the book blurb. As a reminder of their summers together, she also gave him a number of her books, including a copy of *The Verge*, in which she wrote: "You fill the place should be a gate."

Three months after the Langston debacle, Susan was in the news again, this time for joining the protest against the banning of Clifford Odets's political play *Waiting for Lefty*, which had been scheduled to open in the Provincetown Town Hall, but had been cancelled by the board of selectmen, who argued that the play "was about strikes and things and give people the wrong kind of ideas." In her defense of the play, which was printed in the *New York Times*, she complained that theatre was under siege because people were afraid of the truths it offered.[21] In a personal letter to Odets, she praised his play *Paradise Lost* for its "sense of relationships which make it of the very texture of life."[22]

Throughout this period Susan continued to suffer from writer's block, the corner of her study filling with balls of paper torn from her typewriter in frustration. She confided to Dorothy Meyer, "I have to find out if I don't write because I drink or drink because I don't write."[23] Although she would discuss her situation with her close friend, Dorothy never saw her drunk. However the drinkers among the Provincetown group attended parties in her house at which guests sometimes had to support themselves by holding onto the furniture, "like a slowed-up motion picture or an animal act," as Wilson, then a drinker himself, reports it.[24] Susan had known firsthand the dangers alcohol posed for writers. She had seen it take its toll on Jig and contribute to his premature death; she knew others as well from her Greenwich Village days who had been unsuccessful in breaking its hold. Terry Carlin and Louise Bryant had died of it (Louise also of drugs in 1936). But Susan also knew that it was possible to stop drinking; Gene O'Neill had done it. So she struggled over the next year to get hold of her life and to regain her writing voice and her mental and physical equilibrium. During the winter of 1936, she forced herself to start a new novel, working sporadically on and off the wagon, but before she had gotten halfway into the as-yet-unnamed project, she received a letter that changed her plans. It was from Hallie Flanagan, director of the Federal Theatre Project, who asked her to become head of its Chicago-based Midwest Playwrights Bureau. The offer gave Susan exactly what she needed: a fixed purpose, a new location, and a reason to put her struggle with writing aside for the time being. Besides it was a job for which she could once more use the excellent managerial skills she had exercised in helping to run the Provincetown Players. She readily accepted Flanagan's offer.

The Federal Theatre Project was one of four government-funded programs begun in mid-1935 under the Works Progress Administration (WPA). It was designed to get unemployed artists, writers, musicians, and theatre professionals back to work by providing them with federal subsidies. At the same time, the program enriched the general public by offering free or nominally priced cultural activities and performances. It was a daring plan for a country that had no tradition of wide-scale federal support for the arts (and never would again); but because of the exigencies of the depression, the U.S. government was persuaded to go into "the culture business." The Federal Theatre Project was the brainchild of WPA head Harry Hopkins, an Iowa native educated at Grinnell College, where the arts were taught as a central component of everyday life, not as an elitist form. To come up with a specific program, he turned to fellow Iowan and Grinnell graduate Flanagan, a woman of great energy and vision, who was then a professor of theatre at Vassar College. There she had set up one of the most successful educational theatre programs in the country, based on her work with George Pierce Baker at Yale and on her study of theatres she had observed in Europe and Russia during a Guggenheim fellowship, the first awarded to a woman. Building on an earlier outline by yet another Iowan, Professor E. C. Mabie, chair of theatre at the University of Iowa, Flanagan developed a federal network, with the head in Washington, overseeing seven demarcated cities and regions serving in a loose confederation: New York, Los Angeles, Chicago, East, West, Midwest, and South.

Beyond getting people off welfare and back to work, Flanagan dreamed of establishing a permanent Federal Theatre, with offshoots taking root across the country and drawing audiences from all sections of society, particularly people who had never before had the opportunity to see live performances. The government was willing to put up the money— $6,784,036—stipulating that 90 percent of the budget must go for wages, meaning that performances had to generate almost all their own funds, and that 90 percent of those receiving the money had to be on welfare. The rest, like Glaspell, were administrators, whose wages were fixed at $200 a month, a trifling salary for a difficult job. Nevertheless, Susan readily took the assignment. "If I can find some good plays from the soil or from the experiences of recent years, I will feel that we are doing something for the theatre in helping build it up through this part of the country," she wrote to Barrett Clark, when asking if he could suggest any plays for consideration.[25] Her base was to be Chicago, a city she had known in earlier years. Her brother Ray, who had recently developed a debilitating lung disease, now lived there, providing Susan with another incentive to take the job, since she could help his wife, Flossie, care for him. She moved in the middle of September 1936, making the Eastgate Hotel her home for the next two years.

In her first months on the job Susan turned her attention to clarifying her duties and soliciting manuscripts. She immediately made it clear that she would do all she could to further theatre in the West but had no intention of filling out forms and handling the registration of productions and other such onerous work. Hiram Motherwell, in the national office, immediately accepted her job definition. Now she began writing to everyone she knew who might be able to suggest plays that met at least one of the three stated criteria: (1) a midwestern theme, (2) of interest to midwestern audiences, (3) written by a midwestern author. In response Clark sent a rough manuscript by poet Edgar Lee Masters, which Susan found unworkable for the stage. She encouraged him to keep looking, since she knew from her Provincetown years that she would probably not discover an "ideal Midwest play" among the 6,000 unsolicited manuscripts that poured into her office the first year.

A mark of her seriousness was her willingness to attend public events related to theatre and serve on juries for play-writing contests—activities she had shunned in the past, but now undertook in order to develop networks with those in the field. When Professor Mabie invited her to attend the official opening of a new theatre laboratory at the University of Iowa, she enthusiastically accepted. Two plays by members of his faculty—*Within These Walls* by Marcus Bach and *Prologue to Glory* by Elsworth Conkle—eventually became successful Federal Theatre works. There was one playwright in the Iowa program who studied with Mabie, Bach, and Conkle, but whom Glaspell probably did not meet because of Mabie's particular aversion to his work and obvious homosexuality. Tennessee Williams submitted *Candles to the Sun* and *Fugitive Kind* to the Chicago Federal Theatre after Glaspell left the program. They rejected them because the young playwright did not qualify for welfare, a requisite under the program, and, as his biographer argues, because the works were not "radical" enough for the communist-leaning program, an accusation that continued to plague the Federal Theatre, particularly in its Midwest region.[26]

If Glaspell and the Federal Theatre missed Williams, they did not overlook the other great American playwright to emerge in the next decade, Arthur Miller. He, too, was then a student of a midwestern university, graduating in 1937 from the University of Michigan, and he had written a play, which he submitted for consideration for the university's Avery and Julie Hopwood Award in creative writing. In 1936 Glaspell had been asked to serve as a Hopwood reader but declined; she accepted the second invitation in 1937, now that she was actively seeking young writers from the region. From the list of ten plays submitted for the minor awards, under pseudonyms, she gave first place to *Honors at Dawn* by "Corona," a name Miller may have chosen to honor the typewriter on which he composed it. "A faulty play as it stands, but says something in feeling, and here too I found real possibilities in this author," she wrote to the committee.[27] In a personal note she indicated her desire to contact some of the young playwrights to see if they might be able to develop their entries, but she did not include Miller on her list, preferring the work of the second-place winner, although it did not possess Corona's "sense of theatre." Miller, however, did become a Federal Theatre playwright; his second Hopwood Award–winning play, *They Too Arise*, was given one performance in the Detroit Federal Theatre in October 1937.

Continuing her search for playwrights, Susan wrote to William Prichard Eaton, who was now professor of theatre at Yale, having replaced George Baker. He suggested she contact Arnold Sundgaard, a young Wisconsin Rockefeller Fellowship student, who had just graduated from the Yale program and returned to the Midwest. She immediately wrote Sundgaard, asking if he had material. Instead of responding by mail, Sundgaard, then unemployed and with a wife and children to support, hitchhiked to Chicago, portable typewriter and suitcase in each hand, and walked down Erie Street to the offices of the Playwright Bureau, intent on meeting Susan Glaspell and getting a paying job.[28] "My immediate impression of her," Sundgaard later wrote, "was that of a rather frail and somewhat shy woman with the look of an English professor I had known at Wisconsin."[29] Ten days later, after filing for welfare and being accepted, he joined the staff of play readers in her office. Already there was the Chicago playwright Alice Gerstenberg, whose 1915 play *Overtones* had been a model for the kind of experimental form and feminist subject matter Susan used in her early plays. Other readers included University of Iowa graduate Fanny McConnell, who would later marry Ralph Ellison, then part of the Federal Writers Project in New York.

"Under Susan's guidance," Sundgaard recalled, their weekly meetings were "a kind of post-graduate seminar," with each expected to read two manuscripts a day and to say something positive about each, not an easy task.[30] One of the plays she enthusiastically recommended for production was Theodore Ward's *Big White Fog*, a work that forcefully captured the bigotry and hatred a black family confronts when it moves from the South to Chicago, as Ward himself had done. It was the type of play many had dreamed of producing through the Federal Theatre; however, some feared that its ending, with black and white workers banding together, would be considered communistic by the U.S. Congress, already wary of the theatre on precisely these grounds. The administrative locus for the ensuing battle was Glaspell's play bureau, to which various officials dispatched memos trying to decide what stand to take on the play. It was finally staged on April 7, 1937, in the Great Northern Theatre where the project's experimental productions were presented, and it received enthusiastic praise from a racially mixed audience. Flanagan heralded the response, shifting the attention away from charges of communism ("this script carried no political definition," she claimed) to questions of race and historical reactions to Marcus Garvey's Back-to-Africa movement, which the father in the play at first supports.[31]

Glaspell knew that she could not wait for a Theodore Ward to enter and drop a play fully formed on her desk. One day she called her readers together and showed them a photograph she had clipped from a new journal, *Midwest*, showing a vast prairie field. Here was the image of the farm play she dreamed of staging.[32] Sundgaard alone was moved, and he began writing a loose epic work that traced western settlement from its mythic beginnings through the present labor unrest. Susan gave unqualified support for the project, which Sundgaard eventually called *Everywhere I Roam*, a title borrowed from one of his earlier, unfinished plays. Despite her enthusiasm, this time she could not convince regional production head George Kondolf to consider the idea. A few years later, however, the play based on the photograph that had so moved Susan had a short run on Broadway, and the set was executed by Susan's old Greenwich Village friend Robert Edmond Jones.

Susan was persistent in her search for new plays. If "they" didn't like her Midwest idea, she would develop a play using the "living newspaper" format, which the Federal Theatre had developed and which Flanagan called, despite its borrowing from European sources, "as American as Walt Disney."[33] Living newspapers staged news, preferably focusing on a current problem their writers had thoroughly researched and enlivened by the skillful use of actors, music, lighting, effective language, and props. In October 1937 Glaspell and Sundgaard saw a Federal Theatre production of *The Straw*, an early Eugene O'Neill play based on his 1912 hospitalization for tuberculosis at the Gaylord Farm Sanitarium. Walking home afterwards, Susan admitted that she found the subject matter a bit dated, since tuberculosis had abated. However, another scourge-like illness was now threatening large numbers of people: syphilis. Why not write a living newspaper play on that subject, she threw out to Sundgaard, who immediately caught the idea. The two worked closely together, refining the script Sundgaard entitled *Dark Harvest*, out of deference to public sensitivity about even mentioning the disease. Harry Minturn, who had now replaced George Kondolf as production head in the city, challenged him to name the subject directly, so Sundgaard called it what it was: *Spirochete*. It opened at the Blackstone Theatre on April 29, 1938, with the blessing and assistance of the Chicago medical community and the board of health, which provided free syphilis testing in the lobby. Flanagan, in her summary of the accomplishments of the entire Federal Theatre program, cited *Spirochete* as an important milestone.[34]

What she doesn't mention is the battle Susan was forced to wage over the play. This time Susan didn't have to argue for the importance of the work, but rather for the playwright's right to retain the copyright. The Federal Theatre claimed that since Sundgaard had written the play while in its employ, they did not have to pay royalties, because the work belonged to them. Susan, ever sensitive to writers' rights, sent out numerous letters in which she argued that the research may have been done on government time, but the writing took place after hours and that Sundgaard continued to serve as reader, the only position he was paid to execute. Writing directly to Flanagan on April 18, eleven days before the play was scheduled to open, she explained: "I hope you know how strong is my feeling for the Federal Theatre. I think I have shown it in remaining here for more than a year and a half, giving up my own work from which

I make a great deal more, and also weakening my own position, because if you pause too long in the writing world it is a disadvantage to your name. But strong as is my feeling for the Federal Theatre, I think it only right to tell you now that if this matter cannot be arranged with justice to Mr. Sundgaard . . . I shall feel compelled to take it to the immediate attention of the Dramatists' Guild."[35] Flanagan refused to accept her rationale, and Susan made good her threat. She brought the matter to the guild, which issued an immediate injunction stating that unless Sundgaard be allowed to keep his copyright for *Spirochete*, the Federal Theatre would no longer be allowed to produce any plays by guild writers (which meant a majority of the important, established playwrights that they were presenting, including Glaspell and O'Neill). Flanagan relented. The amazing coda to this story is that throughout the furor, Sundgaard, busy with his first produced play, knew nothing about Susan's efforts on his behalf. It was not until the 1960s, when he was reading through the Federal Theatre archives at George Mason University, that he came across her correspondence, too late to ever thank her. She probably hadn't told him, because she wasn't acting on his behalf; she was, as so often in her life, acting on a principle.

Susan won this battle, but relations with Flanagan may have suffered as a result. On July 15, 1938, when Flanagan came to Chicago to attend its yearly meeting, she enumerated the accomplishments of the Midwest group, but made no mention of Susan. Whether she had already tendered her resignation due to the added responsibilities and new management Flanagan instituted or decided to do so after this slight is not certain. By October Don Farran, another Iowan, became head of the Midwest bureau, replacing Susan, whom he said resigned because of illness and overwork. By June 1939 the entire Federal Theatre Project went out of business, due to Congress's refusal to renew its appropriation. In addition to the recurrent charge of communist sympathy, the project was denounced in Congress for its immoral plays. One congressman asked, "Are the people of this country to be taxed to support such vulgar and villainous activities?"[36] Citing the "suggestive and salacious titles" foisted on the public, he gave as an example a play whose title seemed clearly obscene: *Suppressed Desires*. For her two years of hard work for the Federal Theatre, this is the one official government acknowledgement of Glaspell's contribution to the cause.

A Different War

28

Susan's greatest battle took place in a small apartment in Chicago.
It was there she conquered her drinking demon and went on to write
once more.

—Heaton Vorse, interview, August 1988

Susan returned to Provincetown in the summer of 1938 and appeared,
in Edmund Wilson's estimation, "much better for her years in the West,"
although she "seemed to have resigned herself to become an old lady."[1]
At sixty-two, she was grayer, more lined, and frailer than she had been
in the early 1930s, but she was more determined than ever to work. She
was also happy to reconnect with friends, particularly Katie and John Dos
Passos, and she showed her old commitment to activism when, as one of
her first acts, she formed a "defense committee" to block the local beach
club from buying the house next to them and opposite her.[2] If Susan had
forgotten the sea and the special winds of the Cape during her time in
Chicago, she was reminded of the potential fury of both in September,
when one of the most severe hurricanes of the century slammed into land
near New Bedford, throwing out all communication with the Cape. Many
residents believed the Cape to have been flattened by the severity of the
storm. Since the hurricane occurred in the same week that Chamberlain
made his fateful visit to Munich to meet Hitler, Mary Vorse—ever the
political writer—described the two "great disasters" as "contrapuntal to
one another."[3]

Some things had changed in Provincetown during Susan's absence. The
summer before, John Francis, her friend and realtor, who had faithfully
carried out a variety of services for her over the past twenty-five years,

had died. Francis was a man of principle and took his responsibilities seriously. In one of the many testimonial columns his writer-friends published on his death, Susan's friend Phyllis Duganne told of the two schoolteachers who had rented Susan's Truro house one summer, only to discover that several snakes had taken up residence there. Refunding the teachers' money, over her protest that the reptilian invaders could easily be evicted, Francis explained to Susan that houses must be habitable for renters, "And houses with snakes in them aren't habitable."[4]

Before she had gone to Chicago, Susan had spent a good part of each winter in New York, either at the Brevoort or the Holly Arms Hotel in Washington Square. Now New York seemed less appealing to her than Chicago. Her two years there had given her the chance to reconnect with Ray and develop an easy friendship with Flossie, not as intellectually stimulating as with Provincetown friends but, nevertheless, important, since it allowed her to indulge in the everyday conversations she craved after her taxing work. The women would sometimes stroll down Michigan Avenue window-shopping and discuss recent fashion trends, such as women's dyeing their hair to appear younger, something that Flossie was contemplating but that Susan rejected, arguing that gray hairs were "marks of survival not shame."[5] With Flossie and Ray happy to welcome her back, Susan decided to spend the winter of 1939 in Chicago, in order to write.

In *The Glory of the Conquered*, set in Chicago, Georgia, a young newspaper reporter resembling Susan, had remarked on her battle with the city: "You know I had a tough time here, but I won out, and most of us are vain enough to be awfully fond of the place where we've been up against it and come out on top."[6] Susan now conducted a battle in Chicago, not with the city but with the alcoholism that she had not yet gotten completely under control. On her return there in the winter of 1939, without the assistance of any program or drugs, she went "cold turkey" and gave up drinking forever. Friends who knew saw this as Susan's most courageous fight and greatest victory. Floyd Dell, in a 1954 letter to Arthur Waterman, a doctoral student who was at that time working on the first Glaspell dissertation, asked him to include Susan's struggle with drinking in his study: "I think that probably such things should now be told about writers. It is, perhaps, only when the politics of genius are revealed at very great length . . . that they are (as Susan used to say) 'harrowing.' The claims of truth are of uncertain validity, but I think they should not be lightly brushed aside."[7] Leonora Cook, Harl's first wife, also confirmed Glaspell's struggle and triumph, indicating that when she first married Harl, she found Susan difficult because she was drinking so heavily. "But then she realized that she was running out of money and no one was going to take care of her, so she went to Chicago, took an apartment near Ray and wrote a book. She stopped drinking without any help which is very unusual."[8] Cook believed that she could do this because she had the habit of work to fall back on, something, unfortunately, that Harl had not possessed.

It is not clear if the novel Susan began now, *The Morning is Near Us*, was the one she had put aside two years earlier when she went to work for the Federal Theatre. Quite possibly, the "interrupted book" is *Norma Ashe*, published in 1942, since it displays more obvious discontinuity between sections. *Morning*, published in 1940, is far tighter, its sections more seamlessly woven in chronological order, indicating sustained inspiration. A nine-year hiatus separates it from *Ambrose Holt and Family*, twelve years from *Brook Evans*, to which it bears certain similarities. In *Morning* Susan once more focuses on a daughter whose life has been molded by a family secret concerning her birth; but rather than ranging across several generations, two continents, and numerous third-person narrators, this time the story is told from the daughter's point of view. And this time the protagonist, Lydia Chippman, (the name of Susan's great-great grandmother) does not desire to escape the confining circle of family but rather to rejoin the fold and reap the love and comfort they can provide, a telling change in Susan's usual narrative and a sign of her own feelings of closeness to Ray and Flossie. The book is dedicated to them and presents a warm portrait of the ways in which Lydia's brother and sister-in-law assist her in reclaiming her life. The plot—a concoction of equal parts Gothic horror story, Greek tragedy, and midwestern mystery—revolves around Lydia's struggle to unlock the family secret that has made her an outcast, sent away by her parents at an early age and not allowed to return, even for their funerals. Borrowing from *Brook Evans*, Susan once more has her character discover that the man who has raised her was not her father. Hertha, Lydia's mother, had married him—despite the fact she had been adopted and raised by the Chippmans, his family. Since the beautiful and loving Hertha found sex with her husband a defilement of familial ties, he sanctioned the lovers she sought to fulfill her desire for life. Lydia is the product of one of these liaisons, sent away not because she was unloved, but because she represented a love both her parents found too painful to bear.

In a diary dating from her composition of *Inheritors*, Susan had scribbled the name "Hertha" on a single page, indicating that as far back as 1919 she had been thinking about this Scandinavian goddess, representing Mother Earth. Golden-haired Madeline Morton may have been a homegrown variation. In this novel Hertha, who never appears in the story, is thwarted by circumstances and can only express her physical nature in the dark, replicating the mysterious rites to the mythical Hertha, also conducted sub rosa. To shed light on the dark is the central motif of the novel, and Susan's early title was "Let There be Light."[9] During Lydia's struggle to understand the unspoken mystery of the Chippman family, she comes to realize a basic Glaspell tenant: "Life is not of our ordering . . . but chaotic—unpredictable. What we seek we do not find—that would be too trim and tidy for so reckless and opulent a thing as life. It is something else we find."[10] Once she comes to understand and accept her past and finds a place for herself in her family home and community, Lydia recognizes that the best that one can hope to do in life is to go on, keeping some remnants of a belief system in tact—a truth Susan seems to have embraced as well. Survival for the protagonist this time does not include a man. Only three of the novel's 296 pages are devoted to a male lover; the rest describe family and community as providers of the ballast Lydia requires.

The Morning is Near Us drew on Susan's midwestern experiences. When she returned to Provincetown in the summer of 1939, she received two other books that took her back to her past. Nilla's own "road" book, *My Road to India*, covered some of the same Greek terrain Susan had described, but with Nilla now the central figure. Hutch Hapgood, for one, found Nilla's depiction of her father better than Susan's because he felt it captured the irrepressible man rather than the flawed genius. Although in her early chapters, Nilla criticizes her stepmother's strictness with her, at the end she gives credit to Susan, to whom she had grown closer in the past few years. Hutch's own autobiography, *A Victorian in the Modern World*, also appeared in 1939 and caused Susan considerable pain. His Jig is a greater-than-life spirit, somehow unappreciated by his wife, whom Hutch assumes is displaying typical wifely restraint by not allowing the genius his daemonic due. In addition, at one point he writes that Susan "had with the determination of every woman in love, taken him away from his then wife and children."[11] He also peppers his narrative with personal details of the Glaspell/Cook married life, focusing on what he sees as Susan's jealousy of Jig's friends, namely himself. Although Hutch wrote to Neith after the book appeared, "Saw Susan once, full of painful arthritis and complaints about what I wrote of her,"[12] the two continued to be close. Susan was, as Hutch noted in the book, indeed generous to her friends.

Sinclair Lewis, another figure from her past, resurfaced during the summer. Their relationship went back to 1913, when he had worked for Stokes, Glaspell's publisher, and she had provided encouragement for him to leave editing and complete his first book, *Our Mr. Wrenn*. Her copy bears his thanks. Recently Lewis had taken up acting, and he was in Provincetown in August for a performance of O'Neill's *Ah, Wilderness!*, to be given in the Provincetown Playhouse. Susan decided to invite newspaper friends Ernie Meyer and Ted Robinson and their wives to meet America's first Nobel Prize–winning author in order to generate publicity for the production. The evening, however, was a fiasco. Lewis made his entrance through an open window, proceeded to drink everything in sight, and then insulted the guests. As Dorothy Meyer put it: "He talked himself out of a review in Ernie's column."[13] However, for Lewis the visit to Provincetown was auspicious. It was there he met eighteen-year-old Marcella Powers, an apprentice with the theatre group, who became his companion for the next six years. Susan knew the young woman through Lewis, and one fact about her family life may have caught her attention: Marcella's widowed mother supported the family by running a boardinghouse, a detail Susan would appropriate for her next novel, *Norma Ashe*.

The Morning is Near Us, with a flattering Bachrach photograph of Susan on the back cover, was published in London and New York in March 1940. Critics generally dismissed the novel, but the public found it a fascinating story, perfect for diverting attention away from the war now raging in Europe. The Literary Guild, sensing its potential, chose it as their April selection, guaranteeing large sales. A month after its publication, it had already sold 107,500 copies, the greatest initial response to any Glaspell novel. Stokes hosted a cocktail party at the Algonquin Hotel in New York in Susan's honor to mark the success of the book. Ever modest on public occasions, she openly admitted to host Frank Chase that she had long dreamed of attending a literary party at the Algonquin. But before he could congratulate her on her novel, she complimented him on his most recent book. "It was really difficult to make Miss Glaspell stay even on the edge of the limelight," a news article quotes him as saying. "She seemed naturally to begin talking about any subject rather than herself."[14] The novel continued to do well. In May it appeared on the *New York Herald Tribune* book list as tenth in sales, followed by *The Grapes of Wrath* in thirteenth position. A Braille edition appeared in July, and in the same month a rash of stories appeared in newspapers around the country, fueled by gossip columnist Louella Parsons, alleging that Susan had been offered "a record-breaking price" for the film rights to the bestseller and that either Jean Arthur or Irene Dunne would play Lydia. Glaspell eventually received $10,000 from Columbia Pictures, as she had for *Brook Evans*, not record-breaking but a decent sum for a woman who had been paid $200 a month for the past two years. Responding to Jasper Deeter's note of congratulations on the movie sale, she wrote, "I don't know when they're going to do it. Maybe they won't—and maybe that will be as well, though I think it might make a good picture."[15] The film was never made.

If there were old friends surrounding her in the summer of 1940, there were also newer ones. Susan became even closer to the Meyers, who by now were regulars in the Provincetown community. Dorothy was pregnant with her second child in early 1939, and as Susan wrote to a friend: "We're thinking it would be nice if the baby and the book [*Morning*] came out on the same day."[16] When Dorothy gave birth to a daughter, she insisted on naming her after Susan, whom she asked to be godmother. Susan at first hesitated; "I checked and godmothers are charged with protecting the morals of their godchildren. I'm not sure my morals are good enough. In fact I'm not sure I know what morals are." However she took the charge. With a growing family, the Meyers hoped to buy a house, but did not have the money for a down payment and had decided instead to live with Ernie's parents. "It's not a good idea to live with in-laws," Susan advised Dorothy. "I'll lend you the money you need." Dorothy at first refused, but after much persuasion from Susan, she agreed. However, when Dorothy said she wanted to pay interest on the loan, Susan drew herself up and proclaimed, "Madame there will be no interest. I am not a bank," an echo of her great grandfather James's response to a friend a hundred years earlier. With the money, the Meyers were able to purchase a home in Weston, Connecticut. When Susan visited, she was thrilled when Dorothy let her bathe and diaper the baby. The expression on her face reminded Dorothy of the Madonna. No one before had ever let Susan hold a naked baby.[17]

As Susan got older, and no longer had a man who provided the love and connectedness she required in her life, her failure to have children weighed more heavily, and she often discussed the subject with close friends. Miriam Hapgood Dewitt, on one of her visits to her parents in Provincetown, attended a party at Susan's house, given in honor of the granddaughter of John Philip Sousa, who went on at length about her decision not to have children because she was more interested in pursuing a career. Miriam, delighted with her own recent motherhood, noted how uncommonly silent Susan was during the evening and wondered how she must have felt, never having had children.[18] Susan told Dorothy Meyer about her miscarriage in 1914 and her inability to have children after that. She also admitted that in a wooden sea chest Jig had made, she still kept the baby things she had prepared for the birth. Since Nilla's baby had been born in Greece and Harl and her brothers had no children, the clothes had remained there. However, one day when Dorothy visited, she discovered Susan airing the baby things on her outdoor line. "We're having a baby," she gleefully announced.[19] Francelina Sousa Hubbard, who had begun working for her in 1940, had become pregnant by her husband Bill, but wanted to divorce him because he drank. Susan helped her arrange the divorce, paid for it, and took out the clothes for the baby. "I never had a chance to use them," she told Francelina. "I always wanted children but couldn't have any of my own. Take them. It will make me very happy to think someone is putting them to use." "Without her I don't know if I would have made it," Francelina recalled. "She gave me courage to leave my husband, continue on my own, and have my baby." She became devoted to Susan, and worked for her for the next eight years.[20]

As a gift to namesake Susan Marie Meyer and her brother Karl, "lest he be jealous," Susan dedicated a children's story entitled *Cherished and Shared of Old*, first published in *Redbook* in 1940 and then brought out in a miniature-sized edition by Julian Messner, beautifully illustrated by Alice Harvey. To Karl, she signed a copy from "his aunt Susan." To Susan she wrote, "You will not understand the book just now but later you will."[21] The title derives from Jig's 1907 adaptation from Sappho: "Though we know that never a longing mortal / Gains life best—Oh, better it is to pray for / Part in what we cherished and shared of old than / Fail to remember."[22] In a tale simple and direct enough for a child to grasp, Susan creates a beautiful Christmas parable for a world at war. Addie Morrison and Emma Schultz, childhood friends, have not spoken since a land dispute between their fathers long ago caused the families to sever all connections. The women—one a native-born Iowan, the other an immigrant from Germany—still yearn, particularly as each Christmas season approaches, for the companionship they shared and lost; but neither knows how to bridge the gap. When Addie opens her farmhouse to two Dutch refugee children, displaced by the present war, the new arrivals inadvertently bring the women together. Not surprisingly, in a Glaspell story, it the Schultz dog, festooned by the children with ribbons, much like Addie and Emma used to do, that provides the link. He bounds over to the Schultz house, and Emma welcomes him, assuming he is a sign from Addie that it is time for reconciliation. Long-held grievances and animosity quickly fade, or, as Susan puts it, "fear flew out through the window when love came in by the door."

Buoyed by the success of *The Morning is Near Us* and freed for the time being from pressing financial worries, Susan planned to spend the winter of 1941 in Provincetown and begin work on a new novel. However, in January her old problem with arthritis in her foot flared up, and she went to New York for treatment. Back in Provincetown in February, she found she could not move her new novel along and decided to return once more to Chicago in March to see if the city could again unlock her writing. From there she traveled briefly to Davenport in order to meet Harl, who was motoring up from Mexico, where he had spent his honeymoon with his second wife, Carol. The visit also gave her a chance to reconnect with Frank and Hazel, who had continued to live in the family home after Alice Glaspell's death in 1929. The ties between Susan and Frank had never been as strong as those she had with Ray. Frank had had a difficult life, trying a number of jobs in Montana and Texas, but never achieving the financial success he sought. While together, he told her stories of his recent past. To these tales of failed work experiences, she grafted Ray's experiences in the plumbing business and his early dream that oil wells might make him "a millionaire." They became part of the midwestern novel she had been struggling with for some time, *Norma Ashe*—its settings, Davenport and Chicago.

The most important source for the novel, however, was *The Road to the Temple*, which Stokes reissued in April 1941, with a new foreword by Susan. In 1923 in Greece, Jig had written, "The oracle at Delphi, which still speaks to whomso cares to listen, gives Europe till 1941. Europe will then die of Nietzsche's philosophy—as the eagle and lion die, being for themselves alone. Pity their magnificence." Prophetically, the war in Europe seemed to be bearing him out, and Susan used the quotation for her foreword, adding "how triumphant he would be if it develops he was wrong."[23] She describes how his great love and respect for ancient and modern Greece were being vindicated by the heroic battle that country was waging against the Nazi invasion. In this foreword, she omitted those sentences most rankling to Hutch Hapgood. Gone are, "The life of George Cram Cook is a life of achievement which is most distinguished in its defeats" and "He was a great lover and a lusty enthusiastic drinker."

In the process of rereading the text, which she did not alter, she had an opportunity to return to Jig's ideas about the oneness of the universe, the evolutionary thrust of nature toward new life forms, and the possibilities of social evolution in individuals and institutions—ideas even more potent and relevant in 1941, she felt, than they were in 1907, when she first heard them at the Monist meetings in Davenport. These ideas became the central themes of *Norma Ashe*, espoused by a philosophy professor, Joseph Langley, modeled on Jig, who is lured to rural Pioneer College in South Dakota, a version of Morton College of *Inheritors*, by his desire to teach the young. Drawing together five of his brightest students and one young assistant, Langley talks to them about the great thinkers of the past and their own role in the adventure of the future. Dare to dream, he enjoins them, because "The dream comes first; then reality as idea."[24]

Of the five students, three women and two men, Norma Ashe shows the greatest promise, and Langley arranges for her to continue her studies at the University of Chicago after graduation. However, on the train trip back to her Iowa home for summer vacation, she meets Max Utterbach, as committed to business success as she is to education; and almost immediately the direction of her life shifts. They fall in love, marry, and move to Texas, where—like Frank—he takes up land speculation, and she slowly becomes enmeshed in a far different life than the one she imagined. When Max's get-rich-quick schemes become too much for her to bear, she echoes the words of her thwarted namesake Nora in *A Doll's House*, declaring, "I am more than a wife . . . . [I am] myself," but she does not slam the door on her marriage. "Chains of dew" are not easily broken, at least for one who loves, she realizes, just as other Glaspell characters and she, herself, knew.

To illustrate how the hopes of youth often fall painfully short in later years, Susan chooses to begin her three-part novel not with Norma, at the time of her college graduation, but with Norma in 1927, a forty-nine-year-old widow who, since Max's sudden death, has struggled to pay the debts he left and to eke out a living for herself and her grown children by running a dilapidated boardinghouse, which, like its proprietress, has seen better days. So little remains of the old Norma or her dreams that when, near the end of part one, Rosie, one of the five "chosen" students, makes a sudden visit to try to rekindle her own dormant beliefs, she can barely recognize the grotesque woman who greets her and talks only of money. This short first part is one of Glaspell's most detailed, naturalistic pieces of writing, a gritty picture of the sights, sounds, and smells in the decaying house, whose occupants are mostly students at the local "college," patterned after Palmer Chiropractic School in Davenport, where joint manipulation rather than Plato promises the way to a better world.

In parts two and three, Susan breaks the chronology to better illustrate the present loss in comparison to the past hope. She returns to Norma's school years, her meeting with Max, and their life together, and then she moves ahead to 1929, detailing a trip Norma takes to Chicago and her attempt once more to reconnect with the idealism of her past. Stretching credulity, as Glaspell tends to do repeatedly in her fiction, she has Norma find herself at the University of Chicago just in time to attend a lecture given by one of her former classmates, now a business tycoon. As she sits mute, listening to him embellishing a paternalistic speech against unions with snippets of their teacher's words, Norma suddenly finds her voice and rises to denounce his distortion of their shared legacy. So taken with this strange, shabbily dressed woman, the aptly named student Scott Neubolt follows her out of the hall, intent on learning her story. For a short time, the old Norma reappears, but she is soon stripped of her reclaimed idealism by the revelation that her teacher, who preached the sanctity of life, had taken his own. Again bereft, she returns to her Davenport boarding-house, now a thriving establishment run by her daughter and son-in-law and plans to spend her last days there. However, when her daughter gives birth to a girl, Norma recognizes what Lydia discovered in the preceding novel: that life is stronger than death and that even when its route is not clearly marked, it is possible to reach some modicum of fulfillment if one stays true to one's beliefs.

Her new publisher J. B. Lippincott requested she provide a summary for the inside cover of the book. Although she would later admit to Edmund Wilson that she cringed to see words written during the composition process actually appear in the book, her paragraph does offer a summary of the work and does reflect Susan's philosophy at the time, particularly her claim that "The vision and the fight for a better world could not have had so long a life on earth were they not of the very stuff of life itself. The end is not yet. The dreamers who fight will win. So says this book."[25] In the 1940s Susan could no longer focus on a naive, undeterred, and unbent young female hero, like Madeline Morton, moving unblinking into the future. She herself knew only too well the difficulties and defeats facing such dreamers as they grow older. She was also not willing to allow her persona, like Claire, to lapse into insanity as the result of reversals. By situating Norma at the end of her life, rather than at the beginning, or even the middle, she could illustrate, as she had in *Road*, that the greater victory may be the fidelity to the dream rather than its fulfillment. She also illustrates that the past has much to teach the present and the future. It may seem as if Norma's surname Ashe points to destruction; however, from the ruins of her life, Norma continually rises, phoenix-like, or, in another cluster of images, bubbles forth to the surface, an act indicated by her married surname Utterbach, which in German refers to an underground spring.

Although World War II was the unstated backdrop of the novel, Susan chose to set the action much earlier, between 1899 and 1929, only referencing the present date of 1942 in the opening paragraph. Again she stresses that if individuals and societies forget the verities of the past in their rush for material goods and "progress," they do so at their peril— witness the Great Depression, which ends the book, and the great war that hovers in the wings. Susan's attitude toward World War II differed radically from the one she harbored about World War I. Earlier she had called into question all wars and the motivations of those who fought them. In *Norma Ashe* she writes: "When what we know to be good is about to go down before evil: a time to fight! What was it Plato had said? 'The creation of the world—that is to say the world of civilized order—is the victory of persuasion over force.' But if force of evil would not listen to persuasion? Should we keep peace and see the good go down? She did not believe that."[26] Susan seems to have intended that Norma's personal struggles would point to global events, although the connections at best are tenuous and vague in the novel.

To make certain that her earlier stand against war would not be construed as her present position, Susan wrote to Jasper Deeter on December 12, 1941, five days after Pearl Harbor brought America into the war, requesting that his Hedgerow Theatre desist from producing *Inheritors* until the war ended. "I think our country [is] in greater danger than ever before in its history—that all we hold dear, all worth living for, is threatened. The light might go out—and for generations to come. I would not have words of mine—even though unjustly, for those words were not spoken of *this* time—give support to those who oppose this war which has been forced upon us." She hastens to add, "No one has spoken to me about this. The idea is my own. There has been no censorship of the play."[27] She did not rescind the order until the end of the war, even in December 1943, when Deeter requested that a special public reading, not a performance of the play, be given to a Quaker Friends meeting. She also illustrated her belief that force was needed when people were threatened with annihilation by becoming a signatory of a petition, signed in November 1942, by 1,521 government leaders, clergy, professors, and writers calling for the right of stateless Jews of Europe and Jews of Palestine to fight the Nazis, under their own banner. Several of her Provincetown Player friends, including Eugene O'Neill, Edna St. Vincent Millay, and Max Eastman also signed.[28]

Norma Ashe had one of the longest gestations of any Glaspell novel, in part because of an undisclosed illness that required that she be admitted to Lenox Hill Hospital in New York. Lippincott finally published the book in October 1942, and Susan sent a copy to Edmund Wilson, explaining her fears that the publisher might not promote it because it was unlike any novel she had ever written. "I have a divided and somewhat tormenting feeling of being very humble about it, and somewhat proud of it too," she wrote him, a typically modest Glaspell comment.[29] The critical reaction was as divided as her own. The *New Yorker* dismissed it as a Christian Science Tract; the reviewer for the *New York Times* found it one of her most powerful books and gave it an unqualified endorsement. Despite Susan's hopes for the novel, it did not do well. Those who in 1939 had embraced *The Morning is Near Us* because of its happy resolution were, in 1942, flocking to the films of Fred Astaire and Ginger Rogers in order to forget the war. They showed little interest in reading about the failures of an impoverished, middle-aged dreamer.

Writing the novel had depleted Susan's energy and her royalties from *Morning*, and she found herself again in financial trouble. "It's sad that it would be humorous—your asking how much money I can lend Hedgerow," she wrote to Deeter at the beginning of 1943. "A very long and expensive illness about cleaned me out, and I'm worried to death about how to swing certain family obligations (a brother who has been invalided some years now) and also swing things for myself until another book comes out. I indulged myself by writing a book I very much wanted to write, *Norma Ashe*, though knowing it couldn't be a big money maker. I spent a long time on it and am glad I did, only sorry it leaves me unable to do things I would like to do."[30] Some of her financial concerns may have actually colored the scenes of poverty she created for Norma.

Her friends also had money problems, and several, like Katie and John Dos Passos, were now spending the winters in Provincetown, of necessity. As Susan joked to Dorothy Meyer, she and Dos would begin each day exchanging postdated checks that both had asked the other to hold.[31] Sometimes this imposed monotony of life bothered her. One night, walking home with Katie and Eben Given after they had seen *Yankee Doodle Dandy* at the local cinema, Susan muttered, "Gawd, it's getting me! I've got to get out!"[32] But despite her complaint, she continued to stay in her Provincetown house, now that Harl and his wife Carol were living permanently in her Truro home; and she continued to follow the routines she had long ago instituted to provide order in her days. She rose at 8:00 and ate the breakfast Francelina prepared for her, took her daily bath, and then went upstairs once more to work, sometimes still using her pulley elevator.[33] Francelina worked every day until 2:30 and would do the shopping and make Susan's favorite dishes, including cheese soufflé and chocolate mousse. Susan had a sweet tooth, and Francelina gave up her own ration coupons during the war so that she could provide Susan with an extra supply of sugar. Francelina would also make sure that the house was cleaned each day and the sheets changed three times a week, as Susan required. Always a simple dresser, Susan now wore only comfortable dresses and low-heeled shoes, but still kept in her closet the gowns she had once worn to parties. There were few of those now. Social life consisted of visits to and from a few close friend including Harry Kemp, Katie and Dos, Charlie Kaselau, Phyllis Duganne and Eben Given, Ozzie Ball (her lawyer), and the Meyers.

Susan had a special fondness for Harry, leaving her front window open should he be in need of alcohol, which she kept only for him, cigarettes, which they both smoked, or loose change, which she left scattered around the house. Marguerite Kaselau had died suddenly, leaving two small sons. It was Susan who marshaled her friends to help Charlie out and arranged for Katie and Dos to allow them to stay there for a time. In return Charlie sometimes cut her grass. Susan also gave Harry money to work in the garden, but she confided to Francelina that it was worth paying extra if he didn't work there, and she usually got Charlie to put it back in order after one of Kemp's forays. Harl was also a constant visitor, often in need of a loan, since he did not work. Although Susan had stopped drinking, Harl had not. She worried about his health and lack of occupation and sought the assistance of Wilson, who had some connections in Washington, in order to help Harl secure a government position with the United Nations Relief and Rehabilitation Administration in Greece. The agency did not accept him, so Harl spent the war years in Truro. Nilla, after the publication of her book, had returned to Greece with Sirius and served as a correspondent for *Liberty* magazine during the war.

Susan had always believed in public action. She now gratefully accepted an invitation to become a member of PEN, the international writer's association, because "I am interested in what your organization stands for and is doing."[34] With *Norma Ashe* published and no immediate plans for another novel, she also decided to do something for the war effort and joined the Provincetown Public Safety Committee, one of the first organized in the country to provide an early warning station for possible enemy incursions and to meet any civil emergency. For three-hour stretches several times a week, she would go to the report center, housed in a basement, "which seems a good deal like a dungeon," there to receive communiqués from Boston and Hyannis about any suspicious sightings on sea or land. Calls were infrequent, and she even contemplated bringing her writing with her since "no one can come in."[35] Instead she settled for knitting, a hobby she took up during the war years. The monotony was broken, however, on June 16, 1942, when German submarines sank American and British freighters and a passenger steamer off Provincetown, with the loss of ninety-four men, including eighteen soldiers. Susan had been uptown marketing at Bryants when news of the disaster came, and she joined the crowds silently forming a vigil around Chapman's Hotel, requisitioned as a shelter for the forty-two survivors. The disaster—and Provincetown's efficient handling of it—were reported in the local, national, and international press and short-wave broadcasts, many referring to the "pioneering" spirit of the community, because of its history as the first landfall of the Pilgrims and its location, fronting the sea in a place where little grew. Susan attended the ceremony in the Town Hall, in which the national director for the Office of Civilian Defense told the gathering: "You, the people of this village, symbolized what civilians, organized and banded together and willing to work can do." Susan details the event and the speech in a draft of an essay she was preparing for *American Biography* because its message echoes the central theme running through all her works: the power of people who choose to work together for a better society. Privately, in a letter to Martha Robinson, she wrote, "The war makes a difference and it is better to be part of the time, where you feel one of the crowd."[36] This is a very different position than

the one she occupied during World War I, when it was the compact majority whom she most feared.

Susan was willing to do what she could for the war effort; she was not,
however, willing to sacrifice her books unnecessarily because of a government order. In September 1942, a month before *Norma Ashe* appeared,
she received a letter from George Stevens of Lippincott, informing her
that in compliance with a government memo, all the plates of her books,
except *The Road to the Temple* and *The Morning is Near Us*, would be
melted down for ammunition. Lippincott had only recently become her
publisher. When Stokes went out of business, the publisher had shown such
enthusiasm for her writing that she agreed to sign with them in November
1941. She now felt betrayed, since the company was not willing to use its
discretionary rights to withhold certain books, as other publishers were
doing for some of her writer friends. Destroying plates is, she argues, in a
draft letter to George Stevens, tantamount to completely erasing all traces
of the works, since rarely were books reissued after plates were gone.
"We like to think we have done something that remains behind us, that is
not just a question of writing one book and then another, but a cumula-
tive body of work."[37] Besides, she continues, "It is my belief that some
of these novels of mine are one expression of American life in the period
just behind us; and that with the changes that are imminent there may be
'Use' for certain books that give the picture of the life we had so long and
loved so well." She reminds Stevens that such edicts need not be taken as
gospel, just because "somebody in Washington had a brain-storm (you
see I once worked on the Federal Theatre and know about these brain-
storms)." In addition, she claims, "Wholesale book destruction sounds
more like our enemies than us." Her central argument concerns the power
of books and the need to honor the past in the present. At the beginning
of the war, she had voluntarily offered the government Jig's twelve-pound
bronze plaque that the Provincetown Players had returned to her when
the theatre closed. That was one thing; the destruction of her books was
something else. What made the request particularly painful was that it
indicated that Lippincott held out few prospects for *Norma Ashe*—which
Susan believed to be her best—and the possibility that its success might
generate interest in her earlier writing. She requests that Lippincott at
least spare *Brook Evans*, *Ambrose Holt and Family* and *Fugitive's Return*,
in that order. "If *Brook Evans* goes, she writes finally, "something in me
goes with it."

Susan did not let the case end there. She contacted the Authors League;
she also took the unusual step, for her, of agreeing to give a talk to the
National Book Fair in Boston, on October 21, 1942, the eve of the publication of *Norma Ashe*. Her lecture, entitled "The Huntsmen are up in
America," presents a succinct summary of the "hunt" that has engrossed
her throughout her life and which, she argues, the nation must now undertake: "for the feeling, the truth, that will push, not only the light of the
English language but the light of the human spirit a little further against

darkness." The war is terrible, she admits, but it also offers the possibility that "a new energy, new beauty, [can] come into the world." Books can lead the way. Therefore, when asked in a questionaire how a writer can help the war effort, she responded: "to become a better writer." Her character Norma Ashe, she explains, sumarizing the philosophy embedded in her new novel, "is challenged," but continues to fight and to be true to her teacher's idealism and "in the fight the old dream becomes the living reality, and the light that is Norma Ashe goes a little further against the dark."[38] Reporting to Martha Robinson after the talk, she wrote that she had not disgraced herself and had even gotten considerable applause, which was a reward after the talk. In this case the "ordeal" was made worse by Lippincott's advertising manager, who told her backstage that he had few expectations for Norma Ashe, since "it was a story of failure, and people didn't want that now," they preferred "escape."[39] Two months later, she again championed the need for serious literature in times of war. Under the headline, "Susan Glaspell Says We Need Books Today As Never Before," the Chicago Sunday Tribune printed an article in which Susan describes sitting with Katie and John Dos Passos and others in her Provincetown living room during a nightly blackout and reading aloud from André Maurois's I Remember, I Remember, which caused them to share memories of France, now devastated by war. This led Susan to read Whitman's "O Star of France" to the group. Left alone after her friends departed, she describes being comforted by the poem, her rejoinder against those who would burn books or melt bookplates.[40]

Completing the Circle

29

I have never lost the feeling that this [the Middle West] is my part of the country.

> —Susan Glaspell, quoted in "Interview with Florence
> Haxton Bullock," *Chicago Sun Book Week*,
> 28 October 1945

Despite the disappointing reception in the first months of 1943 of *Norma Ashe* and war news that was growing more ominous, Susan was determined to keep working. She now threw herself into a project that she kept secret from her friends until it was completed. It had been thirteen years since she'd written for the theatre, and she decided that she needed to try her hand once more to see if she could still create dramatic plots and dialogue. "Springs Eternal" is the result, a comedy about war, in which three upper-middle class couples banter about love, faithfulness, raising children, philosophies of life, and only parenthetically the carnage abroad.[1] In *Norma Ashe*, Susan had observed, "War could be gallant, but there was nothing gallant about the petty wars of so-called peace, this constant war between people, trying to get ahead of somebody else, when that someone else had a life a good deal like your own."[2] In her play she stages this "other war," but instead of indicting big business or commercialism, she focuses her attention on the love lives and embroilments of her characters and the older generation's moral failures. "We have entangling alliances; we are always busy breaking our pacts," the central female protagonist, Margaret, claims. Owen, her husband is Glaspell's resident philosopher, who has retreated to study dead languages, believing that intellectuals like himself are incapable of exerting a moral force or stopping the present conflagration, an echo of Bernice's father in Glaspell's World War I drama. Bill, a young visiting doctor, is appalled by Owens's abdication of responsibility and by the meaningless conversations around him: "Fellows are dying and you're chewing the rag about your silly little lives." In act 1 Susan shows that the idealists and the realists are equally incapable of providing any leadership to confused youth in troubled times. The problem with the play is that she allows more time for their self-indulgences and banalities than she does for any action that might offer alternatives. Owen's ennui seems little more than an excuse for one-liners about failed values and ageing philosophers.

The play illustrates how far Susan's views concerning war had shifted since *Bernice* and *Inheritors*. Conscientious objection is now portrayed as an excuse for not doing one's duty instead of a moral stance against killing. When Jumbo, Owen's son, claims the status, his father caustically comments, "He never had an objection in his life! And he has no conscience. How does that make him a conscientious objector?" Susan does not jettison her basic belief in human connectedness and the necessity for individual responsibilities to improve society. Hope still springs eternal—as the title indicates—it just takes a little while to arrive. In act 3 Jumbo, now more sure of himself and more convinced that "the only thing that is really ours is the thing that is *in* us—not yet done," decides to join the army; and Owen regains his belief in the efficacy of ideas, after his son reminds him, "if life's all any of us have, that ought to make us feel sort of close together, don't you think?" The comedy ends appropriately with marriage and with the assembled characters offering a toast, not to the brave new world, but to the brave old world, which, despite the mistakes of previous generations, contains, as Jumbo explains, "Feeling [which] stays on—*in* things—in people who weren't even born when it was born. Gee—I just found that out." Such trite, awkward phrasing of her earlier ideas makes it unclear if Susan means to show the superficiality of the characters in the play or is attempting to make her philosophy more accessible to a modern audience, who had rejected *Norma Ashe* because it had not been "entertaining" and clear enough.

To see if her play had merit, Susan turned to an old friend, Lawrence Langner, founder of the Washington Square Players, now active in its offshoot, the Theatre Guild. The guild, like other theatre companies during the war, had suffered, but its mounting of *Oklahoma!*, the musical based on Lynn Riggs' *Green Grows the Lilacs* (the play *Alison's House* beat out for the 1931 Pulitzer Prize), gave them new life and money. In March 1944, during a trip to New York, Susan wrote to Langner asking if he'd be interested in reading "Springs Eternal." "I had fun and an interesting time doing it—and how can I say? Some one else has to say whether it's good!"[3] Langner read the script by May 3 but put off his decision until he could consult other guild members. On May 19, in a carefully worded letter, he informed her that they were not interested in the play, since its ideas seemed to be those of two or three years ago and its form until the middle of act 2 was "so much of a conversation piece." Apologetic about the decision, Langner tries to cushion the rejection: "You know, Susan, I think that you have one of the finest talents in America and it is an impertinence on my part to criticize anything you write. Perhaps I am too much immersed in the practical theatre and you are closer to the truth than I am."[4] One reason that must have influenced the decision was the fact that two months earlier the Theatre Guild had produced a classic in the comedic/wartime genre: Franz Werfel's *Jacobowsky and the Colonel*, adapted by S. N. Behrman. In comparison, "Springs Eternal" falls far short. Still not ready to concede defeat, Susan turned to her friend Eva LeGallienne, who had produced *Inheritors* and *The Verge*. "I've tried to say something I feel, and I want to know whether you think I have said it, she wrote."[5] LeGallienne and director Margaret Webster read the play, liked it, but felt it needed cutting. However, even if rewritten they did not have funding to produce it. Susan responded, "You know me well enough to know I never think I've written the perfect play, and am always ready to do anything I can to see it right. I thought this play had something to say, and would be entertaining. I still think so . . . and wish some one with the wherewithall would like it that way."[6] She was unable to find such a person, and "Springs Eternal" remained unpublished and unproduced.[7]

Susan, in typical fashion, wasted no time over the rejection; instead, in June she immediately launched into a new novel she called *Judd Rankin's Daughter*. It took up the war and generational themes of "Springs Eternal" and grafted them to a story depicting the central battle she had fought in her own adult life: reconciling the Midwest of her birth and the East of her adopted home. Iowa had shaped her practical bent, resiliency, wry humor, and idealist philosophy, legacies from the pioneers from whom she sprung and the Indians they supplanted. Davenport, however, had been a place she fled, because of its smug belief in its own rectitude and its excessive religiosity, which tended to suppress joy and freedom. The East for her had been the corrective—and her emancipation. In Provincetown she had found the culture and intellectual life she craved, with like-minded people who embraced heterodoxy rather than orthodoxy and subscribed to an openness that itself was a type of pioneering—at least as Susan describes it. In *Judd Rankin's Daughter*, her last published work, she does away with her cautionary habit of disguising locales; this time the East is Provincetown, the West is Iowa, although she moves her protagonist's birthplace to a rural farm, in order to strengthen the contrast between the farmland of America, and the eastern establishment. She strives to look objectively at the two regions, portraying their strengths and weaknesses as she sees them during these war years. Her conclusion is that both have failed, since neither seems capable of answering the pressing questions facing America: What are the values for which soldiers are being asked to sacrifice their lives? What kind of a world will they find on their return?

While critiquing the country's direction, Susan also attempts to clarify for herself the ways these two places have failed to fulfill the idealism on which she had based her own beliefs.

Frances, her persona, is the most rounded of her fictional women and the one whose life most nearly follows Susan's biography. Born on a small farm outside Davenport, Frances was educated locally, but moved to Provincetown after her marriage to Len, an Iowa writer and intellectual. Although she has cut her physical ties with her home, she retains a strong bond with her father, Judd Rankin, who was the central shaping force in her early life. Judd is a writer who chronicles his region and its people. Like him, they are hardy and folksy; like him they are also isolationists. In the past Francis had been able to overlook the limitations of her father and her birthplace. However, in 1944 it is no longer possible for her to do so. Her son Judson—named after his grandfather—has come home from the war in a state of mental collapse, unable to face the future because he could find no value system to explain why and for what he has fought. Judd Rankin's world, for all its positive virtues, does not provide answers. "Too much has been left out," Frances feels, and by that she means the sense of connectedness with other people outside of Iowa and a liveliness and desire for life and love, represented in the novel by Judd's cousin Adah, a vital, non-conformist who dies in the prelude to the book.[8]

Although Iowa is her central concern, Susan does not let Provincetown off the hook either. The section set there is twice as long as any of the other three parts, and the writing is her most detailed and successful. She does not hesitate to show her adopted town, like her birthplace, with its limitations as well as its strengths. Susan vividly describes the simple clapboard houses, the vegetation carefully nurtured around them, and the more hardy growth found along the outside, fronting the ocean. She also tells of the friendships of people always "busying themselves with some kind of new form" and sharing this "narrow strip of land out in the sea." Yet, for all the worldliness and culture the town displays, some people there also tend to build walls, which close them off to others' pain. As an example, Susan describes Frances's reaction when she brings together her friend Marianne, who wants to sell the guesthouse she has lovingly restored, and Julia, a social worker from New York, who is in search of a summer retreat. A perfect match of two fine people, Frances thinks, unaware that Marianne suffers from the same attitude Susan had noted among some of her intellectual acquaintances as far back as 1914 and knew only too well from her years with Norman Matson: Julia is Jewish and Marianne is anti-Semitic. Just as the Midwest's isolationism throws blight over the effort of the country to fight, Susan argues in the novel that anti-Semitism at home makes a mockery of the battle fought against it in Germany. "It must be terrible for you," Frances tells Marianne, to have your son "bombing the people who feel just as you do." Although the rift between Frances and Marianne is healed, facilitated by Julia, who argues that patience not violent outbursts is needed to overcome prejudice, Frances comes to realize that even in liberal Provincetown "it comes back to that same old thing: be good to your own, what you think of as your own, then politely but firmly shut the door."

Another subject Susan raises in the novel is the shifting politics of her friends. Frances's husband Len is a socialist, and their son is particularly embittered about his father's global vision, since it could not stop this world war. On his return, Judson temporarily finds refuge with Steve, a family friend, who has drifted far to the right and is now upholding a nationalism more attuned to the isolationism of Judd than to the world-view of Len. Despite her disclaimer to Edmund Wilson that "I did *not* write about any individual—though about the kind of people we know here," and despite her awareness that "I will probably get into trouble,"[9] Susan patterns Steve directly on John Dos Passos, providing her fictional character with Dos's biography and shift of politics. Now Steve "jibed at the things which had once fired him." So did Dos, who had just published *The Ground We Stand On*, a treatise outlining a conservatism that would in later years bring him to embrace the ideology of Barry Goldwater. The exchanges between Steve and his friends at a Provincetown party are some of the best writing in the novel. Frances counters Steve's bantering about liberals with a poem about human relatedness written by a poet from back home, "Someone my father knew—out there, Cook was the name. He's dead now." Although it is hard for Frances to believe that their friend is now a fascist—"we don't *have* them in America," she gasps (an echo of Mabel's disclaimer about suppressed desires in Chicago)—and she continues to like Steve personally, as Susan continued to like Dos, the novel makes clear that Steve has little to provide the Judsons of the world. When Wilson read the novel, he complained that Susan did not offer an equally clear critique of the Midwest. She responds in a letter to him: "Judd Rankin, as I felt it, is isolationism at its most attractive, love of the land that is home, feeling the past of that land, and alliance with the people immediately around him. . . . I am drawn to much in the Middle West, love that country and those people, and think they have been dead wrong in some very important things."[9]

The war and Susan's strong feelings about it were the central motivation for writing *Judd Rankin's Daughter*, but other events also prompted the novel. In 1942, just before launching the project, she had returned briefly to Davenport, after Frank's sudden death. With him gone, and with his wife Hazel preparing to finally sell the family home, Susan lost the final physical connection with her place of birth; and this may have prompted her to once more explore the question of why the region had exerted such a hold on her and to attempt to draw together the two parts of her life that she had always kept separate. The impact of the Midwest on writers who made their reputations in the East was also brought home to her when she read in Wilson's *The Shock of Recognition*, the exchange of letters between Sherwood Anderson, who had died in 1941, and the critic Van Wyck Brooks. To Wilson she wrote: "I read the letters last night with sorrow and understanding. I am sure I did understand them, as Sherwood and I came from about the same time and same kind of place. He would say, 'It's lonely out here' and I knew what he meant—Lord, yes. And I understand, as not all would, that deference for the 'cultivated man'—the Master—the man of letters in the East." In Susan, too, there were elements of deference, as her careful correspondence with Wilson makes abundantly clear; however, her natural tendency toward self-efface-ment never undermined her idealism nor caused her to cut her personality or her writing to fit the fashion of the East or the dictates of critics. She never suffered from a sense of exclusion, as Anderson did, since she never needed, as he did, to be loved by the eastern establishment.

Reversing Glaspell's recent publication pattern, *Judd Rankin's Daugher* appeared first in America, issued by Lippincott in October 1945, followed in March 1946 by Gollancz's British edition, under the title *Prodigal Giver*, since the publisher felt *Judd Rankin's Daughter* sounded too much like "a western."[10] In 1947, Grosset and Dunlap reissued it in the States as one of their "Books of Distinction." The novel generated more interest than *Norma Ashe*, but less than *The Morning is Near Us*. For the most part, reactions depended on what part of the country read it. The *Chicago Sun* ran a full-page, laudatory story on the author and her book on the front page of its book-review section;[11] the *New York Times* gave it a short review commending Glaspell for her detailed description of Judson's con-frontation with the "at-home conservatives who try to corral him into their camp," but faulting her for "wandering in the Iowa cornfields."[12] Susan's Provincetown friends were even less supportive. "Have you read—or are you going to read—Susan's book," Phyllis Duganne inquired of Wilson, reporting that "Sue claims that Katy is no longer speaking to her, which she points out demurely is very silly, since if Kate finds any resemblance between a certain character and Dos, it is really Kate who is . . . insulting her husband—not Susan. She also does a sweet cat-who's-eaten-the-canary approach to Provincetown's anti-Semitism." Duganne proceeded to give her own critique."It's funny—and typical of Sue—books with the usual Iowan homey philosopher who . . . is a cross between Jig and Jesus—mak-ing most of the middle pretty damned dull."[13] She fails to mention that the middle is devoted to Provincetown not Iowa.

Now that her novel was finished, Susan happily turned to reading works of others. Evelyn Waugh's *Brideshead Revisited* made her realize a fun-damental difference between American and British culture: "In caring for the past and the beautiful, those English boys are more unashamed than our boys, and seem to have a finer innocence."[14] Brinton's *Nietzsche* led her to imagine what a fine play, with Wagnerian music, could be writ-ten on this "strange fellow." On Wilson's edition of F. Scott Fitzgerald's, *The Crackup*, she wrote to him: "I don't think I can really understand him without knowing more about his marriage." She was also rereading Henry James: "There has been little companionship here and so I am glad to have had his," she told Wilson. In addition to reading novels, she was also defending them. In a talk at the Nautilus Club in Provincetown, where she read excerpts from *Judd Rankin's Daughter*, she used the occasion to decry the local library's attempt to ban Ayn Rand's *The Fountainhead*. "Censorship by a small group violates a right that is very precious to us, and one that should be guarded at all costs," she argued, as she had consistently in the past.[15]

Although the talk was for a small local group, she prepared seriously, writing long notes in which she tried to answer two central questions: why she wrote and how. For the former, the best she could come up with was "because I want to . . . a real book comes out of an inner compulsion." For the latter, she set out her requirements for what is needed to create good fiction: characters that live and are not simply mouthpieces for the author; form, but not so rigid that it precludes surprise; and story and ideas able to "make us understand better the people around us, and help us in understanding ourselves."[16]

During the winter of 1945–46 Susan remained in Provincetown, entertained by novels but few friends. Her brother Ray had died the preceding April, and she kept in touch with Flossie, who paid her a short visit. "It's rather slim pickings here now as to people; I get lonely, feel the need of more companionship—a more stimulating companionship," she wrote to Wilson, but admitted that she no longer felt up to life in New York. "I'd fall by the wayside." She still continued to write every day, using her usual techniques of jotting down possible titles, writing one or two sentence summaries, or complete scenarios, interspersed with comments or questions to herself. One note contains the title "Bastards I have known," to be used for a short story.[17] Another provides a brief description intended to go into a future novel or story: "The woman whose home is in a town which is a place for others to come in the summer. Too many goodbyes. After they are gone—looking from the window to see someone on the street. Life has gone but she is still there."[18] A variation entitled "Loneliness" reads:" She lives alone. She has work and is thought not to be lonely. The house—how she must get out of it at times. Goes out for many little walks. Hopes she does not look lonely, as others often do to her." These quotations are for an essay she entitled "On Growing Older," a theme Susan continued to work on in various forms over the next year. In one version, she indicates the pleasure found in making an accounting: "Nothing that another can do for us in drama, romance, humor can interest . . . or satisfy as this thing we are able to do for ourselves as the years take us where we can look back on all there has been and sometimes verify what we foresaw and more often contemplate what we wouldn't have believed could happen." In another she creates a scene between two generations, a variation of the opening of *Judd Rankin's Daughter*. However this time the elderly aunt gets a chance to share her message with the younger generation. "I think the reason our lives aren't longer," she reflects, "is that we just wouldn't be able to stand the shock. Finding out we'd learned it all wrong."

In writing the scene of an aunt talking to her college-aged nephew, Susan was taking a page from her own life. In August 1946, Sirius returned from Greece in order to prepare for his entrance into Harvard, and he stayed with her. She had not seen him for ten years and was delighted at the way he had matured and fascinated by his stories of serving, although under age, in the Greek civil war, still being fought. "It's as if Jig's dream of Greece had taken form in our world of today. Here is the future— because there was that past. Nice, don't you think," she wrote to Langston Moffett that Christmas.[19] Sirius's experiences in Greece had made him staunchly anticommunist, and when Susan took him to a Provincetown Town Hall meeting, he shouted down the speaker who supported the leftist struggle. Susan might have been embarrassed by the tone of the outburst but not by the sentiments. She had not moved so far to the right as Dos Passos, but she had certainly shifted away from her earlier socialist positions. Like Frances, her protagonist who had rejected communism— "perhaps because she'd grown up on the prairie and it just didn't seem indigenous"—and had not stayed long a socialist since "it was too allsettled," Susan disliked anything smacking of ideology, which seemed to force people into one set of beliefs at the expense of all others. She still believed a belief should be "nascent, more true this moment than ever before."[20] Although Henry Wallace was a native son of Iowa, Susan had been strongly against his candidacy for vice president on the Democratic ticket, believing that he was too left-wing and would hurt the chances of the party. She supported Roosevelt; in *Judd Rankin's Daughter*, she likens his voice to Christ's.

If the ten years had matured Sirius, they had also changed Susan. At seventy, she was "much frailer and more sedentary" than when he had last visited her, and even her daily walks around Provincetown were becoming fewer.[21] When not writing and reading, she spent a good deal of her time answering letters. In *Judd Rankin's Daughter* she had presented one of the first literary accounts of posttraumatic stress in war. Now as soldiers returned from the war she received letters from families who themselves had sons, like Judson, who bore deep psychological scars. Others wrote to thank her for showing "the real Provincetown." Susan answered them all. She also tried to keep up with old friends. When Hutch Hapgood died in 1944, her letter to his wife Neith Boyce was written on Provincetown Players letterhead. "They were good old days, weren't they? Filled with happy purpose," she observed, adding, "I know that one can be lonely and sad and sometimes lost."[22] She would sometimes hear from Polly Holladay, the former proprietor of Polly's—the center of the universe for early Greenwich Village—who had suffered a mental breakdown in 1927 and was confined to Manhattan State Hospital, on Ward's Island. Susan and Mary Vorse had never been correspondents. To Dorothy Meyer, Susan confided that her relationship with her neighbor was "susanal": sometimes friendly sometimes not.[23] Now, when Mary was in town, she would always stop by. So, too, would Katie Dos Passos, who had evidently decided that Susan had the right to take what literary license she wished in depicting Dos.

Despite her contracting circle, Susan was still capable of action when roused to do so. On June 18, 1946, she fired off a stinging letter to the *Provincetown Advocate* about a New York theatre company that had rented Town Hall from the selectmen in order to present plays during the summer season. She had long supported the work of Catharine Huntington's Provincetown Playhouse, which had been putting on plays since 1940, including several of her own. The problem with this new group was that they were calling themselves the Provincetown Players, something she could not abide. "What's in a Name," she asked and then answered: "Something that keeps things straight. . . . If I wanted to call myself George Bernard Shaw would I ask the London Board of Trade? And if that august body said, why not? It may promote Anglo-American relations, would I then *be* George Bernard Shaw?"[24] She closes by reminding these representatives of a fishing village that a haddock may call itself a mackerel, but that does not make it one. Her protest was picked up by the Associated Press and carried across the country, the *New York Sun* putting it on page one, under a three-column headline—much to the pleasure of an anonymous *Provincetown Advocate* writer who proclaimed that Miss Glaspell had "unexpectedly brought to all hands a lot of excellent publicity," hardly her intention.[25] Later in July, when Huntington's playhouse staged *Alison's House*, Susan attended rehearsals and made suggestions, probably to illustrate her backing of this company and not the interlopers. She even agreed to be present on opening night.[26]

"Do you realize we've made very little impression on this town?" Frances observed about Provincetown in *Judd Rankin's Daughter*, indicating the town's resiliency and seeming indifference to the artists and intellectuals who adopted it.[27] Yet Susan did make an impact on the community. She had become known as "The Lady Who Wrote," someone who would help neighborhood children, like Grace Collinson, with their English.[28] Local historian George Bryant, who took over his father's store, where Susan continued to buy groceries, described her as "a little old lady with gray hair" who came into the public school each year to give an award to the student who wrote the best essay.[29] Of all the writing community, she seems to have been the only one who involved herself in such local activities, perhaps because she came from a small town herself and still believed in people doing practical things to make communal life better. She was a charter member of the Provincetown Civic Association and when plans were published to cut down trees in order to widen a thoroughfare, it was Susan who protested, and the civic association arranged for them to be transplanted, instead, around the Town Hall, adding a Chinese elm in her honor planted near the walk to the Soldier's Monument.[30] It is still growing there.

She could still display indignation over easy exploitation of the past, be it by a theatre or by those who would destroy nature, and she acted upon her anger. However, she was physically declining. At the beginning of 1947, Susan confided to Francelina that she had stomach cancer and asked if Francelina would live with her, since she was now finding it difficult to manage on her own. She kept the news of her illness from her friends and tried to go on as before; but the ravages of the disease were evident in one of the last photos of her, seated in a rocking chair in her living room, with her overflowing bookcase in the background. Not visible was the ivy that had come in through cracks near the fireplace and Susan had trained to run along the length of the living room wall. She still wrote every day but none of the "notes for future works" became completed texts. Sirius's holiday visits roused her, so too did Harl's trips to town. She continued to worry about him and his lack of direction, and would always give him some money when he left. She also gave Sirius $100 toward his Harvard tuition that September, although her own finances were minimal. Since 1940 and her windfall with *The Morning is Near Us*, her yearly net income tended to be around $6,000.[31] Royalties still came in from Lippincott: $2,094 in 1943, $1,113 in 1945. She also got small amounts from the Stokes accounts, which were kept separately, and from Curtis Browne, Walter Baker, and Samuel French, who handled her play royalties. Although occasionally a full-length play would be mounted, for the most part her income from her plays came from *Suppressed Desires* and *Trifles*, the former produced twenty-four times in 1944–45. She had continued to send Ray monthly checks, and Frank some money until their deaths. She also contributed to a number of charities in the 1940s including the Red Cross, Salvation Army, Negro Widows, Animal Rescue, American Legion, various church groups, and the Greek War Relief Association. She had never become rich from her writing, but she was able to sustain herself, as she had since she first began to work in 1894, when she was eighteen.

She was also able to keep up her few close friendships, which meant so much to her. Katie and Dos had been traveling in the first half of 1947, but came back to Provincetown briefly at the end of August. Susan was delighted to see them. While Dos had become more somber over the years, Katie still retained the gaiety that had first drawn Susan to her. He said that his wife was like a wild goose; come the fall and she must take off for distant climes. On September 12, the couple was only going a short distance to visit friends in Connecticut when, just before sunset, they crashed into the back of a parked truck jutting into the road. Katie was killed instantly, partially decapitated by the impact, while Dos sustained facial injuries, including the loss of his right eye. Susan was devastated by the death and attended the funeral. Katie was buried in the Given family plot in Snow's cemetery in Truro, situated on a hill with a view to Provincetown in the background.

Mary Vorse, who had been in Europe, working for the United Nations Relief and Rehabilitation Administration (UNRRA) came back to Provincetown soon after Katie's death and shared with Susan her experiences in war-ravaged Europe. Of all her stories, the ones about Greece most moved Susan, who still retained strong feelings for the country.[32] Another who saw her often was Madie L'Engle who came to regard Susan as a surrogate mother, now that her parents, Lucy and Bill, had moved permanently to St. Augustine. When Madie and her husband rented the Dos Passos house after the accident, she became a daily visitor, often running small errands that Francelina had no time to do.[33] Ozzie Ball, Susan's lawyer, and his wife also came by each day. None knew of Susan's illness, but it soon became difficult to hide. Always thin, she was now skeletal. Joking, she said that no matter how many dishes Francelina learned to prepare from the Fanny Farmer cookbook, which Susan had bought her as a gift, it would not put the weight back on. More and more Francelina became her sole companion. In their discussions that winter and spring of 1948, Susan would range back over her life, talking often of Jig, whose picture she kept in the house, or of Harl. She never spoke of Norman Matson. Francelina sensed her growing sadness, but could not tell if Susan were in pain, since she never complained.

On July 1 Susan turned seventy-two. The Provincetown season was in full swing; new arrivals packed the place in anticipation of the Fourth of July celebrations. Exactly half her lifetime ago, she had first come to the town with Lucy Huffaker for the summer, while waiting for Jig to get his divorce so they could marry. Like her protagonist Ruth Holland in *Fidelity*, she, too, was poised to begin a different life in a place where "It's all new," where "Nothing is mapped out."[34] Nineteen hundred and twelve had seemed that way to many people. The debates in that election year focused on socialism, suffrage for women, conservation of forests, labor movements: all issues Susan would embrace in her writing and life. The 1948 election rhetoric, about to be beamed for the first time on television programs across the country, was filled with arguments for states' rights, post-war economic recovery, jobs for male household providers, and limits on labor's power. It was a different world. Perhaps that is why Susan—foreseeing what was about to happen to the country after the war—ended her 1944 play "Springs Eternal" with a toast to "the Brave Old World!" "It *talked* an awful lot—that brave old world!" one of the younger characters complains, but another defends the past, articulating—albeit awkwardly—one of Susan's central themes that had not changed over the years: "what they *felt*—long gone, but alive then . . . Alive now!"[35] Susan put it better in a talk she once gave on Stanislavski's *The Art of Theatre*:

"Those inner paths of feeling, that conscious road to the gates of the unconscious. This is the sphere of living tradition."[36]

It was colder than usual at the beginning of July and Susan, already frail, caught a summer cold, which she could not shake. Over the next few weeks it turned into viral pneumonia, but she refused to go to the hospital. She was now unable to get out of bed and go downstairs, so Francelina brought a tray up to her, but Susan had stopped eating. On July 26 in the afternoon, as Francelina sat by her bed, Susan looked at her, smiled, and said softly, "I'm dying Frannie." These were her last words. Francelina remained into the evening, and at 10:00 P.M. on the twenty-sixth of July 1948, Saint Anne's Day, Susan Glaspell died.[37] She had grown so emaciated that when Dr. Hiebert arrived, he "carried her down in his arms like a little doll, she weighed so little," Francelina said. Susan's death certificate filled in by Hiebert late at night gives July 27 at 2:10 A.M. as the date of death, the cause a pulmonary embolism and pernicious anemia.

Her death came as a great shock to her friends, who knew nothing about her battle with cancer and assumed the pneumonia would pass. "No one expected she would snuff out like a candle as she did last Tuesday," Mary Vorse wrote her son Joel.[38] The funeral was held in Susan's home on July 29, with the Reverend Richard Kimball of Orleans officiating. The mourners included Harl and Sirius, Mary Vorse, Edy and Frank Shay, John Dos Passos, Phyllis Duganne and Eben Given, Madie L'Engle, and Ozzie Ball and his wife. Norman Matson arrived late. That so few attended bothered Mary. Why "no old Provincetown players" or "the Guild," or "absolutely no townspeople," Vorse wrote rhetorically to her son and answered: "I guess because no one asked them." "Just the Provincetown, Truro, Wellfleet friends everyone looking frayed and older—and as if they had shot their bolt." It was, in Vorse's opinion, definitely not the kind of funeral she wanted or Susan deserved. As she had requested, Susan was cremated, and her ashes were scattered behind her home in Truro. A marble memorial stone was placed in the Snow Cemetery at the back in a wooded section that slopes down to the town, not far from Katie Dos Passos's grave and near the spot where Matson would be buried nineteen years later.[39] In Delphi, on a stone plaque over Jig's grave, Nilla added Susan's name to those of Jig's mother and Mollie Price. In her will, Susan left her house and property jointly to Harl and Sirius. To her sister-in-law Flossie she left $1,000, to Hazel and to Francelina, $500 each.

Obituaries in New York, Iowa, and Provincetown all carried as their headline or subheading references to her Pulitzer Prize award. Each detailed her work with the Provincetown Players, mentioned some of her plays and novels, and her discovery of Eugene O'Neill. The *New York Times* article called her "one of the nation's most widely read novelists."[40] However, a line from the *Provincetown Advocate* notice would probably have pleased her most: "Her mind was as broad in her friendships as in her opinions and she numbered among the former the great and lowly alike, and with equal attachment."[41]

A week after Susan's death, Mary Vorse made an entry in her diary describing a visit Dos Passos had made to Harl. Write a new *Road to the Temple*, he suggested, this time about Susan's life. "It would be wonderful. She was an adventurer, a rebel. . . . It would make a great story."[42]

Notes

UM	University of Michigan, Department of Rare Books and Special Collections (Hopwood Papers, Browne/Van Volkenburg Papers)
UPA	University of Pennsylvania Archives (Theodore Dreiser Papers)
WRLWSU	Walter Reuther Library, Wayne State University (Mary Heaton Vorse Papers)

Private Papers

CE	Cook Estate (Papers of SG and GCC)
CFE	Celia Francis Estate
LME	Langston Moffett Estate
NME	Norman Matson Estate
RBE	Ritamary Bradley Estate
RCC	Regie Cabral Collection
WPC	William Priester Collection

Because so many of the letters that Glaspell and her friends wrote have no dates, I have omitted n.d. to avoid repetition. I have also retained original punctuation.

Preface

1. Details for this scene are taken from Boulton, *Part of a Long Story*, 24–33.

2. Boulton, *Part of a Long Story*, 164.

3. Norman Matson, "Unpublished Autographical Novel," 48, NME. This 111 page unfinished novel, probably written in 1933, describes Matson's meeting with Glaspell, and offers detailed scenes of their personal lives, focusing on their trip to Norway, Paris, and Senlis, France in 1925, and their stay in London and trip to Paris in 1932. In the novel she is named Ruth, he is Peter. Except for changing names and altering a few specifics, the story appears to be taken directly from their lives together between 1924, when they first met, and 1932 when their relationship ended. Glaspell makes reference to the work in several of her letters to Matson, after 1932, so she may have read it. There is also a one-page fragment, headed "To go into Chapter One," that is in same papers and referred to later in the notes.

4. Dorothy Fowler Heald, quoted in Helen Cowles LeCron, "I Remember Young Susan," news clipping, BCNYPL.

5. Langner, *The Magic Curtain*, 70.

6. Luhan, *Movers and Shakers*, 143.

7. Goldberg, *The Drama of Transition*, 471.

8. For the importance of the Provincetown Players, and particularly Susan Glaspell, in establishing modern American drama, see "Susan Glaspell," in Bigsby, *A Critical Introduction to Twentieth-Century American Drama*, 25–35. See also Sarlós, Deutsch and Hanau, *Jig Cook and the Provincetown Players*, *The Provincetown*.

9. James Agate, *Sunday Times*, 4 April 1925; R. Ellis Roberts, *The Manchester Guardian*, 17 July 1925.

10. Elizabeth Robins, quoted in *Time and Tide*, 21 January 1927.

11. Watson, *Strange Bedfellows*, offers a detailed, informative history of many of the people discussed in this study, particularly SG, GCC, and Floyd Dell.

12. SG describes the discovery of Eugene O'Neill in *The Road to the Temple*, 253–54.

13. Selected papers from the symposium are published in Heller and Rudnick, *1915*.

14. Chevigny, "Daughters Writing," 375.

15. Cott, *The Grounding of Modern Feminism*, 151. This book is an excellent study of the development of feminism. The introduction and chapters 1–3 cover the period in which SG was active.

16. Heilbrun, "Letter," *New York Review of Books*, March 1992. See also Heilbrun, *Writing a Woman's Life*, which presents a pattern in the lives of women writers that strikingly resembles SG's.

17. SG, "Norma Ashe Holograph Notbook," BCNYPL.

18. Samuel Beckett, "Dante . . . Bruno. Vico . . Joyce," in *Our Exagmination Round his Factification for Incamination of Work in Progress* (1929; reprint, London: Faber and Faber, 1961), 3.

19. *The Verge*, 77.

20. *The Verge*, 19.

21. Soon after the play was anthologized in Ferguson, *Images of Women in Literature* and Barlow, *Plays by American Women*, critical essays began appearing, most notably Kolodny, "A Map for Rereading."

22. *The Road to the Temple*, (1927), ix. While the texts of the 1927 and 1941 editions are identical, the forewords are different.

Introduction

1. Post, *1876*, 15. The description of the exhibition comes from this source. The publication served as the catalogue for the Smithsonian 1976 exhibition which honored the 1876 Fair.

2. For a description of the Fourth of July celebration, see Slotkin, *The Fatal Environment*, chapter 1.

3. *The Road to the Temple*, 4.

4. Malcolm Cowley, quoted in Rosenstone, *Romantic Rebel*, 104.

5. *The Road to the Temple*, 235–36.

6. SG to Edmund Wilson, BLYU.

7. Luhan, *Movers and Shakers*, 79.

8. SG, quoted in Alice Rohe, "The Story of Susan Glaspell," *New York Morning Telegraph*, 18 December 1921.

9. For background on the settlement period and on Blackhawk, see Wilkie, *Davenport, Past and Present*; Spencer, "Reminiscences of Pioneer Life in the Mississippi Valley"; Burrows, "Fifty Years in Iowa"; and Cowles, "Blackhawk," *Weekly Outlook* 1 (18 July 1896).

10. *Inheritors*, 6.

11. Blackhawk, quoted in Spencer, "Reminiscences of Pioneer Life in the Mississippi Valley," 43.

12. Whitman, quoted in Slotkin, *The Fatal Environment*, 10.

13. Lawrence, *Studies in Classic American Literature*, 160.

14. *Inheritors*, 24.

15. *Judd Rankin's Daughter*, 35.

16. The idea of pollination of corn as a metaphor for social betterment can be found in SG's short story "Pollen," *Harper's* 138 (February 1919).

17. *Inheritors*, 153–54.

18. *Inheritors*, 24.

Chapter 1: A Town Springs Up

1. Burrows, "Fifty Years in Iowa,"105–07. For other details about early Davenport, see Downer, *History of Davenport and Scott County*; Wilkie, *Davenport, Past and Present*; and Spencer, *Reminiscences of Life in the Mississippi Valley*.

2. Plumbe, *Sketches of Iowa and Wisconsin*, 67.

3. Newhall, quoted in F. J. B. Huot, "*History of Davenport*," chapter 1, reprinted in *Weekly Outlook* 1 (13 March 1897).

4. For genealogical materials on the Jewett, Ricker, and Chippman families, see BCNYPL; for the Glaspell family, see Kate Eldridge Glaspell, *Incidents in the Life of a Pioneer* (privately published), found in the Davenport, Iowa, Public Library; and "The Glaspell Family Records written by Eva Glaspy" (Bridgetown, N.J.: Bridgetown Public Library, 1934). For the Glaspell family's connection to the community, see Marie Meyer, *Davenport Democrat*, 27 December 1936.

5. *Fugitive's Return*, 165. Without naming her ancestor, Eleanor (*The Comic Artist*, 13) says, "My people were here long ago. They built this house in seventeen hundred and something. I feel my great grandfather in the old forgotten roads, on the beach[. . .] he lingers in things he had or touched, in my own imagination. . . . He is in me. After long, homesick wandering—in other countries, in New York, he has returned."

6. Quoted in Kate Eldridge Glaspell, *Incidents in the Life of a Pioneer*, 5.

7. Quoted in Kate Eldridge Glaspell, 4.

8. Sister Ritamary Bradley, "Ethnic Pluralism: How We All Got Along," unpublished essay, 3, RBE.

9. Quoted in Roba, *A History of the Quad-Cities, 1812–1960*, 40.

10. Burrows, "Fifty Years in Iowa," 139.

11. Burrows, "Fifty Years in Iowa," 142–43.

12. SG, "Notes for American Biography," SLCC.

13. SG, "Notes for American Biography," SLCC. For other accounts of women's experiences with Indians, see Riley, *Women and Indians on the Frontier*.

14. *Trident* 2.3 (14 January 1904). For church practices in Davenport during this period, see Roba, *A History of the Quad-Cities, 1812–1960*, 37–38.

15. Floyd Dell, *Homecoming*, 80–81.

16. Floyd Dell, *Homecoming*, 170.

17. See C. Ficke, *Memories of Fourscore Years*.

18. For description of cultural life in Davenport at the time, see Roba, *A History of the Quad-Cities, 1812–1960*, chapter 4.

19. SG describes him in *The Road to the Temple*, and his correspondence with Floyd Dell can be found in NL.

20. For background on Nicholas Féjerváry, see Thanet, *In Memoriam*, and Downer, *A History of Davenport and Scott County Iowa*.

21. See Roba, *A History of the Quad-Cities, 1812–1960*, chapters 3 and 4. In 1858, 24 percent of the population was German.

22. Fuller, *Summer on the Lakes in 1843*, 47.

23. When she attended Drake University, SG was elected to the Margaret Fuller Club, established to "emphasize the value of personality through intellectual and social development on a high level of responsibility," quoted in Ozieblo, *Susan Glaspell*, 23.

24. *The Road to the Temple*, 4.

25. *Fugitive's Return*, 110.

26. *The Road to the Temple*, 10.

27. *The Road to the Temple*, 13.

Chapter 2: Families in Fact and Fiction

1. Obituary, *Davenport Democrat*, 26 April 1881. See also Eldridge Glaspell, *Incidents in the Life of a Pioneer*, 38.

2. Obituary, *Davenport Democrat*, 27 September 1923.

3. Addie Mackintosh to Mrs. Susan Glaspell, 6 March 1888, BCNYPL.

4. Elmer Glaspell to Alice Glaspell, 8 October 1882, BCNYPL.

5. Obituary, *Davenport Democrat*, 17 March 1905.

6. SG, quoted in Louise Morgan, "How Writers Work: Susan Glaspell of New England," *Everyman*, 7 January 1932.

7. Mrs. Keating to Alice Glaspell, 6 July, BCNYPL.

8. Mrs. Keating to Alice Glaspell, 21 August, BCNYPL.

9. Elmer Glaspell to Alice Glaspell, 14 July 1872, BCNYPL.

10. SG, quoted by Dorothy Meyer, interview by author, New York City, January 1990.

11. Ricker's diary can be found in the Glaspell Papers, BCNYPL.

12. Unpublished essay, BCNYPL.

13. Inscription quoted in Louis Sheaffer, "Notes on Visiting Glaspell's Truro House," SLCC.

14. SG, "Notes for American Biography," SLCC.

15. Jewett Ricker to Mrs. Susan Glaspell, 6 January 1881, BCNYPL.

16. Elmer Glaspell to Alice Glaspell, 8 October 1882, BCNYPL.

17. Norman Matson, Unpublished Autobiographical Novel," 46, NME.

18. SG to Alice Glaspell, 12 March 1909, BCNYPL.

19. Obituary, *Davenport Democrat*, 17 February 1929.

20. Records come from a transcript made available by the Davenport school district, which I thank for its assistance. E+ was a grade for the highest achievement.

21. SG, "Notes for American Biography," SLCC.

22. Transcript of unpublished play, BCNYPL.

23. SG to Elmer Glaspell, BCNYPL.

24. *Davenport Democrat*, 5 April 1932.

25. Published in *Weekly Outlook* 1 (26 December 1896).

26. *Fugitive's Return*, 111. The accusation "Not much of a housekeeper," hurled against Mrs. Wright in Glaspell's play *Trifles*, may have had its roots in

Susan's own home; but whereas in that play, Mrs. Hale comes to the defense of the doubly-accused woman, saying "Men's hands aren't always as clean as they might be," in *Fugitive's Return* the young Irma feels only shame about her mother's incompetence.

27. *Fugitive's Return*, 138–39.
28. *Brook Evans*, 44.
29. *Brook Evans*, 206–07.

Chapter 3: Society Girls

1. *Fugitive's Return*, 117.
2. Copies of the paper can be found in the Putnam Library, Davenport, Iowa.
3. *Weekly Outlook* 1 (26 December 1896).
4. *Weekly Outlook* 2 (2 January 1897).
5. *Weekly Outlook* 2 (6 February 1897).
6. *Weekly Outlook* 1 (26 December 1896).
7. *Weekly Outlook* 1 (10 October 1896).
8. *Weekly Outlook* 1 (26 December 1896).
9. *Weekly Outlook* 1 (19 December 1896).
10. *Weekly Outlook* 3 (3 July 1897).
11. *Weekly Outlook* 2 (6 March 1897).
12. *Weekly Outlook* 2 (15 May 1897).
13. *Weekly Outlook* 2 (6 February 1897).
14. *Weekly Outlook* 2 (2 January 1897).
15. *Weekly Outlook* 2 (6 February 1897).
16. *Weekly Outlook* 2 (23 January 1897).
17. *Weekly Outlook* 1 (19 December 1896).
18. The term *new woman*, used at the turn of the century, should be distinguished from the term applied to the postsuffrage young woman that SG parodies in *The Verge*.
19. *Weekly Outlook* 1 (17 October 1896). Agnes Boulton, who knew SG well in later years, comments on her ability to talk on an equally wide variety of topics: "economics, the rights of mankind, the theatre, writing people." *Part of a Long Story*, 164.
20. *Weekly Outlook* 2 (19 June 1897).
21. *Weekly Outlook* 3 (3 July 1897).
22. *Weekly Outlook* 3 (13 November 1897).

Chapter 4: Delphic Days

1. Elizabeth McCullough Bray, "Panorama of Cultural Developments Here in Last Half Century," *Davenport Democrat*, 31 March 1929.
2. Heald, quoted in Helen Cowles LeCron, 1928 news clipping, BCNYPL.
3. One of my regrets on researching this biography was my failure to find any new correspondence between Susan and Lucy. Such a correspondence between the two friends during their fifty-year relationship would have added greatly to this study.
4. *Delphic*, February 1899.

5. When SG, for example, revised her 1903 short story "In the Face His Constituents," for publication in *Lifted Masks* nine years later, all references to God were removed. My thanks to Marcia Noe for pointing this out to me.

6. *Des Moines Daily News*, 15 June 1900.

7. *Des Moines Daily News*, 29 November 1899.

8. *Des Moines Daily News*, 19 May 1900.

9. *Des Moines Daily News*, 1 June 1900.

10. *Des Moines Daily News*, 11 December 1899.

11. *Des Moines Daily News*, 1 September 1899.

12. *The Road to the Temple*, 247.

13. SG was not the only woman fiction writer whose early years in the Midwest led from small town to university and city newspaper work. Willa Cather followed a similar route. Three years older, she too grew up in a town that remained at the heart of her writing. At university, both women were drawn to oratory and journalism, wrote for the university literary journal, supplemented their incomes by freelancing for newspapers in the state capital, and, after graduations, became journalists, covering similar stories. Years later in Greenwich Village, they would live in walking distance of each other, but there is no record that they ever met. However, in their love of the Midwest and the shaping force of this love on their subsequent writing, SG and Cather had much in common and deserve some future comparative study.

Chapter 5: The Genesis of *Trifles*

1. See chapter 16, which discusses the play.

2. *Des Moines Daily News*, 4 December 1899.

3. *Des Moines Daily News*, 5 December 1899.

4. *Des Moines Daily News*, 14 January 1900.

5. *Des Moines Daily News*, 5 December 1899.

6. *Des Moines Daily News*, 6 December 1899.

7. *Des Moines Daily News*, 8 December 1899.

8. *Des Moines Daily News*, 12 December 1899.

9. *Des Moines Daily News*, 2 April 1900.

10. *Des Moines Daily News*, 3 April 1900.

11. *Des Moines Daily News*, 2 April 1900.

12. *Des Moines Daily News*, 2 April 1900.

13. *Des Moines Daily News*, 3 April 1900.

14. *Des Moines Daily News*, 8 April 1900.

15. *Des Moines Daily News*, 9 April 1900.

16. *Des Moines Daily News*, 10 April 1900.

17. *Des Moines Daily News*, 11 April 1900.

18. There were seven procedural points upon which the Supreme Court of Iowa based its reversal, the most significant of which were the following: that the hairs found under the corn crib were not proven to be from the murder weapon and had been taken by the county attorney and given to the sheriff and could not, therefore, be introduced as evidence; that the dissension in the Hossack house had abated at least a year prior to the murder and could not, therefore, be introduced in the case. See *State vs. Hossack*, Supreme Court of Iowa, 9 April 1902, *Northwestern Reporter*, 1077–81.

19. Jones, *Women Who Kill*, 231.

20. *State vs. Hossack*, Supreme Court of Iowa, 9 April 1902, *Northwestern Reporter*, 1077–81.

21. Law professors have been particularly interested in the Hossack case and Glaspell's dramatic and literary rendering of the facts. *Trifles* and "A Jury of Her Peers" now regularly appear in the curriculum of courses on Law and Literature, offered in law schools. In addition, several law professors have written on the case. See Patricia Bryan and Thomas Wolf, *Midnight Assassin*, and Marina Angel, "Susan Glaspell's *Trifles* and 'A Jury of Her Peers,'" "Criminal Law and Women," and "A Classical Greek Influence on an American Feminist."

22. Quoted in Kunitz and Haycroft, *Twentieth Century Authors*, 541.

23. SG, "Notes for American biography," SLCC.

24. Elmer Glaspell to SG, 23 October 1897, BCNYPL.

25. For information on Alice French, see McMichael, *Journey to Obscurity*. Those interested in exploring long-term relationships between women will find the partnership between French and her companion Mrs. Jane Allen Crawford significant.

26. Hamlin Garland, quoted in Andrews, *A Literary History of Iowa*, 48.

27. The subject of the child criminal, raised in SG's 1903 *Harper's* short story "In the Face of His Constituents" and later anthologized in *Lifted Masks* as "The Plea," was a highly debated one in Iowa at the time, and SG's position, advocating that the courts consider the background of the child offender, illustrates her already-developed social sense. The story and the political issues it raises are discussed in Noe, "Susan Glaspell's 'Plea' for Juvenile Justice" (unpublished essay). I thank her for sharing it with me.

28. "The Work of the Unloved Libby," *Black Cat*, August 1904.

29. *Des Moines Daily News*, 3 May 1903.

Chapter 6: Chicago

1. SG, notes, BCNYPL.

2. Dell, *Moon-Calf*, 394.

3. Carl Van Vechten, quoted in Kellner, *Carl Van Vechten and the Irreverent Decades*, 19.

4. It is tempting to conjecture that the free-love champion Triggs might have been the unnamed older lover with whom Susan told Jig she had had a serious love affair while in Chicago and perhaps her reason for leaving the university. She identifies the man as an editor (Triggs was), older (he was born in 1865), and married (Laura McAdoo, his wife at the time, was herself reputed to have had a love affair with his friend and Chicago colleague Thorstein Veblen, who was dismissed by the university at the same time as Triggs on presumed charges of moral turpitude). However, whereas Susan claimed her lover died before 1907, Triggs lived until 1930.

5. *The Glory of the Conquered*, 61.

6. Herrick writes in *Chimes* 2, "He liked to think of women as apart from the commonplace of life—as decorative, provocative, mysterious, and how could one when they stuck pencils through their hair and stood on one leg

gossiping with fellow students or bent nearsightedly over a grimy classroom bench?"

7. William Dean Howells, quoted in Duncan, *The Rise of Chicago as a Literary Center, 1885–1920*, xiii.

8. William Dean Howells, "Certain of the Chicago School of Fiction," *North American Review* 176 (May 1903).

9. Dreiser, *A Book about Myself*, 65.

10. H. L. Mencken, *Chicago Sunday Tribune*, 28 October 1917.

11. *Inheritors*, 48.

12. *Inheritors*, 62.

13. *The Verge*, 86.

14. *The Visioning*, 235.

15. Fuller, *The Cliff-Dwellers*, 226.

16. *The Visioning*, 363.

17. *The Visioning*, 365.

18. "For the Love of the Hills," *Black Cat*, October 1905.

19. Quoted in *Trident* (31 July 1904).

20. "From A to Z," *American*, October 1909. The following quotations come from this source.

21. *The Glory of the Conquered*, 232.

Chapter 7: A Greek Out of Time

1. GCC, notebook, BCNYPL.

2. GCC to Neith Boyce, BLYU.

3. GCC to Mollie Price, 15 October 1907, BCNYPL.

4. *The Road to the Temple* (1927), ix.

5. *The Road to the Temple*, 122.

6. Arthur Davison Ficke, "Review of *The Road to the Temple*," *Saturday Review of Literature* 3 (26 March 1927).

7. GCC, "Pendulum Notebook," BCNYPL.

8. Roy Flickinger, quoted in "Iowa Alum No Spicks English," *Daily Iowan*, 9 December 1926.

9. Wilson, *The Twenties*, 277.

10. Floyd Dell, "Memorial," *Davenport Democrat*, 16 January 1924.

11. Dell, *Moon-Calf*, 292.

12. GCC to Floyd Dell, 13 December 1910, BCNYPL.

13. GCC to Mollie Price, 26 September 1906, BCNYPL.

14. Obituary, *Davenport Democrat*, 16 June 1914.

15. GCC to Mollie Price, 23 August 1907, BCNYPL.

16. SG to Edna Kenton, BLUVA.

17. *The Road to the Temple*, 18.

18. *The Road to the Temple*, 17.

19. *Weekly Outlook* 1 (12 December 1896). For other information on the Dodge family, see documents prepared by Edmond M. Cook (September 1978) and by Catherine Newport Sorensen (August 1978), Davenport Public Library archives.

20. *The Road to the Temple*, 18.

21. Ma-Mie Cook to GCC, SLCC.

22. Banks and Everett, assisted by GCC, *American Home Culture and Correct Customs of Polite Society*, 316.

23. GCC, "Harvard Essays," BCNYPL.

24. *The Road to the Temple*, 25.

25. Details from GCC's early life come from his diary and notebook citations, BCNYPL.

26. *The Road to the Temple*, 34–36. See also, GCC, "Balm of Life," BCNYPL.

27. GCC, "Harvard Essays," BCNYPL.

28. Ma-Mie Cook, quoted in *The Road to the Temple*, 47.

29. GCC, quoted in *The Road to the Temple*, 97.

30. For one former student's praise of GCC's teaching methods and his "thoroughly democratic style," see Harry Plum, quoted in "Iowan Alum No Spicks English," *Daily Iowan*, 9 December 1926.

31. GCC, "Class Notes," BCNYPL.

32. GCC to Dr. Shaeffer, 23 April 1898. An earlier letter to Shaeffer when he began teaching was written 27 August 1895, BCNYPL.

33. GCC, "Diary," BCNYPL.

34. *Norma Ashe*, 107.

35. Rudyard Kipling to GCC, 19 August 1895, BCNYPL.

36. Quoted in *The Road to the Temple*, 99–100.

37. For discussions of the play and the published Cook canon, see Kemper, "The Novels, Plays, and Poetry of George Cram Cook, Founder of the Provincetown Players."

38. Undated and unattributed Davenport news clipping, BCNYPL.

39. *The Road to the Temple*, 123.

40. GCC, "Diary," BCNYPL.

41. GCC to Mollie Price, 23 August 1906, BCNYPL.

42. GCC to Mollie Price, 4 September 1907, BCNYPL.

43. GCC to Mollie Price, 5 October 1907, BCNYPL.

44. GCC, "The Balm of Life," BCNYPL.

45. GCC, quoted in *The Road to the Temple*, 178.

46. *The Road to the Temple*, 180.

Chapter 8: The Monist Society

1. *Trident*, 13 July 1904; *Davenport Democrat*, 15 March 1905. The Iowa Women's Archive has the Bushnell-Hamlin Papers.

2. *Trident*, 21 May 1904.

3. Floyd Dell, *Homecoming*, 150–51.

4. Watson in *Strange Bedfellows* accords Dell a central position in the Chicago and New York literary worlds. Six degrees of separation seem to connect Dell with every important figure of the period.

5. Dell's unpublished autobiographical fragment can be found among his papers at the Newberry Library.

6. GCC, quoted in *The Road to the Temple*, 181.

7. Dell, *Homecoming*, 149.

8. Ma-Mie Cook, quoted in Dell, *Homecoming*, 151.

9. Dell, *Homecoming*, 121.

10. GCC, "Evolution Essay," BCNYPL.

11. GCC to Charles Eugene Banks, BCNYPL.

12. *The Road to the Temple*, 191–93.

13. *The Road to the Temple*, 199.

14. Emerson, "Nature," *Essays and Poems*, 41.

15. Haeckel, quoted in Bölsche, *Haeckel*, 28.

16. *The Glory of the Conquered*, 57. The following quotations are from this source.

17. Dell, *Homecoming*, 178.

Chapter 9: Letters from Mollie

1. GCC to Mollie Price, 1 August 1906, BCNYPL. All subsequent letters are in this collection.

2. GCC to Mollie Price, 3–4 August 1906.

3. GCC to Mollie Price, 23 August 1906.

4. GCC to Mollie Price, 18 August 1906.

5. GCC to Mollie Price, 9 August 1906.

6. GCC to Mollie Price, 18 August 1906.

7. Dell, *Homecoming*, 170.

8. GCC to SG, 10 December 1906, BCNYPL. The following quotations are from this source.

9. Dell describes these "free love" discussions. See *Homecoming*, 171.

10. GCC to Mollie Price, 17 December 1907.

11. GCC, "Pendulum Notebook," BCNYPL.

12. GCC, "Pendulum Notebook," BCNYPL. The following quotations are from this source.

13. *The Road to the Temple*, 200.

14. GCC quoted in *The Road to the Temple*, 201.

15. *The Road to the Temple*, 201.

Chapter 10: Travel at Home and Abroad

1. Dell, *Homecoming*, 172–75.

2. Anna Bowman, "Expatriates: The American Colony in Paris," *Bookman*, 27 May 1907.

3. Carl Van Vechten, "Living in Paris on .94 cents a Day," *New York Times*, 4 October 1908.

4. SG, quoted in "Miss Glaspell Back from Paris," *Davenport Democrat*, 8 June 1909.

5. Gertrude Stein, quoted in Watson, *Strange Bedfellows*, 52.

6. *The Glory of the Conquered*, 69.

7. Henri Matisse, "Notes d'un Peintre," *La Grande Revue*, 25 December 1908; reprinted in *Matisse on Art*, translated and edited by Jack Flam (New York: Phaidon, 1973), 35–36.

8. André Antoine, quoted in Cohn, *From Desire to Godot*, 7.

9. Maeterlinck, "The Tragical in Daily Life," 30–36.

10. For Maeterlinck's writing on Emerson in English, see *On Emerson and Other Essays.*

11. Maeterlinck, quoted in Clark, *European Theories of the Drama*, 393.

12. On Nilla Cook's namesake, see GCC, "Diary," BCNYPL.

13. SG to Floyd Dell, Box 5, Folder 161, NL.

14. Mollie Price to Floyd Dell, 16 February 1909, Box 3, Folder 72, NL.

15. *The Visioning*, 398.

16. *New York Times*, 13 March 1909.

17. Alice Glaspell to SG, 4 February 1909, BCNYPL.

18. SG to Alice Glaspell, 12 March 1909, BCNYPL.

19. Mollie Price to Floyd Dell, 16 February 1909, Box 3, Folder 72, NL.

20. Mollie Price to Floyd Dell, Box 3, Folder 72, NL.

21. GCC, "Pendulum Notebook," BCNYPL.

22. *The Road to the Temple*, 207.

23. Mollie Price to Floyd Dell, Box 3, Folder 72, NL.

24. *The Visioning*, 124.

25. *The Road to the Temple*, 207.

Chapter 11: "Though Stone Be Broken"

1. E. A. Sharon, *Davenport Democrat*, 15 February 1910.

2. SG, "Letter to the Editor," *Davenport Democrat*, 16 February 1910.

3. *Davenport Democrat*, 21 February 1910.

4. *The Road to the Temple*, 193.

5. "The Library Controversy," *Davenport Democrat*, 8 April 1910.

6. GCC to Floyd Dell, Box 3, Folder 71, NL.

7. *The Visioning*, 349–50.

8. GCC to FL, Box 3, Folder 71, NL.

9. Dell, *Homecoming*, 201.

10. Floyd Dell, "Daughter of Dreams," 15, Box 22, Folder 179, NL.

11. GCC, "Diary," BCNYPL.

12. Mollie Price to Floyd Dell, Box 3, Folder 72, NL.

13. GCC to Floyd Dell, 18 July 1910, Box 3, Folder 71, NL.

14. William Fineshriber to Floyd Dell, 11 October 1910, Box 4, Folder 132, NL.

15. *The Road to the Temple*, 208.

16. *The Road to the Temple*, 208. SG spells Black Hawk's Tower as three words. In her references to the Indian chief she writes Blackhawk. Both spellings are used to refer to the place and the man.

17. GCC to SG, 2 July 1910, BCNYPL.

18. GCC to Mollie Price, 17 November 1910, BCNYPL.

19. GCC to Mollie Price, 16 April 1911, BCNYPL.

20. Floyd Dell, "Daughter of Dreams" (unpublished manuscript), 14, Box 22, Folder 179, NL.

21. Floyd Dell to Stanley Pagellis, 10 November 1949, Box 2, Folder 92, NL.

22. Nilla Cook to Hutchins Hapgood, BLYU.

23. Nilla Cook to Sirius Cook, 24 May 1960, CE.

24. SG, "Holograph Notebook," BCNYPL.

25. See Arnold Sundgaard, "Susan Glaspell and the Federal Theatre Revisited," *Journal of American Drama and Theatre* 9 (winter 1997).

26. GCC, quoted in *Greek Coins*, 59.

Chapter 12: Staging Area for the Future

1. *New York Times*, 7 May 1911.

2. Francis Hackett, "Review," *Chicago Evening Post*, 19 March 1909. For the Chicago Renaissance, see Duffey, *The Chicago Renaissance*. For the *Chicago Evening Post* and Dell, see Hackett, *American Rainbow*.

3. Anderson, *My Thirty Years' War*, 22, 37.

4. *The Road to the Temple*, 218.

5. For material on Browne and Van Volkenburg, see Browne, *Too Late to Lament*. For discussion on the Little Theatre, see Donald Tingley, "The Chicago Little Theatre," *Illinois Historical Journal* 1, 3 (autumn 1987).

6. Lady Gregory, quoted in Browne, *Too Late to Lament*, 115–16.

7. Original prospectus for the Little Theatre, Maurice Browne and Ellen Van Volkenburg Collection, UM.

8. Tietjens, *The World at My Shoulder*, 19. Several critics, including Steven Watson, indicate a romantic involvement between Tietjens and Cook in 1911–12. However, none offer proof, and I have not found any. See letters from Cook to Tietjens, NL.

9. Anderson to Van Wyck Brooks, April 1918, in Anderson, *Letters of Sherwood Anderson*, 33. See also SG's letter to Edmund Wilson, "On Reading Sherwood Anderson," BCNYPL.

10. GCC to SG, 1 March 1913, BCNYPL.

11. GCC quoted in *The Road to the Temple*, 224.

12. Ray Glaspell, quoted in GCC to SG, 1 March 1913, BCNYPL.

13. GCC to SG, 23 March 1913, BCNYPL.

14. GCC to SG, 23 March 1919, BCNYPL.

15. Patricia Blackman, "Susan Glaspell," talk delivered to the Tuesday Club, 7 April 1991.

16. GCC to Floyd Dell, 13 April 1913, BCNYPL.

17. SG to Charlotte Rudyard, UI.

Interlude 1: Greenwich Village, 1913: The Joyous Season

1. *Fidelity*, 269, 413.

2. Floyd Dell, *Intellectual Vagabondage*, 117.

3. Stieglitz, quoted in Norman, *Alfred Stieglitz*, 178.

4. *The Road to the Temple*, xv.

5. John Reed, quoted in Rosenstone, *Romantic Revolutionary*, 99.

6. Marcel Duchamp, quoted in Green, *New York 1913*, 14.

7. "The Fall of Greenwich Village," in Dell, *Love in Greenwich Village*, 298–99.

8. For a discussion of the various tensions present in the Village community, see Fishbein, "The Culture of Contradiction," in *Greenwich Village*, 212–28.

9. Mary Heaton Vorse, quoted in Garrison, *Mary Heaton Vorse*, 24.

10. For useful books on Greenwich Village during Glaspell's years, see Ware, *Greenwich Village, 1920–30*; Beard and Berlowitz, *Greenwich Village*; and Wetzsteon, *Republic of Dreams*. The latter book, unfortunately, does not have notes.

11. Dell, *Love in Greenwich Village*, 27.

12. John Reed, quoted in Rosenstone, *Romantic Rebel*, 83.

13. John Reed, quoted in Luhan, *Movers and Shakers*, 174–75.

14. Dell, *Love in Greenwich Village*, 17–20.

15. For information about the Liberal Club, see Richwine, "The Liberal Club."

16. Johns, *Time of Our Lives*, 216.

17. Luhan, *Movers and Shakers*, 6.

18. Lincoln Steffens, quoted in Luhan, *Movers and Shakers*, 80.

19. Inez Haynes Irwin, "History of Heterodoxy," SLRI, 414; for recent studies of Heterodoxy, see Schwarz, *Radical Feminists of Heterodoxy*, and Wittenstein, "The Heterodoxy Club and American Feminism, 1912–1930."

20. Quoted in Schwarz, *Radical Feminists of Heterodoxy*, 108.

21. Irwin, "History of Heterodoxy," 416–17, SLRI.

22. GCC to SG, 14 March 1913, BCNYPL.

23. Hutchins Hapgood, *New York Globe*, 27 January 1913.

24. Goldman, *The Social Significance of Modern Art*, 3.

25. Floyd Dell, quoted in Clayton, *Floyd Dell*, 119.

26. John Reed, *The Masses*, June 1913, reprinted in O'Neill, *Echoes of Revolt*, 143–47. For a thorough discussion and analysis of both the Armory Show and the Paterson strike and pageant, see Green, *New York 1913*. For an alternative view of the latter, see Golin, *The Fragile Bridge*. For European antecedents of pageants, see Brown, *Theater and Revolution*. On the history of American pageantry, see Prevots, *American Pageantry*.

27. Luhan, *Movers and Shakers*, 188.

28. See Golin, *The Fragile Bridge*.

29. Golin, *The Fragile Bridge*, 124, mentions that SG was one of the Heterodoxy members who went to Paterson to help the workers and aid in preparing the pageant.

30. Luhan, *Movers and Shakers*, 204.

31. Quoted in Green, *New York 1913*, 201.

32. GCC, "New York Letter," *Chicago Evening Post*, 8 May 1914.

33. *The Road to the Temple*, 250.

34. GCC, "New York Letter," *Chicago Evening Post*, 4 June 1913.

Chapter 13: A Home by the Sea

1. Egan, *Provincetown as a Stage*, 89. See her description of the *Priscilla*, 88.

2. Vorse, quoted in Egan, *Provincetown as a Stage*, 89.

3. GCC to SG, BCNYPL.

4. Vorse, *Time and the Town*, 9.

5. Thoreau, "Cape Cod Beach," quoted in Shay and Shay, *Sand in their Shoes*, 275.

6. Sinclair Lewis to Jack London, 7 August 1911, BLYU.

7. George Readey, quoted in Heaton Vorse, "Provincetown Memories," *Art Association Journal* (summer 1985).

8. SG, quoted in Louise Morgan, *Everyman*, 7 January 1932.

9. Grace Collinson, interview by the author, Provincetown, July 1987.

10. Rachel White, interview by the author, Provincetown, July 1987.

11. Francelina Sousa Hubbard, interview by author, Boston, October 1988.

12. Egan, *Provincetown as a Stage*, 54.

13. SG, *The Road to the Temple*, 228.

14. Goldman, *Living My Life*, 2:584.

15. *The Road to the Temple*, 257.

16. Hutchins Hapgood, quoted in Luhan, *Movers and Shakers*, 230.

17. Quoted by Heaton Vorse, interview by the author, Provincetown, July 1987.

18. *The Road to the Temple*, 236.

19. SG, "Here is the Piece," BCNYPL.

20. SG to Mary Heaton Vorse, 8 May [1914], WRLWSU.

21. *The Road to the Temple*, 235–36.

22. Marsden Hartley, quoted in Farnham, *Charles Demuth*, 19–20.

23. Heaton Vorse, interview by the author, Provincetown, August 1988.

24. For a discussion concerning the shared ideology of the Village women, see Sochen, *The New Woman in Greenwich Village, 1910–1920*.

25. Dell, *Love in the Machine Age*, 72.

26. Dell, *Intellectual Vagabondage*, 139.

27. Floyd Dell, "Feminism for Men," *The Masses*, 5 July 1914.

28. Mabel Dodge to Neith Boyce, BLYU.

29. On the relationship between Neith and Hutch, see Trimberger, *Intimate Warriors* and "Feminism, Men, and Modern Love." The voluminous correspondence between the two is preserved in their papers at BLYU.

30. On Mabel Dodge, see Rudnick, *Mabel Dodge Luhan*.

31. On Goldman's love life, see Falk, *Love, Anarchy, and Emma Goldman*.

32. Hapgood, *A Victorian in the Modern World*, 373–76.

33. Mary Heaton Vorse, quoted in GCC to SG, BCNYPL.

34. *The Road to the Temple*, 238–39.

Chapter 14: War and Peace

1. *Provincetown Advocate*, 14 May 1914.

2. Katharine Dos Passos, "Old Houses and New America," in Shay and Shay, *Sand in their Shoes*, 301.

3. SG, "Notes to go into Plays," BCNYPL.

4. *The Road to the Temple*, 420.

5. Vorse, *Time and the Town*, 33. To read about the relationship between women artists and their private spaces, see Udall, *Carr, O'Keeffe, Kahlo*, particularly 217–24, on O'Keeffe's homes.

6. *The Road to the Temple*, 240.

7. *The Road to the Temple*, 234.

8. Elsie Everts to Emily Farnham, 15 April 1956; Emily Farnham, interview by the author, Provincetown, August 1988. I thank her for making the letter available to me.

9. GCC to SG, 14 March 1913, BCNYPL. Hazel Hawthorne, in an interview by Lewis Sheaffer, indicated that SG posed for the statues on the sundial, SLCC.

10. *The Road to the Temple*, 245.

11. For a description of the house, see Sheaffer, *O'Neill: Son and Playwright*, 456–57, and Dewitt, *Taos*, 66.

12. Luhan, *Movers and Shakers*, 292.

13. For a description of these events, see Hapgood, *A Victorian in the Modern World*, 385–86; Vorse, *Time and the Town*, 100–101; Dell, *Homecoming*, 260; and Watson, *Strange Bedfellows*, 208–10.

14. Vorse, *Time and the Town*, 101.

15. Hapgood, *A Victorian in the Modern World*, 385.

16. GCC, "New York Letter," *Chicago Evening Post*, 7 August 1914.

17. SG to Mary Heaton Vorse, WRLWSU.

18. On Lorber, see Gardner, *Friend and Lover*, 56–57.

19. Emma Goldman received a similar diagnosis from another physician (Falk, *Love, Anarchy, and Emma Goldman*, 22).

20. GCC to SG, BCNYPL.

21. GCC to SG, 26 January, BCNYPL.

22. The hospital no longer has records going back to 1914.

23. *The Road to the Temple*, 239.

24. *Fidelity*, 273.

25. SG, *The Road to the Temple*, 237.

26. SG to Elmer Glaspell, BCNYPL.

Chapter 15: A Theatre on a Wharf

1. GCC to SG, BCNYPL.

2. Jones, *The Dramatic Imagination*, 30, 39.

3. For descriptions of the event, see Sheaffer, *O'Neill: Son and Playwright*, 322, and Gelb and Gelb, *O'Neill: Life with Monte Cristo*, 508–09.

4. Langner, *The Magic Curtain*, 76, 90–104.

5. Quoted in Langner, *The Magic Curtain*, 94–95.

6. Neith Boyce to Hutchins Hapgood, 20 November 1914, BLYU.

7. Sigmund Freud, quoted in Fishbein, *Rebels in Bohemia*, 84. For the impact of Freud's lectures, see Gainor, *Susan Glaspell in Context*, 24–26.

8. Anderson, *Memoirs*, 339.

9. *The Visioning*, 213.

10. *The Road to the Temple*, 250.

11. *Suppressed Desires*, 231–77. The following quotations are from this source.

12. See Ozieblo, "Suppression and Society in Glaspell's Theatre," 105–22.

13. W. David Sievers cites it as such in his book *Freud on Broadway: A History of Psychoanalysis and the American Drama*.

14. Langner (*The Magic Curtain*, 97) describes the scene.

15. *Fidelity*, 301. The following quotations are from this source.

16. See "We Attend an Ibsen Play," in Dell, *Intellectual Vagabondage*, 129–42.

17. Pollitzer, *Lovingly, Georgia*, 20–21.

18. Stieglitz, quoted in Pollitzer, *A Woman on Paper*, 138.

19. *New York Times Book Review*, 16 May 1916.

20. William Carlos Williams, "Letter to the *Egoist*" 3.9 (1915).

21. GCC, "The Third American Sex," *Forum* 50 (October 1913).
22. *The Road to the Temple*, 251.
23. Neith Boyce to Charles Hapgood, Sr., 17 July 1915, BLYU.
24. *The Road to the Temple*, 251.
25. Zorach, *Art is My Life*, 47.
26. See Sarlós, *Jig Cook and the Provincetown Players*, appendix C for a discussion of Wharf Theatre measurements. Mary Vorse provides larger dimensions, which Sarlós challenges (*Time and the Town*, 110, 118).
27. Vorse, *Time and the Town*, 118.
28. Sarlós, *Jig Cook and the Provincetown Players*, appendix C, explains these calculations.
29. GCC, quoted in *The Road to the Temple*, 252.
30. SG, quoted in Vorse, *Time and the Town*, 103.
31. GCC, quoted in *The Road to the Temple*, 249. It is likely, as well, that GCC knew about the Yiddish theatre, then thriving on the Lower East Side of New York, through his friend Hutch Hapgood, who described it in detail in *The Spirit of the Ghetto*.
32. GCC, quoted in Edna Kenton, "The Provincetown Players and the Playwrights' Theatre," 8. The version of Kenton's "The Provincetown Players and the Playwrights' Theatre 1915–1922" used in this book is her draft held at FNYU (folder 3,140.10). A later revised version, edited by Bogard and Bryer, was published in the *Eugene O'Neill Review*, 21.1–2 (spring/fall 1997).

Chapter 16: Summer 1916, Two Playwrights

1. Harry Kemp, quoted in Brevda, *The Last Bohemian*, 143.
2. John Francis, quoted in Ernest L. Meyer, "As the Crow Flies," *New York Post*, 27 August 1937.
3. Goldman, *Living My Life*, 2:583.
4. John Reed, quoted in Rosenstone, *Romantic Rebel*, 239.
5. Heaton Vorse, interview by the author, Provincetown, July 1987.
6. Eastman, *Enjoyment of Life*, 566.
7. Louise Bryant to John Reed, 9 June 1916, bMS Am 1091(240), HLHU.
8. Louise Bryant to John Reed, 12 June 1916, bMS Am 1091 (242), HLHU; see also Louise Bryant to John Reed, 1 December 1916, HLHU.
9. Eugene O'Neill to John Francis, CFE.
10. Eugene O'Neill, quoted in "Editorial Conference," *American Spectator* 1. 11 (September 1933).
11. Dewitt, *Taos*, 85, reports that Hapgood's letter caused a furor. See also Theodore Dreiser to Hutchins Hapgood, 10 October 1933 and Hutchins Hapgood to Theodore Dreiser, 18 October 1933, BLYU. In his letter Dreiser makes his anti-Semitism more overt, and Hapgood challenges his position.
12. SG, "How Do You Begin," BCNYPL.
13. Quoted in Egan, *Provincetown as a Stage*, 156.
14. GCC, quoted in *The Road to the Temple*, 252.
15. GCC, quoted in *The Road to the Temple*, 266.
16. Sarlós, *Jig Cook and the Provincetown Players*, 80. Sarlós indicates that the recipe omits the two quarts of water indicated in bartender guidelines for this drink in this quantity.

17. Kenton, "The Provincetown Players and the Playwrights' Theatre," 10.
18. *Provincetown Advocate*, 8 June 1916.
19. Neith Boyce to Charles Hapgood, Sr., 16 July 1916, BLYU.
20. Edna Kenton, "The Provincetown Players and the Playwrights' Theatre," 10. Glaspell indicates (*Road*, 255) that Cook's letter called for one dollar for the three remaining bills.
21. Bobby Rogers, quoted in Egan, *Provincetown as a Stage*, 170.
22. *The Road to the Temple*, 253–54.
23. Hutchins Hapgood, quoted in Luhan, *Movers and Shakers*, 478.
24. Hapgood, *A Victorian in the Modern World*, 396.
25. For other versions of the discovery of O'Neill, see Harry Kemp, "Out of Provincetown," *Theatre Magazine*, April 1930; Gary Jay Williams, "Turned Down in Provincetown: O'Neill's Debut Re-examined," *Theatre Journal* 37.2 (May 1985).
26. GCC, quoted in Edna Kenton, *Greek Coins*, 18.
27. GCC, "Holograph Essay," BCNYPL.
28. Eugene O'Neill, quoted in Clark, *Eugene O'Neill*, 31.
29. Sheaffer gives this date, but Sarlós argues that the date can be anywhere from 25–28 July. See Sheaffer, *O'Neill: Son and Playwright*, 348, 498; Sarlós, note 51, 210.
30. *The Road to the Temple*, 255–56.
31. *Trifles*, 3–30. The following quotations are from this source.
32. For the connection between quilting and women's solidarity, see Hedges, "Small Things Reconsidered," 49–69; and Showalter, "Common Threads," 145–75.
33. See Gainor, *Susan Glaspell in Context*, for connections with the detective genre, 43–60.
34. "A Jury of her Peers," *Everyweek*, 5 March 1913.
35. *Boston Globe*, 13 August 1916.
36. Minutes of the Provincetown Players, 4 September 1916, BRTC. For a list of the twenty-nine original members, see Deutsch and Hanau, *The Provincetown*, 16–17.
37. GCC to SG, 15 September 1916, BCNYPL.
38. GCC to SG, 19 September 1916, BCNYPL.
39. *The Road to the Temple*, 259.

Chapter 17: A New Kind of Theatre

1. GCC to SG, BCNYPL.
2. Quoted in *World Telegram and Sun*, 11 June 1940.
3. Edna Kenton, "The Provincetown Players and the Playwrights' Theatre," 30.
4. See Sarlós, *Jig Cook and the Provincetown Players*, appendix C, for alternative measurements.
5. Edna Kenton, "The Provincetown Players and the Playwrights' Theatre," 31.
6. Mary Pyne to Mary Heaton Vorse, WRLWSU.
7. GCC to SG, 20 September 1916, BCNYPL.
8. Louise Bryant to John Reed, bMSM Am 1091(245), HLHU.

9. *The Road to the Temple*, 260.
10. Mary Pyne to Mary Heaton Vorse, WRLWSU.
11. Mary Pyne to Mary Heaton Vorse, WRLWSU.
12. Edna Kenton, "The Provincetown Players and the Playwrights' Theatre," 48. For questions concerning the roles women played at the Provincetown, see Black, *Women of Provincetown, 1915–1922*. For women playwrights who were active there, see Judith Barlow, "Susan's Sisters: The 'Other' Women Writers of the Provincetown Players," 259–300.
13. *New York Times*, 9 December 1916. GCC also writes about Mansfield to SG, 13 December, BCNYPL. Edna Kenton describes the Mansfield adventure and tells of his death, "The Provincetown Players and the Playwrights' Theatre," 50–51. The following account is taken from these sources.
14. "Provincetown Players Scrapbook of News Clippings," 1915–22, BRTC.
15. Edna Kenton, "The Provincetown Players and the Playwrights' Theatre," 51.
16. GCC to SG, 11 and 23 December, BCNYPL.
17. SG to Louise Bryant, 21 December, bMS Am 800.52(125), HLHU.
18. *The People*, 31–60. The following quotations are from this source.
19. Jacques Copeau, quoted in Noe, "A Critical Biography of Susan Glaspell," 103; Deutsch and Hanau, *The Provincetown*, 25, refer to *Inheritors* as the play Copeau saw; Norman H. Paul argues that the play is *The People*, see "Jacques Copeau Looks at the American Stage, 1917–1919," *Educational Theatre Journal* 29 (March 1977). In his journal, Copeau describes the visit but not the play, see *Journal, 1901–1949* (Paris: Éditions Claire Paulham, 1991), 47. Heywood Broun also praised her acting in *The People*; see his review in the *New York Tribune*, 18 March 1917. It is interesting to note that even Copeau, with a seasoned professional eye, assumed the actor he saw in the play was "a young woman." SG was then forty-one, three years older than Copeau at the time.
20. Kenton, "The Provincetown Players and the Playwrights' Theatre," 57.
21. Nina Moise to Edna Kenton, 16 October 1933, FNYU.
22. Heywood Broun, *New York Tribune*, 18 March 1917.
23. Ludwig Lewisohn, *Nation* 111 (3 November 1920). See also his book *Drama and the Stage*, in which he offers the same comment (103).
24. Edwin Björkman, *Freeman*, 11 August 1920.
25. Vorse, *A Footnote to Folly*, 154.
26. John Reed, "One Solid Month of Liberty," *The Masses*, September 1917.
27. GCC to SG, 20 September 1917; Boardman Robinson's Cartoon, *The Masses*, July 1916.
28. *The Road to the Temple*, 261.
29. Burns Mantle, quoted in Kenton, "The Provincetown Players and the Playwrights' Theatre," 60.

Chapter 18: Fire from Heaven on MacDougal Street

1. *The Outside*, 97–117. The following quotations are from this source.
2. *Close the Book*, 61–96. The following quotations are from this source.
3. Edwin Björkman, *Freeman*, 11 August 1920.

4. Chloe Arnold, "Susan Glaspell, Author, Playwright by Chance," *Telegram*, 30 December 1917.

5. Alice Rohe, "The Story of Susan Glaspell, *New York Morning Telegraph*, 18 December 1921.

6. See Ozieblo, *Susan Glaspell*, and Noe, "A Critical Biography of Susan Glaspell" and *Susan Glaspell*, who argue for Glaspell's apolitical character. Gainor, however, takes the position outlined in this book, that political activity in its broadest sense can take the form of fomenting for change through one's writing, and that in this sense Glaspell was political and feminist. See Gainor, *Susan Glaspell in Context*, 264–67.

7. GCC, quoted in *The Road to the Temple*, 272.

8. GCC to SG, 24 September 1917, BCNYPL.

9. Heywood Broun, *New York Tribune*, 4 March 1918.

10. Luhan, *Movers and Shakers*, 199.

11. Luhan, *Movers and Shakers*, 484.

12. Hutchins Hapgood to Neith Boyce, March 1918, BLYU.

13. Hutchins Hapgood to Neith Boyce, May 1918, BLYU.

14. Kemp, *Love Among the Cape Enders*, 51. The following quotations are from this source.

15. *Woman's Honor, Plays*, 119–56. The following quotations are from this source.

16. A sixth woman, called the Mercenary One, also appears, but she is looking for a job.

17. John Corbin, *New York Times*, 21 May 1918.

18. Rebecca Drucker, *New York Tribune*, 20 April 1919.

19. *New York Herald*, 21 May 1918.

20. *Dramatic Mirror* 70 (1 June 1918).

21. Edwin Björkman, *Freeman*, 11 August 1920.

22. *Nation*, 1 June 1918.

23. John Corbin, "Who is Susan Glaspell?" *New York Times*, 26 May 1918.

24. John Corbin, *New York Times*, 19 May 1918.

25. See Black, *The Women of the Provincetown*, who takes another position.

26. O'Keeffe, quoted in Lynes, *O'Keeffe, Stieglitz and the Critics, 1916–1929*, 100.

27. Stieglitz, quoted in Pollitzer, *A Woman on Paper*, 48.

28. Udall, *Carr, O'Keeffe, Kahlo*, 47.

29. Norman, *Alfred Stieglitz*, 193, 195.

30. O'Keeffe, quoted in Pollitzer, *A Woman on Paper*, 188.

31. Sarlós, *Jig Cook and the Provincetown Players*, 205–6. He also quotes Nilla Cook as saying that the realization of Jig's "theatre of many domes, of lights and dancers" became her goal, finally realized in the theatre for the Iranian National Ballet, which she established. See also Kenton, "The Provincetown Players and the Playwrights' Theatre," 96–97.

32. Kenton, "The Provincetown Players and the Playwrights' Theatre," 97.

Chapter 19: "Here Pegasus Was Hitched"

1. GCC to SG, 24 May, BCNYPL.

2. SG, notebook 5, BLUVA.

3. GCC, quoted in *The Road to the Temple*, 274.

4. SG to Agnes Boulton, BLYU.

5. Boulton, *Part of a Long Story*, 20.

6. Boulton, *Part of a Long Story*, 163–64.

7. See William Davis King, "The O'Neill of Pulp Fiction," *Eugene O'Neill Review* 26 (2004). See also King, *A Wind is Rising*.

8. Bogard, "Introduction," quoted in O'Neill and MacGowan, *The Theatre We Worked For*, 15–16.

9. See Ben-Zvi, "O'Neill's Cape(d) Compatriot," *Eugene O'Neill Review* 19, 1–2 (spring/fall 1995).

10. SG, "Notes for a Talk," BCNYPL.

11. SG, notebook 20, BLUVA.

12. None of O'Neill's biographers discuss this special connection nor the mutual influence they may have exerted on each other's work.

13. *The Road to the Temple*, 281.

14. *Tickless Time*, 275–315. The following quotations are from this source.

15. GCC to SG, 24 October, BCNYPL.

16. GCC to SG, 24 March 1918, BCNYPL.

17. Ma-Mie Cook, quoted in *The Road to the Temple*, 62.

18. Deutsch and Hanau, *The Provincetown*, use these numbers. Kenton gives the dimensions of the stage as 12-by-26 feet. See Sarlós, *Jig Cook and the Provincetown Players*, appendix C, for comments on these various measurements.

19. Norma Millay, interview by Judith Barlow, tape recording, Steepletop, New York. I thank Barlow for making it available to me.

20. Heywood Broun, *New York Tribune*, 23 December 1918.

21. SG, "Faint Trails," typescript, BCNYPL.

22. *Bernice*, 157–230. The following quotations are from this source.

23. John Corbin, *New York Times*, 30 March 1919.

24. Kenton, "The Provincetown Players and the Playwrights' Theatre," 133.

25. John Corbin, *New York Times*, 30 March 1919.

26. Lewisohn, *Drama and the Stage*, 102, and *Expressionism in America*, 391–97.

27. *The Road to the Temple*, 278.

28. SG, notebook 12, BLUVA.

29. *The Road to the Temple*, 286.

30. Cowley, *Exile's Return*, 72. See also May, *The End of American Innocence*.

31. Dorothy Day, quoted in Clayton, *Floyd Dell*, 183–84.

Chapter 20: *Inheritors*

1. SG, "The Nervous Pig," *Harper's* 140 (February 1920). The following quotations are from this source.

2. John Reed, quoted in *The Road to the Temple*, 302.

3. See Interlude 2, note 47, below.

4. Boulton, *Part of a Long Story*, 296.

5. GCC to Neith Boyce, BLYU.

6. Eugene O'Neill to Agnes Boulton, [1/2 December 1919], HTC.

7. Agnes Boulton to Eugene O'Neill, January 1920 (mislabeled 1919), HTC.

8. Agnes Boulton to Eugene O'Neill, 20 January 1920, HTC.

9. SG, "The Busy Duck," *Harper's* 137 (November 1918). The following quotations are from this source.

10. SG to Arthur Davison Ficke, 16 April, BLYU.

11. Agnes Boulton to Eugene O'Neill, 20 January 1920, HTC.

12. Agnes Boulton to Eugene O'Neill, January 1920 (mislabeled 1919), HTC.

13. For Barnes' reaction to the Players and GCC, see "The Days of Jig Cook," *Theatre Guild Magazine* 6 (January 1929).

14. Alexander Woollcott, *New York Times*, 9 November 1919.

15. Langner, *The Magic Curtain*, 110.

16. Eugene O'Neill to Agnes Boulton, 14 January 1920, HTC.

17. Agnes Boulton to Eugene O'Neill, 16 February 1920, HTC. See also letter of February 25.

18. Eugene O'Neill to Agnes Boulton, [February 1920], HTC.

19. Eugene O'Neill to George Jean Nathan, quoted in Sheaffer, *O'Neill: Son and Playwright*, 464.

20. Eugene O'Neill to Agnes Boulton, 14 January 1920, HTC.

21. SG, notebook 35, BLUVA. See also Agnes Boulton to Eugene O'Neill, 23 February 1920, HTC.

22. Agnes Boulton to Eugene O'Neill, 14 January 1920, HTC.

23. For a summary of the injustices of the period, see Vorse, *A Footnote to Folly*, 302–12.

24. Woodrow Wilson, quoted in Peterson and Fite, *Opponents of the War*, 84.

25. Vorse, *A Footnote to Folly*, 302.

26. GCC to SG, 11 September 1918, BCNYPL.

27. Harold C. Dana and Ralph Bourne, quoted in Diggins, *The Rise and Fall of the American Left*, 103.

28. For the climate in America at the end of World War 1, see Giffin, *Six Who Protested*; Noggle, *Into the Twenties*; Chafee, *Freedom of Speech*; and Peterson and Fite, *Opponents of War*, 262–65. The latter book describes the case of Fred Robinson, 132.

29. *The Road to the Temple*, 17.

30. SG, "His America," in *Lifted Masks*.

31. SG, *Inheritors*, 14. The following quotations are from this source.

32. SG, "Free Laughter," unpublished handwritten manuscript, RCE. The following quotations are from this source. I thank Regie Cabral for making the manuscript available to me.

33. GCC, quoted in *The Road to the Temple*, 292.

34. *The Road to the Temple*, 302.

35. *The Road to the Temple*, 301.

36. *The Road to the Temple*, 286.

37. Kenton, "The Provincetown Players and the Playwrights' Theatre," 162.

38. Agnes Boulton to Eugene O'Neill, 28 April, HTC.

39. "The Provincetown Players Season of 1920–21 Brochure," "Provincetown Players Scrapbook," BRTC.

40. A photo of the production can be found in Deutsch and Hanau, *The Provincetown*, 49.

41. For a precise description of the dome, see, Sarlós, *Jig Cook and the Provincetown Players*, chapter 3, 123–37.

42. Kenton, "The Provincetown Players and the Playwrights' Theatre," 168.

43. Kenton, "The Provincetown Players and the Playwrights' Theatre," 169.

44. Nilla Cook to Hutchins Hapgood, BLYU.

45. Lewis, *Main Street*, 329.

46. Millay, quoted in Norman Brittin, *Edna St. Vincent Millay*, 45.

47. SG to Agnes Boulton, 21 November 1920, HTC.

48. William Archer, *New York Post*, 24 February 1921; Kenneth Macgowan, *Theatre Arts* 5 (March 1921).

49. Eugene O'Neill to GCC, 5 February 1921, BLUVA.

50. Kenton, "The Provincetown Players and the Playwrights' Theatre," 183.

51. Susan indicates in a diary kept sporadically during rehearsals and the run of *Inheritors* that she played Madeline for four performances during the second week of the bill, presumably when Harding was ill, BCNYPL.

52. James Patterson, *Billboard*, 2 April 1921.

53. Alexander Woollcott, *New York Times*, 27 March 1921.

54. Kenneth Macgowan, *Theatre Arts Magazine* 5 (July 1921).

55. Ludwig Lewisohn, *Nation* 112 (6 April 1921). See also Lewisohn, *Drama and the Stage*, 110.

56. Dell, *Homecoming*, 267.

57. Jasper Deeter to SG, 9 December 1936, BU.

Chapter 21: *The Verge* and Beyond

1. GCC to SG, 6 October 1921, BCNYPL.

2. GCC to Agnes Boulton, 28 April 1921, HTC.

3. Kenton, "The Provincetown Players and the Playwrights' Theatre," 194.

4. The story is repeated by Sheaffer, *O'Neill: Son and Artist*, 78, and Gelb and Gelb, *O'Neill*, 492.

5. GCC to SG, 27 August 1921, BCNYPL.

6. Francelina Sousa Hubbard, interview by the author, Boston, October 1988.

7. Chloe Arnold, "Susan Glaspell, Author, Playwright by Chance," *Morning Telegram*, 30 December 1917.

8. Hutchins Hapgood to Mary Berenson, 1941, BLYU.

9. Margaret Sanger, quoted in Chesler, *Woman of Valor*, 98.

10. *The Verge*, 34. The following quotations are from this source.

11. SG, "Notes on *The Verge*," BCNYPL.

12. *The Road to the Temple*, 305–06.

13. Alice Palmer, quoted in Hapgood, *A Victorian in the Modern World*, 323.

14. SG, "Heterodoxy to Marie Album," SLRI.

15. SG, "Notes on Getting Older," BCNYPL.

16. *The Road to the Temple*, 308, 310.

17. Showalter, "Introduction," *These Modern Women*, 13. The seventeen autobiographical essays by leading feminists of the 1920s, reprinted in this collection, were first published in the *Nation* in 1926–27. They provide important insights into many of the issues that Glaspell raises in *The Verge* and her other plays.

18. Isadora Duncan, *My Life*, 356.

19. Malpede, "Reflections on *The Verge*," 126.

20. SG "Notes on *The Verge*," BCNYPL.

21. In the unpublished version of Edna Kenton's "The Provincetown Players and the Playwrights' Theatre," Jig's circular for the 1921–22 season is missing. I have taken it from the published version, edited by Travis Bogard and Jackson Bryer, 143.

22. Percy Hammond, *Herald Tribune*, 15 November 1921.

23. *Greenwich Villager*, 30 November 1921.

24. Weed Dickinson, *New York Evening Telegraph*, 15 November 1921.

25. Arthur Pollock, *Brooklyn Daily Eagle*, 17 November 1921.

26. William Archer, *New York Post*, 19 November 1921.

27. Stephen Rathbun, *New York Sun*, 19 November 1921.

28. Maida Castellun, *New York Call*, 16 November 1921.

29. Alexander Woollcott, *New York Times*, 15 November 1921.

30. Alexander Woollcott, *New York Times*, 20 November 1921.

31. Ruth Hale, "Letter to the Dramatic Editor," *New York Times*, 20 November 1921.

32. Stark Young, *New Republic* 29 (7 December 1921).

33. Barrett Clark, marginal notes, *The Verge*, WPC.

34. Kenneth Macgowan, *New York Globe*, 15 November 1921. For other reviews of *The Verge*, see Papke, *Susan Glaspell*, 64–69.

35. Barrett Clark, marginal notes, *The Verge*, WPC.

36. Hutchins Hapgood, *A Victorian in the Modern World*, 377.

Chapter 22: The End of the Dream

1. GCC to Theodore Dreiser, 15 December 1921, UPA.

2. Howard Irving Young to SG, BCNYPL.

3. Head of the Drama League to GCC, BCNYPL.

4. GCC to Executive Board Provincetown Players, 8 December, HLHU.

5. GCC to SG, HTC.

6. Eugene O'Neill, quoted in Gelb and Gelb, *O'Neill*, 488.

7. Agnes Boulton to Eugene O'Neill, 17 December 1921, HTC.

8. For a comparison between the two plays, see Ben-Zvi, "Susan Glaspell and Eugene O'Neill" and "Susan Glaspell, Eugene O'Neill and the Imagery of Gender."

9. GCC, quoted in *The Road to the Temple*, 309.

10. *The Road to the Temple*, 220–21.

11. GCC, quoted in *The Road to the Temple*, 112.

12. GCC, quoted in *The Road to the Temple*, 309.

13. Charles Kennedy, quoted in Gelb and Gelb, *O'Neill*, 493.

14. Inez Haynes Irwin, clipping, *Philadelphia Public Ledger*, 1922, BCNYPL.

15. Goldberg, *The Drama of Transition*, 481.

16. See, for example, Larabee, "Death in Delphi."

17. For other discussions about the reasons for the end of the Provincetown Players, see Kenton, 191–212; Sarlós, 138–52; and Deutsch and Hanau, 88–93.

18. Kenton, "The Provincetown Players and the Playwrights' Theatre," 206.

19. Kenton, "The Provincetown Players and the Playwrights' Theatre," 208.

20. GCC, quoted in Deutsch and Hanau, *The Provincetown*, 92.

21. GCC, quoted in *The Road to the Temple*, 310.

22. See Black, *Women of Provincetown, 1915–1922*.

23. To see the play in the context of other birth-control plays of the era, see Gainor, "Chains of Dew," 165–93.

24. References to *Chains of Dew* are to the unpublished manuscript in the Library of Congress. The following quotations come from this source.

25. SG, "Notebook 3," BCNYPL.

26. EK to SG, 5 May 1922, BLUVA.

27. SG to EK, BLUVA.

28. SG to EK, BLUVA.

29. SG to EK, BLUVA.

30. Alexander Woollcott, *New York Times*, 28 April 1922.

31. Stephen Rathbun, *New York Sun*, 29 April 1922.

32. *Chains of Dew* will be published for the first time in *The Complete Plays of Susan Glaspell*, ed. Linda Ben-Zvi and Ellen J. Gainor (forthcoming).

Interlude 2: Delphi 1922–24: The Road to the Temple

1. Unless otherwise indicated, the references and quotations for this chapter come from the Greek sections of *The Road to the Temple* or Susan's essay in *Greek Coins*.

2. SG to Alice Glaspell, 23 March 1923, BCNYPL.

3. Sinclair, *Money Writes!*, 169.

4. SG to Hutchins Hapgood, 28 August 1923, BLYU.

5. SG to Alice Glaspell, BCNYPL.

6. SG to Edna Kenton, 4 May 1922, HTC.

7. SG to Edna Kenton, 11 May 1922, BLUVA.

8. SG to Alice Glaspell, 8 May 1922, BCNYPL.

9. SG to Edna Kenton, HTC.

10. Elias Tsakalos, interview by the author, Delphi, August 1997.

11. SG to Edna Kenton, 29 October 1923, HTC.

12. SG to Alice Glaspell, 12 June 1922, BCNYPL.

13. SG, "Dwellers on Parnassos," *New Republic* 33 (17 January 1923).

14. SG to Alice Glaspell, 20 September 1922, BCNYPL.

15. SG to Alice Glaspell, 10 October 1922, BCNYPL.

16. SG to Alice Glaspell, 1 November 1922, BCNYPL.

17. GCC to SG, 15 December, BCNYPL.

18. GCC to SG, 2–15 January, BCNYPL.

19. GCC to William Rapp, 5–18 July 1922, CE.

20. GCC to SG, 10 March, BCNYPL.

21. Nilla Cook to Hutchins Hapgood, BLYU.

22. Cook, *My Road to India*, 4.

23. Cook, *My Road to India*, 9.

24. GCC, *Greek Coins*, 110–15.

25. SG to Hutchins Hapgood, 16 February 1923, BLYU.

26. SG, quoted in Cook, *My Road to India*, 19.

27. SG to Alice Glaspell, 15 July 1923.

28. Cook, *My Road to India*, 23.

29. *The Road to the Temple*, 370.

30. SG, "The Faithless Shepherd," *Cornhill* 60 (January 1926).

31. GCC to Hutchins Hapgood, 28 August 1923, BLYU.

32. GCC to Ida Rauh (unsent), BCNYPL.

33. Hapgood, *A Victorian in the Modern World*, 487.

34. GCC, *Greek Coins*, 123–32.

35. SG to Edna Kenton, 29 October 1923, HTC.

36. GCC to SG, 27 November 1923, BCNYPL. Wording differs in *Road*.

37. SG to William Rapp, CE; for a description of glanders, *see Mosby's Medical Nursing and Allied Health Dictionary*, 4th edition (St. Louis: Mosby's Pub., 1994), 672.

38. SG to William Rapp, CE.

39. Leandros Palamas to William Rapp, 24 June 1924, CE.

40. GCC, *Greek Coins*, 132.

41. GCC, *Greek Coins*, 80.

42. Eleanor Fitzgerald, quoted in Louis Weitzenkorn, "GCC," *New York World*, 20 January 1924.

43. Floyd Dell, "Letter to the Editor," *Davenport Democrat*, 16 January 1924.

44. *Nation*, 23 January 1924.

45. SG to Hutchins Hapgood, 28 January 1924, BLYU.

46. GS to Alice Keating Glaspell, 21 January 1924, BCNYPL.

47. Louise Bryant to Neith Boyce, 28 January 1924, BLYU. In a long scene found in her notes (BCNYPL) and perhaps intended for a future fiction, SG sketches Jack's personality (very like GCC's), his death, and how Louise may have reacted. The description may also reflect Susan's feelings, since she uses some of the same words in her later biography of Jig. "The different times of his life. The playboy-Harvard. What that moment could have opened up but called from it to something quite different. Always on his way. Much believing and always generous. . . . In Russia and when strength left was there no new believing to call him from a desolate moment. Always giving himself to the thing felt at the moment. With more enthusiasm than criticism."

A more detailed scene follows between two women:

> One has been with him in Russia. She knows he died broken disillusioned, hopeless. She must tell the other—his wife [of] what happened. Decides she will not do this—that she will lie to her. There is that in the wife compels truth. Tells her that he lost his strength and pride as a lover. That he died bewildered and bitter. "That was what it comes to." "No that was only that moment." And with Jack—there's always another moment. The next thing. A fine new enthusiasm. He went on to that next moment. . . . "You're not just to him. You loved him as the idealist as romantic. But he faced facts as you never realized. He—your romantic one faced the fact that as a lover he was dead. Then did he coddle himself with thinking there were other things. No faced this last fact." "How romantic of him."

She concludes the section with the words, "But it was another thing to be Brave about. It was—change, the great change to nothingness, change so great it must leave us knowing there is change." There is no date on the fragment, and no specific reference except the words *Russia* and *Jack* to indicate who the characters are.

48. Although SG in *Greek Coins* indicates that the Delphi games would take place in 1925, they were not held until 1927.

49. Cook, *My Road to India*, 60. See also Maynard Owen Williams, "New Greece, the Centenarian Forges Ahead," *National Geographic* (December 1930). This article includes several photographs from the 1930 festival. William Rapp also has notes for an article on Jig, entitled "An American Apollo," that discusses how he had already become a legend among the people of Delphi, CE.

50. Information on Palmer from the Museum of the Delphi Festival.

51. Cook, *My Road to India*, 50.

Chapter 23: Picking Up the Pieces

1. Edna Kenton to SG, 10 July 1923, BLUVA.

2. SG to Edna Kenton, quoted in Edna Kenton to Eleanor Fitzgerald, 9 December 1923, HTC.

3. For a description of this new theatre, see Kenneth Macgowan to Otto Kahn, 18 December 1923, PUA.

4. Edna Kenton to SG and GCC, 17 November 1923, HTC.

5. Edna Kenton to SG, 23 May 1924, HTC.

6. SG to Edna Kenton, BLCOL.

7. Edna Kenton to Eleanor Fitzgerald, 28 October 1924, BLCOL.

8. Agnes Boulton to GS, HTC.

9. SG to Eleanor Fitzgerald, 23 May 1924, HTC.

10. Edna Kenton to SG, 28 May 1924, HTC. The following description comes from this letter.

11. SG to Eleanor Fitzgerald, 31 May 1924, HTC.

12. Eugene O'Neill to SG, 26 May 1924, BLUVA, reprinted in O'Neill, *Selected Letters of Eugene O'Neill*, 186.

13. Prospectus, quoted in Deutsch and Hanau, *The Provincetown*, 136–38, and repeated in brochures for the company until 1929.

14. Eugene O'Neill to Eleanor Fitzgerald, 28 May 1922, SLCC; also quoted, without the last phrase in Sheaffer, *O'Neill: Son and Artist*, 95.

15. Eugene O'Neill to Kenneth Macgowan, quoted in Sheaffer, *O'Neill: Son and Artist*, 114.

16. Eugene O'Neill to Kenneth Macgowan, 28 September 1925, BLYU.

17. Eugene O'Neill, quoted in Sheaffer, *O'Neill: Son and Artist*, 253.

18. Eugene O'Neill to Kenneth Macgowan, August 1924, quoted in O'Neill and Macgowan, *The Theatre We Worked For*, 56.

19. SG, "George Cram Cook: Founder of the Provincetown Players," *Playbill*, 11 October 1924, reprinted in Deutsch and Hanau, *The Provincetown*, 193–96.

20. SG to Edna Kenton, BLCOL.

21. Barrett Clark to Eleanor Fitzgerald, BRTC.

22. SG to Edna Kenton, BCNYPL.

23. On *Greek Coins*, see Kemper, "The Novels, Plays, and Poetry of George Cram Cook, Founder of the Provincetown Players."

24. SG to Edna Kenton, BCNYPL.

25. SG to Edna Kenton, 12 January 1925 (mismarked 1924), BLUVA.
26. Hapgood, *A Victorian in the Modern World*, 499.
27. For a description of this period, see DeWitt, *Taos*, 20.
28. Vorse, *Time and the Town*, 187, 213.
29. Hapgood, *A Victorian in the Modern World*, 499.
30. Heaton Vorse, interview by the author, Provincetown, July 1987.
31. Miriam Hapgood DeWitt, interviews by author, Provincetown, July 1987 and August 1988.
32. Mary Hackett, interview by the author, August 1988.
33. Miriam Hapgood DeWitt, interview by the author, Provincetown, July 1987.
34. SG, *The Morning Is Near Us*, 198.
35. Mary Heaton Vorse, "Diary," March 14, WRLWSU; Garrison, *Mary Heaton Vorse*, 192–95.
36. Joel O'Brien, interview by the author, Provincetown, August 1988.
37. Norman Matson, "40 days on 40 pages," BCNYPL.
38. Neith Boyce to Hutchins Hapgood, BLYU.
39. SG to Norman Matson, BCNYPL. All subsequent letters between the two are in this collection and are not listed unless dated.
40. Norman Matson, "Unpublished Autobiographical Novel" and note for novel, NME.
41. Unfortunately no notes of Goldman's lectures have survived.
42. A. D. Peters, *Daily Telegraph*, 19 June 1924.
43. James Agate, *Sunday Times*, 24 August 1924.
44. Andrew Malone, *Dublin Magazine* 2 (September 1924).
45. "Supplement," *Manchester Guardian*, 10 December 1924.
46. *Bournmouth Echo*, news clipping, BCNYPL.
47. SG to Alice Glaspell, 17 October 1924, BCNYPL. Blanche Hays mentioned to Edna Kenton (16 October 1933, BLCOL) that she was trying to get French director Lugné-Poe interested in *The Verge*, but there is no record it was ever staged in Paris.
48. Sybil Thorndike to Edie Craig, quoted in Roberta Gandolfi, "Susan Glaspell's Debut on the English Stage: *Trifles* and *The Verge*" (a paper presented at the "Suppressed Desires" Conference, University of Glasgow, May 1996), 12. For general information on Craig and Ellen Terry, see Nina Auerbach, *Ellen Terry*.
49. Sybil Thorndike, quoted in *Yorkshire Post*, 13 February 1925.
50. James Agate, *Sunday Times*, 4 April 1925.
51. Deputy Adams, quoted in the *New Age*, 16 April 1925.
52. *Daily Telegraph*, 30 March 1925.
53. *Illustrated London News*, 11 April 1925.
54. R. Ellis Roberts, *Manchester Guardian*, 17 July 1925.
55. *Manchester Guardian*, 28 September 1925.
56. *Liverpool Echo*, 16 October 1925.
57. *Manchester City News*, 7 July 1928.
58. Elizabeth Robins, quoted in *Time and Tide*, 21 January 1927.
59. Clifford Odets, quoted in Brenman-Gibson, *Clifford Odets*, 90.
60. Norman Matson to family, 29 June 1925, NME.
61. Norman Matson, "Unpublished Autobiographical Novel," NME. The following quotations are from this source.

62. SG to Alice Glaspell, 24 November 1925, BCNYPL.

63. SG, quoted in Louise Morgan, "Susan Glaspell of New England," *Everyman*, 7 January 1932.

64. SG to Norman Matson, November 1926, BCNYPL.

65. SG and Norman Matson, *The Comic Artist*, 43. The following quotations are from this source.

66. SG, "The Road to the Temple Notebook," BCNYPL.

67. *The Road to the Temple*, xii.

68. Arthur Davison Ficke, *New York Saturday Review of Literature*, 26 March 1927.

69. Floyd Dell, *Herald Tribune*, 13 March 1927.

70. Hapgood, *A Victorian in the Modern World*, 499–500.

71. Alice Glaspell to SG, 16 July 1928, BCNYPL.

Chapter 24: Novel Times

1. SG, *The Road to the Temple*, xv.

2. SG to Norman Matson, BCNYPL. The following letters are from this archive.

3. SG, "Notes for a Talk," BCNYPL.

4. SG, "Notes for a Talk," BCNYPL.

5. SG, "Notebook," 16 October 1915, BCNYPL.

6. Matson, "Unpublished Autobiographical Novel," 25, NME. The following quotes are from this source.

7. Eva LeGallienne, quoted in Sheehy, *Eva LeGallienne*, 138.

8. R. Dana Skinner, *Commonweal*, 30 March 1927.

9. LeGallienne, *At 33*, 205–06.

10. Arthur Ruhl, *New York Herald Tribune*, 8 March 1927.

11. SG, quoted in Sheehy, *Eva LeGallienne*, 162.

12. Vorse, *Time and the Town*, 260.

13. Thayer, quoted in Vorse, *A Footnote to Folly*, 336.

14. Wilson, *The Twenties*, 385.

15. Hapgood, *A Victorian in the Modern World*, 518.

16. Wilson, *The Thirties*, 24.

17. Neith Boyce, quoted by Miriam Hapgood Dewitt, *Taos*, 56.

18. SG, Diary 16, BLUVA.

19. Miriam Hapgood DeWitt, interview by the author, Provincetown, August 1988.

20. Wilson, *The Thirties*, 24.

21. Neith Boyce to Marguerite Kaselau, BLYU.

22. Norman Matson to SG, 25 October 1927, BCNYPL.

23. SG to Sherwood Anderson, 9 June 1829, Box 5, Folder 72, NL; SG to Theodore Dreiser, 9 June 1928, UPA.

24. *The Statesman*, 28 April 1928.

25. *The Observer*, 29 April 1928.

26. John Chamberlain, *New York Times Book Review*, 1 July 1928.

27. Alice Glaspell to SG, 16 July 1928, BCNYPL.

28. SG, *Fugitive's Return*, 89. The following quotations are from this source.

29. SG to Covici Friede, 19 January 1929, BCNYPL.

30. Ray Glaspell to SG, BCNYPL.

31. Obituary, *Davenport Democrat*, 17 February 1929.

32. Cousin Ruth to SG, 17 February 1929, BCNYPL.

33. SG, quoted in Edith Stiles, "Susan Glaspell in her Cape Cod Farmhouse," *Boston Evening Transcript*, 15 June 1929.

34. Percy Hutchinson, *New York Times*, 10 November 1929.

35. Neith Boyce to Hutchins Hapgood, BLYU.

Chapter 25: *Alison's House*

1. Vorse, *Time and the Town*, 124. For material on SG's composition of the play, see Rodier, "*Glaspell and Dickinson*," 195–218.

2. SG to Barrett Clark, [April 1930], BLYU.

3. For a comprehensive discussion of the connections between *Alison's House* and the Dickinson biography, see Gainor, *Susan Glaspell in Context*, 220–42.

4. On Taggard, see Showalter, ed., *These Modern Women*, 62–67.

5. SG, *Alison's House*. The following quotations are from this source.

6 Dickinson, quoted in Adrienne Rich, *On Lies, Secrets and Silence* (New York: Norton, 1979), 158.

7. Ozieblo, *Susan Glaspell*, 240.

8. *Outlook*, 12 December 1930, reprinted in Rodier, "*Glaspell and Dickinson*," 198.

9. *New York Times*, 5 December 1930.

10. Georges Lewys, quoted in Sheaffer, *O'Neill: Son and Artist*, 341.

11. Responding to the New York Mint Theatre Company's 1999 production, one critic pointed out that "Ms. Glaspell is exploring here the nature of celebrity and the price of fame. When does a private life become public property?" (Nytheatre.com [http://www.nytheatre.com/nytheatre/archweb/ arch_004.htm].

12. *New York Times*, 1 November 1929.

13. Norman Matson, "Unpublished Autobiographical Novel," 106, NME.

14. SG to Norman Matson, BCNYPL. The following letters are from this archive.

15. *Ambrose Holt and Family*, 8. The following quotations are from this source.

16. John Chamberlain, *New York Times Book Review*, 12 April 1931.

17. Theodore Purdy, *Saturday Review of Literature*, 6 June 1931.

18. Wilson, *The Thirties*, 24.

19. Marguerite Kaselau to Hutchins Hapgood, 1930, BLYU.

20. Norman Matson, fragment, NME.

21. SG, notes, BCNYPL.

22. Although this was the official premiere of the play, it had already been produced by the Liverpool Repertory Theatre on November 5, for a limited run.

23. Josephine Hutchinson, quoted in Sheehy, *Eva LeGallienne*, 155.

24. SG to Norman Matson, BCNYPL. The following letters are from this archive.

25. Robert Littell, *New York World*, 2 December 1930; Brooks Atkinson, *New York Times*, 2 December 1930.

26. Burns Mantle, *Daily News*, 2 December 1930.

27. John Mason Brown, *New York Evening Post*, 2 December 1930.

28. Robert Garland, *New York World-Telegram*, 2 December 1930.

29. R. Dana Skinner, *Commonweal* 13 (17 December 1930).

30. Euphemia Van Rensselaer Wyatt, *Catholic World* 132 (February 1931).

31. Inscription, copy of *Alison's House*, WPC.

32. SG to Barrett Clark, BLYU.

33. Norman Matson to Edmund Wilson and Margaret Canby Wilson, BLYU.

34. Up through 2002 only twelve women have been awarded Pulitzer Prizes for drama.

35. Pulitzer Prize citation, quoted in Hohenberg, *The Pulitzer Prize*, 10. For an extended discussion of the prize, see Gainor, *Susan Glaspell in Context*, 238–42.

36. *New York World-Telegram*, 6 May 1931.

37. Robert Garland, *New York World-Telegram*, 12 May 1931.

38. Brooks Atkinson, *New York Times*, 10 May 1931.

39. R. Dana Skinner, "Letter to the Dramatic Editor," *New York Times*, 17 May 1931; R. Dana Skinner, *Commonweal* 14 (20 May 1931).

40. This is despite the fact that Atkinson did have positive things to say about LeGallienne's revival of *Inheritors* in 1927, focusing on Glaspell's presentation of pioneer ideals which he describes as reinforcing the basic tenets of American life.

41. Nancy Cott, *The Grounding of Modern Feminism*, 274, 272.

42. Walter Prichard, quoted in Gainor, *Susan Glaspell in Context*, 239.

43. SG to Mrs. Levy, BCNYPL.

44. Eugene O'Neill to SG, RCE.

Chapter 26: Break Up

1. SG to Norman Matson, BCNYPL. The following letters are from this archive.

2. *New York Times*, 21 January 1932.

3. SG, quoted in Louise Morgan, *Everyman*, 7 January 1932.

4. Norman Matson, "Unpublished Autobiographical Novel," 17. The following quotations are from this source.

5. For a discussion of the flying imagery in *The Verge* and its connection to feminist theory, see Noe, "The Verge," 129–42.

6. SG to Richard Hughes, Richard Hughes manuscripts, LLIU.

7. Anna Matson Hamburger, interviews by author, Wellfleet, Massachusetts, July 1987 and New York City, September 1990.

8. Dorothy Smith to SG, 10 May 1932, BCNYPL.

9. Norman Matson to SG. The following letters are from this archive.

10. Coast guard officer, quoted in SG to Norman Matson, BCNYU. The following events are described in this letter.

11. Ann Walling to SG, 13 September 1932, BCNYPL.

12. SG to Anna Walling, BCNYPL. The letter is reprinted in Noe, *Susan Glaspell*, 63–64.

13. Anna Matson Hamburger, interview by the author, New York City, September 1990.

14. See Papke, *Susan Glaspell*, 81–84, for selected reviews.

15. Joseph Wood Krutch, *Nation* 136 (10 May 1933).

16. Percy Hammond, *New York Herald Tribune*, 30 April 1933.

17. Robert Garland, *New York World-Telegram*, 20 April 1931.

18. SG, quoted in *Des Moines Daily Register*, 1931, reprinted in the *Iowa Historical Society Record*, entry on Susan Glaspell, dated 16 July 1947.

19. SG, quoted in Noe, *Susan Glaspell*, 9.

20. Norman Matson quoted in SG to Norman Matson, BCNYPL.

21. Anna Matson Hamburger, interview by the author, New York City, September 1990.

Chapter 27: The Federal Theatre Project

1. Blanche Hays to Edna Kenton, 16 October 1933, BLCOL.

2. Norman Matson to SG, BCNYPL. The following letters are from this archive.

3. Wilson, *The Thirties*, 307.

4. Information about Langston Moffett and his relationship with Susan are confirmed through interviews by the author with Mary Hackett. Other information about Moffett came from an interview by the author with Claudia Moffett and letters from Langston Moffett. I thank them for their assistance, and thank Gail Cohen for making the connection with Claudia and Langston Moffett.

5. SG, "John Noble," *New York Herald Tribune Magazine*, 13 May 1934.

6. SG to Langston Moffett, LME.

7. *New York Times*, 4 February 1934.

8. Nilla Cook, quoted in Lawrence Griswold, "At 40 and 200 Pounds Plus," *Sunday Mirror Magazine*, 12 February 1950, SLCC.

9. SG to Norman Matson, BCNYPL. The following letters are from this archive.

10. Only nine years after insulin was tested for use in diabetes treatment, Glaspell discussed the disease and injections in her 1931 novel *Ambrose Holt and Family*, probably taking her information from direct observation of Harl's illness and treatment.

11. Leonora Cook, letter to the author, 20 July 1987.

12. *Land of the Whatsit: Stories of Billy and Betty*, ed. C. D. Morris, 1935, 55–56, BCNYPL.

13. Marguerite Kaselau to Hutchins Hapgood, BLYU.

14. Wilson, *The Thirties*, 475.

15. Marguerite Kaselau to Hutchins Hapgood, 16 August, BLYU. The same scene is repeated in Wilson, *The Thirties*, 485, who adds the last quotation.

16. Heaton Vorse, interview by the author, Provincetown, August 1988.

17. Mary Hackett, interview by the author, Provincetown, August 1988.

18. Mary Hackett, interview by the author, Provincetown, August 1988. See also Wilson, *The Thirties*, 477.

19. *Provincetown Advocate*, 22 May 1934.

20. *New York Times*, 24 May 1935.

21. *Provincetown Advocate*, 13 August 1935; *New York Times*, 10 August 1935.

22. SG to Clifford Odets, LLIU.

23. Dorothy Meyer, interview by the author, New York City, January 1990.

24. Wilson, *The Thirties*, 485.

25. SG to Barrett Clark, 7 October 1936, BLYU.

26. Leverich, *Tom*, 267.

27. SG to R. W. Cowden, Hopwood Committee, 14 May 1937, UM. See also Sporn, *Against Itself*, 292.

28. For an extensive discussion of SG's work with the Federal Theatre Project and particularly with Sundgaard, see Ozieblo, *Susan Glaspell*, 255–63.

29. Arnold Sundgaard, "Susan Glaspell and the Federal Theatre Revisited," *Journal of American Drama and Theatre* 9.1 (winter 1997).

30. Sundgaard, quoted in Ozieblo, *Susan Glaspell*, 255.

31. For details about the production and the controversy, see Fraden, *Blueprints for a Black Federal Theatre, 1935–1939*. See also Howard Miller to George Kondolf, 8 November 1937; Howard Miller to SG, 5 November 1937; and Harry Minturn to SG, 20 December 1937, NA.

32. Sundgaard, quoted in Ozieblo, *Susan Glaspell*, 258.

33. Flanagan, *Arena*, 70.

34. For a discussion of the production, see John O'Connor, "*Spirochete* and the War on Syphilis," TDR (March 1977), 91–98.

35. SG to Hallie Flanagan, 18 April 1938, NA.

36. Quoted in Flanagan, *Arena*, 355.

Chapter 28: A Different War

1. Wilson, *The Thirties*, 707.

2. John Dos Passos to Hutchins Hapgood, 8 September 1938, BLYU.

3. Vorse, *Time and the Town*, 329.

4. John Francis, quoted in *Provincetown Advocate*, 2 September 1937.

5. SG, quoted in Phyllis Duganne to Arthur Waterman. The letter offers anecdotes about Susan and Flossie. I thank him for making the letter available to me.

6. *The Glory of the Conquered*, 46.

7. Floyd Dell to Arthur Waterman, 10 March 1954. I thank him for making the letter available to me.

8. Leonora Cook, letter to the author, 20 July 1987.

9. SG, notebook, BCNYPL.

10. *The Morning Is Near Us*, 295.

11. Hapgood, *A Victorian in the Modern World*, 375.

12. Hutchins Hapgood to Neith Boyce 2 October 1939, BLYU.

13. Dorothy Meyer, interview by the author, January 1990.

14. Frank Chase, quoted in *New York Herald Tribune*, 31 March 1940.

15. SG to Jasper Deeter, 27 February, BU.

16. SG to Martha Robinson, 27 February 1940, RCE.

17. Dorothy Meyer, interview by the author, New York City, January 1990.

18. Miriam Hapgood Dewitt, interview by the author, Provincetown, August 1988.

19. SG, quoted by Dorothy Meyer, interview by author, New York City, January 1990.

20. Francelina Sousa Hubbard, interview by the author, Boston, October 1988.

21. Dorothy Meyer, interview by the author, New York City, January 1990.

22. SG, *Cherished and Shared of Old*. The following quotations are from this source.

23. Foreword to *The Road to the Temple*, (1941), x.

24. *Norma Ashe*, 299–300. The following quotations are from this source.

25. *Norma Ashe*, back cover.

26. *Norma Ashe*, 158.

27. SG to Jasper Deeter, 12 December 1942, BU.

28. Petition, YIVO collection. My thanks to Edna Nachshon for calling it to my attention.

29. SG to Edmund Wilson, BLYU.

30. SG to Jasper Deeter, 7 January, BU.

31. Dorothy Meyer, interview by the author, New York City, January 1990.

32. SG, quoted in Phyllis Duganne [Given] to Edmund Wilson, 18 January 1943, BLYU.

33. This and the following information comes from interviews by the author with Francelina Sousa Hubbard, Boston, October 1988 and May 1989.

34. SG to Harrison Smith, 14 March 1942, PUA.

35. SG, "Notes for Biographical Sketch," SLCC. The following description comes from this source. See also *Provincetown Advocate*, 25 June 1942, 16 July 1942, and 17 September 1942.

36. SG to Martha Robinson, RCE.

37. SG drafts of letter to George Stevens, 7 September [1942], BCNYPL. The following quotations are from this source.

38. "Notes for Book Fair Speech," BCNYPL.

39. Lippincott advertising manager, quoted in SG to Martha Robinson, RGE.

40. "Susan Glaspell Says We Need Books Today as Never Before," *Chicago Sunday Tribune*, 6 December 1942.

Chapter 29: Completing the Circle

1. References to "Springs Eternal" come from the unpublished manuscript found in the BCNYPL. The following quotations are from this source.

2. *Norma Ashe*, 158.

3. SG to Lawrence Langner, [March 1944], BLYU.

4. Lawrence Langner to SG, 19 May 1944, BLYU.

5. SG to Eva LeGallienne, 26 May 1944, BRTC.

6. SG to Eva LeGallienne, BRTC.

7. It will be published for the first time in the *Complete Plays of Susan Glaspell*, ed. Linda Ben-Zvi and Ellen J. Gainor (forthcoming).

8. *Judd Rankin's Daughter*, 216. The following quotations are from this source.

9. SG to Edmund Wilson, BLYU. The following letters are from this archive.

10. SG, quoted in the *Provincetown Advocate*, 28 March 1946.

11. Florence Haxton Bullock, *Chicago Sun Book Week*, 28 October 1943.

12. F. W. Leary, *New York Times*, 4 November 1945.

13. Phyllis Duganne [Given] to Edmund Wilson, 28 November 1945, BLYU.

14. SG to Edmund Wilson, BLYU. The following quotations from SG's letters to Wilson are from this archive.

15. *Provincetown Advocate*, 28 March 1946.

16. "Notes on How to Write a Novel," BCNYPL.

17. "Bastards I Have Known," 11 December 1945, BCNYPL.

18. "Notes on Growing Older," BCNYPL. The following quotations are from this source.

19. SG to Langston Moffett, LME.

20. *Judd Rankin's Daughter*, 14–15.

21. Sirius Cook, interview by the author, New York City, October 1987.

22. SG to Neith Boyce, 19 February 1944, BCNYPL.

23. Dorothy Meyer, interview by the author, New York City, January 1990.

24. SG, *Provincetown Advocate*, 18 June 1946.

25. *Provincetown Advocate*, 11 July 1946.

26. Catharine Huntington to Mary Heaton Vorse, 20 March, WRLWSU. The letter describes SG's help on production of *Alison's House* at the Provincetown Playhouse on the Wharf in 1946.

27. *Judd Rankin's Daughter*, 139.

28. Grace Collinson, interview by the author, Provincetown, July 1987.

29. George Bryant, interview by the author, Provincetown, August 1988.

30. *Provincetown Advocate*, 29 July 1948.

31. Bank statements in BCNYPL.

32. Francelina Sousa Hubbard, interviews by the author, Boston, October 1988 and May 1989. The following information comes from these interviews, including details of Susan's death.

33. Madie L'Engle, interview by the author, Provincetown, July 1988.

34. *Fidelity*, 413.

35. "Springs Eternal," 3.34, BCNYPL.

36. "On Stanislavki's *My Life in Art*," BCNYPL.

37. The saint is the mother of Mary, grandmother of Jesus, and is known and worshiped as the protector of children, married women, and those seeking husbands, having married three times herself. Langston Moffett had attached significance to St. Anne's day since it was then Susan and he had visited St. Anne de Beaupré's shrine in Quebec.

38. Mary Heaton Vorse to Joel O'Brien, 29 July 1948, WRLWSU. The following quotations are from this source.

39. She was cremated at the Forest Hills cemetery, Boston, the same cemetery where Eugene O'Neill would be interred five years later. An Associated Press story, printed in the *New York Times* on 30 July 1948, indicated that SG's ashes were to buried in Truro. However, Francelina Hubbard Sousa remembers them being scattered behind Susan's Truro house, the favorite of her homes. An account in the *Provincetown Advocate* indicates the same.

40. *New York Times*, 28 July 1948.

41. *Provincetown Advocate*, 29 July 1948.

42. John Dos Passos, quoted in Mary Heaton Vorse Diary, 7 August 1948, WRLWSU.

Bibliography

The majority of Glaspell and Cook papers—manuscripts, drafts, diaries, correspondence, reviews, and personal items—are located in the Berg Collection of English and American Literature, New York Public Library. The following libraries have additional Glaspell holdings: Clifton Waller Barrett Library of American Literature, University of Virginia: letters to and from Glaspell, poems, notebook, and reviews; Harvard Theatre Collection, Houghton Library: letters to and from Glaspell; Yale Collection of American Literature, Beinecke Rare Book and Manuscript Library: letters from Glaspell; Davenport Public Library: letters to and from Glaspell, genealogy documents; Drake University: *Delphic* short stories and essays; University Libraries, University of Iowa: letters to and from Glaspell; Billy Rose Theatre Collection, New York Public Library for the Performing Arts: miscellaneous materials concerning Glaspell's plays; National Archives, Washington, D.C., Records of the Federal Theatre Project and Works Projects Administration: letters to and from Glaspell and materials concerning the Midwest Bureau she headed; Howard Gottlieb Archival Research Center at Boston University, Hedgerow Theatre collection: letters to and from Glaspell; Rare Books and Manuscript Library, Columbia University: letters to Glaspell; Newberry Library, Chicago: letters from and to Glaspell; Lilly Library, University of Indiana: letter from Glaspell; University of Michigan Special Collections Library, Hopwood Award Archives: Letter from Glaspell.

An essential book for Susan Glaspell study is Papke, *Susan Glaspell: A Research and Production Source Book*, cited below. It contains extensive summaries of her novels and plays and information about their critical reception; an annotated list of most of her short stories, essays, and nonfiction writing; and an annotated list of reviews and secondary critical research through 1992. Additional bibliographies on Glaspell can be found in Ben-Zvi, *Susan Glaspell: Essays on Her Theatre and Fiction*; Black, *Women of Provincetown, 1915–1922*; Carpentier, *The Major Novels of Susan Glaspell*; Gainor, *Susan Glaspell in Context*; Noe, "A Critical Biography of Susan Glaspell"; and Ozieblo, *Susan Glaspell: A Critical Biography*, all cited below.

For bibliography on George Cram Cook, a central source is Tanselle, *George Cram Cook and the Poetry of Living*, cited below, which includes works by and about Cook and reviews of his writings through 1972. See also bibliographies in Kemper, "The Novels, Plays, and Poetry of George Cram Cook, Founder of the Provincetown Players," and Sarlós, *Jig Cook and the Provincetown Players*, cited below.

For material on the Provincetown Players, in addition to Black, *Women of Provincetown, 1915–1922*, and Sarlós, *Jig Cook and the Provincetown Players*, see Bach, *Susan Glaspell und die Provincetown Players*; Deutsch and Hanau, *The Provincetown: A Story of the Theatre*; and Kenton, "The Provincetown Players and the Playwrights' Theatre," all cited below.

Works by Susan Glaspell: American Publications

NOVELS

The Glory of the Conquered. New York: Frederick A. Stokes, 1909.
The Visioning. New York: Frederick A. Stokes, 1911.
Fidelity. Boston: Small, Maynard, 1915.
Brook Evans. New York: Frederick A. Stokes, 1928.
Fugitive's Return. New York: Frederick A. Stokes, 1929.
Ambrose Holt and Family. New York: Frederick A Stokes, 1931.
The Morning is Near Us. New York: Frederick A. Stokes, 1940.
Norma Ashe. Philadelphia: J. B. Lippincott, 1942.
Judd Rankin's Daughter. Philadelphia: J. B. Lippincott, 1945.

PLAYS

Plays. Boston: Small, Maynard, 1920. This edition contains *Trifles, The People, Close the Book, The Outside, Woman's Honor, Suppressed Desires, Tickless Time*, and *Bernice*. (For other editions, see Ben-Zvi, *Susan Glaspell*.)
"Chains of Dew." Unpublished typescript. Library of Congress, Washington, D.C., 1920.
Inheritors. Boston: Small, Maynard, 1921.
The Verge. Boston: Small, Maynard, 1922.
The Comic Artist. New York: Frederick A. Stokes, 1927.
Alison's House. New York: Samuel French, 1930.
Plays by Susan Glaspell. Edited by C. W. E. Bigsby. Cambridge: Cambridge Univ. Press, 1987. This edition contains *Trifles, The Outside, The Verge*, and *Inheritors*.

Complete Plays by Susan Glaspell. Edited by Linda Ben-Zvi and J. Ellen *Gainor.* Jefferson, N.C.: McFarland, 2005. This edition contains *Suppressed Desires, Trifles, The People, Close the Book, The Outside, Woman's Honor, Tickless Time, Bernice, Inheritors, The Verge, Chains of Dew, Alison's House, The Comic Artist,* and *Springs Eternal.*

SHORT STORIES

The following works are in addition to those contained in the annotated list of short stories appearing in Papke, *Susan Glaspell.*

"His Literary Training." *Delphic,* January 1898.
"The Unprofessional Crime." *Delphic.* February 1900.
"The Work of the Unloved Libby." *Black Cat,* August 1904.
"From the *Pen of Failures.*" *Quax,* 1905.
Lifted Masks. 1912. Reprinted *Lifted Masks and Other Works,* edited by Eric S. Rabkin, Ann Arbor: Univ. of Michigan Press, 1993.

POETRY, BIOGRAPHY, AND CHILDREN'S FICTION

"Joe." *The Masses* 8 (January 1916).
Greek Coins: Poems by George Cram Cook. New York: George Doran, 1925. This posthumous collection of Jig's poetry was edited by Glaspell.
The Road to the Temple. New York: Frederick A. Stokes, 1927. Reprint, with a new foreword by the author, New York: Frederick A. Stokes, 1941. Reprint, edited by Linda Ben-Zvi, Jefferson, N.C.: McFarland, 2005.
Cherished and Shared of Old. Illustrated by Alice Harvey. New York: Julian Messner, Inc. 1940.

ESSAYS AND NONFICTION

"In Memoriam." *Delphic* 15 (February 1899).
"Bismarck and European Politics." *Delphic* 15 (March 1899).
"Dwellers on Parnassos." *New Republic* 33 (17 January 1923).
"Last Days in Greece." In *Greek Coins: Poems by George Cram Cook,* edited by Susan Glaspell, 31–49. New York: George Doran, 1925.
"John Noble." *New York Herald Tribune Magazine* (13 May 1934).

Works Cited

For newspaper reviews and news articles, see Notes.

Anderson, Margaret. *My Thirty Years' War.* New York: Covici, Friede, 1930.
Anderson, Sherwood. *Letters of Sherwood Anderson.* Edited by Howard Mumford Jones and Walter B. Rideout. Boston: Little, Brown, 1953.
———. *Memoirs.* Edited by Ray Lewis White. Chapel Hill: Univ. of North Carolina Press, 1969.
Andrews, Clarence. *A Literary History of Iowa.* Iowa City: Univ. of Iowa Press, 1972.

Angel, Marina. "A Classical Greek Influence on an American Feminist: Susan Glaspell's Debt to Aristophanes." *Syracuse Law Review* 52.1 (2002): 81–103.

———. "Criminal Law and Women: Giving the Abused Woman who Kills 'A Jury of Her Peers' who Appreciate *Trifles.*" *American Criminal Law Review* 33.2 (winter 1996): 229–348.

———. "Susan Glaspell's *Trifles* and "A Jury of Her Peers: Women Abuse in a Literary and Legal Context," *Buffalo Law Review* 45.3 (fall 1997): 779–844.

Aston, Elaine. "From Glaspell to Daniels," Common Threads Conference, Tel Aviv University, 1998 (unpublished).

Auerbach, Nina. *Ellen Terry, Player in Her Time.* New York: W. W. Norton., 1989.

Bach, Gerhard. *Susan Glaspell und die Provincetown Players: Die Anfänge des modernen amerikanischen Dramas und Theaters.* Frankfurt am Main: Peter Lang, 1979. This work is in German, with the bibliography in English.

Banks, Charles Eugene, and Marshall Everett [pseudonym of Henry Neil], assisted by George Cram Cook. *American Home Culture and Correct Customs of Polite Society.* Chicago: Bible House, 1902.

Barlow, Judith. Introduction to *Plays by American Women: The Early Years.* 1981. Reprint, New York: Applause Books, 1985.

———. "Susan's Sisters: The 'Other' Women Writers of the Provincetown Players," In *Susan Glaspell: Essays on Her Theater and Fiction*, edited by Linda Ben-Zvi, 259–300. Ann Arbor: Univ. of Michigan Press, 1995.

Barnes, Djuna, "The Days of Jig Cook," *Theatre Guild Magazine* 6 (January 1929): 31–32.

Beard, Rick, and Leslie Cohen Berlowitz, eds. *Greenwich Village: Culture and Counterculture.* New Brunswick, N.J.: Rutgers Univ. Press, 1993.

Ben-Zvi, Linda. "'Murder, She Wrote': The Genesis of Susan Glaspell's *Trifles.*" *Theatre Journal* 44 (1992). Reprint in *Susan Glaspell: Essays on Her Theatre and Fiction*, edited by Linda Ben-Zvi, 19–48. Ann Arbor: Univ. of Michigan Press, 1995.

———, ed. *Susan Glaspell: Essays on Her Theatre and Fiction.* Ann Arbor: Univ. of Michigan Press, 1995.

———. "Susan Glaspell and Eugene O'Neill." *Eugene O'Neill Newsletter* 6.2 (summer/fall 1982): 21–29.

———. "Susan Glaspell, Eugene O'Neill and the Imagery of Gender." *Eugene O'Neill Newsletter* 10.1 (spring 1986): 22–27.

———. "Susan Glaspell's Contribution to Contemporary Women Playwrights." In *Feminine Focus: The New Women Playwrights*, edited by Enoch Brater, 147–66. New York: Oxford Univ. Press, 1989.

Bigsby, C. W. E., ed. *A Critical Introduction to Twentieth-Century American Drama.* Vol. 1: 1900–1940. Cambridge: Cambridge Univ. Press, 1982.

———. Introduction to *Plays by Susan Glaspell.* Cambridge: Cambridge Univ. Press, 1989.

Black, Cheryl. *Women of Provincetown, 1915–1922.* Tuscaloosa: Univ. of Alabama Press, 2002.

Black, Stephen. *Eugene O'Neill: Beyond Mourning and Tragedy.* New Haven: Yale Univ. Press, 1999.

Bölsche, Wilhelm. *Haeckel: His Life and Work.* Translated by Joseph McCabe. Philadelphia: George W. Jacobs, 1907.

Boulton, Agnes. *Part of a Long Story.* London: Peter Davies, 1958.

Brenman-Gibson, Margaret. *Clifford Odets.* Boston: Athenaeum, 1981.

Brevda, William. *The Last Bohemian: The Life of Harry Kemp.* Lewisburg, Pa.: Bucknell Univ. Press, 1986.

Brittin, Norman. *Edna St. Vincent Millay.* Boston: Twayne, 1967.

Brown, Frederick. *Theater and Revolution.* New York: Viking Press, 1980.

Browne, Maurice. *Too Late to Lament: An Autobiography.* London: Victor Gollancz, 1955.

Bryan, Patricia and Thomas Wolf. *Midnight Assassin: The Hossack Case.* Chapel Hill, N.C.: Algonquin Books (forthcoming).

Burrows, J. M. D. "Fifty Years in Iowa." 1888. Reprinted in *The Early Day[sic] of Rock Island and Davenport,* edited by Milo Milton Quaife, Chicago: Lakeside Press, 1942.

Carpentier, Martha. *The Major Novels of Susan Glaspell.* Tallahassee: Univ. Press of Florida, 2001.

Chafee, Zechariah, Jr. *Freedom of Speech.* New York: Harcourt, Brace, and Jovanovich, 1920.

Chesler, Ellen. *Woman of Valor: Margaret Sanger and the Birth Control Movement.* New York: Simon and Schuster, 1992.

Chevigny, Bell Gale. "Daughters Writing: Toward a Theory of Women's Biography." In *Between Women,* edited by Carol Ascher et al., 357–80. Boston: Beacon Press, 1984.

Clark, Barrett. *Eugene O'Neill: The Man and his Plays.* New York: Dover, 1926.

———, ed. *European Theories of the Drama.* 1918. Reprint, revised by Henry Popkin, New York: Crown, 1972.

Clayton, Douglas. *Floyd Dell: The Life and Times of an American Rebel.* Chicago: Ivan R. Dee, 1994.

Cohn, Ruby. *From Desire to Godot.* Berkeley: Univ. of California Press, 1987.

Cook, George Cram. *The Athenian Women.* With the original text and a modern Greek translation by the author and revised by C. Carthaios. Athens: Printing House "Estia," 1926.

———. *The Chasm.* New York: Frederick A. Stokes, 1911.

———. *The Spring.* New York: Frank Shay, 1921.

———, and Frank Shay, eds. *The Provincetown Plays.* Cincinnati: Stewart Kidd, 1921.

Cook, Nilla. *My Road to India.* New York: Lee Furman, 1939.

Cott, Nancy. *The Grounding of Modern Feminism.* New Haven, Conn.: Yale Univ. Press, 1987.

Cowley, Malcolm. *Exile's Return.* New York: Penguin, 1976.

Dell, Floyd. *Homecoming: An Autobiography.* New York: Farrar and Rinehart, 1933.

———. *Intellectual Vagabondage.* 1926. Reprint, edited by Douglas Clayton, Chicago: Ivan R. Dee, 1990.

———. *Love in Greenwich Village.* New York: George H. Doran, 1926.

———. *Love in the Machine Age.* London: Routledge, 1930.

———. *Moon-Calf.* New York: Knopf, 1920.

Deutsch, Helen, and Stella Hanau. *The Provincetown: A Story of the Theatre.* New York: Russell and Russell, 1931.

Dewitt, Miriam Hapgood. *Taos: A Memoir.* Albuquerque: Univ. of New Mexico Press, 1992.

Diggins, John. *The Rise and Fall of the American Left.* New York: Norton, 1992.

Downer, Harry. *A History of Davenport and Scott County Iowa*. Vol. 1. Chicago: S. J. Clarke, 1910.

Dreiser, Theodore. *A Book About Myself*. New York: Boni and Liveright, 1922.

Duffey, Bernard. *The Chicago Renaissance*. East Lansing: Michigan State Univ. Press, 1954.

Duncan, Hugh Dalziel. *The Rise of Chicago as a Literary Center, 1885–1920*. Bedminster, N.J.: Totowa Press, 1964.

Duncan, Isadora. *My Life*. New York: Liveright, 1940.

Eastman, Max. *Enjoyment of Living*. New York: Harper and Bros., 1948.

Egan, Leora Rust. *Provincetown as a Stage*. Orleans, Mass.: Parnassus Imprints, 1994.

Emerson, Ralph Waldo. *Essays and Poems*. New York: Penguin Books, 1996.

Falk, Candace. *Love, Anarchy, and Emma Goldman*. New Brunswick, N.J.: Rutgers Univ. Press, 1990.

Farnham, Emily. *Charles Demuth: Behind a Laughing Mask*. Norman: Univ. of Oklahoma Press, 1971.

Ferguson, Mary Anne, ed. *Images of Women in Literature*. Boston: Houghton Mifflin, 1973.

Fishbein, Leslie. "The Culture of Contradiction." In *Greenwich Village: Culture and Counterculture*, edited by Rick Beard and Leslie Cohen Berlowitz, 212–28. New Brunswick, N.J.: Rutgers Univ. Press, 1993.

———. *Rebels in Bohemia: The Radicals of The Masses, 1911–1917*. Chapel Hill: Univ. of North Carolina Press, 1982.

Ficke, Charles A. *Memories of Fourscore Years*. Davenport: Graphic Services, 1930.

Flanagan, Hallie. *Arena: The History of the Federal Theatre*. New York: Benjamin Blom, 1940.

Fraden, Rena. *Blueprints for a Black Federal Theatre, 1935–1939*. New York: Cambridge Univ. Press, 1996.

Fuller, Henry. *The Cliff-Dwellers*. 1893. Reprint, Ridgewood, NJ: Gregg Press, 1968.

Fuller, Margaret. *Summer on the Lakes in 1843*. Edited by Arthur B. Fuller. 1856. Reprint, New York: Haskell House Press, 1970.

Gainor, J. Ellen. "Chains of Dew and the Drama of Birth Control." In *Susan Glaspell: Essays on Her Theatre and Fiction*, edited by Linda Ben-Zvi, 165–94. Ann Arbor: Univ. of Michigan Press, 1995.

———. *Susan Glaspell in Context*. Ann Arbor: Univ. of Michigan Press, 2001.

Gardner, Virginia. *Friend and Lover: The Life of Louise Bryant*. New York: Horizon Press, 1982.

Garrison, Dee. *Mary Heaton Vorse*. Philadelphia: Temple Univ. Press, 1989.

Gelb, Barbara, and Arthur Gelb. *O'Neill*. New York: Harper and Bros. 1962.

———. *O'Neill: Life With Monte Cristo*. New York: Applause Books, 2000.

Giffin, Frederic C. *Six Who Protested*. Port Washington, NY: Kennikat Press, 1977.

Goldberg, Isaac. *The Drama of Transition*. Cincinnati: Steward Kidd, 1922.

Goldman, Emma. *Living My Life*. 2 vols. 1932. Reprint, New York: Dover Press, 1970.

———. *The Social Significance of Modern Drama*. 1914. Reprint, New York: Applause Theatre Books, 1987.

Golin, Steven. *The Fragile Bridge: The Paterson Silk Strike*. Philadelphia: Temple Univ. Press, 1988.

Green, Martin. *New York 1913*. New York: Charles Scribners' Sons, 1988.

Hapgood, Hutchins. *The Spirit of the Ghetto*. 1902. Reprint, edited by E. Moses Rischin, Cambridge: Harvard Univ. Press, 1967.

———. *A Victorian in the Modern World*. 1939. Reprint, edited by Robert Allen Skotheim. Seattle: Univ. of Washington Press, 1972.

Hedges, Elaine. "Small Things Reconsidered: 'A Jury of Her Peers.'" In *Susan Glaspell: Essays on Her Theatre and Fiction*, edited by Linda Ben-Zvi, 49–70. Ann Arbor: Univ. of Michigan Press, 1995.

Heilbrun, Carolyn. *Writing a Woman's Life*. New York: Norton, 1988.

Heller, Adele, and Lois Rudnick, eds. *1915: The Cultural Moment*. New Brunswick, N.J.: Rutgers Univ. Press, 1991.

Herrick, Robert. *Chimes*. New York: Macmillan, 1926.

Herring, Phillip. *Djuna*. New York: Penguin, 1995.

Hohenberg, John. *The Pulitzer Prize*. New York: Columbia Univ. Press, 1974.

Johns, Orrik. *Time of Our Lives*. New York: Strackpole, 1937.

Jones, Ann. *Women Who Kill*. New York: Holt, Rinehart and Winston, 1980.

Jones, Robert Edmond. *The Dramatic Imagination*. 1941. Reprint, New York: Theatre Arts Books, 1969.

Kellner, Bruce. *Carl Van Vechten and the Irreverent Decades*. Norman: Univ. of Oklahoma Press, 1968.

Kemp, Harry. *Love Among the Cape Enders*. New York: Macauly, 1931.

———. "Turned Down in Provincetown: O'Neill's Debut Reexamined." *Theatre Magazine*, April 1930.

Kemper, Susan. "The Novels, Plays, and Poetry of George Cram Cook, Founder of the Provincetown Players." Ph.D. diss., Bowling Green University, 1982.

Kenton, Edna. "The Provincetown Players and the Playwrights' Theatre" (1931), edited by Travis Bogard and Jackson R. Bryer, *Eugene O'Neill Review* 21.1–2 (fall 1997): 15–160.

King, William Davies, ed. *A Wind Is Rising: The Correspondence of Agnes Boulton and Eugene O'Neill*. Rutherford, N.J.: Farleigh Dickinson Univ. Press, 2000.

———. "The O'Neill of Pulp Fiction," *Eugene O'Neill Review*, 26 (2004): 105–117.

Kolodny, Annette. "A Map for Rereading: Or, Gender, and the Interpretation of Literary Texts." In *The New Feminist Criticism: Essays on Women, Literature, and Theory*, edited by Elaine Showalter, 46–62. New York: Pantheon Books, 1985.

Kunitz, Stanley and Howard Haycroft, eds. *Twentieth Century Authors: A Biographical Dictionary of Modern Literature*. New York: H. H. Wilson, 1942.

Langner, Lawrence. *The Magic Curtain*. New York: E. P. Dutton, 1951.

Larabee, Ann. "Death in Delphi: Susan Glaspell and the Companionate Marriage," *Mid-American Review* 7.2 (1987): 93–106.

Lawrence, D. H. *Studies in Classic American Literature*. 1923. Reprint, New York: Viking Press, 1969.

LeGallienne, Eva. *At 33*. New York: Longmans, Green, 1934.

Leverich, Lyle. *Tom: The Unknown Tennessee Williams*. New York, Crown, 1995.

Lewis, Sinclair. *Main Street*. New York: Harcourt, Brace, and World, 1948.

Lewisohn, Ludwig. *Drama and the Stage*. New York: Harcourt Brace, 1922.
———. *Expressionism in America*. New York: Harpers, 1932.
Luhan, Mabel Dodge. *Movers and Shakers*. Vol. 3 of *Intimate Memories*. 1936. Reprint, Albuquerque: Univ. of New Mexico Press, 1985.
Lynes, Barbara Buhler. *O'Keeffe, Stieglitz and the Critics, 1916–1929*. Chicago: Univ. of Chicago Press, 1989.
Maeterlinck, Maurice. *On Emerson and Other Essays*. Translated by Montrose J. Moses. New York: Dodd, Mead, 1912.
———. "The Tragical in Daily Life." In *The Treasure of the Humble*, translated by Alfred Sutro, 1916. Reprinted as "The Tragic in Daily Life," in *Playwrights on Playwriting*, edited by Toby Cole, New York: Hill and Wang, 1965.
Makowsky, Veronica. *Susan Glaspell's Century of American Women*. New York: Oxford Univ. Press, 1993.
Malpede, Karen. "Reflections on *The Verge*." In *Susan Glaspell: Essays on Her Theater and Fiction*, edited by Linda Ben-Zvi, 123–28. Ann Arbor: Univ. of Michigan Press, 1995.
May, Henry F. *The End of American Innocence*. New York: Knopf, 1959.
McMichael, George. *Journey to Obscurity: The Life of Octave Thanet*. Lincoln: Univ. of Nebraska Press, 1982.
Noe, Marcia. "A Critical Biography of Susan Glaspell." Ph.D. diss., University of Iowa, 1976.
———. *Susan Glaspell: Voice from the Heartland*. Western Illinois Monograph Series, 1983. [This is a shortened version of "A Critical Biography of Susan Glaspell."]
———. "*The Verge*: L'Écriture Féminine at the Provincetown." In *Susan Glaspell: Essays on Her Theatre and Fiction*, edited by Linda Ben-Zvi, 129–44. Ann Arbor: Univ. of Michigan Press, 1995.
Noggle, Bert. *Into the Twenties*. Champaign, IL: Univ. of Illinois Press, 1974.
Norman, Dorothy. *Alfred Stieglitz: An American Seer*. New York: Aperture, 1960.
O'Neill, Eugene. *Selected Letters of Eugene O'Neill*. Edited by Travis Bogard and Jackson R. Bryer. New Haven, Conn.: Yale Univ. Press, 1988.
———, and Kenneth Macgowan. *The Theatre We Worked For: The Letters of Eugene O'Neill and Kenneth Macgowan*. Edited by Jackson R. Bryer and Travis Bogard. New Haven, Conn.: Yale Univ. Press, 1982.
O'Neill, William, ed. *Echoes of Revolt: The Masses, 1911–1917*. Chicago: Ivan R. Dee, 1966.
Ozieblo, Barbara. "Suppression and Society in Susan Glaspell's Theatre." In *Susan Glaspell: Essays on Her Theatre and Fiction*, edited by Linda Ben-Zvi, 105–22. Ann Arbor: Univ. of Michigan Press, 1995.
———. *Susan Glaspell: A Critical Biography*. Chapel Hill: Univ. of North Carolina Press, 2000.
Papke, Mary. *Susan Glaspell: A Research and Production Sourcebook*. Westport, Conn.: Greenwood, 1993.
Paul, Norman H. "Jacques Copeau Looks at the American Stage, 1917–1919." *Educational Theatre Journal* 29 (March 1977): 67–68.
Peterson, H. C., and Gilbert Fite. *Opponents of the War: 1917–1918*. Madison: Univ. of Wisconsin Press, 1957.
Plumbe, John Peter. *Sketches of Iowa and Wisconsin*. 1839. Reprint, Des Moines: State Historical Society of Iowa, 1948.

Pollitzer, Anita. *Lovingly, Georgia: The Complete Correspondence of Georgia O'Keeffe and Anita Pollitzer.* Edited by Clive Giboire. New York: Simon and Schuster, 1990.

———. *A Woman on Paper: Georgia O'Keeffe.* New York: Simon and Schuster, 1988.

Post, Robert C. *1876: A Centennial Exhibition.* Washington, D.C.: National Museum of History and Technology, 1975.

Prevots, Naima. *American Pageantry: A Movement for Art and Democracy.* Ann Arbor: UMI, 1980.

Rich, Adrienne. *On Lies, Secrets and Silence: Selected Prose 1966–1978.* New York. W. W. Norton, 1979.

Richwine, Keith. "The Liberal Club: 1912–1918." Ph.D. diss., University of Pennsylvania, 1968.

Riley, Glenda. *Women and Indians on the Frontier, 1825–1915.* Albuquerque Univ. of New Mexico Press, 1984.

Roba, William. *A History of the Quad-Cities, 1812–1960.* Davenport: Hesperian Press, 1986.

Roberts, Nancy, and Arthur W. Roberts, eds. *"As Ever, Gene": The Letters of Eugene O'Neill and George Jean Nathan.* Rutherford: Farleigh Dickinson Press, 1987.

Rodier, Katharine. "Glaspell and Dickinson: Surveying the Premises of *Alison's House.*" In *Susan Glaspell: Essays on Her Theatre and Fiction,* edited by Linda Ben-Zvi, 195–218. Ann Arbor: Univ. of Michigan Press, 1995.

Rosenstone, Robert. *Romantic Rebel: The Life of John Reed.* New York: Viking Press, 1981.

Rudnick, Lois. *Mabel Dodge Luhan.* Albuquerque: Univ. of New Mexico Press, 1984.

Sarlós, Robert Károly. *Jig Cook and the Provincetown Players.* Boston: Univ. of Massachusetts Press, 1982.

Sayler, Oliver. *Our American Theatre.* New York: B. Blom, 1971.

Schwarz, Judith. *Radical Feminists of Heterodoxy: Greenwich Village, 1912–1940.* Lebanon, N.H.: New Victoria Press, 1982.

Shay, Edith, and Frank Shay. *Sand in their Shoes: A Cape Cod Reader.* Orleans: Parnassas Imprints, 1951. Reprint, 1982.

Sheaffer, Louis. *O'Neill: Son and Artist.* Boston: Little, Brown, 1973.

———. *O'Neill: Son and Playwright.* Boston: Little, Brown, 1968.

Sheehy, Helen. *Eva LeGallienne.* New York: Alfred A., Knopf, 1992.

Showalter, Elaine, ed. "Common Threads." In *Sister's Choice: Tradition and Change in American Women's Writing,* 145–77. New York: Oxford Univ. Press, 1991.

———. *These Modern Women: Autobiographical Essays for the Twenties.* New York: Feminist Press, 1989.

Sievers, W. David. *Freud on Broadway: A History of Psychoanalysis and the American Drama.* New York: Hermitage House, 1955.

Sinclair, Upton. *Money Writes!* New York: Albert and Charles Boni, 1927.

Slotkin, Richard. *The Fatal Environment: The Myth of the Frontier in the Age of Industrialization, 1800–1890.* New York: Harpers, 1994.

Sochen, June. *The New Woman in Greenwich Village, 1910–1920.* New York: Quadrangle, 1972.

Spencer, J. W. "Reminiscences of Pioneer Life in the Mississippi Valley." 1872. Reprinted in *The Early Day[sic] of Rock Island and Davenport*, edited by Milo Milton Quaife, Chicago: Lakeside Press, 1942.

Sporn, Paul. *Against Itself: The Federal Theater and Writers' Projects in the Midwest*. Detroit: Wayne State Univ. Press, 1995.

Sundgaard, Arnold. "Susan Glaspell and the Federal Theatre Revisited." *Journal of American Drama and Theater* 9.1 (winter 1997): 1–10.

Taggard, Genevieve. "Poet Out of Pioneer." In *These Modern Women: Autobiographical Essays from the Twenties*, edited by Elaine Showalter, 62–67. New York: Feminist Press, 1979.

Tanselle, Thomas. "George Cram Cook and the Poetry of Living with a Checklist." *Books at Iowa* 24 (April 1976): 3–31, 35–37.

Thanet, Octave. *The Man of the Hour*. New York: Grosset and Dunlap, 1905.

———. *In Memoriam*. Budapest, 1898.

Tietjens, Eunice. *The World at My Shoulder*. New York: Macmillan, 1938.

Trimberger, Ellen Kay. "Feminism, Men, and Modern Love: Greenwich Village, 1900–1925." In *Forms of Desire: The Politics of Sexuality*, edited by Ann Snitow et al., 131–52. New York: Monthly Review, 1983.

———, ed. *Intimate Warriors: Portraits of a Modern Marriage, 1899–1944*. New York: Feminist Press, 1991.

Udall, Sharyn Rohlfsen. *Carr, O'Keeffe, Kahlo: Places of Their Own*. New Haven: Yale Univ. Press, 2000.

Vorse, Mary Heaton. *A Footnote to Folly*. New York: Farrar and Rinehart, 1935.

———. *Rebel Pen: The Writings of Mary Heaton Vorse*, edited by Dee Garrison. New York: Monthly Review Press, 1985.

———. *Time and the Town*. New York: Dial Press, 1942.

Ware, Caroline. *Greenwich Village, 1920–30: A Comment on American Civilization the Post-War Years*. 1935. Reprint, Berkeley: Univ. of California Press, 1994.

Waterman, Arthur. *Susan Glaspell*. New York: Twayne, 1966.

Watson, Steven. *Strange Bedfellows: The First American Avant Garde*. New York: Abbeville Press, 1991.

Wetzsteon, Ross. *Republic of Dreams: Greenwich Village: The American Bohemia, 1910–1960*. New York: Simon and Schuster, 2002.

Wilkie, Franc B. *Davenport, Past and Present*. Davenport: Lane, Luse, 1858.

Williams, Garry Jay. "Turned Down in Provincetown: O'Neill's Debut Reexamined." *Theatre Journal* 37.2 (May 1985): 155–66.

Wilson, Edmund. *The Thirties*. Edited by Leon Edel. New York: Pocket Books, 1980.

———. *The Twenties*. Edited by Leon Edel. New York: Farrar, Straus and Giroux, 1975.

Wittenstein, Kate. "The Heterodoxy Club and American Feminism, 1912–1930." Ph.D. diss., Boston University, 1989.

Zorach, William. *Art is My Life*. Cleveland: World, 1967.

Acknowledgments

I am pleased to acknowledge and thank the many people who have aided my work over the years. Although several have since died, they are present in the pages of this book.

I first read about Susan Glaspell in Marcia Noe's 1976 dissertation, and she has remained a constant support. My thanks as well to Arthur Waterman. The first time I wrote to him, he responded, "I hope some of this stuff helps; I've been saving it for years hoping you'd come along." That wonderful welcome convinced me I was in the right company. Gerhard Bach also became an important colleague and friend. I am equally indebted to the ever growing number of Glaspell scholars whose studies have enriched my work, particularly Cheryl Black, Martha Carpentier, Christine Dymkowski, J. Ellen Gainor, Veronica Makowsky, Barbara Ozieblo, Mary Papke, and Katharine Rodier. A special thanks to Judith Barlow for her help over the years and her seminal studies of American women playwrights, and to Robert Károly Sarlós an early supporter, who wrote on George Cram Cook. My thanks as well to C. W. E. Bigsby, Travis Bogard, Jack Diggens, Edna Nachshon, Francis Rogers, Alan Wald, and Steven Watson.

This book was made possible by the active cooperation of the Cook/Glaspell estate, and I thank them. Sirius Cook made all Glaspell and Cook materials available to me, and his widow, Valentina Cook, has continued to support my work. I also thank Anna Matson Hamburger and Langston and Claudia Moffett who shared their memories of Susan and allowed me to use their personal papers and materials. It was Gail Cohen who introduced me to the Moffetts, just as she has aided many Glaspell scholars in their work. She has kept Glaspell's memory alive, and we have all benefited from her passion.

In Davenport, I am particularly grateful to Dorothy Adams, Marie Louise LeClaire Anderson, Clarence Andrews, Sister Ritamary Bradley, Charlotte Griggs, Blanche Harrington, Marilyn Jones, Mary Nelson, William Roba, Sandra Tigges, Ida Trauffer, and William Wundrum. I also thank Mary Herr, Lois Leach, and Kay Rundge at the Davenport Public Library; Carol Hunt and Eunice Schlicting at the Putnam Museum Library; researcher Betty Gorshe and Andrea Little and the staff of the Davenport Community School District; Kathryn Hodson, Bob McCowan, Frank Paulka, and David Shoenover at the University of Iowa; Dick Hicks and J. Elias Jones at Drake University; Vernon Tyler and Lowell Webber at the Iowa State Historical Library; and Dennis A. Studer at the State Library of Iowa. In checking the materials for the Hossack murder case in Madison County, I received invaluable assistance from Zoe Blackford, Meryl Davis, Suzanne Null, and Pam Slings.

In Provincetown many enthusiastically supported this study, invited me into their homes, provided materials, told me stories, and showed me great kindnesses. I thank Regie Cabral who opened his Glaspell collection and allowed me to use the materials; Margaret Roberts, executor of the Celia Francis estate, who permitted me to use materials in the Francis collection; Joyce Tager, owner of Glaspell's home who invited me to stay there to gain inspiration; Maurice Tom Moore, the present occupant of Eugene O'Neill's Francis's Flats apartment, who let me inspect the famed carved beams; and local historian Leora Egan who, with Marguerite Young, shared those first heady days of my Glaspell Provincetown adventure. I also thank all those I interviewed, including George Bryant, Grace Collinson, Miriam Hapgood Dewitt, Clive Driver, Theresa Doyle, Madie L'Engle, Emily Farnam, Beatrice Faust, Mary Hackett, Ruth Hiebert, Anna Lewis, Charles Mayo, Charles "Stormy" Mayo III, Joel O'Brien, Francelina Hubbard Sousa, Heaton Vorse, Hazel Hawthorne Werner, and Rachel White as well as the staff of the Provincetown Public library who assisted me.

In New York City I owe a great debt of gratitude to cardiologist and collector William Priester, a native of Davenport, who permitted me to use his Iowa collection, and Dorothy Meyer and her son Karl, who shared with me their memories of Susan. I also thank Hermione Cyr, Kathryn Werling, and especially Polly Masters who responded to my *New York Times* query.

My research trips to Delphi were among the most exciting moments of my work. Armed only with the name Kyrios Kouk and a 1923 photo of Jig and four Delphi men, I walked down the main street of modern Delphi, and in one August morning in 1997 met the relatives of all four, whom I interviewed. I thank Elias Kourelis, the grandson of Elias Scaramouches, Elias Loukas, Elias Tsakalos, as well as Panos Kalthsis, Dimitri Psathas, Tim and Carolyn Sfondouris, and those colleagues and friends who aided and shared in my Delphi research, particularly Leah Levine, Freddie Rokem, Elizabeth Sakelaridou, Yael Shavit, and Nurit Yaari.

Much of my research was done in libraries, and I am grateful for the assistance I received over the years. I thank Isaac Gewirtz, Rodney Phillips, and Lola Szladits, curators of the Berg Collection, New York Public Library; Dorothy L. Swerdlove, curator of the Billy Rose Theatre Collection; as well as Tom Lisanti and Stephan K. Saks, of the Photography Service. I also thank Faye Haun, Museum of the City of New York; Ann Butler, Fales Collection, New York University; Jean Ashton, Butler Library, Columbia University; Michael Plunkett, Barrett Library, University of Virginia; Patricia Willis, curator of American manuscripts, Beinecke Rare Book and Manuscript Library, Yale University; Leslie Morris, Houghton Library, Harvard University; Frederick Woodbridge Wilson, Harvard Theatre Collection, Harvard University; Ellen M. Shea, Schlesinger Library, Radcliffe Institute; Kathryn L. Beam, Special Collections Library, University of Michigan; William LeFevre, Wayne State University Library; Maria Morelli, Boston University Library; Simon Elliott and Genie Guerard, University of California, Los Angeles Library; Martha Briggs, Diane Haskell, and Diana Sudyka, Newberry Library, Chicago; Nancy Shawcross, University of Pennsylvania Library; Laurie Deredita and Brian Rogers, Charles E. Shain Library, Connecticut College; Kathryn Hodson, University of Iowa Libraries; Levi D. Phillips, University of California, Davis Library; Beth Alvarez and Blanche T. Ebeling-Koning, University Libraries, University of Maryland at College Park; Cathy Henderson, Harry Ransom Humanities Research Center, University of Texas at Austin; L. Rebecca Johnson Melvin, University of Delaware Library; Barbara Haase and Rosemary Hogg, Fenwick Library, Lorraine Brown and Sara Neill Davis, Institute of the Federal Theatre Project, George Mason University; and the staffs of the Manuscript Collection, Princeton University Library, the Lilly Library, University of Indiana; and the National Archives, Washington, D.C.

I am pleased to acknowledge the support I received from the following fellowships: National Endowment for the Humanities Fellowship for University Teachers; Library of Congress Fellowship; Newberry Library Fellowship; Colorado State University Research grant and travel grants; and a Tel Aviv University Faculty Research Grant.

My thanks as well to those at Oxford University Press with whom I have been fortunate to work: Elissa Morris, Senior Editor, who enthusiastically supported the project and helped me see it through completion; Eve Bachrach, her able assistant; and Jessica Ryan, efficient Managing Editor. I am also grateful to former editor Susie Chang for her initial interest in my work.

I am equally indebted to those colleagues, friends, and relatives who prodded, encouraged, housed, and assisted me over the years: Ruby Cohn, Mary Crow, Joan Feinberg, Karen Klitzman, Ronnie and Dan Mirkin, and Barbara Mogulescu.

My greatest thanks as always go to my family. My children Oriella and Arik grew up while I was writing this book, and it became part of their world. When they were young, I tried convincing them that cross country journeys from our home in Colorado to New York should include stopovers in Davenport, which they'd find more fun than Disneyland, especially the local libraries. In later years, when I traveled, I wrote them copious memos about what still needed to be done in case something happened and I didn't return. No one is more relieved than they that this book is finally in print and out of their lives. And no one is more responsible for helping me complete the book than my husband, Samuel, to whom it is dedicated. Susan Glaspell was fortunate to have found a partner in Jig, who encouraged her work and took pride in her accomplishments. Samuel has been the great supporter and partner in my life, my best editor and best friend.

Index

Ashcroft, Peggy, 236
Assembly of Gods, The (Triggs, ed.), 54
"At Fifty I Ask God" (Cook), 280, 284–85
Athenian Women, The (Cook), 188, 192, 196, 264, 284
Athens (Greece), 264, 265, 266, 272–75, 277, 280, 281, 282, 284, 286, 287
At 33 (LeGallienne), 320-21
Atkinson, Brooks, 340, 342–44
"At the Turn of the Road" (Glaspell), 58
Authors League, 383
Autobiography (Blackhawk), 6
avant-garde, viii

Babbitt (Lewis), 32
Bach, Gerhard, x
Bach, Marcus, 366
Back-to-Africa movement, 367
Bailey, Nani, 181, 188
Baker, George Pierce, 171, 320, 367
Baker, Martha, 115
Ball, Ozzie, 381, 395, 396
Ballantine, Eddie ("Teddy"), 138
Ballantine, Stella Commins, 138, 166, 167, 168
"Balm of Life, The" (Cook), 75
Bandbox Theatre (N.Y.C.), 154
Banks, Charles Eugene, 29, 33, 63, 69, 73, 80
Barnes, A. C., 201
Barnes, Djuna, 220–21
Barnes, Margaret Ayer, 341, 342
Barnstormers (theatre group), 300
Barrie, James, 213
Barry, Griffin, 304
Barry, Philip, 342
Barthes, Roland, xiv
Beatty, Warren, ix
Beautiful Homes and Social Customs of America (Banks), 69
Beckett, Samuel, x, xiii, 176, 245
Beckhard, Arthur, 356
Before Breakfast (O'Neill), 183
Behrman, S. N., 387
Belardi, Jenny, 123–24, 180, 201, 261, 293

Benn, Ernest (British publisher), 187, 306, 314, 324
Berkman, Alexander, 129, 208, 224
Bernhardt, Sarah, 32, 196
Bernice (Glaspell), 26, 96, 187, 188, 210–13, 217, 222, 231, 246, 255, 259, 300, 306, 309, 328, 333, 344, 386
Bernstein, Aline, 340
Berry (defense lawyer Hossack trial), 43, 46, 47
Berry, Marion, 260
Betrayal, The (Colum), 183
Beyond the Horizon (O'Neill), 210, 219, 222
Bianchi, Martha Dickinson, 331, 332, 334
Bible, 4, 23, 37, 70, 113
Bicknell, Mary, 300
Big White Fog (Ward), 367
Billy and Betty stories (H. Cook), 362
birth control advocates, 124, 126, 127, 128, 159
    Chains of Dew and, 258, 260, 355
Bismarck, Otto von, 37
"Bismarck and European Politics" (Glaspell), 37
Björkman, Edwin, 187, 195, 199
Black Cat (periodical), 51, 59, 342
Blackhawk, 6–7, 8, 225, 228
Black Hawk's Watch Tower, 86, 108, 112
Blackhawk War, 6, 14
Blackstone Theatre (Chicago), 368
Blair, Mary, 322
Blake, William, 65, 283
Bluebird, The (Maeterlinck), 96
Bogard, Travis, 205
Bölsche, Wilhelm, 82
Boni, Albert, 124, 154
Boni, Charles, 124, 154
"Book of Days" (Matson), 305
Borden, Lizzie, 47–48
Boston, 128, 305, 322, 352, 382, 383
Boston Evening Transcript (newspaper), 329
Boston Globe (newspaper), 177
Bouget, Paul, 56

Boulton, Agnes, vii, 22, 204-5, 207, 218, 219, 220, 222, 229-30, 232, 236, 237, 252, 253, 256, 257, 272, 295, 302
    husband of. *See* O'Neill, Eugene
Bound East for Cardiff (O'Neill), 157, 170, 171, 172, 181, 184, 231
Bourne, Ralph, 225
Bowen, Elizabeth, 348
Bowman, Anna, 94
Boyce, Neith, x, 39, 64, 139-43, 148, 149, 150, 154, 157, 160-61, 163, 166, 169, 170, 171, 179, 183, 191, 196, 197, 210, 213, 214, 218, 231, 238, 239, 266, 272, 287, 302, 303, 305, 314, 321, 323, 324, 329, 330, 338, 359, 374, 392
    husband of. *See* Hapgood, Hutchins
Boyd, Fred, 148, 149
Boyesen, Baynard, 148
Bradford, Pricilla, 12
Brancusi, Constantin, 128
Braque, Georges, 95, 128
Bray, Elizabeth McCullough, 35-36
Brevoort Hotel (Greenwich Village), 40, 121, 135, 204, 252, 361, 372
Brewter, Edwin Tenney, 156
Briary Bush, The (Dell), 106
Brideshead Revisited (Waugh), 390
Brill, A. A., 125
Brinton, Crane, 390
Britain, ix, 306-9, 324-25, 326. *See also* London
Brittle Heavens (York and Pohl), 334
Broadway, 213, 232, 235, 236, 242, 246, 253, 260, 320
Brontë, Charlotte, 308
Brook Evans (Glaspell), 26, 27, 318-19, 324-26, 329, 330, 343, 344, 373, 375, 383
Brooks, Van Wyck, 117, 121, 325, 389
Broun, Heywood, 187, 196, 210, 247
Brown, John Mason, 340
Brown, Mabel, 100
Browne, Maurice, 115, 116, 154, 252
Brush, George de Forest, 71
Bryant, George, 393

Bryant, Louise, ix, 22, 166-67, 177, 181, 192, 209, 214, 217, 218, 223, 287-88, 364
    husband of. *See* Reed, John
    O'Neill affair with, 179, 184, 191-92, 197, 204, 213
Buck, Pearl, 329
Burnham, Clara, 57
Burrows, J. M. D., 11, 13-14
Burt, Freddie, 168, 170, 172, 177, 182, 186
Burtis Opera House (Davenport), 30, 33
Bushnell-Hamlin, Ella G., 77, 78
"Busy Duck, The" (Glaspell), 219-20
Bynner, Witter, 115

Cabell, James Branch, 167
Cabin, the (Cook summer home), 69-70, 78, 79, 87, 92, 93, 99, 105-12, 332
Cabinet of Dr. Caligari, The (film), 244, 252
Camelot (Glaspell/Matson cat), 305
Camera Work (journal), 128
Campbell, Mrs. Patrick, 236
Canby, Henry Seidel, 338
Canby, Margaret, 323, 338, 341
Candles to the Sun (T. Williams), 366
Cape Cod School of Art, 136
Captive, The (play), 328
Carb, Dave, 186
Carbon-Copy (Glaspell/Cook cat), 151, 204
Carlin, Terry, 170, 192, 204, 205, 206, 364
Carnegie, Andrew, 49
Cary, Augusta, 115
Cary, Lucian, 115
Castalian spring (Delphi), 269, 272, 280, 282
Castellun, Maida, 247, 249
Cather, Willa, viii, 50, 317, 318, 343
Catholic World (magazine), 340-41
Cattel, James, 225
Century (magazine), 79
Century Theatre (London), 309
Cézanne, Paul, 128
Chains of Dew (Glaspell), 222, 255, 256, 257-61, 337, 343, 355

Dos Passos, Katie, 145, 321, 322, 323, 338, 341, 359, 371, 381, 384, 390, 393, 394–95, 396
Douglass, Frederick, 4
Drake, Francis Marion, 38
Drake University, viii, 22, 34, 37–38, 51, 53, 55, 72, 73, 82, 94, 104, 119, 225
Drama and the Stage (Lewisohn), 233
Drama of Transition, The (Goldberg), 255
Dramatists' Guild, 369
Dreamy Kid, The (O'Neill), 206
Dreiser, Theodore, 56, 58, 115, 123, 167, 168, 251, 253, 324
Drucker, Rebecca, 203
Dublin Magazine, 307
Duchamp, Marcel, 122, 128, 159
Duffey, Bernard, 53
Dufor, Elsie, 249
Dufy, Raoul, 95
Duganne, Phyllis, 323, 372, 381, 390, 396
du Maurier, George, 95
Duncan, Isadora, 243, 275
Duncan, Raymond, 275, 277
Dunne, Finley Peter, 56
Dunne, Irene, 375
Dunsany, Lord, 154
Duse, Eleonora, 196
Dutton (publisher), 231
"Dwellers on Parnassos" (Glaspell), 270, 271–72

Eastgate Hotel (Chicago), 365
Eastman, Crystal, 126
Eastman, Dan, 167
Eastman, Max, 40, 122, 126, 127, 148, 154, 160, 167, 177, 184, 186, 188, 189, 196, 214, 220, 380
  wife of. See Rauh, Ida
Eaton, Walter Prichard, 341, 342, 345, 367
Ebenezer ("Nezer") (Glaspell/Cook dog), 204
Egan, Leora, 168
Egoist (magazine), 159
Eldridge, Miss (archeologist), 263, 271, 326

Elizabeth the Queen (Anderson), 342
Ell, Christine, vii, 160, 195, 204
Ell, Louis, 160
Ellis, Charles, 230, 236
Ellison, Ralph, 367
Emerson, Ralph Waldo, 30, 70, 71, 82, 333, 334, 349
  influence on Glaspell of, 96
Emperor Jones, The (O'Neill), 65, 171, 207, 229–37, 244, 246, 251, 252, 253, 260, 282, 295, 299, 300, 336
Enemy of the People, An (Ibsen), 306
Engels, Friedrich, 126
England. *See* Britain
"Enthusiasm" (Cook), 70
Equal Rights Amendment, 242
Ervine, St. John, 222
Espionage Act of 1917, 195, 208, 222, 223, 224, 226, 227
Ethical Society of Davenport, 104
European Cultural Centre (Delphi), 289
Everyman (periodical), 349, 351
Everyman Theatre (London), 39
Everywhere I Roam (Sundgaard), 368
Experimental Theatre, Inc. *See* Provincetown Players
expressionism, 95, 186, 243–45, 246, 247

"Faint Trails" (Glaspell), 210
"Faithless Shepherd, The" (Glaspell), 270, 276, 278
Fall River Line, 135, 136, 148
Family Pride (Glaspell). *See Close the Book*
Farewell to Arms, A (Hemingway), 304
Farran, Don, 369
Farrar (publisher), 324
Fashion (Mowatt), 295
Faulkner, William, 7
Federal General Intelligence Division, 224
Federal Theatre Project, 359, 364–69, 373, 383
  Midwest Playwrights Bureau, xiii, 364, 367, 369
Federal Writers Project, 367

Gierow, Karl, 221
Gilman, Charlotte Perkins, 127, 188
Gilman, George Houghton, 127
Gilpin, Charles, 230, 231, 236
Given, Eben, 323, 381, 396
Glaspell, Alice Feeney Keating
    (mother), 15, 16, 20–28, 49,
    68, 77, 98, 113, 163, 189, 268,
    269, 272, 273, 276, 287, 293,
    307, 311, 312, 315, 325, 377
    dementia and death of, 327–29, 334
    influence on daughter of, 24, 25,
    26–28
Glaspell, Charles ("Ray") (brother),
    21, 22, 23, 25, 77, 118, 163,
    272, 273, 287, 311, 328, 365,
    372, 373, 377, 391, 394
Glaspell, Elizabeth (great-aunt), 13
Glaspell, Elmer S. (father), 19–25, 49,
    77, 81, 98, 152, 163, 188–89,
    239, 272, 315
    daughter's description of, 25
    daughter's admiration of men like,
    162
Glaspell, Enos (great-great grandfa-
    ther), 13
Glaspell, Florence ("Flossie") (sister-
    in-law), 163, 272, 311, 315,
    329, 365, 372, 373, 391, 396
Glaspell, Frank (brother), 21, 22, 23,
    25, 77, 163, 272, 273, 287,
    315, 329, 377, 378, 389, 394
Glaspell, Hazel (sister-in-law), 163,
    272, 329, 377, 389, 396
Glaspell, James (great-grandfather),
    13, 14, 15, 376
Glaspell, Jane Statham (great-grand-
    mother), 13
Glaspell, Sarah (great-great grand-
    mother), 13
Glaspell, Silas (grandfather), 13, 15,
    16, 17, 19, 20, 22, 226, 239
Glaspell, Susan
    as actor, 37, 39, 161, 173, 181, 183,
    185–86, 193, 195, 197, 209,
    213, 348–49
    annual Davenport visits of, 153,
    163, 184
    appearance of, vii–viii, 205, 303,
    371

birth date discrepancies for, xi, 22
birth of, 3, 21–22
British fame of, 306–9
charitable gifts of, 394
Chicago period of. See Chicago
Chicago stylistic influences on,
    56–57
childhood and youth of, 22–25
childlessness of, 376
children's story by, 376–77
Colorado work experience of, 100–
    101
conformity and, 28, 51
Cook relationship with. See
    Glaspell–Cook relationship
as cultural pioneer, xii–xiii
Davenport library controversy and,
    103–4
death of, 396–97
Dell and, 106–7, 117
Delphi Players and, 280
drinking of, 347, 348, 359–60, 362,
    363, 364, 371, 372, 382
early career of, viii
education of, viii, 24–25, 34, 35–38,
    47, 53–55, 70, 82
European tour of, 94
expressionism and, 95
extent of oeuvre of, x
family background of, viii, 4–8,
    13–18, 19–28
family portrayals in works of,
    26–28
father/daughter relations and, 28,
    151–52
Federal Theatre Project and, 364,
    365–69, 373, 383
feminism and, viii, ix–x, xii, xiii,
    127, 158, 197-201, 242–44,
    255, 256
fiction theory of, 318
finances of, 301, 329–30, 357–58,
    381
Greenwich Village circle of, vii, viii,
    x, xi, 5, 22, 40, 54, 145, 175
Harmonie Society (Davenport) and,
    78
health problems of, 24, 147, 150,
    151, 152, 159, 178, 328, 394,
    395, 396

Heterodoxy club's significance to, viii, 127, 242, 249

homes of. *See* Davenport; Delphi; Greenwich Village; Provincetown; Truro

Hossack case and, 41–47, 48, 127

Huffaker, friendship with, 36, 94, 117

importance of place to, 146

Iowa background of. *See* Davenport

journalistic career of, viii, 30–33, 34, 36, 38–39, 40, 41–47, 48, 50, 56

later years of, 371–96

literary influences on, 96–97, 193, 210

literary subjects of, viii–ix, 26–28, 158, 159

marriage of. *See* Glaspell–Cook relationship

miscarriages of, 144, 150, 152

monism and, 82–83, 384

mother/daughter relations and, 26–28, 49, 98, 325, 327–28, 334

motherhood and, 151, 159, 354, 376

mother-in-law's influence on, 68

Odets and, 364

O'Keeffe compared to, 200

O'Neill and, viii, ix, x, xi, xii, 169, 204–6, 207, 210, 212, 221–22, 237, 240, 245, 295, 298, 302, 307, 345, 363, 396

Paris visit by, 92, 94–101, 106

persona of, viii

as playwright, vii, viii–ix, xiii–xiv, 176. *See also* Provincetown Players

Pulitzer Prize won by, ix, 341–45, 347, 363, 386, 396

refinement and, 241

religious background and, 15

romantic affairs of. *See* Glaspell–Cook relationship; Matson, Norman; Moffett, Langston

routines and, 39, 95, 140, 381

sexuality of, 112, 142–44, 304

social causes and, 7–8, 37, 38, 101, 189, 322, 361, 364, 367–69, 371, 380, 382, 393–94

as stepmother, 166, 231, 237, 357–58, 361–62

Tuesday Club (Davenport) and, 84, 94, 118

World War I and, 7, 36, 159, 189, 196, 383

World War II and, 189, 380, 382–83, 389

writer's block of, 357, 358, 359, 360–61, 364, 377

works of:

"Agnes of Cape End," 178

Alison's House, ix, 26, 246, 300, 328, 331, 332–36, 337, 339–45, 348, 356, 386, 393

Ambrose Holt and Family, 26, 261, 310, 332, 336–37, 373, 383

"At the Turn of the Road," 58

Bernice, 26, 96, 187, 188, 210–13, 218, 222, 231, 246, 255, 256, 257, 259, 300, 306, 309, 328, 333, 344, 386

"Bismarck and European Politics," 37

Brook Evans, 26, 27, 318–19, 324–26, 329, 330, 344, 373, 375, 383

"Busy Duck, The," 219–20

Chains of Dew, 222, 255, 256, 257–61, 337, 343, 355

"Chastening Bug, The," 222

Cherished and Shared of Old, 376–77

"Chicago," 115

Close the Book, 26, 184, 186, 187, 194–95, 259

Comic Artist, The (with Matson), 26, 300, 312–13, 323, 324, 336, 341, 356–57

"Dwellers on Parnassos," 270, 271–72

"Faint Trails," 210

"Faithless Shepherd, The," 270, 276, 278

Family Pride. See Close the Book

Fidelity, 35, 93, 100, 101, 108, 121, 140, 150, 151, 157–59, 293, 307, 318, 324, 333, 395

"Finality in Freeport," 104, 178

Statesman, The (magazine), 325
State University of Iowa (SUI). See
  University of Iowa
Steele, Margaret Thurston, 139, 160,
  161, 191, 219, 272, 302, 311,
  336
Steele, Wilbur Daniel, 139, 160, 162,
  183, 191, 219, 272, 302, 311,
  336
Steffens, Lincoln, 123, 125
Stein, Gertrude, 95, 124, 125, 160
Stein, Leo, 160
Steinbeck, John, 375
Stephen, Leslie, 28
Stevens, George, 383
Stewart, Ralph, 260, 261
Stewart and Kidd Company (publish-
  ers), 231
Stieglitz, Alfred, 122, 128, 158–59,
  200
Stokes, Frederick A. (publisher), 113,
  311, 314, 324, 374, 375, 377,
  383, 394
Stone, Lucy, 78
"Stones That Once Were Temple"
  (Glaspell), 269
Stories of a Western Town (French),
  49
Strand Theatre (London), 356
Strange Interlude (O'Neill), 68, 212,
  240, 248, 329, 335, 342
Straw, The (O'Neill), 368
Streit, Clarence, 281
Strindberg, August, 95, 115, 129, 247,
  248, 295
Strong, Austin, 342
Strunsky, Anna ("Anna Senior"), 349,
  350, 355–56
"Study in Religious Liberty, A" (Fine-
  shriber), 103
suffrage, 123, 124, 126, 139, 141,
  159,
  postsuffrage, 242-43, 249
Summer on the Lakes in 1843 (Fuller),
  16
Sun also Rises, The (Hemingway), 317
Sunday Times (newspaper), 306
Sundgaard, Arnold, 112, 367–69
Suppressed Desires (Cook and
  Glaspell), viii, x, 39, 70,

  155–57, 160, 161, 162, 169,
  177, 183, 184, 186, 189, 194,
  203, 231–32, 235, 259, 283,
  312, 369, 394
Swain, Sara Herndon, 73–74, 77, 78,
  90, 93
Synge, John Millington, 115, 187,
  192, 221
syphilis, 368

Taggard, Genevieve, 332, 333, 334
Tales from Totems of the Hidey
  (Deans; Triggs, ed.), 54
Tannenbaum, Frank, 162
Tattooed Countess, The (Van Vech-
  ten), 54
Tempest, The (Shakespeare), 283
Temple of Apollo (Delphi), 266, 267,
  269
Ten Days That Shook the World
  (Reed), 217
Terry, Ellen, 307, 308
Thanet, Octave. See French, Alice
"That Winter Day" (Cook), 302
Thayer, Webster, 322
Theatre Guild, 215, 222, 236, 246,
  251, 331, 386–87, 396
Themistocles, 263
Theodora (Turkish refugee), 276–77,
  326
They Too Arise (A. Miller), 367
"Third American Sex, The" (Cook),
  159, 224
Thirst (O'Neill), 157, 177
Thomas, Norman, 357
Thompson, Dorothy, 357
Thompson, Hunter, 42
Thompson, P., 285
Thoreau, Henry David, 136, 137, 264
Thorndike, Sybil, 307, 308
"Though Stone be Broken" (Cook
  poem), 112, 302
Three from the Earth (Barnes), 221
Three Plays by Susan Glaspell, 306,
  307
Throckmorton, Cleon, 244, 256, 294,
  295
Tickless Time (Glaspell and Cook), 65,
  206-7, 209, 210
Tietjens, Eunice, 115, 116

Lightning Source UK Ltd.
Milton Keynes UK
UKOW031455091111

181780UK00001B/30/A